RED SEMINARS

RADICAL EXCURSIONS INTO EDUCATIONAL THEORY, CULTURAL POLITICS, AND PEDAGOGY

Peter McLaren and
Compañeras y Compañeros

Critical Education and Ethics
Editors
Barry Kanpol, Indiana University—Purdue University Fort Wayne
Fred Yeo, Southeast Missouri State University

Critical Multicultural Conversations
  Greg S. Goodman and Karen Carey (eds.)

Mediating the Culture Wars
  Eric Bain Selbo

The Academy and the Possibility of Belief: Essays on Intellectual and Spiritual
  Life
    *Mary Louise Buley-Meissner, Mary McCaslin Thompson, and Elizabeth
    Bachrach Tan (eds.)*

Issues and Trends in Critical Pedagogy
  Barry Kanpol

Teachers Talking Back and Breaking Bread
  Barry Kanpol

JOY as a Metaphor of Convergence: A Phenomenological and Aesthetic
  Investigation of Social and Educational Change
    Delores D. Liston

Red Seminars: Radical Excursions in Educational Theory, Cultural Politics,
  and Pedagogy
    Peter McLaren

Body Movements: Pedagogy, Politics and Social Change
  Sherry Shapiro and Svi Shapiro (eds.)

forthcoming

Deconstructing the Oral Eye: Visual Arts/Postmodern Education in an Era of
  Postmodernist Consumption
    Jan Jagodzinski

Talking Leaves: Narratives of Otherness
  Suzanne Soohoo

RED SEMINARS

RADICAL EXCURSIONS INTO EDUCATIONAL THEORY, CULTURAL POLITICS, AND PEDAGOGY

Peter McLaren and
Compañeras y Compañeros

HAMPTON PRESS, INC.
CRESSKILL, NEW JERSEY

Printed in the United States of America

Library of Congress Cataloging-in-Publication Data

McLaren, Peter, 1948-
    Red seminars : radical excursions into educational theory, cultural politics, and
    pedagogy / Peter McLaren and compañeras y compañeros.
        p. cm. -- (Critical education and ethics)
    Includes bibliographic references and index.
    ISBN 1-57273-570-8 -- ISBN 1-57273-571-6
    1. Critical pedagogy--United States. 2. Communism and education--United
States. 3. Education, Higher--Political aspects--United States. I. Title. II. Series.

LC196.5.U6M347 2004
370.11'5--dc22

2004054028

Hampton Press, Inc.
23 Broadway
Cresskill, NJ 07626

This book is dedicated to my past, present and future students.
It is also dedicated to theater and opera director, Peter Sellars, whose work
continues to be a beacon of inspiration.

CONTENTS

RADICALS AND RADICAL IDEAS: GRAMSCI, RORTY, FREIRE, HARVEY AND MENCHU

THE POLITICS OF POPULAR CULTURE

INTERVIEWS WITH PETER McLAREN

FOREWORD

Ramin Farahmandpur

Portland, Oregon

Why should teachers and teacher educators at colleges and universities read Marx? What does *Capital* (Vol. 1), Marx's magnum opus—which took him nearly forty years of his life to complete and covers more than one-thousand pages—reveal to us? More important, why has Marx become so unfashionable among—if not anathema—to scholars and professors in academic circles across the United States? Why it is that universities are eager to offer courses on post-colonialism, postmodernism, post-structuralism, and cultural studies, but are far less willing to provide any serious forums or seminars in which Marx can be critically discussed, debated, and studied? What does Marx, who stood as one of the leading "declassed intellectuals" of the 19th century, reveal that has made him such a pariah in the eyes of the establishment?

From the perspective of the authors of the essays in this volume, a partial response to those questions would be that universities and colleges function as part of the ideological state apparatus that participate in the reproduction and maintenance of capitalist social relations of production. It is precisely because capitalism is able to absorb and neutralize most, if not all, forms of progressive and left-liberal social and political criticism directed against it that we need to reconsider a sustained and renewed Marxist critique of capitalist schooling. As Barbara Foley aptly put it:

> Examining all institutions in capitalist society as part of the ideological state apparatus, Marxism cautions those of us who teach in colleges and universities to have few illusions about higher education as a site for trans-formative pedagogy. The purpose of higher education under capitalism is to ensure the continuation of class stratification and exploitation. Colleges and universities are above all ideology factories—from the humblest vocational programs in community colleges to the most exalted study of liberal arts in the Ivies. Even the most paradigm-shattering pedagogy thus occurs within a context of hierarchical and authoritarian social relations that divests what we do in the classroom of about 90 percent of its radical effects. Indeed, our very existence in the classroom of the bourgeois college or university can

be taken as testimony to the virtues of capitalist pluralism and democracy. (pp. 30-31)

This also holds true for public schools. In the last decade the corporatization and privatization of public schools has become a growing trend among many school districts in the United States. Consider a national organization called Field Trip Factory, which as part of its "Be a Smart Shopper" program, organizes field trips for students who live in the Boston metropolitan area to local chain stores such as Sports Authority. For their homework assignment, students are encouraged to check their local newspaper for Roche Bros. and Sudbury Farms coupons and make a "shopping list."

Corporations have also set foot in the lucrative and profitable market of "branding" adolescent consciousness—literally. In England, for example, the marketing agency Cunning Stunts has developed an innovative approach to advertising commercial brand products. The company has found that students' foreheads can be made into a profitable venture. The advertising agency is hiring students who are willing to wear a corporate logo on their heads for a minimum of three hours a day for £88.20 a week. As John Cassy (2003) of *The Guardian* reports: "The brand or produce message will be attached by a vegetable dye transfer and the students will be paid to leave the logos untouched."

What is evidently clear from the these examples and others is that corporations are not preparing students for critical citizenship, but rather they are preparing them to play their roles as consumer-citizens. Whereas the former encourages students to question, conceptualize, analyze, theorize, and to critically reflect upon their experiences, the latter lures students into an uncritical and blind acceptance of Capitalist market ideology, values, and practices designed to reinforce and reproduce capitalist social relations of production. As Charles Sullivan (2003) noted:

> Of course it is not in the self-interest of capitalism to educate people who can see capitalism for what it is, to think critically about it, and perhaps even do something to change it. Corporate education exists to promote programming consumers and providing an obedient work force to an unfair slave wage system, not to provide society with a well informed and politically active citizenry. In fact these are the things that pose the greatest threat to America's corporate oligarchy.

In spite of the daunting challenge that awaits critical educators in the days ahead, we should not be discouraged and dissuaded from inviting students to participate in ideological and political dialogues regarding the structural contradictions and antagonisms that plague capitalism. But the question is: Where should we begin?

In my own teaching experience as an assistant professor at Portland State University, I invite my undergraduate and graduate students to share their personal experiences by having them write an educational biography paper at the beginning of the course. In the second week of class, students break up into small groups and read each others educational biography. In the course of those readings, I ask students to identify the similarities and the differences of their educational experiences. Here, students begin to explore and examine how race, class, gender, disability, and other forms of identities have been deciding factors in their schooling and their education. By comparing and contrasting their educational experiences, students can begin to recognize how race, class, and gender privileges have a profound influence on their educational opportunities and life chances as well as those of others.

Next, I encourage students to make connections between their experiences and what Iris Marion Young (1990) refers to as the five faces of oppression.[1] Later on in the course, I help students to examine their experiences by introducing them to new concepts and ideas such as alienation, domestication, codification, dialectics, and the banking model of education among others. Throughout the rest of the course, I encourage students to reexamine and rethink the conceptual categories they use to make sense of their experiences and of the world.

Of course, there is no guarantee that all students will be prepared to take such risks. Given that a great many graduate students in education in the United States have cultivated the idea that they will be handed prepackaged teaching tools, frames, and models that they can steadfastly apply to their workplace or teaching environment, they are reluctant to theorize or to critically reflect upon their teaching practices. In some instances, teaching critical pedagogy to students unprepared for the challenges of self-reflections and critique can backfire as in the case of one of my students who wrote in her evaluation of the class the following statement:

> I had a very painful winter quarter in [the] social foundations of education [class]. The direction that the course took was simply problem identification. We talked about problems all quarter, and never even hinted at viable solutions. We didn't even discuss tools, frames or theories that can be used to make decisions. It was so frustrating. I left many classes feeling very depressed that there were too many problems to even try to conquer.

While I would agree that students feel overwhelmed and frustrated by the lack of solutions available for challenging undemocratic educational practices in their workplace environment, I also believe students need to acknowledge that the right questions need to be asked before the right solutions can be developed. Freire talked about problem-posing as the first step, and that developing solutions to these problems has to be a *collective* process that is achieved by engaging the larger community.

---

[1]Marginalization, powerlessness, exploitation, violence, and cultural imperialism.

What needs to be emphasized more than ever in teacher education programs and in graduate schools of education is the dialectical unity between theory and practice, and action and reflection. Here we need to make a distinction between reflection and critical reflection. The former is related to students' awareness of their concrete social and economic circumstances; the latter deals with the investigation of their social location in the world as well as their relationship to the world. Paulo Freire refers to this as a "radical form of being," which he attributes to "beings that not only know, but know that they know."

The essays in *Red Seminars* offer a decidedly Marxian edge to critical pedagogy. The authors—while not all self-identifying Marxists—hold the view that students and teachers are "socially self-critical" political beings. Following in the footsteps of Marx, they maintain that as active self-conscious beings, we have the ability to transform our social environment through cultural and material practices, and that by interacting with the social world through our labor, we can recreate ourselves as "working, thinking, and still-evolving species" (Raines, 2002. p. 2). Thus, part of the project of critical pedagogy in the essays presented in *Red Seminars* is to recognize that we are not only "natural beings," but also "human natural beings" (Raines, 2002, p. 71). In other words, because we have a capacity for self-awareness and self-reflection we are beings for ourselves, and thus, a "species being." Hence, a renewed Marxist approach to critical pedagogy stresses that our human life activities—the way in which we organize and produce our livelihood—is both "sensuous" and "self-reflexive" (Raines, 2002). As Marx reminds us, consciousness is always consciousness of something other than itself. Consciousness is an "in itself," that is, it hurls back upon itself and becomes "for itself," and thus, gains awareness *of* itself.

Marx pointed out that human beings are alienated beings within existing capitalist social, economic, and political arrangements, who must struggle to prevail over their own alienation. In his dialectical approach to labor, Marx asserted that labor is central to our existence. And although it is by the means of our laboring activities that we are able to interact with the social world, we also unwittingly participate in our own alienation through the value form of labor that organizes and shapes capitalist social relations in distinct ways related to race, class, gender, and sexual orientation. Thus, the central task of the critical educator is to encourage students and teachers to become self-reflective practitioners who are willing to take risks by questioning and challenging the ways in which schools participate in the reproduction of capitalist social relations of production. In doing so, students can discuss the individual and collective agency necessary to overcome their own oppression as well as the oppression that is inflicted upon the working class as a whole through capitalist social relations of production. The essays presented in *Red Seminars* invites students and teachers to take such a challenge.

REFERENCES

Cassy, J. Students cash in on "human billboards" plan. *The Guardian.* Available at http://www.guardian.co.uk/Print/0,3858,4600434,00.htm

Foley, B. (2002). Ten propositions on the role played by Marxism in working-class studies. *Rethinking Marxism, 14*(3), 28-31.

Raines, J. (2002). *Marx on religion.* Philadelphia, PA: Temple University Press.

Sullivan, C. (2003). Programming the workforce: The failure of mass education. *Counterpunch.* Available at http://www.counterpunch.org/sullivan02252003.html

Young, I. M. (1990). *Justice and the politics of difference.* Princeton, NJ: Princeton University Press.

PREFACE

Carlos Tejeda

California State University, Los Angeles

Peter McLaren (1991) has written that we are now living in "the future anterior," a space and time in which people have a profound nostalgia for a moment that has yet to take place, in which a naturalized and universalized *we* is disguisedly imposed on a sea of differences. His poetically piercing and politically pounding work has helped those of us working from a decolonizing perspective to argue that we also inhabit an *anterior-less present*, a space and time in which people have an arresting amnesia about a half millennia that has been taking place, in which indigenous and non-white peoples are reduced to ontological foreigners who are ideologically disconnected from the very space and time of their existence, in which the expanse of people's ideological disconnection is colonized by a *difference of domination* (Tejeda, in press). His work (McLaren, 1993) has helped us argue that critical educators must construct a *critical remembrance* that serves to narrate and counter specific histories of oppression and human suffering—a redemptive remembrance that serves as a form of critique and a referent for hope. For those of us thinking and teaching toward a decolonizing pedagogy, who understand that we are direct descendants of people, ideas, and institutions from a genocidal and annihilating colonial and capitalist anterior, little could be more fitting as a preface to McLaren's work than to speak of its significance from the ruminations of a critical remembrance.

Indeed, the past must be excavated with the same insistence that McLaren searches for an understanding of the present. In the *internal neo-colonial* (Tejeda, Espinoza, & Gutierrez, 2003) and capitalist spaces of the United States, the present instantiates the past as it is again common for the machineries of American democracy to be openly employed in attacks against working-class and non-white peoples. In California, for example, these populations have experienced a grinding away of the most basic human rights. In the last decade, voter propositions have sought the following: to deny them medical care and social services (Prop. 187); to expel their children from schools and deny them access to a public education (Prop. 187); to demolish Civil Rights gains that insured greater access to education and employment (Prop. 209); and to deny them the right to learn and be taught in their language (Prop. 227). These voter initiatives have effectively functioned to demolish rights and reconstruct a less equitable condition for non-white peoples—Propositions 187 and 227 were explicitly directed against the demographically expanding (and largely mis-named) "Hispanic/Latino" population, whereas proposition 209 openly targeted the entitlements and opportunities of both the African-American and "Hispanic/Latino" populations (Gutierrez, Asato, Santos, & Gotanda, 2002).

To understand why the machinery of America's capitalist democracy can be employed like a wrecking ball against the human rights of specific popula-tions, it is necessary to focus on happenings in the present while gazing at the horrors of the past. From this vantage, one can recall that the migrating and toil-ing population of unwelcomed "Latinos/Hispanics" targeted by California's propositions largely descended from indigenous populations that have been killed, conquered, converted, and renamed by European conquerors, colonists, and capitalist statesmen throughout the past five centuries. One can also remem-ber that contemporary political processes, legislative mandates, and their sus-taining discourses have a genealogy whose origins can be traced back centuries to the legal, political, and ideological frameworks of the "Indian"-annihilating and African-enslaving imperialisms of a Spanish monarchy and an Anglo-American democracy (Aldama, 2001; Horseman, 1997; Seed, 2001; Spring, 2001; Williams, 1995). What's more, one will recollect that wherever conquest, colonization, and capitalist exploitation found indigenous people in the hemi-sphere, a deculturalizing education that schooled them toward subservience shortly followed. From this vantage, one sees that the past both eerily haunts and imposingly inhabits the contemporary times McLaren's work critically examines and interprets.

In *A Little Matter of Genocide*, Churchill (1997) reminds us of the holo-caust and horrors of that past. He writes that between 1492 and 1892 the popu-lation of approximately 125 million indigenous people in the hemisphere was decimated by more than 90%:

> The people had died in their millions of being hacked apart with axes and swords, burned alive and trampled under horses, hunted as game and fed to dogs, shot, beaten, stabbed, scalped for bounty, hanged on meathooks and thrown over the sides of ships at sea, worked to death as slave laborers, intentionally starved and frozen to death during a multitude of forced marches and internments, and, in an unknown number of instances, deliber-ately infected with epidemic diseases. (p. 1)

And for those who managed to survive, life under the conquering sword was not necessarily better than death at its end. From the very beginning, survivors of what became a centuries-long onslaught of European conquest and colonization were brutally victimized by social practices and institutional arrangements that sought their labor, geographical removal, and/or "civilization"/religious conversion (Brown, 1981; Churchill, 1997; Deloria & Lytle, 1983; Galeano, 1989; Seed, 2001). What they did not eradicate, they attempted to educate.

It is important to remember that if the Natives were not fatally brutalized or banished, they were socialized for subservience. In the 1540s, the Dominican priest Bartolome de Las Casas and the Aristotelian philosopher Juan Gines de Sepulveda debated regarding the most effective methods to "civilize" and convert the "barbarous" and "childlike Indian" within the Spanish Empire (Hanke, 1975). One hundred years later, in the not-too-distant colonies of an expanding British Empire, pressure from England prompted Missionary John Elliot in the colony of Massachusetts to propose that Indians converted to Christianity should be taken from their villages and placed in reservations called *praying towns* (Spring, 2001). That same year, the Massachusetts General Court Declared that any "Christian or pagan [referring to Indians] . . . wittingly and willingly . . . deniing [*sic*] the true god, or his creation or government of the world . . . shalbe [*sic*] put to death" (cited in Spring, 2001). More than two centuries later, having inherited from the British empire the tasks of conquering and converting "Indians," the imperialist democracy of an emerging capitalism in the United States was enacting the Indian Removal Act of 1830 and forcibly removing "Indian" children from their families; the children were placed in boarding schools in an attempt to exterminate "Indian" culture, instill a capitalist ethos, and teach subservience to the U.S. government (Adams, 1995). At about the same time, landowners and government officials in the conquered territories of Texas and California debated the education of Mexicans: Whereas Anglo farmers wanted to keep Mexican children out of schools and ignorant to insure a steady supply of wage-labor, public officials wanted them in segregated schools so they could be "Americanized" (Spring, 2001). Those who survived and became sources of labor had to be schooled.

Gazing down the historical paths of conquest, colonization, and capitalist expansion, we recall that the corporal genocide that massacred the indigenous body was everywhere and always accompanied by a cultural holocaust that annihilated the indigenous mind. What the former accomplished by the swinging of the sword, the latter completed through the schooling of the subject. With the killing, conquest, and conversion came the hegemonic imposition of European worldviews, epistemological traditions, and systems of classification and representation (Deloria, 1997; Tuhiwai Smith 1999; Willinsky 1998), of what Foucault (1972) referred to as the "cultural archive" of the West. Looking at the present from the vantage point of the past, Tuhiwai Smith (1999) emphasizes that the cultural archive that served to train colonial elites and subdue indigenous peoples "has come to structure our own ways of knowing" (p. 59). From a similar positioning, Willinsky (1998) explains that the West's cultural archive was vastly expanded as bodies of knowledge and disciplines were born and developed at the service of imperialist expansion and colonial rule, and that given the enormity of imperialism's educational project (its production and imposition of knowledge) one can only expect that it lives on "as an unconscious aspect of our education" (p. 3). He insists that "we need to learn again how five centuries of studying, classifying, and ordering humanity within an imperial context gave rise to peculiar and powerful ideas of race, culture, and nation that were, in effect, conceptual instruments that the West used both to divide up and educate the world" (p. 2). Speaking specifically about the contemporary consequences of those conceptual instruments, Deloria (1997) explains that regardless of what indigenous peoples say about "their origins, their migrations, their experiences with birds, animals, lands, waters, mountains, and other people," Western science controls the definition of "respectable and reliable human experience" in a manner that allows it to reduce indigenous peoples to "a pre-human level of ignorance" and to reject their knowledges and worldviews as mere "superstition" (p. 7). A *decolonizing* critical remembrance commands that the cultural archive's complicity in the crimes of colonization is committed to memory, and that this memory is called to testify in an indictment against the contemporary inferiorization of the non-European mind in American schools and American imperialism's dealing with non-western countries throughout the world.

Many of the processes and practices of early colonial domination and capitalist exploitation have been altered, abandoned, or legally terminated, but essential features of that domination and exploitation continue to structure the economic, social, political, and cultural relations between differing groups in contemporary capitalist "America." What is more, in various ways the corporal genocide and cultural annihilation of indigenous and non-white peoples is far from over. Although the sounds of the dismantling of educational and linguistic rights implied by the aforementioned propositions loudly remind us of the ongoing annihilation, the sight and smell of rotting corpses force us to recognize the continuing genocide: On June 4, 2003, while reporting the gruesome find of three "illegal" immigrants who had suffocated to death in a Texas rail car, the *Los Angeles Times* (Gold & Kraul, 2003) informed that the number of people found dead from attempting to cross the U.S.-Mexico border during the year was already at 120; a 1999 study found that between 1993 and 1997 the number of possible undocumented migrant deaths on the U.S. side of the U.S.-Mexico Border was 1,034 (Eschbach, 1999). Brown bodies may be dying at the altars of Western Civilization's economic, political, and cultural arrangements in smaller proportions and from different causes than in past centuries, but they continue to be sacrificed nonetheless.

To understand the way things are, it is not only necessary to move firmly grounded in the present while gazing squarely toward the past, but to do so guided by a conceptual compass capable of mapping both the current social terrain and the ways in which the past advances through the concrete circumstances of what McLaren (1991) refers to as the "present era of unspeakable horrors and unnamable pleasures."

It is in the charting of the current social terrain and its educational contours that McLaren's work has been fundamentally important throughout the last two decades. For critical educational theorists and practitioners, McLaren's work has functioned as an analytical and interpretive compass for the contemporary neo-colonial and capitalist contexts of the United States: His committed and uncompromising critique has served like a lighthouse that signals a safe harbor through the dangerous seas of a conservative, corporate-serving educational policy and practice. His trenchant and timely theorization has functioned like a global positioning device that guides through critical social theories that must be explored in the search for an effective resistance to the right-wing stranglehold on U.S. schooling and the appropriate locations for a socially transformative pedagogy.

For those of us working toward a decolonizing pedagogy—scholar-educators who research and reflect as we theorize and teach in the interest of working-class and non-white peoples (Tejeda, in press), McLaren's conceptualizations and critiques have contributed to an understanding of the present that informs our gaze into the past. His discussions and dynamic applications of concepts like ideology, hegemony, discourse, cultural capital, and curriculum (1988, 1998, 1999) have helped us decipher the contemporary workings and effects of educational institutions, curricular contents, and pedagogical practices inherited from the past. Through his work we can seen how *schooling for subservience* perfected during centuries of imperialist expansion and colonial rule effectively functions at the service of today's social domination and economic exploitation, aiding and abetting in the national and international crimes of global capitalism (Allman, McLaren, and Rikowski, 2003; Barton, 2001).

McLaren's staunch critiques and strategic appropriations of postmodernist/poststructuralist theorizations have provided a window to the pitfalls and potentials of the modernist narratives and epistemologies filling the "cultural archive" of the Euro-imperial West and undergirding its current ideological impositions and educational endeavors (1995, 2000). His strategic use of postmodernism/poststructuralism to interrogate and reject notions of an omnipotent positivist science, a unified goal of history, and an autonomous free-thinking subject has offered decolonizing pedagogues access to *conceptual artifacts* (Cole, 1996) from the "the archive" that help deconstruct the culturally crushing façade of Western universality from within; what is more, this access has included a materialist argument that safeguards the use of conceptually double-edged artifacts from the transcendentalization of the linguistic sign and the privileging of the discursive and ideological over the materiality of social relations. Of particular importance to the decolonizing perspective has been that McLaren has employed postmodernist/poststructuralist notions to affirmingly acknowledge the differing localities, positionalities, and specificities of students' experience and knowledge (in terms of race, gender, sexuality, and class) while adhering to a notion of totality that allows for a nonreductive but fundamentally requisite acknowledgement of neo-colonial and capitalist formations that hegemonically structure domination and exploitation at national and international levels. Theorizing the existence of differing existentialities and epistemologies within the hegemonic coherency of larger sociopolitical formations is fundamental to the conception of a decolonizing praxis because it acknowledges the need for struggle from diverse locations and positions against the "totality" of a clearly identified capitalist and neo-colonial formation.

McLaren's theorizations of whiteness as a culture of terror (1993, 1995) and the body as a site of cultural inscription and ideological enfleshment (Cruz & McLaren 2002; McLaren, 1991, 1995) have helped articulate how racist, sexist, and homophobic texts from the past are torturously tattooed on contemporary bodies. In the colonial past, discourses of white supremacist, masculinist, and heteronormative domination were written from Enlightenment reason and religious self-righteousness, and then inscribed on bodies that were beaten, shot, stabbed, scalped, hanged, hacked apart, burned alive, trampled by horses, hunted as game, fed to dogs, infected with epidemic diseases, and starved to death (Churchill, 1997); in the internal neo-colonial present, discourses from the past are plagiarized by the rationality of representative democracy and the religious right wing, re-presented as commonsense legality and conventional morality, and then inscribed on bodies that are brutally beaten or shot dead by police, dragged to death by racists in pickup trucks, beaten and left to die hanging naked on fences by homophobes, branded as "illegal" by national laws, and intentionally made to die crossing imperialist borders. His theorizations of whiteness and culturally inscribed bodies have informed mappings of the spatialities of our present social and educational condition; they help articulate how institutionalized white supremacist discourses construct social spaces in ways that signify European-Americans (white bodies) as a normal and natural extension of national space—as privileged and entitled, while simultaneously signifying indigenous peoples (brown bodies) as alien and unnatural—as undeserving and un-entitled (Tejeda, 2000).

McLaren's call for a *critical multiculturalism* (1993, 1994, 1995) exposes the conceptual and political fraud of "liberal multiculturalisms" that claim to value and affirm diversity and difference while insidiously re-inscribing whiteness and Euro-supremacist narratives through curricular contents. From his critique of the liberal multiculturalism sold to unsuspecting teachers and students "of color" in contemporary schools, we see that the brutalizing benevolence of Bartolome de Las Casas and John Ellliot continues to undergird a *schooling for subservience.* "Culturally sensitive" and "inclusive" curriculums that supposedly soothe the self-esteem of ethnically unaffirmed students—"saving them" from an exile of ethnic festivals and foods—actually function to enforce a *difference of domination* (Tejeda, in press) in which indigenous and non-white people are insidiously inferiorized. We see also that a contemporary consequence of the corporal genocide and cultural annihilation of our colonial and capitalist anterior is that white people and white culture reign as a referential norm against which all other peoples and cultures are defined and assigned a value. More importantly, McLaren's critical multiculturalism insists that difference be understood in terms of asymmetrical relations of power in the larger social formation, that it be situated in real social and historical conflicts, and that it be about *material* relations and not merely a matter of signification. This is fundamentally important because our struggle for decolonization in the contemporary United States is not merely a quest to be represented as equal to whites; it is also and more fundamentally a struggle to dismantle the material foundations that sustain white domination and impose a hierarchy of value and virtue on bodies that pain, hunger, and die crossing borders. The struggle is not about a more equitable racial and ethnic participation in the existing formations of domination and exploitation; it is about a politics and praxis of anti-capitalist, anti-racist, anti-sexist, and anti-homophobic decolonization in the mutually constitutive terrains of material existence that are sowed by and sowing of subjects (Tejeda, Espinoza, & Gutierrez, 2002).

McLaren's recent re-affirmation of the fundamentality of Marxist theory (2001, 2002; Allman, McLaren, & Rikowski, in press) for critical educators insistently emphasizes a materialist conception that has run throughout his body of work and is shared by our decolonizing perspective. He argues that the analysis, interpretation, and struggle against contemporary domination and human misery must be focused on the materiality of everyday life. Although acknowledging the indispensability of analyses and struggles against the discourses and manifestations of racism, sexism, and homophobia and that "racism, sexism and class exploitation reciprocally shape each other," he insists that we not lose focus on the economic structure of society and that we keep "the materiality of human existence squarely in sight" (2001, pp. 705, 701). From the forward-looking, present-focused, and anterior gazing vantage of our decolonizing perspective (Tejeda, Espinoza, Gutierrez, 2002), the condition of our social existence in "American" society is a product of our most fundamental activity as living beings. We live an internal neo-colonial capitalism because we practice neo-colonial capitalist relations of domination and exploitation in the production and reproduction of our material existence and its cultural expressions. We make the history of our domination and exploitation through the practice and *activity systems* (Engeström & Miettinen, 1999) of our everyday lives. Our domination and exploitation do not reside exclusively in an ideological and discursive legacy, nor are these to be found only at the centers of power in "American" society; they reside and can be found in the everyday labor and mundane displacements of our bodies. Our neo-colonial domination and capitalist oppression materialize in the here and now of the material processes and practices of our everyday lives—especially those tied to securing the basic necessities of life. McLaren's re-affirmation of a Marxist materialism for critical educators is affirming and informing for decolonizing pedagogues because his redemptive remembrance of revolutionary theory points to a Marx who reminds us that only having secured "the production of material life itself" do men[/women] position themselves "to live in order to make history" (Marx & Engels, 1970, p. 48). He reminds us that "men[/women] make their own history," but also points out that "they do not make it just as they please; they do not make it under circumstances chosen by themselves, but under circumstances directly encountered, given, and transmitted from the past" (Marx & Engels, 1959, p. 320). Yes, the past that Marx describes as "weighing like a nightmare on the brain [and the bodies] of the living" (p. 320) is far from over for those of us sleeping and waking in the internal neo-colonial and capitalist spaces of the "American dream."

Indeed, from a decolonizing pedagogical perspective, little could be more praising of McLaren's work than to speak of its contribution from the redemptive remembrance of a decolonizing perspective that has argued:

> We also understand that we do not simply choose to engage in processes and practices that make and remake the internal colonialism we experience. We labor and relate to others in the production and reproduction of our social existence with the weight of a colonial and imperialist past squarely on our backs. It is within the circumstances inherited from that past that we reproduce the condition of our social existence and make our history. We are not, however, condemned to continue making and remaking the condition of our existence according to the circumstances imposed by our past. Those circumstances can be changed instead of merely reproduced and made anew. We understand that the very practice that makes possible our existence and characterizes its condition also holds the potential to radically transform them (Tejeda, Espinoza, & Gutierrez, 2002, p. 22)

The pieces in this volume, co-authored with former and current graduate students, are a testament to McLaren's continued commitment to a radical transformation of the social formations inherited from the past. They form a recent part of an impressive body of scholarship that has greatly influenced critical scholars and pedagogues in the notoriously conservative field of education throughout the last two decades. The co-authorship of these pieces represents part of an ongoing struggle for spaces of hope and critique and a commitment to critical scholarship in graduate schools of education.

REFERENCES

Allman, P., McLaren, P., & Rikowski, G. (2003). After the box people: The labor-capital relation as class constitution—and its consequences for Marxist educational theory and human resistance. In S. Allen, J. Freeman-Moir, & A. Scott (Eds.), *Yesterday's dreams: International and critical perspectives on education and social class*. New Zealand: Canterbury University Press.

Adams, D. (1995). *Education for extinction: American Indians and the boarding school experience, 1875-1928*. Lawrence: University Press of Kansas.

Barton, A. C. (2001). Capitalism, critical pedagogy, and urban science education: An interview with Peter McLaren. *Journal of Research in Science Teaching, 38*(8), 847-859.

Brown, D. (1981). *Bury my heart at Wounded Knee: An Indian history of the American West.* New York: Washington Square Press.

Churchill, W. (1997). *A little matter of genocide: Holocaust denial in the Americas 1492 to the present.* San Francisco: City Lights Books.

Cruz, C., & McLaren, P. (2002). Queer bodies and configurations: Towards a critical pedagogy of the body. In S. Shapiro & S. Shapiro (Eds.), *Body works: Pedagogy, politics, and social change* (pp. 187-207). Cresskill, NJ: Hampton Press.

Deloria, V., & Lytle, C.M. (1983). *American Indians, American justice.* Austin: University of Texas Press.

Engeström, Y., & Miettinen, R. (1999). Introduction. In Y. Engeström, R. Miettinen & R. Punamäki (Eds.), *Perspectives on activity theory* (pp. 1-16). New York: Cambridge University Press.

Eschbach, K. (1999). Death at the border. *International Migration Review, 33*(2).

Foucault, M. (1972). *The archeology of knowledge.* New York: Pantheon.

Gold, S, & Kraul, C. (2003, June 4). 3 bodies found in Texas rail car. *Los Angeles Times,* p. A.13.

Gutierrez, K., Asato, J., Santos, M., & Gotanda, N. (2002). Backlash pedagogy: Language and culture and the politics of reform. *The Review of Education, Pedagogy, and Cultural Studies, 24*(4), 335-351.

Hanke, L. (1974). *All mankind is one: A study of the disputation between Bartolomé de Las Casa and Juan Ginés de Sepúlveda in 1550 on the intellectual and religious capacity of the American Indians.* DeKalb: Northern Illinois University Press.

Horseman, R. (1997). Race and manifest destiny: The origins of American racial Anglo-Saxonism. In R. Delgado & J. Stefancic (Eds.), *Critical white studies: Looking behind the mirror* (pp. 139-144). Philadelphia: Temple University Press.

Marx, K., & Engels, F. (1959). *Marx and Engels: The basic writings on politics and philosophy* (L.S. Feuer, ed.). New York: Anchor Books.

Marx, K., & Engels, F. (1970). *The German ideology* (C.J. Arthur, ed.). New York: International Publishers.

McLaren, P. (1988). On ideology and education: Critical pedagogy and the politics of education. *Social Text, 19/20,* 153-185.

McLaren, P. (1991). Postmodernism, postcolonialism, and pedagogy. *Education and Society, 9*(1), 3-22.

McLaren, P. (1993). White terror and oppositional agency: Towards a critical multiculturalism. *Strategies, 7,* 98-131.

McLaren, P. (1994). Multiculturalism and the postmodern critique: Toward a pedagogy of resistance and transformation. In H. Giroux & P. McLaren (Eds.), *Between borders: Pedagogy and the politics of cultural studies* (pp. 192-222). New York: Routledge.

McLaren, P. (1995). *Critical pedagogy and predatory culture: Oppositional politics in a postmodern era.* New York: Routledge.

McLaren, P. (1998). *Life in schools: An introduction to critical pedagogy in the foundations of education* (3rd ed.). New York: Longman.

McLaren, P. (1999). *Schooling as a ritual performance: Toward a political economy of educational symbols and gestures* (3rd ed.). Lanham, MD: Rowman and Littlefield.

McLaren, P. (2001). Bricklayers and bricoleurs: A Marxist addendum. *Qualitative Inquiry*, December, 700-705.

McLaren, P., & Farahmandpur, R. (2000). Reconsidering Marx in post-Marxist times: A requiem for postmodernism? *Educational Researcher, 29*(3), 25-33.

Seed, P. (2001). *American pentimiento: The invention of Indians and the pursuit of riches*. Minneapolis: University of Minnesota Press.

Spring, J. (2001). *Deculturalization and the struggle for equality: A brief history of dominated cultures in the United States* (3rd ed.). San Francisco: McGraw Hill.

Tejeda, C. (2000). Spatialized understandings of the Chicana(o)/Latina(o) educational experience: Theorizations of space and the mapping of educational outcomes in Los Angeles. In C. Tejeda, C. Martinez, & Z. Leonardo (Eds.), *Charting new terrains of Chicana(o)/Latina(o) education* (pp. 131-159). Cresskill, NJ: Hampton Press.

Tejeda, C. (in press). Decolonizing pedagogy and critical multiculturalism in the classroom: Reading the word and the world of American schooling with teacher candidates. *Multicultural Education*.

Tejeda, C., Espinoza, M., & Gutierrez, K. (2003). Toward a decolonizing pedagogy: Social justice reconsidered. In P. Trifonas (Ed.), *Pedagogy of difference*. New York: Routledge.

Williams, R. A. (1995). Documents of barbarism: The contemporary legacy of European racism and colonialism in the narrative traditions of federal Indian Law. In R. Delgado (Ed.), *Critical race theory: The cutting edge* (pp. 98-109). Philadelphia: Temple University Press.

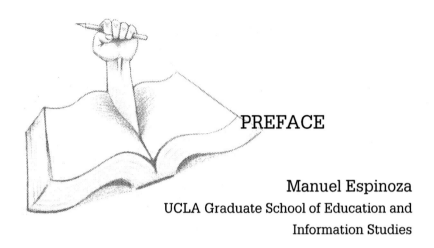

PREFACE

Manuel Espinoza
UCLA Graduate School of Education and
Information Studies

It is often said that men and women do not live by bread alone. We can easily and unproblematically conclude that the person uttering this pop psalm is probably speaking on a full stomach. However, if there is a sliver of truth in this commonsense truism then we might ask what else besides food, oxygen, shelter, and water might a person need in order to live a "human" existence. Specifically as it relates to this context, we could ask the following:

Why *Red Seminars*? Why now?

One of the many tasks before us is determining how *Red Seminars*, or any other liberation project, feeds us in ways that help develop a critical understanding of the historical and economic conditions undergirding the apparently natural pursuit of our daily bread.

Oftentimes, the most crucial questions in our lives are the questions we do not ask. How many times have we been moments away from giving life to a question that would press against the root nerve of our conception of reality and ended up chasing it back down our gut? Speaking personally, too many times to stomach. But perhaps it is for our own good. Those types of questions make it difficult to comfortably deceive ourselves about the kind of world we inhabit and sustain. Those types of questions are dangerous because, if cultivated, they can expand into emancipatory political imperatives.

At some point in our lives, nearly all of us have purposely not asked a question out of fear of reprisal from some authority or simply the desire not to disturb our placid existence. However, there is a danger in using this simple assertion as an explanatory principle for political apathy in our society. Hidden within this negative assertion is a positive logic that would allow one to easily infer that those who do ask those potentially life-altering questions are simply courageous and heroic persons.

Where does that explanation leave the rest of us? We who are far from cowards but have acted cowardly in certain contexts. Perhaps the reasons underlying a non-question are not so ignoble; not every failure to ask an ethically demanding question is a moral collapse. Let me clarify by saying that I do not mean that something like "courage" is unnecessary when asking a question that might rattle existing conceptions of the truth. To borrow from Black liberation theology, in those key moments of conflict we need something to help us cut loose our stammering tongues. What I am saying is that the trope of the heroic individual can only explain so much and that the shadow it casts on the social world is greater than the reality it illuminates. What is obscured is how the individual capability to ask a living, ticking question is a thoroughly social product. In other words, it is more productive to speak of the question-asking practices of political communities. Before doing so let me direct a few words as to the anatomy of the weighty questions I have been speaking of.

There are some questions that knock at our door, sometimes unexpectedly, sometimes at our behest, and beseech us to feed them practical solutions. Provisionally, we can describe them as insurgent operative questions, political queries that are meant to do something. Insurgent because they potentially help us forge long-term political objects, initiate new phases of political thought, activate subjects, and obligate us to work to create qualitatively more humane social relationships. Operative because we use them as a guide for other types of social action. Insurgent operative questions are real insofar as they are used in praxiological activity.

Why don't more people ask insurgent operative questions? A hunch may lead us closer to the cognitive, emotional, and social epicenter of the practice of non-asking. In the most personal aspect, perhaps we are afraid or, even worse, convinced that no one will listen. I think it is here, in the scary silence of non-solidarity that a fuller explanation can be constructed.

The right to ask "deep" questions is not the sole possession of academics. The humblest human beings also ask significant existential and philosophical questions. My *jefita*, Maria Guadalupe Espinoza, works as a janitor cleaning office buildings at night. On a few occasions she has related to me that she thinks about the suffering in the world as she performs her nightly duty of vacuuming the area of half a city block. What my *jefita* and millions of others do not have is an avenue to a stout network of people who are able to work toward creating practical responses to existential and metaphysical inquiries. Insurgent operative questioning practices cannot be done in private; they are exclusively social endeavors.

People need workspaces, where they can hoist and tinker around with questions, hunches, and problems that matter to them. This leads us back to . . .

Why *Red Seminars*? Why now?

The push of a button and the click of a mouse can catapult us into communication with people across the globe. In Los Angeles, it can even hurl us into contact with someone on the other side of the city. Yet, communications technology, in itself, does not guarantee that humans will engage in critical inquiry. It is the human relations, the communities we form, the social action we take, mediated by technology that laughs at time and space, which brings into existence the social practice of shaping the future.

At its best, *Red Seminars* can be a space wherein people can place their own questions-in-formation on a mental clipboard and think about how they can go about making it a social question. In our society, chatter is on the PA system while insurgent questions play on solitary fragmented iPods. Let us not forget that iPods have the potential to network.

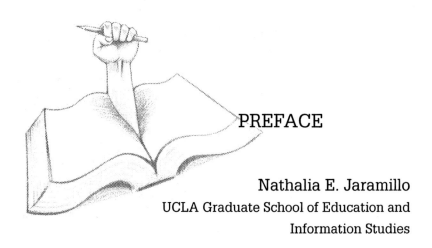

PREFACE

Nathalia E. Jaramillo
UCLA Graduate School of Education and
Information Studies

The collection of essays that make up *Red Seminars* represents important digressions from the standard and standardized political preoccupations of educational theory, politics, and pedagogy. The essays are "radical" in the manner that they compel their audience to critically reflect upon the current historical moment and upon the various manifestations of injustice that tarnish our inner desire and relentless will for a democratic and more humane society. Forging necessary liaisons between the social institution of education and broader economic, political, social, and cultural formations, these works are part of a multifarious and expansive terrain that has been termed critical pedagogy. *Red Seminars* encompasses a myriad of voices—from *compañeras* and *compañeros*—that will influence and inform the ways in which the public-at-large speaks to or remains silent toward education, its attendant social structures, and the pedagogical spaces that question and seek to transform the production of knowledge.

But perhaps most importantly, *Red Seminars* is a reminder of the work that remains ahead of us as we stand witness to an era marked by furious attempts to control and survey the public sphere, by citizenship characterized by unwavering consumerism over critical democracy, by the abject criminalization of poor women and men of color, and by a hyper-masculine project of perpetual warfare and empire-building.

As critical educators we are confronting a timely moment. Whereas decades past have declared the "end of history" (following Francis Fukuyama), the "end of racism," and the "end of feminism," a brief look into the current historical juncture provides us with clear evidence that nothing has truly "ended." Rather, there is a greater need to examine and produce scholarship allied with ongoing social relations in ways that expose the underlying contradictions and subtleties associated with projects of "liberation" and programs of "social justice." Critical pedagogy must continue to move in dynamic directions that reject *en toto* "end-all" claims within the prevailing system of capitalist accumulation and exploitation. It must continue to probe and dispel beliefs and myths associated with the free trade gospel of neoliberal ideology, and it needs to commit itself to a project of humanizing gendered relations that redefine our notions of womanhood and manhood.

The 2004 recipient of the Sydney Peace Prize, Arundhati Roy, emphatically noted in her acceptance speech that "a political struggle that does not have women at the heart of it, above it, below it and within it is no struggle at all." Feminist theorizing in critical pedagogy is functionally imperative to a project that seeks to unearth relations of oppression and to establish transformative projects toward human liberation. This does not mean that all other constructs fall by the wayside to create room for feminist theory, but rather, that the experiences of women are understood and examined from their historically and materially specific standpoints. Languages of critique must be accompanied by an analysis of women's lives in the wider political and cultural sphere. A distinct focus on women's position within the economic structure, and an analysis of the ways that gender is constructed, brings to light the otherwise occluded nature of a patriarchal capitalist system of exploitation and subordination.

Red Seminars merges voices from both women and men and grapples with topics (of sexuality and of culture) in ways that rupture static generational modes of thought. It is a contribution to an existing tradition, but it also generates and points toward new ways of thinking about education and the political sphere without falling prey to presenting social phenomena according to their "proper niches." It compels us to imagine, as Angela Davis once noted, "a more humane future—a future of justice, equality and peace" that can eventually be realized by actively engaging, naming, and fusing the abstract with the concrete in a global, multiracial, gender-balanced and humanizing pedagogical project.

Davis, A. (1990). *Women, Culture, and Politics*. New York: Vintage House.

Roy, A., (2004). Peace and the New Corporate Liberation Theology. Sydney Peace Prize Lecture. (November). Found at: http://sydney.indymedia.org

PART 1

POLICY, POLITICS
AND PRAXIS
IN CRITICAL PEDAGOGY

1

MARX AFTER POST-MARXISM RECLAIMING CRITICAL PEDAGOGY FOR THE LEFT

Peter McLaren and Ramin Farahmandpur

Capital is dead labor which, vampire-like, lives only by sucking living labor, and lives the more, the more labor it sucks.
—Karl Marx

It takes courage and faith to fight the System, that and a dedication to something bigger than one's own self-interest. It is perhaps the quality which the bankerist Overworlders must find it hardest to assess and contain. They start with the premise that every man has his price, and have no difficulty in commanding the allegiance of the selfish and unprincipled on that basis. Satan has his high places, from which to show his prospective adherents all that will be theirs. But men and women of faith are not so easily tempted, and may in fact be somewhat harder to frighten. It has in fact been observed about the god-fearing that, fearing God, they sometimes fear nothing else.
—James Gibb Stuart

THE FIN-DE-SIÉCLE MILLENNIUM AND THE VERTIGO OF GLOBAL CAPITALISM

Regardless of where we position ourselves at the crossroads of history, our location is always precarious and risky. Though we are tempted always to look beyond the agony of the present moment into the sublime abyss of the unknown, we cannot avoid encountering the violent clash between labor and capital. We are at a peculiar juncture in human history that tantalizes us with the promise of redemption and liberation while delivering on its threat of corruption

This chapter originally appeared in *Working Papers in Cultural Studies* No. 25, Department of Comparative American Cultures, Washington State University, Pullman, WA. © 2001 Peter McLaren and Ramin Farahmandpur.

and despair. We are suspended precariously between the revolution and counter-revolution of which Rosa Luxemburg so forcefully referred to as a choice between socialism or barbarism.

We face the future much like the observers of *The Ambassadors*, a masterpiece painted by Hans Hoblein the Younger in 1533 that now hangs in London's British Museum. Below the figures of two ambassadors is a large skull that appears drastically out of proportion when viewed head-on. The distortion corrects itself, however, when viewed at a sharp angle from below the bottom right hand side of the painting. The painting was meant to be viewed from below, possibly as one walked up the stairs to one's bedroom to pray before sleeping. Presumably, the observer would be reminded of one's mortality. The lesson for us voyagers in the new millennium is that we need to position ourselves from below, from the perspective of the suffering masses, in order to see what is happening in the capitalist world system, and how mortality is something that the masses confront on a daily basis, and not because they can afford to commission a painting much less own a house in which to hang it.

Marx's description of capitalism as the sorcerer's dark power that has now become uncontrollable is even more apt today than it was in Marx's time, despite the fact that Marxism has been relegated by the postmodernists to the Icarian status of failed aspirations. No other individual has been able to analyze the Frankensteinian dimensions of capital accumulation with the same intensity and foresight as Marx, who wrote: "If money . . .'comes into the world with a congenital blood-stain on one cheek,' capital comes dripping from head to foot, from every pore, with blood and dirt" (1959, p. 760). Never before has a Marxian analysis of capitalism been so desperately needed than at this particular juncture in history, especially since the global push towards finance and speculative capital. It is becoming increasingly clearer that the quality of life in capitalist nations such as the United States is implicated in the absence of freedom in less developed countries. Global carpetbaggers and "bankerist Overworlders" profiteering from human suffering and bargain basement capitalists with a vision of transforming the environment into Planet Mall are bent upon reaping short-term profits at the expense of ecological health and human dignity and drawing ever more of existence within their expanding domain, cannibalizing life as a whole. On the soil of our former Cold War opponent, a clique of wealthy Russian oligarchs now follow the Western path to redemption, pillaging existing state property—the refineries, steel mills, smelters, pipelines, mineral deposits and factories (Krehm, 2000). The state picks up the bill, while the former proletariats surf the black market for rent money. The World Bank call its "tough love."

James Gibb Stuart notes that "[g]reed has become the seed corn of free-market capitalism" (2000, p. 7) in a period marked by the intensification of class polarization and the upward redistribution of wealth. Capitalism, according to Terry Eagleton, has a "built-in dynamic to universalize itself" and "is bound to ensnare itself in its own strength, since the more it proliferates, the more fronts it breeds on which it can become vulnerable" (1999, p. 37). Marx's prophetic warning against capitalism is no less true for those of us who work in schools of education, where the logic of privatization abounds and where postmodernism has more than encroached on leftist educational discourse; it has taken up permanent residence.

The treacly term "neoliberalism" hides its more invidious characteristics. Neoliberalism ("capitalism with the gloves off" or "socialism for the rich") refers to a corporate domination of society that supports state enforcement of the unregulated market, engages in the oppression of nonmarket forces and anti-market policies, guts free public services, eliminates social subsidies, offers limitless concessions to transnational corporations, enthrones a neomercantilist public policy agenda, establishes the market as the patron of educational reform, and permits private interests to control most of social life in the pursuit of profits for the few (i.e., through lowering taxes on the wealthy, scrapping environmental regulations, and dismantling public education and social welfare programs). It is undeniably one of the most dangerous politics that we face today. As described by Robert McChesney, neoliberalism is "the immediate and foremost enemy of genuine participatory democracy, not just in the United States but across the planet, and will be for the foreseeable future" (1999, p. 11). John McMurtry avers, noting that the restructuring of the United States economy constitutes the "revenge of the rich against those who advocate a more democratic and egalitarian social order" (2000, p. 10). So much has been made of the wonders of the U.S. economic model, yet its so-called success can be measured in its complete rejection of social and environmental capital for the short-term gains of investors and consumers. As McMurtry remarks:

> Cheaper goods and costs come by the loss of tens of millions of secure domestic jobs. Real lower taxes for upper income brackets are achieved by stripping social assistance programs for the poor and unemployed. Equity values are increased by non-productive mergers, laundered drug billions, internet stocks with no earnings, and leveraged debt and asset-flip money. Low unemployment figures are achieved by massive increases in part-time and starvation-wage jobs and a staggering 2,000,000 citizens in prison off the employment rolls (over 12 times the number of US citizens caged as in 1968, and about six times the Western European rate). The new regime rules the globe behind bars of money and iron. (2000, p. 10)

That Marxism appears to have lost its epochal footing and does not yet enjoy a new refunctioned status as the official opponent of neoliberalism and the downsizing of democracy does not mean that educators should remain inactive until history is suddenly served by a wake up call that will make Marxism relevant again. History has already been punched in the solar plexus by the current crisis of capitalism and educators are not taking this warning sitting down. It remains for them to decide how they are going to exercise their political agency. The globalization of capital has occasioned what Mészáros (1999) describes as the "downward equalization of the differential rate of exploitation" where workers all over the world—including those in advanced capitalist countries such as the United States—are facing a steady deterioration of working conditions due to the structural crisis of the capitalist system, a crisis of fast-track, push cart capitalism of the "grab-the-profits-and-run" variety.

Yet at the same time, capitalism has never been so blindly infatuated with its own myth of success. Corporate leaders in the United States and dominant media have inured us into accepting the capitalist marketplace as the only possible social reality. Walter Mosley puts it thus: "The juggernaut of capitalism, having broken the bonds of its imprisonment—national borders—exacts its toll in an equal opportunity manner. It is the nature of capitalism to apply its value system to everything" (2000, p. 11). David McNally writes: "Having vanquished all challengers, having apparently tamed labor, anti-imperialist, and radical social movements, [capitalism] can now calmly go about the business of making us all rich" (1999, p. 134). McNally traces the current capitalist triumphalism to the anti-historical character of bourgeois ideology. He also notes that contemporary pro-capitalist ideology "betrays a remarkable amnesia about capitalism itself: it forgets its bloody past, its recurrent crises; it denies everything that hints at the historically specific limits of the capitalist mode of production" (1999, p. 135). To wit, it naturalizes the exploitation of the world's poor and powerless, reducing workers to the market price of their sweat and blood.

Due to the fast-paced and frenetic changes taking place around us in the wired realms of global technologies and free trade initiatives, we are hard pressed to chart out the vast reach of our daily struggles against oppression and exploitation. As we attempt to flee a psycho-pathological culture of endless acquisition, we find ourselves at the mercy of an even more terrifying corporate culture shaping our subjectivities. We worship at the altar of the Lords of Finance Capital and Transnational Commerce who have been ordained as the world's new global caretakers. Corporate leaders have become the doyens of advanced citizenship, transformed into public icons who rival the status held by athletes and film stars. Bill Gates now masquerades as Dickens' spiritually redeemed Ebenezer Scrooge, offering a gift of one billion dollars worth of scholarship funds to economically disfranchised students of color in the role of Tiny Tim. Education has become reduced to a sub-sector of the economy.

The 1980s and 1990s witnessed the growing economic and political power and influence of corporations. Corporate discourse has increasingly converged with the family values and ideology of the Christian Right (represented by organizations such as Jerry Falwell's Moral Majority and Pat Robertson's Christian Coalition). The Christian Right has openly declared war on the working-class by supporting anti-abortion legislature, school prayer, favorable tax cuts for the rich, privatization of social security, welfare reform, and minimizing government intervention in the free market. It has provided the necessary framework for the alignment of moral and ethical issues with neo-liberal social and economic policies, and has succeeded in decapitating the struggle for economic equality from its moral and ethical foundation (Zweig, 2000).

Immovably entrenched social, political, and economic disparities and antagonisms compel us as educators and cultural workers to create alternatives to the logic of capitalist accumulation. We are struggling and suffering (some of us more than others) through a time when there exists an inordinate and frightening corporate control over job growth and job loss in a capitalist system whose inequalities are becoming more glaringly evident that ever before.

THE CRISIS OF GLOBAL CAPITALISM

In the wake of its triumphant victory over socialism, global capitalism has successfully integrated all types of differences within its borders. The term "liberal democracy" is, for the most part, an oxymoron. Although liberalism lived up to its name by expanding the welfare state after the Second World War, it nevertheless has become more intimately associated with capitalism than with democracy's rule of the majority. Especially over the last several decades, liberal democracy has failed to adequately address the democratic citizenship of marginalized groups, since it has consistently failed to recognize that social inequality is embedded within capitalist property relations (Kelly, 2000).

Neo-liberal free market economics—the purpose of which is to avoid stasis and keep everyone in healthy flux—has become the desideratum of the new corporate barons and continues to advance across the current stage of history, proudly unfurling its laundry list of achievements as the Magna Carta of the New World Order: deregulation, unrestricted access to consumer markets, downsizing, outsourcing, flexible arrangements of labor, intensification of competition among transnational corporations, an increasing centralization of economic and political power, and finally, widening class polarization. The opening of the third millennium represents at once the incalculably expanded scope of the culture of consumption and the implosion of social relations into a universal signifier—namely capital—which Marx metaphorically referred to as the "universal pimp."

For those who believe that the economy is self-regulated by Hayekian archangels who mysteriously ensure that the feedback mechanisms of the unfettered "free" market are "fair," that only democracy will spring forth from its famously spontaneous order, and that the common good will magically advance from its networked complexity, there is reason to be wildly optimistic about the future. But for those, like us, who refuse to fetishize the social system under capitalism as a self-organizing totality, the future appears perilous indeed. We refuse to treat the economy as a thing and endow it with democratic agency. After Marx, we view the economy as a social relation and not a natural entity. Capitalism is not a natural, self-regulating system but rather one overburdened by exploitation, the quest for endless accumulation, and class conflict.

Capital is a social relation; a value relation, in which the source of value is labor and the substance of value is abstract labor. Capital is alienated labor, which manifests itself as exchange value and surplus value (Hudis, 2000). It regenerates by extracting surplus value from the exploitation of workers. the objective of capital is not the accumulation of wealth, but to have commend over objectified labor. Peter Hudis raises an important question which merits attention: Can capital be controlled? In response, he argues that capital does not come with a human face. It cannot be tamed or restrained. Consequently, it must be completely abolished.

THE CHARGE OF THE LITE BRIGADE

Radical theorists such as Paulo Freire and Antonio Gramsci have been disinterred from Marxist soil where they first drew breath, and their graves now sprout the saplings of postmodern theory. It is all part of the postmodernization of the Left and its accompanying retreat from class struggle and latent support of laissez-faire evangelism. this is not to say that postmodernism has been a complete disaster. Far from it. Even in its nascent stage, postmodern theory has made a significant contribution in helping educators grasp the politics that underwrite popular cultural formations, mass media apparatuses, the technological revolution's involvement in the global restructuring of capitalism, the ideological machinations of the new capitalism from Schumpeter to Keynes, and the reconceptualization of schooling practices in the interest of making them more related to (racial, gender, sexual, and national) identity formation within postcolonial geopolitical and cultural spaces. However, its ability to advance (let alone sustain) a critique of global capitalism, corporate anorexia (downsizing and outsourcing), and the contemporary reign of money has been severely compromised. Too eager to take a wide detour around political economy, postmodern educators have been hampered by a number of factors: (a) by their tacit—and often overt—acceptance of a market economy; (b) their joining in the chorus of post-Marxists celebrating the death of universalism and grand narratives; (c) their impatience to strike a novel posture in the theater of educational transgression; (d) their predilection for allowing their politics to be distracted by their postcolonial cultural performances of dissent; and (e) by their failure to recognize that, in the words of Robin D. G. Kelley, "We are hardly in a 'postcolonial' moment. The official apparatus might have been removed, but the political, economic, and cultural links established by colonial domination still remain with some alterations" (1999, p. 18). Teresa Ebert goes so far as to argue that within postmodern theory, the "assumption of the deimperialism of the center is an act of concealed imperialism" (1996, p. 285).

Although postmodern "masters of suspicion" have managed to deftly map the semiotic fault lines of the contemporary *fracture social*, have uncovered the necessity hidden under the appearance of contingency, have challenged stable genres of discourse, have ruptured the Eleatic cohesiveness of master narratives, have transgressed hidebound and sacred binarisms and rent them apart, and have brazenly and percipiently challenged the right-wing philippics of William Bennett-style cultural brokers, they have failed in the main to challenge in any deep or sustained way the engineered misery of neoliberal fiscal regimes and—more importantly—capitalist relations of exploitation. Consequently, the postmodern Left remains hostage to its own strategic ambivalence about capital. Not only have postmodern theorists been woefully remiss in explaining how cultural representations and formations are indentured to capitalism, they have often confused socialism with, at worse, the history of Stalinism, and, at best, the welfare state reformism often associated with Scandinavian countries such as Denmark and Sweden. As James O'Connor notes:

> The theory of capital accumulation and crisis, pioneered by Marx and fine-tuned by three or four generations of Marxist economists, is the baby thrown out with the dirty bath water of totalitarian socialism. Just at the moment that capital triumphs globally, the greatest theorist of capital is relegated to the status of a wrongheaded 19th-century ideologue. . . . This irony, or anomaly, is so pervasive today that we are forced to turn one of Hegel's most famous lines on its head. The great dialectician wrote that "the owl of Minerva spreads its wings only at dusk," meaning that only after a particular historical event or change is it possible for reason to apprehend what has happened and why. (1998, p. 281)

Mocked as a "modernist" form of outmoded phallomilitary and "totalizing" demagoguery, Marxism is now relegated to history's cabinet of lost revolutionary dreams where it is abandoned to those romantic images of guerrillas of the Sierra Maestra. While elegiac hymns to Che Guevara still abound in the courtyards of the diminishing Left, this should not detract from the fact that, when read sharply against Guevarian challenges to imperialism and Marxist challenges to social relations of production and global regimes of capitalist exploitation, postmodernist theory frequently collapses into a form of toothless liberalism and airbrushed insurgency.

While to its considerable credit, postmodern theory—especially through the insights of its pantheon of progenitors such as Nietzsche, Toynbee, Heidegger, C. Wright Mills, Horkheimer, and Adorno—has troubled the primary status of the colonizer, peeled back the horizon of culture to reveal the trace marks of the antipodal, broken the semiotic gridlock of reigning binarisms, prevented the authoritative closure that serves to re-enlist alterity into the ranks of Western imperialism, and revealed how temporal structures of dislocation constitute rather than describe our geographies of identity. It has often reconfirmed as much as contested capitalist relations of exploitation. Although it is important to follow postmodernists in introducing subaltern readers of texts, such texts need to be acknowledged as speaking through the ventriloquism of Western epistemologies linked to imperialist and capitalist social relations. Progressive educators need to ask: How does the semiotic warfare of the postmodern or postcolonial critic reinscribe, repropose, and recohere capitalist social relations of production through decentering and rerouting cultural representations? This is a central question that postmodernists routinely sidestep and to do so at this current historical conjuncture of titanic capitalist forces is, to say the least, perilous. As the dust finally settles we are troubled by the fact that much of what is called postmodern education is freighted with insoluble contradictions that unwittingly push radical critique towards the center.[1]

Capitalism and democracy share a forced intimacy; their marriage has been arranged so that the families of the global ruling class can consolidate their power and set limits on how and what questions concerning equality and emancipation can be raised and in what contexts. The preservation of capital remains entombed within postmodernism's own ineffable logic and "conceals the true contradictions of advanced capitalist societies" (Larrain, 1995, p. 288). This remains the case even though some postmodernists like to imbibe the miasmically iconoclastic aura of Marx without, we might add, necessarily engaging in radical (let along revolutionary) politics. As postmodernists look amusingly as what Charlie Bertsch and Joe Lockard (1999) call "the widely successful repackaging of *The Communist Manifesto* as a pricey fetish object for the upwardly mobile," they can play out their cathartic fantasies of the *guerrillero/a* while continuing to trash the politics that underlies revolutionary praxis.

In many instances, postmodernists have dismissed Marxism as a form of ideological Neanderthalism, or a crusted-over antediluvian memory, and have tried to disabuse progressive educators and other cultural workers of the notion that there are practical and workable alternatives to capitalism worth considering. In their less generous moments they recycle Marxist theory as contemporary farce. We don't want to deny the crimes against humanity committed by regimes claiming to be the heirs of Marx, to ignore the problems associated with Eastern and European Communist parties in the unregenerate Stalinist aspects, or to defend what in certain cases could be called Marxism's recidivistic retreat into bureaucratic authoritarianism, dogmatism, and economic determinism. Nor do we wish to defend what Eagleton calls "the long tragedy of class-society" (1999, p. 35), corporate governance, the ill-gotten gains of financial profiteers and speculators, and the history of imperialism and international terrorism committed by Western "democracies." On the other hand, we don't believe that Marxism should be dismissed because it appears to have reached its apex in the decades before the collapse of the Soviet Union and the appearance of Russia's new gangster capitalism, red bourgeoisie, and forms of primitive accumulation. We admit that Marxist theory may be out of fashion but it has not run out of conceptual fuel for providing the kind of analysis urgently needed at this point in the history of capitalism. Although marked by a depleted vitality in educational research and criticism, Marxist theory is not yet sounding its death rattle. In fact, it appears to be making a comeback, as it is increasingly summoned to the service of the political present. We are confident that Marxist analysis will have a roborant effect on critical pedagogy.

THE POSTMODERN PROMISE

Postmodernism has done more than ensorcell the art of students; it has made impressive advances in helping educators map the hidden trajectories of power within the processes of representation (especially the political optics of mass media), enabling teachers as cultural workers to strip back the epistemological scaffolding that props up essentialist claims to authenticity and to peel away layers of ideological mystification that shroud the assertion of truth and validity made by positivists within the empirical sciences. Postmodern theory's articulations of the epistemic subject have been, for the most part, invigorating and innovatory. In this regard, postmodernism has offered up a veritable cornucopia of research tools for the analysis of identity and has helped uncover ways in which universal narratives are based on masculinist and heteronormative practices of exclusion.

Despite its successes, postmodern dissent is symptomatic of the structural contradictions and problematic assumptions within postmodern theory itself. By too often displacing critique to a field of serial negation without fully grasping its prefigurative or emancipatory potential, postmodern criticism frequently traps intelligibility and meaning internally, that is, inside the texts of culture. In revealing the inconsistencies, aporias, and contradictions within the texts of culture, postmodernism often fails to connect the significance of these contradictions, inconsistencies, and equivocations by comprehending their necessity. As a consequence, it often blunts an understanding of contemporary society and unwittingly agitates for a reenactment of the fate of society that constitutes the object of its critique. This line of fracture is emblematic of the problem that has plagued the postmodern Left over the last several decades. At this moment we are compelled to ask: Is the practice of ignoring these contradictions and inconsistencies of culture structurally advantageous to capitalist relations of exploitation? Do such contradictions left conspicuously unaddressed merely—or mainly—provide ballast to reigning hegemons and the international division of labor? Postmodernists appear loathe to raise such questions yet continue unrepentantly to dismiss an analysis of the so-called economic "base" in favor of the cultural "superstructure." While postmodernists encourage an examination of the cultural discourses of capitalism as open-ended sites of desire, Marxists, by contrast, treat discourses not as sanctuaries of difference barricaded against the forces of history but as always an interpretation naturalized by the libidinal circuits of desire wired into the culture of commerce and historically and socially produced within the crucible of class antagonisms. Marxist criticism uncoils the political economy of texts by remapping and rethinking systems of signification in relation to the material and historical practices that produce them (McLaren, 2000), thus valorizing the "structural endurance of histories" over the "contingent moment" (Ahmad, 1995, p. 15). In doing so it examines not the present's lack of coincidence with itself, or its lack of self-identity, but rather its ability to surpass its own limitations.

The shift towards a postmodernism[2] layered with a thin veneer of cultural Marxism, scaffolded by identity politics and postsocialist ideology, sprayed by aerosol terms such as "difference" and "indeterminancy," and dipped in the gurgling foam of jacuzzi socialism and window-dressing democracy, has witnessed the categories of cultural domination and oppression replace those of class exploitation and imperialism as capitalism's reigning antagonisms. At the same time, a politics of representation has deftly outflanked the issue of socioeconomic redistribution (Fraser, 1997). The postmodernist and postsocialist assumption that culture has suddenly found ways of winning independence from economic forces and that somehow the new globalized capitalism has decapitated culture from the body of class exploitation by constructing new desires and remaking old ones in ways that are currently unmappable and unfactorable within the theoretical optics of political economy has not only contributed to the crisis of Western Marxism, but has effectively secured a long-term monopoly for capitalist market ideology. Gospelized and accorded a sacerdotal status in the temple of the new postsocialist Left, postmodern theory has failed to provide an effective counterstrategy to the spread of neoliberal ideology that currently holds educational policy and practice in its thrall. In fact, it has provided neoliberalism with the political stability it needs to reproduce its most troublesome determinations.

Our purpose here has not been to establish, evidentially, instance by instance, or *in toto*, the dilemmas, pitfalls, and shortcomings of postmodern theory, but rather to sound a rather basic caution with respect to its potential for mounting an effective counter-hegemonic project against global capitalism and its discontents. In doing so we raise the following questions echoed by the epigones of the modernist project: Does returning to Marx reveal the ultimate sources of the patriarchal and colonizing venture of the West's master narratives? Will re-embracing Marxism somehow summon a new coherent identity for the patriarchal West? Is Marxism a quixotically romantic quest for liberation that can only serve as a stimulant for the passion of the Western master narrative? Can Marxist writings today be anything more than a dirge on the death of the communist dream? Will engaging the writings of Marx only exacerbate the theoretical megrims that inflict the anti-theoretical educational left?

The position we take on the issues raised by these questions is unambiguous. We believe that Marxist analysis should serve as an axiomatic tool for contesting current social relations linked to the globalization of capital and the neoliberal education policies that follow in its wake. Educational researchers ignore Marxist analyses of globalization and the quotidian poetics of the everyday at their peril. At the same time, we admit that Marxist theory constitutes a social system of analysis that inscribes subjects and is seeped in the dross of everyday life. As such, it must continually be examined for its underlying trajectories. We believe that a critical reflexive Marxist theory—undergirded by the categorical imperative of striving to overthrow all social conditions in which human beings are exploited and oppressed—can prove foundational in the development of current educational research traditions as well as pedagogies of liberation.

POSTMODERN POLITICS

Following tectonic shifts in the geopolitical landscapes of the 1980s and 1990s, postmodern social and political theory—with its preening emphasis on language, culture, and identity—has become the *de rigeur* conceptual attire among social scientists attempting to make sense of contemporary social life within late capitalism. Mining the terrain of identity politics, consumer fetishism, and privatopia has become a central academic activity and is now considered *theoretical-chic*. In contrast, Marxism has been mummified along with Lenin's corpse, and its scholarly exercise has been likened to tampering with historical relics.

The joint ambition of uncovering the hidden ideologies secreted within Western representations of the "Other" and refashioning the antifoundational self, has disposed postmodern theorists to dampen their euphoria surrounding social transformation at the level of relations of production and to heighten their regard for reforming and decentering dominant discourses and institutional practices at the level of cultural transactions. According to Sam J. Noumoff (1999), postmodern politics attempts (a) to separate culture from ideology, (b) to employ culture as a construct that diminishes the centrality of class, (c) to insert a neoliberal political system of intelligibility and policy agenda, (d) to perpetuate the belief in the ultimate futility of the socialist project, and (e) to promote an assortment of "post" concepts—such as post-structuralism, postmodernism, post-history, post-ideology—as a way of limiting the theoretical direction of inquiry and preempting socialist challenges to new objective realities brought about by the globalization of capital.

Hilary Wainwright (1994) rightly asserts that much of what passes as postmodern politics not only lacks a coherent social and political vision with which to actively challenge the Radical Right, it also endorses a number of the Right's main tenets in progressive and radical discourses. She writes that postmodernism does not "provide adequate tools to answer the radical right . . . the tools of postmodernism produce only a more volatile version of the radical right. . . . Postmodernism cuts the connection between human intention and social outcome" (p. 100).

Postmodern theory's stress on micropolitics transforms what are essentially social struggles into discursive struggles that overvalue economies of desire at the expense of political economy and a philosophy of praxis. Many postmodernists refute the idea that any particular social group or class is capable of transforming the existing social relations of production under capitalism. At the same time, however, they fail to lay the conceptual foundations for building necessary political alliances among oppressed and marginalized social groups. John Ehrenberg underscores this vividly:

> It will not do to claim that knowledge is local, "identity" and "difference" are the key categories in modern social life, human relations are constituted

by language and "discourse," "culture" is the site of struggle, and no single
agent of human liberation can even be theorized. The inexorable concentration and centralization of capital stand in eloquent opposition to the claim
that fragmentation and discontinuity have eliminated all possibilities for collective action toward a common end which can cut across the multiple, shifting and self-defined "identities" that make up the social world. (1998, p. 43)

While postmodern politics tends to focus on particular forms of oppression,
the irrefragable power of Marxist theory resides in its ability to reveal how all
forms of social oppression under capitalism are mutually interconnected (Ebert,
1996; Hennessey, 1993; McLaren & Farahmandpur, 1999; Wood, 1996). While
both Marxism and postmodernism address the "interlocking triumvirate" of
race, class, and gender, Marxist theory attempts to reveal how all of these forms
of oppression are]inked to private ownership of the means of production and
the extraction of surplus labor.

It is a cardinal position in postmodernism to place under suspicion master
narratives, universalism, and objectivity on the grounds that they are particular
epistemological and moral discourses camouflaged under the guise of universal
discourses. Enlightenment ideals come under fire as well since they putatively
aim at creating homogenous discourses which are based on scientific progress
associated with European economic, social, and political dominance
(Thompson, 1997). Postmodernists additionally dismiss the Enlightenment's
claim and appeal to universalism by associating it with European imperialism
and colonialism which, in their view, aided the Spanish, Portuguese, and British
conquest of the "New World." However, history demonstrates that prior
empires did not rely on specific universal discourses similar to the
Enlightenment ideas to justify their atrocities, genocide, and territorial conquest.
On the contrary, Enlightenment thinkers frequently stressed the significance of
other cultures' moral and ethical commitments by comparing and contrasting
them to their own European origins. According to Willie Thompson:

> The Spanish conquistadors did not require the Enlightenment to commit
> genocide upon the populations of the Caribbean, Mexico and Peru and sub-
> ject the remnant to slavery, nor Genghis Khan to do similar things in
> Central Asia during the earlier period. These acts were committed by cul-
> tures with no pretensions to universalism (unless Christianity is to be
> regarded as such, in which case the root of all evil has to be sought a lot
> further back). (1997, p. 219)

Post-Marxists such as Laclau and Mouffe (1985) tend to look at social contradictions as semantic problems whereas Marxists are strongly inclined to see
social contradictions as anchored in the objective nature of everyday life; they
are part of the structural determinations of the social. In rejecting dialectical
thought, and in abandoning the notion that capitalist exploitation is linked to the
law of value and the extraction of surplus value, Laclau and Mouffe reduce

exploitation to a linguistic process in a purely semantic universe. Yet the oppressed know differently. For them, exploitation takes place in a concrete fashion, in the bowels of everyday contradictions which expel relations of equality. Workers might not be able to theorize this, or link it up to a working definition of resistance. But they live such contradictions in their bones. Unlike Laclau and Mouffe, we do not believe that resistance has to be conscious on the part of workers in order to stipulate that exploitation has occurred. Relations of subordination are antagonistic in relation to an ideology (a logic of capital) that rationalizes - hence naturalizes this relationship.

The problem with post-Marxists such as Laclau and Mouffe is that the notion of materiality is often subsumed under or replaced by the signifier, or abstracted out of existence as a form of radical contingency or pure heterogeneity. The material is reduced to an integument that encapsulates a core of preexisting codes. This collapses the material into a type of mediating exteriority that gives birth to the abstract production of ideas. Collapsed in the process is capitalism's mode of production; obliterated is the fundamental tension between labor and capital as the motor force of history. Callinicos has noted that postmodern theory has become so institutionalized in university departments throughout the Western academy that it has become an unchallengeable orthodoxy; in fact, he argues that "postmodernism has become the Parsonian sociology of our fin de siecle" (1999, p. 297). Atilio Boron (2000) has also linked the work of Laclau and Mouffe to Parsons but for a different reason. For Boron, the work of Laclau and Mouffe, far from constituting a supersession of Marxism, is, in effect, reproductive of some of the fundamental conservative expressions of United States sociology of the 1950s, as found in the work of Talcott Parsons.

Postmodern theory's decentering of the 'official' discourses of the dominant culture, while not limited in referential range, is certainly limited in its scope of possible political outcomes in the here-and-now of the ongoing historical process and does little to challenge the unbreakable collective agency of ruling class interests and the superintendence of the state. Such efforts at decentering reigning discourses cannot effectively contest the laws of motion of surplus-value extraction and the systematically exploitative and antagonistic economic order. Class-for-itself action is the only secure and effective means of securing the legal and political apparatuses necessary for controlling the state and its economic hegemony. Of course, the composite consciousness of the working class is not a reflex of large-scale indoctrination of the masses within the social anatomy of the bourgeoisie, but rather is a consequence of rival interpretations of the world. The development of revolutionary consciousness attempts to elaborate the understanding that the working class has of their own interests and capacities. This requires extensive ideological and organizational preparation in sites such as schools. It is within such sites that a critical pedagogy must be born that refuses to compromise with the interests of the capitalist class.

The accusation of some postmodernists (such as Lather, 1998) that classical Marxism leaves virtually untroubled the issue of gender ignores the contributions of Marxist feminists and multiculturalists, not to mention Marxist revolutionaries (Ebert, 1996; Hennessey, 1993). We refer to the programmatic documents on the oppression of women produced by the Fourth International. Trotsky, for example, argued for the liberation of women from unpaid domestic labor as part of the advance towards socialism. And in his criticism of the effects of the Stalinist counter-revolution on the family, he wrote:

> How man enslaved women, how the exploiter subjected them both, how the toilers have attempted at the price of blood to free themselves from slavery and have only exchanged one chain for another—history tells us much about this. In essence, it tells us nothing else. But how in reality to free the child, the woman, and the human being? For that we have as yet no reliable models. All past historical experience, wholly negative, demands of the toilers at least an implacable distrust of all privileged and uncontrollable guardians. (Trotsky cited in Kelly, Cole, & Hill, 1999)

Some postmodern feminists have argued that classical Marxism is shrouded in claims to universal truth and has overlooked the specificity of women's labor. They assert that historical materialism is reductive because it reduces all types of oppression into class exploitation, ignoring racism, sexism, and homophobia. Carol Stabile (1994) responds by describing this attack on Marxism as underwritten by what she calls "theoretical essentialism." Stabile argues that the end to sexual domination does require ending class exploitation. She notes:

> Without considering class position and its centrality for capitalism, social-ist-feminism ceases to exist. Only economic analyses can force academic and similarly privileged feminists to confront the unevenness of gender oppression and undermine its methodological centrality. Only along the frictionless plane—a location where social relations and class antagonisms hold little or no critical purchase can the category of class be so easily dismissed. (1994, p. 157)

Jane Kenway astutely recognizes that in the work of negotiating among competing discourses in pedagogical processes and practices, materialist feminists are more attentive to extra-discursive (that is, economic) factors than are postmodern feminists. She writes:

> University and schools can be seen to consist of fragile settlements between and within discursive fields and such settlements can be recognized as always uncertain; always open to challenge and change through the struggle over meaning, or what is sometimes called the politics of discourse; that is, interdiscursive work directed towards the making and remaking of meaning. Materialist feminists participate in this struggle over meaning but recognize more fully than do postmodernist feminists that this struggle is

overdetermined by the distribution of other resources. It is neither naive nor voluntaristic. (1997, p. 141)

By focusing on identity politics, postmodernists tend to lose sight of the determinate character of global capitalist relations. The challenge posed by theorists like Judith Butler (1993, 1997)—to see identity as performance and as a corporeal exhortation to mobilize against oppression—is undeniably important but must be accompanied by a critique of the cultural formations in which performance as a material practice is produced within existing social relations of production. Otherwise postmodern performance as a "practice of the self" always remains at the level of the cultural disruption of existing discourses instead of the transformation of relations of production—that is, the transformation of the exploited labor power of the proletariat and private ownership of the means of production.

The goal of Marxism is to abolish class society so that every individual—regardless of age, gender, sexuality, race, ethnicity—enjoys the material resources necessary to develop his or her differences and enhance the creative capacities denied to them by capitalism. Many proponents of identity politics fail to situate racism and sexism within the arena of class struggle. Following from this line of argument, we are interested in how racism, sexism and homophobia are implicated in the contradictory and dialectical movement between the forces and relations of production. More specifically, we are interested in how the exploitative social relations of production under capitalism impact the ideological production of racist, sexist, and homophobic cultural identities. In other words, class oppression is linked (in historically specific ways) to other modalities of oppression and together they constitute a dialectically mediated constellation of totality. Identity politics may therefore be said to be conditioned by class struggle but not determined by it. At the same time, we believe that it needs to be located within class struggle.

Take the example of class and gender. In contemporary capitalism, women are objectively "worthless" than men on the basis of exchange-value, on the average. Capitalism systematically discriminates against women, no matter what their (or men's) "subjective" perceptions or feelings or interpretations/justifications, evasions, etc., or the exceptions (growing in number over the last thirty years) that we can point towards. On this basis, capitalism is an abomination for visions of gender equality. Yet it is important not to confuse race or gender with social class. Social class is not the same as gender, race, etc., on the grounds that it is a necessary feature of capitalist society. One could imagine a posthuman future where we are both sexes (or none), where we choose our 'color' (as a fashion statement)—indeed the trans/posthumanists actively seek to bring about such a future. However, this would not invalidate capitalism as such. If, on the other hand, we arranged things such that people did not have to sell their labor powers, then that, in a stroke, would make value an impossibility: as value is based on abstract labor which in turn is based on the labor-time performed at the level of socially average labor power. Hence: no labor power expenditure at all, then the end of value, surplus value and capital. Class, therefore, is different if you maintain this broad definition, i.e. the "working class" is the vast majority who are pressed into selling their labor powers. Of course, a whole set of inequalities arises from whether they can actually sell their labor powers at any point in time. Further inequalities arise from the conditions upon and prices for which they sell their labor powers to capitalist enterprises.

While in an important sense identity politics personalizes in different ways, in different contexts, for different groups, and for different generations of people, the often grinding and impersonal nature of class exploitation, it cannot objectively put an end to class oppression any more than the elimination of class hierarchies can automatically put an end to oppressive discrimination based on race, ethnicity, sexual orientation, etc. Although we argue that class oppression often grounds or anchors other forms of oppression linked to identity politics, we want to underscore the point that, to a large extent, all forms of oppression are important and dialectically interactive with each other. Modes of alienation and anomie resulting from living in a racist, sexist and homophobic society are deeply underlaid by the primary contradiction of class society: the tension between labor and capital. Regrettably, the political emphasis of many of the new social movements within the U.S. left has taken away the primary emphasis on collective class struggle, a struggle linked to the objective requirements of capitalism to accumulate more and more surplus value.

Like graffiti sprayed across the tropes and conceits of modernist narratives, postmodern theory remains a soft form of revolt. It constitutes a transgression of the "already said" in the name of the poetics of the "unsaid." Slouching under the Promethean hubris of avant-garde cosmopolitanism, postmodern theorists privilege the poetics of the sublime over the drab flux of quotidian existence; evanescent immateriality over the raw materiality of lived experience; the imponderability of representations over the historically palpable concreteness of oppression; the autonomy of cultural and political practices over the political and economic determinations of capitalism's law of value; fashionable apostasy over the collective ideals of revolutionary struggle from below (*"bas materialisme"*); the salubriousness of aesthetic subversion over the physical dangers of civil disobedience; the bewitchment and exorcism of signs over the class struggle that shapes their epistemological character; transgressive pedagogy over the pedagogy of revolution.

Lulled into political complacency by their centrist adaptations to the reformist practices of their liberal colleagues, the postmodern left is sharing a bed with mainstream progressive educators whose work remains untroubled by a critique of capitalist social relations and is exhibiting a generic tendency to evade an analysis of schooling from the perspective of political economy. As one of us (McLaren) has written elsewhere:

While not all postmodern theory is to be rejected, there is a species of it that remains loyal to capital's promotional culture where parody can be paraded as dissent and cultural parasitism masqueraded as subversion and where one can avoid putting political commitment to the test. The academy is the a place where Marxism is dismissed as innocent of complexity and where Marxist educators are increasingly outflanked by fashionable, motely minded apostates . . . for whom the metropole has become a riotous mixture of postmodern mestize narratives and hubris shadows of those who remain even remotely loyal to casual thinking. For these vogish hellions of the seminar room, postmodernism is the toxic intensity of bohemian nights, where the proscribed, the immiserated and the wretched of the earth simply get in the way of their fun. (2000, p. xxv)

Mas'ud Zavarzadeh (1995) argues that "post-ality" (a term he uses to refer to discursive modalities within postmodernism) represents "post-ideologies," "post-production," and "post-labor" theories. He offers a powerful critique of post-ality by revealing the mechanisms by which these discourses conceal the logic behind capitalist social relations of production through their stress on language, representation, identity, and structures of feeling. He suggests what is frequently and seriously overlooked by post-al discourses are issues related to economic exploitation, labor, and class inequality. The seduction of post-al theories within academic discourses suggests the existence of a deep-seated pessimism among scholars surrounding the possibility of the working-class becoming the revolutionary agents of social transformation.

Postmodern social theorists maintain that in post-industrial society, consumption is equally as significant as the production of commodities. They fail to focus on how commodities are produced and the relationship each individual has to the means of production, preferring to occupy themselves with how commodities are consumed. Zavarzadeh (1995) suggests that "post-ality attempts to solve—in the theoretical imaginary—the historical and material contradictions of capitalism caused by the social division of labor" (p. 1). He adds that "knowledge, beyond elementary practical everyday problem solving, becomes possible only through the concealed labor of the other—that is, when the social division of labor frees some workers to engage in theoretical analysis" (pp. 11-12). Post-production theorists fail to provide a persuasive critique of property relations and the social relations of production which are at the core of capitalist exploitation (Zavarzadeh, 1995). The shift from production practices towards consumption practices, removes labor and class as the central categories of social organization, and instead replaces them with discourses stressing the politics of desire and consumption. Postmodern theory has both shifted and replaced discourses on economic production and the objective interests of the working-class with the subjective interests of the bourgeoisie. We follow Zavarzadeh (1995) in claiming that: "Class is the repressed concept in all theories of post-ality" (p. 42).

Finally, Zavarzadeh (1995) suggests that postmodernists and post-industrialists confuse employment patterns with class structures. In other words, the

expansion of service industry sectors and the managerial class does not alter the
class composition and class conflict between the two main social classes: those
who are wage earners and those who live off the surplus value of workers. The
existence of a middle class does not change relations of exploitation between
workers and the ruling class. Following Mészáros (1989), he suggests that capitalism must produce new theories to legitimize and justify the existing social
and economic order and to conceal its internal contradictions.

HOME-SPUN DOMINATION AND THE GLOBAL
REACH OF POWER

The presence of capitalism floats in the air like the avuncular aroma of pipe
tobacco wafting through your bedroom window from a neighbor's veranda. It
tickles the nostrils with a mixture of familiarity and security. It instills a capitalist nostalgia, a deep yearning for a time when success appeared inevitable, when
progress was assured, when hunger and disease would be wiped out by the
steady advance of industrial wealth and technological prowess. Mesmerized by
the scent of money, we willfully ignore the ramifications of capitalism's current
capital flight; its elimination of multiple layers of management, administration
and production; and processes such as de-industrialization, the ascendancy of
financial and speculative capital, the expansion of transnational circuits of
migrant workers, and the casualization of the labor force. We ignore the monopolies, the oligopolies, the cartels, the new corporate carpetbaggers, the prophets
of privatization, the Wal-Martization of the global lifeworld, and the transfer of
capital investments to cheaper markets offering higher rates of exploitation. We
pretend we don't see the reduced social expenditures in health, education, and
social services, the business counterattack against labor, the state's growing
indebtedness to corporate bondholders, the privatization of municipal services,
the assault on trade unionism and the draconian attacks on the social safety net.
We want to believe all of this will soon pass, leaving us once again curled up
beside the glowing hearth of the American Dream.

Marx's utopian vision of a democratic society has much to offer today's
educators as it does the world's exploited classes. Its task has been "less to imagine a new social order than to unlock the contradictions which forestall its historical emergence" (Eagleton, 1999, p. 35). We believe that capital has a unique
reifying force and peculiar durability. We agree with Robert Albritton that "capital is the most important single determinant of modem history" (1999, p. 2).

In our view, Marxist social theory's conception of the dynamic and organic
nature of social relations of production under capitalism is more convincing
than the triumphalistic, self-congratulatory and self-centered effusions associated with the "end of-Marxism" claims of neo-liberal ideologues. Ian McKay
(1995/1996) informs us that "Marx's transcendental yet this-worldly vision is at

once ethical, realist and historical" (p. 42). We remain confident that Marxist theory will continue to play a critical role as both theoretical and practical tools in the struggle for social justice.

The unforeseeable future of leftist educational practice is, in part, linked to the outcome of the following questions: Can a renewed, retooled, or conceptually redrawn Marxism—absent its most vulgar and dogmatically rigid trappings—provide the epistemological machinery for explaining and transforming the complex determinations and indeterminacies of culture, as well as theorizing the gap between empirical contingencies and eternal structures, better than a depoliticized and depleted postmodernism can? Can educational theorists escape the vulgarities that compromise the emancipatory potential of Marxism? Can Marxists sufficiently salvage a form of "totalizing" thought within the Marxian optic in such a way that does not forfeit empirical complexity by means of a reductive synthesis? Can educators excise from the grid of casual determination a Marxism that escapes a generalized formalism and monolithic idealism? We believe that these questions can be answered resoundingly in the affirmative. We believe that critical educators can surmount the crisis of credibility of the socialist project. Establishing the conditions of possibility for the restoration of historical materialism will not be easy but the hermeneutical expansion of Marxism that is already taking place in some precincts of the academy is promising (Cole et al., 1997; Ebert, 1996; Hennessy, 1993; Jameson, 1991). We share a guarded optimism about the extent to which educators can become tactically prepared and ideologically predisposed to carry out a "war of position" on sequestered fronts, waged in the interest of building oppositional cultures of revolutionary workers. Recent anti-WTO protests provide us with confidence that future struggles will further point the way to alternatives to the rule of capital.

If anyone doubts the power of collective struggle in the developed Western countries like the United States, they should be reminded of what happened in Seattle on November 30, 1999. On that fateful day, young and old political activists from labor, educational, environment, legal, agricultural, industrial, and trade union groups lay siege to the city—despite a curfew declared by city officials and fierce resistance in the form of 200 National Guard troops, 300 state troopers and State police in riot gear armed with batons, rubber bullets, concussion grenades, and canisters and rubber pellets filled with pepper spray—and prevented the World Trade Organization summit from holding a successful first day in what has become known as the Battle of Seattle. In the same city that hosted the bloody general strike of 1919, the titans of business, the chieftains of corporate finance, neo-liberal global planners, political leaders, and global robber barons were put on notice by tens of thousands of extraordinary ordinary people taking back the streets in the largest export city in the United States that boasts the headquarters of Microsoft, Starbucks, and Boeing.

The all-embracing social revolution of which Babeuf, Marx, Lenin, Luxemburg, Trotsky and others so eloquently spoke is exceedingly relevant today, despite the interminably changing social conditions facing us. History undoubtedly will point us further in the direction of a socialist future but whether we will have the will and the courage to bring it about is quite another story. Capitalism doesn't come equipped with air bags. On its collision course with history, vast numbers of human fatalities are a certainty. No one escapes injury, especially the exploited classes. The answer is not to acquire customized protection for the masses against the ravages of capital but to create a different historical trajectory altogether by cutting capitalism off at the production line. The alternative is to wait for capitalism to drive the human race over the cliff.

If we reduce the past to the postmodern texts that are currently used to write about it or cling to the belief that the future is limited to the post-Marxist discourses currently employed to predict it, we condemn ourselves to the brain-stunting banality and mind-numbing apologetics that are carried by contemporary winds of desperation and, in the long run, we engender a fatal disconnection between hope and possibility.

NOTES

1. Earlier versions of this essay appear under the title "Reconsidering Marx in Post-Marxist Times: A Requiem for Postmodernism?" *Educational Researcher, 29*(3), 25-33.
2 We acknowledge that there are many "postmodernisms" just as there are many "Marxisms." Our criticism is directed against postmodern theories that do not sufficiently contest capitalist relations of production. Our approach to Marxism could be described as classical in that we argue that the root of exploitation is directly connected to private property and the extraction of surplus labor from workers by the capitalist class.
3 Our position as Marxist theorists is not to privilege class over race, gender, or sexual orientation but to see class relations as dealing with the process of producing, appropriating, and distributing surplus value. As such, it is the strongest totalizing force that lies at the very roots of racism and sexism.
4 The Federal Bureau of Investigation brought up Professor Jose Solis Jordán (formerly of DePaul University and now at the University of Puerto Rico) on trumped-up charges of planting two bombs in a military recruitment center and he was sentenced to a lengthy prison term (see McLaren & Solis Jordan, 1999).
5. Third World factories of the transnational corporations.
6. We adopt a classical Marxist position insofar as we recognize class and the forces of production as largely determinant of the social. Unlike postmodernism, which often conceptualizes the social as radical heterogeneity driven by desire and detached from labor and human need, classical Marxism understands difference as determined primarily in relation to private property and to the means of production.

REFERENCES

Ahmad, A. (1995). The politics of literary postcoloniality. *Race & Class, 36*(3), 1-19.

Albritton, R. (1999). *Dialectics and deconstruction in political economy.* New York: St. Martin's Press.

Bertsch, C., & Lockard, J. (1999). Marx without monsters. [Online]. In *Bad Subjects,* no. 45. Available: http://english-www.hss.cmu.edu/bs/45/editors.html. [1999, Nov 30]

Boron, A. (2000). Embattled legacy: Post-Marxism and the social and political theory of Karl Marx. *Latin American Perspectives, 27*(4), 49-79.

Butler, J. (1999). *Bodies that matter: On the discursive limits of sex.* London: Routledge.

Butler, J. (1999). *Excitable speech: A politics of the performative.* London: Routledge.

Callinicos, A. (1993). *Race and class.* London: Bookmarks.

Callinicos, A. (1999). *Social theory: A historical introduction.* New York: New York University Press.

Cole, M., Hill, D., & Rikowski, G. (1997). Between postmodernism and nowhere: The predicament of the postmodernist. *British Journal of Educational Studies, 45*(2), 187-200.

Eagleton, T. (1999). Utopia and its oppositions. In L. Panitch & C. Leys (Eds.), *Socialist Register 2000* (pp. 31-40). Suffolk, England: The Merlin Press.

Ebert, T. (1996). *Ludic feminism and after: Postmodernism, desire, and labor in late capitalism.* Ann Arbor: The University of Michigan Press.

Ehrenberg, J. (1998). Civil society and Marxist politics. *Socialism and Democracy, 12*(1-2), 15-46.

Fraser, N. (1997). *Justice interruptus: Critical reflections on the "postsocialist" condition.* New York: Routledge.

Hennessy, R. (1993). *Materialist feminism and the politics of discourse.* New York and London: Routledge.

Hudis, P. (2000). Can capital be controlled? [Online]. In *News and Letters.* Available: http://www.newsandletters.org/4.00_essay.htm

Jameson, F. (1999). *Postmodernism or the cultural logic of late capitalism.* Durham, NC: Duke University Press.

Kelley, R. D. G. (1999). A poetics of anticolonialism. *Monthly Review, 51*(6), 1-21.

Kelly, J., Cole, M., & Hill, D. (1999, September). *Resisting postmodernism and the ordeal of the undecidable: A Marxist critique.* Unpublished paper presented at the meeting of the British Educational Research Association.

Kelly, D. (2000). Multicultural citizenship: The limitations of liberal democracy. *The Political Quarterly, 71*(1), 31-41.

Kenway, J. (1997). Having a postmodern turn or postmodernist angst: A disorder experienced by an author who is not yet dead or even close to it. In A. H. Halsey, H. Lauder, P. Brown & A. S. Wells (Eds.), *Education: Culture, economy, society* (pp. 131-143). Oxford and New York: Oxford University Press.

Krehm, W. (2000). The co-failure of communism and capitalism in Russia. *Comer, 12*(7), 9, 19.

Laclau, E., & Mouffe, C. (1985). *Hegemony and socialist strategy: Towards a radical democratic politics.* London and New York: Verso.

Larrain, J. (1995). Identity, the other, and postmodernism. In M. Zavarzadeh, T. Ebert & D. Morton (Eds.), *Post-ality: Marxism and postmodernism* (pp. 271-289). Washington, DC: Maisonneuve.

Marx, K. (1959). *Capital* (Vol. 1). Moscow: Foreign Languages Publishing House.

McChesney, R. W. (1999). Introduction. In N. Chomsky (Ed.), *Profit over people: Neoliberalism and global order* (pp. 7-16). New York: Seven Stories Press.

McKay, I. (1995/1996). The many deaths of Mr. Marx: Or, what Left historians might contribute to debates about the "crises of Marxism." *Left History, 3.2 & 4.1*, 9-84.

McLaren, P. (1997). *Revolutionary multiculturalism: Pedagogies of dissent for the new millennium.* Boulder, CO: Westview Press.

McLaren, P. (2000). *Che Guevara, Paulo Freire, and the pedagogy of revolution.* Boulder, CO: Rowman & Littefield.

McLaren, P., & Farahmandpur, R. (1999). Critical pedagogy, postmodernism, and the retreat from class: Towards a contraband pedagogy. *Theoria, 93*, 83-115.

McLaren, P., & Solis Jordan J. (1999). The struggle for liberation! La lucha continua. Jose Solis Jordan's fight for justice. *International Journal of Educational Reform, 8*(2), 168-174.

McMurtry, J. (2000). A failed global experiment: The truth about the US economic model. *Comer, 12*(7), 10-11.

McNally, D. (1999). The present as history: Thoughts on capitalism at the millennium. *Monthly Review, 51*(3), 134-145.

Mészáros, I. (1999). Marxism, the capital system, and social revolution: An interview with Istvan Mészáros. *Science and Society, 63*(3), 338-361.

Mosley, W. (2000). *Workin' on the chain gang: Shaking off the dead hand of history.* New York: The Ballantine Publishing Group.

Noumoff, S. J. (1999). *Globalization and culture.* Pullman: Washington State University.

O'Connor, J. (1998). *Natural causes: Essays in ecological Marxism.* New York and London: The Guilford Press.

Rifkin, J. (2000). *The age of access: The new culture of hypercapitalism where all of life is a paid-for experience.* New York: Tarcher/Putnan Books.

Schuchardt, R. M. (1998). Swoosh! The perfect icon for an imperfect postliterate world. *UTNE Reader, 89*, 76-77.

Stabile, C. A. (1994). *Feminism and the technological fix.* Manchester and New York: Manchester University Press.

Stuart, J. G. (2000). A place for faith. *Comer, 12*(7), 7.

Thompson. W. (1999). *The Left in history: Revolution and reform in twentieth-century politics.* London: Pluto Press.

Wainwright, H. (1994). *Arguments for a new Left: Answering the free market Right.* London and Cambridge, MA: Blackwell Publishers.

Wood, E. M. (1996). *Democracy against capitalism: Renewing historical materialism.* Cambndge, UK: Cambndge University Press.

Zavarzadeh, M. (1995). Post-ality: The (dis)simulations of cybercapitalism. In M. Zavarzadeh (Ed.), *Post-ality: Marxism and postmodernism* (pp. 1-75). Washington, DC: Maisonrleuve.

Zweig, M. (2000). *The working class majority: America's best kept secret.* Ithaca and London: ILR Press.

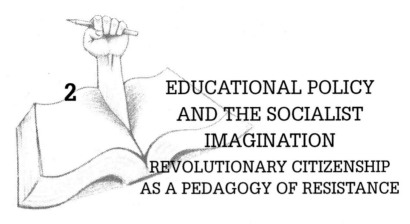

2 EDUCATIONAL POLICY AND THE SOCIALIST IMAGINATION
REVOLUTIONARY CITIZENSHIP AS A PEDAGOGY OF RESISTANCE

Peter McLaren and
Ramin Farahmandpur

> When I was coming up, it was a dangerous world, and you know exactly
> who they are . . . it was us versus them, and it was clear who them was.
> Today we are not so sure who the they are, but we know they're there.
> —George W. Bush (quoted in Ehrenreich, 2000b, pp. 20-21)

> When I give food to the poor, they call me a saint. . . And when I ask why
> they have no food, they call me a communist.
> —Brazilian Bishop Helder Camara (quoted in Galeano, 2000, p. 311)

As we indulge in millennial consumer orgies celebrating the unending promise of 1,000 years of uninterrupted shopping at Planet Mall, we pretend that the social and economic horrors that we have come to associate with Western capitalist democracies have been a temporary spike in global capitalism's blood pressure. We want to believe that in history's long march toward civilization, capitalist exploitation will amount to little more than faint footprints left on the side of the road by Marx's reserve army of labor. But history has proven a worthy opponent in its stubborn refusal to come to an end or to succumb to our best rationalizations. Capitalism's grim legacy of the poverty of the many thriving amidst the wealth of the few is more than just a flicker in the cabinet of lost nineteenth-century memories. It is still the main show in town. In fact, it has enjoyed a record-breaking run ever since the feudal lords were kicked off their estates. But how long can capitalism's vaudeville antics and slapstick financial maneuvering keep us laughing when the ruling class is ensured that it will have the last laugh? As long, it seems, as the march of progress remains obscured by the myths woven into its telling.

This chapter originally appeared in *Educational Policy, 15*(3), 343-378. © 2001 Corwin Press, Inc. Reprinted with permission.

Capitalism has become so intensified that it represses our ability to acknowledge the process of repression itself. It naturalizes repression so completely that the current economic horror has come to be seen as part of the everyday woof and warp of things that we have blithely come to name "the daily grind." Consequently, even progressive educators who are vigorously engaged in the debate over global capitalism and theories that oppose one another within it frequently fail to address the fateful implications of capitalism's confiscation of freedom and kidnapping of hope. Yet capitalism constitutes more than transforming the globe into a version of Minneapolis' Mall of the Americas or a *paradis artificiels* designed after *The Truman Show*; it is a living horror, a total social universe for those who must endure the full force of economic injustice. And the global expanse of capitalism that we have been witnessing over the past few decades has been nothing less than exploitation on stilts. As Alex Callinicos (2000) remarks, "Most of us live in the shadow of the blackmail of capital" (p. 129).

Hypnotized by the silken seductiveness of lingerie capitalism—superexploitation trussed in attire from Frederick's of Hollywood—we are beckoned into a patriarchal mansion of consumer pleasures where fulfillment is untiringly supplanted by the promise of something better. The universe is for sale, and if you can dress it up in a leather corset, so much the better. The serpent *ouroborous* is now chasing investment portfolios instead of its own tail. While capitalism seeks its global advantage, millions of the world's toilers remain captive of the testosterone-fueled dreams of wealth and power as they are forced to mortgage their lives in their futile quest for what has now surely become a tired oxymoron: capitalist democracy. And although U.S. citizens are not indifferent to the salacious thirst of the privileged social classes for power and wealth, they simply find it difficult to imagine a capitalist world where this would not be the case. Callinicos (2000) notes (paraphrasing G. A. Cohen) that the ruling class predicting "that they will produce less, making the poor suffer, unless they continue to be specially rewarded [is like] a kidnapper who predicts that the child he has taken will suffer unless his or her parents come up with the ransom money" (p. 128).

As the tumultuous history of twentiethth-century class struggle is capriciously flung aside to make room for capitalism's victory celebration, littering all paths to the future with hollow triumphs and ticker tape fantasies, we stand as helpless onlookers before one of the most flagrantly vulgar and decadent epochs experienced by Western civilization. Such a statement may seem the flashy product of an overworked Hollywood screenwriter laboring over a low-budget pilot about Pokémon at Armageddon, or of a John Ashcroft dream where he replaces Paul with himself in the pantheon of Christian aristocracy, but we are deadly serious.

The neoliberal formation of the 1980s, whose spinal cord was capital accumulation at the expense of workers' rights, defeated organized labor and left it seriously weakened. The neoliberal offensive—a pugalist Capitalism sporting brass knuckles—has increased its hold over the past decade as the majority of the U.S. voting public appears content to follow leaders who refuse to stand up to the corporate oligopolies. The richest tenth of households in the United States own 83 percent of the country's financial assets, whereas the poorest four fifths own only 8 percent. The Center for the Study of Popular Economics noted, "If a Ford Escort represents the average financial wealth of an African American household, you would need a stretch limousine 300 yards long to show the average for a white household" (Heintz & Folbre, 2000, p. 17). Citing John Roemer, Callinicos (2000) similarly notes that

> to achieve "deep" equality of opportunity with respect to education in the United States, with the objective of ensuring that children in whatever circumstances who expend the same effort will have the same adult earning capacity, would require spending $900 on every white student and $2900 on every black student. (p. 88)

In a broader sense, consider this long list of startling observations: The cost of providing basic education and health care, as well as adequate food and safe water the entire population of the earth, is estimated to be $40 billion (less than the net worth of Bill Gates); the combined wealth of the three richest people in the world exceeds the combined GDPs of the forty-eight poorest countries; the combined wealth of the thirty-two richest people exceeds the total GDP of South Asia; and the combined wealth of the 225 richest people is roughly equal to the annual income of the poorest 47 percent of the world's population of more than 2.2 billion people (Heintz & Folbre, 2000, p. 19).

Governed by a lethal symbiosis of neoliberalism[1] and globalization,[2] the new social and economic global order has met with catastrophic consequences: the Mexican peso devaluation crisis of 1995, the Asian financial crisis of 1997, the Russian financial meltdown of 1998, the Brazilian "Samba effect" of 1999, and the fierce acceleration of Third World debt, among others (Kagarlitsky, 1999).

What has become increasingly clear is that multinational corporations now operate as oligopolies and function as supernational entities. Not only do these oligopolies consolidate and concentrate capital on a global scale, but they also exercise worldwide political influence within the governmental offices of nation-states through lobbying, campaign donations, and unholy business partnerships (Boggs, 2000). The uncomfortable truth of U.S. global hegemony is that it has been secured historically by the ability of the United States to reorganize the world system in its own economic, political, and military dimensions. Samir Amin (2000) summarizes American global strategy as follows:

> To neutralize and subjugate the other partners in the triad (Europe and Japan), while minimizing their ability to act outside the orbit of the United States; to establish military control over NATO while "Latin-Americanizing" the fragments of the former Soviet world; to exert uncon-

tested influence in the Middle East and Central Asia, especially over their
petroleum resources; to dismantle China, ensure the subordination of the
other great nations (India and Brazil), and prevent the constitution of
regional blocks potentially capable of negotiating the terms of globalization; and to marginalize the regions of the South that represent no strategic
interest. (p. 15)

The global military advantage enjoyed by the United States (largely
through its control of NATO) is unprecedented and guarantees the superiority of
the triad (the United States, Europe, and Japan) over the planet and ensures the
formation of a unipolar globalization:

> The strategy employed by the triad, under U.S. direction, takes as its aim
> the construction of a unipolar world organized along two complementary
> principles: the unilateral dictatorship of dominant TNC [transnational cor-
> poration] capital and the unfurling of a U.S. military empire, to which all
> nations must be compelled to submit. No other project may be tolerated
> within this perspective, not even the European project of subaltern NATO
> allies and especially not a project entailing some degrees of autonomy, like
> China's, which must be broken by force if necessary. (Amin, 2000, p. 16)

The post-World War II period has witnessed with dismaying regularity an
obscene concentration and centralization of social, political, and economic
power in the hands of a relatively small number of oligopolies. One of the
recent shifts in capitalist production has been the transference of fiercely competitive capital from Western countries to cheaper markets, giving rise to the
phenomenon known as the "globalization of capital." Globalization is not a new
stage of capitalist development but has intensified some of the most essential
features of imperialism. The term *globalization* has several definitions and has
been associated frequently with social, economic, and political shifts in late
20th-century capitalism. Perhaps a more fitting and close-to-the bone term to
describe contemporary capitalism is *gobbleization*: the hostile takeovers,
megamergers, and aggressive acquisitions of small corporations by larger, more
financially powerful and politically connected corporations. Reports confirm
that by 1997, fifty-one of the world's one hundred largest economies were corporations, and the leading 500 transnational corporations held a monopoly over
42 percent of the wealth generated worldwide (Lasn, 1999).

Capitalist "overworlders" have coined the term globalization to refer to the
expansion of capitalist social relations throughout the globe. However, when
viewed against the backdrop of today's tumultuous political events, such a term
can only be read as a genteel appellation used by the capitalist class as a means
of diverting attention from what is, in effect, an imperialist assault on human dignity throughout the world and a value orientation within which freedom can be
found only in the unmolested core of capital. Lee Dlugin (1999) unhesitatingly
characterizes the relationship between globalization and imperialism as follows:

Globalization is a qualitative development of monopoly capitalism on a world scale. It is based on the free flow of capital. The "free market" is the imperialist code word for the free unimpeded flow of capital of the biggest monopolies seeking maximum prof its, for their freedom to plunder the natural resources of whole nations and capture the biggest share of the world's production and markets. The process develops so that monopoly capital takes over whole industries around the world, agriculture production, transportation, finance operations and other economic spheres. It wipes out all forms of economic competition and it uses both legal and extra-legal measures to achieve its goals, including the use of military force. Through the IMF [International Monetary Fund] and the World Bank, it compels privatization of government services and nationalized industries. From this vantage point it is the able to dominate and usurp these industries. (p. 20)

Contemporary scholars have iterated the protean potential surrounding the concept of globalization and in the process have inflated its coinage but at the same time devalued its explanatory capacity. In his analysis of the recent social and economic shifts in late capitalist economies, István Mészáros (1999) proposes the use of the terms *total social capital* and *totality of labor* instead of globalization as conceptual tools in explaining and analyzing con temporary capitalism and its deformation and reterritorialization of human activity. Mészáros wisely cautioned against the excessive association of "globalization of capital" with its homogenizing tendencies. Capital, as Mészáros notes, cannot be conceived of as a "homogenous entity" because it consists of a "multiplicity of divisions and antagonisms" corresponding to a multiplicity of capitals competing with one another at both the intranational and international levels. In a similar fashion, imperialism (linked to capital) is nonsynchronous and works in contextually and geopolitically specific ways. In fact, globalization is so overwhelmingly triumphant today that it no longer relies on the hierarchical forms of domination associated with industrial capitalist formations, dissolving patriarchal and other fixed forms of domination and replacing them with fluid, hybrid identities, resulting in the unleashing of forces of contradiction and the exposition of capital's crushing machineries of exploitation. Here, forms of subjectivities, even the so-called resistant subjectivities of postmodernism, are able to resignify their own logic to fit the overall frame of capital's voracious logic (Hardt & Negri, 2000).

Finally, and contrary to the views of many social and political theorists, globalization as a social and economic phenomenon cannot be considered to exist apart from its incestuous relationship with the nation-state (McLaren & Farahmandpur, 1999b). In other words, the globalization of capital operates within and cooperates with mechanisms associated with the formation of the nation-state (Wood, 1995). In our view, the popular notion that the state is weakening as a result of the global deregulation of markets signals an erroneous conclusion on the part of social and political theorists. Without the protection of the state, capital becomes a contradiction in terms because existing asymmetrical property relations are protected by various branches of the state apparatus (e.g., law enforcement, the judiciary system).

We also note that the state serves the ruling classes but is not an instrument of the ruling classes in that it is directly controlled by them. Although the state plays little or no role in appropriating a surplus, it protects the private property of capitalists who do not need access to the state to extract surplus value from proletariats separated from their means of production and subsistence (R. Brenner, personal communication, October 30, 2000). The model for global capital's new moral framework is that of the "'network-extender', light and mobile, tolerant of difference and ambivalence, realistic about people's desires, informal and friendly" (Budgen, 2000, p. 153). Of course, such a model of con-nectionist capitalism and entrepreneurial leadership really amounts to little more than giving a "face lift" to the practice of exploitation and in doing so, "a new form of the extortion of surplus value" (Budgen, 2000, p. 155). It is a form of bleeding the workers, hiding the source of the wound, and facilitating the hem-orrhage through treating its victims as disposable pariahs whose lives are not worth confiscating.

TRUTH DECAY IN THE GOVERNMENT OF MISERY

Today, it is impossible to deny the fact that transnational corporations have suc-cessfully conquered the world's economies. This victory has been achieved through a unified strategy that philosopher John McMurtry claims was applied across the cold war divide itself. McMurtry (2000) describes this as a strategy "to defund all social sectors which provide life-serving, non-profit goods into crisis or bankruptcy so that they are forced into private corporate control" (p. 1). Consider the situation in Tijuana's Colonia Chilpancingo, a neighborhood of more than 1,000 families that sits beneath a large industrial park at Otay Mesa. These families live amid the lead waste and corroding batteries of a lead smelter and car battery recycler that closed down in 1994. The waste has contaminated the water that supplies the neighborhood through an open arroyo that passes through the grounds of a local kindergarten. What chance do the inhabitants have of getting help from the Commission for Environmental Cooperation, which was created through NAFTA? After all, labor rights and environmental rights guarantees are unenforceable. Of course, as Ben Ehrenreich (2000a) notes, NAFTA gives corporations recourse to challenge any interference with their abilities to extract surplus labor from workers.

How do transnational corporations avoid paying their way in the very soci-ety on whose infrastructures, resources, and markets they depend for their mate-rial transactions? They manage to thrive because the global market has been reengineered to permit them to sell at high prices anywhere while producing at the lowest cost anywhere else and evading domestic tax contributions, first-world wages and benefits, and compliance with environmental and labor regulations. Transnational corporations operate, under the banner of democracy and in the guise of freedom to sell back to home markets through free trade agreements and corporate-government partnerships. As a result, defunding education achieves the following corporate goals: It lowers corporate costs through depriving social sectors such as school districts of their revenue bases, and it makes schools more dependent on corporate funding (McMurtry, 2000). Privatized public debts are kept intentionally high by through call for more tax cuts. Consider the words of a Citibank (Rockefeller) official: "Nobody's debts are going to be paid. The issue is the borrower remaining creditworthy and able to carry the debt, but not repay it" (quoted in McMurtry, 2000, p. 3). McMurtry adds that, "Government borrowers 'remain creditworthy' for banks and bond-merchants by reducing obligations to non profit programs" (p. 3).

The "big lie" of our time, notes McMurtry (2000), is that blame for the lack of government funding for education (and the social sector in general) is the increased debts on public sector life goods. That is, the blame is placed on sup-posed "out-of-control social spending." This amounts to an obscene distortion, an unvarnished deception. In Canada, for instance, less than 6 percent of the increased government deficit was due to increased social spending, whereas 50 percent was due to increased interest charges, and 44 percent was due to tax cuts for corporations and individuals in high-income tax brackets, according to a Statistics Canada report that was, it is worth noting, engaged by the federal finance ministry and the corporate mass media (McMurtry, 2000).

What rarely gets reported is that the nonprofit sector, which funds social services, is perceived as an untapped market worth trillions of dollars. Big business is salivating. With the assistance of the government, big business is now appropriating social sector funding to help generate corporate profits for the rich. Increased public debt is in effect a corporate-government strategy that ensures that public sector revenues are ripe for corporate appropriation. And, it is all occurring under the banner of freedom. Education is now a for-profit industry.

An "academic gold rush" is in full swing, and the inexorably proliferating corporate-government partnerships are reaping vast benefits through their restructuring of public and higher education for permanent market use

> with the unstated *terminus ad quem* of this process the reproduction of all present and future students as consumers and employees whose desires for commodities and willingness to compete for corporate functions are imprinted reliably into their neuronal processes from the moment they enter school to their graduation. (McMurtry, 2000, p. 6)

We now live in the perfumed world of performance budgets linked to capital's inbred ideology of self-maximization and monetary incentives. McMurtry

(2000) argues that interest-based education is the ruling principle of the corporate market. Rather than requiring educators to address problems independent of their monetary pay-offs, the regulating principle of thought of the corporate management model is the maximization of the private funds of the corporation and "selecting against any knowledge or advance of knowledge which does not fulfill or which conflicts with this goal" (McMurtry, 2000, p. 7). McMurtry's illustration is telling:

> Consider a teacher presenting or a student studying the material of any subject who followed the rules of producing and selling a product for profit in the global marketplace. The anti-educational principles of thought and action would be: Do not address any problem which does not promise Opportunity for profit. Reject contra-indicative evidence to profitable results. Reduce the cost of work input to your product to the minimum possible. Always represent it as unique and without flaw. Treat the customers as always right. In short, the ruling goals of the corporate market subvens knowledge and inquiry itself, closes out critical debate, and blocks any disinterested pursuit of truth by its very nature. (p. 7)

The corporate management model of education demands private patent and copyright control of every piece of knowledge and information that a corporation can accumulate, and "the maximum price people are willing to pay is imposed on every service which can be identified, with no educational or other life service to anyone if it is not money-profitable" (McMurtry, 2000, p. 7). We urge readers to ponder the next illustration proffered by McMurtry (2000):

> Consider a school or university which priced its knowledge transactions, required its agents to do no more than required by commercial contract with student buyers, and sought to privatize more and more of the school's and library's information for its own monetary profit. There could hardly be a more anti-educational regime. Yet all of these requirements are intrinsic to the logic of the market model. Even if the price system is set aside, dissemination in the market is by conditioning and soliciting appetites, as opposed to disseminating what can be substantiated by evidence and reason. (pp. 7-8)

Critical literacy and problem-solving capabilities are jettisoned in the corporate management model in favor of linking individual capability to monetary demand, which establishes all market value. Global market competition becomes the grounds for all skills and competencies. Consider another of McMurtry's (2000) examples:

> If a student or a teacher followed the canonical rules of the global free market and voluntarily exchanged for any price that he or she could get the goods of course essays, tests and assignments, he or she as a student would

be expelled as a cheat, and as a teacher would be dismissed for the grossest moral turpitude. If an educational system as a whole were to develop more and more people with such dependencies on others' work, this regime would undermine education at its foundation. (p. 8)

In the corporate management model, problems of evidence or reason are not open to scrutiny or critical discussion. What gets communicated to students is dictated in a top-down chain of command that "rules out any questions which do not comply with these orders, and repudiates any who transgress this chain of command as employable" (McMurtry, 2000, p. 8). McMurtry (2000) notes,

If principals, teachers, or professors followed this managerial method of top-down command as their model of communication, and decided what was to be thought, said and done with the exclusion of critical dialogue or question on behalf of seeking truth, they would be supplanting education with coercive indoctrination and would be shown unfit to remain in a place of learning. (p. 8)

CORPORATE PHILANTHROPY

The Center for a New American Dream (2000) reported that since 1980, advertising expenditures in the United States have doubled from nearly $ 106 billion to $200 billion in 1998. More than $2 billion alone is spent annually on advertising that specifically targets children, twenty times more than a decade ago. Channel One, the brainchild of Chris Whittle, has a captive audience that is nearly fifty times larger than the number of teenagers who watch MTV. The average child of today is exposed to between 20,000 and 40,000 commercials each year. From age six to eighteen, children view nearly 16,000 hours of television programming and are exposed to 4,000 hours of radio and music programming. Children also spend more time viewing television and commercial programs than they spend in school. Nearly one of four children under the age of 6 has a television set in his or her bedroom. Jean Kilbourne (1999) writes that,

The average American is exposed to at least three thousand ads every day and will spend three years of his or her life watching television commercials. Advertising makes up about 70 percent of our newspapers and 40 percent of our mail. (pp. 58-59)

In 1996, corporate philanthropy funneled nearly $1.3 billion into the education marketplace, constituting 20 percent of the $6.3 billion in total corporate handouts. According to Corporate Watch (2000), the education industry consists of (a) public schools sponsored by corporations such as American Express,

Celebration School, and the American Bankers Insurance Group; (b) corporate charter schools or educational maintenance organizations such as the Edison Project, Advantage Schools Inc., and Educational Alternatives Inc.; (c) marketing and investment companies in the school business, such as Lehman Brothers, EduVentures, and Kid Connection; (d) corporations offering sponsored educational materials, such as Lifetime Learning Systems, Enterprise for Education, the Mazer Corporation, Media Options, Inc., and Youth Marketing International; (e) in-school advertising firms such as Scholastic Inc., Adopt-a-School, and Cover Concepts Marketing Service, Inc.; (f) lunch programs-funded by Pizza Hut, Subway, Arby's, and the American School Food Service Association; and (g) conservative and right-wing think tanks that influence educational policies, such as The Heritage Foundation, the Educational Excellence Network (which is pan of the Hudson Institute, overseen by Chester Finn and Diane Ravitch), and the Landmark Legal Foundation.

In public schools across the country, textbook covers are splashed with corporate logos, and specially designed corporate-sponsored curricula are provided to schools willing to accept free "lessons in a box" in exchange for financial assistance from private corporations. Many poorly funded public school districts are signing contracts that give corporations advertising rights on public school property. For example, the American Passage Media Corporation has installed billboards in high school locker rooms, where their commercial message reaches nearly 3 million students. These "Gymboards" advertise a variety of commercial products, including Tampax tampons. Pizza Hut offers a reading program entitled "Book It," whereby in exchange for a specified period of reading in the classroom, students receive free Pizza Hut coupons. American Express finances "Academies of Travel & Tourism" in four public high schools located in New York City that prepare students for jobs in the tourist industry. Students also learn about world geography and foreign cultures. Lifetime Learning Systems provides free textbook covers that expose 16 million students to advertising and commercials that are largely paid for by corporations such as Nike, McDonald's, and Hershey. The Center for Commercial-Free Public Education (2000) asserted that public schools are signing contracts that permit corporate sponsors such as Burger King and Coca-Cola to place their advertisements on school buses. In New York City, the board of education signed a 9-year, $53 million contract that allows advertisements to be placed on the district's school buses.

Supported by a complex infrastructure, the global empire of McDonald's (which consists of 25,000 restaurants in more than one hundred countries) is aggressively pursuing its ultimate goal of the "McDomination" of the fast food industry. McDonald's has a state-of-the-art university, Hamburger University, located in Oak Brook, Illinois (there are also branches in the United Kingdom, Germany, Japan, and Australia), where it trains its future managers. In a concerted effort to increase consumer loyalty, McDonald's provides public schools with free educational materials. At Pembroke Lakes Elementary School in Broward County, Florida, students are introduced to the world of work by learning how a

McDonald's restaurant is operated and managed, how to complete an employment application, and how to interview for a job at McDonald's. Students are also required to learn about the "nutritional" values of the high-fat, high-cholesterol, low-protein foods served at McDonald's. By providing free educational materials and resources to schools, McDonald's is able to achieve two important goals. First, it expands its market share and influences public school curricula. Second, McDonald's secures the foundation for recruiting future employees from a vast pool of working-class and students of color in urban schools, thus making the transition from school to low-paid work more efficient.

Although there has been vociferous public protest against the corporate takeover of education, corporations have not remained silent and have aggressively fought back against student, teacher, and parent activism. In public schools, colleges, and universities across the country, students have been penalized for resisting corporate colonization. In 1998, Mike Cameron, a senior at Greenbrier High School in Evans, Georgia, was suspended for wearing a Pepsi T-shirt on the day the school was participating in Coca-Cola's "school-sponsored Coke day," a national competition with other schools to win $10,000 (Klein, 1999). Jennifer Beatty, a college student who attended Morain Valley Community College in Palos Hills, Illinois, protested against the growing corporate influence over and commercialization of colleges and universities by chaining herself to the metal mesh curtains of the McDonald's Student Center. Beatty was later arrested and expelled from the college (Lasn, 2000).

In recent years, the profit-driven corporate *coup d'état* has shifted toward a "corporate-sponsored curriculum" supported in part by AT&T, McDonald's, Nike, Coca-Cola, PepsiCo, the Campbell Soup Company, and other corporations that are eagerly seeking new consumer markets. Corporate propaganda has been successful partly because of its ability to associate corporate interests with environmental and health issues. For example, Nike provides teachers with "sneaker-making kits" that teach students how Nike shoes are assembled; the lesson also focuses on how Nike is protecting the environment.

The Center for Commercial-Free Public Education (2000) reponed that in a concerted effort to restore its much-tainted image after the Valdez oil spill in Alaska, Exxon provides free educational videos to classroom teachers. Exxon portrays itself as an environmentally friendly corporation by showing how it is helping protect the wildlife in Alaska. Hershey teaches the nutritional values of its chocolate candies to students and suggests how chocolate can constitute an integral part of a balanced daily diet. Finally, the Campbell Soup Company provides teachers with free science lesson plans that attempt to prove that its Prego spaghetti sauce is thicker than the Ragu brand made by a competitor, Lipton.

Today, the impress of capital is found in the subjectivities of the young and old alike. Children spend $35 billion of their own money annually while influencing their parents to spend another $300 billion. In consumer culture, brand awareness and consumer loyalty are the key ingredients for the successful "cradle-to-grave" marketing strategies of corporations. To lure potential consumers, corporations devise slick advertisement campaigns that frequently involve giving away merchandise and prizes. In short, the commercialization of public schools through campaigns such as Pepsi Stuff, Marlboro Gear, Camel Cash, McDonald's Happy Meals, and the Budweiser frogs attests to the disturbing, growing trend of the privatization of the public life and the increasing transfer of capital from the public to the private sphere.

EDUCATION AND THE RESURGENCE OF THE RIGHT

Prompted by the rise of conservative politics and their impact on school curricula (Apple, 1993, 1996; Brosio, 1998; Spring, 1997, 1998) and the recent blitzkrieg led by the pundits of globalization and their neoliberal counterparts whose economic policies[4] have aimed at creating flexible labor markets, deregulation, downsizing,[5] and outsourcing[6] (Lauder & Brown, 1997; McLaren & Farahmandpur, 1999a, 1999b, 2000), critical educators have grown increasingly active in decrying a free-market economy that reduces politics to the tenuous logic of privatization and to brazenly unapologetic attempts to tie Friedmanian and Hayekian neoliberal economic principles to the production of school curricula (Apple, 1996; Brosio, 1998; McLaren & Farahmandpur, 2000; Spring, 1997, 1998; Tyack & Cuban, 1995). Some have engaged in a spirited counteroffensive to current economic policies aimed at widespread support for standardized tests, mandated textbooks, school-based management, a shared school mission, and the deskilling of teachers' labor (Apple, 1989; Berliner & Biddle, 1995)

Although in no way offering a Marxist alternative, Michael Apple (1996) identifies social policies favoring privatization, centralization, vocationalization, and the differentiation of school curricula as the "conservative restoration." He distinguished between neoliberal and neoconservative politics by correctly pointing out that the former supports economic policies that seek to weaken the role of the state, whereas the latter articulate a morality and an ethics that support a strong state. Apple regards these contradictory social and economic policies as part of what he has called "conservative modernization." In short, the combination of privatization and a relatively strong state has increasingly removed access to education from the public domain.

Educational policies under the influence of neoliberalism aim at controlling school curricula through national standards (Spring, 1998). These standards are geared toward increasing student knowledge by creating a "common curriculum." In the new economic order, students are increasingly urged to acquire basic skills in their journey from school to work and as a pan of their "lifelong learning." Many educational policy makers who seek to employ education as a tool for advancing neoliberal economics believe that the barrier between education and work should be removed without a trace (Banfield, 2000). In their opinion, lifelong learning is synonymous with life long accreditation.

In 1983, the report *A Nation at Risk* famously announced that public schools were to blame for the declining global competitiveness of the United States. Influenced by the report, socioeconomic policies under a burgeoning neoliberalism established control of school curricula by introducing national standards. A common curriculum was believed to be the most effective way of raising overall educational standards (Spring, 1998) and linking educational achievement to increasing the economic competitiveness of the United States (Berliner & Biddle, 1995). Although traditional Republicans viewed economic performance as indissolubly connected to the quality of schools, neoconservatives and their procorporate allies asserted that low academic standards were unequivocally responsible for the poor academic performance of both students and teachers. By the 1980s, the goal of educational performance became synonymous with excellence, and a strong emphasis was placed on increasing the number of school days, providing rigorous academic courses along with back-to-basics teaching methods, and placing increased emphasis and importance on teacher evaluation and accountability and standardized tests (Tyack & Cuban, 1995).

During the Reagan administration, educational policies plunged teachers and students headlong into the abyss of greed. Education's relation to capital was far from an innocent dalliance. Policies were underwritten by a confluence of free-market ideology, conservative Christian ideology, and nationalist sentiments (Spring, 1997). In 1989, the Goals 2000 initiative proposed by President Bush targeted the development of national academic standards and national achievement tests. By 1995, the call for national standards made by the Clinton administration proposed a history curriculum that aimed at concealing issues related to U.S. imperialism, exploitation, and political power (Spring, 1997). A cabal of conservatives (including Chester Finn, Diane Ravitch, and Dick Cheney) launched a national curriculum campaign that unreservedly Supported U.S. foreign policy and unswervingly put education on the path of for-profit schooling.

The far Right, Supported by organizations such as the Heritage Foundation, continues to be represented by powerful conservative political figures such as William Bennett and Newt Gingrich, who blame the government for the declining social and economic status of the United States in the global economy. The goal of these pundits and their corporate allies is to decentralize education and privatize public schools. The Religious Right has accused the government of promoting homosexuality, secular humanism, and scientific creationism; banning school prayer; and downplaying the importance of family values. Neoconservatives supported by the American Enterprise Institute have largely positioned themselves as political centrists who in their frenetic drive for academic excellence advocate a strong role for the federal government and support for private schools. Many of these conservative groups call for a return to the heterosexist patriarchy and still-born democracy of *Leave it to Beaver* and *Lassie*, pop culture's Elysian fields as dreamt by Norman Rockwell on melatonin. We are living Nickelodeon re runs of the American Dream, only in reverse.

A national curriculum and strong educational standards are manifestly viewed by mainstream policy pundits as pan of the modernization of the curriculum. However, an important latent function of such a curriculum is to impose efficient methods of production through the exploitation of labor power. Efforts to build a national curriculum and national standards that emphasize accountability, performance, ranking, and the differential placement of students into educational tracks (Oakes, 1985), is also pan of a larger agenda of steering public schools toward a free-market model that advocates giving a wide range of "choices" to parents (choices that will ultimately decimate the public sphere, morphing education into the structural unconscious of the billionaire boys' club of Bill Gates, Warren Edward Buffet, Paul Gardner, and Steve Ballmer).

TEACHERS' WORK AND THE VALUE FORM OF LABOR

We believe that it is important to engage the issue of educational reform from the perspective of Marx's value theory of labor. Marx's value theory of labor does not attempt to reduce labor to an economic category alone but is illustrative of how labor as a value form constitutes our very social universe, one that has been underwritten by the logic of capital. Value is not some hollow formality, neutral precinct, or barren hinterland empty of power and politics but the very matter and antimatter of Marx's social universe. It is important to keep in mind that the production of value is not the same as the production of wealth.

The production of value is historically specific and emerges whenever labor assumes its dual character. This is most clearly explicated in Marx's discussion of the contradictory nature of the commodity form and the expansive capacity of the commodity known as *labor-power*. To Marx, the commodity was highly unstable and nonidentical. Its concrete particularity (use value) is subsumed by its existence as value in motion or by what we have come to know as "capital" (value is always in motion because of the increase in capital's productivity that is required to maintain expansion). The issue here is not simply that workers are exploited for their surplus value but that all forms of human sociability are constituted by the logic of capitalist work. Labor, therefore, cannot be seen as the negation of capital or the antithesis of capital but as the human form through and against which capitalist work exists (Rikowski, 2000). Capitalist relations of production become hegemonic precisely when the process of the production of abstraction conquers the concrete processes of production, resulting in the expansion of the logic of capitalist work.

Class struggle has now been displaced to the realm of the totality of human relations, as abstract social structures such as labor now exist as the transubstantiation of human life as capital (Neary, 2000). So, when we look at the issue of educational reform, it is important to address the issue of teachers' work within capitalist society as a form of alienated labor, that is, as the specific production of the value form of labor. This becomes clearer when we begin to understand that one of the fundamental functions of schooling is to traffic in labor-power, in the engineering and enhancement of the capacity to labor so that such labor-power can be harnessed in the interests of capital. Rikowski's premise is provocative yet compelling and perhaps deceptively simple. Education is involved in the direct production of the one commodity that generates the entire social universe of capital in all of its dynamic and multiform existence: labor-power. Within the social universe of capital, individuals sell their capacity to labor—their labor-power—for a wage. Because they are included in this social universe on a differential and unequal basis, people can get paid above or below the value of their labor-power. Because labor-power is implicated in human will or agency and because it is impossible for capital to exist without it, education can be redesigned within a social justice agenda that will reclaim labor-power for socialist alternatives to human capital formation.

Helen Raduntz (1999) has made a convincing argument that teachers' work, implicated in the trafficking of labor-power, is fraught with contradictions and is situated on both sides of the labor-capital divide. More specifically, teachers' work is located both on the side of capital and that of wage-labor. It is also an important process of mediation in the class struggle between capital and wage labor, especially as both sides attempt to maximize their margins of surplus value.

Raduntz argues that the major source of contraction in teachers' work arises from the social relations of production. Teachers' work is a productive activity, both structurally and developmentally, and it is constitutive of the reproduction of capitalist social relations. Yet, teachers' work is integral to class struggle. This is because education is fundamental in the process of human development, but such a process becomes dehumanizing when it attempts to regulate education to coincide with and support the interests of capital. Raduntz calls for informed human development by teachers into this process of dehumanization. The struggle entails understanding that teachers' work is productive both for capital and for wage-labor. It is productive for capital in that teachers' work constitutes value transferred to wage laborers' labor-power in the acquisition of knowledge and skills; the value of teachers' work is also embedded as a component of the capital earned from surplus value as well as the wage paid to workers. In producing the use value of labor-power for capital, teachers' work is productive for capital. But, teachers' work is also productive for workers because it adds to the value of workers' labor-power and their ability to attract a wage that will enable them to sustain a livelihood. What is needed is an approach to educational reform that can help teachers understand their relationships to both capital and labor and thus challenge education's embodiment in the value form of labor via corporatization and privatization and push toward reclaiming labor-power for the fulfillment of human needs. Then, it may be possible to develop a model of education outside the current neoliberal agenda that can enable educators and their students to navigate and survive and eventually flourish out side the social universe of capital. This requires exploiting the tensions between the "statist" project of labor-power (human capital) enhancement and the neoliberal "businessification as a site schools underwritten by a view of education as a site for capital accumulation and profit-making (Rikowski, 2000). Of course, to offer an alternative to capitalist social relations is a daunting struggle and one that has untiringly exercised socialists for generations. Once such struggles occupied the efforts of labor unions, but especially since the demise of the Soviet Union and the eastern European bloc countries, unions have been all too happy to coexist with the value form of labor under capitalism.

THE NEW TEACHER UNIONISM

The growing trend in comanagement efforts taking place between teacher unions and school districts could be called the "new teacher unionism." At the core of the new comanagement plan is "peer reviewing," in which experienced or veteran teachers mentor new teachers and teachers who exhibit teaching performance below the standards set forth by their schools or school districts (Jordan, 1999). As many critics have pointed out, however, peer reviewing can work to reinforce deprofessionalization and the disempowerment of teachers, partly because the new teacher unionism aligns the teaching profession closely, and often urgently, with the demands of the global market economy. Nowhere in the new unionism is there a sustained acknowledgment of the theft of teachers' labor-power by the state. Teachers are now required to respond to economic demands for the increased efficiency, productivity, and flexibility of the labor market. Thus, the new teacher unionism not only undermines and weakens the function of more traditional teacher unions, but it also forces teachers to hire and fire other teachers. The new teacher unionism gives ballast to the exploitative, privileging hierarchies of corporate capitalism by further integrating the role of schools into the forces of production and the social relations of capital accumulation.

The panoptic glance of the new neoliberal economic and political order provides the warrant and guarantee for schools to forcibly maintain educational efficiency by incorporating standardized testing, social promotion, and get-tough policies that place the overriding responsibility for the academic achievement of students on schools, teachers, parents, and students themselves instead of addressing sufficiently the role of social and economic relations in the production and unequal distribution of selected forms of knowledge. An unstated contradiction is that school and state bureaucracies are seeking to improve student performance and teaching practices without additional funding for or investment in public schools (Allen, 1999; Leonardo, 2000). Schooling is becoming increasingly addicted to capital's need for the downsizing, outsourcing, and restructuring of the labor force to gain a competitive edge in the global economy. Eugene Plawiuk (1999) suggests that globalization driven by neoliberal economic policies seeks to "recreate public education in the corporate image, to create market driven schools" (p. 20). Here, the capitalist marketplace and democracy function metonymically so that teachers read them off against each other. They "stand in" for each other and have been "homologized" to mean essentially the same thing.

Critical educators must examine how workers' empowerment can be connected to their daily experiences at work and also to their relationships with the forces and relations of production and the "cartelization" of the knowledge industry. Resisting new capitalist production can be achieved by refusing to remain politically passive and by becoming morally and politically active social agents. Gee, Hull, and Lankshear (1997) offer the following strategies in the struggle against the current formation of what they called "fast-capitalist texts." First, critical educators must recognize how the identities of workers are socially and historically grounded. Second, the co-optation of critical ideas and concepts such as "empowerment," "liberation," and "collaboration" by the doyens of the new capitalism compels critical educators to focus on the moral and political aims of teaching. To critique the discourses of fast-capitalist texts in both the workplace and the schools, the development of a critical language becomes fundamentally important. Thus, according to Gee et al.,

> Fast capitalists do not . . . want to promote critical reflection in the sense of questioning systems as wholes and in their political relations to other systems. On the contrary, they are keen to pre-empt this, as we have seen in the case of self-directed learning. (p. 99)

With recent criticisms launched against the failures of public education, conservative and right-wing alliances have increasingly supported the privatization of education through charter schools, school choice, and voucher plans. They support the privatization of public schools because they contend that the private sector can manage schools with much more efficiency and productivity than the public sector. There is, of course, a motivated oversight about the private sector being driven by profit and an engineered silence surrounding the absence of long-term studies indicating that the private sector has produced better schools.

Not only must the struggle waged by teachers on behalf of improved public schools and better working conditions be linked with the labor movements, community activists, progressive organizations, schools of education, and parent and student organizations, but it also must be placed within the broader social and economic relations, specifically those linked to the struggle between capital and labor (Kincheloe, 1998; McLaren, 2000; McLaren & Farahmandpur, 1999a, 1999b, 2000).

Our position takes a cautious step away from the simple assertion that coalitional politics that advance "labor reform" is the favored union strategy, because such an unreflective position tacitly endorses existing arrangements produced by the law of the motion of capital, the forces of production, and the social relations of production. In other words, this position willfully ignores the complex means whereby the schooling process itself is implicated in the historical development of knowledge as a form of private ownership of the intellectual labor of the many for the profit of the few. Through its implication in the historical development of knowledge, labor reform fatefully naturalizes, institutionalizes, legitimizes, and makes hegemonic commonsense understandings of the relationship between schooling and capitalism that serves to refunction and reproduce neoliberal educational ideology.

According to the contemporary wave of pro-capitalist educational reformers, the only way that schools can "outmuscle" corporations that regularly "outsource" to the Third World or offshore labor pools is to transform whatever in education still remains public into a for-profit activity through the mechanics of privatization (Cole, Hill, & Rikowski, 1997; Cole, Hill, Rikowski, & McLaren, 2000). If education can continue to be recast within a "user-pays" optic, then it will be free to fulfill its capitalist destiny by smashing all remaining barriers to the downsizing of education into a consumerist, corporate bunker, or so the neoliberal argument goes. We are warned that if workers in advanced capitalist countries continue to require union protection, contribute to inefficient work practices, demand industry protection, economic regulation, a living wage, and competitive prices, then economic disaster will surely strike.

Educational critics such as Smyth and Shacklock (1998) are aware that the real disaster here for the neoliberals is the falling profit margin of the capitalist class, which desires only to accumulate as much capital as possible in the shortest amount of time. Smyth and Shacklock maintain that globalization has not brought about a fundamental repositioning and reconfiguring of the work of teaching. Although teaching has always served as a technology of discipline through regulating modes of social control (e.g., time and spatial management), it has now manacled itself with new forms of ideological capture through the proliferation of new technologies linked to cyborg visions of a world marketplace. In addition to the old external apparatus of teacher appraisal as a mechanism of social control that gives ballast to the reigning imperatives of capitalist accumulation, we are now confronted by an evolving species of ideational hegemonies created through the administration of the new professionalism, school development planning, marketized forms of management, performance and outcome-based indicators, competencies, skills formation, and the like. Recent moves to transform education into a for-profit, low-trust activity through marketization, the establishment of central inspectorates, and so forth fall squarely within the ideological imperative of the World Bank's recommendation to developing countries: Their curricula and syllabi should be securely tied to performance standards and measures of out come (Cole et al., 2000).

Within the expanded horizon of enterprise culture, under the flagship of economic rationalization, and as part of the prime directive of reconstructing teaching as economic work, Smyth and Shacklock (1998) ask what kind of competencies are invoked for inclusion in the lexicon of the "preferred teacher" (preferred, that is, by the established guardians of the public interest and their corporate comprador counterparts) and required for remaking the global citizen friendly to commerce and hospitable to the directives of the corporate bottom line. Although Smyth and Shacklock clearly reveal that such competencies are designed to mobilize consent for the status quo, they also illustrated how these competencies are being coated in deception through claims that such competencies are disinterested, scientific, and professional. Under the cover of policy hysteria surrounding the future of the global economy and the role that schooling must play in such a future, an "evaluative mode of an economically rational state" has been carefully cobbled out of the detritus of democracy's failed mission. This functions as a "silk glove" form of accountability (tied to technical and nominally "objective" forms of observation and appraisal), requiring individual teachers to implement systemic policy initiatives as a fundamental part of their work, a requirement that allows for a greater external monitoring of the "effectiveness" of teacher work. In the final analysis, educational critics such as Smyth and Shacklock have revealed how competencies that are prefixed and externally circumscribed and administered serve to limit what counts as skilled work in classrooms, undermine indigenous ways of talking about the world in general, and create a hidden blueprint for excluding teachers' active theorization of and experimentation with pedagogical practices. We want to raise an issue of *litem lite resolvere*. Educational policies grounded in the ideology of economic rationalism engineers a view of democratic schooling as premised upon the harmonization of differences among ethnic groups and social classes, thereby mistaking the phenomenon needing explanation for the explanation itself. Racism is a symptom of capitalist exploitation, not the cause of social affliction. Hence teachers are deflected from examining the interrelationship among race, class, and gender oppression within the context of global capitalist relations.

TOWARD A REVOLUTIONARY CITIZENSHIP

Part of the pedagogical project for creating a new revolutionary politics is what we refer to as the praxis of revolutionary citizenship. Such a praxis can be won in the classrooms, in the workplace, in class struggle for ownership of the means of production, and in those volatile and contested spaces of the public sphere where people struggle to redefine the meaning of democratic social life. Because it is a sociopolitical form of praxis, it ventures beyond abstractions and platitudes and refuses to linger inactively in the ambit of the apologists. *Citizenship*, as it is constructed within capitalist democracy, can be described as "a sociopolitical form that isolates individuals from social problems that have their roots in the individualization of goods and their sellers . . . [and] negates real social life by creating a political abstraction that obfuscates the major contradictions of society" (Costilla, 2000, p. 94). By contrast, revolutionary citizenship heeds unflinchingly the intrepid role of the activist and condemns those who would pusillanimously evade the moral issues surrounding neoliberalism's scandalously unbalanced assault on and treatment of the world's poor and aggrieved communities.

The project of revolutionary citizenship works directly against the politics of neoliberalism and seeks to build alliances between unionized workers and political leadership in the interest of increased socialist democracy. Revolutionary citizens work toward a new type of democratic governance and a redistribution of economic and political power that results in an oppositional form of globalization that, according to Costilla (2000), "is not subordinated to capital but humane in its economy, political system, mass media, culture, and citizenship" (p. 87). It works toward bringing all property under the control of the working class (Allman, 1999), with the eventual goal of eliminating private property and capital itself.

We argue that the revolutionary citizenship praxis as a form of creative collective action should be centered on the devalorization of capital as a process of dealienation. That is, the revolutionary citizenship praxis should recognize, following Dinerstein (1997), the contradictory mode of existence of labor; that is, it should grasp that action is a form of alienation and dealienation. Because society fundamentally involves the objectification of subjectivity, revolutionary citizenship becomes the constitution of subjectivity within the class struggle itself and the tension produced between the acceptance and negation of capitalist relationships (Dinerstein, 1997).

In obtaining some necessary political justice for our project, we follow Sam Gindin and Leo Panitch (2000) in arguing for a rethinking and reformulation of socialist utopian goals that exceed what capital and the state will accommodate. Rehabilitating a distinctly concrete Marxist utopianism, Gindin and Panitch addressed an "educated desire" as distinct from a "conservative desire." The former type of desire is described by the notion that "I want to change the world" and the latter by the notion that "I want to change my own place in the world" (Gindin & Panitch, 2000, p. 41). Gindin and Panitch argue that socialist morality

> educates desire toward the goal of realizing our potential to be full human beings and extending that principle to all members of society. Socialist analysis discovers, in the dynamics of capitalist society, the repressed possibility of that new world and the agency that, in the process of "doing-other:' can change both itself (including its dreams) and society, thereby "becoming-other." (p.41)

The utopian Marxism and reenchantment of socialist agency that is articulated in the project of revolutionary citizenship refuses to obliterate liberal democracy's traumatic origin in the production systems of imperialism and capitalist exploitation. It is underwritten by a socialist hope nurtured by particular social capacities that represents the crucial link between the ideal and the possibility of constructing a class collective in which workers "develop the social capacity to dream, to understand, to participate, and to act politically" (Gindin & Panitch, 2000, p. 41). Socialist dreaming is not about the liberation of the individual from the social but is about a collective dreaming through the social in the service of ensuring that workers are able to create a new world on their own terms and in their own voice without seeking permission to narrate their own futures. It enables workers to see the past as (to borrow a phrase from Lukács) "the prehistory of the present." It also enables a vision of the future that interweaves with the objective movement of history itself. The race-based uprising that took place in Los Angeles and that, more recently, occurred in Cincinnati have revealed to us that the melting pot has turned into a meltdown. The ravages of capital—including institutionalized forms of racist violence against African-Americans and Latina/os—have singled out all of the working class as its victim, but the most cruel form of violence and exploitation have been reserved for people of color. Surely, it is among the people of color where the leadership will arise to lead the assault against capitalism and its racist formations and practices.

The most important social capacity is that of acting politically as a class; this serves as the coordinating capacity for other capacities and attempts to make them less sporadic and more cumulative, especially with respect to the role of workers' organizations. Ideals that help steer such a collective vision include overcoming alienation, attenuating the division of labor, transforming consumption, creating alternative ways of living, socializing markets, planning ecologically, internationalizing equality, communicating democratically, and abolishing private property. As Gindin and Panitch (2000) point out, capitalism is "the wrong dream" (p. 50).

Capital agitates out of its productive forces a narrow range of social capacities and human activities. The narrowing of human capacities under global capitalism is due to the fact that they are constitutive of the logic of the corporate regime itself. The underlying structure of the corporate regime is by its very nature life-denying and psychopathic. As McMurtry (2000) asserts,

> The underlying general fact of our condition is that the transnational corporate regime is a profoundly incompetent regime in virtually every capability of life understanding and development. This is because it is based on an engineering paradigm which is in principle life-blind. Its system *has only mastered the methods of machine-manufacture and money-sequencing cost-inputs into greater money outputs, with the through-puts of all of human and environmental life blinkered out as having any value except as mecha-*

> nized means of these money-sequences. This structure of understanding
> civil and planetary life-organization is, from a wider standpoint, insane. As
> a system-decider for ruling the life-world, it is psychopathic, its paradigm
> and practice do not and cannot recognize life or educational values—
> including its vaunted electronic delivery circuits which do not and cannot
> tell the difference between true and false. (p. 9) [italics in original]

Furthermore, problems that do not offer corporate profits as a result of their solutions are no longer defined as problems. The corporate funding of education is about assisting education in solving profitable problems. McMurtry (2000) notes that,

> The fact that corporately directed science and medicine devotes little or no
> research funds to resurgent malaria, dengue fever or river blindness (whose
> many millions of victims lack market demand to pay for cures), while it
> invests billions of dollars into researching and marketing dubious and often
> lethal drugs to treat non-diseases of consumers in rich markets, demon-
> strates this agenda's principle of selection of problems to address. There is
> no reason to suppose that market corporations would behave differently
> with education on unprofitable problems than in their investment in
> researching them. . . . This commercialized research has led to insider trad-
> ing by faculty members, and attack on dissemination of research findings,
> including a University of South Florida filing of criminal charges against an
> M. A. student whose continued research on a patented project was alleged
> as "stealing university property," a charge which resulted in the student's
> sentence to a state chain gang. (p. 15)

Thus, we argue that capitalism instrumentalizes and fetishizes human capacities by truncating and depotentiating what McMurtry (1998) calls the "civil commons," defined as "society's organized and community-funded capacity of universally accessible resources to provide for the life preservation and growth of society's members and their environmental life-host" (p. 24). The civil commons provides the essential backdrop for revolutionary citizenship and socialist dreaming; it provides a space for individuals to participate in social activities that do not follow the logic of the market's exchange value. The civil commons further encompasses such areas as language, education, literacy, and cultural heritage as well as organizations and opportunities traditionally associated with the public sphere. These include but are not limited to public health and education, water and power, the postal service, public access to the media, libraries, and parks (McMurtry, 1998).

The civil commons constitutes assurances that basic human rights such as free health care, education, and employment will be central to the lifeblood of the community. The value system of the civil commons exists in contraposition to the value system of the free market, even though the free market perceives its value system to be identical with that of the civil commons. In reality, the market serves a minority ruling class whose interests are antagonistic to the interests of the rest of society (see also Giroux, 1983, 1992). The civil commons in the United States is afflicted by what the Children's Defense Fund's (2000) terms *affluenza*: "the poverty of having too much that is worth too little" (p. xviii). According to its recent report, millions of American children of all ethnicities in every part of the country

> are given every material thing they desire—cell phones, cars, every latest trendy fashion, CD and electronic gadgets, and live in big houses in well-to-do neighborhoods. But too many are not given enough parental and community attention, limit setting, and moral guidance. (pp. xiii-xiv)

The narrowing of human capacities and capitalism's attack on the civil commons must be transcended by breaking the power of capital and by setting free the human possibilities fostered by democratic community, social collectivity, and political solidarity. Thus, a pedagogy of revolutionary citizenship must stipulate as its primary focus the exposure of the lie of progress that is folded into the promise of neoliberalism. This entails a recognition and overcoming of the multifarious dimensions of deceit that shape the neoliberal utopian agenda. But, a critique of neoliberalism must be accompanied by a broader social revolution of the type described by Marx (Allman, 1999; Neary & Rikowski, 2000).

Revolutionary citizenship as a form of proletarian solidarity refutes the claims made by the supporters of the free market that, under a socialist system, individual rights are sacrificed for community rights. Although the community guarantees individuals rights to universal health care, education, and employment, the value system of the market is unable to meet the social needs of all community members. Consequently, the value system of the civil commons and the market are not identical, because the market is fundamentally rooted in producing profit before meeting the social and economic needs of community members (McMurtry, 1998). We do not hold out as much promise as does McMurtry that capitalist exploitation can be challenged successfully at the level of civil society. Hence, we remain disappointed in those who advocate for a "radical democracy" but fail to explain how workers are to gain the means of capitalist production without a direct assault on the power of the state through oppositional parties and an emphasis on international proletarian hegemony.

We do not advocate legislating for knowledge from a vanguard position from above that hinders its translation into popular action from below. Rather, we support appeals to and conceptions of the knowing, experiencing, and acting subject that claim a descent from Marx and Engels but remain flexibly attuned to the contextual specificity of the present. We draw a conspicuous distinction between critical revolutionary praxis as a real possibility in the advancement of a socialist alternative and the mechanistic and reductionist forms of Marxist theories that consider socialism and communism as historical inevitabilities. Daniel

Singer (1999) wisely remarked, "Socialism may be a historical possibility or even necessary to eliminate the evils of capitalism, but this does not mean that it will inevitably take its place" (p. 272). Although we recognize that we live in different social, historical, and geo-political contexts than the 19th-century world of which Marx wrote, we nevertheless affirm his central claims. For example, we recognize the central role of the working class in the struggle for socialism and the ongoing battle against imperialism worldwide.

Following the demise of socialism in Russia and Eastern Europe, the working class has been relegated to the footnotes of history. The declassing of the working class led by ex-Marxists, post-Marxists, and anti-Marxists who have retreated into the rutted streets of academic ghettos to sell at inflated prices cultural studies, deconstructionism, postmodernism, post structuralism, and various theories of globalization that are often openly hostile to Marxism only prolongs the deferment of revolutionary praxis (Allman, 1999; Cole & Hill, 1995; Hill, 1999; McLaren & Farahmandpur, 2000; Rikowski,2000). Even those radical academics sympathetic to issues on the left often become trapped in the self-referential mystification of their own bourgeois criteria as they attempt to push the boundaries of social critique through the luminous portals of the ivory tower. Michael Burawoy (2000) remarks that,

> One has to wonder to what extent the radicals are giving expression to their own conditions of existence. It is an accident that high-flying academics, hotel-circuiting consultants, conference-hopping professionals, and netscaping virtuosos should develop concepts of the network society, should imagine a manichean world of placeless power and powerless places, should expound on time-space compression or aesthetic cognitive maps? It is perhaps fitting that Giddens should traverse the world from capital to capital as he delivers his Reith lectures, ruminating on risk in Hong Kong, tradition in Delhi, family in Washington, and democracy in London. Their theories of globalization are theories of privileged men, who appear in a privileged airspace above the world they theorize. Their absence from their own accounts aspires to objectivity, but it cannot hide the unspoken, unreflected, stratospheric situatedness of their knowledges. How much of their theorizing is the projection of insulated journeys, unspoken genealogies, self-referential worlds? (p. 340)

It may be as difficult for a high-priced ruling class academic to grasp the exigencies and map the fault lines of working-class struggle as it is for a camel to pass through the eye of a needle or for a rich man or woman to enter the kingdom of heaven (or for Venezuela's president, Hugo Chavez, to spend a night in the Bush's ranch in Crawford, Texas). What is needed is what Paulo Freire (1970, 1998) referred to as a willingness to commit class suicide and a commitment to resist the rule of capital in all dimensions of social life.

Transforming revolutionary praxis into a real socialist alternative necessitates developing a political imaginary that embraces an acute awareness of the social ills induced by capitalism and is capable of producing a political ideology that can unify the oppressed classes into a revolutionary class willing to challenge the relations of capitalist exploitation with the intention of eventually transforming them. Finally, developing a political imaginary means treating "capitalism not as an eternity, but as a historical phase with a distant beginning and a possible proximate end" (Singer, 1999, p. 257).

How do we move beyond nervously twiddling our thumbs while waiting for the next stage of history and merely thumbing our noses at capitalism? After all, unlike some educational leftists and pseudo-leftists, we do not believe that anticapitalist struggle is naive or merely a rhetorical argument. Nor do we believe for an instant that revolutionary pedagogy is a form of "romantic possibilitarianism." Are moderate, reformist ideologies enough? Do we simply carry out the ideology of reform and development? Do we revamp the traditional model of Western parliamentary democracy so that it can be mechanically applied to the peripheral Third World countries of Asia, Latin America, and Eastern Europe? Is there a way to avoid the dangers of both authoritarianism and parliamentarianism?

Boris Kagarlitsky (2000) argues that there is indeed an alternative that is based on creating neither larger nor smaller states but fundamentally different kinds of states that are neither liberal nor bourgeois but place the public sector as an active player in the economy. The public sector is placed in the hands of the workers and their parties such that self-management within state structures will bring about democratic forms of representation. As Kagarlitsky notes, we must change the very nature of our approach to development. We note here by example the efforts of the Workers Party in Brazil to institute participatory budgets and to reinvest in the infrastructures of cities (although at the same time we register our disappointment with Lula).

A revolutionary citizenship must move beyond the centralizing trends of the old statist industrial economy while recognizing the potential role of the state in providing accelerated development in Third World countries. Accumulation and investment policy must be subordinated to the needs of the people. This presupposes a broader notion of the national organization of production. Capitalists began this process; socialists must finish it. Every decision made on behalf of growth must guarantee the rights of the individual. One precondition for this is the social ownership by the workers of the technological base of society. This means struggling for a democratic compatibility between socioeconomic and political structures. We cannot afford to think in phases or that a democratic revolution will naturally precede a socialist one. Development must be driven by socialist institutions, and this includes the schools. As Arthur MacWean (1999) opines,

in a democratic development strategy, it is not enough to expand the
schooling system as a means to promote equality; it is also necessary to
equalize the educational system itself and eliminate the connection between
family income and the quality of education that people receive. (p. 186)

Contemporary approaches to critical pedagogy have bled much of the political praxis capabilities out of it, rendering critical pedagogy ideologically and
conceptually anemic and politically detumescent; in fact, many progressive educators claiming to endorse critical pedagogy have made sure that the questions
posed above are not part of the larger educational agenda. Short-term advances
in educational reform have become impaled on the long term intractability of
capitalist relations of exploitation. Critical pedagogy must do more than paint a
happy face on capitalist social relations of production (Allen, 1999; Leonardo,
2000; McLaren, 2000).

The postmodern Left in education has argued for transgressive forms of
resignification of the symbolic order in the ideological struggle for hegemony.
More specifically, it has attempted a radical transformation of the universal
structuring principle of the existing symbolic order. Yet, in doing so, it has
failed to sufficiently problematize the social universe of capital. Slavoj Zizek
(2000) remarks how post-Marxists such as Judith Butler and Ernesto Laclau
have in their respective critiques of so-called essentialist Marxism neglected to
contest the rule of capital. As Zizek notes,

today's Real which sets a limit to resignification is capital: the smooth
functioning of Capital is that which remains the same, that which "always
returns to its place," in the unconstrained struggle for hegemony. Is this not
demonstrated by the fact that Butler, as well as Laclau, in their criticism of
the old "essentialist" Marxism, none the less silently *accept* a set of premises: they never question the fundamentals of the capitalist market economy
and the liberal-democratic political regime; they never envisage the possibility of a completely *different* economico-political regime. In this way,
they *fully participate* in the abandonment of these questions by the "postmodern" Left: all the changes they propose are changes *within* this economico-political regime. (p. 223)

We are not interested only in palliative damage control measures within the
social universe of capital production and exchange mechanisms. We are interested in the total revolution of which Marx speaks. Here we want to underscore the
importance of autonomous movements such as the Zapatistas. Our Marxian solidarity is not powered by attempts to conscript revolutionary praxis into conformity with a monolithic, Eurocentric *Weltanschauung* premised on Enlightenment
rationality, but by a commitment to multiple forms of organization, human sociality, and solidarity. Such a commitment sets itself against the social, economic,
and spiritual forms of wreckage brought about by those imperialist forces

unchained by the globalization of capital and global neo-liberalism (Grande, 2000, Richardson & Villenas, 2000).

Revolutionary pedagogy examines the conjoined spaces of the pedagogical field to interrogate it in all of its capillary detail. In doing so, revolutionary pedagogy imposes on the educator a new set of obligations, the most important being that of creating revolutionary agency and citizenship. In excavating the planes of practical action that define the space of the pedagogical and the political, as well as their intersection, revolutionary educators recognize that the struggle for educational reform stipulates anticapitalist struggle in both local and global contexts. In doing so, they encourage strategies of conflict and criticism to halt the pretenses of any single conception of the pedagogical.

We cannot afford to be lured by the manufactured daydreams or the halcyon nights of contemporary commodity culture where social agents are reduced to gleeful spectators celebrating the *comédie noire* of capitalism. Democracy cannot be pandered to the demands of a dangerously unrestricted capitalism. In the words of Boris Kagarlitsky (1999), "democracy [under capitalism] . . . is a façade, mere window-dressing" (p. 144). Contrary to the opinion of many postmodern savants and post-Marxist illuminati, we believe that Marx's chiliastic analyses of capitalism will continue to be vital well into the twenty-first century and beyond. The potential of Marxist theory for reinvigorating our understanding of and political resistance to the commodification and corporatization of schooling is only beginning to be fully recognized. As Michael Parenti (1997) so pertinently argues,

> Marx's major work was capital, a study not of "existing socialism:" which actually did not exist in his day, but of capitalism—a subject that remains terribly relevant to our lives. It would make more sense to declare Marxism obsolete if and when capitalism is abolished, rather than socialism. I wish to argue not merely that Marx is still relevant but that he is more relevant today than he was in the nineteenth century, that the forces of capitalist motion and development are operating with greater scope than when he first studied them. (p. 122)

We believe that the time has come for critical educators to answer the following questions or face the consequences: Do we merely fight the excesses of capitalism, or do we work toward overthrowing them? Do we fight against the shrinkage of basic industry and its outsourcing, or do we struggle for workers' rights internationally? Do we participate in the task of increasing shopping opportunities for the rich, or should our efforts be directed at bringing the globalization of capital to an end? Is our task as critical educators to address the inner contradictions within capital-labor relations, or do we in a concrete and even perhaps militant fashion enter the struggle between workers and capitalists? Do we struggle for a redistribution of resources, as most radical educational critics encourage, or do we also develop a socialist future that will serve an unlimitedly developing humankind? Is our goal to manage the crisis of capital or bring down the capitalist system? Will the prime function of critical educators be to articulate and manage conflicts or deepen the development of social struggles? As Samir Amin (2000) aptly puts it,

> The central question, therefore, is how conflicts and social struggles (it is important to differentiate between the two) will be articulated. Which will triumph? Will social struggles be subordinated, framed by conflicts, and therefore mastered by the dominant powers, even made instruments to the benefit of those powers? Or will social struggles surmount their autonomy and force the major powers to respond to their urgent demands? (p. 17)

Do we put our faith in the possibility that abstract labor might negate itself and recompose the relation between capital and labor or between the wage laborers and the bourgeoisie, or do we begin the necessary task of creating a mass revolutionary organization that is aligned with the everyday struggles of the working class and is capable of striking at the heart of the capitalist system? Do we trawl hesitatingly between the Scylla of neoliberalism and the Charybdis of a Third Way politics, or do we move full throttle into the untested waters of mass internationalist movements? Do we retreat into the academic salons of the post-Marxist theorists, or do we rent the vaults of capital with defiant cries from the picket lines with strategies of refusal won on the playing fields of a resurgent Marxist theory? Here we direct our efforts at Rosemary Hennessy's (2001) brilliant work on the renarrating of identities from the standpoint of the collectivity of those whose surplus human needs capitalism has refused to meet. Hennessy emphasizes the historical and material conditions of possibility of identity formation that does not renounce racial, gender, or sexual identities in favor of a class identity but approaches these identities as features of social reality and lived experience that demands a comprehensive historical and materialist explanation. Especially after "The Battle in Seattle," we should be emboldened to accelerate our struggles and recover confidence in our potential capacities and powers. As Alex Callinicos (2000) warns, "The greatest obstacle to change is not, however, the revolt it would evoke from the privileged, but the belief that is is impossible" (p. 128).

Our search must be directed toward new forms of sociality that do not run parallel to the social universe of capital but that are linked to a praxis-driven revolutionary politics dedicated to transforming capitalist social relations of production. Michael Löwy (2000) writes that:

> What alternatives exist to the totalitarian grip of "really existing" world capitalism? The old pseudo-internationalism of the Stalinist Comintern, of the followers of various "Socialist fatherlands" is dead and buried. A new internationalist alternative of the oppressed and exploited is badly needed. . . . It is from the fusion between the international socialist, democratic and anti-imperialist tradition of the labor movement (still much alive among revolu-

tionaries of various tendencies, radical trade unionists, critical communists, left-socialists, etc.) and the new universalist culture of social movements like ecology, feminism, anti-racism, and Third World solidarity that the internationalism of tomorrow will rise. This tendency may be a minority now, but it is nevertheless the seed of a different future and the ultimate guarantee against barbarism. (p.12)

We can no longer afford to remain indifferent to the horrors and savageries committed by capitalism's self-destructive mechanisms, which are steering civilization into a collision course with barbarism. Our deafening silence offers despair a victory and foreshortens the hope necessary for overcoming cynicism in our efforts to create a democratic and egalitarian socialist society. As the gravediggers of capitalism, we must keep our shovels poised to keep digging. History does not end at the doorstep of capitalism, nor is it scripted by the ruling classes. The course of history can be altered by collective struggle. The future remains in the hands of those whose revolutionary activities are directed at creating it. That includes, first and foremost, the workers whose service we dedicate ourselves. We have been handed the red thread that will lead us out of the labyrinth of capital. All that we need is the courage to clutch it and to steel ourselves for the long and winding road to victory.

NOTES

1. Neoliberalism ("capitalism with the gloves off" or "socialism for the rich") refers to a corporate domination of society that supports state enforcement of the unregulated market, engages in the oppression of nonmarket forces and antimarket policies, guts free public services, eliminates social subsidies, offers limitless concessions to transnational corporations, enthrones a neomercantilist public policy agenda, establishes the market as the patron of educational reform, and permits private interests to control most of social life in the pursuit of profits for the few (e.g., through lowering taxes on the wealthy, scrapping environmental regulations, and dismantling public education and social welfare programs). It is undeniably one of the most dangerous politics that we face today. As described by Robert McChesney (1999), neoliberalism is "the immediate and foremost enemy of genuine participatory democracy, not just in the United States but across the planet, and will be for the foreseeable future" (p. 11).
2. To call globalization a form of imperialism might seem a rebarbative exaggeration. But, this identification is necessary because the term *globalization* is calculated by bourgeois critics to render any radical politicization of it as extreme. The ideology of this move is to invisibly frame the concept of globalization within a culturalist logic that reduces it to mean a standardization of commodities. By contrast, we see the process as inextricably tied to the politics of neoliberalism, in which violence asserts itself as stability through a recomposition of the capital-labor relationship. Such a recomposition entails the subordination of social reproduction to the reproduction of capital (Dinerstein, 1999), the deregulation of the labor market, the globalization of liq-

uid capital, the outsourcing of production to cheap labor markets, and the transfer of local capital intended for social services into finance capital for global investment. Also, when we use the term globalization, we are referring to corporate globalization. Free trade is a false term. We use it to refer to oligopolistic trade (see McMurtry, 1998).

3. In a discussion of marketization and educational change, Kari Dehli (1996) argued that the concept of marketization must be made more problematic and must be conceptually differentiated. Dehli identified four forms of marketization: privatization, commercialization, commodification, and residualization. Dehli wrote:

> Privatisation refers to the movement of programs, resources and staff from the public to the private sector, including corporations, families or "voluntary" organisations, as well as the movement of previously "private" services and programs—such as parent "volunteers" social services, and corporate partnerships—into publicly funded schools; commercialisation incorporates exchange-based relations to shape the internal organisation of educational institutions, relations between schools, and relations between schools and their publics; commodification suggests the ascendancy of packaged and quantifiable forms of knowledge and assessment, such as outcome-based curricula, performance indicators and skills testing techniques; while residualisation attends to the structural consequences of individualised choice in public services. These concepts are helpful in sorting through the often confusing and disorienting features and processes of marketisation. They make it possible to tease out the distinctive features of specific practices, and to compare the shape, content and effects of different processes and reactions to them. (p. 365)

4. Business governed by the laws of supply and demand, not restrained by government interference, regulation, or subsidy. According to this point of view, capitalism as an economic system is most efficient and productive when there is regulation or interference by the government.

5. *Downsizing* refers to reducing the total number of employees at a company through terminations, retirements, or spin-offs.

6. *Outsourcing* refers to work done for a company by workers other than the company's full-time employees. A majority of these workers are from Third World nations and are hired by companies contracted by multinational corporations.

7. *Privatization* refers to the transfer of the management of public schools to private or for-profit educational organizations. Privatization emphasizes typical business-oriented concepts such as customer satisfaction and managerial autonomy in running schools.

REFERENCES

Allen, R. L. (1999). The socio-spatial making and marking of "us": Toward a critical postmodern spatial theory of difference and community. *Social Identities, 5*(3), 249-277.

Allman, P. (1999). *Revolutionary social transformation: Democratic hopes, political possibilities and critical education.* Westport, CT: Bergin and Garvey.

Amin, S. (2000).The political economy of the twentieth century. *Monthly Review, 52*(2), 1-17.

Apple, M.W. (1989). *Teachers and texts: A political economy of class & gender relation in education.* New York: Routledge.

Apple, M. W. (1993). *Official knowledge: Democratic education in a conservative age.* New York: Routledge.

Apple, M. W. (1996). *Cultural politics and education.* New York: Teachers College Press.

Banfield, G. (2000). Schooling and the spirit of enterprise: Producing the power top labor. *Education and Social Justice, 2*(3), 23-28.

Berliner, D. C., & Biddle, B. J. (1995). *The manufactured crises: Myths, fraud, and the attack on America's public schools.* Reading, MA: Addison-Wesley.

Boggs, C. (2000). *The end of politics: Corporate power and the decline of the public sphere.* New York: Guilford.

Brosio, R. A. (1998). End of the millennium: Capitalism's dynamism, civic crises, and corresponding consequences for education. In H. S. Shapiro & D. E. Purpel (Eds.), *Critical social issues in American education: Transformation in a postmodern world* (2nd ed., pp. 27-44). Mahwah, NJ: Lawrence Erlbaum.

Budgen, S. (2000). A new "spirit of capitalism." *New Left Review, 1,* 149-156.

Burawoy, M. (2000). Grounding globalization. In M. Burawoy, J. A. Blum, S. George, Z. Gille, T. Gowan, L. Haney, M. Klawiter, S. H. Lopez, S. Riain, & M. Thayer (Eds.), *Global ethnography: Forces, connections, and imaginations in a postmodern world* (pp. 337-350). Berkeley: University of California Press.

Callinicos, A. (2000). *Equality.* Cambridge, UK: Polity.

Center for a New American Dream. (2000, February 22). *Kids and commercialism* [Online]. Available: http://www.newdream.org/campaign/kids/facts.html

Center for Commercial-Free Public Education, The. (2000, February 21). *Commercialism in the schools* [Online]. Available: http://www.commercialfree.org /commercialism.html

Children's Defense Fund. (2000). *The state of America's children.* Boston: Beacon.

Cole, M. (1998). Globalization, modernization and competitiveness: A critique of the New Labour project in education. *International Studies in Sociology of Education, 16,* 165-182.

Cole, M., & Hill, D. (1995). Games of despair and rhetorics of resistance: Postmodernism, education and reaction. *British Journal of Sociology of Education, 16*(2), 165-182.

Cole, M., Hill, D., & Rikowski, G. (1997). Between Postmodernism and nowhere: The predicament of the postmodernist. *British Journal of Educational Studies, 45*(2), 187-200.

Cole, M., Hill, D., Rikowski, G., & McLaren, P. (2000). *Red chalk: On schooling, capitalism and politics.* London: Tufnell Press.

Corporate Watch. (2000, February 21). *The education industry fact sheet* [Online]. Available: http://www.corpwatch.org/trac/ feature/education/industry/fact/html

Costilla, L.F.O. (2000). The reconstitution of power and democracy in the age of capital globalization. *Latin American Perspectives, 27*(1), 82-104.

Dehli, K. (1996). Between "market" and "state": Engendered education in the 1990s. *Discourse: Studies in Cultural Politics of Education, 17*(3), 363-376.

Dinerstein, A. (1997). Marxism and subjectivity: Searching for the marvelous (prelude to a Marxist notion of action). *Common Sense, 22,* 83-96.

Dinerstein, A. (1999). The violence of stability: Argentina in the 1990s. In M. Neary (Ed.), *Global humanization: Studies in the manufacture of labor* (pp. 47-76). London: Mansell.

Dlugin, L. (1999). Globalization. *Political Affairs, 78*(11), 20-22.

Ehrenreich, B. (2000a, October 26-29). Global stench. *LA Weekly*, pp. 19-20.

Ehrenreich, B. (2000b, June 2-8). Terrible waste. *LA Weekly*, pp. 20-21.

Freire, P. (1970). *Pedagogy of the oppressed.* New York: Continuum.

Freire, P. (1998). *Pedagogy of freedom: Ethics, democracy, and civic courage.* Lanham, MD: Rowman & Littlefield.

Galeano, E. (2000). *Upside down: A primer for the looking-class world* (M. Fried, Trans.). New York: Metropolitan Books.

Gee, .J.P., Hull, G., & Lankshear, C. (1997). *The new work order: Behind the language of the new capitalism.* Boulder, CO: Westview.

Gindin, S., & Panitch, L. (2000). Rethinking socialist imagination: Utopian vision and working class capacities. *Monthly Review, 51*(10), 36-51.

Giroux, H. (1983). *Theory and resistance in education: A pedagogy for the opposition.* South Hadley, MA: Bergin & Garvey Publishers.

Giroux, H. (1992). *Border crossings.* New York and London: Routledge.

Grande, S.M.A. (2000). American Indian identity and power: At the crossroads of Indigena and Mesdzaje. *Harvard Educational Review, 70*(4), 467-498.

Hardt, M., & Negri, A. (2000). *Empire.* Cambridge, MA: Harvard University Press.

Heintz, J., & Folbre, N. (2000). *The ultimate field guide to the US. economy: A compact and irreverent guide to economic life in America.* New York: New Press.

Hill, D. (1999). *New Labour and education: Policy, ideology and the Third Way.* London: Tufnell Press.

Hennessy, R. (2001, 31 March). *Building social movement out of unmet needs:Class consciousness, the permanent plantón, and love.* A keynote address at the conference Almost Always Deceived: Revolutionary Praxis and Reinventions of Need. University of Florida, Gainesville.

Jordan, I. (1999). Peer review and the new teacher unionism: Mutual support or policing? *Against the Current, 14*(4), 13-16.

Kagarlitsky, B. (1999). *New realism new barbarism: Socialist theory in the era of globalization* (R. Clark, Trans.). London: Pluto.

Kagarlitsky, B. (2000). *The return of radicalism: Reshaping the left institutions* (R. Clark, Trans.). London: Pluto.

Kilbourne, J. (1999). *Deadly persuasion: Why women and girls must fight the addictive power of advertising.* New York: Free Press.

Kincheloe, J. (1993). *Towards a critical politics of teacher thinking: Mapping the postmodern.* Westport, CT: Bergin and Garvey.

Kincheloe, J. (1998). *How do we tell the workers? The socioeconomic foundations of work and vocational education.* Boulder, CO: Westview Press.

Klein, N. (1999). *No logo: Taking aim at the brand bullies.* New York: Picador.

Lasn, K. (1999). *Culture jam: The uncooling of America.* New York: Eagle.

Lasn, K. (2000). USA TM. *Adbusters, 28,* 52-55.

Lauder, H., & Brown, P. (1997). Education, globalization, and economic development. In A. H. Hasley, H. Lauder, P. Brown, & A. S. Wells (Eds.), *Education: Culture, economy, society* (pp. 172-192). Oxford, UK: Oxford University Press.

Leonardo, Z. (2000). Betwixt and between: An introduction to the politics of identity. In C. Tejada, C. Martinez, & Z. Leonardo (Eds.), *Charting new terrains of chicana(o)/latina(o) education* (pp. 107-129). Cresskill, NJ: Hampton Press.

Löwy, M. (2000). *Nationalism and the new world order* [Working Papers Series in Cultural Studies, Ethnicity, and Race Relations]. Pullman: Washington State University, Department of Comparative American Cultures.

MacWean, A. (1999). *Neoliberation or democracy: Economic strategy, markets, and alternatives for the 21st century.* London: Zed.

McChesney, R.W. (1999), Introduction. In N. Chomsky (Ed.), *Profit over people: Neoliberalism and global order* (pp. 7-16). New York: Seven Stories.

McLaren, P. (2000). *Che Guevara, Paulo Freire, and the pedagogy of revolution.* Lanham, MD: Rowman & Littlefield.

McLaren, P., & Farahmandpur, R. (1999a). Critical multiculturalism and globalization: Some implications for a politics of resistance. *Journal of Curriculum Theorizing, 15*(3), 27-46.

McLaren, P., & Farahmandpur, R. (1999b). Critical pedagogy, postmodernism, and the retreat from class: Toward a contraband pedagogy. *Theoria: A Journal of Social and Political Theory, 93*, 83-115.

McLaren, P., & Farahmandpur, R. (2000). Reconsidering Marx in post-Marxist times: A requiem for postmodernism? *Educational Researcher, 29*(3), 25-33.

McMurtry, J. (198). *Unequal freedoms; The global market as an ethical system.* West Hartford, CT: Kumarian.

McMurtry, J. (2000, March). *Seeing through the corporate agenda: Education, life-value and the global economy.* Paper presented at the annual meeting of the Queen's University Faculty of Education Colloquium, Kingston, Canada.

Mészáros, I. (1999). Marxism, the capital system, and social revolution: An interview with István Mészáros. *Science and Society, 63*(3), 338-361.

Neary, M. (2000). *Travels in Moishe Postone's social universe: A contribution to a critique of political cosmology.* Unpublished manuscript.

Neary, M., & Rikowski, G. (2000, April). *The speed of life: The significance of Karl Marx's concept of socially necessary labour-time.* Paper presented at the annual conference of the British Sociological Association, York, United Kingdom.

Oakes, J. (1985). *Keeping track: How schools structure inequality.* New Haven: Yale University Press.

Parenti, M. (1997). *Blackshirts & Reds: Rational fascism & the overthrow of communism.* San Francisco: City Lights.

Plawiuk, E. (1999). Assaulting public education in Canada: Privalization plague spreads. *Against the Current, 14*(4), 18-20.

Raduntz, H. (1999, November-December). *A Marxian critique of teachers' work in an era of capitalist globalization.* Paper presented at the annual conference of the Australian Association for Research in Education and the New Zealand Association for Research in Education, Melbourne, Australia.

Richardson, T., & Villenas, S. (2000). "Other" encounters: Dances with whiteness in multicultural education. *Educational Theory, 50*(2), 255-274.

Rikowski, G. (2000, September). *Messing with the explosive commodity: School improvement, educational research and labor-power in the era of global capitalism.* Paper presented at the annual conference of the British Educational Research Association, Cardiff, United Kingdom.

Shapiro, S. (1999). Education and the politics of the "Third Way." *Tikkun, 14*(3), 57-61.

Singer, D. (1999). *Whose millennium? Theirs or ours?* New York: Monthly Review Press.

Smyth, G., & Shacklock, G. (1998). *Re-making teaching: Ideology, policy and practice.* London: Routledge.

Spring, I. (1997). *Political agendas for education: From the Christian coalition to the Green Party.* Mahwah, NJ: Lawrence Erlbaum.

Spring, J. (1998). *Education and the rise of the global economy.* Mahwah, NJ: Lawrence Erlbaum.

Tyack, D., & Cuban, L.(1995). *Tinkering toward utopia: A century of public education reform.* Cambridge, MA: Harvard University Press.

Wood, E. M. (1995). *Democracy against capitalism: Renewing historical materialism.* Cambridge, UK: Cambridge University Press.

Zizek, S. (2000). Holding the place. In J. Butler, E. Laclau, & S. Zizek (Eds.), *Contingency, hegemony, universality: Contemporary dialogues on the left.* London: Verso.

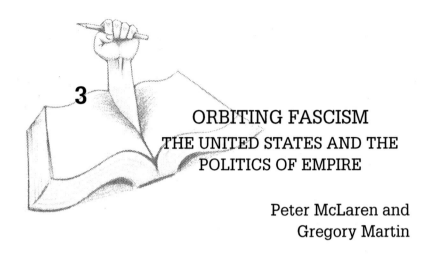

3

ORBITING FASCISM
THE UNITED STATES AND THE
POLITICS OF EMPIRE

Peter McLaren and
Gregory Martin

Following the outbreak of World War II, Trotsky presciently remarked that the reactionary character of imperialism was expressed most clearly by its organic descent into fascism. Faced with internal economic stagnation and decay, those 'civilized hyenas' (Lenin's term) who pompously ride in the saddle of the beast of capital seek to delay its demise by creating conditions for fascism and imperialist war to flourish. How long capital can continue to sustain itself, even as the innocents of entire nations are sacrificed to its unending gluttony for profit, is difficult to predict. But the outcome is not. Capital, in this degenerate and imperialist phase, is no longer concerned with being an internal progressive force— far from it. Indeed, out of absolute necessity, capital becomes a regressive force, a weapon of subjugation, drawing the whole world into its shadowy orbit of deceit and conquest. Likewise, grappling with a sharpening and deepening social crisis, the U.S. ruling class through its supporting state apparatus is today unleashing a raging torrent of reactionary violence, repression, terror and death to create the necessary conditions for its own regeneration. Brandishing its weapons of mass destruction, the wartime U.S. imperialist state led by the Bush gang has emerged as an indispensable guarantor of 'super-profits' for its own wild-eyed imperialist bourgeoisie. Yet, the imperial reach of the U.S. differs from that of Britain a century ago in that the U.S. does not practice colonialism but relies on dependent and satellite states, resorting to armed intervention when the natives get restless and start refusing to buckle down. Whereas the British empire was based on a singularly British purpose, the U. S. is based on a universalist conviction that the rest of the world should follow its example of free market capitalist democracy (Hobsbawm, 2003). Long before Bush W. took power in January 2001, the present architects of U.S. foreign policy at the Project for

This chapter was first published as Peter McLaren and Gregory Martin, America's "Big Lie" Machine, *Socialist Future Review*, Summer 2003, pp. 18-27. www.socialistfuture.org.uk).

the New American Century (PNAC), recognized the need to maintain the dominant position of U.S. capitalism by advancing such American values through a
policy of 'peace through strength.' But the brute reality is that 'one imperialist
state can only expand its power at the expense of another' and what is emerging
today is not 'security' or 'world peace' but new imperialist centers of rivalry as
evidenced by the two-day summit that included Russia, France and Germany in
Russia on 11-12 April 2003 (*Socialist Democracy*, 2002).

Despite the growth of a gigantic, parasitic and militaristic state at the
expense of individual and group freedoms, we really cannot talk about fascism
in the U.S. the same way that Trotsky referred to the term. At the same time, the
conditions that foster fascism cannot be ignored here on U.S. soil, especially
considering the scary success of the Bush gang and its propaganda campaign,
which has led people to forget the actual conditions that make its emergence
and victory possible. Forgotten are the transnationals who are flooding the market with cheap and subsidized food and forcing millions of farmers into bankruptcy, including thousands per week in the U. S. Forgotten are the million of
urban homeless and unemployed and those cannot afford medical insurance.
Forgotten is the environmental degradation in the Homeland, and the toxic
waste we are dumping not just on Native American lands but also exporting to
developing countries as the solution. Forgotten is California' s energy crisis that
was stage-managed by Kenny Boy Lay, the darling of Bush W., who still runs
free even after the collapse of his company, Enron.

All of the above is an old and stale story for 'globalization' theorists, perhaps even for Marxist experts who specialize in the declining rate of profit and
capital's effort to deal with it in a post Keynesian era. But it is rendered excep-
tional by the sheer scale of barbarity and cruelty being waged against humanity
and the planet. What matters here is that without the counterweight of the former
Soviet Union, the U.S., under the Republicans and the 'lesser-evil' Democrats,
has risen rapidly to the top of the imperialist pack and is acting like the world's
bullyboy. Now there was an excuse to crush unforgivingly the remnants of any
progressive consensus that survived the fight with its old adversary, the Soviet
boogeyman. Now neoliberalism could be unleashed unopposed by any super-
power. Now the true enemy—the international working class—could be further
fractured and destroyed. This was expressed in perfect clarity by the brutal military offensive that followed the events of September 11, when a still unproven
force destroyed the World Trade Center and damaged the Pentagon. The tragedy
of 9.11 catapulted infamously the unpopular Bush/Cheney/Scalia/Thomas
rightwing that rode into power by stealing the 2000 U.S. election, onto the stage
of world history (Program Demand Group, 2003). Seizing upon the fear and
sympathy afforded by September 11, Bush & Co. declared an open-ended 'War
on Terrorism,' with the right to wage war on any perceived enemy, domestic or
foreign, for any reason, at anytime, and by any means—including nuclear
weapons. With a jawjutting and arrogant sneer, Bush declared an ultimatum to
the world: "You are either with us or for the terrorists"

The story we are being told here, in the home citadel of U. S. imperialism, is that this unapologetic Crusade, which is being waged on a number of different fronts (e.g., Afghanistan, Colombia, Iraq, the Philippines and United States), is all about protecting 'our way of life' and defending the 'free world' from evildoers (The Editors, 2002). But beneath this overblown rhetoric lurks what Dr. Joseph Goebbels, the notorious Nazi propaganda chief, called the art of the 'Big Lie.' The logic of the 'Big Lie' is that people will accept a lie as truth if it is big enough and is told often enough by authoritative sources. Whereas Goebbels' lie laid the foundations for the Holocaust, the Bush regime is manipulating the U.S. population into an epoch of imperialist war that threatens to kill millions of world's poorest people by the Big Lie. To take just one glaring example, before the invasion of Iraq, the Secretary of State presented evidence from the CIA and U.S. intelligence community to the United Nations Security Council of Iraq's alleged 'Weapons of Mass Destruction.' The so-called 'clear proof' of this stockpile was calculated to create public support for a war, deemed in violation of international law. Yet, not a single chemical, biological or nuclear weapon has been found in its bloody aftermath. But wait: Poll after poll reveals that President Bush is not in any political danger. Over 70 percent of Americans, content with an increased sense of security and a low U.S. casualty count 'victory,' now believe that the war was justified regardless.

Suffice to say, the 24-hour-a-day 'No Spin Zone' ideological manipulation and monopolization techniques of the imperialist rulers and their lackeys in the corporate media (e.g., FOX News) have played a critical role in getting people to identify with ideas that are not objectively in their interests (e.g., nationalism, racism and war). Echoing the rise of fascism in Germany, the Bush regime and its bourgeois apologists are using ultra-nationalist propaganda to create 'public opinion.' Based on generalized fear (e.g., sudden 'Fatherland' terror alerts, stories about duct tape) and programmed ignorance (e.g., formalized schooling and monopoly control over content in the print and mass electronic media), the imperialist's propaganda machine seeks to eliminate dissent in the form of dialectical thinking and critical dialogue by equating it with terrorism. As we have seen, in this claustrophobic, flag-saluting world, a narrow form of patriotism is being used by a cabal of right wingers including media pundits, religious fundamentalists and government officials to witch hunt and brand people who express opinions critical of U.S. policy as unpatriotic, anti-American, and even as traitors who give 'aid and comfort' to the enemy. Steve Rendall (2003) reports in *Extra!* that in a recent tirade, radio talk show host Rush Limbaugh could barely hide his disdain for antiwar demonstrators, 'I want to say something about these anti-war demonstrators. No, let's not mince words, let's call them what they are: anti-American demonstrators' (p. 25). For his part, Bill O'Reilly (Hart, 2003, p. 22), host of Fox's *The O'Reilly Factor*, put it like this:

> Once the war against Saddam begins, we expect every American to support
> our military, and if they can't do that, to shut up. Americans, and indeed
> our allies, who actively work against our military once the war is underway
> will be considered enemies oft he state by me. Just fair warning to you,
> Barbra Steisand, and others who see the world as you do.

Building upon this ultra right-wing sentiment, popular talk show host, Michael
Savage of MSNBC, even called for the restoration of the Sedition Act to silence
dissent (Rendall, 2003, p. 26). Sean Penn has to pay around $125,000 to take
out a full page anti-Bush ad in the *New York Times*, and that is what it costs
now to see dissent appear in the mainstream press. It should not surprise anyone
that the aim of this ideological lockdown on dissent is to create discipline and
support for the totalizing ambitions (e.g., unlimited power, expansionism, military aggression) of the Bush administration and its Likudite advisors from the
Project for the New American Century (PNAC), Dick Cheney, Donald
Rumsfeld, Paul Wolfowitz, Jeb Bush, Francis Fukuyama, and the authors of the
September 2002 'National Security Strategy of the United States of America.'
The U.S. media is so effective that, according to a *New York Times*/CBS News
Survey, 42 percent of the American public believes that Saddam Hussein was
directly responsible for the attacks of September 11 and that 55 percent of
American's believe that Saddam directly supported Al Qaeda. Yet, the crucial
point is that such understandings do not emerge spontaneously, like mush-
rooms, out of the ideological superstructure but are rather deliberately constructed by the capitalist class so that it can pursue its own narrow interests,
albeit popularized by the ideological apparatus (schools, media) as being in the
general interest of "all Americans."

Perhaps the most pathetic lie used to mobilize patriotic solidarity for U.S.
warfare and sacrifice is the shop-worn slogan 'Support Our Troops.' As was the
case in Vietnam, working-class youth are fighting and dying in a war that does
not serve their interests (or recognize their sexuality), let alone the Iraqis. Aside
from the physical injuries, psychological trauma and other long-term health
effects that these young soldiers will undoubtedly suffer, what kind of hellish
fate awaits upon their return? The whole country is a mess, with the ever-grow-
ing ranks of the malingering poor being cast into the pit of pauperism, with
barely enough food to eat. Not only this but Fred Samia (2003), a Vietnam Vet
awarded 7 decorations including the-Purple Heart, reports the difference
between being 'exalted' and 'cajoled' by recruiters and politicians during the
war and his return to indifference and neglect. His experience is not unique with
the plaintive pleas of Vietnam vets for help with PTSD (Post Traumatic Stress
Disorder) and Agent-Orange-caused illness denied for years by the Pentagon,
much the same way the Department of Defense has dismissed Gulf War vet's
complaints of depleted uranium, biological and chemical related illnesses
(Samia, 2003). For thousands of veterans, these wars are never over and continue to take lives. Do not forget, Vietnam War vets not only have the greatest per-

centages of homelessness (the equivalent of 17 infantry divisions on the streets every night), substance abuse and divorce but also, tragically, a suicide rate that has eclipsed in total the number of those who died in actual combat. Tellingly, the Bush administration cut billions from veterans' benefits the same day the illegal invasion of Iraq began but did not hesitate to subsidize the U.S. auto industry by supporting fat tax breaks for purchasers of highprofit, gas-guzzling SUVs and light trucks.

We repudiate this jingoistic and craven form of patriotism, along with its ubiquitous displays of lapel pins, flags, bumper stickers, tee shirts and slogans such as 'United We Stand.' This propaganda campaign is aimed at convincing the broad masses of people to submit to policies that are reducing their civil liberties, including the right to free speech. Of course, the standard line from the bourgeoisie is that the situation in the Homeland—and by imperial extension—the world, is different following the events of September 11. Yet, this claim is not borne out by the facts. September 11 has not stopped police brutality and murder by racist cops, the building of more jails than schools, attacks on affirmative action, Bible Belt bigotry against gays, poverty, job and food 'insecurity,' sexism, animal slavery and slaughter or the flawed and barbaric system of capital punishment. Take for example the recent killing of Alberta Spruill, a quiet church going 57-year-old black woman living in Harlem, under the pretense of fighting the 'war on drugs.' Spruill, a proud union member of DC 37 Local 1549, was preparing for work at 6 a.m. when NYC police, acting on a 'tip' and using a 'no knock' search warrant, set off a deafening concussion grenade in her apartment. After the cops launched an all-out Gestapo-style commando raid, Spruill breathlessly explained that she had a serious heart condition but was dragged out of her home and hand-cuffed anyway before being taken to the hospital, where she was pronounced dead upon arrival an hour and a half later (The NorthStar News Staff, 2003). Make no mistake about it, this outrage was not a 'tragic mistake' or an 'isolated incident.' On the contrary, the use of excessive and deadly force is not a new phenomenon in the U.S. and Spruill's name must be added to the long and growing list of Black, indigenous and immigrant victims who have lost their lives through similar encounters with racist cops, including Amadou Diallo, an example of 'legal lynching,' after the police officers who shot him to death were acquitted in February 2000.

Spruill's death is reflective of the Shock and Awe terror campaign being waged daily in inner-city neighborhoods all across the U.S., which must be understood as a domestic extension of the imperialist's invasion and colonial occupation of Iraq. At the very heart of this is the fact that for the past 25 years, including the period in which Reagan was ranting about an 'evil' Soviet empire, the U.S. has been the world's most aggressive jailer, with a greater proportion of its population in prison than any other country including Communist China—and it is growing, right alongside the prison-industrial complex (Goldberg & Evans, 2002; *The Economist*, 2002; *The Thistle*, 2000). A search for a substantive comparison would take us back to the Stalinist era, when the Soviet Union was under attack from the Nazis. To find a comparison with U.S. imprisonment of black people, one has to look to apartheid South Africa before Mandela became President. It is not a secret that capitalism thrives on divide and conquest strategies and tactics, and when in crisis it ratchets up racism and oppression. But the consequences always have a scale effect and with 'failing' schools, no jobs and no hope, youth in America's segregated inner-city communities are not only being sent to jail in record numbers but are also dying like flies on the blood-soaked streets. In Los Angeles, where the political leadership of much of the black left such as the Black Panthers was assassinated during the 1960s, gang violence has reached epidemic proportions, with over 50 people killed a month, an average higher than in the Palestinian occupied territories (Rampell, 2003, p. 9). When drive-by shootings are not claiming the lives of America's inner-city youth, the toxic emissions from industrial plants surely will. A 2001 Harvard School of Public Health study estimates that there are 2,800 asthma attacks, 500 emergency room visits and 41 preventative deaths a year due to carbon dioxide emissions and high levels of mercury that are poisoning the water. The responsibility for this dangerous assault on human health has been traced directly to Crawford & Fisk coal burning electrical power plants in Chicago, owned by Edison International's Midwest Generation. Chicago's Mayor Daley and the city's Department of the Environment have so far opposed legislation that would clean up most of the pollution generated by Crawford & Fisk plants (*News & Letters*, June, 2003).

So we should not pretend in the aftermath of September 11 that 'everything has changed' when the state is continuing to obstruct the dispensing of justice for its citizens at home, even as it wages multiple and enduring wars of 'justice' and 'liberation' abroad. If anything, the passage of the USA Patriot Act last year by Congress together with the recent slew of executive orders, mandates and Orwellian security measures enacted by Bush, Ashcroft and Co., indicates that we have entered a reactionary period of totalitarian rule, where every thought and activity is subject to pre-emptive action. Authorized by the draconian Patriot Act, the newly created Department of Homeland Security along with its secret police now has the right to wiretap anyone's phone it wants without a court order, to search any home without a warrant, to hold anyone in jail for 30 days or more without filing any charges (with no phone call 'privileges') and to secretly monitor people's finances, purchases, library or internet use with sophisticated electronic and computer eavesdropping equipment. It has even been reported in the press (Sniffen, 2003) that the Pentagon, through the Defense Advanced Research Projects Agency or DARPA, is now soliciting bids to develop a digital super diary, known as Lifelog, that 'records heartbeats, travel, Internet chats, everything a person does.' All of this domestic turmoil is occurring at a time when the U.S. is promising the Iraq people that it will build up the infrastructure of Iraq—schools, hospitals, educational institutions so that it can give the Iraq people what is has been unable to give its own citizens.

Every American should be gravely concerned about the erosion of civil rights in the United States, especially those prepared to speak out against this bloodthirsty system. In the beginning, the government was content to set its sights disproportionately upon immigrants and people of color, especially Muslims, as evidenced by the Department of Homeland Security's plan called 'Operation Liberty Shield,' enacted as bombs rained down on Iraq. Targeting precisely the kind of people who have been victims of regimes that the U.S. was formerly allied with in the past but has now vociferously singled out for condemnation, Operation Liberty Shield authorized immigration officials to detain virtually all asylum seekers from a group of 33 countries including Iraq, Iran, Sudan and Somalia (Amnesty International, 2003). But right now, such repressive measures are quickly being integrated and expanded throughout the entire American judicial system, sharply undermining the democratic rights of U.S. citizens and non-citizens alike. How far is the government prepared to go? The drafting of the 'Domestic Security Enhancement Act of 2003,' dubbed 'Patriot Act II,' threatens to expand the authority of the government's secret police by throwing out a whole set of Constitutional protections under the pretense of 'fighting terrorism.' Amongst other things, Cohen (2003) reports that this draft legislation proposes to empower the Department of Justice to compile a DNA database of 'suspected terrorists' who associate with 'suspected groups' and even to 'expatriate' a U.S. citizen 'if, with the intent to relinquish his nationality, he becomes a member of, or provides material support to, a group that the United States has designated as a 'terrorist organization'" (p. 9). The goal of the Bush administration is to exercise total information control through the consolidation of the corporate media owned by the military industrial complex. Bush's road map to resolution of the Israeli-Palestinian conflict is an attempt to placate the Arab world after the exercise of Bush's imperial ambitions and to deflect attention away from his war against the Homeland's poor, already imposed on the Palestinians, effectively attempting to institutionalize the occupation by the Israeli settler state. Few people are fooled, including a large segment of Israel's own population who agree that the Bush roadmap favors Israel.

Standing silently backstage, the Bush gang is able to exercise the full power of the state to crush every adversary, including organized labor, just like the Nazis did when they formed the government. What this signals is that the ruling class has dispensed with all pretense to bourgeois democracy. Strangely enough, advocates of free-trade and competition such as Bush Jr. have sought to differentiate U.S. capitalism from single-party 'dictatorships' and all sorts of 'totalitarian' regimes, with special attention now turned toward Cuba, where U.S. officials have stepped up their attempt to destabilize the Castro government by increasing the funding of 'dissidents' on the island as well as ruthless terrorist groups of Cuban expatriates who walk the streets of Miami with impunity, and by practically eliminating the visa program for Cuban emigrants wishing to leave (The Editors, 2002). Of course Bush's war against 'totalitarianism' is helped along by leading U.S. intellectuals such as Susan Sontag, who accused Columbian Nobel Prize winning novelist, Gabriel Garcia Marques of lacking integrity and being an apologist of Cuban terrorism. Yet, with the building of this modern Gestapo-like 'security state,' what is exposed is a 'Dictatorship of Capital,' with the Bush regime operating by command rather than by openness and full-fledged participation. By extension, the concept of liberty and freedom for all is turned on its head, with ordinary working people 'freed' from the burden of secure employment, pensions, affordable housing, health care and civil rights, whilst the ruling class rakes in grotesque amounts of money with no limit, regulation or legal obstruction. The plain fact is that the state, which stands "*above* society," is committed to the class rule of the bourgeoisie and that imperialist wars are fought solely to advance only the interests of the capitalist class (Lenin, 1965, p. 9).

Although this shift meshes perfectly with the hegemonic plans of the Bush gang, it is not a question of 'ethics' or 'policy' but of historical and economic necessity (The Editors, 2002). Confronted with a crisis of overproduction, U.S. monopoly capital must override the remnants left of bourgeois democracy in order to re-establish conditions of profitability. Officially, the U.S. fell into recession in early 2001 and the economy is still stagnant, so the state is acting in the immediate interests of its own home-based corporations to produce a loyal and compliant labor force ready to super-exploit. As we have seen, the preference of the ruling class through its neo-liberal agenda is to construct a world with no legal or political barriers to monopoly and finance capital, ensuring its competitive advantage and dominance in the world economy. Domestically, this means doing away with 'old fashioned' democratic freedoms (e.g., individual civil rights and liberties) that were once regarded as necessary to the development of capitalism at a time when Bretton Woods had divided up the world at the behest of the 'victors' of WWII. In constructing such a landscape, the government can flagrantly ignore the wishes of a significant minority of people. Indeed, armed with a vastly expanded police state apparatus, the government has proven its willingness to use the external 'international crisis' as an excuse to break any domestic opposition, under the pretense of national security. Witness the use of militaristic tactics at recent antiwar events such as when riot-equipped police hurled concussion grenades and fired wooden bullets and 'sting bags,' which send out a spray of BB-sized rubber pellets and a cloud of gas, to terrorize and injure anti-war protesters and longshoremen at the Oakland docks (Mendoza, 2003).

As for the Democratic Party, whose views now differ from the Republicans more today in degree than in kind, if you take into consideration their long-standing and egregious loyalty to the military industrial complex, the market economy, and Israel's repression of the Palestinians, its acquiescence to the war in Iraq brings its 'secret alliance' with the ruling class out into the open. In the past, the Democratic Party has situated itself as a viable political alternative to the Republican Party through its advocacy of 'humanist' capitalistic reforms on a whole range of issues such as abortion, education, welfare and civil rights. But lest we forget, the spotlight was already on Clinton's globalization strategy (e.g., the Battle for Seattle) and its cruelties long before Bush came to power (Program Demand Group, 2002). In fact, under Clinton/Gore, the U.S. took a greater share of control over NATO, the IMF, and the World Bank as instruments of ruling class hegemony. Additionally, Clinton was responsible for driving down the standard of living for U.S. workers by signing the welfare reform act in 1996, which forced welfare recipients, mostly women of color with dependent children, into low paying, dead-end jobs that provide no benefits such as childcare or healthcare. Aside from this slave-labor/union-busting measure, Clinton also paved the way for the garrison police state that Bush, Ashcroft and Co., are now gleefully fortifying, by signing into law the Antiterrorism and Effective Death Penalty and Antiterrorism Act in 1996. This deadly piece of 'tough on crime' legislation gutted the writ habeas corpus, which has existed for centuries, by eliminating federal constitutional review of state death penalty cases, and leading to a tripling of the rate of executions. It also authorized the government to deport immigrants based on secret evidence and made it illegal for anyone to support even the lawful activities of an organization labeled 'terrorist' by the State Department (Parkin, 1999).

All this continuality, encapsulated during the 2001 mid-term elections with the bi-partisan hysteria over the 'War on Terrorism,' underscores the reality that electoral politics will never be the basis of social change. Not only was the Democratic Party silent about the dramatic rollback of democratic rights and the whole rotten system of corporate corruption exposed by the collapse of Enron and the telecommunications industry (which amounted to the theft of millions of dollars of working people's pensions), it also offered support for the imperialist war in Iraq. From the outset, the Democratic Party did not oppose this predatory war in principle, with establishment liberals such as Ted Kennedy only wanting a larger coalition of allies to attack Iraq, whilst just about every other Democratic, such as Senate Democratic Leader Tom Daschle, gripped by electoral fear and bourgeois patriotism, adopted a bi-partisan stance of 'unity' to protect the capitalist's interests, albeit by advocating a speedy war of last resort (with fig leaf cover provided by the UN) that minimized U.S. casualties. This 'unity' has an objective class basis: it is founded on the fact that both major parties share the same economic interests. The Democratic Party operatives, along with their think tanks and NGO groups, also played a prominent role in weakening the anti-war movement, especially in red-baiting the ANSWER coalition for being led by the World Worker's Party. Today, even Dennis Kucinich, the strongest rabble-rousing leader of anti-war opposition amongst the Democratic candidates for President during the 2004 elections, who gives voice to the economic predicament of millions of workers, fails to recognize that a truly democratic 'peace' and hope for equality is impossible without challenging the rule of capital. Whereas the Republicans pander to the ruling elite, the Democrats set themselves as defenders of the middle-class. In reality, the middle-class is 'an ideological illusion' that is invented to obscure the fact that we are all wage earners (Ebert & Zavarzadeh, 2003). As Marx said in *Capital Vol. 3*, middle and transitional levels of social differences always conceal the boundaries of classes. They do this 'in order to give ideological stability to the economically insecure and unstable life under capitalism' (Ebert & Zavarzadeh, 2003). If there is any doubt about where the allegiance of the Democratic Party lies, consider the bi-partisan support to imperialist war when, on April 4, the House voted 414-12 while the Senate voted 99-0 to approve the additional 75 billion requested for the military budget. The total amount spent on militarism by the U.S. nearly exceeds that spent by the other 191 countries in the world combined.

One of the deepest and important lessons of the 2000 election was that the electoral system 'stealthily pushes aside the poor' and is 'sufficiently restricted to exclude the lower stratum of the proletariat proper' (Lenin, 1965, p. 105). In the run-up to the elections, Florida Gov. Jeb Bush, Bush the Lesser's brother, and Secretary of State Katherine Harris, who oversaw state elections, hired a private contractor called Database to purge felons from voter rolls (Pierre, 2001). The Democratic Party refused to fight this issue on principle, when the spineless vice presidential candidate Joe Lieberman, caved into mounting pressure and argued that the Democratic Party should stop making a fuss. As in several other U.S. states, Florida law prevents ex-felons from voting. In Florida, this means that 31 percent of all Black men are barred from voting, a state in which Al Gore received more than 90 percent of the black vote. Yet, if this is not disturbing enough, Database botched the felon purge by removing the names of thousands of 'probable felons' (which were really registered voters who had never committed a crime) along with thousands of eligible voters who had only committed misdemeanors. This is capitalist democracy. For those who have been in a cryogenic deep freeze, what this all exposes is the illusion of the U.S. electoral system, which is booby-trapped to spike class struggle, with the Democratic Party acting as a Trojan Horse.

Closely related to this, the glum and muddled leaders of organized labor are engaged in phony opposition to the war in Iraq, criticizing Bush's plans on the basis that he did not build an international coalition similar to one his father led against Iraq during the 1991 Gulf War, killing an estimated 150,000 Iraqis. This deplorable position, adopted by the AFL-CIO, the nation's premier labor organization should come as little surprise, given its unwavering support for past imperialist wars. Despite a lame call for more open debate about the war, AFL-CIO president John Sweeny has clearly betrothed his heart to the Prince of Darkness, George Bush, our Commander-and-Chief, when he labels Iraq a 'global terrorist threat' and asserts, "America certainly has the right to act unilaterally if we need to do so to protect our national interests." This explicit statement of endorsement is shameful and unprincipled given that the Bush administration has brazenly used the so-called war on terrorism as an excuse to advance corporate interests under the cover of 'national security' by repeatedly attacking workers (Walker, 2002). A good illustration of our argument would be Bush's deployment of the anti union Taft-Hartley Act during the Pacific Maritime

Association (PMA) employer lockout at 29 West Coast ports to force International Longshoremen and Warehouse Union (ILWU) workers into compulsory arbitration (Kelber, 2002).

As if that is not dire enough, the Bush gang is sharing the spoils of imperialist war with companies that have close ties to the Republican Party, including the biggest contract so far to Halliburton, a company formerly run by Mr. Cheney, the infamous contract with Betchel to rebuild Iraq's infrastructure, the scandalous, no-bid contract for cell phone service in Iraq to the already bankrupt World Com, and the contract with the union-busting Stevedoring Services of America, the lead company fighting the ILWU on the West Coast docks, for operating the port of Umm Qsar in Iraq, all offering high profits worth billions of dollars (Teather, 2003). This warped tale of justice is accented by the fact that the U.S. government is subsidizing companies with massive bailouts and tax cuts even as Congress passes a law to prevent individuals from getting out of debt through personal bankruptcy. This buttressing of the rate of profit, through the theft of surplus labor from an already besieged labor force, is occurring right when the government is using the economic downturn to justify the shedding of thousands of unionized jobs and to cut key public services, including education and health. But all of this is not enough for Bush's captains of capital, who having exploited the U.S. working class and plundered the nation's natural resources are now out to increase their fabulous riches and profits through a resurgence of imperialist war.

Of course, the Byzantine world of the U.S. labor movement does boost some prominent dissenting voices and a growing number of local unions and wider union organizations have adopted anti-war resolutions such as the one by the Washington State Labor Convention in August 2002 (Socialist Future, 2002). But even a cursory check reveals that, whilst plenty of discontent exists at the base of American society, the U.S. labor movement has not delivered on any of its vague promises, acting only to bargain over the price of labor power. Moreover, aside from its support for Bush's war plans, the pro-capitalist AFL CIO continues to be an instrument of U.S. foreign policy, with its government subsidized international programs sabotaging left wing unions and politics overseas (Shorrock, 2003). Take for example, the AFL-CIO's financial support for the Confederation of Venezuelan Workers (CTV), which is allied with Venezuela's business elite against the leftist government of Hugo Chavez. Such deplorable actions speak louder than words and reflect the labor aristocracy's standpoint of social-chauvinism, demonstrating that it still has absolutely no appreciation for socialist internationalism. Unwittingly or not, this thwarting of expectations (after the euphoria surrounding Sweeny's election in 1995) has lead to widespread demoralization and defeatism, threatening to doom workers to the status of road kill under the wheels of an irresistible historical juggernaut of imperialist war and privatization.

No, people are not dancing in the streets, nor sitting on the stoops of their crumbling tenement houses toasting the Bush administration, they are fighting for their lives. Right here in the bloated white belly of the imperialist beast. Given the blatant contempt of the U.S. ruling class and our so-called political representatives toward the working class, workers must overcome the still persistent illusion that as imperfect and corrupt as it is, bourgeois democracy, U.S.-style, represents the best of all possible worlds. They must organize with more determination than ever to fight the Bush/Cheney junta and its imperialist agenda. Even though the state has assumed a more violent and oppressive character, the situation is not altogether bleak or without opportunities. For example, mass participation in the anti-war movement is just one indication of the latent but explosive potential to create broad opposition to imperialism in the United States. Movements like this provide a glimpse of how a mass uprising of people might be developed to weaken U.S. imperialism and to get rid of production for profit along with its attendant antagonisms including patriarchy, national oppression (e.g., Black, Chicano, Puerto Rican, Native American, Hawaiian and other oppressed and indigenous peoples) and white supremacy.

Yet, in the U.S., many middle class whites and ordinary working class people in the anti-war movement, duped by their own apparatus, became captives of the social chauvinists. As a result, support amongst whites 'withered away' shortly after the bombing campaign in Iraq began in earnest. Against this trend, support for the war remains dramatically lower amongst black Americans who instinctively realize through their own unique experience and history that the government's actions are not altruistic (The Gallop Organization, 2003). Drawing upon the long history of their disenfranchisement, including the mistreatment of black veterans after previous wars, the black community in the U.S. has played a critical role in previous anti-war movements, such as the stance taken by Martin Luther King Jr. against the Vietnam War (The Associated Press, 2003). The lesson is clear, if the U.S. anti-war movement is to grow any larger to curb future wars in Iran, Syria, North Korea or Venezuela, it must confront its real tasks of defeating national chauvinism, racism and attacks on the Third World. The only historic force that can put a stop to capitalism, which has entered a dark and escalating period of imperialist (not just U.S.) war, is the international working class. Along these lines, the only way we are ever going to win 'peace' or the right to a decent education or job is through the linking of our struggles with all the victims of the vicious ruling class and the transnational corporations that our respective heads of government (e.g., Bush, Blair and Howard) speak for.

REFERENCES

Amnesty International. (2003). News Release. Available at: http://www.amnestyusa.org/news./2003/usa03182003_2.html

Coen, R. (March/April, 2003). Another stealth assault on liberties? Muted media response to Ashcroft's proposed Patriot Act II. *Extra!* 16, 2, p. 9.

Clean Air Struggle. *News & Letters*, 48, (5). June, (2003), p. 11.

Ebert, T. & Zavarzadeh. (2002). ABC of Class. *The Red Critique*. Available at: http://www.geocities.com/redtheory/redcritique/NovDec02/abcofclass.htm

Goldberg, E. and Evans, L. (2002). The prison industrial complex and the global economy. Available at: http://www.globalexchange.o!g/campaigns/usa/pic.html

Hart, P. (June, 2003). O'Reilly's War: Any rationale—or none—will do. *Extra!* 16, 3, pp. 22-24.

Hobsbawn, E. (June, 2002). After the winning of the war. *Le Monde Diplomatique*.

Kelber, H. (2002). Taft-Hartley Order ends port lockout: Union blames PMA for Cargo Logjam. *The Labor Educator*. Available at: http://www. laboreducator.org/taftlock htm

Lenin, V. I. (1965). *The state and revolution*. Peking: Foreign Languages Press.

Mendoza, M. (2003). Police open fire at anti-war protest, longshoremen injured. Available at: http://www.truthout.org/docs_03/printer_04090A.shtml

Parkin, J. (1999). Clinton's Effective Death Penalty Act faces Supreme Court Challenge. *The New Abolitionist*. Available at: http://www. nodeathpenalty.org/newab013/clintonAct.html

Pierre, R. (May, 2001). Botched name purge denied some the right to vote. Washtingtonpost.com. Availableat: http://www.washingtonpost.com/ac2/wp-dyn/A99749 2001May30

Policy Statement Issued by Socialist Democracy (January, 2002). The New Imperialism. Vol. 3, No. 1., *Socialist Viewpoint*. Available at: http://www.socialistviewpoint.org/jan_03/jan_03_11.html

Program Demand Group (Winter, 2002). Toward a program of resistance. Los Angeles: Labor/Community Strategy Center.

Rampell, E. (2002). The anti-gangs of L.A. *LA Alternative Press*. 2, 4, May 28-June 10, p. 9.

Rendall, S. (June, 2003). Dissent, disloyalty & double standards: Kosovo doves denounced Iraq War protest as 'Anti-American.' *Extra!* 16, 3, pp. 25-26.

Samia, F. (April, 2003). Support our troops? Voices in the Wilderness. Available at: http://www.nonviolence.org/vitw/pages/analysis_support_troops.html

Shorrock, T. (May 19, 2003). Labor's Cold War. *The Nation*. 276, 19, pp. 15-32.

Sniffen, M. (June, 2003). Super Diary Worries Privacy Activists. Available at: http://www.guardian.co.uk/uslatest/story/0.1282,-2744985,00.html

Socialist Future. (2002). US unions oppose Bush. Available at: http://www.socialistfuture.org.uk/campaigns/tu/awar.htm

Teather, D. (April, 2003). Jobs for the boys: The reconstruction of billions. Available at: http://www.guardian.co.uk/Print/0.3858,4648407,00.html

The Associated Press. (May 22, 2003). Among black Americans, support for war is lower. Available at: http://new.blackvoices.com

The Economist (2002). Prison and beyond: A stigma that never fades. Available at: http://www.economist com/world/na.displayStory.cfm?story_id=1270755

The Editors. (2002). The Dictatorship of Capital. *The Red Critique*. Available at: http://www.geocities.com/redtheory/redcritique/SeptOct02/thedictatorshipofcapital.htm

The Gallop Organization. (2003). Blacks show biggest decline in support for war compared with 1991. Available at: http://www.gallop.com/subscription/?m=f&c_id=13312

The Northstar News Staff (May, 2003). Death by Fear: The case of Alberta Spruill. Available at: http://www.thenorthstarnetwork.com/news/topstories/181948-1.html

The Thistle. (2000). The crime of prisons. Available at: http://web.mit.edu/thistle/www/vl2/1/prisons.html

Walker, C. (2002). AFL-CIO's Sweeney Facing Antiwar opposition. *SocialistViewpoint*. Available at: http://www.socialistviewpoint.org/nov_02_7.html

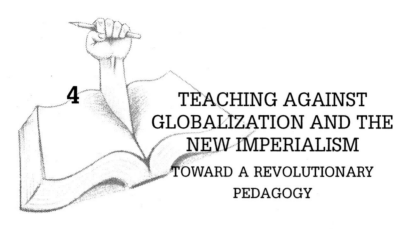

4   TEACHING AGAINST GLOBALIZATION AND THE NEW IMPERIALISM

TOWARD A REVOLUTIONARY PEDAGOGY

Peter McLaren and Ramin Farahmandpur

No teacher giving instruction in any school, or on any property belonging to any agencies included in the public school system, shall advocate or teach communism with the intent to indoctrinate or to inculcate in the mind of any pupil a preference for communism.

In prohibiting the advocacy or teaching of communism with the intent of indoctrinating or inculcating a preference in the mind of any pupil for such doctrine, the Legislature does not intend to prevent the teaching of the facts about communism. Rather, the Legislature intends to prevent the advocacy of, or inculcation and indoctrination into, communism as is hereinafter defined, for the purpose of undermining patriotism for, and the belief in, the government of the United States and of this state.

For the purposes of this section, communism is a political theory that the presently existing form of government of the United States or of this state should be changed, by force, violence, or other unconstitutional means, to a totalitarian dictatorship which is based on the principles of communism as expounded by Marx, Lenin, and Stalin.

—California Education Code, Sec. 51530

This chapter discusses teacher education reform in the United States from the context of critical pedagogy in general and a theory of imperialism and class struggle that is indebted to the Marxist-Leninist tradition. Many of the current discussions of globalization and, for that matter, critical pedagogy have themselves become conceptually impoverished and politically domesticated (McLaren, 1998b, 2000; McLaren & Farahmandpur, 2000). Hence, we have taken pains to offer for public consumption some counter-propaganda to the pronouncements of the corporate Mullahs, aggravating the debate over critical pedagogy before it can accommodate to their supernal demand. We have

This chapter originally appeared in *Journal of Teacher Education, 52*(2). © 2001 American Association of Colleges for Teacher Education. Reprinted with permission.

secured our analysis within a Marxist problematic that takes seriously the imperative of steering critical pedagogy firmly toward anticapitalist struggle (see McLaren, 2000; McLaren & Farahmandpur, 2000). We contend that within critical pedagogy, the issue of class has been egregiously overlooked. Critical pedagogy has, of late, drifted dangerously toward the cultural terrain of identity politics in which class is reduced to an effect rather than understood as a cause and in which a hierarchy of oppression is (usually unwittingly) constituted as a controlling paradigm that frequently leaves the exploitative power of capitalist social relations largely unaddressed. Understanding exploitation as embodied in forms of racist and patriarchal social practices should constitute a central focus of critical pedagogy. On this point we have no quarrel. However, this objective should not be achieved at the grievous expense of understanding how political economy and class struggle operate as the motor force of history and society (Parenti, 1997). With this assertion, we identify the political architecture necessary to contest the enfeeblement and domestication of critical pedagogy and to develop what we call a revolutionary workingclass pedagogy.

FACING GLOBAL CAPITALISM

As we anticipate the ongoing challenges of the new millennium, we bear witness to the unabated mercilessness of global capitalism and the impassable fissure between capital and labor. Today, millions of workers are being exploited by a relatively small yet cunningly powerful global ruling class driven by an unslakable desire for accumulation of profit. Little opposition exists as capitalism runs amok, unhampered and undisturbed by the tectonic upheaval that is occurring in the geopolitical landscape—one that has recently witnessed the collapse of the Soviet Union and the regimes of the Eastern Bloc.

Due to the fast-paced and frenetic changes taking place around us in the wired realms of global technologies and free-trade initiatives, we are hardpressed to chart out our daily struggles against oppression and exploitation instituted by a growing cabal of techno-crazed global robber barons. As we attempt to flee a culture of endless acquisition, we find ourselves at the mercy of an even more terrifying corporate culture shaping our subjectivities. According to Hayat Imam (1997), "Today . . . 'creation of wealth' has become the fundamental value at the center of global society and analyses of economics are devoid of issues of morality, human needs, and social conscience" (p. 13). Mutagenic forms of greed and social relations that permit such greed to flourish have produced severance packages for corporate bosses that exceed the combined salaries of an army of factory workers. Yet there is no authority by which greed can be brought to trial. But when greed is identified as exploitation, that changes the terms of the debate by shifting the concepts from the realm of individualistic psychology to that of historical materialism.

Immovably entrenched social, political, and economic disparities and antago-nisms compel us as educators and cultural workers to create alternatives to the logic of capitalist accumulation. Yet, the creation of alternatives to the logic of capital is a formidable—and what many of our more cynical brothers and sisters in education would deem today an insurmountable—challenge. We are struggling and suffering (some of us more than others) through a time when there exists a dictatorship of the marketplace in a capitalist system whose inequalities are becoming more evident than ever before. This is especially true at this current moment, when the Republican theft of a presidency followed by a continued com-mitment to Disneyland capitalism: the free marketeers meet the Mouseketeers.

THE POLITICS OF NEOLIBERALISM

Neoliberal free market economics—the purpose of which is to avoid stasis and keep businesses in healthy flux—functions as a type of binding arbitration, legitimizing a host of questionable practices and outcomes: deregulation, unre-stricted access to consumer markets, downsizing, outsourcing, flexible arrange-ments of labor, intensification of competition among transnational corporations, increasing centralization of economic and political power, and finally, widening class polarization. Neoliberalism is currently embarking on ways of "re-imagin-ing" democracy through the importation of the market discourse of parasitic financial oligarchies into increasingly domesticated democratic practices and through the valorization of capital and the unrestrained economic power of pri-vate property (Teeple, 1995).

The triumph of neoliberalism represents at once the incalculably expanded scope of the culture of consumption and the implosion of social relations into a universal signifier—namely capital—that Marx metaphorically referred to as the "universal pimp." Marx likened money to a "visible god" that in the gener-alized commodity form

> spreads this illusory perception throughout society, dissolving all previous
> identities and distinctions, and remolding human consciousness in its own
> image. In the fully developed form of capital, money achieves an active,
> self-regulating power through which it shapes the lives of concrete individ-
> uals. (Hawkes, 1996, pp. 101-102)

For those who believe that uninterrupted accumulation and increasing inter-national concentration of capital is a good thing, that the shift from an interna-tional economy to a world economy is a sign of progress that Capital's Vampiric thirst for new surplus value is healthy, that the feedback mechanisms of the unfettered "free" market are fair, that only democracy will spring forth from its spontaneous order, and that the common good will magically advance from its net worked complexity, there is reason to be wildly optimistic about the future. Imagine the possibilities for privatizing public spaces and spreading neoliberal domination over vast exotic populations hitherto unconquered! But for educators who reject the idea that the social system under capitalism is a self-organizing totality and who view the globalization of capital as an irredeemable assault on democracy, the future appears perilous indeed. We refuse to elevate the victimization of the working-class to a regulatory ideal of democracy and decline to treat the economy as a thing or endow it with self- evident democratic agency. After Marx, we view the economy as a social relation and not a self-sustaining natural entity. Capitalism is not powered by a transcendental metaphysic but is a social relation overburdened by its constituent requirement for exploitation, accumulation, endless growth, and class conflict. It remains predicated on the extraction of surplus value from workers (value produced by workers beyond that which the capitalist must pay out in wages so that the workers can reproduce their labor-power).

Unlike its well-known predecessors—slavery and feudalism—capitalism is predicated on the overaccumulation of capital and the superexploitation of rank-and-file wage laborers. The irreversible contradiction inherent within capitalist social and economic relations—those between capital and labor—are taking us further away from democratic accountability and steering us closer to what Rosa Luxemburg (1919) referred to as an age of barbarism. Peery (1997) makes the point that in comparison to the political economy that sustained slavery or feudalism, the social and economic contradictions in the present-day capitalist mode of production are much more virulent and unremitting. This is because the production, distribution, and consumption of commodities are in constant contradiction with labor power and prevents the logic of capital from validating any logic other than its own. Many social and political theorists have studied the phenomenon of globalization extensively and have pronounced it a discomfiting inevitability for some but a powerful, life-enhancing economic tonic for many. Yet, in our opinion, globalization represents an ideological facade that camouflages the manifold operations of imperialism. In fact, the concept of globalization has effectively replaced the term *imperialism* in the lexicon of the privileged class for the purpose of exaggerating the global character of capitalism—as an all-encompassing and indefatigable power that apparently no nation-state has the means to resist or oppose. Furthermore, it deceitfully suggests that capitalism is no longer dependent on the nation-state. This position occludes the fact that a large portion of production in Western European countries takes place within national boundaries. Moreover, the globalization thesis maintains that whereas state power can be used in the interests of the large multinational corporations, it cannot be employed in the interest of the working class.

To call globalization a form of imperialism might seem a rhetorical exaggeration. But we believe that this identification is necessary because the term *globalization* is calculated by bourgeois critics to render any radical politicization of it extreme. The ideology of this move is invisibly to enframe the concept

of globalization within a culturalist logic that reduces it to mean a standardization of commodities (i.e., the same designer clothes appearing in shopping
plazas throughout the world). By contrast, we see the process as inextricably
tied to the politics of neoliberalism, in which violence asserts itself as stability
through a recomposition of the capital labor relationship. Such a recomposition
entails the subordination of social reproduction to the reproduction of capital
(Dinerstein, 1999), the deregulation of the labor market, the globalization of liquid capital, the outsourcing of production to cheap labor markets, and the transfer of local capital intended for social services into finance capital for global
investment.

The new imperialism to which we refer is a combination of old-style military and financial practices as well as recent attempts by developed nations to
impose the law of the market on the whole of humanity itself. Having obscured
the distinction between the sacred and profane, the global aristocracy's new
world order has set out to expand the free market in the interest of quick profits,
to increase global production, to raise the level of exports in the manufacturing
sector, and to intensify competition among transnational corporations. It has
also benefited from part-time and contingent work, reduced the pool of full-time
employment, and accelerated immigration from Third World and developing
countries to industrial nations (Bonacich & Appelbaum, 2000). In addition to
our description of globalization as imperialism we might add the following:
imperialist military intervention primarily disguised as humanitarian aid, the
submission of international institutions such as the United Nations to the social
and economic demands of imperialist conquest, and the instigation of ethnic and
nationalistic conflicts to weaken nations refusing to submit to the rule of the
market (Azad, 2000).

Contrary to popular opinion, wealth depletion among developing nations is
not rescued by capital from advanced capitalist countries. This is because
transnational corporations drain the local capital from poor countries rather than
bring in new capital. Because their savings are often low, banks in developing
countries would rather lend to their own subsidiary corporations (who send their
profits back to advanced nations) than to struggling local businesses in developing nations. Faced with low prices for exports, high tariffs on processed goods,
and a lack of capital and rising prices, local businesses are locked into
entrenched impoverishment because of structural adjustment measures to balance the budget. Such measures are financed through cuts in spending for
human development (Imam, 1997). The World Trade Organization does not
permit poor countries to prioritize fighting poverty over increasing exports or
choosing a development path that will advance the interests of the countries'
own populations. By 1996, the resulting concentration of wealth had "the
income of the world's richest individuals . . . equal to the income of 52 percent
of humanity" (Imam, 1997, p. 13).

THE PRIVATIZATION AND COMMERCIALIZATION OF PUBLIC EDUCATION

Examining education policies within the context of economic globalization and neoliberalism raises a number of critical questions that include the following: What are some of the effects of globalization on public schools and public education? To what extent is the content of teaching and curriculum under the perilous influence of the shifting social, economic, and political relations within global capitalism? Spring (1998) identifies a key paradox that frames education and economic policies pursued in the United States and other advanced capital societies. First, education under globalization is viewed as a vehicle that assists the growing market economy. For many developing countries, an educated and skilled workforce ostensibly would mean higher levels of productivity and economic development. Second, education is viewed as a tool in solving problems associated with economic globalization such as unemployment and poverty. If, however, the market economy (by means of the capitalist law of value) is itself the cause of social and economic inequality, then it would appear a contradiction in terms to argue that the goal of education should be to assist in the expansion of the market economy (Spring, 1998). Economic globalization has not only failed to provide political stability and social and economic equality for many nations around the world, but it has also led to deepening social and economic polarization. Willie Thompson (1997) notes,

> Marx's insights into the nature of capital's reproduction and accumulation have never been bettered or displaced: his prevision of its future was extraordinarily percipient and impressively fulfilled. He was never a better prophet than when he insisted that capitalism was hastening towards its unavoidable destruction, that its internal forces carried it in a certain identifiable direction, which (*contra* Keynes) cannot be reversed or evaded. What capital produces above all is its own gravediggers. Marx meant the working class, and he was mistaken. What looks more likely to be capitalism's executioner is capitalism itself—the problem is that everything else is practically certain to be entombed with it. (p. 224)

As the logic of capital accumulation is shifting toward knowledge-based economies and as new forms of computer technology and biotechnology are being integrated into today's high tech economy, information itself is fast becoming a high-priced new commodity. Transnational corporations are laboring vigorously to privatize the socially produced knowledge associated with the educational system. Decreased government funding of public education has forced an unholy partnership with private corporations who are seeking to create "high-tech knowledge industries" (Witheford, 1997). Transnational corporations are sponsoring research centers in universities across the United States by donating millions of dollars for the research, development, and production of for-profit technologies. This has resulted in the "high-tech colonization of education," transforming public universities into corporate-operated "techopolises" that have little interest in coexistence with the poor (Witheford, 1997).

Under the command of the market economy, not even universities, colleges, and vocational schools are immune from the economic policies favoring capital accumulation. Niemark (1999) reports that the increasing social policies that support for-profit universities have made higher education an extension of the market economy. She writes that social policies that support privatization have moved in the direction of

> establishing for-profit degree-granting institutions (such as the University of Phoenix); outsourcing curriculum, instruction, counseling, operations, and administration (in such areas as bookstores, food services, libraries, computer operations, plant maintenance, security, printing, and payroll); signing campus-corporate research and development partnership and licensing agreements; and selling exclusive on-campus marketing rights to companies that sell products as varied as soft drinks, fast food, computers, and credit and telephone calling cards. The campus is becoming virtually indistinguishable from the marketplace, and both universities and their faculties arc becoming entrepreneurs. (p. 24)

The restructuring of higher education can clearly be seen as reinforcing class inequality and exposing public higher education to social and economic policies governed by the laws of the market economy (i.e., commodification, proletarianization, and capital accumulation). It also visibly functions as an impediment to the education and active participation of citizens in a democratic decision-making process dedicated to coexistence (Niemark, 1999).

The shift toward the privatization and corporatization of public education is best exemplified by the corporate raider Michael Milken, the Wall Street wizard and junk bond king of the mid-1980s who lured investors into high-risk investment schemes. Milken has returned to the business world, this time by focusing on the lucrative $800 billion education market and has decided to create for-profit education enterprises with the help of his powerful—yet comparatively obscure—$500 million company known as Knowledge Universe. Milken has invested heavily in several companies producing educational materials. Knowledge Universe owns companies such as Children's Discovery Centers, Bookman Testing Services, Pyramid Imaging Inc., Nobel Education Dynamics, and Leapfrog, which produces educational tools used at learning centers of the Riordan Foundation (Vrana, 1998). In a recent interview with the *Los Angeles Times*, Milken calculated that if the net worth of the United States is placed at $120 trillion, roughly $75 trillion consists of human capital. This means that every American is worth $400,000 to $500,000 (Vrana, 1998). In short, Milken has discovered that the knowledge business is a profitable commodity.

Recent attempts by corporations to influence policy and curriculum decisions in urban schools abound. According to Kalle Lasn (1999),

> Corporate advertising (or is it the commercial media?) is the largest psychological project ever undertaken by the human race. Yet for all of that, its impact on us remains unknown and largely ignored. When I think of the media's influence over years, over decades, I think of those brainwashing experiments conducted by Dr. Ewen Cameron in a Montreal psychiatric hospital in the 1950s. The idea of the CIA-sponsored "depatterning" experiment was to outfit conscious, unconscious or semiconscious subjects with headphones, and flood their brain with thousands of repetitive "driving" messages that would alter their behavior over time. Sound familiar? Advertising aims to do the same thing. Dr. Cameron's guinea pigs emerged from the Montreal trials with serious psychological damage. It was a great scandal. But no one is saying boo about the ongoing experiment of mass media advertising. In fact, new guinea pigs voluntarily come on board every day. (p. 19)

It is not unusual these days to see school buses in certain states covered with advertisements for Burger King and Wendy's fast food chain restaurants. It has become fashionable for elementary school children to carry books wrapped in free book covers plastered with ads for Kellogg's Pop Tarts and Fox TV personalities. School districts have gleefully granted Coca-Cola and Pepsi exclusive contracts to sell their products in schools. In health education classes, students are taught nutrition by the Hershey Corporation in a scheme that includes a discussion of the important place of chocolate in a balanced diet. A classroom business course teaches students to value work by exploring how McDonald's restaurants are operated and what skills are needed to become a successful McDonald's manager and provides instructions on how to apply for a job at McDonald's. Ecological and environmental education now involves students learning ecology from a Life of an Ant poster sponsored by Skittles candy and an environmental curriculum video produced by Shell Oil that concentrates on the virtues of the external combustion engine. Finally, a new company called Zap Me! lures schools into accepting thousands of dollars worth of computer equipment, including a satellite dish, fifteen top-level personal computers, a furnished computer lab and high-speed Internet access in return for a constant display of on-screen advertisements in the lower left-hand corner of the screen (see Fischman & McLaren, 2000). Lasn (1999) writes,

> Your kids watch Pepsi and Snickers ads in the classroom (The school has made the devil's bargain of accepting free audiovisual equipment in exchange for airing these ads on "Channel One"). . . . Administrators in a Texas school district announce plans to boost revenues by selling ad space on the roofs of the district's seventeen schools—arresting the attention of the fifty-eight million commercial jet passengers who fly into Dallas each

year. Kids tattoo their calves with swooshes. Other kids, at raves, begin wearing actual bar codes that other kids can scan, revealing messages such as "I'd like to sleep with you." . . . A few years ago, marketers began installing ad boards in men's washrooms on college campuses, at eye level above the urinals. From their perspective, it was a brilliant coup: Where else is a guy going to look? But when I first heard this was being done, I was incensed. One of the last private acts was being co-opted. (pp. 19-21)

A math book published by McGraw-Hill is spiked with references to Nike, Gatorade, Disney, McDonald's, Nabisco, Mattel Barbie dolls, Sony play stations, Cocoa Frosted Flakes, Spalding basketballs and Topps baseball cards (Collins & Yeskel, 2000, p. 78). John Borowski, a public school teacher, recently noted in *The New York Times*,

At least 234 corporations are now flooding the public schools with films, textbooks and computer software under the guise of "instructional material." A lesson in self-esteem sponsored by Revlon includes an investigation of "good and bad hair days." In a history lesson, Tootsie Rolls are touted as a part of soldiers' diets during World War II. Exxon provides a video on the Valdez spill playing down its ecological impact. And Chevron, in a lesson for use in civics science classes, reminds students that they will soon be able to vote and make "important decisions" about global warming, which the company then rebuts as incomplete science. (*The New York Times*, 1999, p. A23)

Another example of corporatism in schools is Channel One, a commercially produced news station that now operates in many American schools. As part of a contractual agreement, teachers agree to broadcast Channel One programs in class for ten minutes a day in return for a satellite dish, video cassette recorders, and as many television sets as they want. A study of its effects revealed that the students were no better informed than their contemporaries but that the advertisements broadcast on the channel had a significant effect on their consumer tastes (Aitkenhead, cited in Cole, 1998, p. 327).

On one hand, schools do contribute to the ideals of democratic organizations (in terms of providing access to relevant knowledge and equal opportunities). On the other hand, schools operate at the same time in sustaining and reinforcing the logic of capitalism by functioning as a reproductive force that offers different and unequal kinds of knowledge and rewards based on class, gender, and race (McLaren, 1997). Here we see inequality as having to do with how society regulates the distribution of different types of capital. Perrucci and Wysong (1999) describe these as consumption capital (having to do with wages or salary), investment capital (having to do with a surplus of consumption capital that you can invest and on which you can earn interest), skills capital (having to do with specialized knowledge that people accumulate through their work experience, training, or education), and social capital (having to do with the network of social ties that people have to family, friends, and acquaintances, as well as the collectively owned economic and cultural capital of a group). Educators have long made the case that schools traffic in cultural capital (values, attitudes, dress, mannerisms, personal style, etc.) (McLaren, 1997), but they have rarely linked the production of cultural capital to the international division of labor brought about by uneven development.[1]

RACE, CLASS, OR GENDER? BEYOND THE EITHER-OR IMPASSE

Read against the continuing globalization of capital, the concept of class remains a taboo subject within the guarded precincts of academic discourses. Seldom do politicians, intellectuals, or the media openly discuss class inequality in a language that situates it within the larger problematic of global capitalism and relations of exploitation and oppression linked to imperialism. To understand how educational inequalities are reproduced within schools, it is crucial not to leave class in the shade and to analyze the concept of class and class relations in a contextually nuanced way. Michael Parenti (1994) underscores the importance of class relations when he argues,

> Class realities permeate our society, determining much about our lifestyles and life chances, our capacity to make serviceable things happen, our access to power. How the dynamics and crises of capitalism are handled, and how the state is organized, are core questions for political struggle. They also are inescapably class questions. There are class interests involved in how the law is written and enforced, how political leaders pursue issues, how science and social science are studied and funded, how work is done, how a university is ruled, how the news is reported, how mass culture is created and manipulated, how careers are advanced or retarded, how the environment is treated, how racism and sexism are activated and reinforced, and how social reality itself is defined. (p. 64)

The concept of class expresses the relationship that social groups have to the means of production; it refers to those who own the factories, machinery, media, hotels, hospitals, and so on and those who must sell their labor in exchange for wages (Parenti, 1994). Wages that workers receive in the form of money are equivalent to only part of the value they create by their labor. Wealth so construed constitutes accumulated surplus or the unpaid wages of the workers.

Postmodernists—whose work now composes the fountainhead of radical educational critique—frequently overlook the centrality of class warfare as the overarching mechanism that inscribes individuals and groups in the reproduction of social relations of exploitation under capitalism. Although admittedly an individual's subjectivity or identity cannot be reduced to class interests, nevertheless social oppression and economic exploitation are much more than tangentially linked to class background and the social relations of production. In fact, forms of racial and gender oppression can best be understood against the background of class analysis. Marxists maintain that the eradication of poverty, racism, sexism, and patriarchal exploitation requires an understanding of class struggle. There are two reasons for identifying the working class as the central agent of social transformation. First, the working class continues to possess the ability to halt production lines. Second, a revolutionary working-class politics seeks to abolish all forms of social oppression. Postmodernists, on the other hand, seek to create a radical democracy through new social movements that concentrate on ending particular or local forms of oppression. In the words of Dana L. Cloud (1994),

> While a person's subjectivity is not a simple matter of class determination, his or her oppression and exploitation are directly connected to his/her economic status and position in the relations of production. Marxists believe there is more to liberation than the articulation of alternative subjectivities; an end to poverty, hunger, exploitation and abuse are more central, and require a notion of class position, agency and interests. From this perspective there are two good reasons for privileging working-class struggles. First, the working class has the power to stop production and bring the profit-making system down. Second, the working-class, the group of men and women of all races and sexual orientations whose labour produces profits for the few, has an objective . . . interest in overthrowing capitalism, whereas some members of many cross-class, non-socialist groups organized around other antagonisms (women's rights, environmental issues) have vested interests in maintaining the profit system. (p. 242)

According to E. San Juan, Jr. (1992), identity politics frequently and tragically leads to a privatization of political issues that "recuperates an autonomous will, and indigenous Otherness" (p. 107) and in doing so, voids resistance of its historical density. What identity politics fails to address is the fact that diversity and difference are allowed to proliferate and flourish provided that they remain within the prevailing forms of capitalist social arrangements, including hierarchical property arrangements. E. San Juan, Jr. argues that there is a "blind spot which identity politics cannot apprehend" (p. 107). He refers here to the fact that

> the contingencies of a hegemonic struggle can generate a variety of subject positions which are neither fixed nor shifting but capable of being articulated in various directions according to the play of political forces and the conjunctural alignment of multi-layered determinants. (p. 107)

Along with E. San Juan, Jr. we worry about the engineered collusion between an identity politics that stresses autonomous lived experience and a neoliberalism that encourages the erasure of the public sphere and the ascendancy of a capitalist triumphalism that synchronizes so-called autonomous agency to the hierarchical imperatives of advanced capitalism. What also disturbs us are the denunciations by some radical educators that anti-capitalist struggles can only operate as a foolish rhetorical device and what is needed is an equal distribution of economic resources. Although we favor economic equality, we find that the anti-Marxist sentiments among some radical educators constitutes an egregious capitulation to the value form of labor (often under the banner of a positive populism) and the iron laws of motion of capital accumulation. It is a position innocent of insight into contemporary social relations of production.

What Boris Kagarlitsky (2000) calls a "strategic hierarchy of goals" grounded in the overthrow of the social hierarchy of capitalist society is a measure that we take seriously. We acknowledge that political struggle for race, class, gender, and sexual equality is a tightly interwoven struggle. But, we understand class politics as the engine of our struggle for proletarian hegemony. As Robert McChesney (1996) asserts,

> Radicals are opposed to all forms of oppression and it is ludicrous to debate which of sexism, racism, "classism," or homophobia is most terrible, as if we were in some zero-sum game. Socialists have traditionally emphasized class—and continue to do so today—because the engine of a capitalist society is profit maximization and class struggle. Moreover, it is only through class politics that human liberation can truly be reached. (pp. 4-5)

In acknowledging this, we do not follow postmodernists in calling for an equivalence among various struggles. Rather, we call for a strategic integration of different yet equally important struggles. Recognizing that the legacy of racism and sexism is far from over, we offer possible ways in which race and gender antagonisms can be addressed and overcome within the larger project of class struggle. As Adolph Reed, Jr. (2000) maintains, "Recent debates that juxtapose identity politics or cultural politics to class politics are miscast. Cultural politics and identity politics are class politics" (p. xxii). The ways in which the contradiction between capital and labor is lived at the level of everyday life are almost certainly racialized and gendered. The modalities in which class exploitation are lived have specific consequences related to race, sexuality, age, and religion, and these must be placed at center stage in the struggle against oppression. We want to make clear that we are not subordinating race, ethnic, and gender struggles to class struggle. We simply are saying that without overcoming capitalist relations of production, other struggles will have little chance of succeeding. Yet, to make such an assertion is to identify a structured silence within many postmodernized versions of critical pedagogy: the disappearance of class struggle.

Overcoming racism and sexism are nol sidebar issues but are central to the revolutionary multiculturalism endorsed here. We do not intend to use class relations as a conceptual or political shield for racism or sexism or to make the *jejune* claim that a focus on racial inequality underrnines working-class efforts at organizing against the transnational capitalist oligopolies. Nor do we agree with some of our well-meaning White colleagues that an emphasis on class struggle takes away from the efforts of educators of color in their struggle against racism. This criticism fails to acknowledge that many educators of color have been at the forefront of the class struggle. Although strategically our dependent variable remains that of class, independent variables such as gender, race, religion, sexuality, and political ideology are not seen as cursory sites of antagonisms—they factor in our analysis in very central and distinctive ways.

TOWARD A REVOLUTIONARY WORKING-CLASS PEDAGOGY

One centerpiece of a revolutionary working-class pedagogy is engaging in ideology critique in light of understanding the unseen grammar of commodity logic that serves as the regulatory lexicon of everyday life. Such a pedagogy involves struggle over the production of meaning, a struggle that would enable marginalized social groups to name, identify, and take initial steps to transform the sources of their oppression and exploitation (McLaren, 1998a). It would also encourage them to analyze the myriad ways in which asymmetrical relations of power are both ideologically congealed in and concealed by the dominant discourses of equality, difference, and freedom (Giroux & McLaren, 1986). Although students are admittedly more than unconscious bearers of social structures, we are cognizant of the power of objective social structures to engineer complicity among both students and teachers in relations of exploitation and oppression. Consequently, a revolutionary working-class pedagogy stresses the importance of acquiring a critical literacy—where *literacy* is defined as a practice of reflecting, analyzing, and making critical judgments in relation to social, economic and political issues (see Lankshear & McLaren, 1993; see also Giroux, Lankshear, McLaren, & Peters, 1996). Furthermore, it invites subordinate groups to represent through classroom interaction and dialogue their lived reality in relation to objective social structures that shape their lives. This is done to solidify their beliefs, values, and experiences and also to challenge their everyday beliefs when they are discovered to be hegemonically advantageous (in the sense that they constitute dispositions that lead to concrete social practices or a complicity with certain social arrangements) to the reproduction of capitalist relations of exploitation (Giroux et al., 1996). In addition, this approach challenges students and workers to analyze the various meanings that underlie commonsensical concepts by drawing on everyday understandings that reflect their own social experiences. Teachers as revolutionary intellectuals contest the manufactured meaning of democracy by calling on students, workers, and intellectuals to critically examine socially constructed concepts such as

freedom and democracy, which have been manufactured by neoliberal ideologues in the service of transnational capitalism (Fischman & McLaren, 2000;
McLaren & Fischman, 1998). Students are invited to analyze the stories and
narratives that animate their lives by setting them against a normative back drop
of heterosexist and Eurocentric assumptions (McLaren, 1998a; Ovando &
McLaren, 2000; Sleeter & McLaren, 1995).

Mainstream pedagogy assiduously disregards as crucial a knowledge of
how asymmetrical relations of power become embedded in race, gender, and
class antagonisms that are reinforced through the dominant social and ideological apparatuses of the state. In contrast, a revolutionary working-class pedagogy
sets as its goal the transformation of existing social and economic relations by
encouraging marginalized social groups both to critique and transform capitalist
social relations of production. Here the classroom is conceived as a political
arena for legitimizing the lived experiences of the oppressed social classes without assuming that such experiences are transparent or absent of racism or sexism (Freire, 1970, 1998; Giroux, 1988; McLaren, 1995, 1997).

ATTRIBUTES OF A REVOLUTIONARY
WORKING-CLASS PEDAGOGY

A working-class pedagogy entails struggles over meaning, representation, and
identity in relation to a moral and ethical commitment to social justice (Cole,
1998; Cole & Hill, 1995; Cole, Hill, & Rikowski, 1997). Knoblauch and
Brannon (1993) argue that citizenship within a capitalist democracy

> includes an allegiance to passive consumerism, rather than active engage-
> ment In the construction of social life, and a long-standing hostllity to prac-
> tices of critical inquiry, certainly including llberatory pedagogy but also,
> historically, the challenges of labor unions, feminists, gays, environmental
> actlvists, and anyone else posing a conceivable threat to economic interests
> and managerial hierarchies that the media help to maintain. (p. 31)

This is in marked contrast to a revolutionary working-class pedagogy that underscores the active participation of students and workers in their own self-education as active citizens linked to the struggle for self-realization and coexistence—a process by which workers gain control over both their intellectual and
their physical labor. This also entails promoting among students and workers—
especially in countries where subsistence or state coercion dorninate everyday
life—alternative networks of popular organizing that include revolutionary
social movements (McLaren & Farahmandpur, 2000). A revolutionary working-
class pedagogy aims at transforming the consciousness of being in alienation by
developing a critical consciousness. We should stress that alienation is not root-

ed in the world of Hegelian abstractions but rather embedded within the social and material relations of production. This raises questions as to whether an alienated consciousness is an inert totality and if it can be transcended. According to Mészáros (1989), alienated activity not only produces an alienated consciousness but also a consciousness of being in alienation. Therefore, it is advisable to create those pedagogical conditions that, for the working class, facilitate the development of a critical consciousness to overcome economic alienation and transform the existing social conditions of production through mass political action. Such action must be capable of creating egalitarian structures that are able to achieve—at an increasing level and in an ever-expanding scope—the institutionalization of popular democracy. Of course, this means aggregating diverse constituencies that might be distrustful of one another. We want to be clear that pedagogically we are not arguing for the teacher to serve as the mediator between imputed and factual consciousness, as someone who compels the student to activate or actualize revolutionary consciousness, who imports socialist insight from her rucksack in the Sierra Maestra to student *foco* groups in the United States. Because this position is tantamount to an externally imposed dictatorship of the teacher that relies on the false opposition of ideal type and factual actualization. Rather, our approach is Freirean in that it argues that revolutionary consciousness is a political act of knowing, an active intervention against the barriers that prevent the students from achieving their role as agents of history.

It is critical to remember that as revolutionary educators, we need to identify alternative subject positions that we might assume or counternarratives and countermemories that we might make available to our students to contest existing regimes of representation and social practice. But, we cannot be content to remain here. We need to identify the historical determinations of domination and oppression as part of the struggle to develop concrete practices of counter-representation. The search for external causes of domination and exploitation should not be forgotten in the fashionable rush on the part of some postmodern educators to encounter and explain *différence* in subjective terms.

Emphasizing freedom as the realization of humanity's purpose, by which labor as a social means fulfills its human needs, is an important characteristic of the revolutionary working-class pedagogy that we are envisioning. It engages teachers as reflexive practitioners in their daily lives. To become a critically reflective practitioner requires the ability to engage in complex analyses of social class accompanied by trenchant investigations of other forms of oppression as they are linked to capitalist exploitation—relations linked to race, gender, and sexual orientation. In short, it requires a comprehensive form of political agency that moves beyond the particular struggles of select groups (McLaren & Farahmandpur, 2000).

A revolutionary working-class pedagogy seeks to transgress the boundaries that set high culture apart from popular culture and that privilege the former over the latter. Empowering the working-class and marginalized social groups in society means giving them an opportunity to interrogate theoretically (in the sense articulated by both Marx and Lenin) forms of both high culture and popular culture so that they can analyze, articulate, express, and construct meaning from multiple positionalities located in their lived experiences dealing with racism, sexism, and class exploitation. In addition, disenfranchised groups need to control the means of production of their symbolic economies, not to mention their material existence. Because a revolutionary working-class pedagogy also recognizes that the language and the discourses practiced within the classroom setting as well as in the workplace are ideologically tainted with the values, beliefs, and interests of the privileged social classes so as to conceal asymmetrical relations of power, an important step involves the encouragement of critical dialogues among teachers, students, and workers. The central purpose of such dialogues would be to raise class consciousness and help students and workers recognize how their subjectivities and social identities are configured in ways that are structurally advantageous to the status quo. This requires that students be able to see themselves in relation to their role as workers and to be provided with an opportunity to develop class consciousness. This does not mean that class consciousness excludes other aspects of identity. As Reed (2000) points out,

> The claim that being a worker is not the most crucial identity for members of marginalized groups is debatable. To say the least. But even if that claim were true, what it means simply is that people see themselves in many ways simultaneously. We all have our own sets of experiences fashioned by our social position, our family upbringing, our local political culture, and our voluntary associations. Each of these goes into the mix, modifying crosscutting even at times overriding identities based on race or ethnicity, gender, or sexual orientation. . . . The fact of the existence of a capitalist economic order doesn't automatically tell us how people interpret their positions within it. Class consciousness, no less than other identities, is contingent, the product of political debate and struggle. (p. 137)

It is imperative in our view that the struggles of teachers in schools are linked to the struggles of other workers. A revolutionary working-class pedagogy of labor stresses that the empowerment of workers (i.e., teachers, postal workers, factory workers) can be successfully achieved through organizing labor unions that committed to anticapitalist struggle and a proletarian praxis. Yet, we must also emphasize that the political and economic empowerment of workers will depend on their active participation and self-education. Here we oppose the tradition of "workerism" that is often anti-intellectual and looks on theory with suspicion and often contempt. Instead, we applaud the recent struggles of intellectuals such as Pierre Bourdieu of France to coordinate the efforts of numerous European social movements through his organization, *Raisons d'Agir*. The ability of teachers and prospective teachers to interpret contemporary social relations of production as a set of interconnected social and material practices helps them to understand that success in a capitalist society is not the result of individual capacities but rather is constrained and enabled by asymmetrical relations of power linked to race, class, gender, and sexual economies of privilege. We believe that workers committed to social justice have the opportunity to become liberatory intellectuals (what Antonio Gramsci, 1971, referred to as "organic" intellectuals) who possess the capacity to make meaningful choices and decisions in their lives (McLaren, Fischman, Serra, & Antelo, 1998). Thus, teachers who are central to the process of raising students' political consciousness must themselves become theoreticians of their own teaching practices. Accordingly, our task as organic and committed intellectuals is to create the conditions for the development of a revolutionary consciousness among the working class in general and teachers and students in particular.

In developing a framework for forging solidarity and collective action among workers and students, we find the three conditions that Weinbaum (1998) proposes to be particularly instructive. First, the central role of critical educators must be directed at facilitating dialogues among workers and students concerning every day labor practices at the workplace and teaching practices within schools. Second, teachers and workers must be presented with opportunities for transforming those relationships that link their individual interests and issues at the local and community level to broader social and economic relations at a global level. And finally, Weinbaum stresses the active political role that critical educators in labor unions and schools must play both in their communities and in progressive organizations.

We believe that a revolutionary working-class pedagogy that aims at consciousness raising, political activism, and social empowerment can be a critical tool for self-determination and also for transforming existing social conditions. Yet, we feel it is necessary to stress that working-class pedagogy can be effective only to the degree that marginalized social groups are able to organize into oppositional social and political movements against global capitalism and remain committed to a metanarrative of social justice both inside and outside the classroom. This stipulates that a stress on difference not undercut the possibility of political solidarity. As Reed (2000) notes,

> Insofar as identity politics insists on recognizing difference as the central truth of political life, it undercuts establishing a broad base as a goal of organizing. Its reflex is to define ever more distinct voices and to approach collective action from an attitude more like suspicion than solidarity. (p. xx)

CONCLUSION: TEACHERS AS ACTIVISTS

Capitalism cannot remain a sustainable social and economic system under the guidance of neoliberal free-market economics without periodic wars and financial crises. Following Marx, we believe that the exploitation powered by capitalist social relations can only be overcome by the redistribution of wealth through class struggle and, finally, by the abolition of private property and capital itself.

A revolutionary working-class pedagogy seeks to reclaim revolutionary ideas from the frozen stasis of their exile, an exile that occurred after what John Leonard (2000) calls "the 1989 collapse of the non-profit police states of Eastern Europe" (p. 14). Rebuilding revolutionary ideas and practices can be achieved, in part, by forming coalitions among gay and lesbian organizations, ethnic minority groups, indigenous movements, and labor constituencies of various stripes. Here we are not advancing the revolutionary adventurist rhetoric that Lenin warned against; rather, we are criticizing uncommitted intellectuals in academic circles who constrain rather than enable the advancement of a revolutionary praxis. Such intellectuals too often succumb to a paralysis of the political will.

Struggles against social and economic injustice can effectively be organized and articulated among various anti-imperialist groups when they coalesce around mutual and shared interests. Revolutionary movements can succeed on a global basis only when differences over ideological interests and political goals can be resolved or at least temporarily put aside. This is not an argument for a unification of several political parties under the leadership of one party (e.g., the Rainbow Coalition); rather, we are insisting that a successful revolutionary praxis must occur as the culmination of historical processes in which various social movements with different interests develop an understanding of each others' often conflicting experiences as the victims of societal oppression.

A revolutionary pedagogy requires moving anticapitalist struggles in the direction of a new internationalism that extends beyond the nation-state. Organizing teachers as part of a larger compendium of social movements struggling toward a set of common objective goals (such as the abolition of economic exploitation, sexism, and racism) is necessary for the development of an effective revolutionary politics—one that can effectively and demonstrably create the necessary conditions for marginalized social groups to empower themselves (McLaren, 1998b; McLaren & Farahmandpur, 1999a, 1999b, 2000). This is not a romantic call to don a *bleu de travail* and rush the barricades erected by pro-capitalist ideologues but to understand how the forces of globalization and neoliberalism are not forces in their own right but are connected to a wider system of exploitation that is as old as capitalism itself. This is why the connective tissue that holds the various social movements in place should not be a commitment to counter-hegemonic struggle but a dedication to the achievement of proletarian hegemony.

Revolutionary pedagogy works towards creating a context in which freedom from the enslaving subordination of the individual to the crisis-prone nature of capital accumulation replaces the arid realm of necessity, where the satisfaction of social need replaces the entrapment within the division of labor, where the development of the creative capacities of the individual replaces the laws of capital and landed property, where worker self-rule and the free development of individuals replaces the current entrapment in the burcaucratization and atomization of social life.

Teacher educators as part of a broader revolutionary anticapitalist movement based on the development of a new class politics must be attentive to the
diverse social and political interests as well as the needs of different constituencies in the struggle. Furthermore, Marxist revolutionary theory must be flexible
enough to reinvent itself in the context of current social, economic, and political
restructuring under the economic policies of neoliberalism. Marxist theory is
not set forth here as a universal truth but as a weapon of interpretation. No theory can fully anticipate or account for the consequences of its application but
remains a living aperture through which specific histories are made visible and
intelligible. In this sense, Marxist theory provides the oppressed with the theoretical knowledge for analyzing and challenging capitalist production. It is here
that Marxist theory can be used to advance proletarian hegemony through the
work of organic intellectuals engaged in revolutionary socialist praxis aimed at
the overthrow of the bourgeois state.

The Battle in Seattle can teach educators important lessons (Rikowski, in
press). For instance, we recognize that there are times when anticapitalist struggles require an organized revolutionary class that has, in the course of its protracted political activities, gained a significant measure of class consciousness
and recognizes itself not only as a class in itself but also as a class for itself.
Yet, there are other moments when anticapitalist struggles take the form of what
Jim Hightower (cited in Marshall, 2000) refers to as "spontaneous and unauthorized outbreaks of democracy," as in the case of the anti-World Trade
Organization protests in Seattle. There are moments, too, when class struggle
can consist of isolated individual acts of resistance against corporate colonization and commodification of the life world. A case in point is the French farmer,
José Bova, who protested against genetically modified food by driving his trac-
tor into a McDonald's restaurant under construction in the south of France. All
of these efforts have their importance. Yet our efforts, in particular, are in the
direction of building an organized revolutionary class. Here we struggle against
attempts to decenter and rearticulate contingency in which the social basis of
exploitation is dissolved beyond class politics. In this regard, the concept of
globalization needs to be reformulated so that historical subjects or actors are
granted the potential to challenge the hegemony of international capital in the
defense of justice, solidarity, and the working class. We must not allow our
individual acts of resistance to lead to reformism or economism or to derail the
proletarian movement from its anti-capitalist struggle and its "protracted, all-
encompassing assault upon the state and the capitalist class" (Holst, in press).

Finally, we want to emphasize that although social transformation is
achieved, in part, by structures put in place by historical necessity, to move
beyond these structures requires the exercise of considerable political agency. It
is by means of exercising this agency through collective struggle that the limits
of social transformation set by existing historical structures can be laid bare and
eventually transcended. We are referring to agency as a form of both intellectual
labor and concrete social practice in short, a critical praxis. This requires, in the

words of David McNally (1993), "treating human beings as 'both authors and actors of their own drama'" (p. 153) and situating their actions in the context of the development of their productive forces.

NOTE

1. *Cultural capital*, a term made popular by French sociologist Pierre Bourdieu, refers to "ways of talking, acting, and socializing, as well as language practices, values, and styles of dress and behavior" (McLaren, 1997, p. 193). According to McLaren:

   Schools systematically devalue the cultural capital of students who occupy subordinate class positions. Cultural capital is reflective of material capital and replaces it as a form of symbolic currency that enters into the exchange system of the school. Cultural capital is therefore symbolic of the social structure's economic force and becomes itself a productive force in the reproduction of social relations under capitalism. (p. 193)

REFERENCES

Allman, P., & Wallis, J. (1990). Praxis: Implications for 'really' radical education. *Studies in the Education of Adults, 22*(1), 14-30.

Azad, B. (2000). *Heroic struggle!—bitter defeat: Factors contributing to the dismantling of the socialist state in the USSR.* New York: International.

Bonacich, E., & Appelbaum, R. P. (2000). *Behind the label: Inequality in the Los Angeles apparel industry.* Berkeley: University of California Press.

Borowski, J. (1999, August 21). Schools with a slant. *The New York Times*, p. A23.

Cloud, D. L. (1994). "Socialism of the mind": The new age of post-Marxism. In H. W. Somins & M. Billig (Eds.), *After postmodernism: Reconstructing ideology critique* (pp. 222-251). London: Sage.

Cole, M. (1998). Globalization, modernisation and competitiveness: A critique of the New Labour Project in Education. *International Studies in Sociology of Education, 8*, 315-332.

Cole, M., & Hill, D. (1995). Games of despair and rhetorics of resistance: Postmodernism, education and reaction. *British Journal of Sociology of Education, 16*(2), 165-182.

Cole, M., Hill, D., & Rikowski, G. (1997). Between postmodernism and nowhere: The predicament of the postmodernist. *British Journal of Educational Studies, 45*(2), 187-200.

Collins, C., & Yeskel, F. (2000). *Economic apartheid in America: A primer on economic inequality and security.* New York: The New Press.

Dinerstein, A. (1999). The violence of stability: Argentina in the 1990s. In M. Neary (Ed.), *Global humanization: Studies in the manufacture of labor* (pp. 47-76). London: Mansell.

Fischman, G., & McLaren, P. (2000). Schooling for democracy: Towards a critical utopianism. *Contemporary Society, 29*(1), 168-179.

Freire, P. (1970). *Pedagogy of the oppressed.* New York: Continuum.

Freire, P. (1998). *Pedagogy of freedom: Ethics, democracy, and civic courage.* Lanham, MD: Rowman & Littlefield.

Giroux, H. A. (1988). *Teachers as intellectuals: Toward a critical pedagogy of learning.* New York: Bergin & Garvey.

Giroux, H. A., Lankshear, C., McLaren, P., & Peters, M. (Eds.). (1996). *Counternarratives: Cultural studies and critical pedagogies in postmodern spaces.* New York: Routledge.

Giroux, H. A., & McLaren, P. (1986). Teacher education and the politics of engagement: The case for democratic schooling. *Harvard Educational Review, 56*(3), 213-238.

Gramsci A. (1971). *Selections from the prison notebooks* (Q. Hoare & G. Nowell-Smith, Ed., and Trans.). London: Lawrence and Wishart.

Hawkes, D. (1996). *Ideology.* London: Routledge.

Holst, J. (in press). *Social movements, civil society and radical adult education.* Westport, CT: Bergin & Garvey.

Imam, H. (1997). Global subjects: How did we get here? *Women in Action, 3,* 12-15.

Kagarlitsky, B. (2000). *The return of radicalism: Reshaping the left institutions* (R. Clarke, Trans.). London and Sterling, VA: Pluto Press.

Kincheloe, J. (1998). *How do we tell the workers? The socioeconomic foundations of work and vocational education.* Boulder, CO: Westview Press.

Knoblauch, C. H., & Brannon, L. (1993). *Critical literacy and the idea of literacy.* Portsmouth, NH: Boynton and Cook.

Lankshear, C., & McLaren, P. (Eds.). (1993). *Critical literacy: Politics, praxis, and the postmodern.* New York: State University of New York Press.

Lasn, K. (1999). *Culture jam: The uncooling of America.* New York: Eagle Brook.

Leonard, J. (2000). How a caged bird learns to sing: Or, my life at the *New York Times,* CBS and other pillars of the media establishment. *The Nation, 270*(25), 11-19.

Luxemburg, R. (1919). *The crisis in German social democracy: The Junius pamphlet.* New York: The Socialist Publication Society.

Marshall, S. (2000). Rattling the global corporate suites. *Political Affairs, 79*(1), 6-12.

McChesney, R. (1996). Is there any hope for cultural studies? *Monthly Review, 47*(10), 1-18.

McLaren, P. (1995). *Critical pedagogy and predatory culture: Oppositional politics in a postmodern era.* London: Routledge.

McLaren, P. (1997). *Revolutionary multiculturalism: Pedagogies of dissent for the new millennium.* Boulder, CO: Westview.

McLaren, P. (1998a). *Life in schools: An introduction to critical pedagogy in the foundations of education* (3rd ed.). New York: Longman.

McLaren, P. (1998b). Revolutionary pedagogy in postrevolutionary times: Rethinking the political economy of critical education. *Educational Theory, 48,* 431-462.

McLaren, P. (2000). *Che Guevara, Paulo Freire, and the pedagogy of revolution.* Boulder, CO: Rowman and Littlefield.

McLaren, P., & Farahmandpur, R. (1999a). Critical multiculturalism and globalization: Some implications for a politics of resistance. *Journal of Curriculum Theorizing, 15*(3), 27-46.

McLaren, P., & Farahmandpur, R. (1999b). Critical pedagogy, postmodernism, and the retreat from class: Towards a contraband pedagogy. *Theoria, 93*, 83-115.

McLaren, P., & Farahmandpur, R. (2000). Reconsidering Marx in post-Marxist times: A requiem for postmodernism? *Educational Researcher, 29*(3), 25-33.

McLaren, P., & Fischman, G. (1998). Reclaiming hope: Teacher education and social justice in the age of globalization. *Teacher Education Quarterly, 25*(4), 125-133.

McLaren, P., Fischman, G., Serra, S., & Antelo, E. (1998). The specters of Gramsci: Revolutionary praxis and the committed intellectual. *Journal of Thought, 33*(3), 9-42.

McNally, D. (1993). *Against the market: Political economy, market socialism and the Marxist critique.* London: Verso.

Mészáros, I. (1989). *Marx's theory of alienation.* London: Merlin.

Niemark, M. K. (1999). If it's so important, why won't they pay for it? Public higher education at the turn of the century. *Monthly Review, 51*(5), 20-31.

Ovando, C. J., & McLaren, P. (Eds.). (2000). *The politics of multiculturalism: Students and teachers caught in the cross fire.* Boston: McGraw-Hill.

Parenti, M. (1994). *Land of idols: Political mythology in America.* New York: St. Martin's Press.

Parenti, M. (1997). *Blackshirts & reds: Rational fascism & the overthrow of communism.* San Francisco: City Lights Books.

Peery, N. (1997). The birth of a modern proletariat. In J. Davis, T. Hirschl, & M. Stack (Eds.), *Cutting edge: Technology, information, capitalism and social revolution* (pp. 297- 302). London: Verso.

Perrucci, R., & Wysong, E. (1999). *The new class society.* Boulder, CO: Rowman & Littlefield.

Reed, A., Jr. (2000). *Class notes: Posing as politics and other thoughts on the American scene.* New York: New Press.

Rikowski, G. (in press). *The battle of Seattle.* London: Tufnell Press.

San Juan, E., Jr. (1992). *Racial formations/critical transformations: Articulations of power in ethnic and racial studies in the United States.* New Jersey and London: Humanities Press.

Sleeter, C., & McLaren, P. (Eds.). (1995). *Multicultural education, critical pedagogy, and the politics of difference.* New York: State University of New York Press.

Spring, J. (1998). *Education and the rise of the global economy.* Mahwah, NJ: Lawrence Erlbaum.

Teeple, G. (1995). *Globalization and the decline of social reform.* Toronto: Garamond Press.

Thompson, W. (1997). *The left in history: Revolution and reform in twentieth-century politics.* London: Pluto Press.

Vrana, D. (1998, September 7). Education's pied piper with a dark past. *Los Angeles Times,* p. Al.

Weinbaum, E. S. (1998). Education without paper: Teaching workers to build a labor movement. *Radical History Review, 72,* 68-77.

Witheford, N. (1997). Cycles of circuits and struggles in high-technology capitalism. In J. Davis, T. Hirschil, & M. Stack (Eds.), *Cutting edge: Technology, information, cap-italism and social revolution* (pp. 195-242). London: Verso.

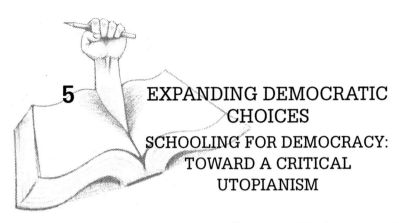

5   EXPANDING DEMOCRATIC CHOICES
SCHOOLING FOR DEMOCRACY: TOWARD A CRITICAL UTOPIANISM

Gustavo Fischman and
Peter McLaren

Our attempt to navigate the murky waters of contemporary definitions of utopia, schooling, and capitalism has been hampered by a mild psychosis of the spirit, brought about by an overly simplified understanding of democracy. In this article, we use the term *democracy* in its pedagogical context. We define *democratic pedagogies* as those that motivate teachers and students, schools and communities to deliberate and shape the choices that they make with the overarching purpose of contributing to increased social justice, equality, and improvement in the quality of life for all constituencies within the larger society. As such, democratic pedagogies are embedded in a web of social relations, where the rights and duties of the learners and educators are evaluated not only for the transmission of knowledge (these days most often reduced to the results of standardized tests) but also for the possible consequences of the participants' actions (those of teachers, administrators, students, and communities) in the ongoing democratization of the larger society.

We believe firmly that a democratic pedagogy should be underwritten by the imperatives of social justice and equality across race, class, and gender divisions. Social justice and equality refer not only to socioeconomic, cultural, and political conditions and relationships but also to equal access to information and tools of critical analysis. Democratic pedagogies are singularly dedicated to creating critical citizens who can analyze the social contradictions that constitute everyday life within capitalist democracy and to transforming relations of exploitation and oppression (McLaren 1997; Giroux 1988). Democratic pedagogies mainly intend to reform capitalist society; more radical versions align themselves with forms of democratic socialism (McLaren 1997a). Democratic pedagogy in both of these senses engages the world within an essentially utopi-

This chapter was originally published in *Contemporary Sociology, 29*(1), 168-179. ©2000 American Sociological Association.

an optic. In fact, we believe that it is first and foremost a discourse of hope and, as such, is ripe with utopic possibilities.

We want to underscore the importance of rethinking public education in an effort to develop schools as utopic-heterotopic democratic spaces. Utopic school spaces are what one could call "perfectible sites" that do not require the negation of difference and dissent for their realization and fulfillment. As Gabriel García Márquez expressed so beautifully in his speech accepting the Nobel Prize in Literature, we need

> a new and overwhelming utopia of life, where nobody can decide for some-
> body else even the way to die, where love can be certain and happiness possi-
> ble, and where the generations condemned to a hundred years of solitude will
> have once and for all a second chance on earth. (quoted in Pizarro 1994: 37)

We also envision schools as heterotopic sites—heterogeneous and relation-al spaces (Soja 1989).[1] In this article we argue that schools that wish to encourage effective democratic participation would then need to be transformed into open sites protected from the disciplinary regimes of market regulation; each "condition" making up the site would necessarily depend upon the other. It is easy to comprehend the need for openness, because it is axiomatic for all forms of democracy. But just as important as accepting the need to embrace and practice different beliefs and ways of looking at the world, and to accomplish different types of educational activities and practices, is the need for schools to be protected from the pressures of the pervasive market.

Here we explore some of the conditions necessary to construct schooling as a utopic-heterotopic democratic experience. To accomplish this task, we visit several themes developed by Ernst Bloch and Paulo Freire that address the creation of the utopian imagination. Next, we present a contemporary example of one urban educational setting in Brazil where progressive educators are engaged in the struggle for democratic schooling. To provide a contrast to the Brazilian experience, we discuss how the increasing presence of corporate sponsorships diminishes the chances of democratizing schools in the United States. Finally, we revisit our main themes and present a series of recommendations for empowering teachers as key actors in the construction of schools as utopic het-erotopic spaces.

RETHINKING UTOPIA

To re-engage the concept of utopia at this current moment within late capital-ism, we turn briefly to the thinking of two of the most significant philosophers of hope of this century: Ernst Bloch and Paulo Freire. Bloch has offered a cre-ative re-imagining of the concept of utopia through his attempt to keep alive a redemptive and radically utopian spirit during a time (the 1930s) when the Enlightenment tradition was under a powerful assault by Fascism. Bloch roundly rejected those who would criticize the idea of utopia as unrealistic, impractical, and other-worldly, or a form of unbridled, unapologetic subjectivism that seeks to make objective reality conform to the irresponsible whims and devices of irrational people.

For Bloch, "utopia extends so far and inputs itself so powerfully to all human activities that every account of man and the world must essentially contain it" (cited in Giroux and McLaren 1997: 146). Bloch argues that reality is determined fundamentally by the future rather than the past. His ontology of possibility, which he called the "not yet" or *anagnorisis* (recognition), claimed that one could ascertain figural traces of the future in remnants of the past. As Giroux and McLaren note: "Hope is given birth in a spectacular sea of possibility. In this view, only the infinitude of possibility can provide the necessary link among past, present, and future (1997: 146).[2]

Bloch's Marxist vision of utopia shares much in common with the philosophy of Brazilian educator Paulo Freire. Freire's influences on our understanding of education are vast and far reaching. Among his many contributions, we want to highlight his ideas that education is a political process, that theory and practice exist as a dialectical unity, and that to exercise radical democratic forms of education, it is essential to reject authoritarian and empty laissez-faire practices. "Just because I reject authoritarianism does not mean I can fall into lack of discipline, nor that rejecting lawlessness, I can dedicate myself to authoritarianism. As I once affirmed: One is not the opposite of the other. The opposite of either manipulative authoritarianism or lawless permissiveness, is democratic radicalism" (Freire 1998: 64).

Real democracy is understood by Freire as something latent in the present, something immanently future-bearing that can be grasped in the flickering moment of anticipatory consciousness. Freire points out that utopia and critical consciousness are mutually inclusive and dialectically reanimating, and that together they synergize new knowledge and new cultural configurations and possibilities for human transformation. Freire points out that "democracy, like any dream, is not made with spiritual words but with reflection and practice. It is not what I say that says I am a democrat, that I am not a racist or machista, but what I do. What I say may not be contradicted by what I do. It is what I do that bespeaks my faithfulness or not to what I say" (1998: 67).

Freire's work underscores the fact that utopian praxis has to include some form of analysis of the real existing circumstances surrounding social contradictions within capitalism, and the most important form of analysis is ideological critique. The utopian disposition of Freire's work is therefore concrete, in that it originates in the living conditions of oppressed social actors, their historical settings, their risks, challenges, and problems, but also their productive and creative energies displayed in the everyday struggles for subsistence (Giroux and McLaren 1997)

One of the most important dimensions of Freire's utopian vision is his demand for changing the oppressive aspects of everyday life in schools and society by engaging in the common struggles of the "here and now," instead of waiting for idealized objective conditions to be realized or for a utopian consciousness to emerge magically among the oppressed. Rather, Freire's utopia is realizable, but only in reading the word and the world in an ever-evolving process of *conscientization*, emerging from the concrete conditions of everyday struggle within capitalist society (Freire 1993). In Freire's utopian vision of schools, the main task is not to liberate others by applying ready-made recipes, but to develop solidarity with the others, by struggling together in classrooms, in schools, and in the streets.

Freire also claimed that for revolutionary praxis to occur, the utopian dimension had to be natural. It is worth quoting Freire in his own words on this issue:

> Revolutionary utopia tends to be dynamic rather than static; tends to life rather than death; to the future as a challenge to man's creativity rather than as a repetition of the present; to love as liberation of subjects rather than as pathological possessiveness; to the emotion of life rather than cold abstractions; to living together in harmony rather than gregariousness; to dialogue rather than mutism; to praxis rather than "law and order"; to men who organize themselves reflectively for action rather than men who are organized for passivity; to creative and communicative language rather than prescriptive signals; to reflective challenges rather than domesticating slogans; and to values that are lived rather than myths that are imposed. (cited in Giroux and McLaren 1997: 150)

What unifies Bloch and Freire in their difficult challenge of transforming schools into more democratic spaces is their active refusal to link hope to a past eschatological event or to a finite historical moment. Hope for changes, improvements, solidarity, and social justice is the guiding force, a force that is grasped "as a pulsating latency of possibility contained in the unity of the immanent and transcendent. As such, hope is to be conscripted by social agents in order to contest the gangsterism of the spirit so common in this era of consumer capitalism, and to fill the empty space of postmodern nihilism" (Giroux and McLaren 1997: 157). We understand utopias, after Freire and Bloch, as providing the conceptual horizon for the development of democratic schooling. This horizon of possibility could also be described as a "critical educational utopia." In the next section we examine a recent educational reform effort in the city of Porto Alegre, Brazil, read against this concept of critical educational utopia.

CRITICAL EDUCATIONAL UTOPIAS OF THE CONCRETE: PORTO ALEGRE, BRAZIL: ESCOLA CIDADÃ[3]

In this section we offer provisional glimpses of a nascent school reform effort that point to some of the utopic imperatives discussed above.[4] In doing so, we discuss a concrete attempt to increase democratic participation in schools, taking place in the south of Brazil and involving an ambitious citywide program. We offer this example not as extensive empirical analysis, but simply as tentative sketches to add some concrete texture to our discussion about the possibilities of encouraging democratic participation in schools.

Located in the south end of Brazil is Porto Alegre, the largest urban district and the city capital of the State of Rio Grande do Sul. The city and its suburban areas have a population of 1,286,000 inhabitants, distributed in 85 neighborhoods. In 1989, the municipal administration adopted a system of participatory decision making to decide the municipality's budget. This program aims to include the population in discussing and elaborating the annual Investment Plan to be held in the city.[5]

This school reform effort is intimately related to and complements the larger participatory budget decision-making process, yet they are separate endeavors. We believe such an effort illustrates the political will and political resolve necessary to combat the type of corporatist colonization of schooling (described below) associated with neoliberal educational reform agendas that provide ballast for globalization.

The *Escola Cidadã Program* (Citizen's School Project) was developed and established by the administration of the *Partido dos Trabalhadores* (Workers' Party) since winning the elections for the Municipality of Porto Alegre in 1989. During the last 10 years, educators, students, parents, community organizations, and individuals have had the opportunity to express their opinions about the role that schools should play in the larger society, and to reflect upon the type of social, political, and educational practices they would like to see in operation in the municipality's schools. This process of educational reform expresses the articulation of democratic ideals, community experiences, the legacy of the popular education movement, and a firm commitment to create a new model of schooling even amid a dramatic financial and economic crisis.

The educational policies implemented by the Secretary of Education of the City of Porto Alegre have attempted to translate into the educational sphere a radical democratic spirit by supporting the direct and active participation of students, teachers, administrators, staff, parents, and the community at large in the formulation, administration, and control of the public policies for the municipality.

The program Escola Cidadã operates from the fundamental premise that democratizing schools requires a collective effort to create an educational project that is open and flexible in its structures while maintaining its goals of radically democratizing classroom practices. Within such a project, schools are transformed into laboratories for the practice of individual and social rights. For example, at the center of the program of Schooling for Citizenship are the following ideals: developing autonomous, critical, and creative individuals; developing citizens who support the daily practices of solidarity, justice, freedom, human respect, and equal relationships between men and women; and informing all curriculum practices with a commitment to the development of a less exploitative relationship with the environment. José Clóvis de Azevedo, the current secretary of education of Porto Alegre, states that to achieve such ambitious goals it is necessary to recover the sense of schools as laboratories of democracy against the technocratic attempts to make markets of schools:

> We reaffirmed our commitment to expand the humanist character of public schools and we oppose the submission of education to the values of the market and Neo-Liberal reforms in education. The market's main concern is to form consumers and customers, to turn education into merchandise submitted to profit-seeking rationales, naturalizing individualism, conformity, unfair competition, indifference and, consequently, the exclusion of those deemed a-priori unsuited to compete. (1999a: 5)

The results of this program are highly impressive, especially when compared to education in other Latin American countries, and when you consider that Escola Cidadã serves the most impoverished population in the city of Porto Alegre.

A recent report illustrates some of the most important advances of this endeavor. In 1989 the number of municipal schools was 37, with 24,232 students enrolled. By 1999 the number of schools increased to 89, serving 49,673 students. In the same period the dropout rate for elementary education descended from 9.02 to 2.43 percent, and retention increased from 71.23 to 85.5 percent. (SMED 1999: 5) Accompanying these changes, new programs were created or expanded. It is worth noting that among these new programs was the amplification services for students with special needs, special programs to reach the educational needs of street children, SEJA (*Serviços Educativos Para Jovems E Adultos*), an educational program for youth and adults, and MOVA (*Movemento de Alfabetizaçaçao*), a program of literacy and popular education.

In 1993, Escola Cidadã implemented a series of Regional Encounters oriented to the establishment of the School Constituent, a collective structure open to the participation of all the segments of the school community. The goal of the School Constituent was to establish the guiding principles that would orient the construction of a nonexcluding, democratic, emancipatory school. The Regional Encounters and the Constituent Congress were attended by elected delegates, guaranteeing the participation of parents, students, teachers, and employees. The discussion was organized around four thematic axes: Curriculum and Knowledge, Administration, Evaluation, and Norms of Coexistence.

After the School Constituent was established, its participants reaffirmed the goals of Escola Cidadã for the democratization of schooling in three primary areas: school administration, access to schools, and access to knowledge.

One of the first actions of Escola Cidadã was to establish mechanisms for the direct election of principals and assistant principals in the schools of Porto Alegre. This step was taken not to link the democratization of schools to the election of the administrative and pedagogical leadership, but to redefine the power relationships inside schools. To be elected, aspiring principals and assistants are required to present programs for the school administration. Successful proposals need the support of staff, teachers, students, and parents, and must be technically and financially responsible. Thus goals, procedures, norms, and guidelines for administrative and pedagogic relationships that are developed inside a given school require the consent of teachers, students, educational authorities, and parents.

Another vital mechanism developed to democratize the exercise of power inside schools was the creation of School Councils. Consisting of elected representatives (parents, students, employees, and teachers), the School Council is the supreme organ of the school, exercising considerable influence in administrative, financial, and pedagogic matters. The Council defines the more global aspects of the school, the basic lines of administration, and resource allocation and application. The Direction, which is part of the Council, is responsible for offering political direction to the project (Azevedo 1999b).

The administrative structures cannot be democratized without the implementation of the program for Planning and Participatory Budget in Schools. The objective of this program is to democratize decision making in the context of each school, as well as to provide financial autonomy in the management of expenses, materials, and services and to develop annual plans for improving educational services.[6] In addition, the district of Porto Alegre implemented participatory research strategies to develop school curricula. One of the most effective tools for resolving the frequent disconnection between the cultural and social frameworks of communities and schools is the use of educational thematic units, built around a central concern for the community. Such a unit is developed after a social-anthropological diagnostic evaluation conducted by teachers with the participation of the involved community. These thematic units become a locally based and locally owned instrument designed to construct and distribute knowledge that is socially relevant for the educational community. The critical incorporation of elements deemed relevant for the school community, complemented with pedagogical practices developed to strengthen the concept of radical democracy within Escola Cidadã, has given a new meaning to teaching and learning in Porto Alegre. Perhaps no other example illustrates this better than the role of the educator as defined by the School Constituent Congress, Principle Number 40:

> The educator's role is to be next to the student, challenging the real and imaginary worlds brought to school by students, contributing to the life-world of the students in such a way that the "world" can be understood and reinvented by the student. The educator should also grow, learn, and experience together with the students, the conflicts, inventions, curiosity, and desires, respecting each student as a being that thinks differently, respecting each student's individuality. (SMED 1999: 57. Our translation from the Portuguese)

This program helps consolidate the mutual responsibility and obligations of the state and civil society, teachers, communities, and students by reinventing the concept of "schools for citizenship" where "achievement for all" is only the first step toward creating more democratic spaces in education.

As Tarso Genro (ex-mayor of the city of Porto Alegre) reflects:

> The truth *about* Escola Cidadã is that fundamentally, it is a rational and undetermined space. In it citizens—teachers and learners are connecting with the values and legacies of the enlightenment, tolerance, respect for human diversity and cultural pluralism, in dialogical coexistence, sharing experiences and knowledge and identifying history as open future. (1999: 11. Our translation from the Portuguese)

To support and extend real, workable democratic reforms in schools such as the ones created by Escola Cidadã would also require that controversial positions be debated fairly within political and social institutions as well as educational systems. The example of Escola Cidadã points to the urgent need for a greater understanding of the sociopolitical conditions facing many aggrieved communities within the social order, and the manifold challenges in cultivating civic responsibility to ensure that public institutions embody community decisions with socially acceptable outcomes.

In short, the case of Escola Cidadã indicates one road leading toward the horizon of possibility charted out by Bloch's and Freire's ideas. The utopian hope inscribed in this educational experiment is present in its promise to implement democratic experiments within schools. These experiments are happening on a large scale in Porto Alegre and on a smaller scale in many more instances around the world.

Democratizing access, knowledge, and relationships in the current context of global capitalism is not easy, but the fact that Escola Cidadã is still operating after 10 years of structural adjustment in Brazil[7] and serving the impoverished communities of greater Porto Alegre reflects the power of community organizing in the struggle for democracy.

At this point, it is worth asking a simple and straightforward question, yet one that cuts a pedagogical swath in the direction of a critical utopianism: In the context of advanced capitalist societies such as the United States, can we imagine systems of high-quality education that are available to everyone and encourage democratic models of organization? In the next section we elaborate on this question.

PUBLIC SCHOOLS IN THE UNITED STATES: THE LAST FRONTIER FOR THE MARKET'S EXPANSION

In the United States—despite the common claims that schools are closed, bureaucratic structures resistant to change—today's schools seem to be more open than ever. They are open to the scrutiny of parents, the federal government, local boards, the news media, lobbying groups (ranging from religious institutions to civil rights organizations), unions, and more recently—also more aggressively—to giant corporations. The opening of new markets inside schools, targeting potential consumers as early as first grade (as if the avalanche of commercials in TV, magazines, food, toys, and clothing were not already securing the allegiance of future buyers), has become an important force in guiding the ethos of the school reform movement.

The pervading sense that public education is in a terminal state of crisis[8] has encouraged educators and politicians to seek newer and more potent remedies not only through vouchers, charter schools, and other school choice initiatives but also through different forms of corporate sponsorships. Without diminishing the importance of globalization in understanding educational reform and change,[9] we want to focus on smaller corporate practices at the level of cultural capital. We contend that in the context of the United States, these corporate practices are nonetheless extremely influential in supporting capitalist globalization while diminishing the democratic-utopic possibilities of schooling.

Cultural capital, a term made popular by French sociologist Pierre Bourdieu, refers to "ways of talking, acting, and socializing, as well as language practices, values, and styles of dress and behavior" (McLaren 1997: 193). According to McLaren,

> Schools systematically *devalue* the cultural capital of students who occupy subordinate class positions. Cultural capital is reflective of material capital and replaces it as a form of symbolic currency that enters into the exchange system of the school. Cultural capital is therefore symbolic of the social structure's economic force and becomes itself a productive force in the reproduction of social relations under capitalism. (1997: 193)

Critics in education have argued for over a decade that schools reproduce distributive norms linked to the larger social order and division of labor; that is, they perpetuate or reproduce the social relationships, pedagogical practices, cultural formations, and attitudes—in short, the *habitus*—needed to sustain the existing patterns of inequality in the larger society (McLaren 1997). They do this—at least in part, and to put it bluntly—by trafficking in pro-capitalist, sexist, and racist knowledge. For students to make meaning out of pro-capitalist, sexist, and racist knowledge, they must possess the cultural tools (capital) to do so. They must be able to decode knowledge. Decoding requires certain competencies linked to the habitus (i.e., cultural capital) of the student, and to unlock the codes of meaning presupposes a familiarity with the processes of encoding and inscription. Such a capability is not universally accessible; it requires prior understanding. By trading in (and trading off) school knowledge that requires students to possess (to be successful) a prior understanding (i.e., cultural capital) of middle-class students, schools can be seen as spaces that "trade" in corporate wares of many colors and stripes (McLaren 1999a, 1999b).

It is not unusual these days to see school buses in some states covered with advertisements for Burger King and Wendy's; elementary schoolchildren carry books wrapped in "free" book covers plastered with ads for Kellogg's Pop Tarts and Fox TV personalities; school districts have gleefully granted Coca-Cola and Pepsi exclusive contracts to sell their products in schools; students are taught nutrition by the Hershey Corporation in a scheme that includes a discussion on the important place of chocolate in a balanced diet; a classroom business course teaches students to value work by exploring how McDonald's restaurants are operated and what skills are needed to become a successful McDonald's manager, and provides instructions on how to apply for a job at McDonald's; students learn ecology from a "Life of an Ant" poster sponsored by Skittles candy and an environmental curriculum video produced by Shell Oil that concentrates on the virtues of the external combustion engine; a new company called Zap Me! offers schools thousands of dollars worth of computer equipment, including a satellite dish, 15 top-level personal computers, a furnished computer lab, and high-speed Internet access in return for a constant display of onscreen advertisements in the lower left-hand corner of the screen.

John Borowsky, a public school teacher, has recently noted in the *New York Times*:

> At least 234 corporations are now flooding the public schools with films, textbooks and computer software under the guise of "instructional material." A lesson in self-esteem sponsored by Revlon includes an investigation of "good and bad days hair days." In a history lesson, Tootsie Rolls are touted as a part of soldiers' diets during World War II. Exxon provides a video on the Valdez spill playing down its ecological impact. And Chevron, in a lesson for use in civics science classes, reminds students that they will soon be able to vote and make "important decisions" about global warming, which the company then rebuts as incomplete science. (*New York Times*, August 21, 1999: A23)

Finally, another example of corporatism in schools is Channel One, a commercially produced news station that many American schools agree to broadcast in class for 10 minutes a day in return for a satellite dish, video cassette recorders, and as many television sets as they want. As Mike Apple notes, Channel One signifies "the officially sponsored opening up of school content to commercial sponsorship and organization" (1998: 136). A study of its effects revealed that the students were no better informed than their contemporaries, but that the advertisements broadcast on the Channel had a significant effect on their consumers' tastes (Aitkenhead, cited in Cole 1998: 327). As Aitkenhead puts it, "big businesses are getting mini-consumers and tailor-made future workers in return for a few thousand quids worth of computers. No wonder they're so keen on the idea" (quoted in Cole 1998: 327).

The pressures for opening new markets with in previously off-limits spaces of learning in school classrooms are disturbingly numerous and gaining vigor by the minute. The existence of these pressures is not surprising, since it is well known that the development of public schooling in much of the West during the last century has resulted from its precarious location at the crossroads of two competing logics. On one hand, schools do contribute to the ideals of democratic organizations (in terms—albeit limited—of providing access to certain forms of knowledge and equal employment opportunities). On the other hand, schools at the same time sustain and reinforce the logic of capitalism by reproducing different and unequal kinds of knowledge and rewards based on class, gender, and race (McLaren 1997).[10]

The strength of these two competing logics is undeniable, yet we want to focus on the conditions necessary for the creation of utopic schools that encourage (but in no way guarantee) effective democratic participation. Following our discussion of Bloch and Freire, the lessons of Escola Cidadã, and our discussion of attempts by corporations to expand their markets into classrooms, we want to argue that it is impossible to propose schools as places that nourish and encourage democratic participation unless they are dramatically reconfigured firmly on two demands. First, it is necessary to establish a set of "certain" means to reach "uncertain" outcomes (Pzreworski 1991: 143). Second, as Atilio Boron (1992) clearly states, democracy implies a definition of the "good society"—some model of society that allows opposition to established practices and that supports the exercise of human agency.[11]

SOME POSSIBLE BUILDING BLOCKS

Schooling for democracy requires clearly and fundamentally the creation of conditions in which the processes and results of the educational experiences "are not 'fixed,' and not always will favor the interests of the dominant class" (Boron 1992: 3). It further demands that individual liberties be recognized in the actual institutional arrangements of the political order. It requires public debate over the direction of social life, and mandates the removal of barriers to free deliberation and disagreements over the direction of the social order. To be recognized as democratic, schools must be transformed into sovereign sites that invite the school community to form reasoned judgments about the ends of school life, and ensure that each member of the school community is accorded equal weight in public deliberation. In other words, school decisions must be based on the judgments of the community as free and equal persons. Autonomy is exercised through the self-governing capacities of understanding, imagining, reasoning, valuing, and desiring (Cohen and Rogers 1983). To claim autonomy for oneself is to recognize the reciprocal claims to autonomy of others (Cohen and Rogers 1983).

Nowadays it appears that for vast sectors of the population, changing the social outcomes of the established pedagogical and political processes seems unrealistic. The lack of confidence about the utopian-democratic possibilities of public schooling is underwritten by a growing feeling of resignation that public schools as part of the democratic system are unable to improve significantly people's everyday quality of life, nor is it destined to do so in the future (see Apple 1998).

In the face of such a growing and persistent skepticism, what is most at stake is not only the chance of increasing democracy, but also the very survival of democratic forms of government, and with them the public educational system. This unravels the following question: "To what extent can democracy take root and consolidate itself amidst the rapid consolidation of poverty . . . which undermines the social and economic citizenship of the newly enfranchised masses just at the moment in which their political citizenship and emancipation are most strongly emphasized?" (Boron 1992: 3).

To merge the concepts of political and social democratization, those social groups in lower socioeconomic and cultural positions in society should have a high level of confidence in the possibility of changing the current situation, in which social outcomes seem fixed in favor of the prevailing dominant sectors. Democracy is not some messianic moment, nor it is a system "naturally" attached to the political, economic, and cultural achievements within the United States, the G-7 countries, and the global financial market. Democracy has not somehow miraculously "arrived" at the current "end of history" and set up shop within the precincts of the business community. Democratic practices and outcomes are fundamentally agonistic: No democratic "essence" precedes our own day-to-day involvement in the task of struggling toward a democratic society.

Democratic practices and rules of governance are not simple procedures that arrive apocalyptically as a final end to a linear march through history. As much as any other term, *democracy* has become a thorny shibboleth, which has only pretensions to an already established and circumscribed state of affairs. And while democracy as it is currently defined appears to depend upon the oxygen of capital to survive, we believe that experiences such as Escola Cidadã indicate that democracy can be rescued from its captivity to corporate interests. It is worth remembering that Antonio Gramsci saw democracy as essentially a dialectical movement between individual agency and structural location:

> But democracy, by definition, cannot mean merely that an unskilled worker can become skilled. It must mean that every "citizen" can "govern" and that society places him, even if only abstractly, in a general condition to achieve this. Political democracy tends toward a coincidence of the rulers and the ruled (in the sense of government with the consent of the governed) ensuring for each non-ruler a free training in the skill and general technical preparation necessary to that end. (1971: 40-41)

The struggle, as we see it, from the stand point of democratic pedagogy, is to work at the macropolitical level against the injustices of global capitalism (a task that we do not have the space to elaborate here) and locally to construct sites—provisional sites—in which new structured mobilities and forces can be made that suture identity to the larger problematic of social justice. In other words, students and cultural workers need to attach themselves to "modalities of belonging" fashioned out of new economies of subjectivity and difference. This requires breaking the power of commodified identities within capitalism as well as the forces and relations that both produce and are products of capitalism.

In our view, one essential way that schools can be more democratic and encouraging of civic life is to offer students and teachers the possibility of dialogical interaction based on a value system that, while not ignoring social realities, will expose the ideological traps of a system that has converted even adults into indifferent citizens or cynical players. The "real world," we contend, is dominated by the frenzied logic of the capitalist market, and so far schools have, with marginal success at best, navigated the messy contradictions between the utopic logic of democracy and that of corporate capitalism. To create school sites that speak to the utopian and heterotopian imperatives of Foucault, Bloch, and Freire, we believe that schools should be detached from the requirements of the "real world," where reality has been collapsed into a function of the market. If we want schools to stress democracy, they need independence from the market.

Finally, we want to argue that imagining schools as utopic-heterotopic spaces is impossible without acknowledging the crucial role of teachers in any educational change. Teacher education in this regard is perhaps a key site for initiating practices aimed at opening new spaces of democratic practice (McLaren 1997a; McLaren and Fischman 1998). Thus, we want to end our discussion in this section by offering some general recommendations that capture the fundamental elements of utopic-heterotopic teacher education. We take these recommendations for teacher education programs from the work of Kincheloe, Slattery, and Steinberg (2000: 251-63):

1. Empowered teachers understand the purposes of education and work to reform schools so they can accomplish such purposes. Teachers must work to develop a coherent philosophical, moral, and political vision of school reform so that they can take the initiative for change from the bottom up.
2. Empowered teachers appreciate the centrality of knowledge production in their pedagogy, since it is the collision of student-teacher experiences with information derived from the academic disciplines that produces knowledge in the classroom.
3. Empowered teachers use that knowledge and those understandings that have heretofore been devalued and excluded: subjugated and indigenous knowledge. Teachers move beyond white, Anglo-Saxon, middle-class, and heterosexual educational norms and explore the subjugated knowledges of women, minority groups, and indigenous groups.
4. Empowered teachers model and teach postformal thinking. Whereas formal thinking involves scientific procedure and the certainty it produces, postformal thinking involves understanding the production of one's own knowledge and includes etymology; the exploration of culturally validated knowledge; and understanding the patterns and relationships that support the lived world.
5. Empowered teachers cooperate with the school and community and facilitate cooperation between them. This includes open forums about race and gender relations and projects that involve parent-student collaborative learning.
6. Empowered teachers build learning networks between schools and communities that employ recent developments and innovations in communications technologies. Students not only learn educational technology and its practical uses, but also investigate how "they modify existing relationships and ways of being" (Kincheloe, Slattery, and Steinberg 2000: 259).
7. Empowered teachers acquire the skills of researchers and, in turn, teach their students sophisticated methods of inquiry. Students are taught to use research-driven powers of analysis: observing, interviewing, photographing, videotaping, note taking, and collecting life histories. In doing so, students not only "polish the traditional skills" that are valued in the curriculum, such as "reading, writing, arithmetic, listening, interpreting and thinking"; but they learn "to uncover the forces that shape their everyday lives: their place in the social hierarchy of their peer groups, their romantic relationships, their vocational aspirations, their relationships with teachers" (Kincheloe, Slattery, and Steinberg 2000: 259).
8. Empowered teachers encourage schools to support their continued learning. Schools must "avoid at all costs the teacher deskilling

authoritarian (top down) management strategies, standardized test driven curricula, and prepackaged (teacher-proof) curriculum materials" (Kincheloe, Slattery, and Steinberg 2000: 260).

9. Empowered teachers recognize the inability of modernist-positivist teaching methods to explain adequately the current world of schooling. Teachers recognize the limitations of current teaching technologies, and employ examples from anthropology, film studies, literacy criticism, and history "to decipher the subliminal codes and detect the intended and unintended effects of computers, television, video games, advertising, earphone stereo systems and other contemporary influences" (Kincheloe, Slattery, and Steinberg 2000: 261).

10. Empowered teachers invent new and appropriate methods of assessment. Objective standardized tests are rejected in favor of giving students a voice in their own assessment; assessment procedures should be an extension of the learning process. Measurement should be less quantitative and should address issues of content.

11. Empowered teachers recognize how power shapes themselves, their students, and the everyday schooling context. Teachers learn to "decipher the power codes, the repressive ways ideological interests invade not only the schools but the popular culture as well" (Kincheloe, Slattery, and Steinberg 2000: 263). The premise here is that "education is a social practice operating within a society characterized by unequal power relations" (2000: 262).

12. We would like to add one recommendation not sufficiently stressed by Kincheloe, Steinberg, and Slattery. Empowered teachers locate schooling both in terms of the larger structure of global capitalism and in terms of the contextual specificity of their own community. While exploring dialectically the relationship between global relations and local antagonisms, empowered teachers are encouraged to re-think the current social order in terms of democratic socialist alternatives to capitalist schooling.

CONCLUSIONS

Returning to the question we raised in the previous section, it appears unlikely that general democratizing reform efforts could take place in schools in the United States at this particular moment in history without a massive effort anchored in the idea of democratic hope and working against the further corporatization of schools. Whereas Porto Alegre is operating under the leadership of the ruling *Partido dos Trabalhadores* (Workers' Party), which has a socialist, democratic, and antiglobalization platform, school boards within the United States are under the ideological sway of a neoliberal, conservative educational restoration linked to creating school-corporate alliances (Apple 1998). Are we suggesting that in the United States any efforts to create radically democratic schools would be limited to experiments by radical educators within single neighborhoods or schools? In the near future, that may well be the case. Yet not to strive to implement ever more democratic classroom practices, transform teacher education programs, and reduce the influence of the corporate sector within public schools would be counterproductive. Even short-lived experiences of democratic schooling—in a single classroom or through district-wide efforts—are worth pursuing. These experiences teach us not only to expect more from schools, but also to improve education by connecting individual and community participation with societal goals of equality and solidarity, the full development of individual skills and potentials, and the improvement of individual and social educational outcomes.

What are the advantages to and gains associated with schools being "detached" from the market? Detachment from the market, in our view, will be axiomatic to creating utopic-heterotopic school spaces. Thus, the exclusionary norm we propose is, first, a concrete and achievable goal. Second, it is a norm that will allow schools to be institutionally eccentric, curious, and able to build heterotopic spaces as part of a new civic utopian vision of democratic life. A renewed openness of schools should warrant socially relevant knowledge, different perspectives on sciences and arts, in a place where disagreement is not punished, where love and a desire to know flourishes, and where a passion for radicalizing democracy and creating more inclusive alternatives is welcomed.

NOTES

1. Foucault describes heterotopias as "Counter-sites, a kind of effectively enacted utopia in which the real sites, all the other real sites that can be found in the culture, are simultaneously represented, contested, and inverted. In this sense, heterotopias differ from utopias, in that they are fundamentally unreal spaces" (Foucault, in Bertsch 1996: 10). Marcks (1995) also points out that besides what we recognize as spatial social heterotopias, Foucault also elaborates heterotopia as an "image of thought." Heterotopic thought, then, is not the exclusive by-product of individual cogito, but also has material and institutional existence and seeks to evade and overcome the boundaries established by images of thought that imprison thinking.

2. Giroux and McLaren elaborate on Bloch's concept of utopia as follows "The possibilities inherent in utopia cannot, claims Bloch, be traced to the repression of bourgeois ideology since there always exists a 'cultural surplus' that 'contains the spark that reaches out beyond the surrounding emptiness,' and that can be directly linked to the utopian function which is expressed as both social and ontological states. For Bloch, our collective dream needs to be translated into the material density of everyday struggle through a dialectical process and ontological unfolding in which 'what is' is constantly being challenged in light of what might be'" (1997: 146-47).

3. While both of us have participated in this project, one of us (Fischman) has had considerably more involvement, working as both researcher and consultant.

4. A more comprehensive study of the impact, problems, and successes of this program is being developed by Gustavo E. Fischman.

5. During this period (1993-99) the secretary of education has organized seven Municipal Encounters of School Councils. These meetings were used to socialize knowledge and successful strategies implemented to administrate schools. At the same time, these encounters allowed open discussion among students, teachers, and parents. These encounters were seen as prime spaces, where the participants were encouraged to develop more universal and less particularistic conceptions related to education.

6. The process of Planning and Participatory Budget in Schools is modeled after the municipal Participatory Budget.

7. In most of the Third World, structural adjustment programs (SAPs) were implemented by combining financial packages that promote economic development and strict compliance regarding payments on the external debt of each debtor country. Under the monitoring actions of the IMF and the World Bank, the implementation of SAPs has required a significant reduction in the size of the state sector as well as in its regulatory functions. This retrenchment of the state has extended to many social services, including education, health, and related forms of welfare; and in most cases SAPs have exacerbated the gap between rich and poor and created important challenges in the provision of basic services that were previously guaranteed by the state.

8. In September 1999, National Public Radio, the Henry J. Kaiser Family Foundation, and Harvard University's Kennedy School of Government broadcast the results of a survey about the public's perception about education. One of the findings was headed "My School Is OK, But Yours Isn't." The survey determined that "Parents give high marks to their children's schools (71% rate them A or B) but are less enthusiastic about schools in their community (60% rate them A or B) and think even less about the nation's schools overall (only 23% rate them A or B; 18% give them a D or F). This means that although parents may have underrated the nation's schools, they clearly tended to overrate their own children's schools and their community's schools as well; not everyone can be above average. Parents think the nation's public schools have more serious problems than schools in their local community.

9. For a thorough discussion of globalization and educational reform, see Davies and Guppy (1997) and Spring (1998).

10. Here we view inequality as having to do with capitalist exploitation (and in its deeply rooted connections with colonialism, racism, and sexism), the international division of labor, and the way society regulates the distribution of different types of capital: consumption capital (wages or salary), investment capital (surplus of consumption capital that you can invest and on which you can earn interest), skills capital (specialized knowledge that people accumulate through their work experience, training, or education), and social capital (the network of social ties to family, friends, and acquaintances as well as collectively owned economic and cultural capital of a group).

11. Larry Grossberg's conception of agency complements our own approach. Grossberg (1999) argues that agency is more than the power to act; it is also "about access to particular places—places at which particular kinds of actions, producing particular kinds of effects, are possible—places at which one can intercede and influence the various 'forces' and vectors that are shaping the world."

REFERENCES

Apple, Michael. 1998. "Selling Our Children: Channel One and the Politics of Education." Pp. 135-49 in *Capitalism and the Information Age: The Political Economy of the Global Communication Revolution*, edited by Robert W. McChesney, Ellen Meiksins Wood, and John Bellamy Foster. New York: Monthly Review Press.

Azevedo, José Clovis de. 1999a. "Escola Cidadã: Construção Coletiva E Participação Popular." Paper presented at The Comparative and International Education Society, Toronto, April 14-19.

_____. 1999b. "A democratização do Estado: A experiencia de Porto Alegre." P. 4 in *Escola Cidadã: Teoria e Práctica*, edited by Heron da Silva Luiz. Petrópolis: Vozes Editora.

Bertsch, Charlie. 1996. "Pedagogy of the Depressed." *Bad Subjects*, no. 27 (September): 8-12.

Boron, Atilio. 1992. "Transition Toward Democracy in Latin America." Mimeograph.

Cohen, Joshua and Joel Rogers. 1983. *On Democracy: Toward a Transformation of American Society*. New York: Penguin.

Cole, Mike. 1998. "Globalization, Modernisation and Competitiveness: A Critique of the New Labour Project in Education." *International Studies in Sociology of Education* 8(3): 315-32.

Davies, Scott and Neil Guppy. 1997. "Globalization and Educational Reforms in Anglo-American Democracies." *Comparative Educational Review* 41(4): 435-59.

Freire, Paulo. 1993. *Pedagogy of the Oppressed*. New York: Continuum.

_____. 1998. *Teachers as Cultural Workers: Letters to Those who Dare to Teach*. Boulder, CO: Westview Press.

Genro, Tarso. 1999. "Cidadãnia, Emancipação e Cidade." Pp. 6-12 in *Escola Cidadã: Teoria e Práctica*, edited by Heron da Silva Luiz. Petrópolis: Vozes Editora.

Giroux, Henry. 1988. *Schooling and the Struggle for Public Life*. Minneapolis: University of Minnesota Press.

Giroux, Henry and Peter McLaren. 1997. "Paulo Freire, Postmodernism, and the Utopian Imagination: A Blochian Reading." Pp. 138-62 in *Not Yet: Reconsidering Ernst Bloch*, edited by Jamie Owen Daniel and Tom Moylan. London & New York: Verso.

Gramsci, Antonio. 1971. *Selections from the Prison Notebooks*. New York: International.

Grossberg, Lawrence. 1999. "Speculations and Articulations of Globalization." *Polygraph* 11: 11-48.

Kincheloe, Joe, Patrick Slattery, and Shirley Steinberg. 2000. *Contextualizing Teaching: Introduction to Education and Educational Foundations*. New York: Longman.

Marcks, John. 1995. "A New Image of Thought." *New Formations* 25 (Summer): 66-76.

McLaren, Peter. 1997a. *Life in Schools*. New York: Longman.

_____. 1997b. *Revolutionary Multiculturalism: Pedagogies of Dissent for the New Millennium*. Boulder, CO: Westview Press.

_____. 1999a. "Che Guevara, Globalization and Leadership." *International Journal of Leadership in Education* 2: 269-92.

_____. 1999b. "A Response to Spencer Maxcy." *International Journal of Leadership in Education* 2: 301-05.

McLaren, Peter and Gustavo Fischman. 1998. "Reclaiming Hope: Teacher Education and Social Justice in the Age of Globalization." *Teacher Education Quarterly* (special 25th anniversary year) 25(4): 125-33.

Pizarro, Ana. 1994. *De Ostras y Canibales: Ensayos sobre la Cultura Latinoamericana.* Santiago de Chile: Editorial Universidad de Santiago.

Pzreworski, Adam. 1991. *Democracy and the Market.* Cambridge: Cambridge University Press.

SMED. 1999. *Cadernos Pedagógicos 9.* Porto Alegre, Brazil: SMED.

Soja, Edward. 1989. *Postmodern Geographies: The Reassertion of Space in Critical Social Theory.* London: Verso.

Spring, Joel. 1998. *Education and the Rise of the Global Economy.* Mahwah, NJ: Lawrence Erlbaum Associates.

6

EDUCATIONAL "ACCOUNTABILITY" AND THE VIOLENCE OF CAPITAL
A MARXIAN READING

Noah De Lissovoy and Peter McLaren

Anyone who follows trends in public education cannot fail to have noticed the rapid increase of so-called "accountability" measures in recent years in the schools. Indeed, the growth of these policies, rules, and regulations seems to be crowding out almost all else, as they come to constitute a new industry, bureaucracy, and language. Students have increasingly been forced to submit to forms of standardized tests and test preparation, as well as interventions to avoid retention. These tests have increasingly come to have perilously high stakes, with no demonstrable educational rationale—although obvious political ones (National Research Council, 1999; Smith, Heinecke, and Noble, 1999). Teachers have found themselves facing new demands for evaluation, new and controversial forms of reward, and new mandates in curriculum and instruction, while administrators face threats of reconstitution of schools if they do not meet achievement standards (Arnstine and McDowell, 1993; McNeil, 2000). We are told that nothing is for free anymore, that the time has come for an end to complacency, that the public demands results. No longer will teachers, students, and administrators be permitted to slack off; from now on their feet will be held to the fire of the righteous demand for superior academic achievement.

It is not mainly our intention in this paper to counter the hegemonic rhetoric of accountability, or to show that it results not in improving schools but in damaging them. This has been done very effectively by others (e.g., Gallagher, 2000; Glovin, 2000; McNeil, 2000; Popham, 1999). Rather, the object of this paper will be to analyze the accountability movement in education with a view to discovering its "deep structure"—its origin in systems of capitalist exploitation and its meaning within these contexts. In the critical exegesis we are undertaking here, we use the term "critical" to designate a strategic reading

---

of accountability which is undertaken from the perspective of the working class. We will show how trends in educational accountability facilitate a violent reification of human consciousness and creativity, serve to inscribe neocolonial assumptions of white supremacy, and derive from a repressive juridical rationality that constitutes students as indebted to the capitalist system by which they are exploited. This will involve an exploration not only of the purpose that is served by these new educational measures in helping to continue to guarantee a society based on oppression and exploitation, but also the ways in which these educational developments can be read as clues to what is particular in the current moment in global capitalism, as well as that which is perhaps not new but which has not been so visible before. In particular we will suggest that it is necessary to conceptualize capitalism as premised on more than a simple logic of interest, and exploitation as operating directly within the field of subjectivity in addition to that of labor.

STANDARDIZED TESTING AND REIFICATION

The furious rhetoric around demands for accountability serves partly to distract attention from the specific mechanisms that proponents seek to introduce in its name. In other words, the rhetoric of accountability itself can to some extent be analyzed as cover for the implementation of large-scale changes in pedagogy and curriculum. More concretely, the linchpin of prevailing accountability systems as they are currently constituted is the standardized test, and appeals to accountability serve in part to facilitate the introduction of these tests into schools. As President Bush put it during a visit to a Washington D.C. elementary school, "Accountability is so important, and by 'accountability' I mean testing children to determine whether or not children are learning" (Gerstenzang, 2001). By positing a series of equations that are never interrogated (learning = absorption of testable material; standardized testing = authentic assessment; accountability = standardized testing) elites are able to justify the wholesale reorganization of curriculum content, teaching methods, and experiences of students in the classroom.

What motivates this tremendous eagerness on the part of elites to intervene on such a large scale to replace local practices with elaborate testing regimes? The key principle at work in the use of standardized tests, which is also what allows them to serve as the mechanism for accountability initiatives, is the reduction of learning and knowledge to a number, i.e. a score. Once this takes place, scores can be compared, statistically analyzed, and variously manipulated. Much of the debate takes place after this process has occurred—for example, in arguments over the fairness of comparisons between schools that have very different resources. Not enough attention, however, is paid to this first step, in which the complexity of human consciousness is reduced to an abstract quantity. Alfie Kohn has noted that a "cultural penchant for attaching numbers to things" valorizes information presented in numerical form as "reassuringly scientific" (2000, p. 3). It is in this very first step, the representation of the human mind and its development in the most reduced form possible, i.e. by a single figure, that the essential process takes place. The damaging consequences that result from "accountability," as it is currently understood, stem from this initial operation.

In reducing learning to a test score, policy makers seek to make the knowledge of disparate individuals commensurable. Never mind that a violence is done to the concreteness of that individual's humanness and particularity; once knowledge is reified in this way, it can be manipulated and described in the same fashion that we are accustomed to manipulating and describing products (commodities) of all kinds. The commodity form, according to Marx, emerges when diverse products can be compared to each other by means of a universal equivalent—in the economy, this is money. As far as standardized tests are concerned, the scoring units represent the universal equivalent (the money indeed) in terms of which students, schools, and districts can be compared. This process of reification is not new, but the subtlety of its hegemony is being stripped away, as complex human and social processes are more and more flattened into crude representations that will conform to the logic of commodity production and exchange. It is a similar tendency that results in "three strikes" laws in the criminal justice system, which abstract absolutely from particular human acts in order to make all felonies count the same, and to make any three felonies count the same. Similarly, in California, a test score improvement could originally be exchanged for a state financial award ("Schools Post Gains," 2000). Two similarly scoring schools, as far as "accountability" is concerned, are considered interchangeable—differences in their locations, student populations, teachers, or curricula mean nothing if their numerical representation is the same.

For Theodor Adorno (1995) this imperative of exchangeability depends upon the violence in the principle of identity: the conceptual act by which we make two different things the same. We enact this principle when we make the student's knowledge identical to the test score that stands for it. The violence in this erasure of particularity and difference then extends outwards, as students are arbitrarily held back, without regard to individual differences in development, and as teachers are given preset curricula, without regard to their own interests and talents and their students' particular needs. "The spread of the principle imposes on the whole world an obligation to become identical, to become total" (p. 146).

His attention to the violence inherent in identitarian, totalizing processes of thought and culture has made Adorno's work a precursor (in part) to the familiar valorization of the concept of difference within poststructural theory. But in Adorno's negative dialectics, the principle of exchange is not to be undone by a principle of "pure" difference. In the educational context, to reject the violent abstraction in standardization is not necessarily to insist on the radical incommensurability of individual consciousnesses. Instead we should ask how students and teachers can find an authentic if provisional *oppositional* unity against their oppression. According to Adorno:

> If comparability as a category of measure were simply annulled, the rationality which is inherent in the barter principle—as ideology, of course, but also as a promise—would give way to direct appropriation, to force, and nowadays to the naked privilege of monopolies and cliques. (1995, pp. 146-147)

Rather, we must seek to imagine a dialectical relationship between identity and nonidentity, and not prioritize one moment over the other. It is precisely the refusal of the fusion of the particulars into the universal that makes possible their authentic relation. Thus, in struggling against the violence of totalizing educational policies and practices we nevertheless ought not to cease to imagine the possibility of a true (dialectical) relationship between individual and collective, or rather between individual and collective moments of being. To take a position against standardized testing, then, is not necessarily to argue that the consciousness of students resides, or should reside, in a realm of perpetual deferral. For Adorno, there is a horizon of commonality and relation that is constituted as possibility in the very negation of alienation. Resistance offers a potential opening against totalitarian logics. In other words, students and teachers coming together to organize against standardized tests, and to seek for alternatives, might begin to construct organic forms of collectivity that create a common space without erasing the real differences between individuals and groups in coalition.

The identitarian tendency in bourgeois thought is of course closely linked to its constitutive violence. "Accountability" contains various senses within it, including the *settling of accounts, accounting to or for,* and of course *being forced to pay up.* In these senses of the word, the stark insistence on individual responsibility to a universal standard, as codified in law and policy, as well as on relentless punishment for those who transgress, is of course deeply connected to old notions of bourgeois morality. In the accountability movement, as in the increasingly repressive criminal justice system, the Kantian doctrines of freedom, duty, and the categorical imperative only attain a monstrousness that was inherent in them from the beginning. The furious tenacity of the belief in personal responsibility in the face of a reality that is in fact overwhelmingly (though not completely) socially determined is what Adorno called "idealism as rage." In his view, bourgeois reason is repression; this view is confirmed not only by educational accountability schemes, but also by drug sentencing guidelines and punitive "welfare reform" measures.

NEOCOLONIALISM AND THE STAGING OF FAILURE

A number of writers (e.g. Berlak, 2001; Kohn, 2000; McNeil, 2000) have pointed out that educational accountability, to the extent that it is based on norm-referenced standardized testing, is racist in a number of ways. Standardized tests
are not neutral in their content; rather, test material is culturally biased in favor
of white middle class students. Tests demand that students reproduce these bias-
es in their responses. On one such test, students were required to give both positive and negative interpretations of the term "Manifest Destiny" regardless of an
individual student's beliefs, or the historical experience of native peoples—in
order to receive full credit, all students had to articulate some positive interpretation of this white settler colonialism (Toussaint, 2000). English Language
Learners are forced to take standardized tests in English without being able to
understand them, a practice that is not only cruel but which also devalues these
students' own languages. Tests are designed so that not all students will succeed; with an initial bias toward white students, this means that students of
color are more likely to do poorly. In addition, in designing specific test items,
questions are formulated so that students who do well overall on the test also do
well on that particular item: this reproduces a structural advantage for those
who are already privileged (Kohn, 2000). It is no surprise then, as is frequently
pointed out, that test results tend simply to mirror already existing socio-economic inequalities, rather than indicating any real distribution of learning or
understanding. The connection of standardized testing to the historical legacy of
scientific racism has also been shown. Standardized testing in the schools is a
direct outgrowth of the IQ testing movement that began in the early twentieth
century, a movement that was vigorously promoted by confirmed eugenicists
such as Lewis Terman (Fass, 1989; Stoskopf, 2000; Valencia 1997).

What we wish to focus on here is less the fact of this racism than the manner of its organization and implementation. If the main tool of accountability
initiatives, the norm-referenced standardized test, is racist in its construction
and in its use, and if these initiatives are touted both as means of restructuring
schools and understanding the truth of what goes on in them, then what we confront in this movement is really a large-scale *staging* of the failure of students of
color. In other words, it is not simply that students of color compete on an
unequal playing field. The field is more than unequal. In fact, the field is constructed so that the responses of certain students will come to *constitute* what is
called failure. The aura of objectivity that the tests seek to attach to themselves
tends to obscure this fact. But once we recognize that this "objectivity" is rather
contingency and bias, then it follows that the success and failure that the tests
pretend to report are actually manufactured by the instruments themselves.
Earnest accountability proposals, stringent standards and tests, and tough-love
retention schemes come then to comprise an insidious performance in which
students, teachers, and administrators are the witting or unwitting participants, a

performance that enacts once again the supposed inferiority of the poor and people of color. This has to be done carefully and covertly. Care is taken by political candidates espousing accountability schemes not to refer to race, and to place the blame on the system rather than on the students; furthermore, the blanket application of the new criteria is recommended as a guarantee of fairness, since *everyone* must submit. But whatever the rhetoric, the script is the same and the narrative will contain no surprises. The (white, wealthy) spectators will get the outcome they paid (voted) for: the aggrandizement of their own class, and the debasement of the (poor, black, brown) Other.

Frantz Fanon's (1968) observation that in the colonialist regime, all that is in the image of the colonizer is exalted and all that is in the image of the colonized is vilified, would appear then to make profound sense even in the context of contemporary public education in the United States. Performance indexes that rank schools and districts according to standardized tests are a medium for a similar picturing: white affluent schools are painted in the triumphant right corners of bell curves, and at the glorious pinnacles of achievement charts, while schools serving students of color are shown in a futile struggle upward and rightward toward the mean. These characterizations don't begin and end with the tests of course. To start with, the student of color arrives with the label "at risk." Later, the student's resistance to a form of schooling that seeks to decide and control him or her becomes for the system another indication of failure, or rather another opportunity to name being and behavior as failure. In any event, once again following Fanon's analysis, the colonial mind behind the educational system refuses to imagine the student of color as anything other than inferior, deficient, disadvantaged, and destined to fail. Accountability schemes are both an assertion of this distorted view and a tool to shore it up.

An anti-colonialist analysis helps us to see the violence that is inherent in these educational "reforms." Common notions of bias and even racism in the U.S. are curiously static. They are imagined as immobile qualities in individuals or more rarely as institutional forces by which people are grouped unfairly into categories. But the process by which this is accomplished is not usually included in the sense of the usual terms (e.g. *discrimination*). Locating racism in a neocolonialist context reminds us of its historicity, its political nature, and the violent means by which it is enacted. Racism in education is likewise a very active process. This analysis also helps us to escape the dangerous abstraction inherent in simple notions of social reproduction, as if it were a question of machinery rather than people, and as if the system did not have to overcome resistance, to actively subjugate in order keep functioning. Within the critique of capitalism as a whole, we must recognize that it is the continuous violent application of force by some against others which permits the processes of appropriation and accumulation to take place and to be naturalized.

The evidence from public schooling predisposes us against the blurring of the boundary between colonizer and colonized that has become common in some cultural theory. For Homi Bhabha (1994), for example, these actors become indistinguishable in the play of mimicry that constitutes them both as "colonial subjects." In his account, the agency of repression, on the one hand, and resistance on the other, cannot be ascribed to one or the other camp, but is rather produced as an effect of the circulation of meanings that transgresses all oppositionalities. E. San Juan Jr. (2000) criticizes this "metaphysical turn" in cultural studies, which frequently leads to the abandonment of any purchase of theory as a concrete political practice on the social in favor of the liberating flights that the imagination of the political as a field of pure discursivity makes possible. Trends in public education, however, show a hardening of the boundaries between oppressor and oppressed (Freire, 1996), indeed an ever-more eager use of ever-more fantastic technologies of repression to reinforce these divisions.

DISCIPLINE AND VIOLENCE

If there is a conceptual violence in the reification of human subjectivity in accountability processes, there is also, we argue, a literal disciplining of the body that is organized in the forced performance by students of their subjection to the State that the *procedure* of testing represents. This discipline and performance are at once the purpose and occasion for a more energetically elaborated technology of *surveillance*, which has itself characterized the operation of state power, according to Michel Foucault, since the time of the plague:

> This enclosed, segmented space, observed at every point, in which the individuals are inserted in a fixed place, in which the slightest movements are supervised, in which all events are recorded, in which an uninterrupted work of writing links the center and periphery, in which power is exercised without division, according to a continuous hierarchical figure, in which each individual is constantly located, examined and distributed among the living beings, the sick and the dead—all this constitutes a compact model of the disciplinary mechanism. (1977, p. 197)

This description of the operation of the quarantine in a medieval town is of course frighteningly apt in relation to contemporary education. It would be difficult to find a more exemplary instance of Foucault's notions of surveillance and *panopticism* than the large-scale implementation of standardized testing in the schools. The intensification and proliferation of the mechanism of control, the economy of its operation, the centralization and invisibility of the authoritative power, which are all aspects of his paradigm, are clearly essential to the testing mechanism. The terrifying and irrational *efficiency* of standardized tests, both in ideological and economic terms, from the point of view of those in power and their functionaries, lends them an irresistible appeal and a tendency to ramify at light speed across administrative and bureaucratic structures. And the mystification of the act and meaning of the surveillance itself, in this case the actual collection and manipulation of test data, which is given a mask of objectivity, is another characteristic attraction of the panoptic principle. In the central observation tower of Bentham's panopticon anyone can come to take the place of the observer or director; likewise, the "neutrality" of the testing regime is apparently guaranteed in the simplicity and mechanical nature of the assessment, as tests are farmed out to firms to be scored by non-professionals for low wages (Glovin, 2000).

On one count, however, it would appear that the contemporary educational accountability movement shows a tendency that is inconsistent with Foucault's society of surveillance and discipline. The principle of surveillance, in his view, in intensifying the scope of power, allows for a softening in the technologies of punishment, as an older juridical procedure (the *inquisition*) is replaced by a modern process of *examination*. The public and brutal destruction of the criminal as the culmination of the investigation is supposed to be replaced by a machinery of rehabilitation that alternates with a pathologizing and ceaselessly extended interrogation: "For the old principle of 'levying-violence', which governed the economy of power, the disciplines substitute the principle of 'mildness-production-profit'" (p. 219). *On the contrary*, however, we believe that contemporary technologies of discipline appear to be correlated with an increased level of state violence, and a greater acceptability in public discourse of such violence. In the penal system, for example, the invention of new systems of registration and surveillance for certain kinds of criminals or alleged criminals (sex offenders, arsonists, gang "affiliates") does not substitute for but rather accompanies the imposition of more ruthless punishments (three strikes laws, tough drug sentencing guidelines, efforts to try youth offenders as adults). Likewise, in education, the machineries of testing, performance awards, retention, or exit examinations do not tend to soften the rough edges of the imposition of power, but rather to facilitate and multiply their cruelty. Draconian "zero-tolerance" disciplinary policies proliferate along with more "academic" accountability initiatives; stern codes of conduct and rigid "gang dress" rules are supposed to make possible the implementation of the scholastic "standards" proper. (And of course these bureaucratic refinements in education are not unconnected to those in the penal system—a very important study would be to examine the precise relationships between educational accountability measures and "get tough" policies in the judicial system, particularly with regard to youth.)

As important, however, as the severity of the regulations governing behavior and responsibility that accompany accountability initiatives, is the violence represented by these new procedures in themselves—testing in particular. It is not merely a question of the degradation of curriculum and pedagogy. It is also a question of the rituals of test preparation and test taking themselves: the training (in a *horticultural* sense) of the body into a posture of subjection before columns of empty bubbles, and the forcing of the will and intelligence against arbitrary, alienating, and demeaning problematics. Teachers can testify to the inevitable reaction—the physical sickness of students forced to apply their bodies and spirits toward a performance by which they feel violated. This violence of course also operates beyond the visible responses. The unconscious damage done to students has to be calculated at a deeper register and over a longer term. It is less a question of "self-esteem" than of the possibility of sense of self at all—by what factor and in which directions does this reduction of the subject take place, this subject suddenly *forced to learn to read itself* as a mere index of effects external to it, as an indifferent sedimentation of technologies, as essentially inhuman?

If the magnification of violence that accompanies the ramification of surveillance in current educational "reforms" appears to contradict the "mildness" of Foucault's panoptic society, it should suggest to us the extent to which the ancient brutalisms are not so ancient. It should also suggest to us perhaps the way in which contemporary capitalism is not only inflected by inherited systems of violence but even deeply constituted by and dependent on such systems. Rather than treating this aspect of capitalism as a distortion, we should pay attention to its immanence in what we usually view as routine. The moment of Marx's "so-called primitive accumulation," in which territory, resources, and bodies are viciously expropriated by colonizing powers to make way for the development of capitalism *per se*, is reproduced as an instant internal to each quotidian iteration of social control and reproduction.

In his model of the panopticon, Foucault displaces the theater of power from the space between subject and object to the subjectless matrix of pure vectors of force. It is perhaps for this reason that he de-emphasizes violence in his account of disciplinary institutions, since violence would seem to imply the intimacy of the space between aggressor and victim. Foucault's anti-humanism cannot abide such simple typologies, which appear to locate power in subjects, and align it with an intentionality that is, in his account, inadequate as a way of understanding sociality. Needless to say, this same prohibition applies as well to the collective subjects represented by classes. As we have described, Foucault's work does provide a useful lens through which to view the ingenuity of the state's technologies of exploitation/repression. However, his hostility to any attempt to work out a *logic* of power, i.e. an account of it that would situate (if not root) it in a non-contingent political economy, seriously undermines the usefulness of his project. In the case of educational reform, while the systematic violence wrought by the state cannot simply be "explained away" by an economistic Marxism (this indeed is our point), it nevertheless takes place within a perspective determined by class hegemony. Though a crude cost-benefit analysis cannot comprehend the complexity of the process and content of this hegemony in education, we cannot understand conservative accountability trends without reference to the founding social rationality of schooling, which is always a calculus, "in the last instance," *in favor of* some and *against* others.

ACCOUNTABILITY, DEBT, AND EXPLOITATION: FROM NIETZSCHE TO MARX

Nietzsche is a figure around whom swirls a great deal of contention within education and critical theory generally. Consider, for example, the contrasting perspectives of Michael Peters (1998), for whom the French poststructuralist reading of Nietzsche is an important bulwark against an atavistically resurgent rational liberalism, and Glenn Rikowski (1997), who, following Geoff Waite (1996), argues that Nietzsche is both the prophet of a more perfectly brutal and hierarchical capitalism and the preeminent proto-postmodernist. It is not our intention here to stake out a place in this controversy, nor to take a position on Nietzsche's relationship to poststructuralist thought. Suffice it to say that in his historical-sociological aspect, Nietzsche, like Foucault, can offer some insights of value to contemporary educationists, provided that we are able to bring them to bear within a dialectical materialist context which, it must be said, is in the main antipathetic to the principal tendencies of Nietzsche as a philosopher.

A useful lens through which to attempt to understand this coincidence of discipline and violence in educational policy is the Nietzschean analysis of justice as arising first of all from the relations between creditor and debtor. According to Nietzsche, the concepts of right and duty arose from the blood-stained species-memory of the brutal punishments, codified by law, exacted by creditors from debtors. Not only the physical suffering of the latter, but the pleasure of the former were involved in this settling of accounts that was the ground of all later concepts of duty:

> Let us be clear as to the logic of this form of compensation: it is strange enough. An equivalence is provided by the creditor's receiving, in place of a literal compensation for an injury (thus in place of money, land, possessions of any kind), a recompense in the form of a kind of *pleasure*—the pleasure of being allowed to vent his power freely upon one who is powerless, the voluptuous pleasure '*de faire le mal pour le plaisir de le faire*,' the enjoyment of violation. (1969, p. 65)

What is important for our purposes here is not so much the idea that violence is deeply embedded in the Western genealogy of morals as a whole, but rather the idea that juridical approaches to debt are historically premised on a logic of violence, suffering, and pleasure. After all, the presumption that underlies educational accountability initiatives is that the state (as the representative of taxpayers) stands in the relation of a creditor to the public school system (including administrators, teachers, and even students) which must be able to produce some return on investment or face being constructed popularly and politically as debtor and delinquent. Once having violated this contract with the state, the persistently low-performing school must face losing its pound of flesh (in

California, these schools are subject to state intervention and sanction; see "Schools Post Gains," 2000). More perniciously, students in general, having failed to live up to standards of performance set arbitrarily and after the fact, are felt to have committed a kind of violation of the public trust and are therefore subject to the host of penalties discussed above in connection to testing and school regulations. The point is that dominant accountability schemes represent less a diagnosis than a punishment, and that they operate on the basis of an unconscious equation according to which students' "failure" will be compensated for by their pain and alienation under a new "reformist" regime.

This Nietzschean insight thus also points to an expanded notion of the profit that capital seeks to derive in the educational arena and elsewhere. His insistence on the "festive" nature of spectacles of violence should emphasize for us the pleasure that infuses the capillaries of power with each new contest for rewards and punishments, each new game of scores and charts, promotion and retention, that the majority are bound to fail at and to suffer by. This pleasure is not personal *per se*, but surges through networks of hegemonic discourse and policy; recognizing it means questioning prevalent views of capitalist exploitation as simply economistic and instrumentalist. However, the recasting of the Nietzschean analysis of justice in terms of the relation between creditor and debtor *within a Marxist framework* is essential, since Nietzsche's formulation by itself is inadequate. After all, under capital, debt and credit never do really cancel each other in violence or punishment as Nietzsche imagines they do. Furthermore, whereas he considers the body to be the ultimate scene and guarantee of justice, we believe that it is the social relationship between capital and labor that mediates, and ultimately refuses, a final settling of accounts.

If individuals are invited by the elite to identify with the subject position "taxpayer" and thus to share in a collective outrage at the inefficiency of public schooling, capital itself feels defrauded at a deeper level, and in a sense more legitimately. Where exactly does this conviction that teachers and students are freeloaders come from? And what exactly provokes the degree of indignant fury that accompanies this idea? While much of the hand-wringing about the schools is clearly a cynical performance, it nevertheless reflects an underlying rage that is real. If the state is a creditor and the student a debtor, in the sense discussed above, this is not only because the public has made an investment in the student's improvement that the latter has an ostensible moral obligation to make good on. It is also because in capitalist society education represents the production of a commodity, namely labor-power, and so the outlay of resources in this enterprise implies a future return. Until the time comes for the consumption of the commodity, i.e. when the student becomes a worker and his or her labor-power is put to use by the employer, the student is indebted (as far as the system is concerned) to those who have invested in the production of his or her abilities.

The problem is that in schooling the production of the commodity, human labor-power, is impossible to separate out from the education of the human being. This represents a paradox for capital. On the one hand, any aspect of the education process that is not strictly commensurable with the logic of commodity production ("human capital" development) is more than a loss; it is actually a criminal wastage of investment. However, the very substance of the objectified commodity labor power is the specifically human capacity to create value, i.e. the creativity, imagination, and energy that makes us human. This creativity, in its humanness and its potentiality, inherently contradicts the logic of objectification to which it is subordinated. In other words, in schooling, the very training of the student toward the production of abilities that will come to have a use in the market involves a mobilization of human creativities that essentially contradict and resist their reduction to objects. In this regard, the worker always owes the capitalist, and the student always owes the system, since neither can ever be wholly absorbed and refigured within the logic of commodity production without the ground of that logic's own possibility being destroyed. Accountability schemes represent the futile attempt to deny or attack those recalcitrant potentialities, to enforce an unceasing transcription of human development into the dehumanizing logics of commodification, and to guarantee that no instant of schooling is available to its alternative conceptualization as a "practice of freedom" (Freire, 1996).

CONCLUSION

Prevailing test-based accountability schemes are attractive to many for their apparent neatness, cleanness and efficiency. They are presented as rational and systematic mechanisms for improving educational quality. Nevertheless, this innocuous surface hides the essential nature of these schemes as technologies of repression and violence. This repression operates simultaneously within social, spiritual, and physical registers. Familiar bourgeois principles of idealism and identity command, by means of these instruments, the reduction of particular human consciousnesses to reified indices (e.g. test scores) which are determined to stand as their sole and perfect equivalents. Neocolonialism finds in this "science" of scales and graphs a new version of an old tool for constructing the colonized black and brown Other as "objectively" inferior. The hegemonic state apparatus organizes, in this hyper-measurement of "success" and "failure," a system of surveillance that is at the same time a subjugation and punishment of student bodies and subjectivities. And the underlying principle of capital itself, now seemingly trapped in an accelerating frenzy of accumulation, vainly seizes upon these schemes in an effort to finally subordinate any remaining margin of human being that resists or contradicts its violent deterritorialization into the abstract commodity of labor-power.

In Marxist critique, we often try our best to counter our natural tendency to think in terms of right and wrong, malice and magnanimity, with a conception of a disinterested oppressor in the form of capital, whose excesses and ignominies can be comfortingly deconstructed into a logic that perpetuates itself beyond the moral register. In this effort to be objective, modern, scientific, and sober, we risk discounting modalities of oppression that escape the instrumental logic of an analysis elaborated purely on the basis of *interest*. The violence, rage and pleasure not merely inherent in, but generative of the process of exploitation are then underestimated in our effort to be clear-headed. An awareness of the libidinal economies within which repression is suffered and enjoyed is important to an understanding of contemporary imperialist capitalism. In this light we can begin to see violence not only as a means to guarantee a mode of production based on exploitation, but also as a moment itself of this exploitation. Our notion of surplus, and value itself, must then expand beyond the sole notion of labor time to include human body, subjectivity, and spirit which are themselves plundered by capital itself as rage and desire.

It is not within the scope of this paper to develop strategies of resistance to this reconceptualized exploitation in general, or to educational accountability measures in particular. Nevertheless, in so far as schooling is premised upon generating the living commodity of labor-power, upon which the entire social universe of capital depends, it can become a foundation for human resistance. Students, as potential sources of labor-power, can engage in acts of refusing alienating work and delinking their labor from capital's value form. However, in order not to reproduce in our own response the process of alienation that defines social life under capitalism, it is important that we recognize as well the reality of the *sense of violation* that we experience under its regime. These experiences are not mere signals that have to be transcended to arrive at a correct and dispassionate appraisal of the abstract logic of capital. Rather, to the extent that this process is embodied, these experiences are themselves forms of understanding of it. Therefore, we must be attentive to the way that forms of praxis develop within the physical, emotional, and spiritual registers, and how they can enrich interventions in the realms of policy and practical politics (California Consortium for Critical Educators, 2001). Networks of solidarity (e.g. critical teacher support groups) and cultural practices (e.g. resistant youth movements) are not secondary accompaniments to authentic resistance; rather, they represent action on crucial fronts against a form of oppression that offers no quarter in its assaults on human subjectivity. The business of capitalism is to reduce us in every dimension; in resisting, we must not, in naming who we are, accede to a definition of ourselves as simple instruments. Rather, we must risk a claim to a ground of imagination and possibility within the framework of a humanist solidarity that refuses to be recuperated into the logics of exchange, punishment, consumption and cruelty.

REFERENCES

Adorno, Theodor (1995). *Negative Dialectics* (E.B. Ashton, Trans.). New York: Continuum.

Arnstine, Donald; and McDowell, Judith A. (1993). "Unfair Rewards: Merit Pay, Grades, and a Flawed System of Evaluation." *Teacher Education Quarterly*, vol. 20, no. 2, pp. 5-21.

Berlak, Harold (2001). "Race and the Achievement Gap." *Rethinking Schools*, vol. 15, no. 4, pp. 10-11.

Bhabha, Homi K. (1994). *The Location of Culture*. New York: Routledge.

California Consortium for Critical Educators (2001). "Study Groups."

Fanon, Frantz (1968). *The Wretched of the Earth* (Constance Farrington, Trans.). New York: Grove Press.

Fass, Paula S. (1989). *Outside In: Minorities and the Transformation of American Education*. Oxford: Oxford University Press.

Foucault, Michel (1977). *Discipline and Punish* (Alan Sheridan, Trans.). New York: Pantheon Books.

Freire, Paulo (1996). *Pedagogy of the Oppressed* (Myra Bergman Ramos, Trans.). New York: Continuum.

Gallagher, Chris (2000). "A Seat at the Table: Teachers Reclaiming Assessment Through Rethinking Accountability." *Phi Delta Kappan*, vol. 81, no. 10, pp. 502-507.

Gerstenzang, James (2001). "Bush Defends Annual Tests as Key Reform for Schools." *Los Angeles Times*, Friday, January 26, p. A14.

Glovin, David (2000). "Welcome to Measurement, Inc." In Kathy Swope and Barbara Miner (eds.). *Failing Our Kids: Why the Testing Craze Won't Fix Our Schools* (pp. 20-23). Milwaukee, WI: Rethinking Schools.

Kohn, Alfie (2000). *The Case Against Standardized Testing*. Portsmouth, NH: Heinemann.

McNeil, Linda (2000). *Contradictions of School Reform: Educational Costs of Standardized Testing*. New York: Routledge.

National Research Council (1999). *High Stakes: Testing for Tracking, Promotion, and Graduation*. Washington, D.C.: National Academy Press.

Nietzsche, Friedrich (1969). *On the Genealogy of Morals* (Walter Kaufmann, Trans.). New York:. Vintage Books.

Peters, Michael (1998). *Naming The Multiple: Poststructuralism and Education*. Westport, CT: Bergin and Garvey.

Popham, W. James (1999). "Where Large Scale Educational Assessment Is Heading and Why It Shouldn't." *Educational Measurement: Issues and Practice*, vol. 18, no. 3, pp. 13-17.

Rikowski, Glenn (1997). "Nietzsche's School? The Roots of Educational Postmodernism." Unpublished manuscript.

San Juan, E. Jr. (2000). "Cultural Studies—A Reformist or Revolutionary Force for Social Change?" *Tamkang Review*, vol. 31, no. 2, pp. 1-29.

"Schools Post Gains on Academic Performance Index— Eastin Announces Monetary Awards Eligibility." (2000). California Department of Education.

Smith, Mary Lee; Heinecke, Walter; and Noble, Audrey J. (1999). "Assessment Policy and Political Spectacle." *Teachers College Record*, vol. 101, no. 2, pp. 157-191.

Stoskopf, Alan (2000). "The Forgotten History of Eugenics." In Kathy Swope and Barbara Miner (eds.). *Failing Our Kids: Why the Testing Craze Won't Fix Our Schools* (pp. 76-80). Milwaukee,WI: Rethinking Schools.

Toussaint, Reggie (2000). "Manifest Destiny or Cultural Integrity?" *Rethinking Schools*, vol. 15, no. 2, p. 11.

Valencia, Richard R (1997). "Genetic Pathology Model of Deficit Thinking." In Richard R. Valencia (eds.). *The Evolution of Deficit Thinking: Educational Thought and Practice* (pp. 41-112). Washington D.C.: The Falmer Press.

Waite, Geoff (1996). *Nietzsche's Corpse: Aesthetics, Politics, Prophecy, or, the Spectacular Technoculture of Everyday Life*. Durham, NC: Duke University Press.

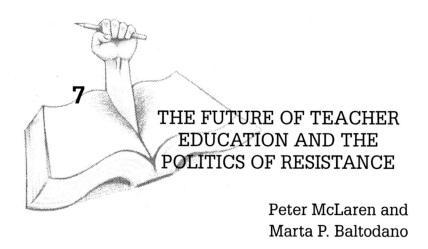

7

THE FUTURE OF TEACHER EDUCATION AND THE POLITICS OF RESISTANCE

Peter McLaren and
Marta P. Baltodano

The authors argue that teacher education reform is becoming increasingly aligned to the imperatives of the capitalist marketplace. They describe current initiatives in California that attempt to reclaim schools and teacher education as sites for democratic socialist struggle.

THE GLOBAL CONTEXT

As declared "allies of the state" schools work as an ideological apparatus to "shape advantage" for those who are in the best position to push the levers of capitalist accumulation. Therefore, any discussion of the future of teacher education would be remiss if it did not include a discussion of recent global economic developments. Mike Cole and other educators (McLaren, 1999; McLaren & Farahmandpur, 1999) have positioned educational reform within the larger context of globalization or the international unification of capital in which capitalists are becoming free to move their capital anywhere in the world, most often under the stewardship of multinational corporations and in the wake of a retreating nation state whose functions are becoming increasingly transformed. Cole stresses the primacy of *finance capital over manufacturing capital* by noting that since the 1970s, there has been little profit to be made from expanding the capacity to produce goods.

When the United States renounced the convertibility of the dollar into gold in 1971, because of huge deficit in the balance of payments resulting from the war in Vietnam and Cold War expenditures, there occurred an outflow of dol-

This updated chapter was originally published in *Teaching Education, 11*(1), 47-60. © 2000 Taylor and Francis. http://www.tandf.co.uk.

lars, reinforced by a jump in oil prices in 1973, and the creation of a large international pool of petrodollars. International banks created an international capitalist market consisting of Eurodollars, a market that lent heavily to countries and corporations in search of new markets. Cole notes how offshore banking centers—set up to free banks of the regulatory activities of their national governments—provided loans to developing countries. This led to the debt crisis of the 1980s.

Financial capital then turned its predatory gaze towards underwriting the merger and acquisitions craze of the 1980s, creating Las Vegas superstar status for big banks, brokerage firms and junk bond dealers. As the dollar floated in relation to other international currencies, speculation in exchange rates became another major theater of operations for finance capital that by mid-1995 generated a trillion dollars a day. The biggest arena for finance capital in the 1990s was the global equities markets (the buying and selling of stocks) mostly in the so-called "Third World", where there exist 35 stock exchanges, and in former communist bloc countries. Cole (1998) writes:

> The fact that capitalist enterprises are increasingly operating on a global scale creates an international unity of capital. Accompanying the international unity of capital is the weakening and fragmentation of organised labor and of the working class as a whole. In being free to move their capital anywhere in the world, capitalists are able to avoid employing any expensive and/or militant labor which still exists. Within what remains of individual nation states, in the geographical location they inhabit, it is incumbent on workers, given this globalised market, to be flexible in their approach to what they do and for how long they do it, to accept lower wages and to concur with the restructuring and diminution of welfare states. (p. 316)

Although globalization has brought about "new forms of capitalist integration and cooperation across nation states" it has also brought about competition between national and regional capitalists. And while a common definition of working class includes only those workers directly exploited by labor in the production process (i.e., whose surplus labor yields surplus value), there is a wider definition of working class that includes all those who are obliged to sell their labor in order to survive (most of whom are at least indirectly exploited since they don't produce goods). Individuals and groups who fall into this wider definition include those employed in business services, in the growing service sector, and "workers in the central state and in the local state who are necessary for the political stability of capitalism" (Cole, 1998, p. 319) such as civil servants and local authority office workers/bureaucrats. The final sector includes health and education service workers (teachers) who are "engaged in producing new workers and/or maintaining the working class" (p. 319) .

We agree with Cole that globalization has not been followed by the demise of the working class but rather by its recomposition. Accompanying this reconfiguration of class has been the fragmentation of organized labor, a decline in trade union membership and a "disparate, low-waged and weakened labor force" (Cole, 1998, p. 319). Multinational capital depends upon the ability of nation states to discipline the labor force and to provide economic stability (i.e., sometimes, as in the case of Mexico and elsewhere, by use of military force). As Smyth and Shacklock (1998) observe, schools are continuing their role as a disciplinary force of the capitalist class through the corporate managerialisation of teacher education.

The United States now has a protected privileged class and a divided working class consisting of core workers, temporary workers, and contingent workers (Percucci & Wysong, 1999). Core workers have the greatest job security and possess skills that can be traded in the external labor market. Temporary workers lose their jobs when there is a need to cut production because of weak sales. Contingent workers are employees of an agency that contracts with a firm for their services. We are suffering (some of us more than others) through a time in which there exists an inordinate and frightening corporate control over job growth and job loss in a capitalist system whose inequalities are more glaringly evident that ever before:

> The real problem posed by the global economy is that it has increased the influence of large corporations over the daily lives of most Americans. This influence is revealed in corporate control over job growth and job loss, media control of information, and the role of big money in the world of national politics. At the same time that this growing influence is revealed on a daily basis, it has become increasingly clear that the major corporations have abandoned any sense of allegiance to, or special responsibilities toward, American workers and their communities. (Perrucci & Wysong, 1999, p. 100)

If it is true that, according to Perrucci and Wysong (1999), "one in five Americans is doing very well indeed, enjoying the protection that comes with high income, wealth, and social contacts" whereas "the remaining four out of five Americans are exploited and excluded" (p. 100), then we have serious reason to be concerned about how schools are providing ballast to this division of labor, and how they are functionally advantageous to perpetuating these asymmetrical relations of power and privilege.

The following section attempts to show how the corporate model of education has realigned teacher education in California to serve its own ideological interests.

THE THREE REVOLUTIONS OF TEACHER EDUCATION

According to Sarason (1993), there have been three revolutions in the history of education in the United States. The first revolution took place when public schooling became universal and mandatory; the second occurred when the Supreme Court declared racial segregation unconstitutional; and the third revolution happened when Congress passed Public Law 94-142, "Education for All Handicapped Children's Act". These three turning points in the history of US public education reflect the contradictory nature of schooling: the need for society to assure the reproduction of its values through a controlled and homogenous school system, and the paradox of creating access and integration for historically excluded social groups. It is in the context of those contradictions that the cries for educational reforms have to be examined.

After the last educational revolution—as defined by Sarason—took place in the United States in the early 1970s, a new political period arrived characterized by "an economic crisis in government, a conservative political shift, the development of an ideology that more clearly integrate[d] industrial needs with educational policy, and a belief that the previous era of centralized social and educational reforms ha[d] failed" (Popkewitz, 1987, p. viii). This period (1980s) marked the end of the welfare state—i.e., capitalism with a "human face"—and the transition to a global economy. It was the beginning of "Reaganomics" and signaled a major momentum in the US economy. Schools again became scapegoats and the criticism centered almost exclusively on teacher education.

Never before has teacher education received so much attention and been so deeply scrutinized as in that last 24 years. The publication of several reports on the state of teacher education and the release of new legislation surpasses the ability of the public to process the suggested changes. The consecutive release of reports like *A nation at risk: The imperative for educational reform* (National Commission on Excellence in Education,1983); *A nation prepared: Teachers for the 21st century* (Carnegie Forum on Education and the Economy, 1986); *Tomorrow's teachers* (Holmes Group,1986); *Time for results: The Governors' 1991 report on education* (National Governors Association, 1991); *Goals 2000* (US State Department of Education); and the Bush-sponsored Act "No Child Left Behind (NCLB) that symbolizes the culmination of one of the most convervative trends in education, clearly conveys the message about society's need to realign teacher education with the needs of the globalized market. The NCLB fascination with standardized testing, school accountability, reading standards, and rigorous teacher certification sheds light on the use of educational institutions to advance the hegemonic transmission of social inequalities.

The common recommendations includes the following: (1) an imposition of higher standards for the accreditation of teacher preparation programs; (2) an enforcement of greater requirements for teacher credentialing; (3) the establishment of rigid assessment instruments in schools; and (4) an imposition of higher test scores for high school graduation and admission in higher education institutions. These reports represented a glorification of the "ideology of improvement" (Hollingsworth & Sockett, 1994) and excellence that has pervaded the entire educational system of our time.

The development of teacher education in the last two decades has been shaped by these recommendations in light of the current economic transition to a ruthless globalized economy (Smyth & Shacklock, 1998). Yet the question that emerges here is how teacher education in California has been affected by those reports and in what ways they will determine its future?

In the last decade most of the political and educational accomplishments of the cultural revolution of the 1960s has been systematically dismembered in states such as California. The endorsement of Proposition 187 (the anti-immigrant initiative), the approval of Proposition 209 (marking the end of affirmative action) and the passage of Proposition 227 (dismantling bilingual education) is a clear indication that California has become the "bellwether" for the rest of the nation and the political laboratory for anti-democratic legislation in Washington, DC[1] and other states.[2]

In this sense, the education of teachers has been affected by those initiatives and has been translated into greater restrictions on the ability of teachers to utilize their pedagogical spaces for emancipatory purposes. In the last few years, teacher education has become the primary arena chosen by the dominant society to refine its mechanisms of control through an "ideology of improvement and excellence". The end of bilingual education in the state "coincided" with the imposition of new standardized tests administered in English only. The obligation to use those test scores to determine whether a student will be retained or promoted to the next grade level dangerously overlapped with the end of social promotion and the imposition of new high school graduation exams. The enforcement of a new RICA test for elementary teachers assured the return of the "Back to Basics" movement and the implementation of literacy practices that conform to Freire's banking concept of education. The control over *what* is taught at schools and *how* that knowledge is *communicated* has been strictly exerted by state agencies and credentialing commissions. The opportunity for teachers to design their own curriculum has been elipsed by a new accountability system that will measure teachers and schools' performance based on students' test scores. The imposition of new certification requirements for teacher education programs that include the creation of a three-tier[3] certification system—similar to the suggested by the Holmes Report in 1986—leaves little doubt about the direction of teacher education programs and its impact on the teaching profession.

One of the major trends and challenges that teachers face in the new 1999-2000 academic year is the imposition of "test-based student retention" that are penalizing working class and second language learners. These "test-based reforms" (Caputo-Pearl, 1999) are clearly leading to increasing inequality in "low income communities of color resulting in higher dropout rates, more tracking and retention, and the thread of punitive measures like identifying the '100 Worst' schools in the city—as already practiced in Chicago" (Caputo-Pearl, 1999, p. 1).

The devastating impact of these standardized tests has alerted the federal government. In response, a presidential advisory commission directed the US Department of Education to investigate whether "making children with limited English skills take tests written only English and using the results to decide such pivotal questions as promotion or graduation may violate their civil rights" (Cooper, 1999).

The strong reliance on standardized tests is manifested in a recent initiative proposed by Governor Davis in California that would give schools a bonus of $150 per pupil for improving their test scores at least 5 percentile, and would give teachers a bonus up to $25,000 for proving extraordinary success in boosting the test results of their students. This nearly sacerdotal veneration of testing has become problematic not only because it penalizes students and glorifies teachers who "teach to the test", but because of the faulty data they generate. In New York City (that has one of the largest school districts in the nation) 8600 students were forced to attend summer school in order to be promoted to the next grade level. Such action was traced to the faulty results of standardized tests (Colvin, 1999). Obviously, this is something that the highly lucrative testing industry keeps hidden and that school administrators try to keep from public scrutiny.

Another concern is the recent judicial decision that allows parents to enact lawsuits against teachers and school administrators who refuse to implement the English-only initiative. Decisions made in federal courts could open the doors to a series of punitive measures against bilingual educators who speak a language other than English in the classroom.

What teachers are witnessing at the end of the century is the consolidation of a cycle of control over the process of schooling and particularly over the certification of teachers in order to realign education to the needs of the globalized economy.

ALLOCATING WORKERS TO THE GLOBAL MARKET

According to Antonia Darder (1991), "American schools strongly reinforce an acceptance of differential roles in the economy and society as a just and democratic way of organizing social relations. In this manner, the class system of education provides an effective vehicle for the dominant culture to civilize [working class and culturally diverse] populations to ensure that society remains orderly and safe" (p. 6). Darder states that one of the major mechanisms that schools have utilized to "naturalize" this distribution of hierarchical roles in the job market is tracking.

Dennis Carlson (1999) defines tracking as "the separation of students and classes into differentiated curriculum programs based on their expected adult statuses and occupational location in the labor force . . . and (in an overlapping manner) the hierarchical ability grouping of students based on their presumed intellectual capabilities and development levels" (p. 15).

Carlson (1999) argues that in spite of educational reforms that speak to the importance of "detracking", the dualistic view of student identity that has historically permeated tracking practices (manual laborers versus mental laborers, failure prone versus success oriented, high achievers versus low achievers) has been strengthened and extended throughout urban schools across the United States. Carlson warns:

> Curricular tracks are not disappearing in public high schools, despite all the talk of detracking. Tracks are still very much implicated in the production and reproduction of unequal identities. The rules of the game that organize tracking structures and practices have been altered and rewritten a bit, but not substantially altered. As we face a new century and millennium, we risk becoming a formally democratic nation, but a nation in which the democratic spirit, as part of the living culture of everyday life, is slipping away. Democracy cannot long survive or prosper in a two-tiered, two-tracked society. (1999, p. 31)

Carlson claims that the traditional three tracks of college-bound, general, and vocational education have been reformulated and replaced by two major tracks: basic skills and what he calls "the new vocationalism". The new basic skills track has been cobbled out of the old general academic track and is closely integrated with remaining vocational and school-to-work programs. This new track, according to Carlson, is directed toward learning basic functional and occupational literacy, passing a high school proficiency test, and graduating into the new, post-industrial workforce. In this track there is greater use of computer-based individualized instruction that facilitates heterogeneous grouping. The curriculum is narrowly linked to basic skills mastery in the core subject areas, with an emphasis on computer-guided instruction.

The other track identified by Carlson is the college preparatory track that is "spatially distanced from the basic skills track through relocation to specialized 'magnet schools' and special school-within-a-school programs" (1999, p. 17). These two tracks are functionally linked to the urban job market and the development of a two-tiered and inequitable labor force associated with global capitalism and the new service industry. It is also linked to the deepening fiscal crisis of the liberal welfare state. While vocational programs have been deemed too expensive, a basic skills curriculum offers what Carlson calls "a stripped-down, no-frills education delivered in a cost-effective way" (1999, p. 18).

The rapid growth of the general, basic skills track is closely associated with recent shifts in the post-industrial economy, mainly growth in service sector jobs such as waiters, household workers, janitors and maintenance workers, security guards, food service workers, and computer data processing. Functional literacy and technological literacy is stressed in this program and is also linked to the discourse of corporate management and outcomes-based learning for students that stress collaborative learning as "team players". This is plainly an economic discourse rather than a democratic discourse, stressing the adaptation of young people to the needs of the economy and "socializing them to docility" (Carlson, 1999, p. 20). There is a stress on courses that are organized around occupational and work themes and youth apprenticeship programs. Here there is a stress placed on industry and education to become "equal partners".

The new college preparatory tracks are also underwritten by an economic rationale, preparing students for new high wage, high skilled, high tech professional, scientific, and managerial jobs. College preparatory students who are enrolled in magnet schools often must pass admission requirements and their instruction is frequently organized around specialized programs such as performing arts, math science, communications, the humanities, etc. Magnet schools are exempt from central office and state regulations with respect to course offerings, class schedules, and student evaluation, and there increasingly exist concerted efforts to separate neighborhood schools from magnet schools in terms of who will more effectively serve college-bound students.

According to Carlson, magnet schools are much more likely to receive a greater share of financial aid from school districts and to be linked to corporate and foundation partners who provide further financial support. He argues that current trends involving magnet schools and the new vocationalism "raise disturbing prospects of a two-tiered system of public education, one (for those bound for college and middle-class jobs) well-financed with the help of corporate capital, and one (for those bound for the new working and underclasses) fiscally starved" (1999, p. 28). While some magnet schools governed by boards composed of teachers, students, and community groups have sought to serve low income students, and have been used by progressive groups to reinvent education in democratic ways, Carlson argues that such schools are the exception rather than the rule. While most magnet schools currently serve as privileged educational sites for college preparatory students, evidence is accumulating that suggests that magnet schools can serve a broader audience.

Carlson refers to the case of El Puente Academy for Peace and Justice, which mainly serves students from Williamsburg's Latino south side and teaches them to become community activists. According to Carlson,

> if magnet schools are a mechanism for "saving" some students at the expense of the vast majority of others in urban school systems, then support for them has to be very limited and qualified. The challenge is to reconstruct the idea of specialized small schools within the context of a more democratic discourse and practice. (1999, p. 31)

Carlson notes that if vocational or occupational education "are to have any place in a democratic education" (1999, p. 32), they must shift their focus from functional literacy to workplace literacy and critical work education. He concludes that all of these reform efforts "are only palliative so long as the underlying forces that perpetuate tracking practices remain unaddressed" (p. 33). In other words, what is needed is a "democratic progressive discourse that is serious about detracking" and that can be "integrated with a new economic policy discourse that begins to talk seriously about countering the growing inequalities that divide us as a society and as a people" (p. 33).

Another example of the realignment of the educational system to the needs of the global market is offered by Joe Kincheloe, who argues that the School-to-Work Opportunities Act signed by President Clinton in 1994 is simply another educational initiative designed to facilitate the reproduction of global capitalist relations in spite of its putative support for democratic goals (i.e., worker-led problem-solving teams, contextualized cooperative learning opportunities that stress interpersonal communication skills). Kincheloe (1999) remarks:

> Those of us concerned with economic justice may become enamored with such postmodern managerial changes until hit with the fact the realization that often the purpose of such humanistic innovations still involves the traditional managerial effort to adjust students to the inequalities of the economic sphere. At this level, post-Fordist worker empowerment becomes little more than a Taylorist (or post-Taylorist) disempowerment. (p. 410)

Consider the case of Tech Prep programs. These advocate workplace literacy and applied academics in the last 2 years of high school and are tied to student immersion in an occupational cluster curriculum. After high school graduation, students enroll in 2-year occupational training programs in a community college that prepare them for "middle-range occupations" such as law enforcement, nursing, computer processing, engineering technology, and office-machine maintenance. Kincheloe is critical of the Tech Prep programs for permitting themselves to be "too shaped by corporate values and business needs" (1999, p. 411). He writes that "a critical pedagogy of vocational education teaches vocational teachers, vocational students, and workers to identify the ways that ostensibly neutral programs like Tech Prep are inscribed with corporate values" (1999, pp. 411-412).

INTEGRATING POLITICAL ECONOMY IN SCHOOL LITERACY

Transforming schools into democratic public spheres requires educators to take seriously the type of worker civics and critical vocational education advocated by Carlson (1999), Kincheloe (1999), Simon, Dippo and Schenke (1991), and

Kincheloe, Slattery and Steinberg (2000). These approaches are similar in purpose to many of the classroom teaching strategies that fall under the rubric of "critical pedagogy" and "critical literacy" (see McLaren, 1997a, b). Of course, the success of worker civics, critical pedagogy, and critical vocational education is fundamentally shaped by the socioeconomic context in which schools function. Even magnet schools cannot completely escape—and often promote—the social practices and relations of capital accumulation and exchange that are driving the public educational system further and further into a two-tiered apparatus, with one tier tracking students into future occupations of limited opportunities, and the other reproducing the cultural and social capital of the capitalist class and their cadres of the elite.

Kincheloe calls for unionists and vocational educators to collectively struggle for what he calls "industrial democracy" through a critical pedagogy of worker self rule. Kincheloe (1999) writes:

> Critical vocational teachers stimulate students' social imagination via their engagement with alternative democratic models of economic and political community development. The imaginative is therefore integrated with the pragmatic, as teachers induce students to study the particulars of worker managed companies such as the I.G.P. Insurance company in Washington state, several timber cooperatives in the Pacific Northwest, and Valley Care Cooperative (a Waterbury, Connecticut-based home health care enterprise). Workers at Valley Care Cooperative not only own their own company and earn a living but are constantly learning and improving their literacy through Freirean educational strategies. The cooperative consists of thirty African American and Latina home care aides who administer the health needs of elderly people in the local area. The woman workers study labor-management concerns and examine the workings of cooperative business ventures. (p. 364)

Kincheloe (1999) also advocates what he calls "worker civics" which refers to "both a pedagogy and a political vision that struggles to provide vocational students and workers with an understanding of the social, economic, political, philosophical, and ethical context in which labor and schooling for it takes place" (p. 385). For Kincheloe, worker civics centers around a politics of student questioning:

> [T]eachers induce students to question the ways public and corporate decisions shape their work futures: Will students be able to gain steady, long-term jobs? Will they be able to achieve economic security? Will they have access to career advancement and financial mobility? Will the attainment of good work be possible? How as worker-citizens can they help shape political and economic policies to benefit themselves and their fellow workers around the world? (1999, p. 385)

Simon et al. (1991) offer a similar approach to that of Kincheloe when they advise students to

> broaden the base of their knowledge by gathering information from want ads, friends, relatives, co-workers, and strangers, and then challenging them to think critically about the issue of pay in relation to their own working lives and the working lives of others. We want to encourage them to ask questions about the limitations and possibilities of existing structures of exchange relations. And we want them to consider what kinds of changes would be required to make fairness the basis of the exchange. (p. 167)

THE FUTURE OF TEACHER EDUCATION IN A TIME OF "GLOBAL ECONOMIC APARTHEID"[4]

The struggle to reclaim schools as public spheres and teacher education programs as sites for social transformation seems to gradually dissipate in the presence of the latest threats and punitive measures against students and educators. The process of deskilling teachers and stripping their teaching practices of any liberatory purpose is consistent with the current government practice of utilizing the teaching force to prepare the workers of the future for their roles in the new post-Fordist service economy. Thus, the question that emerges here is whether teacher education can become a truly emancipatory project in the forthcoming century in spite of its current alienating structures and its compatibility with the authoritarian turn of the capitalist classes resulting in a deepening social polarization and heightened class conflict.

If the political struggles of the 1930s and 1960s gave inception to some of the most important social gains in education, it is clear that only through a similar process of social unrest and organized protest schools can be reclaimed and teacher education transformed.

What became more and more evident with the endorsement of the latest antidemocratic initiatives in California (Propositions 187, 209, 227) is that media advertising funded by powerful corporations clearly targeted and attracted first and second generation immigrants and other racialized populations for the purpose of reproducing existing relations of power and privilege that favored the Euro-American majority. Thus, the current challenge consists of how to counteract these strategies while recognizing that the escalation of global economic exploitation is robbing society of important educational sites from which to begin a dialogue of social transformation. Such a dialogue should be centered around the issues of what kind of society we are forming, what kind of schools we want, and what kind of teachers our current struggle for social justice demands.

What is at stake in this discussion is not a bureaucratic visualization of the future of teacher education, but an critical analysis of and a programmatic strategy for the future of education and society in times of "global economic apartheid". Such an analysis implies a number of important features: a recognition that active democratic citizenship must be deeply connected to the struggles that teachers and schools face; a willingness of everyday citizens to take part in the struggle for democratic schooling; and a clear commitment on the part of teachers and other cultural workers to create active dialogue and historical blocs where political awareness and civic action can flourish. It is clear that reclaiming schools must involve anti-capitalist struggle on both a local and global basis, and a new fight for socialist ideals and practices. School activists can learn a great deal from the anti-World Trade Organization protests known as 'The Battle in Seattle'.

Reclaiming schools and teacher education as arenas of cultural struggle and education in general as a vehicle for social transformation in conservative/capitalist times is premised upon a clear commitment to organize parents, students and communities. It stipulates that society needs to develop critical educators, community activists, organic intellectuals, and teachers whose advocacy of social justice will illuminate their pedagogical practices. The future of teacher education will be determined by how effectively a critical mass can be organized in order to begin reshaping the public discourse over schooling, a discourse that acknowledges that capitalism is the 'wrong dream'.

In this regard, it is necessary to mention that some initiatives are already on the way. Second Opinion—"an alternative voice" of UTLA[5]—is currently forming a broad-based teacher movement in order to resist the implementation of the Stanford 9 test and proposing "an alternative reform plan" that includes the institutionalization of new assessment methods, smaller class sizes, resistance to test-based tracking, the retention and reinstatement of bilingual education, the elimination of merit pay based on test scores, and the redirection of prison funding to the Los Angeles School District (Caputo-Pearl, 1999).

Another similar initiative has evolved with the formation of the California Consortium for Critical Educators (CCCE) that is comprised of teachers, teacher educators, professors and community activists across the state who seek to "create both intellectual and political support for classroom teachers within their schools and communities" (CCCE, 1999). CCCE is forming regional study groups across the state to develop political spaces for teachers and community members to initiate dialogues on school issues. Because the current conservative movement has seriously damaged the organizational ability of teachers, parents, students and community activists to halt the latest pro-capitalist and anti-democratic reforms, CCCE is developing itself as an action movement. This organization operates as an educational community that seeks to create alliances for other political movements for the purpose of reversing the conservative trend in education, refusing to accede to the corporate capitalist diminution of education to the extraction of surplus labor, and denying allegiance to the idols of state, class, patriarchy, and whiteness.

The future of teacher education and the future of public schooling in the United States will depend upon initiatives like the ones implemented by Second Opinion and CCCE. Only through an organized and politically motivated citizenry can schools and teacher education be reclaimed as sites for social transformation.

NOTES

1. The endorsement of Proposition 187 in California facilitated the quick enactment of a new restrictive Immigration Law in Washington, DC in 1996.
2. The major proponent of Proposition 227 in California, Ron Unz, has been invited to Arizona to begin a similar campaign.
3. The requirements of the new California teaching credential (SB2042) has created a 3-tier system that will advance candidates through three different stages: preliminary credential, clear credential (induction), and professional development.
4. John Cavanaugh's words expressed in a speech aired by Alternative Radio in Boulder, Colorado. Cited in CCCE (1998).
5. United Teachers-Los Angeles.
6. Critical approaches such as those advocated by practitioners of critical pedagogy programs are crucial to reform efforts within teacher education.. The following recommendations for the creation of critical teacher educators developed by Kincheloe et al. (2000) constitute an effective challenge to the current emphasis on making teacher education functionally advantageous for the current service economy. (1) Empowered teachers understand the purposes of education and work to reform schools so they accomplish such purposes. Teachers must work to develop a coherent philosophical, moral, and political vision of school reform so that they can take the initiative for change from the bottom up. (2) Empowered teachers appreciate the centrality of knowledge production in their pedagogy. The collision of student—teacher experiences with information derived from the disciplines produces knowledge in the classroom. (3) Empowered teachers make use of that knowledge and those understandings that have heretofore been devalued and excluded: subjugated and indigenous knowledge. Teachers move beyond white, Anglo-Saxon, middle class and heterosexual educational norms and explore the subjugated knowledges of women, minority groups and indigenous groups. (4) Empowered teachers model and teach postformal thinking. Formal thinking involves scientific procedure and the certainty it produces. Postformal thinking involves understanding the production of one's own knowledge and includes etymology—the exploration of culturally validated knowledge; pattern—understanding the patterns and relationships that support the lived world (p. 257); and process—"the cultivation of new ways of interpreting the world that make sense of both ourselves and contemporary society" (2000, p. 287). (5) Empowered teachers cooperate with school and community and facilitate cooperation between them. This includes open forums about race and gender relations and parent-student collaborative learning. (6) Empowered teachers build leaning networks between schools and communities that make use of recent developments and innovations in communications technologies. Students not only develop an understanding of educational technology

and its practical uses, but also investigate how "they modify existing relationships and ways of being" (2000, p. 289). (7) Empowered teachers become researchers and teach their students sophisticated methods of inquiry. Students need to use research-driven powers of analysis observing, interviewing, photographing, videotaping, note-taking, and collecting life histories. In so doing teachers not only "polish the traditional skills" that are valued in the curriculum such as "reading, writing, arithmetic, listening, interpreting and thinking" but students learn "to uncover the forces that shape their everyday lives: their place in the social hierarchy of their peer groups, their romantic relationships, their vocational aspirations, their relationships with teachers" (2000, p. 259). (8) Empowered teachers encourage schools to support their continued learning. Schools must "avoid at all costs the teacher deskilling authoritarian (top-down) management strategies, standardized test driven curricula and prepackaged (teacherproof) curriculum materials" (2000, p. 269). (9) Empowered teachers recognize the inability of modernists-positivist teaching methods to explain the current world of schooling. Teachers recognize the limitations of current teaching technologies, and seek to employ examples from anthropology, film studies, literacy criticism and history "to decipher the subliminal codes and detest the intended and unintended effects of video games, advertising, carphones, computers, television, stereos systems and other contemporary influences" (2000, p. 261). (10) Empowered teachers invent new and appropriate modes of assessment. Objective standardized tests are rejected in favor of giving students a voice in their own assessment and should be an extension of the learning process. Measurement is less quantitative and addresses issues of content. (11) Empowered teachers recognize how power shapes them, their students and the everyday schooling context. Teachers learn to "decipher the power codes, the repressive ways ideological interests invade not only the schools but the popular culture as well" (2000, p. 263). The premise here is that "education is a social practice operating within a society characterized by unequal power relations" (2000, p. 262). (12) Fischman & McLaren (in press) have added an additional recommendation to the 11 that we have summarized above from the work of Kincheloe, Slattery and Steinberg. They argue that empowered teachers must locate the schooling process in both local and global socioeconomic and political contexts, while exploring the relation between them. This mandates situating the process of schooling within the structures, social relations and processes of advanced capitalism.

The struggle for critical teacher education is a daunting task, and while we may be discouraged by the difficult battles ahead, we should not be paralyzed by them.

REFERENCES

California Consortium for Critical Educators. (1998). *CCCE working vision paper.* Claremont, CA: Claremont Graduate University.

California Consortium for Critical Educators. (1999). *CCCE working paper on capitalism.* Claremont, CA: Claremont Graduate University.

Caputo-Pearl, A. (1999). *Fight racism at "low performing" schools! We want civil rights, not retention or more standardized tests!* Los Angeles: Second Opinion Caucus of United Teachers-Los Angeles.

Carlson, D. (1999). The rules of the game: Detracking and retracking the urban high school. In F. Yeo & B. Kanpol (Eds.), *From nihilism to possibility: Democratic transformations for the inner city* (pp. 15-35) Cresskill, NJ: Hampton Press.

Carnegie Forum on Teaching and the Economy, Task Force on Teaching as a Profession. (1986). *A nation prepared: Teachers for the 21st century. The report of the task force on teaching as a profession.* New York: Carnegie Forum on Education and the Economy.

Cole, M. (1998). Globalization, modernisation and competitiveness: A critique of the new labour project in education. *International Studies in Sociology of Education, 8*(3), 315-332.

Colvin, R.L. (1999, September 25). Schools learn perils of using a single test. *Los Angeles Times*, front page.

Cooper, R.T. (1999, September 16). Inquiry into English-only tests ordered. *Los Angeles Times*, A3.

Darder, A. (1991). *Culture and power in the classroom.* New York: Bergin & Garvey.

Fischman, G., & McLaren, P. (in press). Reclaiming hope. *Contemporary Sociology.*

Hollingsworth, S., & Sockett, H. (1994). *Teacher research and educational reform.* Chicago: University of Chicago Press.

Holmes Group. (1986). *Tomorrow's teachers.* A report of the Holmes Group. East Lansing, MI: Holmes Group.

Kincheloe, J. (1999). *How do we tell the workers? The socioeconomic foundations of work and vocational education.* Boulder, CO: Westview Press.

Kincheloe, J., Slattery, P., & Steinberg, S. (2000). *Contextualizing teaching: Introduction to education and educational foundations.* New York: Longman.

McLaren, P. (1997a). *Life in schools.* New York: Longman

McLaren, P. (1997b). *Revolutionary multiculturalism: Pedagogies of dissent for the new millennium.* Boulder, CO: Westview Press.

McLaren, P. (1999). Che Guevara, globalization and leadership. *International Journal of Leadership in Education, 2*(3), 269-292.

McLaren, P., & Farahmandpur, R. (1999). Contraband pedagogy, postmodernism and the retreat from class. *Theoria, 93*, 83-115.

National Commission on Excellence in Education. (1983). *A nation at risk: The imperative for educational reform.* Washington, DC: United States Department of Education.

National Governors Association. (1991). *Time for results: The governors' 1991 report on education.* Washington, DC: National Governors Association.

Percucci, R., & Wysong, E. (1999). *The new class society.* Boulder, CO: Rowman & Littlefield.

Popkewitz, T.S. (Ed.). (1987). *Critical studies in teacher education: Its folklore, theory and practice.* New York: Falmer Press.

Sarason, S.B. (1993). *Schooling in America: Scapegoat and salvation.* New York: Free Press.

Simon, R., Dippo, D., & Schenke, A. (1991). *Learning work: A critical pedagogy of work education.* New York: Bergin & Garvey

Smyth, J., & Shacklock, G. (1998) *Re-making teaching: Ideology, Policy and practice.* London: Routledge.

The No Child Left Behind Act. Public Law 107-110 (January 8, 2002).

United States Department of Education. (1985). *Goals 2000. A progress report.* Washington, DC: US Department of Education.

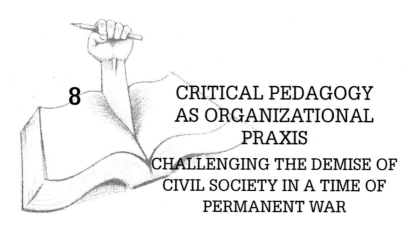

8 CRITICAL PEDAGOGY AS ORGANIZATIONAL PRAXIS

CHALLENGING THE DEMISE OF CIVIL SOCIETY IN A TIME OF PERMANENT WAR

Peter McLaren and
Nathalia E. Jaramillo

Dedicated to Rachel Corrie

THE CRISIS OF THE EDUCATIONAL LEFT IN THE UNITED STATES

Critical educators today are struggling assiduously to defend the public sphere from its integration into the neoliberal and imperialist practices of the state and the behemoth of globalized capitalism. While no one is seriously talking about seizing the state on behalf of workers struggling against the "petrolarchs" in Washington, there are promising indications that social movements in the United States will become more active in the days ahead. With administration hawks such as Defense Secretary Donald Rumsfeld, Vice President Dick Cheney, Deputy Defense Secretary Paul Wolfowitz, Undersecretary of State John Bolton, and Defense Policy Board member, Richard Perle, leading the White House charge for "preventative war", it is clear that their fanatical allegiance to the imperialist Project for the New American Century is fuelled by U.S. triumphalism, unipolar political consolidation and dominion, and the conquest of new markets. The bacchanalia of patriotism that has overtaken cities and towns throughout the country has blinded U.S. citizens to the thousands of innocent civilians killed in the "liberation" of Iraq. The slogan dripping red and black from anti-war posters that reads "No Blood for Oil" has, if anything, increased in relevance since the U.S. military invasion of Iraq. As it stands, OPEC resides outside the ambit of complete U.S. control. Total U.S. influence over the vast untapped oil reserves would demonstrably change the power equation. Iraqi opposition to the U.S. "free market" looting of their country was a

This chapter originally appeared in *Educational Foundations, 16*(4), pp. 5-32. © 2002 Caddo Gap Press. Reprinted with the permission of the publisher.

major factor in the Bush administration's decision to invade Iraq. The drive to obtain "free markets" and to open up investment for U.S. corporations is now accompanied by the most formidable military presence ever known to humankind, one that is fundamentally unopposed. Iraq is now "liberated" for U.S. corporate investment and control, having been "pacified" as a client state. Judging from recent U.S. history, the future will no doubt require that millions more will die in the oil-rich Middle East and elsewhere around the planet on behalf of the U.S. empire. The Bush *junta* has serious lessons to learn. You can't bomb democracy into being. Democracy's universal egalitarian values require the reciprocal acceptance of mutual perspectives.

Just as in the case of the last two centuries, when U.S. troops invaded Cuba, Nicaragua, Guatemala, El Salvador, Haiti, Colombia, Grenada, and Panama, the recent U.S. invasion of Iraq not only tells us a lot about the history of Western democracy and the imperial roots of U.S. foreign policy, but also about the symbiosis between capitalism and imperialism. Aside from the illegality of the invasion and the imperialist ideology that drives the Bush doctrine of "preventative war", we need only look at the 7,000 years of human history that has been defenestrated, stolen, or otherwise pulverized to dust to understand what kind of democracy is in store for Iraq. Displaying a symbolic violence more wretchedly powerful than when a blue curtain was hung over Picasso's *Guernica* outside the UN Security Council Chambers so that a photo-op with Colin Powell would not be tarnished by the anti-war masterpiece, or when Laura Bush cancelled a White House poetry symposium when informed by her advisor that some of the poems might reveal anti-war sentiments, the U.S. enthralled the world once again by failing to prevent—some have even said by encouraging—the wanton theft and destruction of 170,000 priceless treasures of antiquity in the Baghdad Archaeological Museum as well as a museum in the northern city of Mosul (treasures that included the tablets of the Code of Hammurabi). Multimillionaire art collectors from the advanced capitalist states wait in air-conditioned anticipation for receipt of priceless artifacts whose planned theft was just another facet of the U.S. invasion of Iraq. Whose secret office vault now contains the statue of King Entemena, or the Assyrian god Ashur, or the golden harp from Ur? In a movie reminiscent of the destruction of Teotihuacan, the Roman pillage of Carthage, or the devastation visited upon Constantinople during the Fourth Crusade, the U.S. has facilitated the liquidation of what has been called the cradle of civilization. Perhaps the U.S. military leadership could learn something from a senior at Trumbell College, Susannah Rutherglen (2003), who, commenting on the "murder of Iraq's national museum", writes:

> The work of art is the bearer of our cultural memory; it is the only trace we keep of the fact that we have lived at all. Long before Sigmund Freud compared the ruins of Rome to the layers of the human unconscious, the work of art came to stand as a lasting storehouse for the ephemeral contents of human lives, a place where we might recover the meaning of our culture and ourselves through time.

Perhaps the Iraqis would have been better off by placing their museums inside their oil fields which are—by stark contrast carefully guarded by the U.S. military. While the oil fields were being protected by tanks and armored personnel carriers, citizens were freely looting and burning the National Archives, the Koranic library, the Ministry of Irrigation, the Ministry of Industry, the Ministry of Foreign Affairs, the Ministry of Culture, the Ministry of Education, the Ministry of Planning, the Ministry of Information, and the Ministry of Trade (not to mention three hospitals). In fact, every one of the city's ministries has been burned except the Ministry of Interior (with its wealth of intelligence information on Iraq) and the Ministry of Oil as well as UN offices, embassies and shopping malls (Fisk, 2003a, 2003b).

As if the looting and burning of Baghdad were not enough, the citizens of Iraq have been put on lockdown. The command of the 1st U.S. Marine Division recently issued its "Message to the Citizens of Baghdad" to "please avoid leaving your homes during the night hours after evening prayers and before the call to morning prayers. During this time, terrorist forces associated with the former regime of Saddam Hussein, as well as various criminal elements, are known to move through the area . . . please do not leave your homes during this time. During all hours, please approach Coalition military positions with extreme caution" (Fisk, 2003). Iraqis are locked up from dusk to dawn in homes without electricity or running water. But mostly the media reported on the cheering Iraqis in the streets, welcoming the conquering heroes. Yet, as Alexander Cockburn notes:

> There's cheering in the streets now. No big surprise. Saddam was not a popular guy, and anyway, people know which side their bread is buttered on. Never forget, upstanding citizens of Nagasaki sponsored a festive Miss Atomic Bomb contest almost at the onset of the US occupation at the end of World War II. As I'm sure Martha Stewart would tell us, the art of living is learning to adjust briskly to changed circumstances. (2003, p. 12)

Accompanying the cheers of "liberation" are the frenetic and accelerating cries against a long-term U.S. presence. Only days following the recalcitrant removal of a month-old Saddam Hussein statue whose images flooded T.V. stations across the country, hundreds if not thousands of Iraqis occupied the streets to demonstrate a grim resolve against a long-term U.S. occupation. Greeted by M-16 rifles that left at least a hundred wounded and roughly a dozen dead, the Iraqi people continue to bear signs reading "Occupiers Go Home" and "No US and UK in Iraq" (Keane, 2003).

When Colin Powell was advocating cuts to the U.S. military budget in 2001, he was quoted as saying: "Think hard about it. I'm running out of demons. I'm running out of villains" (cited in Gibbs, 2002, p. 15). A year earlier, Condoleezza Rice clearly was pushing for a completely different agenda:

> The United States has found it exceedingly difficult to define its "national interest" in the absence of Soviet power. . . . That we do not know how to think about what follows the U.S.-Soviet confrontation is clear from the continued references to the "post-Cold War period." Yes such periods of Transition are important, because they offer strategic opportunities. During these fluid times, one can affect the shape of the world to come.

The opportunities to which Rice was referring could be summed up as transforming U.S. foreign policy into a motor of economic modernization that could move the world inexorably towards economic openness—clearly, Rice was supporting at that time a foreign policy initiative that advocated neoliberal globalization as the means to export democracy throughout the globe. In this regard, she argued that "the United States and its allies are on the right side of history." It is equally telling that, several years later, Rice would take an even harder line, echoing the unipolar perspective of the administration hawks. In an interview with Nicholas Lemann for *The New Yorker* magazine, she spoke about what the attacks of September 11th afforded U.S. foreign policy initiatives:

> "I think the difficulty has passed in defining a role," she said immediately. "I think September 11th was one of those great earthquakes that clarify and sharpen. Events are in much sharper relief." Like Bush, she said that opposing terrorism and preventing the accumulation of weapons of mass destruction "in the hands of irresponsible states" now define the national interest. . . . Rice said that she had called together the senior staff people of the National Security Council and asked them to think seriously about "*how do you capitalize on these opportunities*" to fundamentally change American doctrine, and the shape of the world, in the wake of September 11th." (*The New Yorker*, 1/4/02, emphasis added; this quotation was taken from The Research Unit for Political Economy, 2003)

According to India's Research Unit for Political Economy (2003), the quotation by Rice reveals that the target of U.S. foreign policy is not terrorism. On the contrary: "The supposed suppression of terrorism worldwide merely offers 'opportunities' for the U.S. to pursue its strategic agenda without geographic or temporal limits." It is therefore no surprise to see the link between neoliberal globalization and an aggressive U.S. military posture, especially when the military-industrial complex has become such an important economic actor (Gibbs, 2001). As Richard Friedman has pointed out: "The hidden hand of the market will never work without a hidden fist—McDonald's cannot flourish without McDonnell Douglas, the designer of the F-15. And the hidden fist that keeps the world safe for Silicon Valley's technologies is called the United States Army, Air Force, Navy, and Marine Corps" (Cited in Gibbs, 2001, pp. 33-34). Neoliberal globalization gives a powerful competitive advantage to developed countries and benefits the U.S. especially through the liberalization of international finance and the unique function of the dollar in an international economy (Gibbs, 2001). In the process it exacerbates a class and ethnic stratification of the world economy. Grandin offers the following succinct description:

> Along with neoliberalism, we have a neo-civilizing mission. The West will deliver free-market democracy, one way or another, to the rest of the world, whether through the proper mix of technology, markets, constitutions, consumer goods or out of the barrel of a smart weapon. (2003, p. 29)

The strategic agenda of the free-market democratic reconstruction of which Rice speaks is really another way of describing an assault on the forces that are trying to build a more just and equitable society: the working-classes of the underdeveloped countries:

> While the apparent targets of the US assault are the *regimes* of these countries, that would hardly make sense, since none of them poses a threat to the US, and in fact some of them, such as Saudi Arabia and Egypt, are its client states. Rather the real targets are the anti-imperialist masses of the region, whom certain regimes are unwilling, and others are unable, to control. It is these anti-imperialist masses of West Asia, not their rulers of whatever hue, who have always constituted the real threat to US domination. The US appears to believe that its overwhelming and highly sophisticated military might can tackle the masses effectively if they come out into the open. That is why it even contemplates *provoking* mass uprisings so as to have occasion to crush them. (Research Unit for Political Economy, 2003)

The case of Latin America offers a convincing example. We are witnessing the recolonization of Latin America through militarization as new U.S. bases are installed in Manta (Ecuador), Tres Esquinas and Leticia (Colombia), Iquitos (Peru), Rainha Beatrix (Aruba), and Hato (Curacao). The U.S. is training Latin American militaries from Chile, Brazil, Bolivia, Ecuador, Peru, and Uruguay as part of Operation Cabanas in Argentina. In addition to the infamous Plan Colombia, the U.S. is installing the System of Surveillance of the Amazon that can monitor 5.5 million square kilometers, as well as a mammoth radar facility in Argentina (Mendonca, 2003). While struggles against U.S.-supported fascist dictatorships by the Latin American left eventually ended in the restoration of constitutional rule in a number of countries, the United States continues to dissuade political parties there from mass mobilization; the U.S. would prefer that these parties adopt a more "modern" democratic politics of "passive representation and elite negotiation" (Grandin, 2003, p. 29). Furthermore, there has been an ongoing assault on direct democracy by curtailing regional and domestic grassroots efforts at regulating the economy:

> Washington has crafted a number of antidemocratic measures—such as international treaties that limit the ability of local states to implement regulations, and the establishment of independent central banks that remove monetary policy from public debate—restricting popular will. (Grandin, 2003, p. 29)

While civilians continue to cheer and die in Iraq with ominous regularity, a private contractor with close ties to the Republican Party, Betchtel Corporation, has been tapped by the U.S. State Department to be the primary contractor in rebuilding Iraq's infrastructure, including power facilities, electrical grids, municipal water and sewage systems. This must be seen as good news by Donald Rumsfeld, since Rumsfeld worked closely with Saddam Hussein from 1983 to 1987 to secure an oil pipeline contract for Betchtel. David Moberg (2003, p. 17) writes that a "new report from the Institute for Policy Studies, using previously unpublished government papers, documents how Rumsfeld and other Reagan aides worked closely with Saddam from 1983 to 1987—after public revelation of his use of poison gas in his war with Iran—in an ultimately failed bid to help Bechtel Corporation construct a new pipeline for Iraqi oil." The new Bechtel contract is worth up to $680 million, and the logic here is that the more infrastructure the U.S. destroys, the more lucrative it becomes for the San Francisco-based contractor, whose board includes former Secretary of State, George Shultz. The U.S. Agency for International Development (USAID) has invited other U.S. multinationals to bid on Iraq's "reconstruction." In line with the reconstruction efforts is a focus on ensuring that 8 million Iraqi children return to school in the fall. A for-profit company, Creative Associates International, has landed the $65 million bid for reopening a battered school system, largely the product of 12 years of UN sanctions that led to plunging literacy rates for a country that boasted the highest quality education in the Middle East prior to 1991. Charged with instilling "politically neutral studies" by removing the former Ba'ath party nationalist curricula, Creative Associates International will be under close scrutiny by critical educators who will want to see how politically neutral the curriculum will be towards the U.S. Creative Associates currently enjoys multi-million dollar contracts for "rebuilding" Afghanistan's school system along with other USAID-funded "liberatory" projects in Lebanon, Jordan, El Salvador and Guatemala, leading to an excess of $200 million in signed contracts.

That capitalism, education and technology go hand-in-hand is a truism captured—if only symbolically—in the efforts by California Republican Congressman Darrel Issa to introduce a bill that would require the Defense Department to build a CDMA cellphone system (developed by Qualcomm, one of Issa's most lucrative donors) in postwar Iraq that would benefit "US patent holders." According to Naomi Klein (2003), "by the time the Iraqi people have a say in choosing a government, the key economic decisions about their country's future will have been made by their occupiers." Of course, the U.S. will partially privatize the oil industry, and sell off Iraq's oil reserves to ExxonMobil and Shell. Iraqi exiles will be given posts in Iraq's interim government in exchange for implementing privatization "in such a way that it isn't seen to be coming from the United States" (Klein, 2003). Klein (2003) writes:

> Some argue that it's too simplistic to say this war is about oil. They're right. It's about oil, water, roads, trains, phones, ports and drugs. And if this process isn't halted, "free Iraq" will be the most sold country on earth.

Our point is that the logic of capital itself is what prohibits democracy from being realized as the achievement of individual freedom and self-determination. The free cheese is always in the mousetrap. What we are seeing talking place in Iraq is not the triumph of democracy. Klein (2003) asserts:

> Entirely absent from this debate are the Iraqi people, who might—who knows?—want to hold on to a few of their assets. Iraq will be owed massive reparations after the bombing stops, but without any real democratic process, what is being planned is not reparations, reconstruction or rehabilitation. It is robbery: mass then disguised as charity; privatization without representation.

But isn't the current situation in Iraq—and the events which led up to it—precisely a metaphor for globalized capitalism worldwide? The United States is advocating struggle for freedom and democracy in Iraq—indeed, a struggle that arcs across the firmament like a Fourth of July Roman candle. Yet the very democracy that it has mandated for Iraq has failed miserably to materialize in the United States. As critical educators, we are not convinced that democracy can be sustained in a world ruled by capitalism's law of value—with or without the imposition of empire. The prospect of democracy looks especially bleak these days, as the Bush administration puts the country on ideological lockdown in an attempt to return to the halcyon days of the McKinley era when the fat cats of industry ran a retrograde financial kingdom that enshrined private property rights and supported the annexation of foreign interests.

In a social universe pock-marked by the ravages of capitalism's war against the working-class and people of color, there are few places in which to retreat that the global market does not already occupy. Clearly, the United States has not faced up to capitalism's addiction to injustice, and its politicians have provided little space in educational debates for teachers to question the structurally dependent relationship between the standard of living in developed countries and misery and poverty in the underdeveloped ones. Early in the twentieth century, this country failed to heed the advice of one of its greatest philosophers, John Dewey (1927), who, mindful of "the extended meaning which has been given to the Monroe Doctrine," warned: "The natural movement of business enterprise, combined with Anglo-American legalistic notions of contracts and their sanctity, and the international custom which obtains as to the duty of a nation to protect the property of its nationals, suffices to bring about imperialistic undertakings."

Employing a politics that counts on the stupefaction of a media-primed electorate, the Bush administration has marshaled the corporate media in the service of its foreign policy such that the environment is literally suffused with its neoliberal agenda, with very little space devoid of it's ideological cheerleading. Where classrooms once served as at least potentially one of the few spaces of respite from the ravages of the dominant ideology, they have now been colonized by the corporate logic of privatization and the imperial ideology of the militarized state. Teachers are left suspended across an ideological divide that separates reason and irrationality, consciousness and indoctrination, as they are reminded by their administrators and government officials that to bring "politics" into the classroom is unpatriotic. Consider the case of Bill Nevins, a high school teacher in New Mexico who faced an impromptu paid leave of absence following a student's reading of "Revolution X," a poem that lends a critical eye toward the war in Iraq.

If the President is to be believed, it was Jesus who first approved of the current Pentagon plan to expand the U.S. empire into the Middle East, as Bush *hijo* shamelessly exploits his policy objectives with frequent Biblical references and overtures of solidarity to Christian evangelical fundamentalists. Through direct presidential orders that circumvent congressional debate and bypass public debate, the White House has launched faith-based initiatives which provide millions of dollars in state funds to right-wing Christian groups who run job-training programs requiring a "total surrender to Christ," or who oversee childcare programs or chemical-dependency recovery programs, or who offer spiritual and moral regeneration to troubled families.

All of this has not gone unnoticed by critical educators. Though they have become used to the academic marginalization that often follows in the wake of attacks by the more churlish and reactionary conservative educationalists among us, proponents and practitioners of critical pedagogy have long feared being cast into the pit of academic hell for being perceived not only as dangerously irrelevant to United States democracy but also as politically treasonous. At this current historical juncture in U.S. history, when fighting a "permanent war" against terrorism, and expanding the American empire while we're at it, one would think that such a fear is duly warranted. This is partly due to the fact that critical pedagogy earned its early reputation as a fierce critic of U.S. imperialism and capitalist exploitation. However, times have changed. Today critical pedagogy is no longer the dangerous critic of free market liberal education that it once was. Rather, it has become so absorbed by the cosmopolitanized liberalism of the postmodernized left that it no longer serves as a trenchant challenge to capital and U.S. economic and military hegemony. Of course, we believe that this can change. There are numerous developments on our campuses related to the anti-war and anti-globalization movements that give us hope that the voices of our youth—and among them those who will be attending our teacher education programs will be much more politicized or open to what Freire called "conscientization" than in previous years. No doubt this has been encouraged by the worldwide mobilization against Bush and his de facto military/oil *junta*. There will be pressure on critical educators (whom in the United States are mostly liberal, not revolutionary) to respond to the voices of a new generation of politicized student teachers. But it won't be a simple case of preaching to the converted. There are now more than 80 right-leaning newspapers and magazines circulating on college and university campuses throughout the country. Clearly, there is a concerted effort by conservative organizations to silence progressive voices. There is a need for teacher educators to bring a more radical discourse into the educational literature as well as directly into their teacher education programs. Even in the field of critical pedagogy these attempts have been disappointing.

Written as a counterpoint to the onslaught of neoliberal globalization and its "civilizing mission" for the oppressed of developed and developing countries alike, this article is both a commentary on the domestication of critical pedagogy, and a challenge for revivifying its political roots and role in the civil societarian left. It is meant to initiate a dialogue and conversation among progressive educators. Especially for those of us living in the belly of the beast in *gringolandia*, we are inhabiting a time when citizenship has become marked by a lived historical presence blindingly uncritical of its own self-formation, when residents inhabiting the nation's multifarious geoscapes are racially marked so as to render them educationally segregated, and when the working-class has become deputized by capital to uphold the neoliberal market ideology of the ruling class against any and all other alternatives—all of which legitimates the subordinate status of the working class within the existing division of labor.

This article is written at a time of permanent war, which is not only a war against the enemies of the United States (which today seems like just about every other country or dissenting organization/persons) but also a war against the working-class, people of color and women (a war that dates back to the violent founding of the country itself). This is not to say that times haven't changed. For instance, Bush *hijo* , a beneficiary of the so-called "good breeding" of the "Episcopacy", made it into Yale in the days when "character" (read as the cultural capital of rich white "silver spoon" families) was a singular badge of merit. Today, increasingly egregious forms of "testocracy", scores from scientifically invalid and unreliable aptitude tests that correlate well with social class, race and linguistic background—serve as the primary route to the academy. The overt racism and class privilege of the ruling elite now enables the bourgeoisie to shirk off the notion of "good breeding" and hide themselves beneath the "objectivity" of high school test scores and university entrance criteria at a time in which meritocracy is presumed to have been secured. Of this is reflected in Bush *hijo's* condescending and patronizing attitude towards ethnic populations, both at home and abroad. As William Saletan (2003) has pointed out, President Bush likes to use the term "gifted" when addressing the Iraqi people on their TV screens. "You are a good and gifted people," he conveyed to them while Arabic subtitles appeared below his face during a broadcast that followed in the wake of the destruction of Baghdad. Saletan notes that Bush has used the term "gifted" seven times during his presidency, once to refer to Bill Cosby, once to Martin Luther King Sr., and four times to Iraqis and Palestinians. The other time was when he was reading from a script at an arts award ceremony. He has referred to Iraqis and Latinos as "talented" people. The Chinese have been referred to by Bush as "talented, brilliant, and energetic" while Russians are singled out as possessing "entrepreneurial talent." Irish Americans betray an "industry and talent" while Cubans display "determination and talent." Saletan correctly notes that such descriptions is tantamount to the obscenely patronizing and condescending discourse that white people often use to refer to "ethnic" people who need to be told that they are capable. Saletan remarks:

> If you're black, Hispanic, or a member of some other group often stereotyped as incompetent, you may be familiar with this kind of condescension. It's the way polite white people express their surprise that you aren't stupid. They marvel at how "bright" and "articulate" you are. Instead of treating you the way they'd treat an equally competent white person—say, by ignoring you—they fuss over your every accomplishment.

At this current historical juncture, as the right seizes every chance it gets to replace the social wage with the free market system, as conservative think tanks game out plans for privatizing what remains of the devastated public sphere, thousands of teachers and teacher educators throughout the country look to the left for guidance and leadership. Stunned by the results of a New York Times/CBS News survey that revealed that 42 percent of the American public believes that Saddam Hussein is directly responsible for the attacks of September 11, and that 55 percent of Americans believe Saddam Hussein directly supports al Qaida, U.S. educators are feeling powerless against the hegemonizing force of the rightwing corporate media. Under cover of democracy, Bush's carney lingo about saving civilization from the terrorist hordes rings the air. Americans old enough to remember the anti-Communist propaganda of the late 1940s and 1950s are experiencing a political *deja vu*. Millions read the books, *Is This Tomorrow: America Under Communism!*, *Blood is the Harvest*, and *Red Nightmare*. In 1948, the Chamber of Commerce of the United States published A Program for Community Anti-Communism which contained a phrase eerily reminiscent of a remark that President Bush made weeks after the attacks of September 11: "You know that they hate us and our freedom." Those too young to remember the McCarthy era get to experience the sequel first hand. Some see this as democracy in practice. Not everybody is fooled.

But even when we are detoxicated of the shadowed obscurity surrounding the current war on terrorism and disabused of the calls for the primitive patriotism of flags and bumper stickers that is part of Bush *hijo's* petulant crusade for a decent America (i.e., an America devoid of its critics), there still remains a glaring absence within the liberal academy of challenging capital as a social relation. While there exists plenty of talk about income redistribution, surprisingly little is said about setting ourselves against the deviances and devices of capital's regime of profit-making other than prosecuting the CEOs of the latest round of corporate offenders. The stunted criticism of the Bush administration's fascist assault on democracy is not so much a refusal of political will among liberal educators as much as a realization that if we persist with an internationalized market economy, the introduction of effective social controls to protect the underclass, marginalized and immiserated will create overwhelming comparative disadvantages for the nation state or the economic bloc that seeks to institute such policies. If, as liberal educators (begrudgingly) and conservative educators (demagogically) insist, there effectively is no alternative to working within institutionalized market economy, then admittedly neo-liberal policies that champion free market capitalism and that undermine what is left of the welfare state make sense. And while surely the punishment exacted against the poor can be staggered by parceling out the conditions for mass poverty in more discreet—yet no less lethal—policies and practices, there remains the question of how to cope with the havoc that will eventually be wreaked on the poor and the powerless in the absence of a socialist alternative. It is in this context—of breadlines, overcrowded hospitals, and unemployment lines longer than those at the polling stations—that the question of organization becomes imperative for the left in a search for a socialist alternative.

THE POLITICS OF ORGANISATION

This brings us face-to-face with the thorny question of organization, a problem that has exercised both the revolutionary left and the progressive left for over a century. Max Elbaum (2002) notes that organisations are crucial in the struggle for social justice. He writes that "[w]ithout collective forms it is impossible to train cadre, debate theory and strategy, spread information and analysis, or engage fully with the urgent struggles of the day. Only through organisations can revolutionaries maximise their contribution to ongoing battles and position themselves to maximally influence events when new mass upheavals and opportunities arise" (2002, p. 335). Yet at the same time, Elbaum warns that we must avoid what he calls "sectarian dead-ends" in our struggle for social justice. Reflecting on his experiences with the New Communist Movement of the 1970s, he explains that when a movement becomes a "self-contained world" that insists upon group solidarity and discipline, this can often lead to the suppression of internal democracy. The rigid top-down party model is obviously a problem for Elbaum. On the one hand social activists need to engage with and be accountable to a large, active, anti-capitalist social base; on the other hand, there are pressures to put one's revolutionary politics aside in order to make an immediate impact on public policy. There is the impulse to "retreat into a small but secure niche on the margins of politics and/or confine oneself to revolutionary propaganda" (2002, p. 334). Elbaum cites Marx's dictum that periods of socialist sectarianism obtain when "the time is not yet ripe for an independent historical movement" (2002, p. 334). Problems inevitably arise when "purer-than-thou fidelity to old orthodoxies" are employed to maintain membership morale necessary for group cohesion and to compete with other groups. He reports that the healthiest periods of social movements appear to be when tight knit cadre groups and other forms are able to coexist and interact while at the same time considering themselves part of a common political trend. He writes that "diversity of organisational forms (publishing collectives, research centers, cultural collectives, and broad organising networks, in addition to local and national cadre formations) along with a dynamic interaction between them supplied (at least to a degree) some of the pressures for democracy and realism that in other situations flowed from a socialist-oriented working class" (2002, p. 335). It is important to avoid a uniform approach in all sectors, especially when disparities in consciousness and activity are manifold. Elbaum notes that Leninist centralized leadership worked in the short run but "lacked any substantial social base and were almost by definition hostile to all others on the left; they could never break out of the limits of a sect" (2002, p. 335). The size of membership has a profound qualitative impact on strategies employed and organisational models adopted. Elbaum warns that attempts to build a small revolutionary party (a party in embryo) "blinded movement activists to Lenin's view that a revolutionary party must not only be an 'advanced' detachment but must also actually represent and be rooted in a substantial, socialist-leaning wing of the working class" (2002, p. 335). Realistic and complex paths will need to be taken which will clearly be dependent on the state of the working-class movement itself.

It is axiomatic for the ongoing development of critical pedagogy that it be based upon an alternative vision of human sociality, one that operates outside the social universe of capital, a vision that goes beyond the market, but also one that goes beyond the state. It must reject the false opposition between the market and the state. Massimo De Angelis writes that "the historical challenge before us is that the question of alternatives . . . not be separated from the organisational forms that this movement gives itself" (2002, p. 5). Given that we are faced globally with the emergent transnational capitalist class and the incursion of capital into the far reaches of the planet, critical educators need a philosophy of organisation that sufficiently addresses the dilemma and the challenge of the global proletariat. In discussing alternative manifestations of anti-globalisation struggles, De Angelis itemises some promising characteristics as follows: the production of various counter-summits; Zapatista Encuentros; social practices that produce use values beyond economic calculation and the competitive relation with the other and inspired by practices of social and mutual solidarity; hor-

izontally-linked clusters outside vertical networks in which the market is protected and enforced; social cooperation through grassroots democracy, consensus, dialogue, and the recognition of the other; authority and social cooperation
developed in fluid relations and self-constituted through interaction; and a new
engagement with the other that transcends locality, job, social condition, gender, age, race, culture, sexual orientation, language, religion and beliefs. All of
these characteristics are to be secondary to the constitution of communal relations. He writes:

> The global scene for us is the discovery of the "other", while the local
> scene is the discovery of the "us", and by discovering the "us", we change
> our relation to the "other". In a community, commonality is a creative
> process of discovery, not a presupposition. So we do both, but we do it hav-
> ing the community in mind, the community as a mode of engagement with
> the other. (2002, p. 14)

But what about the national state? According to Ellen Meiksins Wood, "the
state is the point at which global capital is most vulnerable, both as a target of
opposition in the dominant economies and as a lever of resistance elsewhere. It
also means that now more than ever, much depends on the particular class
forces embodied in the state, and that now more than ever, there is scope, as
well as need, for class struggle" (2001, p. 291). Sam Gindin (2002) argues that
the state is no longer a relevant site of struggle if by struggle we mean taking
over the state and pushing it in another direction. But the state is still a relevant
arena for contestation if our purpose is one of transforming the state. He writes:

> Conventional wisdom has it that the national state, whether we like it or
> not, is no longer a relevant site of struggle. At one level, this is true. If our
> notion of the state is that of an institution which left governments can "cap-
> ture" and push in a different direction, experience suggests this will con-
> tribute little to social justice. But if our goal is to transform the state into an
> instrument for popular mobilisation and the development of democratic
> capacities, to bring our economy under popular control and restructure our
> relationships to the world economy, then winning state power would mani-
> fest the worst nightmares of the corporate world. When we reject strategies
> based on winning through undercutting others and maintain our fight for
> dignity and justice nationally, we can inspire others abroad and create new
> spaces for their own struggles. (2002, p. 11)

John Holloway's premise is similar to that of Gindin. He argues that we must
theorise the world negatively as a "moment" of practice as part of the struggle to
change the world. But this change cannot come about through transforming the
state through the taking of power but rather must occur through the dissolution of
power as a means of transforming the state and thus the world. This is because

the state renders people powerless by separating them from "doing" (human activity). In our work as critical educators, Holloway's distinction between power-to do (potentia) and power-over (potestas) is instructive. Power-to is a part of the "social flow of doing," the collective construction of a "we" and the practice of the mutual recognition of dignity. Power-over negates the social flow of doing thereby alienating the collective "we" into mere objects of instruction.

Holloway advocates creating the conditions for the future "doing" of others through a power-to do. In the process, we must not transform power-to into power-over, since power-over only separates the "means of doing" from the actual "doing" which has reached its highest point in capitalism. In fact, those who exercise power-over separate the done from the doing of others and declare it to be theirs. The doers then become detached from the origin of thought and practice, dehumanized to the level of instructed "objects" under the command of those that have assumed power-over. Power-over reduces people to mere owners and non-owners, flattening out relations between people to relations between things. It converts doing into a static condition of being. Whereas doing refers to both "we are" (the present) and "we are not" (the possibility of being something else) being refers only to "we are." To take away the "we are not" tears away possibility from social agency. The rule of power-over is the rule of "this is the way things are" which is the rule of identity. When we are separated from our own doing we create our own subordination. Power-to is not counter-power (which presupposes a symmetry with power) but anti-power.

Holloway reminds us that the separation of doing and done is not an accomplished fact but a process. Separation and alienation is a movement against its own negation, against anti-alienation. That which exists in the form of its negation—or anti-alienation (the mode of "being" denied) really does exist, in spite of its negation. It is the negation of the process of denial. Capitalism, according to Holloway, is based on the denial of "power-to", of dignity, of humanity, but that does not mean power-to (counter-capitalism) does not exist. Asserting our power-to is simultaneously to assert our resistance against subordination. This may take the form of open rebellion, of struggles to defend control over the labour process, or efforts to control the processes of health and education. Power-over depends upon that which it negates. The history of domination is not only the struggle of the oppressed against their oppressors but also the struggle of the powerful to liberate themselves from their dependence on the powerless. But there is no way in which power-over can escape from being transformed into power-to because capital's flight from labour depends upon labour (upon its capacity to convert power-to into abstract value-producing labour) in the form of falling rates of profit.

We are beginning to witness new forms of social organization as a part of revolutionary praxis. In addition to the Zapatistas, we have the important example of the participatory budget of the Workers Party in Brazil. And in Argentina we are seeing new forms of organized struggle as a result of the recent economic collapse of the country. We are referring here to the examples of the street protests of the *piqueteros* (the unemployed) currently underway and which first emerged about five years ago in the impoverished communities in the provinces. More recently, new neighborhood *asambleas* (assemblies) have arisen out of local streetcorner protests. Numbering around 300 throughout the country, these assemblies meet once a week to organize *cacerolas* (protests) and to defend those evicted from their homes, or who are having their utilities shut off, etc. The *asambleistas* (assembly members) also co-ordinate soup kitchens to feed themselves and others. This anti-hierarchical, decentralized, and grassroots movement consisting of both employed and unemployed workers, mostly women, has taken on a new urgency since December, 2002, when four governments collapsed in quick succession following Argentina's default on its foreign debt. Canadian activist Naomi Klein (2003) captures the spirit surrounding the creation of the *asambleas* when she writes:

> In Argentina, many of the young people fighting the neo-liberal policies that have bankrupted this country are children of leftist activists who were "disappeared" during the military dictatorship of 1976-'83. They talk openly about their determination to continue their parents' political fight for socialism but by different means. Rather than attacking military barracks, they squat on abandoned land and build bakeries and homes; rather than planning their actions in secret, they hold open assemblies on street corners; rather than insisting on ideological purity, they value democratic decision-making above all. Plenty of older activists, the lucky ones who survived the terror of the '70s, have joined these movements, speaking enthusiastically of learning from people half their age, of feeling freed of the ideological prisons of their pasts, of having a second chance to get it right.

A recent report in *News and Letters* adds to this description:

> What is remarkable is how ferociously opposed the *asambleas* are to being controlled, and to any hint of a vertical, top down hierarchy. They insist on independence, autonomy self-determination, encouraging all to learn how to voice their opinions and rotating responsibilities. They are explicitly for individual, personal self-development at the same time as they are for fighting the powers that be with everything they've got at their disposal. (2002, p. 6)

The larger *asambleas interbarriales* (mass meetings of the various *asambleas)* elect rotating delegates from the *asambleas* to speak and vote on issues that their local communities generate. In addition, workers have occupied a number of factories and work sites such as Brukman, Zanon, and Panificadora Cinco. Workers have also occupied a mine in Rio Turbio. Clearly, new revolutionary forms of organization are appearing. As Ernesto Herrera notes:

> The experiences of the piquetero movement and neighborhood assemblies
> allow the possibility of the construction of a revolutionary movement, a
> democratic popular power with a socialist perspective. The "great revolt"
> has put on the agenda the question of a strategy that links resistance and the
> struggle for power, representative democracy and/or the principle of revo-
> cability, the "saqueos" as acts of self-subsistence in food. (2002, p. 10)

Currently Brukman, a garment factory composed of 55 female workers,
aged 45-50, has proved symbolic in the struggle against the Argentine state.
Brukman workers are demanding public ownership of the factory, setting a dangerous precedent for the bourgeoisie. In fact, approximately twenty-five other
factories in Argentina are occupied by workers who are also demanding public
ownership. Workers in approximately two hundred and fifty other factories are
demanding some kind of state intervention for a type of workers' control (such
as forming cooperatives, etc.). They have formed a popular front to resist
assault from the state. However, assaults from the state continue. Over twenty-
five thousand people surrounded the Brukman factory recently to defend workers that had been expelled by the police, leading to numerous injuries and
arrests.

Of course, the *asambleas* confront many problems in that they are composed of members of different class fractions, with their many different political
agendas. Yet all of the *asambleas* hold the restratification of recently privatized
industries as a top priority (even as they reject vanguardist parties). At the same
time, in this new rise of popular mobilisation, as subjectivities become revolu-
tionized under the assault of capitalism, there needs to occur a programmatic
proposal for a political regroupment of the radical and anti-capitalist forces.
There must be more options available for organizers of the revolutionary left.
Herrera writes:

> In Mexico, the Zapatista movement could not translate its capacity of mobi-
> lization in the Consultas and Marches into a political alternative of the left.
> There was no modification of the relationship of forces. The theory of the
> "indefinite anti-power" or "changing the world without taking power" has
> produced neither a process of radical reforms, nor a revolutionary process.
> (2002, p. 13)

We are more optimistic about the possibilities of the Zapatista movement
than Herrera, but we do believe that whatever shape the struggle against imperialism and capitalist globalization will take, it will need to be international. We
believe in a multiracial, gender-balanced, internationalist anti-imperialist struggle. What appears promising are the rise of the Bolivarian Circles in Caracas,
Venezuela, a mass mobilization of working-class Venezuelans on behalf of
President Hugo Chavez. The Bolivarian Circles (named after Simon Bolivar)
serve as watchdog groups modeled after Cuba's Committee for the Defense of

the Revolution and function as liaisons between the neighborhoods and the government as well as fomenting support for Chavez. They are important in combating business leaders and dissident army generals whom, with U.S. support, are trying to overthrow the Chavez government. Members of the Bolivarian Circles bang on hollow electricity poles to warn against mobilizations by the opposition and to rally supporters across the city's working-class neighborhoods. They are an example of self-determination for sovereignty as evidenced by the Bolivarian declaration "Nuestra America: una sola patria" (Our America: one motherhood) which rejects an ideological loyalty to "America" as an America defined by a capitalist laden value system that favors imperialism and exploitation for increased profit margins. According to "Nuestra America" the people will not succumb to neoliberal modernity at the expense of becoming "scavengers of the industrial extravagance" (translation, Jaramillo). This movement is a clear signal that the present can be rewritten, there is an alternative, and the people can search for their own "America" (Nuestra America, 2003). In the spirit of this declaration we urge critical educators to pressure the International Monetary Fund (IMF) and World Bank to open their meetings to the media and to the public and to cancel the full measure of the debt they claim from underdeveloped counties, since such debts were accrued by dictators who used their IMF and World Bank loans to oppress their own people in the service of capital accumulation.

In the struggle against capitalism and its state formations, Alex Callinicos (2003) discusses two options: reformism within the anti-capitalist movement (as a result of the pressure posed by capital flight and currency crises, or in reaction to "rebellions of the rich" as seen recently in Venezuela)—a move that has witnessed center-left state bodies surrendering without a fight to the Washington Consensus. Here, the state is considered to be a vehicle through which social change can be successfully achieved. Callinicos, however, makes the important point that the state simply can't be used as an instrument of social transformation since it is already too implicated in the social relations of production and the bureaucratic apparatus centered on the means of coercion. Callinicos minces no words:

> Recent historical experience thus confirms the judgement made long ago by Marx and Lenin that the state can't simply be used as an instrument of social transformation. It is part of the capitalist system, not a means for changing it. The economic pressures of international capital—reflected particularly in the movements of money across the globe—push states to promote capital accumulation. Moreover, in the core of the state itself is a permanent bureaucratic apparatus centred on control of the means of coercion—the armed forces, police, and intelligence services—whose ultimate allegiance is not to elected governments but to the unelected ruling class.

A second option discussed by Callinicos is the one that is propounded by the autonomist wing of the anti-capitalist movement. This position renounces a reliance on the existing state and also eschews the objective of taking power from capital. Callinicos cites Tony Negri and John Holloway as perhaps the best known exponents of this position. Holloway's position is described by Callinicos as "an extreme form of commodity fetishism, in which all the apparently objective structures of capitalist society are simply alienated expressions of human activity, based on the separation of subject and object . . . doer and done." Holloway's "movement of negation" or "anti-power" suggests to Callinicos that "any attempt to understand capitalism as a set of objective structures implies the abandonment of Marx's original conception of socialism as self emancipation. Accordingly, virtually the entire subsequent Marxist tradition is dismissed as 'scientistic' and authoritarian."

Holloway's project of dissolving the fetishistic structures of alienated human activity and liberating the human qualities that are denied by capitalism is regarded by Callinicos as extremely troubling. For instance, he argues that the work of Holloway and Negri is being used in Argentina as a way of justifying "the idea that the small network of factories abandoned by their bosses and taken over by the workers represents the beginning of a new post-capitalist economy." While it is clear that Holloway realizes that the struggle against alienation must not leave productive processes in the control of capital, his approach suffers from a central contradiction. In the final analysis, Holloway's cry that "we do not struggle as working class, we struggle *against* being working class, against being classified" really amounts to attempting to abolish capitalist relations of production by pretending that they aren't there. If we are really determined to abolish capitalist social relations, it makes less sense to disidentify with working-class struggle than to build more effective forms of working-class struggle and organization. The point here is not to remain paralyzed by the fear that capitalism cannot be defeated but to help to cultivate an alternative source of power in capitalist society—what Callinicos describes as "the extraordinary capacities of democratic self organization possessed by the mass of ordinary people." While one route for this is trade unionism, such self organization against capitalism is not the sole preserve of workers' organization. Other possibilities include anti-capitalist, anti-war and anti-imperialist movements. The key to all attempts to organize social movements, argues Callinicos, is to develop and cultivate forms of organization that unite the working-class at local and national levels in the forms of workers' councils (here Callinicos is thinking about the forms of organization that emerge during mass strikes and popular upheavals of the working class). We have seen such forms of organization during the Russian Revolutions of 1905 and 1917, the Spanish Revolution of 1936, the Hungarian Revolution of 1956, the Iranian Revolution of 1978-79, and the rise of Solidarity in Poland in 1980-81. According to Callinicos:

> These workers' councils embody a more advanced form of democracy than
> is practiced in liberal capitalist societies. They are based on rank and file
> participation, decentralized decision making where people work and live,

and the immediate accountability of delegates to higher bodies to those who elected them. The councils represent an alterative way of running society to the centralized and bureaucratic forms of power on which capitalist domination depends.

The overarching goal is to develop the capacity of social movements to challenge successfully the core apparatuses of capitalist state power, and eventually replace the state altogether. Social movements can serve as points of departure and shed glimmers of hope for an alternative to the governing force of capital. The challenge for us is to recognize that the United States is as much a product of globalized capital as it is a producer of it and to translate social movements incubated within national borders into a widespread movement against capital. As Michael Löwy points out, in an unprecedented time when capital permeates lines of demarcation and casts its oppressive force through institutions such as the World Bank, International Monetary Fund, the World Trade Organization and the U.S. empire, what is lacking "is a network of political organizations—parties, fronts, movements, that can propose an alternative project inside the perspective of a new society, with neither oppressor nor oppressed." The multiplicity of social movements (albeit heterogeneous in composition and diverse in their beliefs on how to combat capital) do identify the same enemy—the transnational capitalist class. They recognize the broad scope of the current crisis, which encompasses a crisis of overproduction, a crisis of legitimacy of democratic governance, and a crisis of overextension that has dangerously depleted the world's material resources.

To address this point, we focus attention on the important work of James Petras and Henry Veltmeyer (2001) who challenge the egregious inequalities produced by transnational corporations and demand living wages for workers, food production for the urban poor, and land reform for peasants. Such a transformation points towards the importance of "development from below" which can be achieved through the democratization of the workplace by way of workers' and engineers' councils across international borders, accompanied by a "development from the inside." This refers to a major shift of ownership of production, trade and credit in order to expand food production and basic necessities to the poor who inhabit the "internal market". In order to bring about socialism— what Petras and Veltmeyer refer to as "an integral change based on transformations in the economic, cultural, and political spheres and based on understanding the multidimensional domination of imperialism" (2001, p. 166)—so-called Third World workers will face multiple obstacles that hinder their path. To face this challenge successfully, Petras and Veltmeyer argue that we must move from a globalized imperial export strategy towards an integrated domestic economy. It is important not to delink from world production on the basis of being self-reliant or because one believes it is possible to achieve "socialism in one country". It would be equally misguided, they note, to embrace a market socialism because it is unreasonable to assume that market forces, private ownership, and foreign investment directed by the government can build the basis of socialism. All economic exchanges—external and internal—must be subordinated to a democratic regime based on direct popular representation in territorial and productive units.

We argue that what needs to be emphasized and struggled for is not only the abolition of private property but also a struggle against alienated labor. The key point here is not to get lost in the state (nationalized capital) versus neoliberalism (privatized capital) debate. As the Resident Editorial Board of *News & Letters* have made clear, the real issue that must not be obscured is the need to abolish the domination of labor by capital. Capital needs to be uprooted through the creation of new human relations that dispense with value production altogether. This does not mean that we stop opposing neoliberalism or privatization. What it does mean is that we should not stop there.

One of the major tasks ahead is the breaking down of the separation between manual and mental labor. This struggle is clearly focused on dismantling the current capitalist mode of production and setting in motion conditions for the creation of freely associated individuals. This means working towards a concept of socialism that will meet the needs of those who struggle within the present crisis of global capitalism. We need here to project a second negativity that moves beyond opposition (that is, opposition to the form of property, i.e., private property)—a second or "absolute" negativity that moves towards the creation of the new. This stipulates not simply embracing new forms of social organization, new social movements, etc., but addressing new theoretical and philosophical questions that are being raised by these new spontaneous movements. We need a new philosophy of revolution, as well as a new pedagogy that emerges out of the dialectic of absolute negation (McLaren, in press).

Over the years we have made modest efforts to revive the fecundity of Marxist critique in the field of education. In contrast to many liberal educators who see Marxist theory as synonymous with much of the hidebound, box-trained, reductionistic discourse produced by the Second International, we believe that Marxist theory, in all of its heteronomous manifestations and theoretical gestation for well over a century, performs an irreplaceable analytical and political function of positing history as the mediator of human value production. Keening the death of Marxism will do little more than momentarily stir the ghost of the old bearded devil. Clearly, present day left educationalists need to "suspend the stale, existing (post)ideological coordinates" (Zizek, 2002, p. 195) in order to rethink the state as a terrain of contestation while at the same time developing a multiracial, gender-balanced, anti-imperialist and internationalist popular front. We have to keep our belief that another world is possible. We need to do more than to break with capital or abscond from it; clearly, we need to challenge its rule of value. One necessary (but not sufficient) way to proceed, in our view, is to develop a revolutionary critical pedagogy that will enable multiracial and gendered working-class groups to discover how capital exploits the use-value of their labour-power but also how working class initiative and power can destroy this type of determination and force a recomposition of class relations by directly confronting capital in all of its multi-faceted dimensions. This will require critical pedagogy not only to plot the oscillations of the labor/capital dialectic, but also to reconstruct the object context of class struggle to include school sites. Efforts also must be made to break down capital's creation of a new species of labour-power through current attempts to corporatise, businessify, and moralise the process of schooling and to resist the endless subordination of life in the social factory so many students call home (Cleaver, 2000; see also Rikowski, 2001). Novel ingressions towards rebuilding the educational left will not be easy, but neither will living under an increasingly militarised capitalist state where labour-power is constantly put to the rack to carry out the will of capital. As McLaren (2003) has noted elsewhere, while critical pedagogy may seem driven by lofty, high-rise aspirations that spike an otherwise desolate landscape of despair, it anchors our hope in the dreams of the present. Here the social revolution is not reborn in the aerosal insights of anti-foundationalist scholars which only increases ballast for the reigning liberal consensus, but emerges from the everyday struggle on the part of the oppressed to release themselves from the burdens of political detente and democratic disengagement. It is anchored, in other words, in class struggle (McLaren, 2003).

CRITICAL PEDAGOGY AND THE CIVIL SOCIETARIAN LEFT

We are living at a time in which civil society is being colonized by the bilious sentiments and hawkish political propaganda of right-wing media pundits, many of whom advocate for pre-emptive war against any country that impedes the continuation of the "American Way of Life" and who regularly denounce anti-war activists as traitors. While the media are often thought to play a key role in defending democracy, it is clear that today the U.S. corporate media largely serve the interests of the ruling elite, crippling what remains of civil society in the process. While Fox TV has been identified in the mainstream press as an "infotainment" vehicle for promoting and defending the agenda of the reactionary wing of the Republican Party, considerably less controversy has been stirred by the role of Clear Channel Communications, the nation's largest radio chain of about 1,200 radio stations (50 percent of the U.S. total). In one of his first acts as President, Bush *hijo* appointed the son of Secretary of State Colin Powell, Michael Powell, as chairman of the Federal Communications Commission. Powell controls the agency that regulates the domestic news and entertainment networks at a time in which the telecommunications industry is in the throes of unimpeded deregulation following the Telecommunications Act of 1996. And while Powell appears concerned about the possibility of anti-trust violations in the radio industry, the most concentrated ownership of all broadcast media, Clear Channel's acquisitions, led by a former Bush *hijo* business associate, Lowry Mays, continues unabated, despite current congressional investigations of its business practices. According to Stephen Marshall, since 9.11 Clear Channel "has been the most sycophantic and pro-militarist Big Media corporation" (2003, p. 24). All of its radio stations were issued songs to be blacklisted including "Peace Train" by Cat Stevens and "Imagine" by John Lennon. During the invasion of Iraq, Clear Channel began sponsoring pro-war, "support our troops" rallies across the United States they referred to as "Rally for America"—not so surprising, perhaps, for a corporation that supports Rush Limbaugh, but disturbing nonetheless for peace activists and critics of the Bush administration. Marshall reports: "Using its 1,200 stations, Clear Channel pummeled listeners with a mind-numbing stream of uncritical 'patriotism'" (2003, p. 24). Marshall further warns that "with Michael Powell, George W. Bush and Clear Channel the lines between political, military and corporate media power have become blurred into one authoritarian impulse" (2003, p. 24). Of course, other television and radio stations are following this lead. We wish to offer one case in point.

Defending its decision to give a weekly television program to Michael Savage, a controversial radio talk show host who specializes in racist, misogynistic, and homophobic diatribes against various groups, the MSNBC cable network—co-owned by Microsoft and General Electric/NBC called hiring Savage—whose show premiered on Saturday, March 8—"a legitimate attempt to expand the marketplace of ideas" (FAIR, 2003). Among other supreme acts of hatred, Savage has dismissed child victims of gunfire as "ghetto slime," referred to non-white countries as "turd ("turd" is a synonym for "shit") world nations," and calls homosexuality a "perversion" while at the same time he violently asserts that Latinos "breed like rabbits." And while MSNBC's formal report declared that its decision to hire Savage "underscores its commitment to ensuring that its perspective programming promotes no one single point of view" (see FAIR, 2003), the network chose to announce that a program hosted by liberal anti-war advocate, Phil Donahue, had been cancelled, even though the show received the highest ratings on the network.

A study commissioned by NBC described Donahue as "a tired, left-wing liberal out of touch with the current marketplace" and as such, he would be a "difficult public face for NBC in a time of war" (FAIR, 2003). The report stressed a fear that Donahue's show could become "a home for the liberal anti-war agenda at the same time as our competitors are waving the flag at every opportunity" (FAIR, 2003).

Savage has publicly asked the government to arrest the leaders of the anti-war movement in the case of war. And he has threatened to use his influence to put those who have complained about his upcoming show in jail. He has said that he would make an effort to have his enemies investigated and that he would use to his advantage the fact that the U.S. has a Republican Attorney General.

As critical educators, we condemn the double standards of the U.S. media, particularly in the case of MSNBC's hiring of Savage. We do not believe in a First Amendment (via the U.S. Constitution) absolutist position—a doctrine of pure, indiscriminate tolerance—that advocates the *de jure* right to express any opinion in public an abstract and indiscriminate defense of the right of any citizen to express any opinion in any way, regardless of its content or meaning or repressive societal impact. Not only must there be a consideration of content, there must also be standards of rationality (see Reitz, forthcoming). To advocate an "anything goes" approach rewrites anti-racism and anti-sexism as bigotry. We all participate in discussions as rational beings, and this obliges us to know the grounds of our convictions. Any authentic political culture must presuppose an educational and cultural context that does not try to wrest control of ideas but that honors opposing positions as a precondition for the pursuit of truth (see Reitz, 2003). In the case of Michael Savage, his *de jure* right to express his hate speech is contradicted by the *de facto* condition within the U.S. that left opinions challenging the ruling class are suppressed within the oligopolistic corporate media that "dramatize consciousness" (in the sense used by Raymond Williams) through sanitized abstractions and the management of meaning. Tolerance must become a liberating force, and not a repressive force, and as such pure tolerance of "free" speech must be challenged when it impedes the chances of creating a context in which people can live free of fear and violence. As Charles Reitz (2003) notes, drawing upon Herbert Marcuse, the First Amendment cannot be used to protect the speech and action of those intent upon destroying the right to liberty and civil rights of others. It appears that within the dominant logic of the corporate media and government institutions that support the media, prohibiting the hate speech of Michael Savage is a threat to democracy whereas the crimes of the right—imperialist attacks on sovereign nations, the exploitation of human labor, the support and training of terrorist groups in the name of U.S. interests—are tolerated in the name of democracy.

This brings us to a crucial question: How can critical educators reinvigorate the civil societarian left precisely at a time when we are creating a world where elites are less accountable to civil society than ever before? Takis Fotopoulous writes: "This new world order implies that, at the center, the model that has the greatest chance of being universalized is the Anglo-Saxon model of massive low-paid employment and underemployment, with poverty alleviated by the few security nets that the '40 per cent society' will be willing to finance, in exchange for a tolerable degree of social peace which will be mainly secured by the vast security apparatuses being created by the public and private sectors" (1997, p. 358).

If we persist with an internationalized market economy, the introduction of effective social controls to protect the underclass and the marginalized will create overwhelming comparative disadvantages for the nation state or the economic bloc that seeks to institute such policies. Additionally, if we accept that there is no alternative to working within the institutionalized market economy, then the neo-liberal policies of the ruling class make sense to the elites and under these circumstances there is a logic in rejecting the imposition of social controls by the civil societarian left. The only answer is one from without—we need to make our choice between socialism or barbarism. If we choose the latter, then we truly have no alternative than to sleep in the neoliberal bed that we have made for ourselves. If we choose socialism, then we must never abandon a vision for the radical transformation of society. As critical revolutionary educators who seek to transform the existing capitalist state into a socialist alternative, we can begin by revisiting our notions of democracy, by extending the traditional public realm to include the economic, ecological and social realms as well as the political realm (Fotopoulous, 1997). Democracy here is seen as a process of self-institution, where there exists no divinely or objectively defined code of human conduct.

A number of positions illuminated by Takis Fotopoulos (1997) on the creation of a revolutionary transition to socialism proves exceedingly instructive here for reconquering the notion of democracy and providing a politically robust concept of social justice. According to Fotopoulos, we need to develop a deeper conception of political democracy or direct democracy that includes economic, political, cultural, social, and ecological democracy. This falls under the rubric of what Fotopoulos calls "confederal inclusive democracy" and refers to the equal sharing of power among all citizens through the self-institution of society. This means that democracy is grounded in the choice of its citizens, mandating the dismantling of oligarchic institutionalized processes and eliminating institutionalized political structures embodying unequal power relations. Economic democracy must be institutionalized by eliminating oligarchic processes and giving over macro economic decisions to the citizen body whereas micro decisions at the workplace and household are taken over by the individual production or consumption unit. Here, the focus is on the needs of the community and not growth per se; where satisfaction of community needs does not depend upon the continuous expansion of production to cover the needs that the market creates.

Within this model of deep democracy, unequal economic power relations are structurally eliminated by assuring that the means of production and distribution are collectively owned and controlled by a multiracial citizen body. Democracy in the social realm refers to an equality of social relations in the household and in the social realm in general such as the workplace and the educational establishment. Cultural democracy means the creation of community controlled art and media activity. Democracy must also be ecologically sensitive, developing an expanded level of ecological consciousness which will work to create the institutional preconditions for radical change with respect to society's attitude toward nature, making it less instrumentalist and less likely to see nature as an instrument for growth within a practice of power creation. In sum, Fotopoulous's notion of inclusive democracy implies a new conception of political citizenship and the return to the classical concept of direct democracy; where economic citizenship involves new economic structures of "demotic" ownership and control of economic resources; where social citizenship involves self-management structures at the workplace, democracy in the household and new welfare structures where all basic needs are democratically determined and served by community resources; where cultural citizenship allows every community worker to develop their intellectual and cultural potential. Here Fotopoulous combines democratic and anarchist traditions with radical Green, feminist, and liberation traditions. In our view, such a reworked notion of citizenship is compatible with building independent working-class political action involving teachers and students and other cultural workers. As the basis of the self-organization of the working class, this transitional stage would include the confederation of workplace assemblies as part of a broader democratic movement directly linked to communities.

For critical revolutionary educators, the struggle for inclusive democracy stipulates working with students to build revolutionary consciousness and collective action as a means whereby we can resist our insinuation in the ugly truth of capital: that it is designed to separate the laborer from her labor. The fetishization and unequal distribution of life chances produced by capitalist social relations of production must be challenged by dialectical praxis. The center-left liberal covenant which enshrines resource distribution as the site of resistance, and seeks to calibrate social transformation according to how easily it can be integrated into a more "compassionate" capitalism with a human face, must be directly challenged by a coherent philosophy of praxis that directly confronts globalized capital with a socialist alternative. It can pitch this challenge within the framework of an intergenerational, multiracial, transnational and anti-imperialist social movement. This will not be an easy task, especially at this current moment of political despair that has infected much of the educational left. It will require radical hope.

Hope is the freeing of possibility, with possibility serving as the dialectical partner of necessity. When hope is strong enough, it can bend the future backward towards the past, where, trapped between the two, the present can escape its orbit of inevitability and break the force of history's hubris, so that what is struggled for no longer remains an inert idea frozen in the hinterland of "what is", but becomes a reality carved out of "what could be". Hope is the oxygen of dreams, and provides the stamina for revolutionary struggle. Revolutionary dreams are those in which the dreamers dream until there are no longer dreamers but only the dreams themselves, shaping our everyday lives from moment to moment, and opening the causeways of possibility where abilities are nourished not for the reaping of profit, but for the satisfaction of needs and the full development of human potential.

The days ahead will witness furious attempts by the petrolarchs of the Bush administration to justify its political and military occupation. They will say that they are making the world safe for freedom and democracy and providing opportunities for other countries to benefit from "the American Way of Life." This will be accompanied by attempts by the Bush administration to get a whole new generation of nuclear weapons into production in order to meet their expanded "national security objectives." And they have most of the evangelical

Christian communities behind these initiatives. It looks as though the American public will be left out of the debate. Why should Bush care about what the American people think? They didn't vote for him.

Currently the most important front against capitalism is stopping the U.S. from invading more countries, since the administration's National Security Strategy of the United States of America establishes an irrevocable connection between U.S. global domination and the neoliberal Washington consensus (Callinicos, 2003a). Callinicos warns that

> If the U.S. is victorious in Iraq, then it is more likely to go on the offensive in Latin America, the zone in the south where resistance to neoliberalism is most advanced. Even if the B-52s and Special Forces aren't directly deployed against Brazilian landless laborers or Argentinian piqueteros, victory for U.S. military power will weaken the struggle against poverty and hunger everywhere.

Commenting on imperialistic sentiment of the American people (with specific historical reference to Mexico), John Dewey (1927) wrote that "it is only too easy to create a situation after which the cry 'stand by the President,' and then 'stand by the country,' is overwhelming. . . . Public sentiment, to be permanently effective, most do more than protest. It must find expression in a permanent change of our habits." Addressing U.S. imperialism since September 11, 2002, Gilbert Aschar (2002, p. 81) portentously warns: "The real, inescapable question is this: is the US population really ready to endure even more September 11s, as the unavoidable price of a global hegemony that only benefits its ruling class?" Perhaps it's time to give consideration to comments coming not from the theater of war but the theater of playwrights and actors. Recently, Peter Ustinov observed: "Terrorism is the war of the poor, and war is the terrorism of the rich" (cited in Berger, 2003, p. 34).

We reject the notion, advanced by Foucault and other post-structuralists, that posing a vision of the future only reinforces the tyranny of the present. Similarly, we reject Derrida's insistence that the fetish is not opposable. It is self-defeating in our view to embrace the advice of many postmodernists: that all we can do is engage in an endless critique of the forms of thought defined by commodity fetishism. In contrast, we believe that we can do more than enjoy our symptoms in a world where the subjects of capitalism have been endlessly disappearing into the vortex of history (see Hudis, 2003). As Peter Hudis (2003) notes, such defeatism arises as long as critics believe that value production within capitalism is natural and immutable. We believe that the value form of mediation within capitalism is permeable and that another world outside of the social universe of capital is possible. We are also committed to the idea that revolutionary critical pedagogy can play a role in its realization. The voices and actions of critical educators will become more crucial in the days ahead. Whatever organizational forms their struggles take, they will need to address a global audience who share the radical hope that a new world outside the social universe of capital is possible.

REFERENCES

Aschar, Gilbert. (2002). *The Clash of Barbarisms: September 11 and the Making of the New World Disorder*. New York: Monthly Review Press.

Berger, John. (2003). Fear Eats the Soul. *The Nation*, vol. 276, no. 18 (May 12), pp. 33-35.

Callinicos, Alex. (2003). State of Discontent. *Socialist Review*, no. 272 (March). http://www.swp.org.uk/SR/272/SR2.htm

Callinicos, Alex. (2003a). War Under Attack. *Socialist Review*, no. 273 (April). http://www.swp.org.uk/SR/273/SR2.htm

Cleaver, Harry. (2000). *Reading Capital Politically*. Leeds: Antitheses and Edinburgh: AK Press.

Cockburn, Alexander. (2003). Yes, War Really is Hell. *The Nation*, vol. 276, no. 16 (April 28), p. 12.

De Angelis, Massimo. (2002). From Movement to Society. *The Commoner*. no. 4 (May). http://www.commoner.org.uk/01-3groundzero.htm

Dewey, John (1927). "Imperialism is Easy." *The New Republic* 50 (March 23). http//www.boondocksnet.com/ai/ailtexts/dewey.html. In Jim Zwick, ed., *Anti-Imperialism in the United States, 1898-1935*. http://www.boondocksnet.com/ai/

Elbaum, Max (2002). *Revolution in the Air: Sixties Radicals turn to Lenin, Mao and Che*. London and New York: Verso.

Fairness & Accuracy In *Reporting, activism update*. (March 7, 2003). "MSNBC's Double Standard on Free Speech "Turd World" is OK—"anti-war, anti-Bush" is not."

Fisk, Robert. (2003). For the people on the streets, this is not liberation but a new colonial oppression. *The Independent*. (April 17). http://argument. independent.co.uk/commentators/story.jsp?story=397925

Fisk, Robert. (2003a). Library Books, Letters and Priceless Documents Are Set Ablaze in Final Chapter of the Sacking of Baghdad. *The Independent*. (April 15). http://argument.independent.co uk/commentators/story.jpp?story=397350

Fisk, Robert. (2003b). Americans Defend Two Untouchable Ministries From the Hordes of Looters. *The Independent*. (April 14). http://162.42.211.226/article2918.htm

Fotopoulos, Takis. (1997). *Towards an Inclusive Democracy: The Crisis of the Growth Economy and the Need for a New Liberatory Project*. London and New York: Cassell.

Gibbs, David N. (2001). Washington's New Interventionism: U.S. Hegemony and Inter Imperialist Rivalries. *Monthly Review*, vol 53, no. 4 (September), pp. 15-37.

Gindin, Sam. (2002). Social Justice and Globalization: Are They Compatible? *Monthly Review*, vol. 54, no. 2 (June), pp. 1-11.

Grandin, Greg. (2003). What's a Neoliberal to Do? *The Nation*, vol. 276, no. 9 (March 10), pp. 25-29.

Greider, William. (2003). The Right's Grand Ambition: Rolling Back the 20th Century. *The Nation*, vol. 276, no. 18 (May 12), pp. 11-19.

Herrera, Ernesto. (2002). Latin America: The Current Situation and the Task of Revolutionaries. *Fourth International Press*. pp. 1-16. Wednesday, July 17. Fl-press—I@mail.comlink.apc.org.

Holloway, John. (2002). Twelve Theses On Changing the World Without Taking Power. *The Commoner*, no. 4 (May). http://www.commoner.org.uk/04holloway2.pdf

Kean, Fergal. (2003). A dangerous groundswell of resentment is building up on the streets of Baghdad. *The Independent*. (April 19) http://argument.independent.co.uk/low_res/story.jsp?story=398447$host=6&dir=154

Klein, Naomi. (2003). Privatization in Disguise. *The Nation*. (April 15). In AlterNet.org. http://www.altanet.org/story.html?StorvID= 15638

Klein, Naomi. (2003). Demonstrated Ideals. *Los Angeles Times*. (April 20). http://www.calendarlive.com/books/bookreview/cl-bk-klein20apr20.story

Lemannn, Nicholas. (2002). The Next World Order. *The New Yorker*. (January 4). http://www.newyorker com/fact/content/?020401fa_FACT1

Löwy, Michael. (2002) Debate: Towards a New International? *Revista Rebeldia*, no. 2, (December). http://www.revistarebeldia.org

Marshall, Stephen. (2003). Prime Time Payola. *In These Times*. vol. 27, no. 11-12 (May 5), pp. 23-24.

McLaren, Peter. (2003). Critical Pedagogy and Class Struggle in the Age of Neoliberal Globalization. *Democracy and Nature*, vol. 9, no. 1 (March), pp. 65-90.

Mendonca, Maria Luisa. (2003). New Challenges for Brazilian Grassroots Movements. *Economic Justice News*, Vol. 6, no. 1 (April), pp. 3, 14-15.

Moberg, David. (2003). The Road from Baghdad. *In These Times*, vol. 27, no. 11-12 (May 5), pp. 16-18.

Nuestra America: una sola patria. (2003). Found at http://www.unasolapatria.org/documento.html

Petras, James and Veltmeyer, Henry. (2001). *Globalization Unmasked: Imperialism in the 21st Century*. Halifax, Canada and London, England: Fernwood Publishing and Zed Books.

Reitz, Charles. (2000). *Art. Alienation. and the Humanities: A Critical Engagement with Herbert Marcuse*. Albany: State University Press of New York.

Reitz, Charles. (forthcoming). Herbert Marcuse and the New Culture Wars: Campus Codes, Hate Speech, and the Critique of Pure Tolerance. *New Political Science*, vol. 25, no. 2 (June 2003).

Research Unit for Political Economy, The. (2002). The Real Reason for the US Invasion: The Current Strategic Agenda of the United States. *Aspects of India's Economy*, nos. 33 & 34 (December). http://rupe-india.org/34/reasons.html and http://www.rupe-india.org/34/agenda/html

Resident Editorial Board, The. (2002). *News & Letters*, vol. 47. no 6 (July), pp. 5-8.

Rice, Condoleezza. (2000). Campaign 2000: Promoting the National Interest. *Foreign Affairs*. (January/February). http://www.foreignaffairs.org/2000010faessay5/condoleezza-rice/campaign2000-promoting-the-national-interest.html

Rikowski, Glenn. (2001) *The Battle in Seattle: Its Significance for Education*. London: Tufnell Press.

Rutherglen, Susannah. (2003). The Violent Obliteration of Art and Memory. *Yale Daily News*. (April 15). http://www.yaledailynews.com/article/asp?AID=22603.

Saletan, William. (2002). The Soft Bigotry of Loose Adulation. *Slate* (April 10). http://www.slate.msn.com/id/2081213/

Wood, Ellen Meiksins. (2001). Contradictions: Only in Capitalism. In L. Panitch and C. Leys, eds. *A World of Contradictions, Socialist Register*. London: Merlin.

Zizek, S. (2002). *Repeating Lenin*. Unpublished manuscript.

PART 2

THE POLITICS OF
MULTICULTURAL
EDUCATION

9 DIS-INVESTING WHITENESS TOWARD A COMMON STRUGGLE FOR SOCIAL JUSTICE

Peter McLaren and Juan S. Muñoz

There is nothing positive about white identity. As James Baldwin said, "As long as you think you're white, there's no hope for you." Whiteness is not a culture. There is Irish culture and Italian culture and American culture; there is youth culture and drug culture and gear culture. There is no such thing as white culture. Shakespeare was not white; he was English. Mozart was not white; he was Austrian. Whiteness has nothing to do with culture and everything to do with social position. Without the privileges attached to it, there would be no white race, and fair skin would have the same significance as big feet. (Ignatiev, 1998, p. 199)

INTRODUCTION

Increasingly, the context in which race, ethnicity and identity is being evaluated is shifting with staggering intensity underscoring the need to establish critical but provisional conceptions which are discernible without being essentialist, but not so completely de-essentialized so as to become meaningless. The interactive and routinely synergistic affects of race, ethnicity and identity are multidimensional and play out on a fieldtypically unexamined by the social actors that are most affected by these categorical processes. Indeed, these three fields comprise unambiguous efforts to construct categories of humanity which the untrained observer may presume ebb and flow across entirely indistinguishable boundaries. Race, ethnicity and identity are, for all intent and purpose presented for public consumption as not simply co-informants but completely inter-change-

Sections of this paper appear in Peter McLaren, *Revolutionary Multiculturalism* (Boulder, Colo.: Westview Press, 1997). We want to thank Carlos Ovando for his excellent editorial suggestions and for his support and encouragement.

able. Cloaking the social construction of race, ethnicity, and identity, while further conflating these significant characterizing paradigms as synonymous, serves to undermine aggressive efforts by critical thinkers and cultural workers to disaggregate the political nature and white supremacist ideology which these imposed and proscriptive demarcations have historically represented. Moreover, the ability to cover and conceal the epistemological impulses distinctive to race, ethnicity and identity minimize the potential for these paradigms to be rearticulated, and yield significant sources of critique and analysis to understanding how they act in the service of power and privilege.

Among the various constituents of identity, race and ethnicity Whiteness is rarely assailed as a racialized practice of power and privilege, exactly because of its ubiquitous and invisible presence. That is, whitness as a racialized practice within social conventions has been expressed and interpreted as the perpetual and uncontested anchor of normality. Whitness has been positioned—and subsequently serves to re-position the *Other*—as the backdrop against which alternative or unconventional social practices and cultural formations are judged, thus ascribing an unprecedented degree of authority and power to its membership and their ethnocentric cultural social and ideological expressions. However, even among criticalist and other cultural workers there is considerable inattention to the various ways in which ethnicity and race informs white identity. Whiteness is universalized as an identity that both supersedes and transcends ethnicity. Rarely are we provided in public discussions of race opportunities to recognize the epistemological, phenomenological, metaphysical, political, or ethical implications of racialized social practices in our everyday experiences as racialized subjects. These dilemmas are symptomatic of an image of identity that forecloses consideration of its broader political dimensions. Within increasingly globalized commodity cultures, such "cultural" differences become transformed into consumer "lifestyle" choices. In other words, the cultural characteristics associated with different ethnic groups begin as distinctions between cultural traditions and expressions, however, after time these distinctions assume economic dimensions justifying the manipulations of ethnic groups for profit and power. Another phase to transforming cultural difference to consumer practices involves re-covering the original discourse used to establish different groups according to cultural difference, and understanding how this logic is reformulated to introduce economic motives to cultural difference which did not exist originally. Thus, in a sophisticated reversal of politics of culture and identity, the dominant cultural environment responsible for imparting ethnic groups with their sense of identity becomes inseparable from a record of economic manipulations. Rarely are ethnic discourses and practices interrogated for the interests that they serve and the social arrangements that they privilege.

ORIGINS OF MULTICULTURAL EDUCATION

Multicultural education originated in the 1960s as an offspring of the civil rights movement and its fundamental concern with freedom, political power, and economic equality (Sleeter and McLaren 1995). It was as much a political and ethical response to conflagrations of power as it was an educational reaction to the growing concerns of teachers and parents who aligned themselves with the social, political, cultural, and economic struggles of besieged and embattled ethnic groups during the tumultuous struggles over integration. While much of the direction of multicultural education can be traced to African American activism and community involvement in struggles over the curriculum, multicultural education today has multiplied its vision, and its constituencies now include broad participation and leadership from Asian American, Latino/a, and other communities. Discussing the origins of the term *multicultural education*, Sleeter and McLaren (1995) write:

> The prefix "multi" was adopted as an umbrella to join diverse groups of color. . . . The term "multiethnic education" was used to bridge racial and ethnic groups; "multicultural education" broadened the umbrella to include gender and other forms of diversity. The term "culture" rather than "racism" was adopted mainly so that audiences of white educators would listen. (12)

Mainstream liberal multiculturalism with its signature stress on diversity and its "normative grammar" of inclusion has given way in the 1990s to more heterogeneous strands on the periphery of the educational establishment that call for stronger links with workers' and women's movements, bilingual education associations, indigenous rights groups, and gay and lesbian organizations (see McLaren 1997a, 1977b). And while the increasing politicization of multicultural education has resulted in what has sometimes been seen as the "culture wars" surrounding political correctness and ethnic separatism, multicultural education in the main has remained quarantined within a fairly domesticated political project that has focused on a vociferous yet relatively nonthreatening call for ethnic diversity and inclusion. While by no means has this mainstream project congealed into a fully articulated, all-encompassing theory, it has been given a greater command than the more critical "multiculturalisms" (i.e., Grant 1998; Kincheloe and Steinberg 1997; May 1999; McLaren 1997; Sleeter and McLaren 1995) in the public arena of programs and policy.

While our emphasis in this chapter is mainly on issues of class exploitation in the present global economy and its relationship to racism, whiteness, color-blindness, and multicultural education, we acknowledge a fundamental interrelationship among struggles involving race, class, gender, and sexual orientation. We would like to underscore at the outset that we are not attempting to place the importance of class above race, or race above issues of gender or sexuality, but rather we are resituating the project of multicultural education in general from a point of view that takes seriously the current restructuring of capitalism on a global basis and is willing to consider what this might mean for challenging the hegemony of white privilege. In doing so we assume the explanatory primacy—not exclusivity—of economic determinations as our major premise.

MULTICULTURAL EDUCATION AND CAPITALIST SOCIAL RELATIONS

Multicultural education has received more attention over recent years since demographic studies now indicate that people of color will constitute the majority of the United States population during the twenty-first century (McLaren 1995; Sleeter and McLaren 1995). Multicultural educators recognize that the relationship between marginalized and disenfranchised groups of U.S. citizens and public education has been dramatically affected by the social, political, and economic influences texturing the communities in which they live and the schools they attend (La Belle and Ward 1994).

Mainstream multiculturalism's quest for the elusive holy grail of cultural diversity has at times offered tantalizing promises, but in our view, can unwittingly prove functional for the reproduction of capitalist relations of power and privilege and the international imperialist order and an ultimate barrier to the task of erecting a broader social movement that also includes struggles over class, gender, and sexual orientation. In fact, from the bourgeois standpoint, mainstream multicultural education has served as an educational diversion from the theoretical and programmatic contributions of leftist critiques of capitalist social relations and exhibits a generic tendency to evade the political implications of the anticapitalist struggle in general. We believe that multicultural education has in the main ignored relations of class exploitation. We are especially troubled by this structured silence because we now inhabit a historical conjuncture of globalized capitalism in which neoliberal economics and social policy are greatly exacerbating as well as racializing the social division of labor.

The work of David Theo Goldberg is instructive in this regard. Goldberg states that among the multi-layered challenges facing those committed to exposing the interested and privileged social arrangement in the West is an ubiquitous epistemology of exclusion predicated on racist assumptions dating back to the birth of modernity. We believe that it is time to go beyond current positions on multiculturalism and their mutual anathemas and move toward a supersession of past divisions. What multicultural education above all needs today is an advance beyond the threshold of the division between race and class, toward the point where the transformation of capitalist relations of exploitation becomes the practical terminus.

The multicultural left in the United States is caught in the powerful pincers of current economic history. The top jaw is the deregulation of the global economy, and the bottom jaw is the neoliberal philosophy that emphasizes an acceleration of cuts in social spending, including deep reductions in education spending. Abetted by their centrist adaptations to the reformist forces of progressive educators and policy makers, and under camouflage of cheap, carnival barking for liberal democratic values, much of the multicultural left is busy feathering a nest with mainstream liberals and conservatives whose work remains devoid of any substantial critique of capitalism. Having imbibed the comforting aroma of capitalism's inevitability, even some erstwhile members of the radical left are dancing on the grave of the former Soviet Union, overtly disavowing their once highly esteemed socialist ideals. The rightward lunge of the pseudo-multicultural left and its unquestionable thirst for capitulation to the disintegrative character of bourgeois liberal reforms is disheartening. The educational swamp of liberal reformism into which most educational progressives now sink is infested with the world-historical arrogance of a neoliberalism that sees the untrammeled free market as the answer to all social programs, including education, even as neoliberal reforms call for a frontal assault against public education, support a voucher system, and encourage the privatization of schooling. Liberal reformism conduces to a partial counterconstrual to its own democratic premises: By incanting "diversity" as a solution to inequality, it fails to target the underlying matrix of power relations upon which such diversity will rest, namely, the social relations of white supremacist capitalist patriarchy.

More specifically, multicultural education has been impoverished by proponents who fail to link racism to capitalist social relations but instead perceive it to be primarily a problem confined to the realm of psychological disposition, pathological attitude formation, or epistemological claims. Such proponents have gutted multicultural education of its most profound political implications such as the anticapitalist struggle and the struggle against white supremacy. In our view, multicultural education can be transformed in a satisfactory way only if it adopts a fundamental stance against capitalist relations of exploitation and addresses the process of imperialism, the social relations of production, and the construction of white privilege. Here we take the position that systematic racism is an ideology and set of social and cultural practices that grew out of slavery in which the act of discrimination created categories and criteriologies of difference and hierarchical systems of classification that served to universalize and naturalize imperialist aggression and dominant social relations of exploitation.

The ideological charter of public schooling that grounds contemporary educational practice throughout the United States is the same today as it was during the early nineteenth century: to socialize students and to assimilate them into the labor market and international division of labor. We live in a world in which the material production under capitalism is subordinate to the production of surplus value (or profit) and those who monopolize the ownership of the means of production are able to appropriate this surplus value. Rather than educate people to question their social location within the market economy, education was designed by the employer class to inculcate specific industrial skills necessary for individuals to perform within a heavily dominated manufacturing labor market so that their surplus value could be extracted by the capitalist class. And while today's global marketplace has seen sweeping new adjustments, along with vast and accelerated changes with respect to the skills necessary to succeed within it, the exploitation of the many by the few has remained a disturbing constant. We argue that critical educators need to acknowledge the process of disorganized and uneven capitalist development and commit themselves to anti-imperialist struggle against global hierarchies of power and privilege whose chief western guardian is the United States.

Capitalism's worldwide structural crisis is linked to the internal logic of the capitalist system itself and is manifested in overaccumulation and failure to utilize fully its productive capacity. The reorganization of the labor process has significantly altered the relation between capital and labor. Capital is eliminating multiple layers of management, administration, and production to lower costs. Deindustrialization, capital flight, the ascendancy of financial and speculative capital, the expansion of transnational circuits of migrant workers, and the deproletarianized surplus labor force have created radically new social conditions throughout most of the globe. We are witnessing in unprecedented scope the globalization of capital; the domination of the economy by monopolies, oligopolies, and cartels as capital investment hurriedly moves to cheaper markets offering a higher rate of exploitation; the decline of corporate taxes; tax increases on the working class in the form of state-run gambling and lotteries; and reduced social expenditures in health, education, and social services. We are also witnessing the development of "free" economic zones; a powerful business counterattack in response to sporadic minor victories by labor; the relieving of the state of any barriers that might restrict private accumulation; the state's growing indebtedness to corporate bondholders; the constitutional enshrinement of the rights of private property; the discouragement of social redistribution policies; the privatization of municipal services; a massive assault on trade unionism; draconian attacks on social assistance; a conviction that capital is self-regulating; and the drastic reduction of state interventions in the economy and social life that have grown with the development of capital (Teeple 1995). The move toward deregulation has been described as one that is tantamount to progress. For example, the *New York Times* reported that Russian free-market advocates "faced the mammoth task of civilizing their country" (Parenti 1998, 178). Of course, in reality, the globalization of the economy has brought nothing but massive unemployment and misery to Russia and the former Eastern bloc countries as well as to countries within Latin America (McLaren 1999; 1998). In the case of Latin America and Asia, the International Monetary Fund has put together multibillion-dollar bailouts in return for austerity measures that mandate major spending cuts and accelerate liberalization and deregulation in economies that are still characterized by strong state interventions.

Unfettered capitalism—what some have called "casino capitalism," "fast capitalism," or "tycoon capitalism"—is not only objectionable on ethical grounds. It does not work even within the terms of its own logic. Brenner (1998) notes, "If, after more than two decades of wage-cutting, tax-cutting, reductions in the growth of social expenditure, deregulation and 'sound finance,' the ever less fettered 'free market' economy is unable to perform half as well as in the 1960s, there might be some reason to question the dogma that the freer market, the better the economic performance" (238).

The United Nations reported that in 1996, the assets held by the world's 358 billionaires exceeded the combined incomes of countries with 45 percent of the world's people, exacerbating the rich-poor divide in the most grotesque form imaginable (Gates 1998). Manning Marable (1998) notes that between 1973 and 1989, the overall average annual income of all wage earners living in U.S. cities dropped by 16 percent. For instance, in 1990, the median annual incomes of the poorest fifth and the wealthiest fifth in Los Angeles were, $6,821 and $123,098, respectively. In Chicago, the gap was $4,743 versus $86,632. In Detroit, it was $3,109 versus $63,625. Forty million U.S. citizens today lack any form of medical insurance (5-6).

Critical multicultural education and critical pedagogy historically have set out to contest vigorously the persistence of race, class, and gender inequalities, whether they are based on the ownership of property, the possession of credentials, or the persistence of patriarchy and homophobia. Education was often criticized by multicultural educators as a way of adjusting young people to the inevitability of these inequalities rather than motivating them to claim their own historical agency by struggling against them. As a means of contesting the fact that schooling in the United States is functionally advantageous to the reproduction of class and cultural assimilation, critical educators introduced "political literacy" to students through Paulo Freire well-known practice of "conscientization." "Conscientization" involves learning to perceive, resist, and transform the social, political, and economic contradictions within the learner's everyday world as well as within the macrostructure of social life in general (Freire 1970). And while the agenda of "conscientization" still prevails among many multicultural educators, it is undeniably the case that critical education in general has become politically domesticated. That is, it has been toned down so that it poses no significant threat to the status quo (McLaren in press a, in press b). The continued assault on public education as well as the ascendancy of neoliberal educational policy and practices have undercut the foundation for transforming multicultural educational into a larger political project that could transform structures of oppression on a wide scale. Another reason for the domestication of critical pedagogy and multicultural education has been its alignment with conservative forms of postmodern educational critique (McLaren 1995; McLaren in press a). This follows from a recession of Marxist critique in the former heartlands of educational theory—the sociology of education and curriculum studies—which have now been overtaken by the voguish apostasy of post-structuralist and postmodernist critiques with their emphasis on "power/knowledge relations" and their disabling abstention from social relations of production.

While critical pedagogy and critical multicultural education advocates do not always agree with one another on the extent to which critical education should be linked to wider social movements, they are in general agreement that the educational system should reflect the concerns of diverse groups and that individuals must learn to collaborate and organize to bring about social change even at the expense of a radical alteration of current social arrangements. More specifically, critical pedagogy and critical multicultural education offer insight into the possible dismantling of white privilege and hegemony and a counter-hegemonic position to mainstream educational positions on educational "success." According to Christine Sleeter and Carl Grant (1994), conventional educational approaches assume that all students will be guaranteed social and economic opportunities commensurate with their level of education regardless of race, class, gender, and ethnicity. As individuals increase their "human capital" through an accumulation of educational experiences, they will appreciably affect their quality of life and social standing through a "bootstrap effect." Or so the story goes. The notion that the market will reward the degree to which individuals are presumed to obtain higher levels of human capital displays the temper, if not the letter, of the mainstream position. Schools are targeted as critical junctures where human capital (knowledge and skills), is transmitted or withheld. While critical pedagogy and critical multicultural education challenges these mainstream assumptions, what rarely accompanies such critiques is a sustained critique of capitalism. Of greater significance than this lapse is its facilitating condition: the supposed separation of educational "success" from the perpetuation of those conditions disabling to the elimination of race and class privilege.

THE RELATIONSHIP BETWEEN CAPITALISM, RACISM, AND MULTICULTURAL EDUCATION

Antiracism is, of course, one of the key components of virtually any multicultural curriculum. However, in our view, racism is inextricably linked to capitalism. So for multicultural educators to address racism, they must also address the reality of capitalism. Ultimately, to abolish racism, we need to abolish global capitalism.

Racism occurs when the characteristics that justify discrimination are held to be inherent in the oppressed group. This form of oppression is peculiar to capitalist societies; it arises in the circumstances surrounding industrial capitalism and the attempt to acquire a large labor force. Callinicos (1993) notes the way in which Marx grasped how racial divisions between "native" and immigrant workers could weaken the working class and make it easily susceptible to exploitation. U.S. politicians take advantage of this division, which the capitalist class understands and manipulates only too well. George Bush, Jesse Helms, Pat Buchanan, Phil Gramm, David Duke, and Pete Wilson have effectively used racism to divide the working class.

Today the globalization of capital has put so much pressure on the working and middle classes in general that the dominant Anglo-European population is trying to hold on to its advantage by abolishing all initiatives that assist minority populations. Symptomatic of such contemporary racism in the capitalist economy, multicultural education today is coming under a powerful assault by anti-immigration organizations, conservative Christian fundamentalist groups, and conservative politicians who are interested in promoting a neo-liberal economic and cultural agenda. In California, the backlash from the right has led to the abolition of affirmative action for minority groups and women. It has also led to public initiatives that have abolished bilingual education, limited medical provisions and schooling for undocumented immigrants, and restricted immigration. It has also led to a growth of white supremacist organizations and citizen militia movements that support and practice racist agendas.

What is so pernicious and feral about the dominant class position is that proponents replicate one of the generic vices of mainstream education in arguing that affirmative action should be abolished on the grounds that race should not be a factor in one's ability to secure a job. They argue instead that jobs should be acquired on the basis of one's "merit" or "qualifications" alone. But what the Anglo-Europeans do not recognize when they enjoin U.S. citizens to be "color-blind" is that European Americans securely hold the structural advantage in all levels of society. They do not recognize that racism and class exploitation is still widespread in U.S. society. And what is even worse is that some conservative African Americans and Latinos/as have joined forces with the European American power elite in calling for an end to affirmative action programs. What the power elite fails to acknowledge publicly is that there has always been affirmative action for European Americans—an advantage that was secured (and is still secured today) through colonization, imperialism, and racism. Consequently, without affirmative action for people of color, the dominant European American population will function virtually uncontested. The myth of color-blindness suggests that the cultural sphere in the United States has been fully integrated and that social and economic equality have been realized. This is patently false, of course, but serves as a convenient lie, and it is in the interest of the dominant power elite to keep it alive.

Racism, which is alive and well in the United States, has had a long and deeply ingrained history. For example, more than two hundred years ago, Benjamin Franklin wrote:

> Why increase the Sons of *Africa*, by planting them in America, where we have so fair an Opportunity, by excluding all Blacks and Tawneys, of increasing the lovely White and Red? (cited in Perea 1995, 973)

Woodrow Wilson, considered by many to be one of the most unblemished presidents of the twentieth century, was an unrepentant white supremacist who believed that black people were inferior to white people. In fact, Wilson ordered that black and white workers in federal government jobs be segregated. Among other things, he vetoed a clause on racial equality in the Covenant of the League of Nations, and his wife told "darky" stories in cabinet meetings (Loewen 1995). The next president, Warren G. Harding, was inducted into the Ku Klux Klan in a ceremony at the White House (Loewen 1995). How many students can boast knowledge of these facts? How can U.S. history books cover up these events and hundreds of others, including the 1921 race riot in Tulsa, Oklahoma, in which whites dropped dynamite from an airplane onto a black community, destroying eleven hundred homes and killing seventy-five people (Loewen 1995)?

The experience of Latinos/as in the United States provides another example of deeply rooted racist attitudes. In his eighteenth-century study of Mexico, the historian William Robertson (1777) offered a distorted presentation that tainted the colonists' perceptions of Mexicans for generations to follow. The assessment that Robertson offered of Mexicans was fundamentally informed by his repugnantly low estimation of the character of Spaniards as well as of Mexican aboriginals, whose racial fusion gave rise to the modern biological Mexican archetype. For Robertson,

> the Mexican stood as the fiercest and most detestable of the New World peoples, inferior culturally to the Incas and in qualities of character to the North American native. By also arguing that the Spaniards who were attracted to America were the most undesirable elements of their society, Robertson offered to his readers a Mexico populated by two extraordinary breeds of scoundrels already mixing their blood. (Paredes 1978, 156).

Negative stereotypes of the Mexican continued into the twentieth century. Even as Chicanos were fighting with distinction in World War II throughout Europe, the Pacific, and North Africa, another war was raging in the United States. On the home front Chicanos/as were continuously denied the civil rights accorded to other members of American society. The Sleepy Lagoon case acutely captured this subjective application of the law. It involved the discovery of a young Anglo man's murdered body on the morning of August 2, 1942. Twenty two Chicanos, members of the 38th Street Boys gang, were arrested and charged with the murder. The defendants were portrayed as incorrigible criminals and convicted in the court of public opinion long before they reached a court of law. Chicano historian Rodolfo Acuña (1972) offers the following summary of a report issued during the case by the Los Angeles Sheriff's Department.

> Chicanos were inherently criminal and violent. . . . Chicanos were Indians . . . Indians were Orientals and . . . Orientals had an utter disregard for life.

Therefore, because Chicanos had this inborn characteristic, they too were violent. [The report further alleged] that Chicanos were cruel for they descended from the Aztecs who supposedly sacrificed 30,000 victims a day! Chicanos . . . could not change their spots . . . and had an innate desire to use a knife and let blood, and this inborn cruelty was aggravated by liquor and jealousy (255).

Today the image of the undocumented worker as an illegal alien, as a "migrant" living in squalor, spreading disease, raping white women, extorting lunch money from white school children, creating squatter communities, hanging out in shopping centers, forcing Anglo schools to adopt bilingual education programs to accommodate the offspring of criminals and to appease the foreigner living on U.S. soil has served to identify Mexicans with dirt, filth, and unnatural acts, while symbolically constructing European American citizens as pure, law-abiding, and living in harmony with God's natural law (Gutierrez 1996). These images are unambiguous extensions of racist and nativist nineteenth- and early twentieth-century Anglo-American representations of Mexicans and continue to influence Anglo perceptions about Mexicans. This is despite the substantial contribution of Mexicans to the economy as laborers and consumers, their disproportionately low use of social welfare programs, and their increasing presence among the middle-class voting public (not to mention their rich contribution to literature, the arts, and education).

Looking more recently, the Los Angeles uprisings of 1992 can be traced to extreme poverty in African American and Latino communities brought on by the effects of globalization and neoliberal economic policies and practices. The structural changes associated with the emergence of the postindustrial economy had reconfigured the city's social relations. As Los Angeles County's largest population, Latinos cannot strictly be categorized as a "race," a nationality, or an ethnic grouping since they constitute a cross section of Latin American immigrants, most of whom are "racially" mixed Mexicans and Central Americans. As a mixed or *mestizo* people, Latino ethnicities are woven from indigenous, African, Iberian, and European, as well as Asian strands. Culture, language, gender, and history, in addition to class, must be integrated when attempting to grasp multiple, overlapping racialized identities. During the uprising, however, the media's reliance on a racialized language of blacks vs. Asians vs. Latinos precluded the use of alternative explanatory categories (Valle and Torres 1995). The media lacks a semantic category—as well as a general "problematic" with which to identify and conceptualize Latino racial ambiguity as well as an analysis of class exploitation.

In the United States, neither the media nor its audiences have created a language with which to adequately reveal the nation's heterodox ensemble of racialized ethnicities and cultures. Rather, the suppression of this cultural dialogue has been conveniently institutionalized. The Census Bureau, for example, has had a very difficult time trying to figure out how to classify

Latinos/as by color. In the 1940 census, Latinos/as were classified as "black" or a "racial" nonwhite group. In the 1950 and 1960 censuses, the term "white person of Spanish surname" was used. In 1970, the classification was changed to "White person of Spanish surname and Spanish mother tongue." Then in 1980, Mexican Americans, Puerto Ricans, and other Central and Latin Americans of diverse national origin were reclassified as "nonwhite Hispanic." Latinos were back to square one. Because the census used a "white/black" paradigm to classify its citizens, it has shuttled Latinos back and forth between these two extremes. In each case, the organizing principle behind the labels is the perceived presence or absence of color (Valle and Torres 1995).

THE CONCEPT OF WHITENESS

Much of the discussion about identity formation in the multicultural literature has focused on those groups whom the dominant culture has characterized as "ethnic." Such populations are almost invariably described as visible "minorities" and most often appear under the term "people of color." This has perpetuated the idea that phenotype, skin color, and temperament are permanently fixed and "natural" attributes of different ethnic groups. Although we recognize biological markers of race such as phenotype, skin color, and hair texture as "floating signifiers" that acquire different meanings according to shifting sociocultural, historical, and political contexts, it remains the case that race matters. Race creates significant negative effects in the lives of people of color.

Our attention has been drawn to the fact that the term *ethnic* is rarely applied to populations commonly described as "white." If you are white, you occupy a space that seemingly transcends ethnicity. Whiteness miraculously becomes the "oneness" without which otherness could not exist—the primogenitor of identity, the marker against which otherness defines itself. Whiteness functions as a frozen state—a dead zone where "traits" associated with skin color, phenotype, race, class, and gender characteristics historically associated with Anglo-Europeans are held to be perpetually raceless. Whiteness has been positioned as the backdrop against which alternative or unconventional social practices and cultural formations are judged, thus ascribing an unprecedented degree of authority and power to its membership and its ethnocentric cultural, social, and ideological expressions, while at the same time repositioning the "other" as deviant. White has become the laboratory where ethnicities are given defining characteristics, assembled, and categorized. Schools are the clinics that "treat" these ethnic groups, police their behavior, and assimilate them.

THE ABOLITION OF WHITENESS

We argue, after Theodore W. Allen (1994; 1997) and Scott (1998) that white-ness is, first and foremost, a "sociogenic" (having to do with social forces and relations) rather than a "phylogenic" (having to do with phenotype or skin color) phenomenon. Historically, whiteness was an invention of the seventeenth century Anglo-American and United States ruling class—largely the oligarchy of owners of large colonial plantations—who endowed indentured Europeans (who were *de facto* slaves) with civil and social privileges that greatly exceeded those of their fellow African bondsmen. This was a political and economic maneuver designed to secure control of the plantocracy. The invention of the white race was primarily a means of preventing Anglo-Americans who existed in a state of chattel bond-servitude from joining forces with african bondsmen and overthrowing the plantocracy. That is, whiteness was an historical process of homogenizing the social statuses of Anglo-European tenants, merchants and planters into membership in the white race.

Within New England's system of equitably distributed small land holdings, freedom for bond-laborers (six thousand Europeans and two thousand African Americans) would have effectively terminated the plantocracy's super-exploita-tion of the African and European bond laborers since the eight thousand bond-laborers would then have become part of a diversified small holder economy. The chattelization of labor became a necessity for strengthening Virginia's tobac-co monoculture. In colonial Virginia, roughly between 1676 and 1705, there was no initial status distinction between 'black" and "white" bond-laborers. However, the small landholders of colonial Virginia had begun to oppose changes in Virginia land policy that allocated the best land to wealthy capitalist investors, and laws that forbade them from trading with the Indians. More and more land-less laborers began to fight against their chattel bond-servitude. Africans and Europeans fought side by side against the plantation bourgeoisie who would rou-tinely punish runaway laborers by adding years to their servitude, and who ordered severe restrictions on corn planting and a ban on hunting for food in the forests so that the rebelling chattel bond laborers would starve to death.

The aim of the Anglo-American continental plantation bourgeoisie was to prepare the ground for a system of lifetime hereditary bond-servitude. But the African American and European bond-laborers began to "confederate" and together they were too strong for the tiny colony elite to defeat. Indentured Anglo-Americans were consequently recruited into the middle classes through anomalous white-skin privileges. White skin privilege was an acknowledgment of their loyalty to the colonial land and property-owning class. There were sim-ply too many laboring-class Europeans who had no social mobility and were thus a constant threat to the plantocracy. The white race had to be invented in order to diffuse this potential threat to ruling class hegemony. Racial oppression was systematically put into place and European Americans were brought into the white "middle class." This saved the ruling class the money that it would have cost them to put down constant rebellions.

As Allen (1994, 1997) notes, the social function of whiteness in this respect was social control, a practice which has colonial origins that can be traced back to the assault upon the tribal affinities, customs, laws and institutions of Africans, Native Americans, and Irish by English/British and Anglo-American colonialism. Practices of social control reduce all members of oppressed groups to one undifferentiated social status beneath that of any member of the colonizing population. With the rise of the abolitionist movement, racial typologies, classification systems, and criteriologies favoring whiteness and demonizing blackness became widespread in order to justify and legitimize the slavery of Africans and ensure the continuation of lifetime chattel bond-servitude. Today "whiteness" has become naturalized as part of our 'commonsense' reality.

As an identity formation, whiteness is rarely assailed as a racialized practice of power and privilege, exactly because of its ubiquitous and invisible presence. That is, whiteness as a racialized practice within social conventions has been expressed and interpreted as the perpetual and uncontested anchor of normality. Michael Parenti (1998) raises a series of questions about the media that progressive educators need to take seriously: How often do television newscasters or newspapers talk about "white-on-white" violence? Why have the media lavished attention on the Ku Klux Klan, magnifying its visibility, yet consistently failed to report the Klan's alignment with racism, fascism, anticommunism, and anti-Semitism? Why do the media fail to report the role played by the FBI in organizing and financing chapters of the Klan, on the pretext of infiltrating their ranks? Why do the media not give as much exposure to leftist organizations such as the National Alliance Against Racism and Political Repression headed by Angela Davis and Charlene Mitchell as they do to conservative groups? Why did the media give more national attention to Nazi-Ku Klux Klan member David Duke in his unsuccessful bid for a seat in the Louisiana state legislature than to socialist Bernard Sanders who ran for the U.S. Congress in Vermont and won? Why do the U.S. media often attribute political instability in Latin America to the nature and the culture of the Latin Americans themselves? Why do the media report a typical "Arab style" of thinking or describe the Russian people as having an "urge for order"? Can you imagine the media talking about a typical "white" way of thinking? (Parenti 1998).

Even among critical educators, little attention is given to the formation of whiteness. Whiteness is universalized as an identity that both supersedes and transcends ethnicity. Rarely in public discussions of race are we provided opportunities to recognize the many implications of racialized social practices in our everyday experiences as racialized subjects. This dilemma is symptomatic of an understanding of identity that largely forecloses consideration of its broader political dimensions. Rarely are discourses and practices that we attribute to "ethnicity" questioned beyond their expression as individual or group "attitudes" and seen instead for the economic interests that they serve and the social arrangements that they privilege.

Our policies of multiculturalism and invocations of diversity are, for the most part, grounded in an integrationist universalism that links truth to the transcendence of racial categories and status. Within such a liberal tradition, white people, as mentioned previously, are encouraged to become "color-blind," not to recognize the specificity of their own white ethnicity because to do so would reveal whiteness as an invisible market for conceptualizing normative arrangements of social practices. Current legal definitions of race embrace the norm of color-blindness and thus disconnect race from social identity and race-consciousness. Within the discourse of color-blindness, blackness and whiteness are seen as neutral and apolitical descriptions reflecting skin color. They are seen as being unrelated to social conditions of domination and subordination and to social attributes such as class, culture, language, and education. According to Harris (1993)

> To define race reductively as simply color, and therefore meaningless . . . is as subordinating as defining race to be scientifically determinative of inherent deficiency. The old definition creates a false linkage between race and inferiority, the new definition denies the real linkage between race and oppression under systemic white supremacy. Distorting and denying reality, both definitions support race subordination. As Neil Gotanda has argued, color blindness is a form of race subordination in that it denies the historical context of white domination and Black subordination. (1768)

We need to recognize that most attempts at practicing a form of multiculturalism actually reconfirm existing relations of power and privilege. This is because social practices of whiteness are rarely, if ever, named, let alone interrogated in the clarion call for increasing cultural diversity. There remains a limited amount of critical discussion of the history, construction, and representation of whiteness, particularly with respect to its ability to remain the presumed default setting for so much of mainstream American culture, social relations, and intellectual activity. This has been the case from the advent of compulsory education in the United States, which was designed to provide socializing programs to train individuals both to accept and to further reify whiteness as an immutable reference point constituting normality. Within the current call for diversity in our schools and wider society, there exists little acknowledgement of, let alone complex engagement with, the processes by which racialized difference is grounded in dominant social relations of production and consumption and the existing social division of labor.

It is possible that a half century from now whites might be a minority in the United States. As they continue to feel that their civil society is being despoiled and to blame immigrants for their increasing downward mobility and the disappearance of "traditional" American values, whites fall prey to the appeal of a reactionary and fascist politics of authoritarian repression. The kindling of fascism lies in the furnace of U.S. democracy waiting for a spark to ignite a firestorm of state repression. Previous firestorms have occurred in the Watts rebellion of August 1965, the civil rights movement, and the antiwar movement of the 1960s. More recently, we have witnessed the Los Angeles uprising of April 29, 1992, and the East Los Angeles high school walkouts of 1994 over Proposition 187. The same heat has found expression in several other initiatives in California aimed directly at constituencies of color, in particular Latinos. These initiatives include Proposition 209 (the abolition of affirmative action programs) and Proposition 227 (the repeal of bilingual education). Likewise, Propositions 187, 209 and 227 constitute a "three strikes and you're out" assault on Latino/as, who presently constitute the fastest growing community in California.

In the United States, we are living at a time of undeclared war. Each day we negotiate our way through mine-sown terrains of confrontation and uncertainty surrounding the meaning and purpose of identity. American democracy faces Janus-like in two directions simultaneously: toward a horizon of hope and coexistence and toward the burning eyes of Klansmen in sheets soiled with blood. While this current historical juncture is witnessing an unprecedented growth of white supremacist organizations living on the fringes of social life, establishment conservatives are stridently asserting nativistic and populist sentiments that barely distinguish them ideologically from their counterparts in racialist far-right groups and citizen militias. The Ku Klux Klan, Posse Comitatus, The Order, White Aryan Resistance, Christian Identity, National Alliance, Aryan Nations, American Front, Gun Owners of America, United Citizens of Justice, and militia groups have organizations in most, if not all, of the fifty states.

Social policies, drafted without the conscious contribution by disenfranchised peoples, have created the conditions for white communities to feel as if they are under siege. As social welfare spending increased from 11.2 percent to 18.7 percent of the U.S. gross national product from 1965 to 1980 (Jencks 1992), conservative writers began to assail social welfare programs as counterproductive and wasteful. If economically disenfranchised people of color are to be helped, they vociferously argued, then it should be done by private individuals or organizations and not the government. But wealthy private organizations have benefited from the hegemony of white privilege in the government and the marketplace for centuries. Unbridled capitalism in our present service economy is ruthlessly uncharitable to the poverty-stricken. Transferring the challenge of economic justice from the government into the hands of philanthropists who feel "pity" for the poor is certainly not the solution.

As attitudes toward social welfare changed, a new rhetorical strategy developed to bind the spirit and restrict access to social welfare programs. The debate over social supports became a competition between the deserving poor (elderly and the disabled), and the undeserving poor (single mothers). Benefits would be allocated according to a subjective standard of merit and deservedness. Categories of "deserving" and "undeserving" poor, designed to feed the anger of whites demanding accountability from those receiving financial assistance, were presented for public consumption.

Not surprisingly, the "deserving" sector of Americans were often the offspring of an aging white baby-boom middle class concerned with retirement and health benefits. Those members of the American "family" who were deemed undeserving were the racialized "welfare mothers or parasitic immigrants." Thus, the historical past that middle-class whites clamor for and the present that confronts them and quickens their pulse are informed by a racialized logic. This position remains steadfast regardless of significant data indicating that, historically, social welfare programs have benefited white Americans to a greater extent than any other ethnic group. The notion of who constitutes the deserving and undeserving poor marked an important shift in how people of color were perceived. The social condition of poverty has become inseparable from individual volition. According to Jencks (1992), "The popularity of the term thus signals a political shift: instead of blaming poverty on society, as we did in the late 60's, we are now inclined to blame poverty on the poor" (120).

MULTICULTURAL EDUCATION AND THE CHALLENGE TO WHITENESS

As we survey the contemporary landscape of global capitalism, racism, and poverty, we can conclude that the challenge to multicultural educators is to choose against whiteness. We believe that an emphasis on the social and historical construction of whiteness will put a different and important focus on the problem surrounding identity formation at this particular juncture in US. history. When North Americans talk about race, they inevitably refer to African Americans, Asians, Latinos/as, and Native Americans, to the consistent exclusion of European Americans. We want to challenge the prevailing assumption that to defeat racism, we need to put our initiatives behind the inclusions of minority populations—in other words, of nonwhites. We want to argue instead that in addition to making an argument for diversity, we need to put more emphasis on the analysis of white ethnicity and the destabilization of white identity, specifically white supremacist ideology and practice. As David Roediger (1994) notes:

> Whiteness describes, from Little Big Horn to Simi Valley, not a culture but the absence of culture. It is the empty and therefore terrifying attempt to build an identity based on what one isn't and on whom one can hold back. (137)

One would think that the choice against whiteness would be morally self-evident. However, precisely because whiteness is so pervasive and yet built on "what one isn't," it remains difficult to identify, challenge, and separate from our daily lives.

Our critique of whiteness is not an all-out assault on white people.Our central argument is that we must create a new public sphere where the practice of whiteness is not only identified and analyzed but also contested and destroyed when it subverts the opportunities of those who are not white. For choosing against whiteness is the hope and promise of the future. One of the tasks ahead for those of us who wish to reclaim the dignity offered by true justice is to revive democratic citizenship in an era of diminishing returns. It is to create critical citizens who are no longer content in occupying furtive spaces of private affirmation but who possess the will and the knowledge to turn these spaces into public spheres through the creation of new social movements aimed at the deconstruction of de jure and de facto white privilege.

Rather than stressing the importance of diversity and inclusion, as do most multiculturalists, we think that significantly more emphasis should be placed on the social and political construction of white supremacy and the dispensation of white hegemony. Whiteness needs to be recognized and acted upon by multicultural educators as a cultural disposition and an ideology linked to specific political, social, and historical arrangements.

In particular, a neoliberal democracy, performing under the banner of diversity yet actually in the hidden service of capital accumulation, often reconfirms the racist stereotypes already prescribed by European American nationalist myths of supremacy. In the pluralizing move to become a society of diverse voices, neoliberal democracy has often succumbed to a recolonization of multiculturalism. It has done this by failing to challenge ideological assumptions surrounding difference that are installed in its current positions regarding anti-affirmative action and welfare "reform" initiatives. In this sense, people of color are still excluded from full U.S. citizenship.

One of the most hated groups among the poor in the Southwest and southern California is Mexican migrant workers. Stereotyped as *"crimmegrantes,"* they have become the object of xenophobia par excellence. Ron Prince, one of the architects of Proposition 187, has remarked: "Illegal aliens are a category of criminal, not a category of ethnic group" (Gomez-Peha 1996, 67). The process of "Mexicanization" has struck fear into the hearts of the European Americans who view this inevitability as an obdurate political reality. And this fear is only exacerbated by the media and anti-immigration activists.

Latinos have responded to the heterophobic rhetoric that has dominated California's public debate over the last several years. Through *banda* music, *quebradita* dance, and the surge of rock *en Español*, Latinos are very consciously exercising culture as a form of resistance to the pejorative stereotypes imposed by white hegemonic institutionalized structures and practices. These fashion and music trends are an indication of the many signals that the Southwest and beyond will continue to experience a substantial Latinization of major American urban hubs. Latinos have substantially influenced mainstream European American culture, a reality that flies in the face of the frequent charge that the Latino community represents a passive target of assimilation. We consider it a mark of ingenuity and courage that Latinos/as have managed to develop creatively independent cultural alternatives—as well as oppositional strategies—to dominant cultural arrangements that fuel extant mythologies surrounding Latino populations. Martinez (1994), writing from the point of view of a Latino addressing European Americans, states:

> You must accept that the Latinos of California aren't going anywhere. . . . You must stop thinking and acting with the arrogance of a culture that sees itself as the arbiter of life in the city: your culture will become less and less dominant. . . . And I must accept that you aren't going anywhere either. . . . You must allow yourself to be transformed even as we are being and have been transformed. It is a process that is at the heart of America's democracy. (39)

Often the terrain inhabited by groups of native and immigrant people results in a creative experiment and eventually involves some degree of culture contact where both subordinate and dominant groups are transformed. This is precisely the point that Martinez is making. Perhaps no other geopolitical space offers an opportunity to view this phenomenon of cultural and ideological confluence more saliently than metropolitan Los Angeles, which has become a metaphor for the new urban frontier—a place where renegades still run wild, gun in hand, and where (as the prevailing discourse requires) the "good" guys still wear white.

Throughout the history of public education, the official school charter has been to socialize the children of recent immigrants into Americans and future workers possessing the habits and attitudes required of an industrialized economy. Schools were openly a means of indoctrinating the children of subordinate social groups. Not surprisingly, Latinos living in the United States carried with them from Latin American countries the idea that education is a fundamental necessity. Moreover, contrary to current myths, Latinos—then and now—clearly recognize the importance of higher education. An appalling and undeserved misrepresentation of Latinos/as as intellectually indifferent has led to their being stigmatized as academically docile and intellectual passive. This false image contradicts an abundance of evidence that portrays a vigorous history of academic participation, school-based activism, and resistance to unequal treatment. Given the importance that Latinos attach to education, the need to maintain a critically informed and representative curriculum is significant. However, conventional pedagogical and curricular approaches fail to substantively engage activities and topics that are most pressing to a community that still experiences pronounced levels of racial discrimination, economic oppression, and popular misrepresentation—not to mention exclusion and demonization on the part of the wider educational community.

Contributing to the situation whereby racialized relations become normalized is the aversion of whites to critically examine the processes responsible for white identity. They remain historically unwilling to consider their own processes of self-identification and how these processes are linked to other racialized groups. Furthermore, there exists a motivated amnesia with respect to acknowledging that the United States has been built by downtrodden immigrants of all hues, by Native Americans, and by southern blacks. The very mortar that holds its cities and towns in place has been stirred by the hands of minority workers. To negate this vital multiethnic presence is not simply factually incorrect. It is a serious abdication of the democratic impulse that is fundamental to the principles on which this country claims to rest.

The powerful but hidden force of whiteness has provided the context for our distorted views of history. However, it is difficult to clearly define the character of whiteness because cultural practices considered to be white are historically produced and transformable (Frankenberg 1993). White culture is not monolithic, and its borders are malleable and porous. It is a historically specific confluence of economic, geopolitical, and ethnocultural processes. According to Alastair Bonnett (1996), whiteness is neither a discrete entity nor a fixed social category. White identity is an ensemble of sometimes contradictory discourses. Whiteness is always in a state of flux. Bonnett notes that "even if one-ignores the transgressive youth or ethnic borderlands of Western identities, and focuses on the 'center' or 'heartlands' of 'whiteness,' one will discover racialized subjectivities, that, far from being settled and confident, exhibit a constantly reformulated panic over the meaning of 'whiteness' and the defining presence of 'nonwhiteness' within it" (106).

Whiteness is a sociohistorical form of consciousness, born at the nexus of capitalism, colonial rule, and the emergent relationships among dominant and subordinate groups. Where whiteness operates, the white bourgeois appropriates the right to speak on behalf of everyone who is nonwhite, while denying voice to these others in the name of civilized. Whiteness demarcates ideas, feelings, knowledge, social practices, cultural formations, and systems of intelligibility that are invested in by white people as "white." Whiteness is also a refusal to acknowledge how white people are implicated in relations of domination and subordination. Whiteness, then, as we mentioned before, can be considered as a form of social amnesia. Whiteness constitutes the selective tradition of dominant discourses about race, class, gender, and sexuality. Whiteness is not a unified, homogeneous culture but a *social position.*

Whiteness in the United States can be understood largely through the social consequences it provides for those who are considered to be nonwhite. Such consequences can be seen in the criminal justice system, in prisons, in schools, and in the boardrooms of corporations such as Texaco. It can be defined in relation to immigration practices, social policies, and practices of sexism, racism, and nationalism.

Ignatiev (1998) writes that while poor whites have been historically exploited, many of these "slaves" believe that they are part of the "master class" because they partake of the privilege of white skin. In actual fact, whiteness has become a substitute for freedom and dignity in the case of the majority of European Americans who live in the United States. What identification with white privilege does is to reconnect whites to relations of exploitation. The answer to this plight, notes Ignatiev, is for whites to cease to exist as whites. Whites "must commit suicide as whites to come alive as workers or youth or women or artists or whatever other identity will let them stop being the miserable, petulant, subordinated creatures they now are and become freely associated, developing human beings" (200). He goes on to say:

> The task at hand is not to convince more whites to oppose "racism"; there are already enough "antiracists" to do the job. The task is to make it impossible for anyone to be white. What would white people have to do to accomplish this? They would have to break the laws of whiteness so flagrantly as to destroy the myth of white unanimity. They would have to respond to every manifestation of white supremacy as if it were directed against them. (202)

Whiteness is so pervasive in our social, political, and economic structure that people tend to be unaware of its powerful and damaging presence. López (1996) cites an incident at a feminist legal conference in which participants were asked to pick two or three words to describe themselves. All of the women of color selected at least one racial term, but not one white woman selected a term referring to her race. This prompted Angela Harris to remark that only white people in this society have the luxury of having no color. An informal study conducted at Harvard Law School underscores Harris's remark. A student interviewer asked ten African Americans and ten white Americans how they identified themselves. Unlike the African Americans, most of the white Americans did not consciously factor in their "whiteness" as a crucial or even tangential part of their identity.

Given the elusiveness of whiteness, the educational left has failed to address the issue sufficiently. Consider the case of the insecurities that young whites harbor regarding their future during times of diminishing economic expectations. With their racist and divisive rhetoric, neoconservatives may be able to enjoy tremendous success in helping insecure young white populations develop white identity along racist lines. Consider these comments by David Stowe (1996):

> The only people nowadays who profess any kind of loyalty to whiteness qua whiteness (as opposed to whiteness as an incidental feature of some more specific identity), are Christian Identity types and Aryan Nation diehards. Anecdotal surveys reveal that few white Americans mention

whiteness as a quality that they think much about or particularly value. In their day-to-day cultural preferences—food, music, clothing, sports, hairstyles—the great majority of American whites display no particular attachment to white things. There does seem to be a kind of emptiness at the core of whiteness. (74)

CONCLUSION: DECENTERING WHITENESS THROUGH REVOLUTIONARY MULTICULTURALISM

López (1996) argues that one is not born white but becomes white "by virtue of the social context in which one finds oneself, to be sure, but also by virtue of the choices one makes" (190). But how can one born into the culture of whiteness, one who is defined as white, undo that whiteness? López addresses this question in his formulation of whiteness. He locates whiteness in the overlapping of *chance* (e.g., features and ancestry that we have no control over, morphology); *context* (context-specific meanings that are attached to race, the social setting in which races are recognized, constructed, and contested); and *choice* (conscious choices with regard to the morphology and ancestries of social actors) in order to "alter the readability of their identity" (191).

In other words, López (1996) maintains that chance and context are not racially determinative. He notes:

> Racial choices must always be made from within specific contexts, where the context materially and ideologically circumscribes the range of available choices and also delimits the significance of the act. Nevertheless, these are racial choices, if sometimes only in their overtone or subtext, because they resonate in the complex of meanings associated with race. Given the thorough suffusion of race throughout society, in the daily dance of life we constantly make racially meaningful decisions. (193)

López outlines—productively, in our view—three steps in dismantling whiteness:

> First, Whites must overcome the omnipresent effects of transparency and of the naturalization of race in order to recognize the many racial aspects of their identity, paying particular attention to the daily acts that draw upon and in turn confirm their whiteness. Second, they must recognize and accept the personal and social consequences of breaking out of a White identity. Third, they must embark on a daily process of choosing against whiteness. (193)

We are acutely aware that people of color might find troubling the idea that white populations can simply reinvent themselves by making the simple choice of not being white. Of course, this is not what López and others appear to be saying. The choices one makes and the reinvention one aspires to as a race traitor are not "simple," nor are they easy choices for groups of whites to make. Yet from the perspective of some people of color, offering the choice to white people of opting out of their whiteness could seem to set up an easy path for those who do not want to assume responsibility for their privilege as white people. Indeed, there is certainly cause for concern. David Roediger (1994) captures some of this when he remarks: "whites cannot fully renounce whiteness even if they want to" (16). Whites are, after all, still accorded the privileges of being white even as they ideologically renounce their whiteness, often with the best of intentions. Yet the possibility that whites might seriously consider nonwhiteness and antiwhite struggle is too important to ignore, dismiss as wishful thinking, or associate with a fashionable form of code-switching. Choosing not to be white is not an easy option for white people, for it implies the recognition of a profound existential pain, a heightened sense of social criticism, and an unwavering commitment to social justice (McLaren 1997a; Roediger 1994).

Does this mean that white people can become black or brown? No. In discussing the position of the "new abolitionism" (the name is taken from the abolitionists who fought against slavery in the United States and refers to a movement calling on whites to renounce their possessive investment in whiteness), Ignatiev (1998) writes:

> Abolitionists realize that no "white," as an individual, can escape from the privileges of whiteness. But they also understand that when there comes into being a critical mass of people who look white but who do not act white, the white race will undergo fission, and former whites, born again, will be able to take part with others in building a new human community. (203)

The key, George Yudice (1995) maintains, is to center the struggle for social justice around resource distribution rather than identity:

> Shifting the focus of struggle from identity to resource distribution will also make it possible to engage such seemingly nonracial issues as the environment, the military, the military-industrial complex, foreign aid, and free trade agreements as matters impacting local identities and thus requiring a global politics that works outside of the national frame. (280)

REVOLUTIONARY MULTICULTURALISM

Given the axiomatic role of capitalism in the perpetuation of racism, whiteness, and, consequently, social injustice, we propose a reorientation of educators toward revolutionary, or critical, multiculturalism. Revolutionary multiculturalism recognizes that the objective structures in which we live and the material relations tied to production in which we are situated are all reflected in our everyday lives. In other words, our lived experiences are always mediated through ideological configurations of discourses, political economies of power and privilege, and the social division of labor. The following characteristics offer a brief summary of the major position of revolutionary multiculturalism:

1. Revolutionary multiculturalism is a socialist-feminist multicultural-ism that challenges the historically sedimented processes through which race, class and gender identities are produced within capital-ist society. Therefore, revolutionary multiculturalism is not limited to transformng attitudinal discrimination. Racism is not simply understood as a "wrong way to think" in the sense that it is politi-cally incorrect. Racism is a complex process and is implicated in social relations of production and their valoration and naturaliza-tion through systems of classification produced historically in reli-gious, anthropological, and scientific texts. Revolutionary multicul-turalism is dedicated to reconstituting the deep structures of politi-cal economy, culture, and power in contemporary social arrange-ments. It is not about *reforming* capitalist democracy but rather transforming it by cutting it at its joints and then rebuilding the social order from the vantage point of the oppressed.

2. Revolutionary multiculturalism, as we envision it, is not a general theory but rather uses general categories that can capture the lived experiences of oppressed groups so that explanatory concepts can be developed and explanations mustered that have a historical con-creteness. Too much theory preempts the development of knowl-edge and forecloses empirical speculation; too little theory, howev-er, ends up on the cutting-room floor of banal, descriptive analysis that makes insufficient links to the social media and forces of which our categories for description are but ideal abstract expressions.

3. Revolutionary multiculturalism acknowledges the importance of identity politics but puts such politics in perspective. Identity poli-tics—that is, social movements based on feminism, or Afrocentrism, or ecology, or gay or lesbian issues—are important (even those that are single issue movements) as a self-defense against heteronomous control by the capitalist class. But such movements should be seen in terms of formulating a concrete multicultural universal that arches toward an organic whole. Rather than keep the larger movement against the social injustices of capitalism and a common class enemy fragmented, identity politics are valuable as transitional phases toward a multicultural universality (Katsiaficas, 1998).

4. A revolutionary multicultural pedagogy will creatively respond to the needs of marginalized groups of learners, and it will prepare

educators to consciously assist in reconciling pervasive social and economic inequities (Darder 1992; Moraes 1996). The struggle for liberation on the basis of race and gender must not remain detached from anticapitalist struggle. More directly, the decentering of whiteness and the privileges it enjoys within the ideological mystifications of capitalism can serve as the basis of a new revolutionary multiculturalism (McLaren 1997a).

For Ignatiev (1998), the school system is a major institution of white supremacy that "is doing more harm than the Nazis and the Klan and all the-other 'racist' groups combined by directing millions of black children into low-wage jobs, the military, and prison" (200). Consequently, school practices need to address more than ever before the objective, material conditions of the workplace and labor relations in order to prevent the further perpetuation of the neoliberal corporatist state.

5. A revolutionary multiculturalism links inequality on the basis of race, class, and gender to the vicissitudes of U.S. transnational capitalism and its neocolonial clientele and to the alienation and racism that overwhelmingly characterize everyday cultural practices. It is committed to freeing society from the alienation and exploitation endemic to a market-based system of profit. Revolutionary multiculturalism is not premised on creating diversity and inclusion—although it recognizes that such an effort is immensely important. Revolutionary multiculturalism does not begin with bringing the margins into the center but rather with criticizing the existing center of power—the power that inheres in white supremacist capitalist patriarchy. On this issue Paulo Freire (1998) writes:

> The criticism of capitalism I put forth, from an ethical point of view, derives as much from the educator as it does from the activist, which I seek to continue to be in my own way. My activism can never become dissociated from my theoretical work; on the contrary, the former has its tactics and strategies formulated on the latter. The moment we recognize that food production around the world could be sufficient to feed twice its population, it is desolating to realize the numbers of those who come into the world but do not stay, or those who do but are forced into early departure by hunger.
>
> My struggle against capitalism is founded on that—its intrinsic perversity, its antisolidarity nature.
>
> The argument has been destroyed of scarcity as a production problem that capitalism would not be able to respond to and that would represent an obstacle to the preservation of this system. Capitalism is effective in this and other aspects, but it has shown its other face—absolute insensitivity to the ethical dimension of existence. (88)

Revolutionary multiculturalism is not only about teaching about forms of social inequality but also about helping to transform that inequality. It is about reconstructing a society in which diversity, equality, and social and economic justice become organic parts of the life forms we invent for ourselves in our pursuit of democratic public life. But revolutionary multiculturalism goes further than this. It is international in scope and is part of a worldwide struggle for social emancipation from capital accumulation and its ideology of white patriarchal supremacy.

6. The ethics of revolutionary multiculturalism are not premised on a universally valid way of being human but rather fluctuate from rage against oppression to a joyous celebration and love of life (Welch 1999). According to Sharon Welch,

> Multicultural education is deeply disturbing, as disturbing to the myths of a common culture as it is to the myths of a revolutionary vanguard. It is also profoundly rewarding and exhilarating, a rush of creative energy that takes us out of the paralyzing trap of endlessly denouncing and analyzing forms of injustice and oppression. We can do so much more. The first step is to recognize that social cohesion is created by contact, by working with other people, and does not require uniformity or total agreement. The second step is focusing on the power we have and using it to create relationships of mutuality and respect. Universal human solidarity is not our birthright, not a gift, not an essence, but a task. (117)

7. Schools in the United States should provide students with a language of criticism and a language of hope. They should prepare students to conceptualize fully the relationship between their private dreams and the collective dreams of the larger social order. Yet in doing so teachers cannot retreat to an extrahistorical, Archimedean vantage-point and must cancel their pretension to "neutral" analysis. Analysis itself is a political practice that is always mediated by the positionality of those undertaking it. How analysis imparts ballast to conditions of exploitation or supplies validation for it is a challenge that must be addressed rather than avoided. Students must further be capable of analyzing the social and material conditions in which dreams are given birth, realized, diminished, or destroyed. More important, students need to be able to recognize which dreams and which dreamers are dangerous to the larger society and why this is the case. Schools need to foster collective dreaming, a dreaming that speaks to the creation of social justice for all groups and the eventual elimination of classism, racism, sexism, and homophobia. This can only occur if schools help students analyze the ways in which their views or per-

ceptions have been ideologically formed within the exploitative forces of globalized capitalism. Schools also need to help to foster a critical praxis that can eventually transform the conditions that are responsible for the exploitation of the subordinate classes. Schools need to help citizens resist the American business plutocracy, which pursues speculative international financial markets at the expense of international democracy.

One might argue that current school reform efforts are already addressing such issues of social justice. However, such measures most often provide only limited insurance against intractable sociopolitical conflicts. Most are forms of concessionary state policies, forms of state-mandated accords (Teeple 1995). Such reforms, in other words, are only limited concessions to people who continue to have no control over their lives. They are temporary reprieves. Reforms are always provisional and conditional and simply serve to postpone resolutions to class conflicts. As Teeple (1995) notes, reforms both resist the capitalist mode of production and maintain existing capitalist social relations. They impose amelioration of the worst effects of capitalism, but they do not fundamentally transform the contradictions of contemporary capitalism. However, revolutionary multiculturalism acknowledges that reforms, while admittedly temporary and insufficient, are often necessary first steps in the struggle for social justice, and in this case the dis-investment of whitness.

We must, nevertheless, go far beyond the current reform movement in education. We must continue to wage new struggles of liberation, creating new identities both global and local—along the way. We must begin to rethink identity more in terms of what we can do for each other (a question of ethics) rather than in terms of who we are (a question of epistemology). Both questions are important, certainly, but we believe that coalition-building requires us to begin our struggle with an ethical commitment to each other while at the same time understanding that both the "self" and "other" are forged out of historically determinate social relations of production. Only by committing ourselves to the "other"—to our "brother and sister outsiders"—can we discover the "other within." And only by discovering the "outsider within" can we discover who we are in our hearts. We cannot discover who we are separately from our common struggle with, against, and beyond each other, for only through such a struggle can we recognize that there exist no boundaries separating ourselves from others. We are all bound together in our humanity and in our struggle for peace and justice.

STUDY QUESTIONS

1. Since its inception, what has been the general aim of multicultural education and how does this chapter depart from, or perhaps modi-

fy, the conventional scope of multiculturalism? What are the conceptual and practical limitations of traditional multiculturalism, if any? What are the conceptual and practical limitations of the arguments presented in this chapter, if any?

2. In what ways and for what reasons does the chapter advocate a more sophisticated and complex linkage between multicultural education and related campaigns for social justice? Provide examples of the role multicultural education may yet serve in the pursuit of social justice.

3. The chapter offers several examples of historical information not typically available in conventional textbooks. Give some examples that you found particularly interesting and explain why. To the extent possible, describe how this information was instructive to your understanding of critical/revolutionary multiculturalism.

4. How does the absence of a critical/revolutionary multicultural agenda contribute to a cultural landscape that permits inequities to proceed unabated? According to a critical/revolutionary multicultural framework, what responsibility does an individual have to contest unequal relations of power? In particular, what are some areas in which whites can substantially contribute to the destabilization of white privilege and to the struggle for social justice?

5. The chapter examines the usefulness of deconstructing "whiteness" in shaping a reconceptualized notion of multiculturalism. How is whiteness defined and examined? What do the authors mean by "social amnesia" in relation to whiteness? How does social amnesia contribute to the preservation of whiteness?

6. Critical/revolutionary multiculturalism advocates an extreme personal commitment to the abolition of social inequalities and to the formation of a new human community through challenging capitalist social relations. How can one become committed to "others" without embracing a paternalistic or self-serving missionary attitude? In light of the chapter's general call for personal action, what concrete steps can you take to defend the interests of "others" (i.e., marginalized groups), while also contesting the privileged status of the ruling elite?

7. What type of society can we begin to envision and work toward that challenges the exploitative premises of so-called "capitalist democracy"? Can socialism be rescued as a viable alternative to capitalism? What would a democratic socialist society look like?

KEY CONCEPTS

Color-blindness
Connection between racism, capitalism, and multicultural education
Conscientization
Critical/revolutionary multiculturalism
Decentering whiteness
Hegemony
Liberal and neoliberal multiculturalism
Marginalized communities
Multicultural left
Neoliberal global capitalism
Whiteness as a privileged social position

REFERENCES

Acuna, R. 1972. *Occupied America: A History of Chicanos.* New York: HarperCollins.

Allen, T. 1994. *The Invention of the White Race, Volume One: Racial Oppression and Social Control.* London and New York: Verso.

Allen, T. 1997. *The Invention of the White Race, Volume Two: The Origin of Racial Oppression in Anglo-America.* London and New York: Verso.

Bonnett, A.1996. Anti-racism and the critique of white identities. *New Community,* 22(1): 97-110.

Brenner, R. 1998. The economics of global turbulence. *New Left Review,* 229: 1-262.

Callinicos, A. 1993. *Race and Class.* London: Bookmarks.

Darder, A. 1992. *Culture and Power in the Classroom.* South Hadley, MA: Bergin and Garvey.

Frankenberg, R. 1993. *The Social Construction of Whiteness: White Women, Race Matters.* Minneapolis: University of Minnesota Press.

Freire, P. 1970. *Pedagogy of the Oppressed.* New York: Continuum.

Freire, P. 1998. *Pedagogy of the Heart.* New York: Continuum.

Gates, J. 1998. Twenty-first century capitalism: To humanize, ownerize. *Humanist* 58(4): 9-14.

Grant, Car, Ed. 1999. *Multicultural Research: A Reflective Engagement with Race, Class, and Sexual Orientation.* London: Falmer Press.

Gómez-Peña, G. 1996. *The New World Border.* San Francisco: City Lights Bookstore.

Gutierrez, R. 1996. The erotic zone: Sexual transgression on the U.S.-Mexican border. In *Mapping Multiculturalism*, ed. A. Gordon and C. Newfield, 253-262. Minneapolis: University of Minnesota Press.

Harris, C. I. 1993. Whiteness as property. *Harvard Law Review* 106(8): 1709-1791.

Ignatiev, N. 1998. The new abolitionists. *Transition*, 73: 199-203.

Jencks, Christopher. 1992. *Rethinking Social Policy: Race, Poverty, and the Underclass.* New York: HarperCollins.

Katsiaficas, G. 1998. The latent universal within identity politics. In *The Promise of Multiculturalism*, ed. G. Katsiaficas and T. Teodros, 72-81. New York: Routledge.

Kincheoe, J., and S. Steinberg. 1997. *Changing Multiculturalism*. Philadelphia: Open University Press.

La Belle, T. J., and C. R. Ward. 1994. *Multiculturalism and Education: Diversity and its Impact on Schools and Society*. Albany: State University of New York Press.

López, F. H. 1996. *White by Law*. New York: New York University Press.

Loewen, J. W. 1995. *Lies My Teacher Told Me: Everything Your American History Textbook Got Wrong*. New York: Touchstone.

Marable, M. 1998. The left. *Social Policy*, 28(93): 4-9.

Martinez, R. 1994. The shock of the new anti-immigrant fever is at a fever pitch, but the real issue is this: Will the old (Anglo) join the new (Latino) LA., and learn to dance the *quebradita*. *Los Angeles Times Magazine*, January, p. 12.

May, Stephen, Ed. 1999. *Critical Multiculturalism: Rethinking Multicultural and Antiracist Education*. London: Falmer Press.

McLaren, P. 1995. *Critical Pedagogy and Predatory Culture*. New York: Routledge.

McLaren, P. 1997a. *Revolutionary Multiculturalism: Pedagogies of Dissent for the New Millennium*. Boulder, Colo.: Westview Press.

McLaren, P. 1997b. *Multiculturalismo Crítico*. São Paulo: Cortéz.

McLaren, P. 1998. The pedagogy of Che Guevara. *Cultural Circles*, vol. 3, Ricardo Romo and Raymund Paredes, eds.

McLaren, P. 1999. Traumatizing capital. In *Critical Education in the new Information Age*, ed. M. Castells, R. Flecha, Paulo Freire, H. A. Giroux, D. Macedo, and P. Willis, pp. 1-36. Boulder, Colo.: Rowman and Littlefield.

Moraes, M. 1996. *Bilingual Education: A Dialogue with the Bakhtin Circle*. Albany: SUNY Press.

Paredes, R. 1978. The origins of anti-Mexican sentiment in the United States. In *New Directions in Chicano Scholarship*, 139-165. San Diego: University of California.

Parenti, M. 1998. *America Besieged*. San Francisco: City Lights Books.

Perea, J. F. 1995. Los olvidados: On the making of invisible people. *New York University Law Review*, 70(4): 965-991.

Robertson, W. 1777. *The History of America*. New York: J. Harper.

Roediger, D. 1994. *Towards the Abolition of Whiteness*. New York: Verso.

Scott, J. 1998. "Before the White Race was Invented." *Against the Current*, vol. 72, pp. 46-49.

Sleeter, C. E., and C. A. Grant. 1994. *Making Choices for Multicultural Education: Five Approaches to Race, Class, Gender*. Columbus, Ohio: Merrill.

Sleeter, C. E., and P. L. McLaren, eds. 1995. *Multicultural Education, Critical Pedagogy, and the Politics of Difference*. Albany: State University of New York Press.

Stowe; D. W. 1996. Uncolored people: The rise of whiteness studies. *Lingua Franca* 6(6): 68 77.

Teeple, G. 1995. *Globalization and the Decline of Social Reform*. New Jersey: Humanities Press.

Valle, V., and R. D. Torres.1995. The idea of *Mestizaje* and the "race" problematic: Racialized media discourse in post-Fordist landscape. In *Culture and difference. Critical perspectives on the bicultural experience in the United States*, ed. A. Darder, 139-153. Westport, Conn.: Bergin and Garvey.

Welch, S. 1999. *Sweet dreams in America: Making ethics and spirituality work*. New York: Routledge.

West, C. 1998. I'm ofay, you're ofay. *Transition*, 73: 176-198.

Yudice, G. 1995. Neither impugning nor disavowing whiteness does a viable politics make: The limits of identity politics. In *After political correctness: The humanities and society in the 1990s*, ed. C. Newfield and R. Strickland, 255-285. Boulder, Colo.: Westview Press.

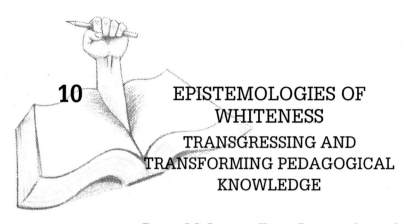

10   EPISTEMOLOGIES OF WHITENESS
TRANSGRESSING AND TRANSFORMING PEDAGOGICAL KNOWLEDGE

Peter McLaren, Zeus Leonardo and Ricky Lee Allen

In California, the white empire is striking back. Neo-Nazis, skinhead surfers, the Ku Klux Klan and their acolytes, and the White Aryan Resistance are just a few of the racist groups whose memberships are on the rise, a trend that is disturbing but not altogether surprising. Yet these groups are on the fringes of a significantly more coherent, broad-based, and influential whiteness movement that threatens to sever many of the lifelines that people of color have created throughout the years. The passage of California's Propositions 187, 209, and 227 in the 1990s marked more than a mere round of mean-spirited political victories for the radical right, but was alarmingly suggestive of the political coalescence of white identity formation that has been fomenting in the swamps of racial intolerance at least since the civil rights movement. These California propositions succeeded not because they were an example of *bien trouvé* legislation, but because they were able to effectively invest in a white subjectivity whose *point d'appui* hinges on the desperate fear of losing control of moral, economic, and cultural space. These propositions reflected the secret teeth of racist formations and were expressive of the "angry white male" narrative that views whites as being summarily "imposed upon" by people of color. For example, the visual images used to cultivate support for Proposition 187, the "anti-illegal alien" legislation (i.e., the attack on undocumented immigrants), were selections from a security camera videotape of Mexicans dashing through an opening in the fence at the highly militarized U.S.-Mexico border. Pro-187 television ads expressly avoided representations of the many whites from countries such as Canada who work without documents throughout the southwestern United States. Imagine trying to muster white support for Proposition 187 by televising Air Canada flights unloading more Anglo Canadians at Los Angeles International Airport! The new California politics of whiteness, with its public spectacles of white power, even placed former Klansman David Duke in the mainstream of political discourse. During a debate on Proposition 209, a referendum on affirmative action, Duke expressed his moral concern that California was beginning to "look like Mexico" (Bernstein 1996; McLaren 1997). Many white Californians were enthusiastic about the new admissions policies at the University of California that ended decades of affirmative action. In abolishing affirmative action, the University of California regents effectively mandated that "minority taxpayers subsidize the educations of those who successfully discriminate against them" (Lipsitz 1998).

In what follows, we trace much of the mounting insecurity among whites to that *fons et origo malorum* known as global capitalism, a condition that has encompassed a judicious slice of history, one that predates the transatlantic slave trade and encompasses today's "capitalist globalization, neoliberalism, unregulated speculative financial markets, monstrous indebtedness and impoverishment of the Third World, environmental degradation, [and the] gravely menacing ecological crisis" (Löwy 1998).

Recent public displays of white nationalism, as instanced in these racially inflamed California propositions, weaken what little institutional credibility multiculturalism has managed to create over the years, particularly among white teachers. A long-standing concern of the multiculturalist movement has been the fact that white teachers, who comprise approximately 86.5 percent of the nation's teachers (Acuna 1997), exercise overwhelming control over the environment of most urban schools. Historically, most multicultural curricula in teacher education programs have focused on educating white teachers about the cultural histories and knowledge of students of color as an indirect way of battling white racism. More radical versions of multiculturalism move beyond simple "color blind" and "nonracial" thinking. Radical multiculturalists argue that the ethical fate of the United States hinges on the success of the decolonization of the white population as well as the fulfillment of the aspirations of the oppressed to embody history (Sleeter and McLaren 1995; McLaren 1995, 1997; McCarthy 1990). As the white nation continues its agenda of recolonizing its lost historical horizons, it would be judicious and circumspect for multicultural scholars to pay increased attention to the critical study of whiteness.

This chapter seeks to examine the emerging social context of whiteness through its intersections with production and expenditure. The production of whiteness is discussed in terms of a Marxist geography of white racial identity. It also examines the significance of Georges Bataille in the critical study of whiteness and outlines how whiteness even colonizes those features of social life that are distinct from processes of production and consumption.

PRODUCING WHITENESS

In the *Communist Manifesto* (1848/1964), Karl Marx and Friedrich Engels state that the bourgeoisie "creates a world in its own image" (64-65). That is to say, the bourgeoisie seeks to manufacture and regulate a hospitable environment for its own plans for humanity. One of the modalities of place-making for the bourgeoisie has been the racialization of material, discursive, and social spaces associated with the human body. To a significant extent, the image that the bourgeoisie has created for itself is an image of whiteness. After all, the bourgeoisie was not and is not without material bodies, and for much of the world the bodies of the bourgeoisie are imagined and experienced as white. In essence, global capital is white capital in that the bodies of most capitalists are seen as white— or some thing close to white.

As capitalism has deepened around the globe, the racial signifier of "white" has grown exponentially in value, and, like any other overly valued product, it is closely inspected for quality control during the production process to ensure its purity to the consumers of whiteness. The capitalist technology of racial production and consumption, particularly in the Western world, is "whiteness," an ideological system of racialization and power that constructs racial identities as it simultaneously bestows privilege to those identified as "white" (McLaren 1997; Lipsitz 1998; Kincheloe et al. 1998). As an oppressive, socially constructed system, its processes and consequences must be named and elaborated in order to transform the spaces it manufactures.

The key to producing whiteness, of course, is not to refer to it explicitly, but to make it an all-encompassing field of communication, to have it so visible that it is not noticed. For critical multiculturalists, the methodological apprenticeship needed for dismantling whiteness is to learn to see what is visible and to denaturalize it. Whiteness produces itself with built-in elevation so that it is always more than it signifies. It signifies its own preexistence to the other. It knots together a popular reciprocity: If you aren't recognized here, you don't really count! Its message is its milieu. It is a constant transmission around which social life is both organized and hierarchized. But whiteness as backdrop is simultaneously a protective screen—it "screens out" as well as colonizes meaning. We forget that the world of whiteness has a materiality, a history, and proceeds apace only by virtue of its ability to erase itself, its history of genocide or horror.

What is a white racial identity, or any identity, without a space to which it refers? The survival of whiteness in global capitalism requires the continual production and reproduction of spaces in which its order and existence is organized. One of the primary organizers of capitalism is the idea that social spaces are interpreted or planned as "markets" based on their perceived value or potential value for economic exploitation. The production of markets in capitalism has been dominated by whites, and this domination has situated the bodies of most people of color as a market of cheap labor.

The social spaces of whiteness are those of power, territories that confer privilege and domination for whites. As such, the actual social and spatial rituals that form white racial identity in global capitalism might best be revealed through the politically and spatially focused lens of human territoriality. According to Robert Sack (1986), territoriality is a spatial matter "of transmitting energy and information in order to affect, influence, and control the ideas and actions of others and their access to resources" (26). Territoriality is essential to understanding the construction of any type of domination at the level of human interactions since it is the spatial practice of attempting to control the materials and discourses of others. Territoriality is the spatial manifestation of what Michel Foucault describes as "governmentality." Governmentality is a territorial strategy for the control and disciplining of bodies and thoughts on a microgeopolitical scale. For Foucault, most theorizations of power underconceptualize the impact of activities and interactions of social agents in constructing social compliance on microgeopolitical scales (Hesse 1997). In order for power to be structured across time and space in the modern nation-state, it must be surveilled through the disciplined rationales of individual agents (Foucault 1978). Whiteness exists through the territoriality of white agents whose consciousnesses are informed and infected by the rubric of white governmentality, a social and psychological condition that scripts the behavior of whites. The territoriality of whiteness draws breath from the processes of white governmentality that turn the spaces of the human body into a readily identifiable signpost of differential social value and location. These signposts guide the surveillance of white domination in white territories.

To be a person of color in white territory is to be monitored, marked, and excluded. To be white in white territory is to be able to pass the gaze of its bourgeois sentries and traverse its social space as an included, or at least properly subjugated, member. Beverly Daniel Tatum (1997) uses Rosabeth Moss Kanter's (1980) social psychology model of the experience of differentness in an organization to outline the spatial practice of surveilling whiteness. As Tatum explains, "In a Tale of *O*, psychologist Rosabeth Moss Kanter . . . highlights what happens to the *O*, the token, in a world of *X*s. In corporate America, Black people are still in the *O* position. One consequence of being an *O* . . . is heightened visibility. When an *O* walks in the room, the *X*s [white people] notice. Whatever the *O* does, positive or negative, stands out because of this increased visibility. It is hard for an *O* to blend in. When several *O*s are together, the attention of the *X*s is really captured" (89).

Membership in the white community can be revoked, at least in the eyes of other whites, if the warning sensors are triggered under the watch of white governmentality, as white territoriality is essentially a geography of racial selectivity. White governmentality operates in a regulatory mode where as long as people and property are fulfilling their idealized roles in the logic of white capitalism they will be allowed to move about within the given constraints. Among whites, there are codes that determine whether another white person is in line with white governmentality and keeping territorial order. Like some sort of secret handshake, these codes form racial bonds that are difficult for some dissenting whites to see until they themselves experience being surveilled. For example, a group of white girls in the farm town of Morocco, Indiana, went to their mostly white school dressed in the hip-hop style of baggy jeans, dreadlocks, and combat boots (Ignatiev and Garvey 1996). They were physically harassed and threatened at school by other whites for "acting black." In the following months, the school received bomb threats and a visit from the Ku Klux Klan. White territoriality in this case was quite visibly enacted in a public space for all to see.

Yet the maintenance of white territoriality is typically more subtle than this. One of its subtleties has to do with the connectivity among whites or the white community that forges the governmentality for making whiteness. Many times, the testing of bonds in the white community is hidden away in the private spaces of whiteness. Multicultural educator Christine Sleeter (1996) describes a feature of whiteness called "white racial bonding" that acts to "affirm a common stance on race-related issues, legitimating particular interpretations of oppressed groups, and drawing we-they boundaries" (216). As evidence, she tells the story of a conversation she had with a white neighbor whom she barely knew. Almost immediately after exchanging their greetings, the neighbor commented on how pleased she was that the federal government was sending welfare mothers back to work. Sleeter says that racial bonding among whites often works through this type of discursive engagement—a tactic that we call "baiting"—around social issues. Discursive baiting is a common interaction among whites who are acquaintances. It begins with a simple exchange of pleasantries and quickly moves into a test of white solidarity. One of the consequences for giving the wrong answer to discursive bait is to have an extended, oddly antagonistic debate whereby the instigator, or "white sentry," attempts to discipline the logic of the resistor, or "white infidel," and bring her back into the order of whiteness. Of course, another possible consequence for a white infidel is to be socially shunned altogether and made an outsider to the white polity.

Produced through time and space at the nexus of racial oppression and white territoriality, the logic of white governmentality is coded by whites as a means of minimizing the material effects of what is perceived to be a multicultural invasion of the United States—that is, of the white nation. Though whites often do not wish to discuss their own privilege, their recognition of and responses to broad social issues are replete with racial rhetoric and representative of a definite group identity, or "white community." In an important empirical study of white college students, Gallagher (1997) found that the white students he surveyed felt that people of color are or will be responsible for lowered standards of living for whites. Their fear of material deprivation is also located in a white victimization narrative whereby they believe that whites are unfairly attacked by equity programs, such as those of affirmative action. Contradicting the typical notion in whiteness research that whites do not think of themselves as white, Gallagher's research suggests a different trend. As he explains, "The majority of whites in this study have come to understand themselves and their interests as white. Many of my respondents now think about themselves as whites, not as ethnics; they see themselves as individuals who are members of a racial category with its own particular set of interests" (7).

The students expressed an interest in making a new white identity that is non-demonized. One antidemonization strategy currently used by white students to territorialize their white identities in discursive space is to strip away all sense of historical and material reality while representing the white race as simply "equal" to all other races. In spite of the current realities of real oppression, whites argue that society is a utopia of equality, with one exception: whites are now an oppressed class. They contend that true equality can be achieved by eliminating affirmative action, being blind to race, and wiping out "reverse racism" against whites. Within this strategy of white governmentality, whites readily adopt "color blindness" because they see it as a way of promoting their agenda of white victimization, dismissing further criticisms of whiteness, and presenting an image that they are humane for not wanting to refer to others in racial terms.

White racial identity sees the material lives of people of color, and thus, of themselves through the smoke of a historical illusion. In particular, urban spaces such as the inner city, ghetto, barrio, and suburbia are racial signifiers in that their material conditions are inscribed in the logic of white governmentality as readily understood or "plain to see." To most whites, the inner city is a place of dirt, filth, chaos, incivility, and laziness whereas the suburbs are envisioned as orderly, productive, civil, comfortable, and secure. In the logic of white capitalism, the Manichean distinctions between the inner city and suburbia are supposed evidence that a pure and just meritocracy governs social life. Whites morally rationalize the unevenness of urban space through a puritanical work-ethic narrative: those who work hard get to live in the comfort of suburbia while those who are lazy and inept are exiled and then quarantined in the inner city. Douglas Massey and Nancy Denton (1993) describe in great detail how the federal government, banking institutions, and real estate agencies constructed whiteness in its urban form. At the turn of the century, Blacks and whites were more likely to live in integrated neighborhoods than they are today. Starting in the 1930s, the federal government initiated mortgage insurance policies so that banks would accept a lower down payment for purchasing a home, in order to spur the housing market. These programs, however, served to support white racism by institutionalizing a system called "redlining" that identified the neighborhoods that were considered suitable or unsuitable locations for investment. As part of its institutional policy, the Federal Housing Administration (FHA), Veterans Administration (VA), and commercial banks seldom gave federally insured mortgage loans to buyers, who were almost exclusively people of color, in redlined neighborhoods. Additionally, the FHA considered racial segregation as a necessary tactic to maintain stable housing values, at least in white areas.

For example, a 1933 FHA report written in conjunction with realtors concluded that the English, Germans, Scottish, Irish, and Scandinavians were good for neighborhood stability while Mexicans and Blacks were not. Five years later, the FHA warned bank-loan officers in its underwriting manual that they should beware of "incompatible" racial groups that might invade and devalue a neighborhood. Meanwhile, whites were receiving federal backing for a historically unprecedented residential construction project—the building of American suburbia. Today, most of these homes are still owned by whites and continue to increase in value, and unfair banking practices persist. Current studies of banking practices reveal that banks across the country create surplus capital by taking more in deposits *from* Black communities than they invest in them. Banks then shift the surplus toward investment in white ventures (Lipsitz 1995). Many whites remain oblivious to the very real institutional processes that continue to help make their privileged place in the world.

To this day, government institutions are responsible for placing landfills, hazardous waste sites, and chemical manufacturers close to abandoned low-income minority communities. Government institutions single out minority communities for toxic waste sites, as Robin D. Kelley (1997) points out, since it is estimated that "three out of five African-Americans live dangerously close to abandoned toxic waste sites and commercial hazardous landfills" (148). Women of color often take the lead in community-based organizing. For instance, South Central Los Angeles in the 1960s witnessed the growth of the Watts Women's Association, the Avalon-Carver Community Center, the Mothers of Watts Community Action Council, Mothers Anonymous, the Welfare Recipients Union, the Central City Community Mental Health Center, the Neighborhood Organization of Watts, and the South Central Bureau of Los Angeles as precursors for such contemporary groups as Mothers Reclaiming Our Children, and the Mothers of East Los Angeles. In 1984 the Mothers of East Los Angeles won a protracted battle against the prison-industrial complex that wanted to build a prison in East Los Angeles; they also defeated attempts at constructing an oil pipeline and hazardous waste incinerator in the heart of their community. Still, the largest hazardous waste landfill in the country is located in Emelle, Alabama, whose population is nearly 80 percent Black. Kelley also notes other disturbing facts: that the greatest concentration of hazardous waste sites is in the mostly Black and Latino south side of Chicago; federally sponsored toxic cleanup programs take longer and are less thorough in minority neighborhoods; and polluters based in minority areas are treated less severely by government agencies than those in largely white communities. White capitalism as a practice of oppression resides in its ability to spatialize race as well as racialize space.

Ironically, most whites do not see themselves as privileged and, as previously mentioned, have even come to see themselves as social victims. Whites have a problematic construction of privilege primarily because they come to know the world within the boundaries of white territoriality. Peggy McIntosh (1997) argues that privilege is relational and not absolute. One group can only become unprivileged through the privileging of another group. She summarizes the essence of white privilege when she says, "Being white, I am given considerable power to escape many kinds of danger or penalty as well as to choose which risks I want to take" (297).

For people of color, their stories about the organization of privilege in white capitalism are certainly not the same as those of whites. As people of color encounter alienation in the territories of whiteness, survival depends on the ability to construct counterterritorialities that are resistant to white governmentality and provide a spatially productive experience for the recovery and assemblage of nonwhite racial identities. Stephen Nathan Haymes (1995) makes the argument that Black identity coincides with the (re)production of Black public spaces that challenge the moral order of whiteness in urban space. Rather than reading the inner city as a site of Black passivity and victimization, Haymes situates it as a homeplace for the Black counterpublic.

In particular, if power is linked to the production of urban meaning, then those public spaces located at the center of city life dominate its meaning, and in so doing, define the cultural and political terrain in which marginalized public spaces—in this case Black public spaces—resist, form alternative identities, and make culture in the city (Haymes 1995, 113).

The culturally specific institutions of Black public spaces are being disassembled through white territorial practices like gentrification and the production of desaturated spaces of whiteness known as "urban renewal." The gaze of white governmentality situated in the mind of whites perceives Black urban spaces as places of decay, ineptitude, and dysfunction. Whites fantasize about ritualistically purifying Black urban space through the ceremony of urban renewal. White capitalistic desires are satiated when defiled Black spaces are morally laundered by the invisible hand of the market. All of this transpires while Black communities in the inner city have been forced to live in steadily more concentrated quarters. We agree with Haymes when he argues that educators must have a critical understanding of the place-making practices of white institutions that continually attempt to turn the city into a safe space for whiteness under the guise of "reform."

White teachers must also develop an understanding of how students of color experience the territoriality of whiteness at school in ways that form their racial identities. William Cross (1991) has put forth a model that codifies the structure of the psychological process of becoming Black in a white-dominated context. According to Cross, Black people begin with the belief that they are part of the dominant culture until their experiences with racism raises their consciousness about their social status and location. Black children who have reached this stage of "encounter" typically seek out other Black children who share a similar racialized experience. As Black children form friendships with those that they perceive to be similar to themselves, informal groups crystallize and serve as a space for Black racial identity formation. Around the age of adolescence, Black children immerse themselves in differentiated and particular public spaces that act to organize their new identities as representations of their lived struggles with white culture, or as we would argue, with and against white territoriality. On a similar note, John Ogbu (1992) casts this resistance aspect of the encounter stage as a "cultural inversion" of whiteness. Black students that assimilate to white models of educational success run the risk of being tagged as "acting white" by other Black students. Regardless of the strategies employed by students of color, the bottom line is that whiteness affects, influences, and controls the identity formation of people of color through the territorial manipulation of the discursive and material spaces of schooling.

A critique of epistemologies of whiteness necessitates interrogating the ways regimes of white knowledge produce white privilege and reproduce the social conditions that exploit racialized "others." The production of whiteness is simultaneously the creation of racial hierarchies by institutionalizing white-centric norms. But this only works through the control of institutions and social formations, without which white culture becomes one signifier among many. As an institution concerned with producing knowledge, education becomes a prosthesis—the long arm of whiteness—in its quest to reterritorialize social life. Transforming pedagogical knowledge becomes that much more urgent.

WHITENESS AND THE THEORY OF EXPENDITURE

Transforming labor, and consequently student work, requires a revolutionary disposition toward relations of production. In particular, it is imperative that educators link the transformation of the economy with a critique of whiteness. However, theories of whiteness must be linked to the idea that capitalism is not only the exploitation of knowledge for profits, but the simultaneous repression of expenditure, or what Georges Bataille (1997, 1991, 1988, 1985) describes as the human proclivity to expend energy and not to accumulate it. Transformation of labor produces social relations that flourish in conditions free of alienation and exploitation. A discourse on production must also consider alternative theoretical frameworks to explain students' inner experiences and the knowledge they gain from them. Transforming relations of production allows students, as concrete subjects, to experience schooling in new ways, but Bataille's theory of expenditure provides a general framework that explains how we come to know these inner experiences themselves, a theory that functions not within the logic of production, but within that of waste. As Bataille (1988) explains,

> On the surface of the globe, for *living matter in general*, energy is always in excess; the question is always posed in terms of extravagance. The choice is limited to how the wealth is to be squandered. . . . The general movement of exudation (of waste) of living matter implies him [*sic*], and he cannot stop it; . . . it destines him, in a privileged way, to that glorious operation, to

useless consumption. The latter cannot accumulate limitlessly in the productive forces; eventually, like a river into the sea, it is bound to escape us
and be lost to us. (23; emphasis in the original)

Schools accumulate useful knowledge to the point where they cannot hold it.
Students memorize, tabulate, and synthesize knowledge for future-oriented purposes. Eventually, unproductive student behavior erupts and then spreads as students resist and rebel against work as a guiding principle. The conventional
explanation for disruptive student behavior is "unproductivity." Resistant students are either alienated or lazy, and they willfully opt out of work. Bataillean
pedagogy understands this to be a state of wasteful activity that cannot be fully
explained by a productivist logic. It represents the "blind spot" of the discourse
on work. Bataille's pedagogy attempts to transgress the utility of current school
knowledge. Educators isolate unproductive students from their peers to ensure
that they "do their work" or detain them after school to give them extra work.
Meanwhile, what escapes our understanding is the principle of expenditure, or
how students squander schoolwork for no apparently useful or productive reason.

The theory of expenditure does not deny the presence of work, let alone the
importance of liberated labor. It acknowledges the production of life for purposes of subsistence, survival, and improvement of the species. Furthermore, the
modified theory of expenditure we are presenting recognizes the importance of
revolutionizing student work as part of an overall transformation of social life.
In fact, Bataille (1997) clarifies, "Class struggle . . . becomes the grandest form
of social expenditure when it is taken up again and developed, this time on the
part of the workers, and on such a scale that it threatens the very existence of
the masters" (178).

It is at this intersection between work and nonwork that we locate a revolution both of student work and waste. Injected in this dialectic is the indictment
of whiteness as an ideology that alienates students from real knowledge as well
as preventing them from rejoicing in the event of knowing, unfettered from utilitarian concerns.

School knowledge has become not only a commodity in the Marxian sense,
but has taken on the quality of a thing that exists for other things. And as things
go, school knowledge is deemed useful for something outside of itself, to fulfill
a destiny that has been predetermined, such as grades or higher education.
Bataille's perspective decries this utilitarian condition wherein students are subjected to schoolwork that apparently has no intrinsic worth but an exchange
value in the markets of white capitalism.

A radical education understands that combating capitalism is the call for
unalienated student work, but it also recognizes that liberated work then affords
students the opportunity for leisure, or luxurious work. As Herbert Kliebard
(1986) notes, the etymological root of *school* finds itself in the word *leisure*.
This is to say that as much as capitalism exploits labor, it also reduces our
capacity to celebrate nonwork life. This mode of celebration is not to be found

in white societies but expresses itself in what Jean Baudrillard (1975) calls "primitive" societies. As Bataille (1997) describes it, one finds the "festival" or "potlatch" in social arrangements that function under the sign of the gift exchange. Euro-white societies, which function under the sign of classical economics, find the gift exchange rather foreign and irrational. In his endorsement of the gift principle imported by Marcel Mauss, Bataille (1997) writes,

> The "merchants" of Mexico practised the paradoxical system of exchange I have described as a regular sequence of gifts; these customs, not barter, in fact constituted the archaic organization of exchange. Potlatch, still practised by the Indians of the north-west coast of America, is its typical form. Ethnographers now employ this term to designate institutions functioning on a similar principle; they find traces of it in all societies. Among the Tlingit, the Haida, the Tsimshian, the Kwakiutl, potlatch is of prime importance in social life. . . .
>
> Potlatch is, like commerce, a means of circulating wealth, but it excludes bargaining. More often than not it is the solemn giving of considerable riches, offered by a chief to his rival for the purpose of humiliation, challenging and obligating him. The recipient has to erase the humiliation and take up the challenge; he must satisfy the obligation that was contracted by accepting. He can only reply, a short time later, by means of a new potlatch, more generous than the first: he must pay back with interest. (202)

Expenditure is a form of social obligation between subjects who exchange "gifts" and then transcend their limits. A "countergift" raises the stakes. Seen this way, expenditure is inherently intersubjective and anti-individualistic. It binds, for example, teachers and students with one another as each benefits from the other's challenge. The gift is an alternative form of exchange opposed to classical economic transactions. The gift is ruled by the principle of loss, not profit or accumulation. Accumulating gifts without offering countergifts violates the exchange and institutes power in favor of the giver over the receiver. To maintain the equilibrium, it is necessary to perpetuate the exchange, and more important, to raise the stakes with more extravagant gifts. Indeed, in some cases the gift object is produced, but it is produced only to be squandered.

In schools, the moment of learning is subjugated to the utilitarian economic principle of saving the concrete knowledge gained, for an abstract, future purpose. This is the pathological consequence of autocapitalism, which becomes obsessed with "growth for growth's sake" (Ashley 1997), a process with no end in sight. Student curiosity and spontaneity are forsaken, and the excitement—the Aha!—of learning is deferred. What results is the alienation of student subjectivity for utilitarian goals. In short, the gift of knowledge is violated.

Bataillean pedagogy reinstitutes the challenge involved in transgressing the current regimes of school knowledge surveilled by white governmentality through considering schooling as a gift to be returned. Furthermore, this intersubjective process is guided by the principle of expenditure rather than accumulation for utilitarian purposes.

A critical perspective on epistemologies of whiteness considers the general terrorism of the Protestant ethic to negate nonwork life in schools. Within our framework, we suggest that Max Weber's immanent insight neglects the evolution of the spirit of whiteness along with the coevolution of capitalism and Protestantism. In its search to procure salvation through work and accumulation of things, the parallel evolution of Protestantism, whiteness, and capitalism suppresses students' capacity to enjoy the fruits of their work. Students' immediate gratification from work is always either denied or deferred. Salvation through work becomes the only good, against which all other endeavors are measured (Richardson 1994). A student quickly learns that one's worth becomes coextensive with one's work. Human identity becomes the kind of work one takes up: *I am* an attorney! *I am* a doctor! Take note of the dejection a person feels when he loses his job. Over and beyond the feeling of improvidence, he feels worthless. Extending Weber's thesis, we argue that capitalism is also linked with the *Protestant ethnic*, or the hyperutilitarianism found in white patriarchal capitalism. That is, Weber's findings neglect the *construction of whiteness* with respect to work and utilitarianism, or the making of a *Protestant ethnic*. We suggest that any discourse that negates white capitalism as the exploitation of labor for profit must also critique the way it exploits all facets of learning as determined by utilitarian labor.

Homogeneous societies, or social formations determined by utility, are characterized by limits because their imagination is bound by a foreseeable end that turns any form of waste into what Bataille calls the "accursed share," or the cursed portion of society. On the other hand, heterogeneous societies, or social formations determined by expenditure, know no bounds since they are driven by transgression of the sacred. The accursed share, those denigrated discursive and material spaces of people of color in white territories, is jettisoned by the mechanisms of white capitalism since it is seen as unproductive by white governmentalities. The high unemployment of people of color is considered a natural residue of competition and ameliorating homelessness an inefficient endeavor. In Donnie Brasco's words, "Forget about it." Learning-disabled students, gang members, children with physical exceptionalities, and high school dropouts represent the cursed parts of schooling and are grouped under the sign "unproductive." Yet their heterogeneous existence points to their alternative way of being, an experience that can be explained through its contrast with utilitarian work. This does not suggest that these subjects do not want to work, or do not work hard for that matter. Often, as Paul Willis (1977), Peter McLaren (1999), and Jay MacLeod (1987) have shown, some of the most alienated students are the ones who valorize work. But it goes without saying that their perceived incompatibility with production is responsible for labeling them as part of the accursed share of white capitalism. Bataillean pedagogy speaks up for the oppressed segments of our schools, the heterogeneous other of the workaday world (Pefanis 1991).

Much has been said about white fascism (see, e.g., McLaren 1995, 1997). For Georges Bataille (1997), fascism's renegade morality represents something of the order of the heterogeneous and warrants critical attention from the perspective of expenditure. In his studies of German and Italian fascism, Bataille writes,

> Opposed to democratic politicians, who represent in different countries the platitude inherent to homogeneous [i.e., productive] society, Mussolini and Hitler immediately stand out as something other. Whatever emotions their actual existence as political agents of evolution provokes, it is impossible to ignore the force that situates them above men, parties and even laws: a force that disrupts the regular course of things, the peaceful but fastidious homogeneity powerless to maintain itself (the fact that laws are broken is only the most obvious sign of the transcendent, heterogeneous nature of fascist action). (128)

Bataille does not promote fascists and their human atrocities. This is unequivocal, and his unrelenting critique of fascism is well documented (Richardson 1994). What captures his interest is fascism's utmost heterogeneity and extreme authority, which exists for itself before it exists for any useful or productive reasons. To Bataille, the psychological structure of fascism exceeds any conventional ideas about morality involving good and bad. There seems to be no boundary to fascist atrocities. "Evil" just does not seem to suffice as a descriptor. What can we call Adolf Hitler's disgusting campaign of death? What signifier fits the image, the punishment for the crime? Fascism is driven to extreme social hypnosis as a way of concentrating the people's affective flows before it is linked with any productive ends. It is wasteful in all its manifestation, and fascism—etymologically tied to "uniting" or "concentrating" (Bataille 1997, 135)—becomes the hoarding of human energy for the fascist leader. In short, what was originally explorable in terms of expenditure becomes a convenient story about accumulation of power, of energy, and ultimately of homogeneous purpose.

White fascism is not only the enforcement of white territorial control of the means of production. It is also the simultaneous policing of excess, of curbing expenditure and revelry (not to mention ribaldry) where these may threaten the puritanical code of white governmentality. How many examples do we have of the carnivalesque activity, outlawry, and social brigandage of student behavior quelled by the repressive power of state or local police? Celebration is confused for lawlessness as the antiriot unit marches into the potlatch to subdue its energy. School classrooms function under this sign of general repression where quietude is valued over movement and vitality. Yet shift the scene to a crowded hallway or students on their way to their lockers and the noise deafens even the hard of hearing. White fascism is as much about the control of expenditure as it is the control of the means of production. As an apparatus of whiteness, schools become places of the saving of energy rather than the spending of it.

It should be plain to see that white capitalism has encoded the colored body as a site of excess. To the white fascist, black students (especially males) have become the site of supersexuality and the Latina body a site of superreproduction. On the other hand, the white body has been constructed as the site of rationality and savings. The white body is almost nonsexualized. This erotic economy of "excess" is linked to a genocidal tendency in the history and geography of whiteness to the extent that white ideology has been involved in consistent crimes against the eroticized other. The oppression of the sexual other is evidence of a certain repression of the expenditure that whiteness represses in itself. That is, whiteness recognizes an excess beyond productivity but fails to squander it, fearing the ecstatic consequences of such a waste.

It is a vicarious living of sorts that robs whiteness of any life of its own. It is a mitigated, *surreptitious* experience that partitions the erotic—that is, the irreducible experience—into fantasies rather than participating in its flows. It is a projection of what whiteness fears about itself and fails to understand: a certain excessive drive. This may sound like the eroticization of the racialized subject represented in the white imaginary. For it seems a standard white discourse to portray the other as a site of excess. However, remaining consistent with Bataille's theory, expenditure is a general economy that inheres in all humans. It is not an economic drive particular to non-Western societies, but one that finds its expression in them, and its repression in whiteness.

Simple life forms excrete waste, factories spew smoke, and stars explode as supernova only to give birth to new star formations from leftover stellar material. Inasmuch as capitalism commodifies any and all social spaces for profit, whiteness refuses to divest itself of excess but saves it for further growth, forestalling its inevitable and disastrous expression. Wars, riots, and civil unrest are today's social potlatch.

CONCLUSION

The theory of expenditure proposed here is a modified Bataillean pedagogy. It represents an alternative theory to production that nevertheless depends on the transformation of labor to realize its luxurious goals. A modified theory of expenditure recognizes the value in school experiences promoting knowledge that serves no master. But it also realizes that a master currently exists and must be deposed strategically. The double helix of whiteness and capitalism is the conspiratorial first cause. Pushing the contradictions of white capitalism to their extreme exposes the weak joints of the economy. Only then can we approach what Bataille calls "unknowing," or knowledge divorced from utilitarian ends, because it reconciles student interests in work as these evolve in their liberated form and not as they (re)produce certain outcomes. Bataillean pedagogy, as Jurgen Habermas (1987) suggests, appears like a form of fantastic anarchism because it lacks a rational basis for valuing one form of student work over another (since this is beyond linguistic representation). Moreover, Bataille is involved in a performative contradiction that uses reasoned arguments to reject the metanarrative of rational knowledge (Jay 1993). However, it is also possible to construct Bataille's suggestions not as anarchistic, but as an opening up of knowledge to all possibilities. Transforming student labor and transgressing utilitarian experience represents the double move out of alienated school knowledge.

A revolutionary multicultural education entails teaching students and teachers about the productive basis of schools and social life. It calls for white teachers to pay attention to how they manifest their whiteness through their territorial control over production and expenditure. Revolutionary multiculturalists assist students in constructing a concrete education by exposing the contradictions found in their encounters with the normative spatial orders of whiteness. Revolutionary multiculturalism encourages young minds to link their critique of school knowledge with the white exploitation of racialized labor. However, revolutionary multiculturalism also recognizes the importance of a theory of expenditure in order to guard against the uncritical valorization of utilitarian labor coextensive with whiteness. Squandering knowledge without return or profit is not the opposite of production but rather its completion. Revolutionary multiculturalism is involved in planning the counterterritorial construction of spaces for forging liberating relationships between expenditure and production. But we should problematize those relationships between expenditure and production that serve the interests of white capitalism. For example, a certain factory in Los Angeles employs mostly Mexicans for the production of audio speakers. On Cinco de Mayo, the mostly white administration of this factory hires mariachi bands to perform for the workers during their lunch break. In this scenario, expenditure has been folded into capitalist production. The mariachis are hired not to promote the resistance of labor, but to make the laborers more productive and loyal to the company. This is not the kind of relationship between production and expenditure that is counterhegemonic. A revolutionary multiculturalism calls for whites to be allies with people of color in authoring spatialities that intervene in the normative functioning of white privilege in white capitalism.

A revolutionary multiculturalism sharpens on the whetstone of liberation. Bataille's vision of excess and Marx's imperative of class struggle can help us to formulate such a revolutionary project in order to sever both the economic thralldom through which the oppressed are imprisoned by the capitalist class as well as the systems of classification and intelligibility that are used to justify the current social and spatial division of labor. We need not wait to be given the gift of solidarity from the gods of progress nor expect it to be produced by the inevitability of revolution. Rather, we must take that first step toward revolutionary praxis. That is one gift we can bestow on ourselves.

REFERENCES

Acuña, R. 1997. *Anything but Mexican: Chicanos in Contemporary Los Angeles.* London: Verso.

Ashley, D. 1997. *History without a Subject.* Boulder, Colo.: Westview Press.

Banks, J. 1989. "Multicultural Education: Characteristics and Goals." In *Multicultural Education: Issues and Perspective*, edited by J. Banks and C. M. Banks, 2-26. Needham Heights, Mass.: Allyn Bacon.

Bataille, G. 1985. *Visions of Excess: Selected Writings 1927-1939*, translated by A. Stoekl. Manchester: Manchester University Press.

_____. 1988. *The Accursed Share.* Vol. I, translated by R. Hurley. New York: Zone Books.

_____.1991. *The Accursed Share.* Vols. 2 and 3, translated by R. Hurley. New York: Zone Books.

_____.1997. *The Bataille Reader*, edited by F. Botting and S. Wilson. Cornwall: Blackwell.

Baudrillard, J. 1975. *The Mirror of Production.* St. Louis: Telos Press.

Bernstein, S. 1996. "The Storm Rises Over Ex-Klansman in Debate." *Los Angeles Times*, 11 September, A3, A14.

Cross, W. E. 1991. *Shades of Black: Diversity in African-American Identity.* Philadelphia: Temple University Press.

Foucault, M. 1978. *Discipline and Punish: The Birth of the Prison*, translated by A. Sheridan. New York: Pantheon Books.

Gallagher, C. 1997. "White Racial Formation: Into the Twenty-First Century." In *Critical White Studies: Looking Behind the Mirror*, edited by R. Delgado and J. Stefanic, 6-11. Philadelphia: Temple University Press.

Habermas, J. 1987. *The Philosophical Discourse of Modernity*, translated by F. G. Lawrence. Cambridge, Mass.: MIT Press.

Haymes, S. N. 1995. *Race, Culture, and the City: A Pedagogy for Black Urban Struggle.* Albany: State University of New York Press.

Hesse, B. 1997. "White Governmentality." In *Imagining Cities: Scripts, Signs, Memory*, edited by S. Westwood and J. Williams, 86-103. London: Routledge.

Ignatiev, N., and J. Garvey. 1996. "Free to Be Me." In *Race Traitor*, edited by N. Ignatiev and J. Garvey, 1. New York: Routledge.

Jay, M. 1993. *Downcast Eyes.* Berkeley and Los Angeles: University of California Press.

Kanter, R. M. 1980. *A Tale of "O". On Being Different in an Organization.* New York: Harper and Row.

Kelley, R. D. G. 1997. *Yo' Mama's Disfunktional! Fighting the Cultural Wars in Urban America.* Boston: Beacon Press.

Kincheloe, J., S. Steinberg, N. Rodriguez, and R. Chennault, eds. 1998. *White Reign: Deploying Whiteness in America.* New York: St. Martin's Press.

Lipsitz, G. 1995. "The Possessive Investment in Whiteness: Racialized Social Democracy and the 'White' Problem in American Studies." *American Quarterly* 47, no.3: 369-87.

Lott, E. 1993. "White Like Me: Racial Cross-Dressing and the Construction of American Whiteness." In *Cultures of United States Imperialism*, edited by A. Kaplan and D. E. Pease, 47-98. Durham, N.C.: Duke University Press.

Löwy, M. 1998. Globalization and Internationalism: How Up-to-Date Is the *Communist Manifesto*?" *Monthly Review*, 50, no. 6: 16-27.

MacLeod, J. 1987. *Ain't No Makin' It*. Boulder, Colo.: Westview Press.

McIntosh, P. 1997. "White Privilege and Male Privilege: A Personal Account of Coming to See Correspondences through Work in Women's Studies." In *Critical White Studies: Looking Behind the Mirror*, edited by R. Delgado and J. Stefanic, 291-99. Philadelphia: Temple University Press.

McCarthy, C. 1990. *Race and Curriculum*. London: Falmer Press.

McIntyre, A. 1997. "Constructing an Image of a White Teacher." *Teachers College Record* 98, no. 4: 653-81.

McLaren, P. 1999. *Schooling as a Ritual Performance*, 3rd ed. Boulder, Colo.: Rowman and Littlefield.

_____. 1995. *Critical Pedagogy and Predatory Culture*. London: Routledge.

_____. 1997. *Revolutionary Multiculturalism*. Boulder, Colo.: Westview Press.

Marx, K., and F. Engels. 1964. *The Communist Manifesto*, translated by S. Moore. New York: Simon and Schuster

Massey, D., and N. Denton. 1993. *American Apartheid: Segregation and the Making of the Underclass*. Cambridge, Mass.: Harvard University Press.

Ogbu, J 1992. "Understanding Cultural Diversity and Learning." *Educational Researcher* 21, no. 8: 5-14.

Pefanis, J. 1991. *Heterology and the Postmodern*. Durham, N.C.: Duke University Press.

Sack, R. 1986. *Human Territoriality: Its Theory and History*. Cambridge: Cambridge University Press.

Sleeter, C. 1996. "White Silence, White Solidarity." In *Race Traitor*, edited by N. Ignatiev and J. Williams, 257-65. New York: Routledge.

Sleeter, C., and P. McLaren, eds. 1995. *Multicultural Education, Critical Pedagogy, and the Politics of Difference*. Albany: State University of New York Press.

Tatum, B. D. 1997. *"Why Are all the Black Kids Sitting Together in the Cafeteria?" and Other Conversations about Race*. New York: Basic Books.

Willis, P. 1977. *Learning to Labor*. New York: Columbia University Press.

11

LABELING WHITENESS
DECENTERING STRATEGIES OF WHITE RACIAL DOMINATION

Peter McLaren, Aimee M. Carrillo-Rowe, Rebecca L. Clark, and Philip A. Craft

The term 'whiteness' has become a voguish buzzword in academia, having secured at least a temporary place of honor in the lexicon of the new multiculturalists. Increasingly, this itinerant and unstable term has been put on exhibit at the wine-and-cheese salons of postmodernist academics where the concept of 'white trash' has suddenly taken on new scholarly dimensions. A burgeoning fascination with the social construction of whiteness has spawned a giddy rush of conferences, books, articles, and courses dedicated to its analysis and critique. Recently, in an attempt to lend legitimacy to white studies, following the recent surge of interest in critical race theory, Temple University Press has issued a collection of essays entitled, *Critical White Studies* (Delgado and Stefancic 1997). But what exactly is 'whiteness'? Is it multiculturalism's latest effort at rhetorical camouflage? Is it a *foramen magnum* to a new way of understanding racism? A *force majeure* in advancing new theories of subjectivity? Is it simply an academic ruse that will enable white theorists to steal some of the limelight in the ongoing culture wars? Is it a mere quasi-theoretical residue of more complex analyses of racialized identity? Will the topic of whiteness be of interest to a wider public? Can whiteness be addressed pertinently, in a way that delves deeper than the out-of-context cut-and-paste treatises we have come to expect from crackpot 'race' theorists in the media? (After all, such pundits of the airwaves more often than not reduce race and ethnicity to little more than a market-driven, self-serving saturnalia of ill-defined ethnic celebrations—for example, Cinco de Mayo or Black History Month—while acting as stand alone moralists and unashamedly extolling the commodity character of racial traits.) More importantly, is this label at all useful, or does its racial specificity merely replicate the logic of racism by reifying and dialectically reinitiating 'chromatic' differences, as its critics claim?

This chapter originally appeared in Glenn P. Hudak and Paul Kihn (Eds.), *Labeling: Pedagogy and Politics*, pp. 203-224. © 2001 RoutledgeFalmer. Reprinted with permission of the publisher.

We intend to demonstrate—albeit in abbreviated form—that the term 'whiteness' serves as a useful vehicle for contesting and altering the existing and persistent racial power relations within the United States. While traditional discussions of race focus on non-whites, analyses of whiteness examine white people, the dominant racial group, who have heretofore escaped public and academic scrutiny of their racist, sexist and heterosexist practices. Labeling whiteness provides a sociopolitical optic through which the practices that produce structural privilege and exploitation can be examined and addressed. Using whiteness as a label broadens and deepens more traditional explanations of racism by mapping racist characteristics that are specific to the dominant racial group in this nation: white people.

Largely because public opinion in the United States defines racism 'psychodynamically' as interpersonal acts of hatred and because there has been a decline in overt forms of racial violence, the dominant white society has all too often, jumped to the conclusion that the problem is almost completely resolved. To support this argument one need only cite California's recent abolition of affirmative action measures and its elimination of bilingual education. Another strong indicator of the unacknowledged presence of white supremacy is the manner in which whiteness has become institutionalized as the key marker or measure against which identity is defined. For an example of the hereditary invisibility of whiteness, we need look no farther than Senate majority leader Trent Lott, a politician from Mississippi well known to the general public for his conservative ideals and his role in the impeachment proceedings of president William Jefferson Clinton. Although Lott has been described in a recent issue of *The Nation* as one of 'the pinstriped mafiosi of the culture wars' (Shapiro 1999: 4), he continues to be invoked by the mainstream media as a principled actor in the cause of family values. Despite his past participation in and alleged continuing relationship with Mississippi's white supremacist Council of Conservative Citizens (CCC), Lott is frequently portrayed by the mainstream media as a courageous example of moral impeccability and national leadership.

With white supremacy so invisible in today's society—with the exception of a smattering of stories about growing numbers of militia groups throughout the United States—is it any wonder that racial injustice rages on? Recent analyses of whiteness address some of the numerous oversights that result from this conceptually truncated definition of racism by interrogating it instead as an institutionalized system of economic, political, social, and cultural relations that ensures that one racial group maintains power and advantage over all others. While there is nothing inherently 'white' about racism, the status of white people in the United States as the dominant 'race' demands that we specifically examine the structural relationship between racism and white privilege. It is precisely this structural relationship between white people and racial domination that needs to be 'marked' and examined because, as we will argue, it is a relationship that has nourished a specific form of social and political invisibility in mainstream United States culture.

In order to explore how and why the study of whiteness provides a useful conceptual framework for interrogating racism, we first examine how 'whiteness' functions. In so doing, we identify three strategies through which white people are assured continued racial privilege, strategies that we consider related to the remarkably 'unmarked' character of whiteness. We follow with an examination of the conjunctural relationship among whiteness, capitalism, and neo-imperialism. We suggest that within the spatial boundaries of the United States, whiteness cannot be reduced to racism, but must be considered as a function of those colonial legacies and contemporary imperialist and racist practices through which white power and social position is hegemonically secured. We conclude with a sketch of possible tactical maneuvers aimed at decentering whiteness in our own daily practices.

DEFINING WHITENESS

[T]he vision of a world of intelligent men [sic] with sufficient income to live decently and with the will to build a beautiful world . . . will not be easy to accomplish . . . but the quickest way to bring the reason of the world face to face with this major problem of human progress is to listen to the complaint of those human beings today who are suffering most from white attitudes, from white habits, from the conscious and unconscious wrongs which white folks are today inflicting on their victims.
(Du Bois 1968: 172)

If whiteness is never articulated, then it is people of Color, as a group, who can be scrutinized and blamed in order to exalt the perfection of that which is natural and left unexamined.
(Hurtado 1996: 139)

We cannot talk intelligently about 'whiteness' unless we introduce the dynamics of political economy. Too often critical race theory, critical pedagogy, and whiteness studies decapitate or degut the study of race from the history of capitalist social relations. According to Alex Callinicos (1993), racial differences are invented within specific political economies associated with the mode of production. Racism occurs when the characteristics which justify discrimination are held to be inherent in the oppressed group. The institutionalized forms of this type of oppression are peculiar to capitalist societies; they arise in the circumstances surrounding industrial capitalism and the attempt to acquire a large labor force. Racism is no mere epiphenomenon of a determinant social process, but a fundamental component of that process. Callinicos points out three main conditions for the existence of racism as outlined by Marx: economic competition between workers; the appeal of racist ideology to white workers; and efforts of the capitalist class to establish and maintain racial divisions among workers. Capital's constantly changing demands for different kinds of labor can only be met through immigration. Callinicos remarks that 'racism offers for workers of the oppressing "race" the imaginary compensation for the exploitation they suffer of belonging to the "*ruling* nation"' (1993: 39). He also underscores the profound manner in which Marx grasped how racial divisions between 'native' and immigrant workers could weaken the working class.

What George Lipsitz refers to as 'the possessive investment in whiteness' has always been influenced by its origin in the history of United States racist practices, involving the demonization of the *faex populi* (the lower orders), slavery, segregation, and the wholesale extermination of indigenous peoples. In North America, slavery took on distinctive racial formations that reduced African Americans to permanent, hereditary, chattel-bond slaves. According to Lipsitz (1998: 3):

> White settlers institutionalized a possessive investment in whiteness by making blackness synonymous with slavery and whiteness synonymous with freedom, but also by pitting people of color against one another. Fearful of alliances between Native Americans and African Americans that might challenge the prerogatives of whiteness, white settlers prohibited slaves and free blacks from traveling in 'Indian country.' European Americans used diplomacy and force to compel Native Americans to return runaway slaves to their white masters. During the Stono Rebellion of 1739, colonial authorities offered Native Americans a bounty for every rebellious slave they captured or killed. At the same time, British settlers recruited black slaves to fight against Native Americans within colonial militias. The power of whiteness depended not only on white hegemony over separate racialized groups, but also on manipulating racial outsiders to fight against one another, to compete with each other for white approval, and to seek the rewards and privileges of whiteness for themselves at the expense of other racialized populations.

If we wish to get at the roots of whiteness, we need to focus on the social, political, economic, and historical actualities that sustain it. And while we do not have space here to cut a large clearing in the dense thicket of capital's relationship to whiteness, we can still explore a few possibilities. Our principal claim is that we cannot discuss whiteness in abstraction from material circumstances or the practices of exploitation that capitalism provokes in its train. We support the claim that whiteness and capitalism interweave and that whiteness is fundamentally linked to the practice of Anglo-European and United States colonialism. Its concrete historical facticity can be traced to the trans-Atlantic slave trade. Following Theodore W. Allen (1994, 1997), Jonathan Scott (1998), and McLaren and Munoz (2000), we proceed on the prevailing assumption that whiteness is, first and foremost, a 'sociogenic' (having to do with social forces and relations rather than a 'phylogenic' (having to do with phenotype or skin color) phenomenon. We start from the premise that the concept of a separate white race did not exist prior to the seventeenth century. For instance, in colonial Virginia, roughly between 1676 and 1705, there existed little distinction in status between 'black' and 'white' bond-laborers who were essentially *ejusdem generis*. Whiteness was a false totality imperiously imposed on the heterogeneous population of the colony so that the Anglo-American continental plantation bourgeoisie could keep the colonial tobacco monoculture from being diversified or threatened by rebellious landless laborers (as in the famous case of the Bacon Rebellion). Whiteness was a status position introduced by seventeenth-century Anglo-American and United States ruling class—largely the oligarchy of owners of large colonial plantations—who for purely political and economic purposes endowed indentured Europeans (who at the time were *de facto* slaves) with civil and social privileges that greatly exceeded those of their fellow African bondsmen and granted those with white skin an inscrutable unity (Allen 1994; Scott 1998).

Within New England's progressive system of equitably distributed small land holdings, freedom for bond-laborers (6,000 Europeans and 2,000 African Americans) would effectively have created a condition of economic *écroulement*, ending the plantocracy's super-exploitation of the African and European bond-laborers. Freedom for these 8,000 bond-laborers would have transformed the colony into a diversified smallholder economy. This would have been ultimately disastrous for the tobacco monoculture, which essentially depended upon chattel or bond labor. The chattelization of labor thus became a necessity for strengthening Virginia's tobacco monoculture. However, the small landholders of colonial Virginia had begun to oppose changes in Virginia land policy that allocated the best land to wealthy capitalist investors, and laws that forbade them to trade with the Indians. More and more landless laborers began to fight against their chattel bond-servitude. In the Bacon Rebellion Africans and Europeans fought side by side against the plantation bourgeoisie, who would routinely punish runaway laborers by adding years to their servitude, and who ordered severe restrictions on corn-planting and a ban on hunting for food in the forests so that the rebelling chattel bond-laborers would starve to death (Allen 1994; Scott 1998).

The aim of the Anglo-American continental plantation bourgeoisie was to prepare the ground for a system of lifetime hereditary bond-servitude. But the 'confederation' of African American slaves and European bond-laborers made their military power too strong for the colony elite to defeat with its small force of only 500 fighters. Indentured Anglo-Americans were consequently recruited into the middle classes through anomalous white-skin privileges. White-skin privilege was an acknowledgement of loyalty to the colonial land- and property-owning class. Africans were not brought into the middle class because there were simply too many laboring-class Europeans who had no social mobility and were thus a constant threat to the plantocracy. The white race had to be invented in order to diffuse this potential threat to ruling-class hegemony.

In summary, the invention of the white race was a political and economic maneuver designed to secure control by the plantocracy. It was primarily a means of preventing Anglo-Americans who existed in a state of chattel bond-servitude from joining forces with African bondsmen and overthrowing the plantocracy. That is, whiteness was an historical process of homogenizing the social statuses of Anglo-European tenants, merchants and planters into membership in the white race. Racial oppression was systematically put into place and European Americans were brought into the white 'middle class.' This saved the ruling class the money that it would have cost them to put down constant rebellions. Whiteness in this sense was a type of hideous abstraction, a dead 'second nature' invented by capitalism in order to falsely resurrect the putative natural superiority of the plantation bourgeoisie and the necessity of lifetime servitude for those who were not admitted into the white race.

With the rise of the abolitionist movement, racial typologies, classification systems, and criteriologies favoring whiteness and demonizing blackness became widespread in order to justify and legitimize the slavery of Africans and ensure the continuation of lifetime chattel bond-servitude. As Euro-Americans were called to imperialistically impute their categories and criteriologies everywhere, African Americans were forced to subordinate their lives to historically specific external criteria—imprinted with Eurocentric discourses of superiority—designed to usurp their autonomy and to separate their labor from a free collective exercise of will. Whiteness as an affirmation of power did not emerge from some transcendent intertwining with the immanent, but is thoroughly sinewy and historical; whiteness has no absolute, but only historical relevance as a specific mode of oppression. Today 'whiteness' has become naturalized as part of the national envelope of 'commonsense' reality.

Within this historical context, whiteness can be conceptualized as a social location that offers white people a structurally privileged position in current US society in relation to people of color. This social location constitutes a particular 'standpoint' or racial referent against which white people interpret themselves, others, and the world, a standpoint that can be maintained only by burying the historical memory of slavery, sealing it in a vault of silence, a shimmering alabaster monument to the Great White Lie. In talking about whiteness we need to outlaw transhistorical categories. Whiteness is a context-specific social construction, a fictional identity that facilitates and ensures that social privilege is maintained for those who are positioned as white. Accordingly, as well as being a social location or a standpoint, whiteness is also a set of strategies that operate to maintain white supremacy. There is no *Aufhebung* of whiteness, no logic of totality or dialectics of transformation that can contain it within the social universe of capital.

McLaren (1997) and McLaren and Muñoz (2000) articulate whiteness as an essentially mystifying and self-naturalizing discourse intrinsic to capitalism, a sociohistorical form of consciousness born at the nexus of capitalism, colonial rule, and the emergent relationships among dominant and subordinate groups.

Wherever whiteness operates, the bourgeoisie appropriate the right to speak on behalf of everyone who is non-white, while denying voice to 'others' in the name of 'civilization.' Whiteness is born in a context where increased wealth for the few means impoverishment or marginalization for the many. Whiteness demarcates ideas, feelings, knowledge, social practices, cultural formations, and systems of intelligibility that are invested in by white people as 'white.' Whiteness is also a refusal to acknowledge how white people are implicated in relations of social domination and subordination and instances of economic exploitation. Whiteness, in this sense, as we mentioned before, appears ubiquitous and stable yet at the same time can be considered as a form of historical amnesia. Whiteness constitutes the selective tradition of dominant discourses about race, class, gender, and sexuality. Whiteness is not a unified, homogeneous culture but a social position, one that 'unvoices' or 'unpeoples' the Other. As Ignatiev (1998: 199, 233) comments:

> There is nothing positive about white identity. As James Baldwin said, 'As long as you think you're white, there's no hope for you.' Whiteness is not a culture. There is Irish culture and Italian culture and American culture; there is youth culture and drug culture and gear culture. There is no such thing as white culture. Shakespeare was not white; he was English. Mozart was not white; he was Austrian. Whiteness has nothing to do with culture and everything to do with social position. Without the privileges attached to it, there would be no white race, and fair skin would have the same significance as big feet.
>
> The problem with white people is not whiteness, but our possessive investment in it. Created by politics, culture, and consciousness, our possessive investment in whiteness can be altered by those same processes, but only if we face the hard facts openly and honestly and admit that whiteness is a matter of interests and attitudes, that it has more to do with property than with pigment. Not all believers in white supremacy are white. All whites do not have to be supremacists. But the possessive investment in whiteness is a matter of behavior as well as belief.

Referring to California as the 'Mississippi of the 1990s,' George Lipsitz criticizes the University of California regents for abolishing affirmative action, a practice he refers to as a 'possessive investment in whiteness.' He argues

> The violent upheaval in Los Angeles in 1992 reflected only a small portion of the rage, despair and cynicism permeating California as a result of the racial effects of the transformation from a national industrial economy to a global postindustrial economy. The possessive investment in whiteness plays an insidious role in these realities: it occludes the crisis that we all face as a result of declining wages, environmental hazards, and social disintegration, while it generates racial antagonism as the only available frame for comprehending how individuals imagine themselves as a part of society.

Whiteness is not an essential category. For example, we oppose the belief that race is genetically determined, and can be sorted neatly by phenotype. Rather, we insist that whiteness as an *ideology* functions as an ongoing social, historical, cultural, and political practice in which meanings are secured that ensure the reproduction of white racial supremacy. It is absolutely important that we recognize that there are material benefits involuntarily accrued by persons with perceived white racial status, and that the meaning of whiteness and who counts as white entails a social, discursive process. Recent scholarly attention devoted to the topic of whiteness delineates several social practices on which the maintenance of a system of racial domination by whites depends. We outline three here.

The Definition of Difference

First, through their dominant racial position, white people have been able to construct themselves as 'central' because of their ability to construct 'others' as marginal and different, with difference from whiteness judged as inferior. White people have been able to secure a privileged 'standpoint' manifested in their ability to define cultural common sense, because whiteness has been consciously and unconsciously measured *against* racialized 'others.' This means that the category 'white' is not construed as racialized, while other 'races' serve to define the 'outer limits' of whiteness. Whiteness, in this sense, functions through defining what is different. And difference *never designates neutrality.* As soon as difference is marked, it is evaluated according to the overarching standards of whiteness and is always found to be lacking. Within a logic of hierarchy, where one race dominates the other, difference cannot, by definition, ever be equal to whiteness if white people are to maintain their dominant social position. Hence, we must remain skeptical about a great deal of contemporary rhetoric that advocates 'embracing difference.' Without a critical examination of how whiteness functions through difference as superiority, such claims to equality are premature and serve only to prolong racial disparities. For example, anti-affirmative action bills such as Proposition 209 in California and I-200 in Washington—which effectively terminate financial aid to women and ethnic minority groups—gain support by coopting the rhetoric used in Civil Rights efforts to 'end discrimination.' In the case of these anti-affirmative action bills, the supposed 'victim' in whose interest we are to 'end discrimination' happens to be white and male. Claims that white men are victimized by what they see as 'racial favoritism' in affirmative action policies are only credible if we assume that differences are equal, that is, that white males experience the same kind of economic disadvantage and discrimination on the basis of skin color and phenotype as people of color who are also 'different'.

The Significance of Difference

The ability of white people to arrange social perception highlights our second point, that whiteness is really a type of social contract, a social construction and organization which works only if social subjects accept both that racial differences exist and they provide a valid means to interpret or understand ourselves and others. Because racial differences are visible to social subjects as a text to be read, they take on a semblance of reality or facticity. Differences seem factual because we trust our eyes to provide us with 'accurate' information about our world. We see differences, as Du Bois would say, of 'skin, hair and bone' (1968). But what is important is not that differences merely *exist*, but that such differences are associated with certain meanings or endowed with a special significance (a significance always populated with the intentions of others). How do we make sense of the differences we see? The differences that make a difference? Culture—ranging from the popular (movies, books, newspapers) to the institutional (schools, families, government)—has been described as the 'terrain' upon and through which social meaning occurs. As social subjects, we make sense of the world through the values and norms expressed through the cultural production of knowledge. But culture is also the quilting point where nature intersects with labor, and in this regard it is important to consider how people are reduced to the commodification of their labor-power to be bought and sold in the expanding capitalist marketplace. Race 'matters' to us because we are ideological subjects and whiteness, as a dominant ideological formation and social position, informs and deforms our actions and our interactions in and on the world—whether we realize it or not.

The Inferiority of Difference

Third, it is important to recognize that whiteness is a category that operates and 'succeeds' precisely because it remains itself 'unmarked'. Because whiteness externalizes and labels difference as inferior, its 'gaze' is always directed outward. In other words, white people reserve for themselves the privilege of 'officially' defining racial understandings with the mainstream culture. This outward 'gaze' what white people project on others serves to maintain the white center as 'unmarked.' This allows whiteness to escape the scrutiny of and definition by people of color. People of color have, of course, historically theorized whiteness both academically and culturally in an attempt to call a halt to the historical dialectic of white oppression, but the dominant position of white people ensures that this discussion is not publicly sanctioned in our schools, the press, the entertainment industry, or government. Because whiteness is the ideology of the center, those who operate within its precincts are not obliged to examine the power and privilege that their whiteness affords them. Not engaging in or 'not hearing' criticisms against whiteness has been an insidious strategy for neutralizing challenges to the system initiated by people of color. While not a direct rebuttal of attacks on the racial status quo, this strategy functions as a 'trick' of whiteness. Typically, dismissals of racial critique may be brief, but the subtext, according to Hurtado (1996: 152), reads as follows:

> I will listen to you, sometimes for the first time, and will seem engaged. At critical points in your analysis I will claim I do not know what you are talking about and will ask you to elaborate ad nauseum. I will consistently subvert your efforts at dialogue by claiming we 'do not speak the same language.'

This trick prompts the erasure of whiteness as a category.

Because whiteness resists labeling, it is also able to resist linkages to racial domination, colonialism, imperialism, racialized labor exploitation, and violent assimilation. For example, contemporary discourses on immigration define the 'problem of illegal immigration' around 'illegal aliens' who are constructed by means of racist terminology as a threat to the integrity of the nation. This outward gaze in the direction of the 'other' protects white subjects from a critical self-examination of the racism evident within these discourses, because such racism is naturalized within an ideology that cloaks difference in the mantle of inferiority. In addition, the policies and practices of imperialism directed by the First World against the so-called 'Third World' is effectively erased from our view. As long as whiteness instantiates a universal center and the basis for all forms of 'truth,' white racial domination will continue. Hence, labeling and thus exposing the socially 'invisible' matrix of privileges and strategies of the white dominant class as 'whiteness' is a necessary, albeit insufficient, counter-strategy in the fight for social justice.

Linking Whiteness to the Neo/Colonial

> Operationally, the maintenance of boundaries between 'politics' and 'non-politics' and the casting of certain 'political' acts into the 'non-political' domain, are themselves political acts, and reflect the structure of power and interest. These acts of labeling in the political domain, far from being self-evident, or a law of the natural world, constitute a form of continuing political 'work' on the part of the elites of power; they are, indeed, often the opening salvo in the whole process of political control. (Hall, 1996)

In the previous section we demonstrated why we need a chromatic analysis of contemporary relations of inequality. In this section, we argue that we are not 'just' talking about race when we talk about whiteness. Rather, we expand our concept of whiteness beyond the confines of a discussion of race as discourse and social position to include social relations linked to transnational capitalism.

President Clinton introduced the nationally televised 'Town Meeting on Race' with the following argument: the United States has shown an ability to overcome adversity (in war, economic depression, natural disasters, etc.) and it should utilize that ability in addressing the issue of race. He cited the nation's strong and prosperous economy as evidence of the continued innovation and determination of the population and the hard work of the country's citizens. His justification of the town meeting was his commitment to the idea that open discussion of 'racial issues' would help the country move beyond its racialized history and would promote, in turn, continued prosperity and leadership in the world economic and political order. Clinton's position with respect to 'racial issues'—we quote this term to highlight the absence of the word 'racism' in much of the town meeting—is representative of a larger problem underlying current efforts to address relations of power and racial injustice within the contemporary conjuncture of neo-liberalism and global capitalism, of which the Clinton administration is the world's leading representative. Clinton is certainly not the main agent of whiteness; rather, his appeal arises, at least in part, out of his powerful articulations of whiteness. Our point is not to foreground Clinton as 'the problem,' but to examine our own attachments to his political strategies. In analyzing absences in Clinton's introduction of the 'Town Meeting on Race,' the following section focuses on how whiteness centers and privileges those perceived as white, gazing outward to define and defend differences and transcend those differences by remaining unmarked.

In his town hall remarks, Clinton willfully ignored the processes through which the United States has been able to secure 'the strongest economy in the world.' He did not mention the country's history of transnational labor exploitation, advocacy for unbalanced trade negotiations, or its role in creating unfair development loans and structural adjustments, through global lending agencies such as the World Bank and the International Monetary Fund. Many scholars have analyzed the role of United States corporate and governing bodies in a variety of development policies that continue to organize privilege and oppression on massive scale. Others have tied those policies, more specifically, to racial ideologies. Yet the commonsense understanding about Third World economic crises that was largely exhibited in President Clinton's remarks at the town hall meeting focuses blame and responsibility on those so-called 'Third World' countries, while celebrating the United States as a leader in global politics and capitalist production. This inability to implicate the United States capitalist elite in analyses of global capital flows stems, in our view, from an inability to recognize the ways in which whiteness constitutes relations of power in our neo/colonial present.

Clinton's focus on racial issues remained almost exclusively on United States history and the country's *internal* cultural politics. Clinton's approach to race assumes it is a cultural or 'lifestyle' issue that involves the exercise of prudent citizenship skills and does not challenge dominant class arrangements and institutional class interests. In its imposed ignorance, Clinton's conception of race suggests that 'culture' is somehow autonomous from social relations of production. As a result of his magisterial incomprehension of, or motivated neglect with respect to, the racialized characteristics of development economics, transnational capitalism, and neo-colonial relations, Clinton cordoned off the possibility of larger analysis of the role of whiteness in organizing social formations at both national and global levels. Further, by restricting the concept of racism to irresistible impersonal forces and attitude formations that occur within the cultural borders of the United States, Clinton foreclosed an important opportunity to analyze racism in relation to broader social forces such as global systems of trade and production, as well as international political relations and 'orientalist' ideologies. His perspective tramples historical context under the heel of bourgeois humanism, an approach that has more to do with opinion polls than scientific social analysis.

Deploying spatial borders around the politics of race (so that racial antagonisms in the United States are assumed to be about black-white histories, while inequalities around the world are assumed to be about the underdeveloped nature of Second and Third World countries) remains one of the most powerful and pervasive strategies for resecuring privilege based on race and class. Gayatri Spivak emphasizes the possible repercussions of critical work that neglects the position of the United States within larger systems of power 'To simply foreclose or ignore the international division of labor because that's complicit with our own production, in the interests of the black-white division as representing the problem, is a foreclosure of neo-colonialism operated by chromatist race-analysis'. We present our analysis of 'whiteness' as part of a counter-strategy against the frequent reductionist discourses linked to identity politics that increasingly fleck the landscape of multicultural education, and the often apolitical discourse that informs the pedagogy of development studies.

Dominant development models operate from the misguided and exceedingly Eurocentric assumption that Western nations are more advanced in economic, political, and cultural formation than so-called 'Third World' countries. Although development models have earned the counter-attacks of leftist scholars who consistently point to the massive influences of industrialized nations on the economies of the Third World, many of these scholars have neglected to interrogate further the assumption that industrialized nations have 'healthy,' 'prosperous,' and 'model' economic and cultural systems. In part, this lacuna in critical scholarship has resulted from too little attention being paid to the mutual imbrication of whiteness and transnational relations. However, by focusing one's critique on the mechanisms of whiteness that variously constitute global systems of exploitation—mechanisms that we expose as largely dependent upon myths of the Third World 'Other' as inferior—we contend that new and fecund possibilities will emerge for unsettling the reigning assumptions of developmental models. Exploring global economic histories and development policies through the optic of whiteness studies can address the complexities of power relations and their racialized modalities across modernity.

If destabilizing the Eurocentric and orientalist models in development economics is a prime necessity, the same type of decentering has also to take place when analyzing the internal cultural politics of the United States, a politics that implicitly persuades public opinion in the direction of supporting a market economy as the only sane and responsible position. We agree with Ellen Meiksins Wood's observation that 'wherever market imperatives regulate the economy and govern social reproduction, there will be no escape from exploitation.' There can, in other words, be no such thing as a truly 'social' or democratic market, let alone a 'market socialism' (1999: 119). Woods' perspective is worth quoting at length.

> Today it is more obvious than ever that the imperatives of the market will not allow capital to prosper without depressing the conditions of great multitudes of people and degrading the environment throughout the world. We have now reached the point where the destructive effects of capitalism are outstripping its material gains. No third world country today, for example, can hope to achieve even the contradictory development that England underwent. With the pressures of competition, accumulation, and exploitation imposed by more developed capitalist economies, and with the inevitable crises of overcapacity engendered by capitalist competition, the attempt to achieve material prosperity according to capitalist principles is increasingly likely to bring with it only the negative side of the capitalist contradiction, its dispossession and destruction without its material benefits—certainly for the vast majority.

Revealing that a discourse of 'whiteness' exists at the very heart of reigning constructions of race and citizenship displaces the assumption of the nation as a taken-for granted boundary separating ideological systems and histories. Prevailing forms of racial analysis in the United States displace a global frame that could articulate the hegemonizing role 'whiteness' in organizing new forms of capital accumulation and new modes of oppression with respect to specific social collectivities as well as differentiated forms of exploitation linked to both different social sectors and the differential composition of the labor force. In effect, nation-centered expositions of racial politics allow celebratory claims about the economic prosperity of the United States to stand unfettered by doubt and discrimination and unburdened by challenges from more critical perspectives. In failing to respond adequately to causal claims about the economic success of the United States in relation to the stagnated economies of Asian Pacific, South Asian, and South American countries (causal claims that link success to the hard work, initiative, and the innovation of United States corporations and entrepreneurs), dominant models of multiculturalism give balance to prevailing development explanations of inequality in the United States and worldwide. Dominant explanatory frameworks on poverty, for instance, argue that poverty is exacerbated by low-income groups' 'dependency' on the welfare state, declines in the moral character of the poor, and a massive breakdown of 'family values.' Viewing the nation-state as a concept-metaphor populated by changing meanings and functions, rather than as a final organizer of various forms of cultural politics, provides a working context for initiating heuristic critiques of whiteness that partake of a discursive, material and political effectivity and are productive of a re-visioning of experiences of people and groups in their local and global relation to capital. The key point here is that material relations of production are not liquidable from racialized social practices. It is the exploitation of human labor, not consumer culture, that remains the dominant mechanism in capitalist society (Cleaver 1999). And while to a certain extent it is true that the labor force has been outstripping the relative growth rate of jobs (via downsizing and layoffs), we still need to consider the redistribution of work from waged to unwaged in the informal sector. If we truly want to fight racism, we need to fight capitalism and we need to push beyond this struggle in order to bring about the abolition of capital itself.

Deconstructing Whiteness

> Mujeres, a no dejar que el peligro del viaje y la immensidad del territorio nos asuste—a mirar hacia adelante y a abrir paso en el monte. Women, let's not let the danger of the journey and the vastness of the territory scare us— let's look forward and open paths in these woods.] . . . Caminante, no hay puentes, se hace puentes al andar. [Voyager, there are no bridges, one builds them as one walks]. (Anzaldúa, in Moraga and Anzaldúa, 1981: v)

> Humility is not thinking less of yourself, but rather, thinking of yourself less. (Anon.)

Deconstructing whiteness essentially involves submitting it to the type of critical examination that is has long avoided, inverting the white hegemonic gaze, in order to reveal the strategies by which racial inequality is tenebrously secured. This entails analyzing the relations of production, the privileges, and the affective energies that enable a possessive investment in whiteness.This also suggests that deconstructing whiteness is not so much the rejection of racialized social practices as a rigorously honest appraisal of the ways in which white individuals benefit from and contribute to preserving social inequality.

Because they have suffered the vicissitudes of history in perilously unambiguous ways, it has been the particular charge of people of color to contest racism, to prove that it exists in multifarious formations and practices, to translate it to the theater of the mundane and everyday practices of ordinary citizens, and to do something about it—particularly now, when the rotting corpse of civil rights has been disinterred and reanimated by Republican lawmakers eager to bring about a new conservative restoration (i.e. calling for civil rights for white people). Examining and challenging whiteness is, however, not just an ambitious political project but a deeply personal one. It is also a project in which white people especially need to participate, because, as Hurtado says, 'it takes psychological work to maintain privilege; it takes cognitive training not to empathize or feel for your victims—how individuals get socialized to accomplish the abnormal should be at the core of a reflexive theory of subordination' (1996: 130). Thus the deconstruction of whiteness promises more than 'equality;' it offers freedom from the contract that binds both oppressor and oppressed.

Hamani Bannerji registers a signal insight when she maintains that 'there is no better point of entry into a critique or a reflection than one's own experience'. Such a move enjoins us to focus on whiteness as a product of the constitution of the subject under capitalism by way of the phenomenon of lived experience rather than to relegate 'whiteness' solely to the category of 'race.' Individual experience is a productive site for the interrogation of whiteness precisely because it is framed by the specular structure of ideology that sutures or chains the subject into the flow of discourse or to 'structures of meaning.' Hence, Bannerji advocates that we engage in 'textual mediation,' by which she means a critical examination of the relationship between individual experience and social relations in our daily lives. Because white people occupy a privileged structural location, mediated self-reflexivity entails a critical examination of how ideological and institutional structures ensure the continued, unearned, and race-based privilege white people enjoy at the expense of people of color. The insidious nature of whiteness is precisely that it disguises itself as 'natural,' especially to white people who, voluntarily or not, continue to benefit from a social position marked by whiteness. White people in particular need to be vigilant, to take an active role in decentering whiteness, and to call for its mystifications to be done away with. They can begin by examining their own affective investments in whiteness and how such investments add ballast to the hegemonic relations of white supremacist patriarchy.

Because the very structure of whiteness presents it as an excess of recognizability, as beyond symbolization, as too-real in the sense that it has the power to create itself, decentering whiteness is destined to provoke a profound defensiveness on the part of many white people, and here we do not refer simply to the reactionary charges of political correctness by conservative politicians but to generalized feelings of victimization on the part of the white population. The vexing question that remains to be uncoiled in all of this is not the *meaning* of whiteness, but why the discourses of whiteness reverberate so much as to go unnoticed and why representations of whiteness continue to remain so zealously unproblematized. A provisional answer would be that discourses and representations of whiteness go unnamed and unmarked and yet remain powerful sites for investment because their continued deployment is functionally advantageous for the prevailing structures of capitalism and for the advancement of white people. The characteristics we attribute to whiteness are a function of the 'social capital' (the informal and formal rules that govern human interaction) within which they are embedded. White identity does not operate out of a contextualizing transcendence, but involves the exercise of privilege determined—at least in part—by the social relations prevailing at the time. Although the middle class is shrinking in the United States, the promise of escaping poverty by joining the white race has continuing appeal for Euro-Americans, just as it did when the colonial plantocracy promised chattel bond-laborers that by becoming part of the white race they could rise above the economic and social status of African slaves. A fraught example of the conspiracy of whiteness occurred recently when some of us attended a reading group with several white communication scholars. The focus of the group was a study of whiteness by Nakamaya and Krizek. The article concludes with an 'invitation to communication scholars to begin to mark and incorporate whiteness into their analyses and claims—an invitation to become reflexive' (1995: 305). Many members of the reading group perceived this 'invitation' as threatening and expressed exasperation at the 'angry' tone of the article. Instead of engaging the 'invitation,' they wondered if *all* essays *had* to address race, and if their work was irrelevant if they failed to do so. They wanted to know *how much* engagement with whiteness would be *enough* to absolve them of their whiteness. The request seemingly threatened the relevance of their scholarly training, since they had no formal background in anti-racist education. When it came to the 'critical point' in the discussion where white scholars were asked to deconstruct whiteness, suddenly no one knew what the authors were talking about, and they proceeded to attack the authors of the article for not being specific enough, or for not clarifying their theoretical citations.

Because whiteness is based fundamentally on exclusion, there is a fear associated with decentering whiteness that white people will be excluded from a 'post-whiteness' world. This attendant fear of exclusion is often accompanied by anger and operates out of a perception of 'individual justice' that is fundamental to the ideology of whiteness. Many white people believe that the American ideals of 'liberty' and 'justice' mean that they have a right to be anywhere they want to, and to do anything they want. Confusedly clinging to such a perception, white people feel that anything that is for 'people of color only,' that puts any restrictions on unlimited white access, constitutes an 'injustice.'

However, the practice of social justice exclusively for white people has deep historical roots. As Cheryl Harris (1993) has detailed, US law has conflated property rights with legal rights from its inception. But property ownership, like freedom and access to social resources, is deeply racialized. For instance, the democratization of the nineteenth-century United States, in which political participation was extended to non-property-owning white men, was *de facto* a political strategy of the elite to gain support for slavery in exchange for the promise of economic opportunity. Thus a true democracy, a socialist democracy (socialist because it includes everyone), would have to transcend historical conceptions of liberty that are founded on racial injustice. In their efforts to move towards dismantling whiteness, white people therefore need to relinquish their own need for inclusion so as to let new possibilities for inclusion develop.

Another pervasive defensive strategy on the part of white people that arise in anti-racist discussions is their impulse to discuss race only in a 'safe space.' While having safe spaces in which to question one's identity formation is important, this insistence by white people on safety has often functioned to disavow responsibility for discussing and disinvesting in whiteness.

In a country where the word 'crime' has become almost completely interchangeable with 'African Americans', 'Latinos', 'inner cities', and 'illegal immigrants,' it is impossible to extricate the term 'safety' from a racialized understanding. Because our sense of safety has been thoroughly racialized, 'safety' needs to be a focal point for a dismantling of whiteness. This rhetoric of 'safety', usually accompanying campaigns against violence, can be found in almost any public high school in the United States. Rather than address the reasons for violence among high school students, teachers often emphasize, for example, Eurocentric notions of 'decency' and 'civility' in order to frame how youth must conduct themselves, and with what language they may discuss their experience of oppression. Among students of color, it is often their very claims of oppression and racism, both in and out of the classroom, both verbally or visually (through graffiti, clothing, music, colors, haircuts, and especially violence), that make white people feel threatened and unsafe. It is through a mainstream and racially determined definition of safety that counter-voices raised in opposition to social injustice are largely silenced.

Inverting the white gaze means moving beyond a 'closet' critique of whiteness; it entails a fundamentally painful process, especially for those white people who pride themselves on their liberal values of equality and social justice but fail to see how their own assumptions undermine such values. Marking whiteness as hegemonic involves partaking in the discomfort that accompanies the inversion of the white gaze—a discomfort which this hegemony imposes on its 'others.' For female or working-class white people in particular, this means recognizing that they occupy a contradictory space vis-à-vis oppression that isn't easily resolved.

CONCLUSION

> Labels are invented and maintained by institutions on an ongoing basis, as part of an apparently rational process that is essentially political. Although the whole process has at times devastating effects on the labeled groups— through stereotyping, normalizing, fragmentation of people's experience, disorganization of the poor—it also implies the possibility of counterlabeling. (Escobar 1995: 110)

Critical work on whiteness should specify the ways in which unmarked racial tropes, cultural formations, and social relations of production, and social and institutional practices organize both our social and political structures as well as the microprocesses of our daily lives. In arguing that whiteness is a *learned* set of ideologies, behaviors, and practices, we mean to emphasize the profoundly contextually specific processes through which whiteness is reproduced and transformed. In conclusion, we argue for the specific ways in which labeling whiteness can contribute to redefining the content of this ideological formation. In doing so, we argue that the racism that contemporary forms of whiteness enable may be successfully challenged.

First, the label 'whiteness' aims to reconfigure the 'unmarked' aspect of this racial location by redefining its contents. As we argued earlier, whiteness 'succeeds' as a dominant discourse that privileges white people because it is conflated with universal Western ideals. Because 'white' is delinked from the idea of a racial formation, other 'races' thus serve to define the outer limits of whiteness. This means that, as a hegemonic discourse embedded in a set of cap-italist social relations and practices, whiteness secures power for whites by *uni-versalizing* whiteness. Universalized conceptualizations of whiteness function to center the white racial formation, because the universal is privileged as the standard of measure for 'appropriate' ways of life, behavior, rules for society, *et cetera*. The move to label whiteness seeks therefore to *specify* whiteness and is designed precisely to counteract its universalizing functions. To articulate whiteness as a specific set of qualities and strategies serves to unhinge it from its universal social location. This, we argue, undermines the ability of discursive practices inscribed as 'white' to define what is deemed 'appropriate' and 'com-monsensical.' In the process, whiteness may no longer be conflated with propri-ety and the strategies by which it has maintained this definitional power can be unmasked and challenged.

As elaborated above, the second and related point we wish to foreground is that whiteness is a category that 'succeeds' precisely because it is 'unmarked' (Frankenberg 1993; Kincheloe and Steinberg 1997). The outward gaze of white-ness serves three vital functions in maintaining white privilege: it externalizes difference; it defines difference from whiteness as inferiority; and it resists self-examination and critique. Each of these functions of white hegemony is enabled by the outwardly directed gaze of whiteness. Because labeling whiteness 'inverts the gaze' of the white center and provokes an examination of that cen-ter, white people are presented with a proactive framework for examining the modes through which white privilege is secured. The very process of marking these three functions of the outward gaze of whiteness is an important step in the direction of dismantling whiteness. As we point to the specific discursive strategies through which whiteness remains centered and unexamined, we invert the outward gaze and *label* whiteness as a strategic discourse of privilege. This is the first and necessary step in examining the meanings that get attached to whiteness and in raising our awareness of how this discourse serves to insulate white people from acknowledging their own privilege, even where they want to.

Next we argue that whiteness functions within an international context by means of neo-imperialist practices and ideologies that must be examined with respect to the inscription and marking of whiteness. This focus is consistent with deconstructionist moves to examine the silences produced within the discourses of the white Western logic of phallocentrism and its metaphysical search for 'truth,' in which the white heterosexual Christian male figure is continually reinscribed as the standard measure of 'mankind.'

We must recognize that the task of labeling whiteness is but one step in a much larger project of defetishizing whiteness, of showing how the givenness of whiteness is not a natural fact but is socially and historically constituted and conjuncturally embedded within capitalist social relations of production. We want to emphasize that because whiteness is ideological, and not 'natural,' because it is socially constituted, fluid, changing, and not permanently fixed, then it can be transformed. As we have mentioned in the previous section, due to the complex and contradictory nature of this particular formation, this represents very challenging work. If whiteness secures power for white people by means of its capacity to remain unmarked and to maintain its.outward gaze, then redressing these conditions will not be easy. Attempting to resist and transform these relations may even feel 'wrong' and 'gravely uncomfortable,' particularly to white people themselves. We must begin to recognize such feelings as productive of change, as evidence of success, and as a positive indicator for a more just future.

We conclude, along with Lipsitz (1998), that free market policies reinforce rather than ameliorate the possessive investment in whiteness. We also support the observation by Howard Winant that at a time where we are witnessing growing diasporic movements—as former colonial subjects immigrate to the Western metropoles, challenging the majoritarian status of European groups—we need to focus our attention on the racialized dimensions of capital and the mobilization of white racial antagonisms. Whiteness is being implicated on a global basis in the internationalizaton of capital, which can only lead to the internationalization of racial antagonisms.

We want to underscore the fact that North American workers have, for the most part, embraced ideologies of whiteness and in doing so have failed to turn their partial consciousness of the economic depravations of capitalism into a revolutionary political project aimed at transforming the current social division of labor. Their whiteness has been purchased at the faultline that separates them from the ownership of the conditions for the realization of their labor. The baptism of workers in the Sacred White Trust denies them an opportunity to create both strategic as well as tactical alliances with people of color. As workers assume the mantle of whiteness, they become at the same time fully integrated into the process of self-expanding profit-making. Whiteness in this instance serves as a 'cover' for the collusion of corporate and financial groups in the promotion of financial integration, deregulation, trade liberalization, and the internationalization of production. We believe that the more surplus labor becomes regulated at a global level, with consequent urgent 'adjustments' to entitlements and welfare spending in the quest for national competitiveness,the more implications arise for the racialization of capital (Cole, Hill, Rikowski and McLaren).

The globalization of trade is similarly fraught with dangers, often related to indigenous cultures and local networks of production and subsistence. The corporate drive to reduce the cost of production and to create new markets invariably leads to plant closures and, whenever unionized labor poses a threat to profit, to frequent and rapid shifts to 'emergent economies.' Globalization is leading to increased global poverty among unskilled and skilled workers, at a time when capitalist reification is extending into spheres of life previously unsubjected to capitalist exploitation or rationalization. Global institutions such as the World Trade Organization and the World Bank and the International Monetary Fund frequently exercise their power in order to undo national and regional legislation designed to create some barriers over environmental, labor, and social issues (De Angelis 1999). The current internationalization of labor that occurs in the wake of these conditions depends upon the structural fragmentation of the working class. The division of workers within an income hierarchy that offers the most economic mobility and security to white workers is functionally advantageous to capital because it keeps the working class racialized and decentered. The figuration of racial and ethnic specificity remains entombed within the governing discourses and tropes of globalization and the enthralling media apparatuses that promote them. Furthermore, the sacrosanct character of the unfettered free market is divinely invoked to overwrite the voices of the indigenous and the demands of the minoritized racial and ethnic groups who constitute those most marginalized by globalization. Within the fractal geometry of today's capitalist production, the threat to the white working class is so great that whites are doing everything in their power to maintain their advantage, from attempts at dismantling affirmative action and bilingual education, to militarizing the border, to demonizing Mexican immigrants when they are permitted to enter the country. The social function of the economic rationale of neo-liberalism is to keep white workers from creating alliances with aggrieved communities of color. It is in the interests of capital to keep 'race' and 'class' separate.

It is also functionally advantageous for capital if corporations expropriate the residual power that workers once had in the Keynesian era: the power to negotiate conditions of work, wage, and social entitlements through trade unions or political parties (Taylor 1999). The social process of recomposing civil society through social movements is a forbidding possibility for the corporate barons of globalization, that international cadre of renovated carpetbaggers and overworlders who remain bent on keeping working people vulnerable and dependent. Because capitalism takes the form of a self-constituting reality, the continuing rationalization of the labor process involves attempts to prevent the working class from conceptualizing the social totality. Identity politics is one way to promote the sectionalism necessary to mystify the relationship between the globalization and racialization of labor, and the universal objective of human emancipation. What is needed is not identity politics but a revolutionary multiculturalism that is able to confront the relationship between the reification of everyday labor and the possessive investment in whiteness.

Read in this light, revolutionary multiculturalism, with its enthrallment with open-endedness, its resistance to fixity, and its quest for flexible identities, offers us a serious challenge to certain trajectories of postmodernist theory. Revolutionary multiculturalism calls attention to the bourgeois outlawry, fashionable philistinism, and aristocratic brigandism that characterize those forms of postmodern criticism that betray a civil inattention to issues of relations of production and a motivated amnesia towards history (McLaren 1997).

A limited praxis—a praxis that does not take into account the totality of social relations—only reproduces the given social order or dialectical contradictions in their inversion. Especially at this less than quiescent political moment, revolutionary or critical praxis must do two things: it must critique the resulting ideological explanations, and it must transform those relations which constitute the social contradictions. In so doing it reveals that a pedagogy of liberation looks like, one that moves from the liberal humanist notion of 'traditional democratic freedom' to the Marxist-humanist concept of freeing oneself and others from a relationship of dependency to capital.

A nagging question facing the left around the globe can be pitched as follows: how can the left protagonize a process of structural change that goes beyond state intervention and its goal to achieve internal redistribution and and a tacit acceptance of the neo-liberal model of free market integration into the global economy? One cannot of course ignore the important contributions of organized left parties such as the Sandinista National Liberation Front in Nicaragua, The Workers Party in Brazil, the Farabundo Liberation Front in El Salvador, the party of the Democratic Revolution in Mexico, the Broad Front in Uruguay, the National Solidarity Front in Argentina the Fuerzas Armadas Revolucionarios de Colombia—Ejército del Pueblo (FARC), the Causa-Rin Venezuela, the Communist Party in Cuba, and the Communist Party in Chile. But one also has to recognize and emphasize the importance of grass-roots social movements that operate outside of state structures and organized left parties, such as Christian-based communities, solidarity groups, the Landless Workers of Brazil, and revolutionary groups such as Mexico's Zapatistas (Robinson 1998/99). How can these new social movements mediate between the state and the popular masses? How can these struggles be made within a transnational space that can challenge and contest the hegemony of the transnational elite and their local counterparts? How can a transnationalism from below—from the civil society as distinct from the political society—occur that is capable of challenging the power of the global elite? How can relations of capitalist exploitation be engaged so that the ideologies of racial superiority, of unmarked whiteness, that support them can finally be overcome and thrown into the dustbin of history? These are questions that cannot be ignored or pushed aside in our universal struggle for a world unfettered by racism and unmarked by exploitation.

REFERENCES

Allen, Theodore W. (1994) T*he Invention of the White Race* vol. 1, 'Racial Oppression and Social Control,' London and New York: Verso.

Allen, T. (1997) *The Invention of the White Race, Volume Two: The Origin of Racial Oppression in Anglo-America*, London and New York: Verso.

Bannerji, H. (1995) *Thinking Through: Essays on Feminism, Marxism and Anti-Racism*, Toronto: Women's Press.

Callinicos, Alex (1993) *Race and Class*, London: Bookmarks.

Cleaver, Harry (1999) 'Work is Still the Central Issue,' unpublished paper.

Cole, Mike, Dave Hill, Glenn Rikowski, and Peter McLaren. (2000) *Red Chalk*, London: The Tufnell Press.

Du Bois, W. E. B. (1968) *Dusk of Dawn: An Essay Toward an Autobiography of a Race Concept*, New York: Schocken Books.

De Angelis, Massimo (1999) 'Globalization, Work, and Class: Some Research Notes,' unpublished paper.

Delgado, Richard and Stefancic, Jean (eds) (1997) *Critical White Studies: Looking Behind the Mirror*, Philadelphia: Temple University Press.

Escobar, A. (1995) *Encountering Development: The, Making and Unmaking of the Third World*, Princeton, NJ: Princeton University Press.

Ferguson, J. (1996) *The Anti-Politics Machine: 'Development,' Depoliticization, and Bureaucratic Power in Lesotho*, Minneapolis: University of Minnesota Press.

Frankenberg, R (1993) *White Women, Race Matters: The Social Construction of Whiteness*, Minneapolis: University of Minnesota Press.

Hall, S. (1996) 'Gramsci's Relevance for the Study of Race and Ethnicity,' in D. Morley and K H. Chen (eds) *Stuart Hall Critical Dialogues in Cultural Studies*, New York: Routledge.

Hall, S (1996) 'The Problem of Ideology: Marxism without Guarantees,' in David Morley and Kuan-Hsing Chen (eds) *Stuart Hall. Critical Dialogues in Cultural Studies*, New York: Routledge.

Harris, C. (1993) 'Whiteness as Property,' *Harvard Law Review* 106(8): 709-91.

Hurtado, A. (1996) *The Color of Privilege: Three Blasphemies on Race and Feminism*, Ann Arbor: University of Michigan.

Ignatiev, N. 1998. 'The New Abolitionists,' *Transition* 73: 199-203.

Kincheloe, Joe and Steinberg, Shirley (1997) *Changing Multiculturalism*, London: Open University Press.

Lipsitz, George (1998) *The Possessive Investment in Whiteness*, Philadelphia: Temple University Press.

Lowe, L. (1996) *Immigrant Acts: On Asian American Cultural Politics*, Durham and London: Duke University Press.

McLaren, Peter (1995) *Critical Pedagogy and Predatory Culture*, London and New York: Routledge.

_____ (1997) *Revolutionary Multiculturalism*, Boulder: Westview Press.

McLaren, Peter and Muñoz,Juan (2000) 'Unsettling Whiteness' in Carlos Ovando and Peter McLaren (eds) *The Politics of Multiculturalism and Bilingual Education: Students and Teachers Caught in the Crossfire*, New York: McGraw-Hill.

Moraga, C. and Anzaldúa, G. (1981) *This Bridge Called My Back: Writings by Radical Women of Color*, New York: Kitchen Table.

Morrison, T. (1992) *Playing in the Dark: Whiteness and the Literary Imagination*, New York: Vintage Books.

Nakayama, T. and Krizek, R (1995) 'Whiteness: A Strategic Rhetoric,' *Quarterly Journal of Speech* 81: 291-309.

Robinson, William (1998/1999) 'Latin America and Global Capitalism,' *Race & Class,* 40(2 & 3): 111-31.

Saxton, A. (1990) *The Rise and Fall of the White Republic*, New York: Verso.

Scott, Jonathan (1998) 'Before the White Race Was Invented, *Against the Current* 72: 46-9.

Shapiro, Bruce (1999) 'The Guns of Littleton,' *The Nation* 268(18): 4-5.

Spivak, G. (1987) 'French Feminism in an International Frame' in G. Spivak (ed.) *In Other Worlds: Essays in Cultural Politics*, New York: Routledge.

_____ (1990) *The Post-Colonial Critic: Interviews, Strategies, Dialogues*, New York: Routledge.

Taylor, Graham (1999) 'Labor and Subjectivity: Rethinking the Limits of Working Class Consciousness,' unpublished paper.

Tsing, A. L (1993) *In the Realm of the Diamond Queen: Marginality in an Out of the Way Place*, Princeton, NJ: Princeton University Press.

Winant, Howard (1994) *Racial Conditions*, Minneapolis: University of Minnesota Press.

Wood, Ellen Meiksins (1999) *The Origin of Capitalism*, New York: Monthly Review Press.

PART 3

RADICALS AND
RADICAL IDEAS:
GRAMSCI, RORTY, FREIRE,
HARVEY AND MENCHU

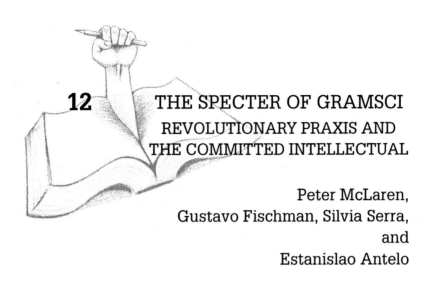

12   THE SPECTER OF GRAMSCI
REVOLUTIONARY PRAXIS AND THE COMMITTED INTELLECTUAL

Peter McLaren,
Gustavo Fischman, Silvia Serra,
and
Estanislao Antelo

INTRODUCTION

The posthumous birth of Antonio Gramsci in the works of the British and North American New Left theorists over the last twenty years has left an impressive and important legacy. The contemporary debates that it has provoked—about the saliency of the term "articulation"; the conceptual status of the term "ideology" in relation to that of discourse; the political import of the "new times" project of analyzing and regulating capitalism via the flow of finance and post-Fordist capitalist formations and the concomitant changes these formations have brought about in social, political, and cultural life; the rise of the metropolitan service class and the overall decomposition of social class as the main axis of politics; the question of whether the social totality is an open field or structured by the determining lines of force of material relations; the positionality of politics within a network of strategies and powers and their articulations—are as variable as they are important (see Harris, 1992). However, it is not the purpose of this chapter to map the shifting trajectories of these debates, except to note a general one that has emerged from them: Given current structural and conjunctural conditions such as the capitalization of global culture, the privatization of subjectivity, and the moral collapse of social democracy after the defeat of communism, should the role of Gramsci's "organic" intellectual primarily be restricted to practicing "cultural politics," or should the Gramscian agent challenge the pernicious power of capital? In other words, to what extent has Gramsci's work remained at the level of methodological idealism with respect to a neo-Gramscian privileging of culture over structure? To what extent have

This chapter originally appeared in Carmel Borg, Joseph Buttigieg, and Peter Mayo (Eds.), *Gramsci and Education*, pp. 147-178. © 2002 Rowman & Littlefield. Reprinted with the permission of the publisher.

the entire dynamics of subjectivity been commodified, including those very faculties of self-reflexivity that might enable the masses to disturb official culture and rebel against such commodification? In this essay, we shall argue that (in the face of the global restructuring of accumulation, the financescape of "high octane" capitalism, and the blandishments of "free market authoritarianism," and in the midst of the current embattlement of the culture/ideology of consumerism and individualism within neocapitalist technoculture) revisiting Gramsci's ideas can provide important resources and inspiration for teachers as they attempt to transform schools into sites of radical reform within "real existing capitalist societies."

Today's commodity culture provides an urgent backdrop for revisiting Gramsci, especially his work on the role of the intellectual. De Azua (1996) has described the intellectual as someone who consults the dead. However, in the light of current metropolitan life, does this not necessarily imply several paradoxes? Haven't present-day intellectuals spent more time and energy trying to get an "advertising" spot in tabloids, instant sound-bite news commentary, and television talk shows instead of using those media as forums for critique and analysis? A second paradox results from the rather simple observation that talking with the dead is impossible. It is impossible because death implies closure and ending. Death "does not conceal any mystery, does not open any door. It is the end of the human being. What survives [. . .] is what is given to other human beings, what remains in their memories" (Elias, cited in Eribon, 1992, p. 100). Yet, what is not considered in Elias's remark is the presence of the dead through their ability to haunt and influence the living, and thus the tremendous and tremulous power of their spectral essence. What do we make of such specters haunting us as intellectuals, teachers, and activists, as we struggle with the limitations of contemporary social theory and social activism?

HAUNTING AND TALKING TO SPECTERS

In *The Communist Manifesto* (1848), Karl Marx and Friedrich Engels write that "the specter" of communism is haunting Europe; 148 years later, Jacques Derrida (1996) defines the term "specter" as the frequency of a certain visibility—the visibility of the invisible, as if the specter were projected on an imaginary screen (for our purposes this screen is composed of the pedagogical discourses of the contemporary educational left). The specter sees us before we see it. It pre-exists our consciousness, puts us under surveillance, and can violently repay us a visit. It occupies a social mode or style of haunting that demands to be understood in the singularity of its temporality or historicity (which for us seems too eerily close to Nietzsche's eternal return of the same).

Whereas Marx and Engels call for the specter of communism to become a living reality, a concrete presence on the stage of world history, Derrida examines the "specters of Marx" as "the persistence of a present past, the return of the dead which the worldwide work of mourning cannot get rid of, whose return it runs away from, which it *chases* (excludes, banishes, and at the same time pursues)" (1995, p. 101). For Derrida, Marxism is a discourse whose finality is interrupted by its own haunting of the present. Derrida believes that Marx wanted to replace the ghost of communism with the living presence of communism. Just as capitalist states feared the ghosts of communism, so Marx apparently fears the ghost of communism's "other." In *Specters of Marx*, Derrida accuses Marx of fearing spectrality, of wanting to rid society of its ghosts altogether in order to raise his own philosophy to the status of ontology (Lewis, 1997). Derrida wishes to replace Marxist ontology with hauntology—yet, paradoxically, the entire project of *Specters of Marx* is to exorcise the ghost of Marx, to blast Marx from the rock of living history. In this deconstruction as exorcism, Derrida disavows class struggle and establishes an International built on the unfinalizability of discourses and the impossibility of political coordination. It is here that Derrida betrays a voguish dissidence, a fashionable apostasy, an insurgent posturing in his preoccupation for celebrating the incommensurability of discourses. Uninterested in class politics, Derrida forecloses the possibility of mounting a program of anticapitalist struggle. Marx saw vividly in a way that Derrida does not that discourses always converge and pivot around objective labor practices and that global capitalism has a way of reshaping, reinflecting, and rearticulating dissent. Consequently, Derrida's cosmopolitan deconstructionist efforts to establish a "hauntology" fit securely within the manageable compass of business interests and a corporate-sponsored rebellion. And, while they unsettle and decenter the dusty elitism of canonical tomes of Western Enlightenment thinking, aloof and posturing on varnished bookshelves, the conditions of life and action that structure our everyday lives through exchange value and labor are rarely, if ever, deeply challenged.

Fixation on the dead can embalm the spirit of the living and often signals the other face of the cynicism we harbor about the living. We need not be impeccably reverential in our role as translators of the dead since our unswerving loyalty is neither to the dead nor to the living; our role is to disinter the unsaid so as to provoke an awakening of critical self-consciousness. Avery Gordon (1997) develops a "spectral sociology" that takes such "structuring conditions" of everyday life more seriously than Derrida. She maintains that "haunting" is a "constituent element of modern social life," a "generalizable social phenomenon of great import." Hers is a spectral sociology or hauntology that "looks for a language for identifying haunting and for writings with the ghosts any haunting inevitably throws up" (p. 7). For Gordon, ghosts are the remains of a history of unaddressed social injustices that have been spectacularly and systematically suppressed in mainstream sociological thinking. Gordon describes haunting in a haunted society as an objective force. It is the moment of mediation that she believes exceeds both psychoanalysis and Marxism. She writes:

> Haunting [. . .] is precisely what prevents rational detachment, prevents your
> willful control, prevents the desegregation of class struggle and your feelings,
> motivations, blind spots, craziness, and desires. A haunted society is full of
> ghosts, and the ghost always carries the message—albeit not in the form of
> the academic treatise, or the clinical case study, or the polemical broadside,
> or the mind-numbing factual report—that the gap between personal and
> social, public and private, objective and subjective is misleading in the first
> place. That is to say, it is leading you elsewhere, it is making you see things
> you did not see before, it is making an impact on you; your relation to things
> that seemed separate or invisible is changing. This is not to say that the gap
> or the reification is not an enormously powerful real experience. Nor is it to
> say that haunting somehow transcends the actually existing social relations in
> which we live, think, and think up new concepts and visions of life. Quite the
> contrary. But these questions remain: what effectively describes the gap as an
> organized and elaborate symptom, and what describes the moment when we
> understand that it is, in fact, misleading us? (p. 98)

Hauntings, as we intend the term, have little to do with the ectoplasm of
Ouija board conjurers in rhinestone turbans, but rather refer to dangerous memories that live in the structural unconscious of humanity. It is the task of the intellectual to set these ghostly memories on fire so that they irrupt to haunt the social
consciousness of the living. That is, the intellectual does not function to exorcise
ghosts but to give ghosts the necessary materiality so that we recognize them and
have the opportunity to understand their meaning. An intellectual is an artisan
and a laborer who works with inherited memories, recollections of that stuff of
which we are constituted. Yet, death and memory only speak about heritage.
Heritage, however, has been described by Derrida (1994) as something not related to what is given and easily transmitted but is a neverending labor. Heritage
involves infinite operations of acquisition. We agree with Derrida on this point.
But let us now bring the conversation closer to our main theme: that of education.
We recognize that if heritage implies intellectual labor and operations of acquisition, these tasks must, at the same time, be eminently pedagogical. In this sense,
then, an educator is a carrier of culture, a dealer, a "smuggler of memories"
(Hassoun, 1996)—a smuggler who testifies, gives testimonies, and shapes words.
An intellectual speaks through the lips of the dead and serves as the medium
through which subjugated histories are released into the present. Yet, it is precisely the intellectual who is most at risk for failing to give voice to the specters of
history. This is because, for Derrida, scholars feel that looking is sufficient and
are singularly incapable of entering into a dialogue with a ghost. Derrida writes:

> As theoreticians or witnesses, spectators, observers, and intellectuals, schol-
> ars believe that looking is sufficient. Therefore, they are not always in the
> most competent position to do what is necessary: speak to the specter. [. . .]
> A traditional scholar does not believe in ghosts—nor in all that could be
> called the virtual space of spectrality. (1995, p. 11)

The dead are not only visited by us; their ghosts also attempt to be haunt-ingly present among us. To talk to the dead is not to visit them and reverentially offer their ghosts our most sincere homage. It is to press them for answers, for explanations; it is to demand that they give us reasons for why they haunt us. The dead to whom we wish to speak—not as scholars but as social agents who care about education—are the spirits of Antonio Gramsci, for it is certainly true that Gramsci is not one but many spirits. There are the Gramscian spirits that haunt the cultural Marxists, the orthodox "manifesto Marxists," the "post-Marxists," and the "other than Marxists" who occupy the North and South American educational Left. The ghosts of Gramsci haunt teachers working in public schools who have been reduced to a fetishized form of hypostasized pub-lic service clerks. And they haunt us, the educators of the educators, those of us who are paid by the State to teach the clerks of the new internal colonies of hegemonized memory. For some of us, the surviving ideas of Gramsci become the ghosts of memory that we must confront in order to understand our own his-tories. For others, they represent a ghoulish voice from the past that threatens the foundations of our moral, ethical, and political lives and our studied compla-cency as citizens. As critical educators, we are concerned with speaking to both the ghosts and the ghouls of Gramsci on specific issues surrounding the role of the educator as intellectual, as activist, as someone engaged in organic praxis, and in revolutionary struggle.

TALKING TO THE SPECTER OF GRAMSCI

Gramsci studied historical linguistics at Turin University, but abandoned his studies in favor of working full time on the paper *Avanti!* Inspired by the Russian Revolution, he became involved with the Turin factory council move-ment (at a time when thousands of workers from Italian industrial cities occu-pied their factories), and was greatly influenced by the work of Italian idealist philosopher Benedetto Croce. In 1919, he helped to found the socialist paper *L'Ordine Nuovo*, with its motto: "Pessimism of the intellect, optimism of the will." Determined to break with the Second International Marxism and social Darwinism, Gramsci became involved with rethinking Marxist philosophical formulations that were developing from the Third International. He spent the 1920s involved in the Italian revolutionary movement as leader of the Communist Party. In 1922, he was an Italian Communist Party delegate on the Executive Committee of the Communist Third International in Moscow. In 1922, Mussolini took power, began arresting Communist leaders, and, in a rela-tively short time, defeated the Italian proletariat drive for a Soviet style revolu-tion. In the general election of April 1924, Gramsci was elected parliamentary deputy and eventually became the general secretary of the Italian Communist Party. He worked from the conviction that the greatest potential for overthrowing fascism lay with the peasantry and helped to organize the party on the basis of workplace cells. His inaugural speech in 1924 exhibited an uncompromising and fearless commitment to antifascist struggle, and several years later, in November 1926, he was arrested along with other Communist deputies on charges of conspiracy, insurrection, agitation, inciting class war, and subverting the State. Sentenced on June 4, 1928, to over twenty years of imprisonment, he spent the 1930s—"the long Calvary of Antonio Gramsci" (Fiori, 1973)—in Mussolini's prison. His prosecuting attorney, Michele Isgro, is reported to have exclaimed, "For 20 years we must stop this brain from working" (cited in Ledwith, 1997, p. 84). Moving from Rome, to exile on the island of Ustica, to Milan to await trial, back to Rome for sentencing in May 1928, to a special prison in Bari in July 1928, and then to a clinic in Formia in 1933, Gramsci remained a prisoner of the State until his death from a cerebral hemorrhage on April 27, 1937. It is a testament to his indomitable will and fearless optimism that his brain did not stop functioning during his confinement in prison, which saw him produce thirty-three notebooks or 2,848 dense pages of writing that constitute his *Quaderni del carcere* or *Prison Notebooks* (Ledwith, 1997, p. 84).

Throughout his intellectual life, Gramsci sought ways to oppose the idealist conception of consciousness common to neo-Hegelian and neo-Kantian philosophy through an encounter with Saussurean linguistics and Russian formalism (Brandist, 1996, 1996a). Perhaps the two Gramscian concepts that have exercised (and exorcised) the North and South American educational Left the most over the last two decades have been those of ideology and hegemony. For Antonio Gramsci, as well as for many of his followers (Aronowitz, 1992; Eagleton, 1991), there exists a continuous interplay—a dialectical reinitiation of sorts—between the workings of ideology and hegemony. Terry Eagleton (1991) indicates that for the Italian revolutionary, the concept of "ideology"—based on Marx's "solidity of popular beliefs"—refers to the way that power struggles are developed in any given society at the level of signification. The view of ideology presented by Stuart Hall and James Donald (1986) is quintessentially Gramscian. For Hall and Donald, ideology refers to

> the framework of thought which is used in society to explain, figure out, make sense of or give meaning to the social and political world [. . .] without these frameworks, we could not make sense of the world at all. But with them, our perceptions are inevitably structured in particular directions by the very concepts we are using. (pp. xi-x)

For this reason, it is possible to say that ideologies serve as a collective embrace or cajolery that seductively corrupts the civic culture, or that is perhaps imposed upon the people (an obvious condition of any colonial project), such as in the case of white supremacist ideologies in South Africa or national security doctrines that predominated during long periods of dictatorial rule in Latin

America, Asia, and Africa. These historical examples illustrate what Gramsci meant when he stated that "the function of 'domination' without that of 'leadership': dictatorship without hegemony" (1971, p. 106) occurs when a dominant class resorts to coercive means of control rather than adopting a strategy of hegemonic consensus building.

Hegemony is a broader concept than ideology, as it requires the use of ideological forms but at the same time cannot be reduced to them. Hegemony invents a coincidence among four relevant sites of ideological production: identity politics, "imagined" communities, the State administration, and social relations of production. Hegemony points to the essential caducity of ideology. Not only does hegemony eluviate over time, it also enlists new forms and assemblages; it is able to permute new social relations and formations; it functions as a public regulatory agency that embargos certain ideas and promotes others. In other words, hegemony points to the constitutive nature of ideology.

The relationship between ideology and hegemony is further elucidated in Dick Hebdige's (1996) discussion of the two dominant and potentially opposed tendencies that have emerged from debates (primarily among the British Left) surrounding Gramsci's work. First, there exists the tension between populism and the national-popular. Second, there exists the tension between ideological discourse in the shaping of historical subjectivities and the world outside of discourse (sites of extradiscursivity). The imaginary community of the "we" has itself become a reflection of these tensions. Stuart Hall's use of the term "articulation" is heralded as a theoretically fecund means by which the "double emphasis" of Gramsci—that is, the emphasis on culture and structure, on ideology and material social relations—can be linked together. What this "double movement" through the concept of articulation has achieved has been to conceptualize class and cultural struggles as interwoven and complexly articulated as a "range of competing populisms" (Hebdige, 1996). According to this formulation, groups and classes exist in a shifting and mediated relationship, in a structured field of complex relations and ideological forces stitched together out of social fragments and privileging hierarchies, in structured asymmetries of power, in contending vectors of influence, and in emergent, contingent alliances. When one examines ideology, one does not look for smooth lines of articulation; rather, one conceives of a regime of culture not stitched together as a set of canonical ideas but rather existing as a palimpsest of emergent and residual discourses. Hebdige offers a summary of the Gramscian conception as follows:

> From the perspectives heavily influenced by the Gramscian approach, nothing is anchored to the "grand recites," to master narratives, to stable (positive) identities, to fixed and certain meanings: all social and semantic relations are contestable hence mutable: everything appears to be in flux: there are no predictable outcomes. Though classes still exist there is no guaranteed dynamic to class struggle and no "class belong": there are no solid homes to return to, no places reserved in advance for the righteous. No one

"owns" an ideology because ideologies are themselves in process: in a state of constant formation and reformation. In the same way, the concept of hegemony remains distinct from the Frankfurt model of a "total closure of discourse" (Marcuse) and from the ascription of total class domination which is implied in the Althusserian model of a contradictory social formation held in check eternally (at least until "the last (ruptural) instance") by the work of the RSAs and the ISAs. Instead hegemony is a precarious, "moving equilibrium" (Gramsci) achieved through the orchestration of conflicting and competing forces by more or less unstable, more or less temporary alliances of class fractions. (1996, p. 198)

In order to grasp the nuanced relationship between ideology and hegemony, we recommend that they be seen in parallax, that is, from the perspective of the positionality of the social agent at the present moment, with the understanding that this location or site of enunciation is in itself dialectically conditioned by this interplay. Gramsci underscored the fact that to obtain hegemonic power, a dominant class or class alliance necessarily requires two forms of control: coercion (sustained by politically regulated repression) and consent. These forms of control work together to stipulate an ethical domain tied to the forces of production. According to Gramsci,

every State is ethical in as much as one of its most important functions is to raise the great mass of the population to a particular cultural and moral level, a level (or type) which corresponds to the needs of the productive forces for development, and hence to the interest of the ruling classes. The school as a positive educative function, and the courts as a repressive and negative educative function, are the most important State activities in this sense. (1971, p. 258)

Not only are hegemonic relationships ethical, but they are also pedagogical. Gramsci (1971, p. 350) clearly stated that "every relationship of hegemony is necessarily a pedagogical relationship" because

a class is dominant in two ways, i.e. leading and dominant. It leads the classes which are its allies, and dominates those which are its enemies [. . .] one should not count solely on the power and material force which such position gives in order to exercise political leadership or hegemony. (Gramsci, 1971, p. 57)

These perspectives stress the importance of cultural, political, and pedagogical aspects in the construction of hegemonic orders. However, as a Marxist intellectual, Gramsci never failed to stress the importance of economic relations, because he insisted that the economy determines (in the last instance) the extent of the compromises and agreements that can be achieved among the dominant groups and the popular sectors. He further clarifies this point as follows:

Undoubtedly the fact of hegemony presupposes that account be taken of the interests and the tendencies of the groups over which hegemony is to be exercised, and that a certain compromise equilibrium should be formed—in other words, that the leading group should make sacrifices of an economic-corporate kind. But there is also no doubt that such sacrifices and such a compromise cannot touch the essential; for though hegemony is ethical-political, it must also be economic, must necessarily be based on the decisive function exercised by the leading group in the decisive nucleus of economic activity. (1971, p. 161)

Richard Brosio (1994, p. 48) emphasizes Gramsci's realization that "hegemony must be ultimately anchored in economic strength—and ultimately physical power." Brosio also reminds us that while the State uses a combination of force and consent in order to maintain hegemony, we must not forget "that the exercise and maintenance of hegemony over subaltern groups is still a variation of class struggle." Brosio further cautions us not to forget the relationship of power to the educative aspects of hegemony: "There is a tendency to stress Gramsci's important development of hegemony, the role of persuasion and consent, the seemingly willing participation by subaltern groups in their own domination; however, he was not naive about the relationship of power to this persuasive hegemony" (1994, p. 49). The characteristics of consent and coercion that underwrite Gramsci's model of hegemonic domination are fundamentally dynamic categories. Because they are dynamic and not static relationships, they admit the possibility of rearticulation into alternative or counterhegemonic practices. We must not forget Gramsci's firm conviction that "ordinary men and women could be educated into understanding the coercive and persuasive power of capitalist hegemony over them" (Brosio, 1994, pp. 49-50). One of the merits of Gramsci's framework is that it makes a vital departure from the conception of ideology as a somewhat outdated system of static and fixed ideas—such as in Althusser's conceptualization that is often recited by orthodox leftists with great condescension toward the very possibility of new forms of resistance—to ideology as embodied, lived, dynamic sets of social practices that are constructed and carried out by individuals as well as institutions.

The notion of hegemonic rule, however, was not well developed in Gramsci. Walter Adamson notes that the relationship among hegemony, State power, and forms of political legitimization was at times ambiguous and was used in several different (and sometimes contradictory) senses:

It is used, first of all, in a morally neutral and instrumental sense to characterize those bourgeois regimes that have proved capable of organizing mass consent effectively. But it is also used in an essentially ethical sense to characterize the functioning of a proletarian regulated society. Here is another instance in which the attempt to incorporate Machiavellian and ethical state traditions raises perplexing and unresolved questions. Is the sort of consent

being obtained the same in both cases? Or is consent in a bourgeois hegemony somehow passive and noncritical, while under proletarian auspices it
would be active, participatory, and philosophical? If so, what more fully is
the institutional basis of this latter sort of control? (1980, p. 242)

We find that the Gramscian dichotomy of force and consent is not nearly
sufficient or comprehensive enough to allow us to examine the complex character of hegemonic rule since these two terms do not permit a detailed and
nuanced analysis of forms of political legitimization. Consequently, it makes
more sense to view the terms "force" and "consent," in Adamson's terms, as
"endpoints of a continuum that includes such intermediate positions as con-
straint (e.g., fear of unemployment), co-optation, and perhaps even Arendt's
category of 'authority'" (Adamson, 1980, p. 243).

Whereas Gramsci often stressed as a defining attribute the spirit or the will,
Marx gave pride of place to production. Gramsci emphasized human consciousness as a defining attribute of humanity. Consciousness was akin to spirit,
which was linked to the notion of history as a form of "becoming." Organized
will becomes the basis of his philosophy. While Gramsci acknowledges the link
between humanity and production, he does not sufficiently emphasize the most
important aspects of humanity's "complex of social relations": the satisfaction
of human needs and the human necessity to produce (see Hoffman, 1984). The
satisfaction of human needs is the primary historical act, and must be satisfied
before men and women are in the position to make history. The human necessity to produce thus underwrites all social relationships. For Gramsci, humanity is
defined by concrete will (will plus historical circumstances); for Marx, will is a
response to social and historical circumstances independent of human will.
Human relationships thus exist independently of the way in which people
understand them (Hoffman, 1984, p. 112). Here we agree with Brosio (after
Mandel) that "classical Marxism examined closely the repressive function of
the class State, and that Gramsci and Lukacs stressed the integrative function"
(1994, p. 50).

Eagleton (1991) points out that Gramsci, "with certain notable inconsistencies," associates hegemony with the arena of civil society, a term used by the
Italian revolutionary to indicate an extensive range of institutions that serve as
intermediaries between the State and the economy: the church, schools, press,
family, hospitals, political parties, and so on. In this regard, Perry Anderson
(1977) asserts that Gramsci was wrong when he exclusively located hegemony
within the realm of civil society, because, by doing so, he diminished the importance of the capitalist State as a vital organ of hegemonic power. However,
Torres (1992), also referring to Anderson's work, points out that Gramsci's distinction between civil society and political society is basically methodological.
In addition, Gramsci's attention to culture and the relatively autonomous institutions of civil society enabled him to reject the pitfalls of a monodeterministic
base-superstructural model:

Although Gramsci did adhere to the Marxist premise of one hegemonic center (i.e., the social relations generated by the mode of production), his attention to culture and to the relatively autonomous institutions of civil society amounted to a rejection of the monodeterministic base-superstructure argument of classical Marxism. Unlike Leninism, which ignored the democratic forms of culture needed to sustain autonomous movements, Gramsci's focus on a "war of position" resonates with the efforts of social movements to create new political spaces within civil society and alter the content of hegemony. The Gramscian concept of "historic bloc" has its counterpart in the coalition-building notions prevalent in NSM [New Social Movement] theory. The emphasis on the unification of class with popular-democratic struggles can be viewed, positively, as offering an analytic basis for exploring historical continuities between "old" and "new" social movements, a continuity otherwise obliterated by the atemporality of identity politics. (Carroll & Ratner, 1994, p. 21)

For our own purposes, it should be stressed that hegemony is as much related to antagonistic processes as it is to consensual individual and social practices of negotiation and/or exchange that take place, not only in the realm of the civil society but also in the everyday actions of families, the State, and the various political arenas. Ernesto Laclau and Chantal Mouffe (1985) explain that the concept of hegemony was originally tied to an essentialist logic in which only one authentic historical subject, "the working class," was able to develop truly counter-hegemonic policies and practices. Such a logic, rather than advancing the project of social change and social justice, covered over and obstructed multiple forms of struggles developed by several groups and social movements (such as those developed by indigenous peoples, ethnic groups, women, ecologists, human rights activists, and the like), which could not be reduced or categorized on the exclusive basis of the class position of their members. However, instead of throwing the baby out with the bathwater, Laclau and Mouffe propose to free "hegemony" of any kind of essentialism and reappropriate the potentially emancipatory characteristics of the concept. Best and Kellner maintain that, for Laclau and Mouffe, "hegemony entails a detotalizing logic of articulation and contingency that refuses the conception of the a priori unity or the progressive character of the working class or any other subject position. Rather, cultural and political identities are never given in advance, but must be constituted or articulated, from diverse elements" (1991, p. 195).

Similar to the position articulated by Laclau and Mouffe, Stuart Hall situates the Gramscian challenge as the struggle for a new social order. Hall's eloquent summary is worth quoting at length:

Gramsci always insisted that hegemony is not exclusively an ideological phenomenon. There can be no hegemony without "the decisive nucleus of the economic." On the other hand, do not fall into the trap of the old mechanical economism and believe that if you can only get hold of the economy, you can move the rest of life. The nature of power in the modern world is that it is also constructed in relation to political, moral, intellectual, cultural, ideological and sexual questions. The question of hegemony is always the question of a new cultural order. The question which faced Gramsci in relation to Italy faces us now in relation to Britain: what is the nature of this new civilization? Hegemony is not a state of grace that is installed forever. It is not a formation that incorporates everybody. The notion of a "historical bloc" is precisely different from that of a pacified, homogeneous, ruling class. It entails a quite different conception of how social forces and movements, in their diversity, can be articulated into strategic alliances. To construct a new cultural order, you need not to reflect an already-formed collective will, but to fashion a new one, to inaugurate a new historical project. (1988, p. 170)

Contemporary social scientists such as Hall and Laclau and Mouffe have developed a conception of hegemony as an ever-evolving political, economic, ideological, and cultural set of processes by which the dominant social sectors (hegemonic bloc) elicit consent from the popular sectors. And yet, hegemony is inseparable from conflicts and struggles over it. In this process, the struggle for control over the symbolic and economic means of any given society and the role the State plays in such struggles cannot be diminished. Nevertheless, we have some reservations about the analysis advanced by Laclau and Mouffe, as well as by Hall, in terms of their penchant for de-emphasizing the totalizing power and function of capital. In their inauguration of a new collective will, post-modernists and post-Marxists such as Laclau and Mouffe often theorize or abstract out of existence the working class, even as they seek new positions of popular will from which to struggle and wage war against the hegemonic order. We believe this is a major mistake and misappropriation of hegemony. In our view, Gramsci's work can help us in understanding the class contradictions that structure the subjectivities of oppressed classes. Such an understanding enables us to resist the formation of the comprador intellectual, who simply (and often unwittingly) resecures the consent of the subaltern classes for the relations of domination that structure and exploit them. It is a major error, we contend, to use Gramsci's concept of hegemony in such a way as to depotentiate class analysis by reducing class to a series of unstable "negotiations" among all and every political position. Hegemony does not take place in an indeterminate terrain (Katz, 1997). The concept of hegemony as articulated by many post-Marxists often serves as a type of *trompe d'oeil* whereby forces of domination are willfully misrecognized as the structured equanimity of inevitability, fate, chance, or irreversibility. Built into a number of theories of hegemony is the notion of the "reversibility" of cultural practices, as if such practices are asocial or ahistorical or have otherwise been severed from the chains of class determination. According to Katz (1997), this is clearly a misunderstanding of Gramsci and evacuates the entire problem of domination. Misappropriations of Gramsci's work have caused domination, in effect, to virtually disappear into a storm of relational "negotiations" in which certain ideological positions are "won" through "consent." Here we need to be reminded that intellectuals themselves are always the products of new forms of collective labor power brought about and consolidated by the forces of late capitalism.

FROM RESISTANCE TO AGENCY

In Gramsci's work, the distinctive presence of the notions of collective will and consciousness are closely related to the concepts of resistance and agency. Gramsci described resistance as largely passive and unconscious, and suggested that as a political movement develops, agency replaces resistance:

> if yesterday the subaltern element was a thing, today it is no longer a thing but a historical person, a protagonist; if yesterday it was not responsible because "resisting" a will external to itself, now it feels itself to be responsible because it is no longer resisting but an agent, necessarily active and taking the initiative. But even yesterday was it ever mere "resistance," a mere "thing," mere "nonresponsibility"? Certainly not. (1971, p. 337)

Gramsci also argued that some intellectuals, particularly those that may be described as traditional, mistakenly understand the popular sectors as merely resisting hegemonic processes, "when they don't even expect that the subaltern will become directive and responsible" (1971, p. 337). Gramsci deeply understood the importance of the articulation of knowledge with passion and commitment. He reminds us that:

> The intellectual's error consists in believing that one can know without understanding and even more without feeling and being impassioned (not only for knowledge in itself but also for the object of knowledge): in other words that the intellectual can be an intellectual (and not a pure pedant) if distinct and separate from the people-nation, that is without feeling the elementary passions of the people, understanding them and therefore explaining and justifying them in the particular historical situation and connecting them dialectically to the laws of history and to a superior conception of the world, scientifically and coherently elaborated—i.e., knowledge. (1971, p. 418)

For Gramsci, "resistance" was a sign of (subaltern) discontent, rather than a conscious effort to promote social change. How is it possible, then, to turn mere resistance into agency? The organic intellectual (specialized intellectuals that each class develops) was Gramsci's answer. According to Carl Boggs, Gramsci helped to synthesize Lenin's Marxist Jacobinism (harnessing the State apparatus to the task of social reconstruction) and the radical spontanaeism of Luxemburg and Lukács.

It was Kautsky who first set forth the rationale for an intellectual vanguard. He argued that "since socialist ideas were first coherently articulated within the bourgeois intelligentsia, mass revolutionary consciousness depended upon the tutelary function of an educational and politically committed elite" (Boggs, 1993, p. 41). Boggs affirms that

> Kautsky's thesis, inspired by a naturalistic and positivist view of conscious-ness, justified a rigid separation between the "scientific" knowledge of intellectuals and the limited, partial ideology of the average worker. It fol-lows that only when the proletariat finally grasps the necessary "laws" of historical development (as formulated by intellectuals) can it become an active revolutionary force. (1993, p. 42)

Lenin similarly felt that the ideology of the worker, confined to the realm of production, could only be partial and that workers needed intellectuals to teach them the laws of historical development and disseminate among them the socialist ideals necessary to move beyond the logic of bourgeois reformism and towards a class political consciousness. This could be achieved most produc-tively through the efforts of a disciplined and highly organized vanguard party that, through forms of bureaucratic centralism, would serve as a repository of political knowledge and the agency of collective will capable of seizing State power. Unmediated popular self-activity was flatly rejected. According to Boggs (1993),

> Leninism, therefore, was able to "resolve" the problem of mass conscious-ness that had troubled Marxism for so long: a centralized, professional, and disciplined party would be the main repository of political knowledge. Intellectuals, fiercely dedicated to the party's historical mission, impose their own conception of totality upon the chaotic flow of disparate popular experiences and struggles. (p. 43)

Yet, Lenin's vision of intellectual leadership demanded coercion, force, and manipulation in order to be successful. More than this, it demanded the type of instrumental rationality and rationalizing ethos based on an internal division of labor that was constitutive of the very logic of capitalism. This situation was as precarious as it was perilous:

> Leninism found itself trapped in a dilemma. As it strove to consolidate power in a way that was bound to turn the masses it claimed to "represent" into manipulated objects, it was sure to gravitate toward an instrumental rationality wherein the methods and tools of politics took precedence over ultimate objectives. This suppression of the teleological element permitted Lenin to employ the very logic of capitalism in the service of its overthrow: hierarchical organization, mass assembly-line production, material incen-

tives, strict forms of labor discipline. It also meant that socialist goals would be deferred to a "future" that bore little resemblance to the actuality of the present. Ultimate aims were scarcely discussed or questioned, meaning in effect that organizational methods became ideological ends. (Boggs, 1993, p. 45)

Marxists such as Rosa Luxemburg, Emma Goldman, and Georg Lukács supported a more voluntarist or spontaneous approach, as did the worker-centered syndicalism of Sorel. From the spontaneist perspective, radical consciousness was immanent and organic to proletarian social relations. Boggs writes:

Luxemburg, like Lukács a few years later, sought to locate her critique of Jacobinism squarely within a Marxist framework: pitting Marx against Lenin, she anticipated massive worker upheavals growing out of the ever-widening global crisis of capitalism [. . .] Luxemburg waged a protracted fight against elitism, bureaucracy, and authoritarian manipulation that, in her view, was too often justified by appeals to "scientific" truth and the need for an intellectual vanguard. She understood democracy as being central to the revolutionary process, following the 1905 Russian model of the mass strike. Both the social Democrats and Bolsheviks had erred seriously in their tendency to dismiss mass spontaneity and in their fetishism of leadership. (1993, p. 51)

Gramsci took up the challenge of articulating the extent to which the working class could generate its own intellectual force, building on his well-known conviction that "All men are intellectuals [. . .] but not all men have in society the function of intellectuals" (1971, p. 9). His solution—the "organic intellectual"—took a collective character within a working-class formation in which the role of theory was organically linked with the ebb and flow of daily proletarian life. In this view, intellectuals should become an elaborate, historical expression of traditions, culture, values, and social relations. As Boggs (1993) notes, quasi-Jacobin ideological functions were still important intellectual tasks but now were required to be centered within the proletarian milieu (factories, community life, and culture). In this regard, intellectuals would be organic to that milieu only if they were fully immersed in its culture and language. Intellectuals, therefore, carried out "universal" functions that situate social activity within local and specific class struggles and in the defense of class interests. In effect, Gramsci was able to transcend the mechanical separation between the intellectual and popular realms that was upheld by both spontaneism and vanguardism. According to Gramsci:

The popular element "feels" but does not always know or understand; the intellectual element "knows" but does not always understand and in particular does not always feel. The two extremes are therefore pedantry and philistinism on the one hand and blind passion and sectarianism on the other. Not that the pedant cannot be impassioned; far from it. Impassioned pedantry is every bit as ridiculous and dangerous as the wildest sectarianism and demagogy. [. . .1 One cannot make politics-history without this passion, without this sentimental connection between intellectuals and people-nation. In the absence of such a nexus the relations between the intellectual and the people-nation are, or are reduced to, relationships of a purely bureaucratic and formal order; the intellectuals become a caste, or a priesthood. (1971, p. 418)

In a similar fashion, Paulo Freire also proposed transcending the antimony of populism and vanguardism through a synthesis of various types of demands and the development of reflective knowledge. Aronowitz remarks:

Freire's solution to [the] antimony of populism and vanguardism is to find a "synthesis" in which the demand for salaries is supported but posed as a "problem" that on one level becomes an obstacle to the achievement of full "humanization" through workers' ownership of their own labor. Again, workers pose wage increases as a solution to their felt oppression because they have internalized the oppressor's image of themselves and have not (yet) posed self-determination over the conditions of their lives as an object of their political practice. They have not yet seen themselves subjectively. (1993, pp. 16-17)

Aronowitz describes the role of the Freirean intellectual as sharing the power over knowledge. He writes:

Reporting on a conversation with workers' leaders in São Paulo, Freire defines class consciousness as the power and the will by workers and other oppressed and exploited strata to share in the formulation of the conditions of knowledge and futurity. This demand inevitably alters the situation of power: intellectuals must be consistent in the translation of their democratic visions to practice. In other words, they must share the power over knowledge, share the power to shape the future. (p. 21)

Gramsci, like Freire, urged intellectuals to develop a relational knowledge of and with the masses in order to help them become self-reflective. His unsurpassed understanding of the relationship between theory and practice stipulated an active participation in their quotidian struggles and an investment in their future well-being. Hence, Gramsci enjoined intellectuals to live intellectual life praxiologically, that is, in a state of ongoing praxis: "The mode of being of the new intellectual can no longer consist in eloquence, which is an exterior and momentary mover of feelings and passions, but in active participation in practical life, as constructor, organiser 'permanent persuader' and not just a simple orator" (1971, p. 10). In other words, Gramsci believed that intellectuals need to develop not only intellectual capital to distribute to the masses, but also the social capital of trust and collective will necessary to bring about community-based liberatory praxis (Richards, 1998).

Gramsci was concerned that popular revolt would be absorbed into the prevailing hegemony or else mobilized into the direction of reactionary fascism. Gramsci did not believe, as did the anarchists and syndicalists, that common sense was innately rebellious. For Gramsci, mass consciousness was contradictory and rather formless by necessity, and the construction of a collective political will is always gradual, uneven, and part of a counterhegemonic movement where intellectuals play an increasingly important role (Boggs, 1984). Leadership was indirect, as spontaneity was refracted through cultural formations and organizational and institutional sites. The challenge for Gramsci "was how to move beyond social immediacy without at the same time destroying spontaneous impulses" (Boggs, 1984, p. 208) to a point where common sense became good sense and spontaneity was transformed into critical consciousness. Boggs describes the democratizing character of the organic intellectual as follows:

> It seems clear that Gramsci, with the Turin council movement of 1918-1919 always in mind, saw the organic intellectual as a democratizing force who, virtually indistinguishable from the average worker in many ways, could articulate the values and goals of proletarian revolution. It was in this spirit that Gramsci could refer to theory as a "popular" enterprise and could champion the subversive idea that all persons are in some sense intellectuals insofar as they carry out certain forms of mental activity, enter into social relations, express opinions and make cultural choices. (1993, pp. 58-59)

INTELLECTUALS: FROM ORGANIC TO COMMITTED

For Gramsci, organic intellectuals were a fundamentally important expression of working-class life, an interrogation of emergent patterns of thought and action, the radicalization of the subaltern strata, the translation of theory into strategy, and the creation of revolutionary subjectivity through the formation of continuous and multifaceted counterhegemonic activity and the development of a revolutionary historical bloc where divergent interests converge and coalesce around shared visions and objectives. Gramsci did resign himself, however, to a commitment to some form of mass party, given the conjunctural events within Italy. Boggs writes:

> Gramsci's anti-Jacobinism gave way to certain historical pressures: he soon concluded that the Communist party ought to be the repository of theory, with its leadership the final arbiter of strategy. Gramsci himself was a founder and leading figure in the Italian Communist party. Yet his view of

> the party, like his concept of intellectuals, differed profoundly from Lenin's in many ways, beginning with Gramsci's emphasis on the ideological-cultural role of the party (the "myth prince") in contrast to Lenin's zeal for organization and power. Gramsci's idea of a "national-popular" movement required jettisoning the strict Leninist boundary between political and social realms best exemplified by the professional cadre—the hallmark of Bolshevik-type parties. Even in his later Jacobin phase, Gramsci approached critical consciousness as the product of an ongoing dialectical relationship between intellectuals and masses. This synthesis, however flawed, did go beyond the polarities of Marxist theory in the period 1890-1930: it was more compatible with the aims of popular self-emancipation than was vanguardism, more attuned to the indeterminate nature of mass consciousness than spontaneism, and more suitable to the condition of advanced capitalism than either. (1993, pp. 59-60)

While Gramsci considered all individuals to be intellectuals, not all of them had the function traditionally assigned to and developed by intellectuals (1971). Most importantly for Gramsci, organic intellectuals of the working class not only resist hegemonic processes, but attempt to displace the old hegemonic order by leading their class or popular front into more elaborated forms of understanding of the capitalist system of exploitation. At the same time, organic intellectuals serve as role models that open the horizons of their class or popular front in order to secure a more equitable system of societal organization, which Gramsci believed must take the form of a socialist society.

The role of the organic intellectual was to mediate between the good sense of subaltern groups and the formation of a counterhegemonic consciousness able to read the contextually specific and historically conjunctural contradictions that suffuse the social formation. According to Carroll and Ratner, Gramsci

> held that all people are intellectuals in capacity, if not function. He believed that counter-hegemonic leadership emanates from intellectuals whose organic ties to subaltern groups enable them to achieve a unity of theory and practice and of thinking and feeling, thus mediating between the abstract and concrete in a manner foreign to traditional scholastic, ecclesiastic, and political elites. For Gramsci, the role of the intellectual is that of organizer and facilitator: instead of bringing correct consciousness to the masses "from without," the organic intellectual facilitates the practical movement from "good sense" (which resistant subordinates already possess) to a broader, counterhegemonic consciousness that is sensitive to the specific conditions of a social formation at a given conjuncture. (1994, p. 12)

In the search for the limits of what it means to be an intellectual, there exists a lucid mistrustfulness in Gramsci's materialism. He maintains that an intellectual activity is not outside of a relational logic; therefore, to think about the role of an intellectual is to think about its very limits. If, as Ernesto Laclau (1993) points out, to see the limits of something is to see what is beyond those limits, then the criterion of distinction of what is and what is not, in strict terms, an intellectual task becomes constitutively opaque.

Gramsci knew that to say "all men" or "everyone" is the same as saying "no one." He was more concerned with the intellectual "function" than the function of the intellectual. Laclau (1993) has pointed out that "the intellectual for Gramsci is not a segregated intellectual group but one that establishes the organic unity among a group of activities that, if left to themselves, would remain fragmented and dispersed. A union activist, in that sense, would be an intellectual" (p. 204). As Laclau emphasizes, this is not about the function of the intellectual but about the intellectual function. It is not focused on a class; it cannot be the exclusive place of an elite: it emerges at all points of the social net—and consists of the practice of articulation. Priests, physicians, notaries, lawyers, teachers, nurses, dropouts, and gang members; schools, court, houses, hospitals, churches, and streetcorners: once we accept the intellectual task as a function, does it matter who and what they are? For Gramsci (and also for Paulo Freire), political-pedagogical actions are not an exclusive problem of having the right knowledge, but also of faithfulness to the event; in other words, to be in the right place at the right time.

Let us remember a passage of a rural educator's tale, which Freire mentions in his *Pedagogy of Hope*: "We need to tell you, friend, something very important. If you came here thinking you were going to teach us that we are being exploited, you do not need to, because we know that very well. Now, what we want to know about you is whether you are going to be with us at the time we are hit" (Freire, 1995, p. 67). Is this a popular expression of the rejection of intellectual tasks? Not necessarily. It deals with the ethical privilege of being "there" over being "something." By focusing on the relationships developed through hegemonic and counterhegemonic practices, Gramsci highlights the paradoxical practices in which the popular sectors engage, showing only one way out of this paradox. The organic intellectuals of the popular classes have the knowledge and the solutions that must be exercised if society is to become democratic. Gramsci saw democracy as essentially a dialectical movement between individual agency and structural location.

> But democracy, by definition, cannot mean merely that an unskilled worker can become skilled. It must mean that every "citizen" can "govern" and that society places him, even if only abstractly, in a general condition to achieve this. Political democracy tends towards a coincidence of the rulers and the ruled (in the sense of government with the consent of the governed) ensuring for each nonruler a free training in the skill and general technical preparation necessary to that end. (1971, pp. 40-41)

On the one hand, Gramsci believed that the popular classes are the only historical subjects able to effectively resist, challenge, and transform the hegemonic position of the bourgeoisie—even though the working class and the peasants (i.e., popular classes) have developed a contradictory consciousness which ultimately does not allow the elaboration of autonomous decisions. On the other hand, organic intellectuals, on their own merits, are able to construct other models of consciousness in political and cultural arenas, and it is this process that, for Gramsci, constitutes the key to overcoming the shortcomings of the popular classes:

> Critical self-consciousness means, historically and politically, the construction of an élite of intellectuals. A human mass does not "distinguish" itself, does not become independent in its own right without, in the widest sense, organizing itself; and there is no organization without intellectuals, that is without organizers and leaders, in other words, without the theoretical aspect of the theory-practice nexus being distinguished concretely by the existence of a group of people "specialized" in conceptual and philosophical elaboration of ideas. (Gramsci, 1971, p. 334)

One of the main challenges of Gramsci's framework, and one that is repeated by many in the field of education, is that there exists a categorical assumption that organic intellectuals must develop some sort of supranatural level of consciousness, avoiding or overcoming the contradictory personal and social struggles present in everyday life. At the same time, this hypervalorization of the role of one small group of leaders and organizers replicates the heroic myths of romantic idealism of the last century, which in turn reflects its positivistic heritage, and a firm belief in the existence of a normal and teleological line of progress for all societies (i.e., from backward societies, to capitalistic forms, to socialist and finally communist societies). Additionally, it is worth noting that ideology, hegemony, and resistance are also concepts that have been developed and employed in deeply gendered frameworks. For this reason, the important criticisms of feminist scholars must be taken seriously (i.e., Alcoff & Potter, 1993; Butler, 1993; Hill Collins, 1990). Margaret Ledwith (1997) points out that Gramsci's work often "fell foul of the public-private divide" (1997, p. 91). For example, Gramsci largely overlooked the support of his sister-in-law, Tatiana Schucht, during his prison years, especially in relation to her assistance with his prison notebooks. Gramsci's thinking, however, did capture at least some of the issues confronting gender equality. Ledwith notes that Gramsci

> was not confronted with the feminist awareness that has developed over the last few decades. There seem to be some contradictory issues here: Gramsci accepted as natural the roles of the women in his personal life without recognizing their political implications. However, there is a glimpse that he was aware at some deeper level of the complex subordination of women. In

his discussion of Americanism and Fordism [. . .] he not only acknowledges women's exploitation in the public domain, but also recognizes our vital function in the reproduction of the workforce, thereby identifying sexuality as a focus of oppression. [. . .] he saw economic independence as only part of the story; true emancipation involves freedom of choice in relation to sexual relationships. What he referred to as a "new ethic" [. . .] is the transformative moment gained from a war of position, which frees women in a truly liberatory way. Gramsci's feminist consciousness therefore connects women's sexual rights not only with women's liberation, but also with the total transformation of society as a whole. (1997, p. 91)

Some Gramscian scholars and activists have pointed out that the very distinction between domination and resistance has often been misunderstood by contemporary social scientists, because it is only when resistance is performed as a violently explicit act, or as an act of direct opposition, that it is given validity or conceptualized as the true voice or will of subjects expressing their agency. Yet, counterhegemonic practices do not necessarily result in violent acts. They partake of many genres and modalities of "performance," ranging from decentering dominant discourses in a spectrum of public practices (such as political journalism, political theatre, insurrectionary artistic endeavors, or acts of scholarship) to actively resisting repressive State apparatuses (through strikes, walk-outs, political demonstrations, armed struggle and the like). Furthermore, counterhegemonic resistance among feminist intellectuals carries its own set of special challenges. Boggs notes that feminist intellectuals

are immersed in the world of collective action, in the language and values of women struggling to change their lives. The gulf between intellectual work and everyday life, between thought and action, is greatly narrowed where it is not eliminated altogether. With few exceptions, feminist intellectuals of this sort carry no Jacobin illusions, no global or "imported" theories, no fixation on a single privileged agency of change. Nor do they adhere to prevailing technocratic norms. At the same time, the always shifting social bases and fortunes of women's movements and projects means that long-term organic attachment of intellectuals to local communities is problematic. In this sense the "organic" character of intellectuals in new social movements can be expected to have a provisional status. (1993, p. 178)

Perhaps the main problem in this Gramscian inspired framework is that it presents a categorical assumption that agents of change (organic intellectuals, teachers, or social activists) should be able to develop a supranatural level of consciousness.

RETHINKING CRITICAL PEDAGOGY IN THE SPIRIT OF GRAMSCI

While we agree with Boggs (1986) that today's critical intellectuals also embody some elements of Gramsci's organic model, we are concerned about the lack of interest in class politics and class struggle on the part of the emerging strata of postmodern intellectuals and their relationship to new social movements, including global movements. We further believe that Gramsci's appropriation by educational postmodernists has too often emphasized the priority of language and representation in the hegemonic processes of identity formation to the detriment of acknowledging how the social construction of race, class, and gender are implicated in the international division of labor. Postmodern educators have not sufficiently grasped the importance of understanding and challenging the totalizing power of capitalism. Capitalism totalizes like nothing else—it is its totalizing character that renders capitalism unique (Carroll & Ratner, 1993). According to Marx:

> [I]t is not values in use and the enjoyment of them, but exchange value and its augmentation, that spur [the capitalist] into action. Fanatically bent on making value expand itself, he ruthlessly forces the human race to produce for production's sake [. . .]. Moreover, the development of capitalist production makes it constantly necessary to keep increasing the amount of the capital laid out in a given industrial undertaking, and competition makes the immanent laws of capitalist production to be felt by each individual capitalist, as external coercive laws. It compels him to keep constantly extending his capital, in order to preserve it, but extend it he cannot, except by means of progressive accumulations [. . .]. To accumulate, is to conquer the world of social wealth, to increase the mass of human beings exploited by him, and thus to extend both the direct and the indirect sway of the capitalist. (Marx, 1967, p. 592, cited in Carroll & Ratner, 1994, p. 17)

We argue for a counterhegemonic coalition of social formations composed of committed intellectuals whose political links are connected and articulated through the unification of demands in heterogeneous, multifaceted, yet focalized anticapitalist struggles. This is not to limit counterhegemonic struggles to the productivist framework of unilinear labor struggles or Marxist "workerism," but rather to forge new links between labor and new social movements without dismissing the potential of "politically" unorganized social sectors (such as the growing numbers of the unemployed and homeless) (Boggs, 1986).

One of the main goals of these multivaried coalitions should be to suffocate the authoritarian power of the State and curb its ability to support other structures of oppression. This demands moving beyond the radical autonomy of localized struggles or the creation of a network of micropolitical struggles. It does not mean that we reject community-based multiform politics; rather, we need to coordinate our single-issue and micropolitical efforts so that the power of State apparatuses are not underestimated and can be effectively challenged. Of course, we also acknowledge that the State is not the all-encompassing structure of domination that orthodox Marxists have often made it out to be. But we recognize that State formations, while more fluid in the context of global markets and the internationalization of capital, have not become obsolete. Too often radical pluralism does not sufficiently acknowledge the extent to which relations of subordination are connected to State formations, through which capitalist power circulates and becomes legitimate.

While we agree with Boggs that "a reconstituted definition of organic intellectuals emphasizes movement as opposed to class or social identity" (1993, p. 179), we worry that such a renovated dialectic between intellectuals and social forces or movements is unlikely to overturn the highly integrated power structures of global capitalism associated with the economic exploitation of the masses, ecological genocide, and bureaucratic domination. We maintain that it is imperative to move beyond a monodeterministic base-superstructural argument. Consequently, we reject, as did Marx (in the *Grundrisse*), the establishment of a mechanical one-to-one "mimetic" relation of determination between the social relations of production and cultural formations. Yet we still urge the recognition of the priority of labor relations in social processes and the "logic" inherent in the productive processes of capital—the expropriation of the labor of the many by the few.

While it is surely the case that economic and cultural relations can be and often are—decoupled within capitalist society, we call for the need to acknowledge that objective surplus labor grounds cultural practices and social institutions. Here we follow Hoffman (1984) in arguing that to avoid a mechanical hypostatization and organic splicing apart of the Gramscian couplet of coercion and consent, all political action must be premised on the idea of the coercive character of all social relationships. Failure to do this has led post-Marxists who champion the new social movements to overemphasize contingency at the expense of structural determination. The cabaret avant-gardism of many postmodernist critics confirms rather than contests the authority of the sovereign discourses in a way that reduces the desired exchange with the specters of the unsaid. While their gravitational center constitutes a cultural politics that attempts to locate culture as a terrain where social justice is contested and where victory for the subaltern needs to be won, it is too often the case that dominant images, symbols, and representations are portrayed as establishing the most fundamental conditions of daily action, structuring daily life in the most immediate and important ways. This is not to say that cultural discourses are secondary to economic relations, or to maintain that symbolic production (as in the work of Walter Benjamin) has no revolutionary significance or potential; nor are we suggesting that resistance at the level of culture is merely epiphenomenal (we are thinking, for instance, of the Chicano school walkouts in East Los Angeles over Proposition 187, the art of Barbara Kruger, and project ACT-UP). What we are saying is that in much postmodern criticism, the world of class struggle linked to the social division of labor and relations of production is theoretically dissolved into a world composed of unstable constellations of meanings and indeterminate and incommensurable discourses that appear severed from the messy terrain of capitalist social relations. In this scenario, class struggles are too often rewritten as a political economy of conjunctural antagonisms or a type of crosshatching of determinations that do not intersect neatly in terms of class location.

Post-Marxist or postmodernist critics do not see consent as a moment conceived within social coercion brought about by productive practices. By contrast, the committed intellectual recognizes that so-called autonomous acts of consent are always already rooted in the coercive relationships of the realm of necessity. Since coercion is the "ethical expression of the fact that people have to produce" (Hoffman, 1984, p. 212), it makes sense to view the dialectical relationship between coercion and consent as a unity in distinction. Hoffman asserts that "consent has to respond to coercion in order to 'negate' it. We have to avoid [. . .] a fatalistic social determinism [. . .] and a voluntaristic postulation of situations in which 'social' pressures are non-existent" (1984, p. 210). Without acknowledging coercion, we are faced with a pedagogy grounded in an antipolitics of free-floating critique. As Carroll and Ratner remark: "Politics becomes an anything-goes adventure—as exhilarating as it is strategically rudderless" (1994, p. 14).

TOWARDS A CRITICAL PEDAGOGY OF THE COMMITTED INTELLECTUAL

We wish to extend the role of the organic intellectual by suggesting that the resisting, hegemonized, and fragmented subaltern needs to function not only as a critically superconscious "organic intellectual," but also as a committed one (Fischman, 1998). The committed intellectual is sometimes critically self-conscious and active, but at other times is too confused about, or even unaware of, his or her limitations or capacities to be an active promoter of social change. Or, as Paulo Freire has noted: "Conscientization is not exactly the starting point of commitment. Conscientization is more of a product of commitment. I do not have to be already conscious in order to struggle. By struggling I become conscious/aware" (Freire, 1988, p. 114).

Consciousness always implies that the subject has some awareness of the immediate world that concerns him or her. As Freire (1989) came to recognize, a deep understanding of the complex processes of oppression and domination is not enough to guarantee personal or collective praxis. What must serve as the genesis of such an understanding is an unwavering commitment to the struggle against injustice. Only by developing an understanding that is born of a commitment to social justice can such an understanding lead to the type of conscientization necessary to challenge the hegemonic structures of domination and exploitation. The globalization of capital can be challenged and defeated not only by understanding its formation but also by developing the will and the courage—the commitment—to struggle against it.

The committed intellectual is not someone who is interested only in resisting and defeating forms of cultural domination, but rather someone for whom the end of all forms of exploitation is the focal point of his or her commitment to transform the world. We do not endorse the view that conflicting or competing claims are ultimately, or "in the last instance," unsolvable, nor do we wish to articulate a view of the intellectual that merely invites the subaltern to add his or her recipe to the existing pot so that the clenched fists of history can label them into an apocalyptic meltdown of final consensus. This would be a politically ambiguous stance, as well as an intellectually dishonest one.

The point is not to initiate a "face off" between two equally dogmatic assertions: between advocates of structural determination and proponents of universal contingency; or between supporters of Leninist reflectionism and those who support a poststructuralist relativism. We believe that a better strategy is to follow Gramsci's stress on acquiring a critical understanding of the hegemonic structures (civic, social, and State) that constrain human action, while at the same time emphasizing a commitment to revolutionary agency that will permit collective re-definitions of social change and enable freedom from capitalist exploitation. Following Carroll and Ratner (1994), we need a more dialectical view of revolutionary praxis that acknowledges that systems of intelligibility and relations of signification (i.e., cultural politics) are reciprocally reenacted in social relations in the material world.

We recognize, of course, that the situation today is far different from the milieu of Turin in which Gramsci struggled. With the pervasiveness of ideological and social diversity that exists today, and with the lack of an integrated working class, it is more likely that intellectual labor for the cause of social justice will take place outside a single global system of thought (such as Marxism), although we believe such a system to be indispensable for achieving the conditions of liberation of which Gramsci spoke. Boggs remarks on the growth of critical, free-floating intellectuals that has accompanied the pluralization of social life-worlds and political opposition. As we noted in the case of feminist intellectuals, the new "critical intellectual" associated with the new social movements and the struggle for radical democracy

> articulates oppositional values but does so in something of a free-floating manner, alone or in small groups, removed from the sphere of popular movements or constituencies. The organic type, on the other hand, engages in a more collective, transformative activity where the old distinction between intellectuals and masses is broken down, so that "theoretical" and other mental functions are no longer imported from the outside, in Jacobin style. From a Gramscian standpoint, organic intellectuals are counter-hegemonic precisely to the extent that their contribution takes place within a democratized struggle for social change. (Boggs, 1994, p. 175)

The committed intellectual recognizes that self-reflexivity (or the capacity to engage in critical self-consciousness) is not enough to resist both the repressive and integrative functions of hegemony. It is necessary to find ways to actively intervene in the capitalist world order. Such strategies entail combining aspects of the free-floating intellectual with those of the organic intellectual. In other words, the committed intellectual works in diverse spheres, in which new social movements intersect with more organically traditionalist socialist movements. What links the two groups of intellectuals is a common commitment to anti-capitalist struggle and a provisional model of socialist democracy. As Brosio warns:

> The fact that working-class consciousness has not yet overcome this hegemony in the West causes one to think that becoming aware may not be enough, when one considers the advances which have been made by capital in its colonization of the quotidian, lived experiences of the masses since the time in which Gramsci wrote. Moreover, there are many persons in Gramsci's native country and elsewhere who understand the nature of their sophisticated oppression, but are unable to muster the power to stop it and finally overcome it. (1994, p. 50)

LEGACIES OF GRAMSCI'S SPECTER: REVOLUTIONARY PATIENCE AND COMMITTED INTELLECTUALS

The figure of the committed intellectual that we are developing never forgets that we live in a world of messy material relations that not only structures our consciousness and shapes our subjectivities but frequently exploits human labor and strips subaltern subjects of their fundamental humanity and self-worth (McLaren, 1995, 1997). Exploitation not only alienates, it also destroys; it forces people to work and live in dangerous workplace environments, it pollutes the earth with toxic, life-threatening chemicals, it forces people to endure long hours of indignity, job insecurity, and low wages.

The objective world produces our social intelligibilities and our discourses about it. These discourses often function in ways that naturalize and legitimize objective labor practices (Ebert, 1997). They help to win approval for the extraction of surplus labor from the working class. The textuality of the world enables us to know it primarily through narratives. Our engagement with the discourses of everyday life are relational because knowledge is never pristine or stable. Discourses themselves have a materiality about them by the very fact that they are uncontainable by any theory or explanation. As narratives, they are immune from ultimate closure. Even though the arena of signification is always already an undecidable social text, this is not the same thing as claiming that meanings constitute nothing more than the relations among signs or the free play of significant difference. The committed intellectual does not view these discourses as seamless but rather views all discourses as fundamentally contradictory and conflictual; further, discourses are never immune from the larger context of objective labor practices or disentangled from social relations arising from the history of productive labor. Recognizing that the international division of labor is refracted through race, class, and gender antagonisms, the committed intellectual confronts the capitalist world order with a race, class, and gender consciousness and a politics of respite and renewal. The committed intellectual does this without succumbing to a right-wing anti-statism of backlash populism (as in the case of agrarian fascists or Christian militia movements), an organic communitarianism, populist nostalgia, possessive parochialism, or militant cultural particularism.

Walter Adamson remarked that although Gramsci's world "is no longer our world, his experience remains a critical moment in the development of Western Marxism from which we can all continue to learn" (1980, p. 246). Gramsci's work is highly suggestive for understanding how the regime of capital functions through historically specific ethnic and gender differentiation, and for understanding how the law of value is refracted through the culturally specific character of labor power. His work on the contradictory aspects of ideological formations can give us a much needed critical understanding of the nature of "the 'subjection' of the victims of racism to the mystifications of the very racist ideologies which imprison and define them" (Hall, 1996, p. 440). His concept of the organic intellectual offers a fecund beginning for understanding the possibilities inherent in critical agency. We have attempted to build on these potent ideas in our nascent formulation of the committed intellectual. We believe that Gramsci's conception of the relationship between the role of the intellectuals and ideology and hegemony provides contemporary educators with a basis to forge a critical pedagogy capable of meeting the challenges of the new millennium.

REFERENCES

Adamson, W. L. (1980). *Hegemony and Revolution: A Study of Antonio Gramsci's Political and Cultural Theory.* Berkeley: University of California Press.

Alcoff, L., & Potter, E. (Eds.). (1993). *Feminist Epistemologies.* New York: Routledge.

Anderson, P. (1977). *Las Antinomias de Antonio Gramsci.* Barcelona: Fontana.

Aronowitz, S. (1993). Paulo Freire's Radical Democratic Humanism. In P. McLaren & P. Leonard (Eds.), *Paulo Freire: A Critical Encounter* (pp. 8-24). London: Routledge.

Berger, J. (1988, January 4). How to Live with Stones. An Open Letter to Subcommandante Marcos in the Mountains of Southeast Mexico. [Book Review]. *Los Angeles Times,* 3.

Best, S., & Kellner, D. (1991). *Postmodern Theory: Critical Interrogations.* New York: Guilford.

Boggs, C. (1996). *Social Movements and Political Power*. Philadelphia: Temple University Press.

Boggs, C. (1993). *Intellectuals and the Crisis of Modernity*. Albany: State University of New York Press.

Boggs, C. (1984). *The Two Revolutions: Gramsci and the Dilemmas of Western Marxism*. Boston: South End.

Brandist, C. (1996). Gramsci, Bakhtin and the Semiotics of Hegemony. *New Left Review*, 216, 94-109.

Brandist, C. (1996a). The Official and the Popular in Gramsci and Bakhtin. *Theory, Culture & Society*, 13 (2), 59-74.

Brosio, R. A. (1994). *A Radical Democratic Critique of Capitalist Education*. New York: Peter Lang.

Butler, J. (1993). *Bodies that Matter: On the Discursive Limits of "Sex."* New York: Routledge.

Butler, J. (1990). *Gender Trouble: Feminism and the Subversion of Identity*. New York: Routledge.

Carroll, W. K., & Ratner, R. S. (1994). Between Leninism and Radical Pluralism: Gramscian Reflections on Counter-Hegemony and the New Social Movements. *Critical Sociology*, 20 (2), 3-26.

De Azua, F. (1997). Para que leer? *Cuadernos de Pedagogia*, 1 (1).

Derrida, J. (1994). *Specters of Marx: The State of the Debt, the Work of Mourning, and the New*. London: Routledge.

Donald, J. (1992). *Sentimental Education: Schooling, Popular Culture, and the Regulation of Liberty*. London: Verso.

Eagleton, T. (1991). *Ideology. An Introduction*. London: Verso.

Ebert, T. (1997). (Oc)Cult of the Post-al. *Rethinking Marxism*, 9 (3), 103-18.

Eribon, D. (1992). *Foucault*. Barcelona: Editorial Anagrama.

Fischman, G. (1998). Donkeys and Superteachers: Popular Education and Structural Adjustment in Latin America. *International Journal of Education*.

Fiori, G. (1990). *Antonio Gramsci: Life of a Revolutionary* (T. Nairn, Trans.). London: Verso.

Fraser, N. (1997). Heterosexism, Misrecognition, and Capitalism: A Response to Judith Butler. *Social Text*, 52-53, 279-89.

Freire, P. (1989). *Education for the Critical Consciousness*. New York: Continuum.

Freire, P. (1988). *Pedagogia, Dialogo y Conflicto*. Buenos Aires: Ediciones Cinco.

Freire, P., & Gadotti, M. (1995). We Can Reinvent the World. In P. McLaren & J. Giarelli (Eds.), *Critical Theory and Educational Research*. New York: State University of New York Press.

Gordon, A. (1997). *Ghostly Matters: Haunting and the Sociological Imagination*. Minneapolis: University of Minnesota Press.

Gramsci, A. (1971). *Selections from the Prison Notebooks*. New York: International.

Hall, S. (1996). Gramsci's Relevance for the Study of Race and Ethnicity. In D. Morley & K-H Chen (Eds.), *Stuart Hall: Critical Dialogues in Cultural Studies*. London: Routledge.

Hall, S., & Donald, J. (Eds.). (1986). *Politics and Ideology: A Reader*. Philadelphia: Open University Press.

Harris, D. (1992). *From Class to Class Struggle to the Politics of Pleasure: The Effects of Gramscianism on Cultural Studies*. London: Routledge.

Hassoun, J. (1996). *Los contrabandistas de la memoria*. Buenos Aires: Ediciones de la Flor.

Hebdige, D. (1996). Postmodernism and "the other side." In D. Morley & K-H Chen (Eds.), *Stuart Hall: Critical Dialogues in Cultural Studies* (pp. 174-200). London: Routledge.

Hill Collins, P. (1990). *Black Feminist Thought*. New York: Routledge.

Hoffman, J. (1984). *The Gramscian Challenge: Coercion and Consent in Marxist Political Theory*. Oxford: Blackwell.

Katz, A. (1997). Postmodern Cultural Studies: A Critique. *Cultural Logic: An Electronic Journal of Marxist Theory and Practice*, 1 (1).

Laclau, E., & Mouffe, C. (1986). *Hegemony and Socialist Strategy*. London: Verso.

Laclau, E., & Mouffe, C. (1990). *New Reflections on the Revolution of Our Time*. London: Verso.

Ledwith, M. (1997). *Participating in Transformation: Towards a Working Model of Community Development*. Birmingham: Venture.

Lewis, T. (1996/97). The Politics of "Hauntology" in Derrida's *Specters of Marx*. *Rethinking Marxism, 9* (3), 19-39.

McLaren, P., & Lankshear, C. (Eds.). (1994). *Politics of Liberation: Paths from Freire*. London: Routledge.

McLaren, P. (1995). *Critical Pedagogy and Predatory Culture*. London: Routledge.

McLaren, P. (1997). *Revolutionary Multiculturalism: Pedagogies of Dissent for the New Millennium*. Boulder, CO: Westview.

Richards, L. (1998). *The Heart of Knowledge: An Epistemology of Relationship*. Unpublished doctoral dissertation, The Fielding Institute, Santa Barbara.

Torres, C. A. (1992). *The Church, Society and Hegemony*. London: Praeger.

13 RICHARD RORTY'S SELF-HELP LIBERALISM
A MARXIST CRITIQUE OF AMERICA'S MOST WANTED IRONIST

Peter McLaren,
Ramin Farahmandpur
and Juha Suoranta

INTRODUCTION

The fireworks displays ushering in the new millennium have long subsided, but the smoke has not-yet cleared. We haven't noticed that capitalism's "Goliath" roller-coaster ride has no destination, only repetition. Like a Möbius strip, the exit transforms into the entrance and the ride begins again. In this reengineered era of "no exit" capitalism, the future has already arrived. And to the philosophically inclined, the future is also beginning to look more and more like Richard Rorty playing a toga-clad ambassador from outer space in an early *Star Trek* episode. Presumably the future will take care of itself as long as Americans like Rorty are around to ensure that the universe is run by "liberal gentlefolk" ready and willing to make the necessary incremental efforts to transform the world's globobosses and corporate managers into a fraternity of happy campers determined to "be all that they can be." Precisely at the time when we are witnessing the capitulation of Eastern bloc regimes to the capitalist law of value, attention has waxed with respect to those "reform" discourses of which Rorty is the liberal academy's prime *anitmateur*.

While capitalism is becoming more and more like Hal the Computer, and taking on a life of its own, we remain unclear as to whether or not it's programmed to self-terminate or destined to rejuvenate. So far nobody has been able to identify the "gene" for capitalism in the human species. No doubt that discovery will soon be announced with considerable corporate fanfare. In which case, genetic material from Milton Friedman and Ronald Reagan will likely be carefully sifted from their corpses and put in petri dish displays in a future mon-

This chapter originally appeared in Michael A. Peters and Paulo Ghiraldelli, Jr. (Eds.), *Richard Rorty: Education, Philosophy, and Politics*, pp. 139-162. © 2001 Rowman & Littlefield. Reprinted with permission of the publisher.

ument to capitalism—something of a rude counterpoint to Lenin's embalmed flesh in Red Square.

The labor-capital contradiction is today the most fundamental and all-encompassing relation of exploitation—the last of the Russian Matryoshka dolls in the larger social totality of Western capitalist countries. The more that people are hurt by capitalism, the more frenetically they try to fasten themselves onto the global economic grid. The more that capitalism defeats them, the more they desire to become capitalists. Capitalism no longer requires the tutelage of the state to promote it; it is now self-justificatory. Its internal logic is unassailable. It has insinuated itself into the pores of our psyche; it jumps across our synapses, commanding us to loathe communism and uphold the promise of the American Dream. As Michael Parenti notes, "capitalism is not just an economic system, but a political and cultural one as well, an entire social order" (1997, 133).

Enter philosopher Richard Rorty, a staunch defender of neoliberalism and free-market democracy. Despite the abundance of evidence that capitalist democracies, guided by a neoliberal politics, are condemning the world's laboring class to a life sentence of poverty not only for themselves but for generations to follow, Rorty continues to cling to a Malthusian conviction that the forces that foster equality and political freedom within liberal social democracies far outweigh those that foster inequality and restrict political freedom. True to his staunch and steadfast antiempiricism, Rorty offers no convincing evidence that this is indeed the case.

RORTY THE REBEL:
THE ANTIPHILOSOPHER'S PHILOSOPHER

Over the years, Richard Rorty's reputation as one of the most influential philosophers in current literary and philosophical circles has provoked considerable scholarly attention. With an Argus eye on John Dewey's armoire of pragmatist pronouncements on self and society, Rorty's ascentional commentaries on current developments in intellectual and political history are eagerly anticipated by the Left academy and its beleaguered opponents. Rorty's philosophical touchstone has remained his unflinching pragmatism, his fulsome attention to social issues, and his remonstrative opposition to rank-and-file ultra leftists (i.e., Marxists, anarchists).

Richard Rorty is considered one of the most influential, yet controversial, philosophers of our generation. According to John Smith, "Rorty stands out as the most vocal and at the same time the most quixotic" philosophers of the pragmatic school (1992, 5). Rorty has shaken the foundations of the West's analytic tradition in philosophy so violently that Plato's bones can be heard rattling through the four corners of his cave. In fact, Rorty has participated with delinquent relish in the most urgent moral and political debates of the last twenty

years. These debates have ranged from commentaries on contemporary literature to debates on globalization and the future of liberal democracies that are
trying to free themselves from the grip of "socially accepted sadism." Rorty can
be described as a philosopher-chameleon, an argumentative magician of many
rhetorical faces whose epistemological platform sags under the weight of its
own contradictory dualism, even as he mightily describes his philosophical
view as antidualism. Rorty may also be considered an unrepentant academic
outlaw who has sought to destabilize the entire Western tradition of analytic
philosophy by accusing it of becoming co-opted by a pragmatically detumescent academic discourse (Von Wright 1992).

We agree with David Hall that it is difficult to criticize Rorty in ways other
than participating in an *excursus ad hominum.* This is because Rorty understands that his poetic nominalism is closed to internal critique and that his shifting position on issues is not open to rational analysis. Hall writes that:

> Eschewing historical and rational reconstructions in favor of geistes-
> geschichten permit Rorty, by recourse to a series of strong misreadings, to
> insulate himself against the standard philosophical criticisms. His quite
> plausible claim that beliefs change not only rationally, but casually, as well,
> through recontextualizations stimulated by novel metaphors renders this
> insulation well-nigh complete. (1994, 169)

Rorty's fellow philosophers are not amused with his immodest claim as the
most pristine heir to the Deweyan philosophical and political tradition. In their
opinion, Rorty's philosophical pluralism (or what his critics would identify as
"philosophical relativism") has greatly oversimplified Dewey's pragmatism and
has discredited pragmatism in general. John Smith (1992) condemns Rorty for
reducing the pragmatist tradition to antifoundationalism, engendering what could
be called "post-philosophical culture". Such reductionism, claims Smith, sorely
overlooks contemporary social issues, not to mention all the other disciplinary
arenas to which pragmatists have contributed over the course of history: religion,
ethics, social and political thought, the history of science, and aesthetics.

Rorty's reinterpretations of the American pragmatist tradition have been
criticized by a broad range of pragmatists and philosophers of various stripes
(Pihlström 1996). However, much of the criticism against Rorty could be
described as disciplinary border skirmishes that concern only the philosophical
academic elite. Much of the debate against Rorty from within the philosophy
community itself stems from the fact that he has confused things unnecessarily;
his detractors continue to hope that he will not make things any more complicated than they already are. That appears to be a terminal case of wishful thinking,
given that, throughout his academic career (at least since *Philosophy and the
Mirror of Nature*), Rorty has strategically taken cover in counternarratives ranging from the benign to the hostile—while brazenly identifying himself as an
antiphilosopher. As Ree puts it: "In the Seventies he curried disfavor with ana-

lytic philosophers by accusing them of blinkered vanity; in the Eighties he leveled the same accusation at philosophers in general; and during the Nineties he
has extended it to his allies on the cultural left" (1998, 11). While Rorty con-
fesses that he is not amused, it is difficult to fathom the extent to which—if
any—he is actually affected by the intemperate comments and irremovable
objections of his fellow philosophers. Cryptically, he states:

> I am sometimes told, by critics from both ends of the political spectrum,
> that my views are so weird as to be merely frivolous. They suspect that I
> will say anything to get a gasp, that I am just amusing myself by contradict-
> ing everybody else. This hurts. (1999, 5)

THE FOUNDATIONS OF RORTY'S ANTIFOUNDATIONALISM

Although Rorty's *Philosophy and the Mirror of Nature* (1979) is accepted as a
modern classic in philosophy, many philosophers have failed to understand the
logic behind Rorty's work. It could be said that his book has effectively explod-
ed the contemporary frames of analytic philosophy. While *Philosophy and the
Mirror of Nature* was not warmly received by most of Rorty's fellow philosophers, its ideas were unflaggingly supported by many social scientists and educational theorists. Its success was, in part, due to the fact that it provided some
answers to seemingly eternal problems with respect to the relationship between
scientific explanation and humanistic understanding, between the natural sciences and the humanities.

Social and educational scientists took Rorty's basic message seriously: that
the researcher's task is not so much to explain social phenomena as to facilitate
"edifying conversations" of various kinds. Rorty states: "I shall use 'edification'
to stand for this project of finding new, better, more interesting, more fruitful
ways of speaking" (1980, 360). Relying on Gadamer's *Truth and Method*, Rorty
draws a dividing line between the desire for edification and the desire for truth.
In Rorty's interpretation, the former is more interesting and needed to understand and cope with the world as well as to reach for a decent society in which
institutions do not humiliate: "From the educational, as opposed to the epistemological or the technological, point of view, the way things are said is more
important than the possession of truths" (Rorty 1980, 359)

Rorty learned two important lessons from the enthusiastic reception of
Philosophy and the Mirror of Nature. On one hand, it gave him the self-confi-
dence he had previously lacked. On the other hand, it taught him that there was
no point in reaching for his youthful dream of a single vision which would keep
both the explanation of reality and the fundamentals of justice together.
Keeping epistemological and ontological questions separated from moral ones,
he has turned more and more towards Darwinism. For Rorty, there is no criteri-

on, either for growth or for education. Requesting such a criterion "is like asking a dinosaur to specify what would make for a good mammal or asking a fourth-century Athenian to propose forms of life for the citizens of a twentieth-century industrial democracy" (Rorty 1999, 120). Thus, education is always a type of experiment, a choice of nature.

As human beings, we can, of course, hope "that the future will be unspecifiably different from, and unspecifiably freer than, the past" (Rorty 1999, 120). And if hoping does not help, we can, claims Rorty, give natural growth a helping hand. When reflecting on the larger-than-life question that will save us from ecological, economic, and social destruction, Rorty—representing us "Northern gentlefolk"—offers the following meditation on education:

> The only things we know of which might help are top-down techno-bureaucratic initiatives like the cruel Chinese only-one-child-per-family policy (or, literalizing the top-down metaphor and pushing things one monstrous step further, spraying villages from the air with sterilizing chemicals). If there is a happy solution to the dilemma created by the need of very poor Brazilians to find work and the need of the rest of us for the oxygen produced by the Amazonian rain forest, it is going to be the result of some as yet unimagined bureaucratic-technological initiative, not of revolution in 'values'. (Rorty 1999, 227-28)

Although Rorty identities himself as an antifoundationalist, Rockmore proclaims that "the terms 'antifoundationalism' and 'foundationalism' are not natural, but normative, there is no one way to draw the distinction between them" (1992, 4). We should also note that different types of antifoundationalisms abound. For instance, metaphysical antifoundationalism referred to the denial of ultimate reality or a fundamental kind of being. Epistemological antifoundationalism, for its part, refers to the view that there are no secure foundations for knowledge. Thus, antifoundationalism is not a philosophical miracle invented by Rorty, but one discursive position out of several others (institutionalism and foundationalism) that makes philosophical and methodological discussion possible.

Rockmore reminds us that Rorty did not coin the term "antifoundationalism," although he sometimes seems to credit himself (1992, 3). The debate over the foundations of knowledge, including the antifoundationalist point of view, can be traced as far back as early Greek thought. Furthermore, Rorty's use of the term "antifoundationalism" is uncharacteristic because he limits its use to criticize an analytic approach to epistemology and thus mistakenly equates the analytic approach with a theory of knowledge. Rorty's philosophical worldview is impressively captured in the words of Carey:

> Reality must be repaired for it consistently breaks down: people get lost physically and spiritually, experiments fail, evidence counter to the representation is produced, mental derangement sets in—threats all to our mod-

els of and for reality that lead to intense repair work. Finally, we must, often with fear and regret, toss away our authoritative representations of reality and begin to build the world anew. (1975, 10-17)

Rorty is mainly interested in the question which has captured the imagination of philosophers throughout history: how to begin to repair and build the world anew. Rorty's epistemological antifoundationalism casts aside representations as more or less accurate pictures of the world. He also wants to do away with scientific and ideological authorities—but only some of them—in his metaphysical antifoundationalism. Both Jesus and Marx, claims Rorty, should be relegated to the rag-and-bone shop of passé perspectives, while Darwin and Dewey deserve canonization in the liberal think tanks (whose intellectual capital Rorty celebrates). In other words, not everyone is invited to dinner; history's banquet is, for Rorty, reserved for the select few. So much for Rorty's pluralism.

Darwin and Dewey are among those who purposefully follow Rorty's extremely naive and idealistic methodological imperative: "the habits of relying on persuasion rather than force, of respect for the opinions of colleagues, of curiosity and eagerness for new data and ideas, are the only virtues which scientists have" (Rorty 1991, 39). It is as if Rorty did not know that, from time to time, academic life is nasty, messy, not to mention Machiavellian.

Rorty's effort in revitalizing America's national pride parallels his dream of keeping the academy squeaky clean while ignoring the "multicultural" voices from outside. Here Rorty's thinking is internally contradictory and thus self-defeating. On one hand, Rorty proclaims that:

> All the universities worthy of the name have always been centers of social protest. If American universities ever cease to be such centers, they will lose both their self-respect and the respect of the learned world. It is doubtful whether the current critics of the universities who are called 'conservative intellectuals' deserve this description. For intellectuals are supposed to be aware of, and speak to, issues of social justice. (1998, 82)

On the other hand, Rorty wishes to quarantine political movements outside the campus lest they infect academia. According to Rorty, these movements state nothing original; what they do is to "simply add further concreteness to sketches of the good old egalitarian utopia" (Rorty 1999, 235).

However, nagging questions surrounding Rorty's politics remain unanswered: What are the criteria, beyond "growth itself" in Rorty's Dewey-laden vocabulary, to decide who will be inside or outside of the academy? Who, in the end, collects the social and economic capital?

RORTY'S ANTIREVOLUTION

Achieving Our Country (1998) is Rorty's latest—and most—ambitious project in the field of political philosophy. He begins the book with the following conviction: "National pride is to countries what self-respect is to individuals: a necessary condition for self-improvement" (3). He is eager to set forth the essential ingredients of national pride. Rorty begins his narrative by claiming that almost all "American" stories are written and told "in tones either of self-mockery or of self-disgust" (4). Some cultural heroes are urgently needed to change the current tone. Self-evidently, Rorty wants to be recognized as one of the "chosen".

In Rorty's narrative of salvation, there are several key distinctions. The main one is between the "good" old reformist Left and the "bad" new cultural Left. For the old reformists, "American patriotism, redistributionist economics, anti-communism, and Deweyan pragmatism went together easily and naturally" (Rorty 1998, 61). At one time leftist politics was associated with antimilitarism, and with a need for laws and bureaucratic initiatives in order to redistribute the wealth produced by the capitalist mode of production. In Rorty's opinion, those days are long gone. Rorty has a warm heart for the reformist Left. They never doubted "that America was a great, noble, progressive country in which justice would eventually triumph" (59).

On the other hand, there is the current cultural Left, whom Rorty believes is guilty of two cardinal sins. First, the current cultural Left does not participate in the struggle for a just society (Rorty 1998). Even worse, it privileges the theoretical over the practical and is guilty of possessing a "spectator" point of view. Rorty suggests that the cultural Left needs to grind their fancy theories to a halt and instead try to figure out "what remains of our pride in being Americans" (1998, 92). Rorty criticizes the new cultural Left's search for its one-size-fits all standard for truth. The Left seek such a standard, Rorty claims, in the spirit of "eschatologies like Hegel's and Marx's, inverted eschatologies like Heidegger's, and the rationalizations of hopelessness like Foucault's and Lacan" in order to "satisfy the urges that theology used to satisfy" (1998, 38).

Although Rorty is more than willing to criticize the radical Left for its Hegelian Marxian eschatology, his utopian lexicon lacks a social and political agenda and offers little in the way of meaningful commentary on social change. In his recent work, Rorty fails to map out strategies for working towards economic and social justice.

Rorty's philosopher-hero is basically an intellectual historian who perceptively documents ways of living and thinking and how the self-portraits of individuals change in the course of time (Kunelius 1999). Rorty believes that without the speculation of Hegel, Heidegger, Marx, or Dewey, humankind would be much poorer than it is now. On the other hand, this kind of critical storytelling is not something in which Rorty considers himself genuinely competent: "Although I think that historical narrative and utopian speculation are the best sort of background for political deliberation, I have no special expertise at constructing such narratives and speculations" (Rorty 1999, 234).

However, despite the unguarded naivetes and bellicose expostulations of Rorty's political philosophy, his latest texts may well turn out to be, as Rée suggests, "signs of a long-delayed breaking of the ice in socialist politics following the end of the Cold War" (1998, 9). In his latest volumes, Rorty (1998; 1999) offers a standard critique of global capitalism. Yet he ends up supporting the political foundations that make such a capitalism possible.

RORTY ON MARXISM

Rorty continues to cast a vituperative eye on political theory—Marxism especially—and banishes it from the Holy Liberal Empire where he enjoys a refunctioned mandarin status as the ruling elite's *Chico Malo* "Bad Boy". Rorty trawls superficially through the works of Marx, Lenin, and Trotsky. The cover story in all of this is, of course, that "leftist theory is not necessary." He does not believe leftists need deep theories or cause-and-effect relationships and in this sense indulging in Marxist theory is simply an excuse for not involving oneself in the pressing daily tasks of ameliorating suffering (Melkonian 1999).

It is difficult to take Rorty's criticism of Marxism seriously, especially when he so disdainfully rejects the politics of those who write about the dilemmas surrounding life in a white male Anglo-Saxon heterosexist culture, a culture, by the way, that he feels doesn't exist. The pathetic nature of his "angry white man on the left position" is deftly summarized by Alan Johnson, who asserts: "His failure to distinguish the spectorial academic left from the more general phenomenon of the new social movements; his tendency to counterpose economics to culture, and trade unions to groups organized on the basis of their identity, his implicit blaming of the desperate state of the left on identity politics, makes for a blunderbuss of a polemic which, as Martin Duberman has pointed out, sends the message 'Shut Up!' to a wider group of people" (2000, 105).

Rorty suggests that since there are no foundations to human knowledge, Marxist concepts such as "ideology" along with its "reality-appearance" distinction, is useless. Rorty believes that communities of people understand the social world by using vocabularies. However, Rorty warns us that the vocabularies we use are incommensurable because each community uses different vocabularies. In addition, Rorty's antiessentialism refutes claims that there exists a human nature or a "true self" since there are no singular traits or characteristics that can be identified as "human" (Melkonian 1999). He acknowledges that the self is fundamentally provisional; it consists of a constellation of beliefs, attitudes, and values accumulated through the arduous process of socialization. He insists that individuals are socialized to act and behave in certain ways while lacking "essential" human traits. Rorty also claims that since there is no "true self," concepts such as "alienation" have little or no utility. He argues that "[t]here is only the shaping of an animal into a human being by a process of socialization, followed (with luck) by the self-individualization and self-creation of that human being through his or her own later revolt against that very same process" (Rorty 1999, 118). It is hardly surprising that Rorty would reject universal human rights since, in his opinion, there are no objective truths. Instead, he proposes that human rights should be based on localized consensual agreements.

Rorty (1999) believes that democracy is a "promising experiment" grounded in a "shared knowledge" of a community of individuals. He believes that theories that have not been substantiated using his pragmatic criteria should be summarily abandoned. As an antiphilosophy philosopher, Rorty (1999) believes that theory should serve practical purposes. He suggests that the reduction of practice into theory (as with Marxism) leads to empty promises. Thus, Rorty (1998) recommends that Marxists abandon their dependence on theory and philosophy, reexamine the work of Whitman, Dewey, and Lincoln, and ask themselves how the country that they prognosticated can be built.

Rorty (1999) draws a bold line between knowledge and hope. He explains that hope is grounded in prediction while knowledge is grounded in experience. Claiming that Marxists' fixation on hope constitutes a philosophy of "false predictions" and "failed prophecies," he likens Marxism more to a religion than to a vehicle for social transformation. In his comparison of the *Communist Manifesto* to the New Testament, Rorty claims that both documents are premised on the hope of creating a better world by claiming to have access to "superior knowledge." Both documents merely possess "inspirational value" for Rorty. We Marxists, by contrast, appreciate the social and analytical content of the *Communist Manifesto*, including Marx's notion that "all that is solid melts into air"—a brilliant rendering of the experience of modernity in our view.

Rorty fails to recognize that most Marxists deny that progress is firmly secured by the iron laws of historical materialism (Sunker 1997). Marxism is not equipped with "cruise-control" mechanisms that will automatically transport civilization towards a socialist utopia. Marxists, however, hypothesize that under certain social conditions in which the working class succeeds in recognizing itself not only as a class for itself but a class in itself, the working class can transform itself into a revolutionary class capable of ending the exploitative relations of power under capitalism.

Rorty (1998) believes that the struggle for a classless society is neither natural or rational since society is a collection of social experiments lacking a teleological destination. He maintains that the effort in creating a Marxian classless society, although desirable in itself, remains only a detached and whimsical notion since there exists no empirical evidence supporting it. It comes as no surprise when Rorty recommends that the "Left vs. Liberal" distinction be abandoned since the old Left (meaning classical Marxists) now constitute the reformist Left. In the end, Rorty's pragmatic politics remains firmly in support of social reformism, since social revolution is no longer a viable option for him.

Finally, Rorty (1998) distinguishes between "spectatorship" and "agency" and identifies Marxists as "spectators" that have merely criticized and not transformed what is wrong with America. Rorty proposes that the Marxists transform themselves to "agents" by participating in a constructive political discourse: in short, a pragmatic Rortyan-style politics.

A MARXIST CRITIQUE OF RORTY'S POLITICS

Rorty's resilient attempt to bury Marxism has unwittingly provided the grounds for rejecting his own liberal democratic politics. A recent comment by Michael Burawoy is apposite when he warns: "Before hastening to the funeral parlor, one should remember that although Marxism may have been a specter that haunted the twentieth century, by the same token it also inspired some of the century's greatest and most creative thinking—for and against Marxism—in philosophy, history, economics, and politics, not to mention sociology. Intellectuals who celebrate the end of Marxism may be digging their own graves, too" (2000, 151). Marx's ghost, hovering high above its grave site in London, continues to observe crimes routinely committed against millions of innocent men, women, and children on behalf of a New World Order with the United States at the helm.

THE NATURE OF HUMAN NATURE

A Marxist approach to the question of human nature has some points in common with Rorty and some that are in bold distinction. Rorty believes that human nature is a myth, that it is really a process of socialization devoid of distinguishing characteristics that can be identified as singularly "human". Marxists believe that human nature is neither fixed nor predetermined. They reject the claims of Social Darwinists that human nature is biologically determined and the metaphysical position that human existence depends on some form of spiritual essence. Marxists fundamentally posit a dialectical relation between biology and human agency. We agree with C. J. Arthur who asserts: "There is . . . a dialectically conceived relation between his [sic] nature as determined by the conditions of his life, and the practical transformations of those conditions. The link between the two is labor" (1995, 21).

We espouse a Marxian notion of human nature that is grounded within the social relations of production (Geras, 1983). In our view, human beings share a set of common traits such as the ability to produce their means of subsistence. In his *Philosophical Manuscripts*, Marx makes a case in support of human nature by writing that: "A being which does not have its nature outside of itself is not a natural being and does not play no part in the system of nature. A being which has no object outside itself is not an objective being. A being which is not itself an object for a third being has no being for its object, i.e. it has no objective relationships and its existence is not objective" (1975, 390).

Marx views human nature processually, as a type of flux shaped by human beings acting externally on the world at the same time as it shapes human beings. Human needs are decidedly not transhistorical; rather, they are relative insofar as they are shaped by social forces in different ways at different historical moments. Rorty seems to accept this position when he says that people are "children of their time and place, without any significant metaphysical or biological limits on their plasticity" (cited in Sayers 1998, 150). Yet he makes the gross claim that there is no such thing as human nature. True, one cannot step outside of the social, or beyond socialization. Nevertheless, it is important to understand the dynamic relation between the social and the biological, otherwise one is left with the untenable notion that human beings exist as some kind of tabula rasa. We engage in productive activity in order to satisfy our needs, but as historical beings we create new needs in the process. The social relations out of which these needs are created are shaped by the development of new forms of productive activity and productive powers.

We defend the social and historical character of human nature against Rorty's antiessentialism. We need to oppose the false antimony he postulates between the social and human nature. Human will and desire are still intertwined biosocially, even if the specific character of social life is determined in the last instance by the development of the level of productive forces.

As Marxist educators, we believe that Rorty's antifoundational views are inherently flawed and misleading. In the absence of universal principles, there is no injustice, since there would be a multitude of definitions of justice and injustice by different communities (Geras 1995). Thus, an absence of an agreement on universal human rights leans towards social, cultural, and political relativism. We maintain that without any form of objectivity, anything goes.

Rorty's invitation for celebrating the achievements of Western liberal democracies is exceptionally plagued with problems. Referring to liberal democracy in the United States, Rorty proudly claims that it "slowly and painfully, threw off a foreign yoke, freed its slaves, enfranchised its women, restrained Robber Barons and licensed its trade unions, liberalized its religious practices, broadened its religious and moral tolerance" (1999, 121). However, Rorty suffers from classic Reaganesque amnesia, leaving unmolested dominant arrangements of power and privilege. He appears to have forgotten that the robber barons of yesterday have now been replaced by the global carpetbaggers of today; that white supremacy is alive and well throughout the United States; and that violence against women, gays, and lesbians remains widespread (particularly in the military). One of the more glaring lacunae in Rorty's corpus of works is his failure to link racism to wider capitalist social relations, those very social relations that he feels have liberated the United States from tyranny and hatred.

In contrast to Rorty's decapitation of racism from political economy, Marxists stress its indissoluble link. Parenti writes:

> Marxists further maintain that racism involves not just personal attitude but institutional structure and systematic power. They point out that racist organizations and sentiments are often propagated by well-financed reactionary forces seeking to divide the working populace against itself, fracturing it into antagonistic ethnic enclaves. (1997, 133-34)

We agree with David Sidorsky (2000) who argues that Rorty fails to criticize right-wing politics primarily by focusing on the retreat of the Left. While Rorty claims that Marxists have failed to fulfill their dreams of a classless society, he neglects to discuss the emergence of right-wing and conservative politics in the 1980s and 1990s which took the offensive by attacking welfare programs, affirmative action, and bilingual education. Rorty fails to adequately distinguish between right-wing and left-wing politics. While the Right has avidly defended the interests of the private sector and transnational corporations, Marxists, on the other hand, have supported working class struggles. Finally, Sidorsky points out that Rorty fails to propose an alternative economic model to neoliberalism. In short, Rorty's pragmatism is actually little more than pluralism in disguise: a tolerance of diverse opinions and views that we believe signals an ongoing *individualisierangsprozess*.

We believe that Rorty's pragmatism retains its class character as a liberal extension of bourgeois ideology. Rorty's biased advocacy of democratic consensus implies that the democratization of capitalism remains a possibility. He claims that regardless of class antagonisms and class interests, communities of people divided along racial, gendered, and class lines can work side by side in an ever-expanding democracy.

However, we find that advancing democratic ideals, while at the same time ignoring class interests, amount to little more than a reactionary form of populism. Rorty's pragmatism glaringly sidesteps issues related to class, the exploitation of labor, and capital. He fails to address with either verve or vision the politics of property relations, the globalization of capital, neoliberalism and the new global imperialism, and the class character of American society. As a consequence, he fails to recognize that the inhuman face of socialism and the human face of capitalism are the obverse of each other.

We wonder what Rorty thinks of the recent revelations—first by the European press followed by the North American press—that PSYOPS (Psychological Operations) specialists from the U.S. Army had worked as interns at CNN's Atlanta news headquarters and at National Public Radio. PSYOPS is a division of the U.S. Army that has been created to develop propaganda that lowers the morale of "enemy forces" and is designed to "build support among the civil population" in other countries for U.S. objectives (Ackerman 2000, 1). Its illegal domestic operations were first exposed during the Iran

Contra scandal when the now defunct Office of Public Diplomacy (formerly part of the National Security Council) was operated by the 4th Army PSYOPS Group stationed at Fort Bragg. This group—that successfully demonized Nicaragua's Sandinista government—is the same group that later produced the CNN and NPR interns. A high ranking PSYOPS officer recently "called for greater cooperation between the armed forces and media giants" (Ackerman 2000, l). Is this an example of Rorty's liberal democracy in action?

Rorty has replaced God with "democratic consensus," thereby substituting good, old-fashioned, issues oriented politics for the scholarly exegesis of Marx, Engels, Trotsky, Lukács, and Lenin. In other words, he wants to banish the church in favor of tobacco-chewing veranda conversations for ragtag members of the polis, and sherry-sipping, cigar-puffing dialogue among the literati.

Rorty evades debating political economy not only by failing to undress his own bourgeois assumptions about capital, but also by barricading himself within the very impenetrable walls of academic philosophy that he himself has criticized. Were we to take Rorty's pragmatism seriously, we would have to question whether it provides the best explanatory framework not only for understanding neoliberalism, but also for strategically reducing the immense social, economic, and political inequalities under global capitalism. We believe that Rorty's pragmatism fails to provide a convincing argument against the widening disparities between the rich and the poor.

Finally, we disagree with Rorty's claim that "Marxism was not only a catastrophe for all the countries in which Marxists took power, but a disaster for the reformist Left in all countries in which they did not" (1998, 41). Although socialism has been temporarily set back in the former Soviet Union and Eastern European socialist countries, these countries succeeded in making some substantial strides towards social and economic equality. In addition, Rorty cannot simply ignore achievements made by socialist Cuba during the last forty years, especially in the areas of health care, literacy, and employment. The struggle for socialism is far from over. In fact, we may be witnessing a new beginning.

Our position is grounded in the premise that surplus extraction within capitalist exchange practices are all-pervasive within capitalist economies and mediate the production of the constitutive structures of the "lifeworld" in profound and politically defining ways. It is only by recognizing the all-pervasive influence of capitalist exchange and by culturally producing catalytic agency through subjectivities able and willing to work collectively in order to resist and transform capitalist accumulation, that a pedagogy of liberation can be formed. Terry Eagleton argues that "it is possible for certain forms of social life to drive a wedge between these two dimensions of the self, individual and communal, and this, in effect, is what the young Marx means by *alienation*" (1999, 273). Here Marx is referring to a particularly profound form of alienation, especially when you consider the ontological position taken by Marx on the issue of the productive powers and capacities that human beings possess—powers and capacities that enable them to transform the world. Eagleton summarizes

Marx's position thus: "My product is my existence for the other, and presupposes the other's existence for me" (1999, 27).

Our naturally productive species-being is constrained by the "minority of the opulent" who own and control the means of production so that the production of the masses becomes instrumental to the self-development of the elite capitalist class. We do not simply mean "production" in the economic sense, but also in the cultural/symbolic sense. This is consistent with Marx's position on the unfolding of an individual's productive powers. According to Eagleton:

> We are free when, like artists, we produce without the goad of physical necessity; and it is this nature which for Marx is the essence of all individuals. In developing my own individual personality through fashioning a world, I am also realizing what it that I have most deeply in common with others, so that individual and species being are ultimately one. My product is my existence for the other, and presupposes the other's existence for me. This for Marx is an ontological truth. (1999, 97)

We do not have time to rehearse this notion of self-development except by way of brief description. According to David Bernans, class exploitation within capitalist societies occupies a strategic centrality in organizing those very activities that make us human. Bernans follows Volosinov in maintaining that speech genres themselves are determined by production relations and sociopolitical order. This is an important assertion especially in view of the fact that the market system is being applied to democracy itself, where democracy is seen as occurring at the sites that market intervention occurs the least, where abstract law overrides concrete determinations and abstracts real existence into nothingness, where distributive principles overrule concrete struggles for new freedoms, where a successful democracy is defined in terms of its ability to become self-legitimating and self-justificatory, where the market is permitted to remain impersonal and omnipresent and is encouraged and facilitated in its efforts to totalize the field of social relations in which it has become a central force (McMurtry 1998). Speech genres and language games facilitate the interdictions and injunctions of the Big Other so that their authorial voice remains invisible so that interdictions against regulating the "natural" and "free" market seem freestanding (McMurtry 1998; 1999).

Bernans is correct in maintaining that surplus extraction occurs through processes that are dialogical and simultaneously economic, political, and ideological. We agree with him that these are not ontologically privileged processes but rather become central in the way that they organize the constitutive processes of everyday life. In other words, class struggle is also a language game, perhaps the most fundamental game in town. It is not just a piece in an autonomous chain of equivalence but rather a language game that organizes all the other language games. All language games are accented by class power. Bernans makes the important point that, by virtue of their organizing function, dialogical processes of surplus extraction have a certain primacy with respect to other forms of social interaction. As part of the constitutive activities that make up social life, the dialogical processes of surplus extraction factor forcefully and foundationally. Not only are they central in organizing other dialogical forms, but they also play a major part in imposing material limitations on human social interaction. In fact, Bernans argues that because the dialogical processes of surplus extraction organize speakers and addressees in particular ways, a radical transformation of all social hierarchies (i.e., those of race, class, gender, sexuality) demands the continual affirmation of a working-class struggle against capital (1999, 30). Following Volosinov, Bernans maintains that the sign becomes the very arena of class struggle because the continual accumulation of capital can only continue through an exchange that favors one partner while the other is reduced to "mere survival." Of course, capital accumulation is also functionally integrated with nonclass hierarchies such as racism and sexism since it is obvious that white male workers derive material benefits from sexist and racist exploitation even while they are exploited themselves. It is at this point that we welcome Carspecken's materialist understanding of cultural production that he derived from the work of Paul Willis (1977). For Carspecken, cultural production is constitutive of praxis in that it serves as both the medium and the outcome of action and constitutes the "action conditions" or "structures" for self-production through work. Praxis also includes the social-communicative preconditions for the emergence of a self and the motivational structures that are created along with these preconditions.

Bradley Macdonald looks to the practices of the self from the perspective of a historical materialist conception of desire. According to Macdonald's prescient observations, Marx relates desire to "the totality of ways in which sensuous beings attempt to engage and objectify their world, in the process aspiring towards plenitude and singularity" (1999, 32). Such desires and pleasures are diverted from their full potential because of seemingly insuperable constraints of diverse kinds resulting from capital accumulation. As Macdonald puts it, desire exists as an ontological horizon but is taken up in specific historical formations; its ontology does not exist outside of history but is wrapped up in it through its embodiment in the sensuous materiality and potentialities of pain and joy, suffering and well-being.

As Sayers notes, there exists a dialectic of needs and productive powers; each develops in relation to each other (1998, 152). Capitalism is to be condemned not just for failing to satisfy universal biological needs but the needs that it itself has created (134). Needs—be they biological or psychological— are always modified by certain social conditions. Needs are always social— even the need for food—because satisfaction and the quest for satisfaction take on specific cultural, historical, and social forms within certain contexts. Socially modified needs are the only needs that exist concretely—the rest, notes Sayers, are abstractions. True needs are those that are necessary for a minimum standard of social life and happiness. But it would be a mistake to designate all new needs as "false" because, as our powers and capacities change, as they develop in and through history, new needs and desires emerge. Human potentialities are not unchanging. As Sayers notes, even alienation, in certain contexts, can help to increase self-development and lead to a new stage of individuation (137). Thus, capitalism has both a positive and a negative aspect to it. In the movement of historical reality, we look beyond capitalism, and indeed, beyond capital itself.

We want to be clear here that we are not trying to limit or reverse economic development but to control such developments in the interests of workers. We object to the fact that the human potentialities under capitalism can be realized only by a small number of the world population. Our conception of economic justice is not based on transhistorical principles that are externally self-evident or to a universal standard of reason. Justice, admittedly, is always held hostage to lived historical experience. Justice cannot be realized in relation to the logic of ideas themselves, but only in terms of the social formations that give rise to these ideas and that emerge historically out of human struggle. We are arguing for the formation of what we call "revolutionary subjectivity" that works the fissures of the self, that connects across the private spaces of splintered political agency and the public spaces of collective struggle.

We believe that the fact that we are not fully transparent to ourselves suggests that we become conscious of our own embeddedness in the theoretical assumptions that guide our everyday praxis. We do this as a means of providing a better guide in our attempts to make warrantable choices in how we act in, on, and through the world. We do this as a way of identifying and surmounting the historical continuities and discontinuities that constrain our efforts at promoting social justice. This runs counter to Rorty's position that there exists no theoretical defense for one's actions other than how they relate to existing political and moral traditions of public life. In the final analysis, Rorty appears to be supporting Nietzsche's "Eternal Recurrence of the Same" when he advocates for a form of liberalism that returns the same set of hierarchical discourses and social practices—only shrouded by the empty promise of an ever-renewed "Otherness". It is in this sense that Rorty lapses into a fibrillating hopelessness. Alan Johnson writes that "when the tensions in his thought—between his acceptance of the free market and his revolt against its results, his hatred of the bosses and his despair about the workers, his attention to protectionism and its honor at its implications—overwhelm Rorty, he slips into hopelessness" (2000, 115).

While he accuses Marxists of being part of a state religion, denigrates the history of social movements, and vehemently exercises contempt of Marxist leaders such as Lenin for, among other things, his stress on political analysis, Rorty views class struggle itself as simply a drama orchestrated by leftists who want to feel they are part of some world-historical drama. Rorty believes that people, regardless of their class interests, can work together for the common welfare, and his unrestricted relativism and particularism denies the importance of any general laws of development. Rorty is disinclined to relegate class to an important part of his project, nor does he pay attention to the means by which the forces of production (means of production and human labor), and their level of development, impact social, cultural, and institutional formations. Instead, he takes an unreserved stance in protecting bourgeois liberal interests.

In the face of Rorty's reformist and redistributionist politics and his eschewal of ontologies of each and every stripe, we support an unblushingly Marxist ontology, grounded in a scientific understanding of the social totality, a realistic analysis of capitalist society, and the view that the interests between labor and capital are essentially incompatible.

Rorty finds the acme of liberal autonomy in a box of metaphors to be used in the process of self-fashioning; how this academic game of performative Scrabble helps campesinos craft a collective agency capable of preventing their skulls from being crushed under the jackboots of paramilitary death squads is quite another matter. Rorty's project of metaphoric self-fashioning does little to address the fact that liberal democracies have been engaged since their inception in degrading acts of imperialist violence and oppression.

Rorty's dream of self-creation through recursively articulated descriptions and redescriptions set against the conventions of mainstream social discourse turns on his belief that socialization will be superceded by edification—and an opportunity to privately redescribe oneself at will. In our view, such an antidialectical and antidialogical approach to knowledge is delusional. His sheltered and favored position in the academy—what Johnson refers to as "a bold-as-brass elitism" (2000, 114)—appears to have erected a partition between him and the masses that has disabled his ability to experience the contradictions inherent in the capitalist enterprise itself. If we are seeking guardians of democracy in this current era of late capitalism, then it is less likely that we will find them in university seminar rooms and more likely that they will be found among the struggling masses in the streets.

While Rorty may see himself as luxurious champion of the Left—as he urges academic leftists to embrace pluralism, move beyond their bovine leftism as immaculate spectators in the safe precincts of the seminar room where the culture wars are fought, and give up their pretentious claims to objectivity and truth—we see him caught in an assiduous avoidance of substantive engagements with political economy in favor of grazing in the lush fields of literary conceit, or musing with fellow cognoscenti along the philosopher's ivy-covered walkway. And while his call for homelessness studies and economic redistribution in *Achieving Our Country* (1998) is a step in the right direction, we believe that his larger struggle to redirect professional irony to the cause of public activism as "Americans" rather than as human beings—is misguided. We believe the main game is to rethink the nature of capital as a social relation within the larger capital labor antagonism.

In mounting his oppositional politics, Rorty appears to bear his opponents little open rancor. Why should he? His is comfortably ensconced in the salons of the bourgeois academy where he thrives capriciously on the succulence of the discourses of consensus and manipulates his nihilism as an alibi for a groundless defense of human freedom. David Hall writes that: "Like Nietzsche, Rorty is a Benign Nihilist. And that nihilism expresses itself directly in Rorty's provincialism, ethnocentrism, and heroism. It also shapes his attitudes towards poetry and prophecy—issues central to his narrativist posture" (1994, 170).

Rorty's notion of the decentered subject that emerges from his expostulations about antifoundationalism, in our view, corresponds nicely with the desiring subject produced by capitalism. His antifoundationalist agent itself remains embedded in an economic matrix. In denying alternative possibilities of subject formation in opposition to capitalism, he participates in a reconditioning of the subject so that it becomes functionally advantageous for the reproduction of the capitalist class. In fact, he does more than this; he insaturates a new elitism, a neoaristocratic wing of the academy that exhibits pretenses towards social transformation yet leaves unmolested current capitalist relations of exploitation. Rorty's procapitalist and neoliberal politics offers little more than a mild countervailing force to the conservative mainstream and a conceptual dalliance with Left liberalism. As such it enfeebles anticapitalist struggle and pauperizes the educational Left. Melkonian (1999) notes that Rorty

> cannot accommodate the suggestion that liberal institutions be recast within the context of working.class state power . . . [because] he is committed not merely to . . . several liberal institutions . . . but also to "the institutions of large market economies." "Large market economies," he believes, constitute the "economic determinants" of liberal democracies: The North Atlantic has achieved its measure of decency and equality by relying on "a free market in capital and on compromises between pressure groups." In this respect, he is once again backing away from Dewey's New Liberalism to a position closer to that of the English classical liberals who associated liberty with laissez-faire economic policies. (143)

As an effete advocate of Left reformism, a pragmatist panjandrum whose raised fist carries inside of it the condensed power of Walt Whitman and John Dewey, Rorty stumbles into an enfeebling vortex of relativism. We need more than Rorty's white-knuckled promise for a petit-bourgeois revitalization of democracy but rather the permanent revolution of which Trotsky spoke. In this respect, the words of Geoff Waite are apposite:

> world communism has always come into being at moments of counterrevolution and defeat (as exemplified by the USSR and by Gramsci's Italy of the early twenties). Born in defeat, communism never guarantees victory, only ongoing struggle. As such, it may be the most realistic counter-movement against Capital Triumphant in postcontemporary times. (1996, 3)

CONCLUSION: THE RENEWED IMPORTANCE OF MARX

Out of the bloody tumult of capitalist social relations and the wounds of political disappointment, Marxism has cancelled democracy's promissory note, replacing it with the demand that it effect a political breach with capitalism and a move towards socialism. Yet most Americans recoil at the mere mental touch of Marx, giving Marxism little compass today. As the United States waves its wand of instant rebuttal, capitalism is embraced, sustaining a promise of democracy that entails its denial. As Marxism attempts to put some spine into the politics of the Left, postmodernists and conservatives alike decry its stress on class struggle. The effect of such a denunciation advances a conciliatory spirit towards the established order and acts in unreflective accord with ruling-class interests. According to Aijaz Ahmad:

> Theoretically, the possibility of socialism arises from within the contradictions of capitalism. Morally, opposition to capitalism is its own justification since capitalism is poisoning human survival itself, let alone human happiness. in the present circumstances, the resolve to overturn this globally dominant system does not indeed involve what Ernest Bloch once called 'utopian surplus'; but the Utopian aspect of the communist imagination need not translate itself into 'the messianic'. (1999, 95)

We need to rethink the nature of capital as a social form; we need to transform both the mediatory forms (property relations and class formations) and their essential determinants. The abolition of private property is not an end in itself but rather a step towards the transformation of the labor process. It is fruitless to call for the abolition of private property without the abolition of the value-form of labor. Marx's underlying dialectic of negativity makes this clear. The major issue is not the abolition of private property but to abolish capital itself, through the creation of freely associated labor (Hudis 2000). The first negation is the negation of the external forms (private property). The negation of the negation that follows is the negation of external barriers to self-movement towards a transcendence of alienation. The second negation is absolute negativity or self-reflected negativity that pervades the positive transcendence of alienation, and positive humanism beginning from itself (Hudis 2000). This is what brings about a permanent revolution.

One promising sign on the horizon is that the political fade-out of Marx has been temporary; the old bearded devil is coming back with a vengeance, having been summoned by those who both recognize and rage against the fact that "the inexorable march of privatization [is] leading England (and a good part of the Western world) forward to the social hierarchy of the 17th century" (Morris 2000, 67).

While Marx might not have anticipated the specific trajectory capitalism would take at this particular moment in history, his work was most certainly premonitory of the current crisis of capitalism. What is so significant about Marx's analysis is that it stresses above all the underlying systemic dynamics of capitalism in all of its capillary detail. No doubt Marx would have recognized the current crisis of capitalism as implicated in the global capitalist economy as a whole, inextricably tied to the laws of motion of capital and the ways in which capital and wage-labor reproduces itself (McNally 1999). While it fails to offer ready to-wear strategies for social struggle in the arena of critical education, Marxist theory is congruent with left multiculturalists and bilingual educators who recognize the relationship between the exploitation of human labor and systems of classification and mythologies linked to the demonization of certain groups on the basis of race, ethnicity, phenotype, etc. (McLaren 1997). It is also helpful in efforts by multiculturalists to tease out the labyrinthine complexities that scaffold race, class, gender, and sexual antagonisms and their co-constitutivity (McLaren and Farahmandpur 1999b).

Even in moments of defeat, Marxism has never ceased undermining capitalism's unrelenting logic of profiteerism, with unparalleled tenacity, revitalizing itself in the space of its own isolation, drawing nourishment from its own marginalization and abandonment. Marxists acknowledge that the best substitute for not having "pragmatic" solutions to the pressing problems of our planet is to acquire a deep understanding and intimate and robust relationship with the questions while developing an informed grasp of the frame in which such questions are asked.

Critical pedagogy cries out for a critical Marxist consciousness, one that moves beyond a scenario where Rorty's Athenian polis meets redistributive socialism. The critical pedagogy that we seek is driven more by a larger project of socialist democracy linked to the abolition of capital and to revolutionary movements than to the uncorked effervescence of Rorty's Jacuzzi populism (McLaren and Farahmandpur 2000; 1999a; 1999b). We believe that philosophy can play a part in the project of critical pedagogy. We are joined in solidarity with Adorno when he writes that:

> The only philosophy which can be responsibly practiced in face of despair is the attempt to contemplate all things as they would present themselves from the stand.point of redemption: all else is reconstruction, mere technique. (1951, 247)

NOTE

For a description of what distinguishes our approach to critical pedagogy from its more liberal, domesticated variants, see Peter McLaren (2000), *Che*

Guevara, Paulo Freire, and the pedagogy of evolution. Boulder, Colo.: Rowman & Littlefield.

BIBLIOGRAPHY

Ackerman, S. (2000, June) PSYOPS in the newsroom. EXTRA! *Update*, 1.

Adorno, T. (1951) *Minima Moralia.* London: Verso.

Ahmad, A. (1999) Reconciling Derrida: 'Spectres of Marx' and deconstructive politics. In M. Sprinker (ed.): *Ghostly demarcations: A symposium on Jacques Derrida's Specters of Marx* (88-109). London: Verso.

Arthur, C. J. (ed.) (1995) *Introduction. The German Ideology.* New York: International Publishers.

Bernans, D. (1999) Historical materialism and ordinary language: Grammatical peculiarities of the class struggle "language game." *Rethinking Marxism* 11(2), 18-37.

Burawoy, M. (2000) Marxism after Communism. *Theory and Society* 29(2), 151-174.

Carey, J. (1975) A cultural approach to communication. *Communication* 2(1), 1-22.

Carspecken, P. (1999) *Four scenes for posing the question of meaning and other explorations in critical philosophy and critical methodology.* New York: Peter Lang.

Eagleton, T. (1999) *Marx.* New York: Routledge.

Feyerabend, P. (1993) *Against method.* Third Edition. London: Verso.

Geras, N. (1983) *Marx and human nature: Refutation of a legend.* London: Verso.

___ (1995) *Solidarity in the conversation of humankind: The ungroudable liberalism of Richard Rorty.* London: Verso.

Hall, D. L. (1994) *Richard Rorty: Prophet and poet of the new pragmatism.* Albany: State University of New York Press.

Hudis, P. (2000) The dialectical structure of Marx's concept of 'revolution in permanence'. *Capital and Class* 70, 127-43.

Johnson, A. (2000) The politics of Richard Rorty. *New Politics* 8(1), 103-21.

Kunelius, R. (1999) Philosophy today: waiting for the revolution. Richard Rorty's interview. *niin & näin—Finnish Philosophical Journal* 6(2), 22-27. (Original in Finnish.)

MacDonald, B. (1999) Marx and the figure of desire. *Rethinking Marxism* 11(4), 21-37.

Marx, K. (1975) *Early writings* (R. Livingstone and G. Benton, trans.). New York: Vintage Books.

McLaren, P. and R. Farahmandpur. (1999a) Critical pedagogy, postmodernism, and the retreat from class: Towards a contraband pedagogy. *Theoria* 93, 83-115.

___ (1999b) Critical multiculturalism and globalization: Some implications for a politics of resistance. *Journal of Curriculum Theorizing* 15(3), 27-46.

___. (2000) Reconsidering Marx in Post-Marxist times: A Requiem for Postmodernism? *Educational Researcher*, 29(3), 25-33.

McLaren, P. (2000) *Che Guevara, Paulo Freire, and the pedagogy of revolution.* Boulder, Colo.: Rowman & Littlefield.

McMurtry, J. (1998) *Unequal freedoms: The global market as an ethical system.* West Hartford, Conn.: Kumarian.

___. (1999) *The cancer stage of capitalism.* London: Pluto Press.

McNally, D. (1999) The present as history: Thoughts on capitalism at the Millennium. *Monthly Review* 51(3), 135-145.

Melkonian, M. (1999) . *Richard Rorty's politics: Liberalism at the end of the American century.* New York: Humanity Books.

Morris, S. L. (2000) Boys R Us. *LA Weekly.* March 17-23, 67.

Parenti, M. (1997) *Blackshirts and Reds: Rational fascism and the overthrow of commu-nism.* San Francisco: City Lights.

Pihlström, S. (1996) Structuring the world: The issue of realism and the nature of onto-logical problems in classical and contemporary pragmatism. *Acta Philosophica Fennica* 59. Helsinki: The Philosophical Society of Finland.

Rée, J. (1998) Strenuous unbelief. *London Review of Books* (20), 7-11.

Rockmore, T. (1992) Introduction. In *Antifoundationalism old and new.* T. Rockmore and B. Singer, eds., 1-12. Philadelphia: Temple University Press.

Rorty, R. (1980) *Philosophy and the mirror of nature.* Princeton N.J.: Princeton University Press.

___. (1989) *Contingency, irony, and solidarity.* Cambridge: Cambridge University Press.

___. (1991) *Objectivity, relativism, and truth.* Philosophical papers, vol. 1. Cambridge: Cambridge University Press.

___. (1998) *Achieving our country: Leftist thought in the twentieth-century America.* Cambridge, Mass.: Harvard University Press.

___. (1999) *Philosophy and social hope.* London: Penguin Books.

Sayers, S. (1998) *Marxism and human nature.* London: Routledge.

Sidorsky, D. (2000) Does the left have the power to speak? *Partisan Review* 67(1), 122-30.

Smith, J. (1992) *America's philosophical vision.* Chicago: University of Chicago Press.

Sünker, H. (1997) Heydorn's bildungs theory and content as social analysis. R. F. Famen and H. Sünker, eds., 113-28. *The politics, sociology, and economics of education: Interdisciplinary and comparative perspective.* New York: St. Martin's Press.

von Wright, G. H. (1992) *The Owl of Minerva.* Keunuu: Otava. (Original in Finnish.)

Waite, G. (1996) *Nietzsche's corpse: Aesthetics, politics, prophesy, or, the spectacular technoculture of everyday life.* Durham: Duke University Press.

Willis, P. (1977) *Learning to labor: How working class kids get working class jobs.* Westmead, U.K.: Gower.

14

THE REVOLUTIONARY
LEGACY OF PAULO FREIRE

Peter McLaren and
Valerie Scatamburlo-D'Annisale

> The emotion of hope goes out of itself, makes people broad instead of confining them. . . . the work of this emotion requires people who throw themselves actively into what is is becoming. . . . Hopelessness is itself, in a temporal and factual sense, the most insupportable thing, downright intolerable to human needs.
>
> —Ernest Bloch, *The Principle of Hope*

> I could never think of education without love and that is why I think I am an educator, first of all because I feel love . . .
>
> —Paulo Freire

Paulo Reglus Neves Freire uttered these words to a friend just days before his untimely death on May 2, 1997. The tragic loss robbed us of one of the most radical, politically engaged, public intellectuals of our time, but that tragedy could never rob us of his legacy nor could it diminish the promise and insights of his life's work. With every line Freire's writings emanated a spirit, a sense of urgency, and an intensity which was as rare as it was refreshing. He was a passionate pedagogue and activist—someone who took the theory/praxis nexus seriously, someone who was engaged in struggle all his life, someone who was much more than an armchair academic.

As a courageous scholar and cultural worker, Freire was able to develop an anti-imperialist and anti-capitalist literacy praxis that served as the foundation for a more broadly based struggle for liberation. Freire's internationally celebrated work with the poor began in the 1940s and continued unabated until 1964 when a right-wing military coup overthrew the democratically elected

This chapter was originally published in *Democracy & Education, 13*(1), Spring 1999, pp. 16-17. © 1999 Institute for Democracy in Education. Reprinted with permission of the publisher.

government of President Joao Goulart. Freire was accused of preaching communism and arrested. He was imprisoned by the military government for seventy
days and exiled for his work in the national literacy campaign of which he had
served as director. According to Moacir Gadotti (1994), the Brazilian military
considered Freire an "international subversive," "a traitor to Christ and the
Brazilian people," and accused him of developing a teaching method "similar to
that of Stalin, Hitler, Peron, and Mussolini." He was further accused of trying to
turn Brazil into a "bolshevik" country.

Freire's sixteen years of exile were tumultuous and productive times: a
five-year stay in Chile as a UNESCO consultant with the Research and Training
Institute for Agrarian Reform; an appointment in 1969 to Harvard University's
Center for Studies in Development and Social Change; a move to Geneva,
Switzerland in 1970 as a consultant to the Office of Education of the World
Council of Churches where he developed literacy programs for Tanzania and
Guinea-Bissau that focused on the re-Africanization of their countries; the
development of literacy programs in some post-revolutionary former
Portuguese colonies such as Angola and Mozambique; assisting the govern-
ments of Peru and Nicaragua with their literacy campaigns; the establishment of
the Institute of Cultural Action in Geneva in 1971; a brief return to Chile after
Salvador Allende was assassinated in 1973, provoking General Pinochet to
declare Freire a dangerous subversive; a summer stint at the Ontario Institute
for Studies in Education in 1975; and his brief visit to Brazil under a political
amnesty in 1979 before his final return to Brazil in 1980 to teach at the
Pontifica Universidade de Campinas in Sao Paulo. These events were accompanied by numerous works, most notably *Pedagogy of the Oppressed*, *Cultural
Action for Freedom* and *Pedagogy in Process: Letter to Guinea-Bissau*. In more
recent years, Freire worked briefly as Secretary of Education of Sao Paulo, continuing his radical agenda of literacy reform for the people of that city. Freire's
literacy programs for disempowered peasants have since been employed in
countries all over the world. In fact, Freire was preparing for a trip to Cuba to
receive an award from Fidel Castro for his pedagogical efforts and accomplishments when he passed away.

By linking the categories of history, politics, economics, and class to the
concepts of culture and power, Freire managed to develop both a language of
critique and a language of hope that work conjointly and dialectically and which
have proven successful in helping generations of disenfranchised peoples to liberate themselves. Although Freire's work is most often taken up in education
circles, his inspirational thought provides a depth and richness that should not
be restricted to any one discipline or field, and his democratic, socialist vision
and revolutionary humanism provide a source of radical hope in an age marked
by postmodern despair and Nietzschean nihilism. While postmodern prophets
have, for the last two decades or so, been busily proclaiming the implosion of
subjects or treating them as mere functions of discourse, as entities which float
aimlessly in a sea of ever-proliferating signifiers, Freire reminded us of the liv-

ing, breathing, and bleeding subjects of history; the children of the damned; the wretched of the earth; the victims of the culture of silence. Unlike those that would have us believe that the cart of history marches forward on its own without the agency and will of embodied social actors, he reminded us that people do in fact make history, although not always in conditions of their choosing. In Freire's narratives, social agents were firmly rooted in historical struggle and never lost their capacity for effecting social transformation. His dialectical posturing, where the world and action are intimately intertwined, revealed the potency of human enterprise and human knowledge as both products of, and forces in, shaping social and political reality.

Moreover, his dialectical understanding of the subjective and the objective, the culture of everyday life and the broader matrices of capitalist social organization bear mentioning, especially at a time when many seek to bury objective reality beneath the priority of significations, discourses, and texts. Freire, however, reminds us that the polarization of wealth and the rampant poverty, exploitation, alienation, and misery engendered by the ravages of global capitalism are historical realities whose material and objective existence can hardly be denied. This is a strand of Freire's work that speaks volumes in an intellectual climate that is, as Kincheloe (1994: 217) aptly points out, "blind to the political but hypersensitive to the cultural." Indeed, in the rush to avoid the "theoretically incorrect" sins of totalization and economism, many have elided even a minimalist concern with political economy. As a result, many have replaced the economic reductionism of orthodox Marxism with a new form of reductionism—that of culturalism. The current romance with the cultural and the concomitant ignorance of political and economic conditions has helped to advance the importance of cultural identification, especially for marginalized constituencies, but at the same time has obfuscated the political and economic roots of their marginalization and underminded an exploration of the ways in which difference is actively produced in relation to the history and social organization of capital—inclusive of imperialist and colonialist legacies. Freire's insights become all the more crucial given this context, for he insists upon a deep connection between the culture of everyday life and the machinations of capital. His approach is aimed at transforming the underlying economic structures that produce relations of exploitation.

Finally, at a time when the narrative of humanism has been relegated to the dustbin of history, Freire's revolutionary humanism (as opposed to bourgeois liberal humanism) provides a constant reminder that the project of humanity remains unrealized in the most profound sense. Freire's commitment to human emancipation and the extension of human dignity, freedom, and social justice to all people—a commitment to realize the values and promises in concrete, practical terms rather than merely giving them lip service in some abstractly delineated discourse of rights—reminds us that one must remain dedicated to the struggle for democratic socialism precisely because (to paraphrase Eagleton, 1996) these values have not yet been universalized. Freire reminds us, in short, that in a world where too many do not eat, where too many are denied justice, and where too many are deprived of their humanity, it is still too early to write the obituaries of revolutionary humanism and the project of democratic socialism. It is now up to progressives everywhere to actively embrace Freire's radical spirit, see his vision through, and above all to keep hope alive.

REFERENCES

Eagleton, Terry. *The Illusions of Postmodernism.* Cambridge, Massachusetts: Blackwell Publishers, 1996.

Kincheloe, Joe. "Afterword," *Politics of Liberation: Paths from Freire.* Eds. Peter McLaren and Colin Lankshear. London and New York: Routledge, 1994, pp. 216-218.

15

SPACES OF CAPITAL
TOWARDS A CRITICAL
GEOGRAPHY
(DAVID HARVEY)

Gregory Martin and
Peter McLaren

Although he is not well-known among educators, David Harvey is one of geography's best-known social theorists and one of the most important voices on the academic left in the United States. He is an ardent defender of the Marxist theory of class, whose interdisciplinary work on capitalist accumulation and the production of space and uneven geographical development has genuine implications for those fighting for social justice in urban spaces. A British import, Harvey was a professor of geography at Johns Hopkins University when he stumbled onto Marxist theory in 1971, after graduate students asked him to help organize a reading group to study Capital. The rest is history, so to speak, particularly as Harvey has now accepted a position in the anthropology program at the City University of New York. Thus, it seems fitting that Harvey has put out his latest book, *Spaces of Capital*, an assortment of essays written over the past thirty years, which constitute a blistering indictment of contemporary capitalism.

After the prologue (which consists of an interview with the editors of *New Left Review*), the essays are divided into two parts. In the first set of essays, Harvey examines how geographical knowledges have served to naturalize and reproduce existing political-economic power structures. What is important here is the development of a critical geography, which is not only capable of "deconstructing" certain kinds of knowledge and spatial forms but also transforming them. Mollifying the gnashing anti-theory critics, Harvey moves beyond mere abstractions. For example, in *A view from Federal Hill,* he acts as our anti-tour guide in his former adopted home of Baltimore, pointing out all the horrors that lurk beneath the carnival of capitalism. Here, the Baltimore that emerged as a tourist mecca during the 1980's, after a slick marketing campaign, is a paradise only to the oblivious tourists. The reality is that since the deadly race riots of the

This chapter originally appeared as a book review on TCRecord.org (www.TCRecord,org). © 2003 Teachers College.

1960s and a series of economic convulsions in the 1970s, conditions (including access to employment, education and health) have changed little for the majority of Baltimore's inner-city residents, proving that the city's celebrated achievement in urban renewal (Baltimore was featured twice in *Time* magazine) is really just another example of public subsidy for private gain.

For Harvey, challenging such social inequality and uneven development requires recognizing how capitalism is dependent upon certain kinds of geographical understandings in the public domain. Implicit in this idea is the notion that such geographical knowledges do not emerge autonomously but are rather deliberately constructed and maintained by the capitalist class so that it can pursue it own narrow interests, albeit in the name of universal goodness. For example, in *Cartographic Identities*, Harvey (p. 211) eerily reminds us of how access to certain forms of geographical knowledge in the public domain has been responsible for constructing various "demonized" spaces in the global economy such as Cuba, China, Libya, Iran, Iraq and the Evil Empire of the former Soviet Union. The tragedy here is that "A recent poll in the US showed that the more knowledgeable people were about conditions and circumstances of life in a given country, the less likely they were to support US government military interventions or economic sanctions" (p. 211). Thus, the exercise of military power requires keeping the American public in a chronic sate of geographic ignorance about the role of the United States as a bearer of a "global ethic," when it is really imposing a "rational" spatial order that opens up the possibility for capital accumulation (p. 211).

In the second set of essays, Harvey's central task is the reconstruction of Marxist theory, in light of contemporary conditions and historical-geographical experience. Indeed, for Harvey, it is clear that capitalism has failed to deliver its promise of equality and freedom for all, when material conditions are just as inhumane today as when Karl Marx wrote the *Communist Manifesto* in 1847. Witness not only spiraling social inequality in the home citadels of imperialism such as the United States but also the trade in human misery and despair in the neo-colonies, where the majority of the world's gendered and raced proletariat remain physically or economically shackled in factories (producing commodities such as Nike shoes and Gap clothing) and in the fields, almost 150 years since slavery was officially abolished. In fact, despite the claims of "globalization" theorists such as Anthony Giddens (1999), the world imperialist economy is not becoming homogenous, far from it. This is hardly surprising as Marx points out in *Capital*, "Accumulation of wealth at one pole is . . . the accumulation of misery, agony of toil, slavery, ignorance, brutality, mental degradation, at the opposite pole, i.e. on the side of the class that produces its own product in the form of capital" (p. 645). It is little wonder that for Harvey the working out of this contradiction constitutes one of the major forms of motion that will inevitably determine human history and geography.

Deriving his analysis from the labor process, Harvey argues that it is precisely within this context that it is possible to point to the limits and reversibility of changes in the world economy. For example, in *The Geography of Class Power,* he points out that as capital perpetually turns to a "spatial fix" to resolve it internal contradictions, it not only expands productive relations on a progressively larger scale but also the bases for socialist revolution (p. 369). Thus, even as the bourgeoisie are driven to reorganize geographical space over time to create economic and social surpluses, uneven development ultimately threatens to wreck the whole system. Although the *Communist Manifesto* implies that capitalist development produces a homogenous working class, the communist movement must begin to recognize the differentiating power of capital, which has often absorbed class struggle by exacerbating place-bound loyalties including all manner of gender, religious, ethnic and cultural divisions. Thus, Harvey argues that just as uneven development itself is shaped by particular geographical re-orderings, spatial strategies and geo-politics, class struggle also unfolds differentially across this varied landscape.

What is more, Harvey argues that labor organizing must move beyond the traditional starting and measuring point for class struggle, the factory. After all, the geographical basis of such organizing is changing as factories "disappear" by moving to another locale and as the workforce becomes increasingly contingent, temporary, and casualized. As an example, Harvey points to the campaign for a living wage in Baltimore, a citywide movement for all workers, that brings various activist groups together at the metropolitan scale. What matters here for Harvey is that the fight against the ability of the bourgeoisie to command and control space for capital accumulation requires learning how to bridge the gap between the place specific and the universal, by dialectically integrating struggles at different spatial scales (e.g. local, metropolitan, regional and national).

To sum up, Harvey's analytical work is not always easily grasped but it deserves to be taken up amongst critical educators, particularly as we witness the current deforming of schools into precincts of free enterprise. After all, the basic premise throughout these essays is that capital must restrict and deny working and oppressed people access to space, both physical and mental, if it is to maintain the division of labor, which is necessary to the production of value. In such a context, people choose what side they are on.

Unfortunately, the academic left is not in the best condition to appreciate Harvey's work, as avant-garde theorists make a career out of promoting the "proper" uses of theory. Today, the academic left is more likely to spurn the clarion cry of class struggle as a shop-worn phrase and the contributions of Marxism as burdened by economism, essentialism, determinism, totalization, liberal humanism, and teleology. The liberalized, postmodernized left appears less interested in class struggle than in making capitalism more compassionate to the needs of the poor, but in the process they unwittingly naturalize scarcity. Capitalism *is* an overarching totality that is, unfortunately, becoming increasingly invisible in postmodernist narratives that eschew and reject such categories *tout court* or else resignify them in the doxology of the establishment left so that instead of the determinate category of capitalist exploitation, we are given the subjective notion of "oppression." Postmodern normativity inheres in its assertion that ambiguity and difference leak incessantly from the seams of totalizing axioms.

In an attempt to challenge the "totalitarian certainties" of the Marxist problematic, and to dismember larger "totalities" (such as capitalism), by theoretically in-worming them (through processes of resignification) and opening them up to multiple destinies other than those analyzed by Marxists, academic postmodernists have too often distracted attention from capital's global project of accumulation. What this approach exquisitely obfuscates is the way in which new capitalist efforts to divide and conquer the working-class and to recompose class relations have employed xenophobic nationalism, racism, sexism, ableism, and homophobia. This conveniently draws attention away from the crucially important ways in which women and people of color provide capitalism with its superexploited labor pools a phenomenon that is on the upswing all over the world. Postmodernist educators tend to ignore that capitalism is a ruthless totalizing process that subjects all social life to the abstract requirements of the market. Or that it forms the material basis of racism and sexism. The art school trangressiveness and anti-Marxist high-mindedness of educational postmodernists that gives primacy to incommensurability as the touchstone of analysis and explanation has diverted critical analysis from the global sweep of advanced capitalism and the imperialist exploitation of the world's laboring class. This is the class that has been at the mercy of what has been known as "lean production," and the creation of a two-tiered workforce—the speeding up of the work process; and deskilling of the workforce; the increase in multitasking and outsourcing work previously done by unionized workers; and the increased flexibility for management in setting hours and tasks; and the elimination of replacements for workers who are absent or who retire.

The point is not that theoretical performances exercised in the bourgeois salons of the postmodernists have not made some important contributions in the area of cultural politics, or that they have not exerted some influence (albeit proleptically) in the arena of social justice reform efforts, but that, in the main, their efforts have helped to protect the bulwark of ruling class power by limiting the options of educational policy in order to perpetuate the hegemony of ruling class academics. The succulent criticism of postmodernism is bereft of the power to challenge the liberal-democratic consensus.

Harvey is not a captive of such professionals of post-ideological consensus. Clashing over the most basic issues of theory and practice, Harvey argues that the immediate task today is not "the play of signification" or a politics of "undecidability" but rather the creation of geographical knowledges that will lead to the creation of alternative geographies. Here, improving the lot of working people and the oppressed, while building support for a broader revolutionary movement, requires thinking dialectically, applying knowledge to concrete situations and working in an organized way for liberation. At a time when the fashionable abstractions of the bourgeois left just do not seem cute anymore, Harvey's historical geographic materialist analysis offers a refreshingly real-and-imagined geography of radical hope.

REFERENCES

Giddens, Anthony (1999). *Runaway world: How globalization is reshaping our lives.* New York: Routledge.

Marx, Karl (1992). *Capital: A Critique of political economy.* New York: International Publishers.

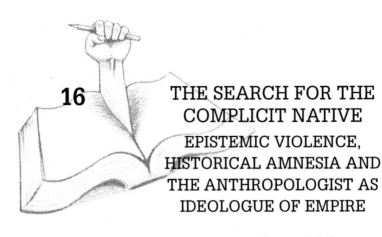

16   THE SEARCH FOR THE COMPLICIT NATIVE
EPISTEMIC VIOLENCE, HISTORICAL AMNESIA AND THE ANTHROPOLOGIST AS IDEOLOGUE OF EMPIRE

Peter McLaren and
Jill Pinkney- Pastrana

This essay analyzes a number of issues surrounding the Menchú/Stoll dispute. In locating Stoll's criticism of Rigoberta within a larger referential arena that includes an attack on the North American academic left and an unbridled anti-Marxism, the authors attempt to reveal how Stoll's ideological agenda is functionally compatible with the larger political agenda of the New Right. The authors also attempt to reveal Stoll's distortions of Guatemalan guerrilla history as well as problems with his analysis and collection of the data.

INTRODUCTION

What a world! Being upside down, it is now discussing whether Rigoberta deserved the prize instead of asking whether the prize was worthy of her! (Galeano, 1999, p. 11)

The history of all hitherto existing society is the history of class struggle. (Marx & Engels, 1952, p. 40)

Although he has been scathingly described as the Matt Drudge and Kenneth Starr of contemporary anthropology—and no doubt considered little more than a counter-insurgency agent by some of his more militant critics on the left—David Stoll presents himself as a sympathetic and earnest scholar troubled yet undaunted in his search for truth. He is troubled in the sense that he has had to

This chapter was originally published in *International Journal of Qualitative Studies in Education*, *13*(2), pp. 163-184. © 2000 Taylor and Francis. http://www.tandf.co.uk. Reprinted with the permission of the publisher.

challenge the almost sacerdotal status accorded to Rigoberta Menchú—the K'iche' Maya woman who won the 1992 Nobel Peace Prize—by her many admirers around the world. Yet he remains undaunted in the metropolitan anthropologist's categorical imperative of boldly seeking out alien worlds and in the process sifting objective fact from subjective opinion. What troubles him in his mission is revising our understanding of the conditions that brought about the genocide in Guatemala. For Stoll, this means exposing the role of left propagandists who, in the theater of the Western academy, hold a rigid monopoly on how events transpired. It also means uncovering the role that Rigoberta played as a pawn in the hands of the Marxist guerrilla movement. After all, before her performance as the Maya Everywoman, Rigoberta committed what in Stoll's searching eyes amounted to cardinal sins: she joined the political apparatus of the Guerrilla Army of the Poor (EGP) and apparently cooperated with the guerrillas in demonizing all *Ladinos*. Furthermore, she had the temerity and bad judgement to transform herself into a living advertisement for guerrilla warfare in a countryside already foundering in blood and chaos. Stoll appears haunted by the specter of the international left whose bellicose activities he perceives as wildly complicitous in the "backlash" against indigenous peoples by the Guatemalan government.

The cynosure of Stoll's accusations is the verve and high energy they add to the current culture wars with their sharply drawn battle-lines surrounding the canon, and the ammunition they have given the sworn enemies of Marx and Lenin (not to mention Che Guevara) in their continued assault on the political sympathies of the beleaguered academic left. Despite his fervent protestations that his work was being unfairly exploited by right-wing opportunists in the still ongoing debate over political correctness and multiculturalism, Stoll's disavowals appear glaringly hypocritical when read in light of the cagily disguised conservative polemic that he penned for the dust jacket:

> Stoll authored a provocative, anti-P. C. polemic for the book's dust jacket that was virtually tailor-made for conservative writers. And in the book's splashy and excerpt-friendly preface and final chapter, Stoll departed significantly from his stated purpose of reexamining *I, Rigoberta Menchú*. He waxed at some length about his categorical opposition to armed guerrilla movements and his extreme distaste for their romantic leftist allies abroad. (Cohen, 1999, p. 52)

In a letter published in a recent issue of *The Nation*, Stoll unwittingly gives the main game away with his comment: "One of the dangers of Menchú's story is that as the expression of a novice cadre, it enshrined a rationale for guerrilla warfare that continues to enchant the latte left in New Haven long after it has lost its appeal in rural Guatemala" (1999, p. 2). Stoll is more concerned, it seems, with haute bourgeoisie academics who harbor romantic fantasies of rebellion than with real rebels who engage in the struggle for freedom out of necessity. He wants at all costs to implode the image of the guerrilla as a stalwart who rouses the people to free themselves from all those who betray a sublime indifference to the suffering poor; and he desires to render detumescent the image of the guerrilla as a warrior who can supply the wretched of the earth all the courage, leadership, and vision that is needed to bring about political emancipation. Clearly Stoll holds in considerable contempt those belletristic dilettantes who have become fearless advocates for Rigoberta's work and who, from Starbuck cafes and university bookstores afar, glamorize and lionize the path of the *guerrillero*. Stoll is set against the left amplifying Rigoberta's voice, because he fears her iconic presence in the political unconscious of the academic left as a vehicle for perpetuating a neo-romantic notion of the subaltern as the noble savage held in thrall to *Guevarismo* and "bolstering the misguided cause of Che Guevara-style revolutionary violence" (Cohen, 1999, pp. 53-54). Above all, Stoll abhors the "latte left" whose bohemian dissent takes place in the secure precincts of the seminar room where acolytes, epigones, and fashionable apostates of cultural studies can vomit up their own discursive excess in the form of cafe conversations on guerrilla strategy and publications in avant-garde journals—all in total capitulation to capitalist consumerism—while Mayan *campesinos* die ignominiously in the fields. After all, not all *campesinos* (not even those with a seventh grade education like Rigoberta) have the option of hoity-toity revelling in the liminal space of the cosmopolitan salon, deconstructing texts with fellow graduate students. Decrying any guerrilla strategy that attempts to dredge *campesino* thought to the fertile banks of revolutionary consciousness, Stoll favors a temporary abatement of antagonisms and incremental concession from the government as opposed to revolutionary struggle. Stoll believes that during the *guerra sucia* (the dirty war), the Mayan *campesinos* articulated a protest of the particular set against the unrelenting universalism of Marxism (its revolutionary laws seemingly folded into time, its code of dissent apparently fixed at the moment history was born, ensuring an inscription in eternity) which could not be reconciled with it. Stoll perceives a danger in emancipating the subject through a form of self-legitimization, which in his view is precisely as totalitarian in its grounding as the practices of oppression from which Marxism hoped to emancipate modern humanity.

That Rigoberta is villainized by the lubricity of Stoll's orientalist and counter-revolutionary gaze should come as little surprise to students of post-colonialist studies, but what is equally as distressful as the nervous and precarious trajectory of his thought is the flawless and impeccable timing of his text. Why did he choose to release his findings just prior to the report by the Guatemalan Truth Commission? And why would he choose to take a position so in keeping with the politics of Guatemala's homicidal military at a time when global capitalism is in a crisis of insuperable complexity?

BLAMING THE VICTIM

"They killed the dogs with sticks and said, 'This is how we're going to kill the guerrillas.' They cut off their heads and gave us the blood and said, 'This is how you'll drink the blood of the guerrillas.'

"Soldiers who showed their fear of eating dog-flesh were forced to eat uncooked human flesh, and drink human blood. They would make us watch as they cut out the flesh from people held there in the torture center on the army base . . . In the torture center when they killed someone, they bled them into a container beneath the body and that way saved all the blood. We never knew who these people were. From the look of their clothes and their faces they seemed to be poor ladinos. Only Ladinos live there in Zacapa. All of the soldiers on the base went there to see them." (Forster, 1999, p. 18)

Among some ten soldiers I interviewed from different regions, the details remained the same. Depending on the year, foot soldiers were taken one-by-one to the torture cells and forced to practice burning and cutting civilians imprisoned there. "Gringo" advisors were present according to the soldiers and knew how the foot soldiers were being trained. (Forster, 1999, p. 18)

We have all heard Stoll's principal charges with references to the main debates and recent rapprochements: Most Maya Indians were not motivated by economic necessity or ideological conviction in their resistance to oppression by the Guatemalan military but were irresponsibly coerced into the ranks of the *guerrilleros* during the 1970s; the struggles of Rigoberta's impoverished father with land-baron *Ladinos* (mestizo or non-Indian Guatemalans) over land issues was in reality part of an intrafamilial conflict between her relatively affluent "homesteader" father (who cooperated with Peace Corps volunteers and Heifer Project staff) and other K'ich' Maya in-laws (e.g., with the family of Rigoberta's mother); Rigoberta did not work on coastal export plantations a a child or work as a maid for a wealthy Guatemalan woman; she did not witness her younger brother die of malnutrition on a coastal *finca*; contrary to her own account, she received a convent education that included years of Spanish-speaking education in Catholic boarding schools (e.g., the Colegio Belga in Guatemala City, the Colegio Búsico Nuestro Señora de Candelaria in Chiantla, Huehuetenango where she finished the seventh grade); she did not witness her brother, Petrocinio, being burned alive by the military in the town square of Chajul; and her father was possibly responsible for his own death during a peasant protest at the Spanish Embassy in Guatemala City in January, 1981, after taking part in a revolutionary suicide that included the murdering of hostages and fellow protesters.

Yet the soft register of these acerbic revelations in Stoll's book does little to assuage the perniciously reactionary temper of his ideological agenda. Stoll's manner of authorizing himself in his reading of Rigoberta's text is not ideologically ambiguous but signals its place on the most Northern extremities of the hermeneutic map. His exercising of an essentialist power in order to stage himself as an "objective observer" in search of the Less Militant Mayan is relayed from the "us" side of the "us versus them" dyad and redolent of so many imperialist tracts. Should we be surprised? Yet, although there may exist embellishments and contrivances to Rigoberta's text, and while Rigoberta surely made choices in her presentation of the book's material that were designed to protect people or to create a composite portrait, Grandin and Goldman's comments underscore what really matters: "the undisputed facts of Menchú's story are horrible enough: She *did* have two brothers who died of malnutrition at an early age; her mother and brother *were* kidnapped and killed by the army; and her father was burned alive" (1999, p. 26).

In Stoll's universe, the anthropologist is able to see clearly. In the case of Stoll's proclamations, however, any critical ethnographer worth her salt could make a case that Stoll's imagination is ideologically out of focus such that what might appear to him as disinterested observations and analysis is, in effect, ideologically and politically charged. Rather than viewing knowledge from within a Manichean divide of subjective/objective knowledge, contemporary critical ethnography asserts that all knowledge is refracted rather than transparent; it pushes the anthropologist's gaze away from some pristine vantage point from which to assess the truth (McLaren, 1999a; Kincheloe, 1991).

What, then, is Stoll's central ideological claim? Stoll is terrified to come face to face with his own tortured conscience, which is primed to defend the morally and politically impermissible judgement that there exists a terrain of neutrality out of which innocent indigenous peoples have been dragged, their feet kicking, by the warring factions of guerrillas and the army. His major claim in our view is that the guerrillas worsened the violence in Guatemala by bringing the peasants into the struggle and then abandoning them when the going got rough. Stoll sees the forced conscription of peasants into the EGP (Guerrilla Army of the Poor) as a fatal strategy that apparently foreclosed political and economic reform through peaceful and conciliatory means. Recourse to armed struggle at the helm of a ship commandeered by Marxist guerrillas is about the worst possible option imaginable for Stoll in any political arena, least of all the political climate of Guatemala. Stoll believes that only a response from domestic and foreign Communist insurgents would have occasioned such swift and deadly reprisals from the Guatemalan military; horrific acts the sheer scale of which are shocking and riveting beyond compare, are for the most part indisputable (an admission even Stoll makes) in Rigoberta's unnervingly graphic text. It is true that the politics of Mayan peasants is far from homogeneous, and that the popular left with center of gravity located in Marxist revolutionary politics shared its differences with localized pan Mayan groups influenced by the

tradition of the K'amal B'ee and the ajq'iij shaman priests, traditionalist saint
societies, and sacremental Catholic groups (Warren, 1998). Pan-Mayanists for
the most part stress cultural issues and the politics of difference language, education, religion, and development strategies—whereas the popular left stresses
issues of class inequality. For example, in the early 1990s, the popular left and
the pan-Mayanists differed around the issue of federalism. Many members of
the popular left were wary of the idea of administrative regionalization proposed by the pan-Mayanists whereas popular organizers "were viewed as exter-
nalizing injustice by focusing their critiques on U.S. imperialism and colonialism—and more recently on global 'neoliberalism'—rather than giving high priority to patterns of Guatamalan racism, internal colonialism, and cultural dis-
tinctiveness" (Warren, 1998, p. 198). Regardless of the divisions that existed
during the *guerra sucia*, there was still an overwhelmingly popular sentiment in
favor of the guerrilla movement over the terror and-rampage tactics of the military. The military were not only executioners, but exploiters of the very heart
and soul of Guatemala. We know, for instance, that military expansionism
affected not only the Guatemalan economic base but also the control of culture
and education. Corruption occurred on a massive scale such as arms purchasing.
George Black writes that:

> In the most celebrated case of Mafia-style activity—an arms-buying racket
> controlled by eight generals—runaway sums were involved. Young officers
> reported that between 1975 and 1981, the Guatemalan military registered
> $175 million worth of arms purchases from Israel, Italy, Belgium, and
> Yugoslavia. The generals reported the value of the sales as $425 million,
> salting away the difference in private bank accounts in the tax haven of the
> Cayman Islands. (1997, p. 362)

Cindy Forster's observations are poised in stark opposition to those of Stoll:

> Indigenous participation was the backbone of the guerrilla insurgency and
> remains the lifeblood of the popular movement . . . In my reading of the
> evidence it was thousands of grassroots activists who risked their lives to
> move forward the machinery of a just peace, rather than the dissident guer-
> rillas in exile after 1983, or the Christian Democrats with their hands in the
> till after 1985, or the first Protestant president Jorge Serrano, who fled to
> Panama in 1993 with every cent he could extract from the National
> Treasury. (1999, p. 17)

Hal Cohen's comments also prove instructive:

> [T]he broad claims in Stoll's conclusion rely on some sleight of hand. He is
> eager to make sweeping statements abut the nature of rural insurgencies
> ("at bottom rural guerrilla strategies are an urban romance, a myth pro-

pounded by middle class radicals who dream of finding true solidarity in the countryside"), the international left ("it is time to face the fact that guerrilla strategies are far more likely to kill off the left than build it"), and Guatemalan society ("Guatemalans are also less likely [than Menchú's foreign admirers] to feel the need to vindicate the left's tradition of armed struggle, just as few of them wish to justify the Guatemalan right's history of repression"). But evidence for these speculative claims eludes him: His book, after all, is a study of a particular region. (1999, p. 53)

While it is true that there were few women and Indians in high-level leadership positions in the Guatemalan guerrilla movement, this surely is no reason to support Stoll's claim that Indians were not historical agents who joined the guerrilla movement with a clear agenda that included fighting racism, sexism, and economic exploitation (Chinchilla, 1999). Though it is disturbing to read Stoll's infantilizing of the Maya, it is equally as disturbing to consider Stoll's blaming of the government massacres of Indians on communists-at-large and the historical memory of Guevaristas and Fideslistas. Stoll claims that if it were not for the specter of communism, the military would not have murdered the Indians because the murderous acts of the military were due to fanatical anticommunist sentiments (Smith, 1999). (We should not forget that the military were supported by the Reagan administration who were equally as fanatical in their condemnation of communists everywhere as evil.) There is no reason to support Stoll's "symbolic impeachment" of Rigoberta's testimony, since so many of his reconstructions of history lack credible sources (Sanford, 1999).

MULTICULTURALISTS BEWARE

Stoll's book has served as a clarion call for the lay culture of well-educated nonspecialists with an ideological predilection for conservative politics and Marxophobia. Upon publication of Stoll's book, neoconservatives jumped quickly to his defense and attempted to use his research as a means for reenfranchising constituencies of the right whose political lights had been dimmed with the advent of the Clinton administration. Until the publication of *Rigoberta Menchú and the story of all poor Guatemalans* (1999), Stoll's anthropological career had been uncrowned with major acclaim, consisting of several competent but largely unremarkable books: *Is Latin America turning Protestant? The politics of evangelical groups* (Berkeley: University of California Press, 1990), and *Between two armies: in the Ixil towns of Guatemala* (New York: Columbia University Press, 1993. Yet in a rhetorical sortie by a salivating right-wing propagandist, David Horowitz, Stoll is described as "one of the leading academic experts on Guatemala" (1999, p. 1) while Rigoberta's text is summarily decried as a "hoax" and a "classic Marxist myth" created by the Guatemalan "terrorists", the French left, and the international community of human rights activists. Horowitz fulminates thus:

> Unfortunately for her case, everything that Menchú has written is a lie—and the lies are neither incidental nor accidental. They are lies about the central events of her story and have been concocted for specifically political purposes, in order to create a specific political myth. . . . The fictional story of Rigoberta Menchú is a piece of Communist propaganda designed to incite hatred of Europeans and Westerners and the societies they have built, and to build support for Communist and terrorist organizations at war with the democracies of the West. It has become the single most influential social treatise among American college students. Over 15,000 theses have been written on Rigoberta Menchú the world over-all accepting her lies as gospel. The Nobel Peace Prize committee has made Rigoberta an international figure and spokeswoman for "social justice and peace." (1999, p. 1)

Horowitz ends his breathtakingly naive diatribe by imploring the international left to "leave the third world alone" (p. 3) without ever alluding to the barbarous decades of Washington-condoned fascism in much of Latin America or recognizing that it is precisely the United States government officials who share his own reactionary political ideology who have been responsible for overthrowing democratically elected governments in Latin America, for rendering Guatemala as a "laboratory test case" for hemisphere-wide U.S. counterinsurgency to battle *Guevarismo*, for providing skills to Latin American military officers at torture-training centers on United States military bases, and for supporting the ruthless counterinsurgency policies of military dictatorships. Horowitz fails to recognize the political context of Guatemala in relation to what E. San Juan (1996, p. 186) refers to as "the habitus of dependency produced by U.S. colonial tutelage" and the fact that, as early as the 1960s, the capitalist class turned away from national industrial development to join with the transnational banks and corporations. Together they worked to open up their domestic markets to foreign investment (Harris, 1995). The results have been disastrous for all but the wealthy classes (see McLaren, 2000).

BLUSTERING HISTORICAL AMNESIA

The salty paean of Horowitz—"leave the third world alone"—not only rings hollow but is complicit with the very violence he decries. Horowitz displays the same convoluted logic as does Stoll, who explains the complex sociopathy of the Guatemalan military as a backlash against provocation by the Marxist-Leninist guerrillas. Consider these inflammatory observations in the face of a military machine that has been condemned and held responsible for 93 percent of a mind-numbing total of 200,000 massacred indigenous peoples (these figures are contained in the four volume report by the Catholic Archbishop's Human Rights office based in Guatemala as well as the Guatemalan Truth Commission (a joint venture of the United Nations and the Guatemalan government). The military, in other words, is made out by Stoll to be the real victim. He blames the guerrilla movement for foisting upon the public the romantically heroic imagery of the guerrilla peasant—in this case, Ixil Maya *campesinos*—as a way of camouflaging their nefarious Marxist intentions. Stoll appears to believe that if somehow the passive and simple-minded Mayan peasants had only minded their own business, such detachment was bound to have nonviolent consequences: to prevent a collision "between two armies" that was bent on bringing about mutual annihilation, to serve as a prophylactic to the genocide of the "rural pacification" campaign, and perhaps eventually to yield an end to the *guerra sucia* and usher in a radiant future. Comments by Richard Gott in the *London Review of Books* are apposite and worth quoting at length:

> Stoll puts much of the blame on the guerrillas for unleashing these events. Like the Guatemalan Communist Party, he deplores the recourse to armed struggle by sections of the Guatemalan left. It would have been far better, he seems to suggest, if the Indians had been left to negotiate their own way out of their historic difficulties, taking advantage of what political opportunities (perhaps the Christian Democracy Party) or administrative paths (the Land Reform Institute) were open to them. This argument must sound plausible to anyone unfamiliar with Guatemala, yet it ignores not only five hundred years of history but even the five years that preceded the Central American explosion of 1978-82. Two potentially reformist politicians, Alberto Fuentes Mohr and Manuel Colom Argueta, were assassinated at the beginning of 1979. (1999, p. 18)

Grandin and Goldman would concur with Gott's assessment, maintaining that Stoll's formulation reveals a "deep ignorance of Guatemalan and Latin American history" (1999, p. 27). They write:

> [Stoll's] formulation reveals a deep ignorance of Guatemalan and Latin American history. In the century before the cold war, dictators throughout Latin America, like the nineteenth-century Argentine despot Juan Manuel de Rosas, used terror to hold on to power. If a democratic transition was under way in Guatemala prior to the left's decision to pick up arms, how does Stoll account for the violent 1954 overthrow of Jacobo Arbenz Guzmán, Guatemala's best chance at democracy? Or the 1963 military coup aimed at preventing Juan José Arévalo, a former reformist president, from again running for president? If guerrillas are responsible for Latin American political violence, how does Stoll explain Pinochet's Chile, where military repression took place despite the absence of armed rebels? Or the systematic state violence directed at union activists and independent

reporters in Mexico before the Zapatista uprising? Or the 1968 massacre in
Tlatelolco plaza? (1999, p. 27)

Stoll's position that the Indians were the innocent victims, caught between the
guerrillas and the military, and forced to align themselves with the former group
has provoked Greg Grandin to respond: "any scholar could go to Birmingham,
Alabama, and find plenty of African-Americans who say that the civil rights
movement placed them in danger. In Stoll's moral universe, Martin Luther King
Jr. is responsible for Bull Connor's dogs" (1999, p. 67).

In a similar fashion, anthropologist Cindy Forster opines:

> Stoll's method explains why his analyses share so much in common with
> those of the Guatemalan government and military. He sees peasants and
> Indigenous people as "mute" or disengaged. So in his view organizers bear
> the burden of guilt for unleashing the violence and the guerrillas sacrificed
> tens of thousands of Maya in a futile war. (1999, p. 16)

With respect to Stoll's accusation that the guerrillas were responsible for the
carnage in Guatemala, Jorge Rogachevsky writes:

> I must say, with all due respect to Stoll, that I find that proposition obscene.
> . . . It is ludicrous to use the action of the guerrillas as a rationale for the
> atrocities of the army. The army's behavior would suggest that within
> Guatemala—contrary to the image of the upwardly mobile peasantry that
> Stoll wishes to promote—the indigenous population was seen by the
> Guatemalan power structure as an expendable group that mattered little
> more than the cattle exterminated after it contracted mad cow disease; why
> not send Indian soldiers to slaughter Indian peasants? (1999, p. 98)

Peter Canby concurs with this assessment, adding his own observation that:

> During the dictatorship of General Fernando Romeo Lucas García between
> 1978 and 1982, for instance, government-sponsored death squads killed a
> great many trade unionists, peasant organizers, and Catholic "catechists," or
> activists. For their own protection, some of the opponents of the govern-
> ment joined what had been, until that time, an insignificant guerrilla force.
> It seems clear, however, that an army that had already been assassinating its
> political opponents for well over a decade would not have hesitated to
> attack members of such opposition groups even if the guerrillas had never
> emerged in the countryside. Other than his account of Rigoberta's region,
> Stoll presents no evidence to the contrary. (1999, p. 30)

Perhaps Stoll received the willing consent and support of the Guatemalan military to do his research in the "conflict zones" because he is closely affiliated

with right-wing protestant evangelical sects who were instrumental in convert-ing a quarter of the indigenous population to Protestantism (the military was extremely pleased with the prospect of thousands of Mayans renouncing their Catholic faith because the military equated Catholicism with guerrilla sympa-thies; see Forster, 1990), undoubtedly because of the influence of the liberation theology movement within the Catholic Church and terms like "the preferential option for the poor" and the "social gospel of Jesus Christ" which became sub-liminally attached to it.

In contrast with Stoll's conservatively varnished account of Guatemala, we have Cindy Forster's research. While Stoll believed that the army had won on the battlefield and in the political arena by 1982, and that the country was a ver-itable wasteland by this time, Forster reports that by 1983 a new guerrilla front had already opened and that by 1984 it was making active alliances with a resurgent union movement. During the time that Stoll saw a Guatemala already in the iron grip of military control and *campesino* passivity, Forster deftly argues that the Committee for Campesino Unity was busy organizing major strikes while networks of indigenous farmworkers fought for and achieved—in the face of helicopter surveillance, Israeli-designed intelligence, riot police, attack dogs and landowner paramilitaries—an increase in the minimum wage for the entire country. Richard Gott supports Forster's account, claiming that:

> Stoll ignores, or skates over, the context in which the strategy was elaborat-ed. The Guatemalan EGP was an heir to the group that killed the Spanish ambassador in 1968. It had worked quietly among the Indian population in the mountains along the Mexican border ever since 1972, and was one of the first left-wing movements in Latin America to try to make common cause with indigenous peoples, an essential precondition of success for any political movement in country with a majority Indian population. The guer-rillas only opted for armed action towards the end of the decade, when the conditions both at home and abroad looked promising. Although the victory of the Sandinistas in Nicaragua in July 1979 gave a much needed fillip to the guerrillas in Guatemala, they were also spurred on by the growth of mil-itary repression after 1978, during the dictatorship of General Romeo Lucas García. The famous Panzos massacre of peasants in Alta Verapaz, the adja-cent province to El Quiché, had occurred in May 1978. In 1980, with the Sandinistas in power and the guerrillas in El Salvador planning a major offensive (which took place in January 1981), the strategy of the EGP seemed reasonable enough. (1999, p. 19)

Canby (1999, p. 30) underscores Stoll's failure to support his assertion that things were getting better for the Maya before the arrival of the guerrillas. In fact, he cites evidence directly to the contrary: That there were, in fact, worsen-ing land shortages among the Maya as well as an increasing dependence on unpaid seasonal Maya laborers by coastal agribusiness plantations.

Stoll makes a number of further dubious assumptions, one being that intraethnic conflict among Mayan peasants is proof that their slaughter by the army was not motivated by racism. Since 83 percent of the dead are indigenous, we find this assertion ludicrous. We also find Stoll's comment that Mayan governments do not comprise impoverished peasants, but rather comprise the bourgeoisie, to be similarly flawed. We are concerned about any researcher who does not take a firm position against the poverty inflicted upon the indigenous population by the government ruling class, or who casts the Maya into the category of the mute subaltern (perhaps Stoll believes the Maya have survived five centuries of oppression and still remain the majority population by some weird accident of fate). While it is the case that Stoll "rewrites history by simply ignoring the crimes of the right" (Forster, 1999, p. 20), it is also the case that his telescoping and simplifying of historical depth enables him "to dilute the reader's understanding of the racial divides that were sharpened by debt peonage and forced labor on the plantations" (1999, p. 19). While the centerpiece of Stoll's book is about land reforms, it is telling to consider why, notes Forster, Stoll chose to overlook the 1952 Agrarian Reform legislated by President Jacobo Arbenz, whose left liberal regime was toppled by a CIA-led invasion (even the monumental centrist, Bill Clinton, apologized for the clandestine support the United States government gave to the murderous Guatemalan dictatorship). Stoll's case of historical amnesia—what Forster refers to as "breathtaking misreadings of the historical record" (1999, p. 20)—also neglects to discuss the U.S. training on Guatemalan soil for the Bay of Pigs invasion that Forster argues "inspired many nationalist junior officers to desert and form the first wave of guerrillas" (1999, p. 20). Stoll fails to mention as well the use of Guatemala as a site to carry out a "'laboratory test case' for counterinsurgency in the hemisphere to battle the ideas of Che and Fidel" (1999, p. 20).

COLLECTION OF EVIDENCE

John Beverley states that Stoll's own "basis for questioning Menchú's account are interviews years later with people from the village where the massacre occurred. That is, the only things he can put in the place of what he considers Menchú's inadequately representative testimony are other testimonies: other texts, narratives, versions, and voices" (1996, pp. 225-226). Forster blames Stoll's research skills as much as his conservative ideology for the egregious misrepresentations of the state of affairs in Guatemala in the early 1980s. She writes that Stoll's position is hobbled by the way he has conducted his research:

> Stoll criticizes faulty evidence but he doesn't seem to practice the rudiments of scholarship. He changes the argument at will. His footnoting is haphazard. He surveyed combatants and conducted studies of particular

cases but we learn nothing of his methodology. Often, we do not know the socioeconomic status of the speaker (see e.g. 196, 102, 116). He presents conflicting stories with no resolution (150-151), apparently as a strategy to argue that truth is unknowable and action ill-advised. (1999, p. 17)

Similarly, in a recent article in the *Chronicle of Higher Education*, Joanne Rappaport is quoted as criticizing Stoll for veering away from accepted procedures in cultural anthropology which Rappaport argues "no longer advocates studying indigenous people as objects" (see Wilson, 1999, p. A16). Similarly, Arturo Arias is quoted in *Lingua Franca* as claiming: "Stoll did a reductive analysis" and adds: "And now everything Rigoberta's *testimonio* defends becomes tainted, and it becomes the basis for undermining the credibility of what happened—genocide, massacres, personal losses for many people. It becomes a whitewashing of history that is similar to discourses that deny the Holocaust" (1999, p. 52). While the latter accusation is overstated (Stoll never denies the atrocities of the Guatemalan military), it is true that Stoll's attack on the credibility of Rigoberta's testimony helps put the murderous right-wing fascists in the position of deniability.

Hal Cohen reports on some telling criticisms of Stoll's research. He offers some comments by Paul Yamauchi, the founder and former director of the International Center for Human Rights, who criticized Stoll for conducting an interview in a *pension* (a Ladino and gringo-controlled environment) claiming that he lacked the familiarity with the intimate details of life in the village, that he failed to work in the native tongue of most of the population, and that he did his interviewing in public spaces. Yamauchi contends that "No one will give you accurate information about how they feel unless you meet in secrecy" (Cohen, 1999, p. 53). He further notes: "In my experience, anyone who is interviewed in a public space will say they were not for the guerrillas or the army—exactly Stoll's thesis" (1999, p. 53). Cohen also offers the following commentary from Carlota McAllister, a graduate student who has recently completed two years of fieldwork in Guatemala:

"It is impossible to ask a more loaded question in the Guatemalan highlands than 'To what degree did you willingly support the guerrillas?' Not least because it's the question soldiers would ask prior to beginning a massacre or a torture session. . . . In my community, the same people can easily give me ten radically different answers to that question, depending on how I ask them and how well they know me. Stoll's big thing is 'just the facts,' but he confuses people's subsequent interpretations of their experiences with strictly referential statements." (Cohen, 1999, p. 53)

It would appear that Stoll wants readers to believe that his informants were telling the truth, whereas Rigoberta was a lying Indian, someone who, despite her claims, is not representative of the Mayan attitude towards the guerrillas—

in other words, she is only really a "Maya" in inverted commas. Although Stoll organizes his work around tropes of sympathy and empathy, he offers precious little evidence about how he encountered the alterity of Guatemalan life and his efforts to identify embryonic Guatemalan ideas on guerrilla movements fall short of convincing. He offers little reflection on the epistemological assumptions that guide his own questions. He betrays little appreciation for the manner in which the heterotopicality of Rigoberta's *testimonio* can complicate, interrupt, and displace the Orientalism of the Western observer.

Stoll (1999c) accepts the recent suggestion of Gary Gossen that Rigoberta's text be considered an epic, rather than a *testimonio*, because a *testimonio* "carries a strong connotation of eyewitness truth" (p. 78). Stoll prefers to follow Gossen in describing Rigoberta's book as epic narrative because it is "about a time of tribulation, has a basis in historical fact, and is told from a very partisan point of view yet becomes a charter for national identity" (1999, p. 79). Gossen writes:

> Now all the Maya have *I, Rigoberta Menchú*, complete with its own political biases. It may indeed be a partisan propaganda document, as Stoll alleges; it may be a conflation of the stories of many into the voice of one, even as she, Rigoberta, now acknowledges; and it clearly does not incorporate the point of view of all modern Maya people. Nevertheless, it stands as the most important Maya literary document of the modern era. In my effort to appreciate its singular stature, I prefer to approach it not as testimony or as history or as autobiography or as biased political propaganda. It should be evaluated in the domain where it belongs: epic literature. (1999, p. 65)

Gossen's categorization of *I, Rigoberta Menchú* as epic literature suits Stoll's conservative agenda because it dulls the point where history as event intersects with history as interpretation, generically transforms Rigoberta's story into the realm of national myth, and turns it into an iconographic national charter of sorts. This leaves more room for Stoll to claim that his own research is where the real facts can be gathered and interpreted in a nonpartisan manner. This is interesting in light of Stoll's recent assertion that Rigoberta's text should be taught, but only when read against Stoll's own work, which he announces "complicates the task of teaching it" (1999c, p. 78). One is left to wonder if one of Stoll's purposes in attacking an esteemed Guatemalan figure (who gave her testimony when she was only 22, and after her parents and brother had been tortured and killed) was because he wants to complicate the picture of the relations the Maya had with the guerrillas or because he seeks to make his work a companion piece to Rigoberta's best-selling book.

THE PLURAL SUBJECT OF *TESTIMONIO*:
EPISTEMIC MURKINESS AND THE QUEST FOR TRANSPARENCY

E. San Juan Jr. captures the essence of Stoll's accusations when he condemns them as shamelessly underwriting one side in the debate over objectivity versus human interest. According to San Juan Jr., the Menchú/Stoll confrontation:

> . . . serves as a timely reminder that the dispute over truth and its representation is transnational in scope and perennial in nature. It evokes the memory of some durable controversies that have assumed new disguises. Should the tale be trusted over the teller? Or is it the case that if there is no teller, there is no worthwhile tale? (1999, p. 4).

San Juan recognizes that what is at stake is understanding the consequences that the struggle over knowledge presents for those who—especially in times of urgency and crisis—are in a position to speak truth to power. E. San Juan has posed the following question in relation to Menchú and the Western scholar: "How can we so easily shift from the paradigm/worldview of the K'iche' people that refuses to recognize the separation of humans from nature, of individual from the community, to the central premises of a liberal party centered on possessive, exclusivist racializing individualism?" (1998, p. 12) . The singularity of Menchú's text—a text that questions "the innocence of the Judaeo-Christian tradition"—counterpoints the standpoint of the West. According to San Juan, "this tradition [of the West] has legitimized the conquest of the continent and the genocide of its aboriginal peoples, and today sanctions their continued repression by an oligarchic government and supported by various United States administrations" (1998, pp. 12-13). San Juan lucidly describes Rigoberta as a courageous activist who valiantly performs the inventory of her life "in the act of surpassing the past, of valorizing the transitional moment of decision and existential becoming" (1998, p. 51). In effect, Rigoberta links Guatemala to us here in the West; she scalds the history of repression and Western complicity with that repression into our popular unconscious. She provides "a strategy of popular anticolonialism premised on historical retrospection and narratives of 'belonging' and 'solidarity'" (1998, p. 52). Fredric Jameson places Rigoberta's testimonio in the category of Bakhtin's concepts of dialogue and polyphony. According to Jameson, testimonio "both dispels authorship of the old centered-subject private property type and institutes some new collective space between named subjects and individual human beings" (1996, p. 1 85). Beverley argues, convincingly in our view, that the "I" of Rigoberta's *testimonio* has the linguistic status of a "shifter" such that the meaning of the *testimonio* "lies not in its uniqueness but in its ability to stand for the experience of her community as a whole" (1996, p. 35). Rigoberta does not lose her identity in speaking for others, far from it. She is not turned into "the faceless sociological average or sam-

ple or least common denominator, but the association of one individual with a
host of other names and other concrete individuals" that are specific to the Third
World (Jameson, 1996, p. 186). Beverley makes an important distinction
between testimonio and autobiography in the following comment:

> Testimonio represents an affirmation of the individual subject, even of indi-
> vidual growth and transformation, but in connection with a group or class
> situation marked by marginalization, oppression, and struggle. If it loses
> this connection, it ceases to be testimonio and becomes autobiography, that
> is, an account of, and also a means of access to, middle-or-upper-class sta-
> tus, a sort of documentary bildungsroman. (1996, pp. 35-36)

According to Doris Sommer (1997), the plural subject of Rigoberta removes her
from the role of the inimitable person, disclaims her particularity, situates her
testimonio as a power-inflected act, and places her in a position representative
of her people. This is an important attribute of the *testimonio*. It captures the
relationship between the one and the many; voices converge like friends in a
restaurant who choose to sit at the back table because they have secrets to share.
Essentially Rigoberta's *testimonio* promotes an expression of personal "embodied" or "enfleshed" experience. According to George Yudice, "in contrast with
the hegemonic postmodern text, in which the 'I' is expelled as vomit, in which
the body transforms into vomit that which is expelled, separating it from nature
(mother and father), thus making dialogue impossible . . . Menchú's text is,
rather, a testimonial of incorporation, embodiment" (1996, p. 56). Yudice
locates Rigoberta's text not as part of the struggle to deconstruct representation,
but as part of the struggle for hegemony under the flagships of Marxism and liberation theology (Yudice, 1996, p. 57; see also McLaren, 2000) and as part of a
practical and performed aesthetics of community-building and solidarity. Marc
Zimmerman notes that Rigoberta's narrative voice has a latent metonymic function that in a single voice evokes "an absent polyphony" of other voices and
experiences and marks the reader with desire. It is the voice of an individual
decentered by the collective (Zimmerman, 1996, p. 112) who becomes, in
effect, "a new, deterritorialized, organic intellectual of the subaltern, capable of
acting effectively in global circuits of power and representation" (Beverley,
1993, p. 16). According to San Juan, Rigoberta's text surpasses the past and
replaces the ambivalence of the postmodern text with "resolve, commitment,
determination to face specific problems and crisis" (1998, p. 51). Instead of the
postmodern attention to the local, "we have a striving for coalitions and
counter-hegemonic blocs to prefigure a universal public space" (1998, p. 51).
Instead of the syncretic and the hybrid, often associated with postmodern texts,
Rigoberta gives us an architectonic of the new, and instead of the polyvocal,
Rigoberta develops an "articulation from the silenced grassroots, the loci of
invention and resourceful innovation" (1998, p. 51). Further, San Juan explains
how Rigoberta's text replaces the trope of "difference" with the trope of "possi-

bilities." Her materialist critique is able to move beyond the "binary impasse of reified hegemonic culture" (1998, p. 51). It represents a shriek of collective anguish, an utterance of the masses rather than a solipsistic or private narrative; it is not heteroglossic but rather triangulated; it is not contingent but "charted by cognitive mapping and provisional orientations" (1998, p. 51). For Rigoberta, the act of *testimonio* is "a culminating life ceremony, as embedded in the life of the community, just as her 'I' is embedded and absolutely tied to a 'we'" (Zimmerman, 1996, p. 113). The *testimonio* for Rigoberta is a ritual or embodied metaphor of transformation (see McLaren, 1999b). In essence, Rigoberta reveals how the residual characteristics of Mayan culture overlay with contemporary philosophy of revolutionary movements in Guatemala. Zimmerman describe the results as "a dynamic future-oriented syncretism" (1996, p. 115), a revitalization process that partakes of both the ceremonial and the communal and is infused with the imperatives of restoring political and cultural dimensions to their central place in Maya culture.

Rigoberta's text does not derive its imprimatur from the expanding archive of postcolonial orthodoxy any more than it does from the authority of tradition. This is because, as John Beverley notes, "it is an appeal that is being activated *in the present*" (1996, p. 278, italics original). Beverley notes further that "it is a response to the conditions of proletarianism and semiproletarianism, which subjects like Menchú and her family are experiencing in the context of the same processes of globalization that affect our own lives" (1996, p. 278). The power and the promise of Rigoberta's text is its power to disidentify with the seigneurial bourgeoisie and convert the "other" into us through a metaphoric identification with the other (Moreiras, 1996, p. 199). This is not as easy as it sounds since in order for us to develop feelings of solidarity we need to be able to engage in a form of prosopopoetic mediation in which the abject other is incorporated into us, "for only the abject, which lives in the unlivable, requires solidarity" (Moreiras, 1996, p. 211). Given that Rigoberta's text is able to interpellate marginality and subalternality through the collective, it is possible to see how Stoll's criticism has become epistemologically fetishized precisely through its reabsorption into "objective" and detached science. The tremulous tropology of Stoll's study transforms itself into the false consciousness of the colonizing gaze that is functionally advantageous as an instrument of colonial domination by refunctioning contestatory power into imperial representational self-knowledge. After all, what were the consequences of not speaking? For Rigoberta, the consequences of not speaking meant certain death for her people at the hands of the military death squads. The personal risk of not speaking—of remaining silent—held out the real possibility of ending up like her fellow *campesinos*: mutilated, butchered, gutted, and left to die an agonizing death. But there was also a risk entailed in the act of speaking out. Such a risk could very likely mean ending up like Guatemalan anthropologist Myrna Mack, who had been researching the return and integration of the Mayan population that had been driven out by the counterinsurgency of the early 1980s and who died after suffering 17 stab wounds outside her office in Guatemala City. Or it meant the possibility of following in the final footsteps of Monsignor Juan Gerardi Conedera, who had been bishop of El Quiché when the military unleashed its scorched earth tactics in the early 1980s and who later directed the report, *Never again*, by the Catholic Archbishop's Human Rights office. (The group who wrote the report was called REMHI, or Recuperación de la Memoria Histórica.) Gerardi was murdered in his parish-house garage on April 26, 1998, two days after he held the press conference to announce the completion of the report. Or it is possible that Rigoberta would end up like a Catholic nun from the United States "who was raped, thrown into a rat-infested pit with dead and dying bodies, and scarred by over 100 cigarette burns" (Forster, 1999, p. 18). In the early 1980s alone, some 5,000 Catholic lay catechists were assassinated (Forster, 1999). Forster notes:

> The Guatemalan military has been charged with causing ninety-three percent of the human rights violations among some 200,000 political murders. Yet Stoll, with the permission of local military commanders, collected interviews in the heart of the conflict zones in El Quiché. (1999, p. 17)

Could Rigoberta have spoken out without embellishing some of the details of her life and still received the international attention she so desperately sought for her work? Perhaps. But under wartime conditions and with the extermination of family members and friends occurring with such fiendish regularity and impunity—in fact, with the encouragement of and often with direct orders from the state—it was important to get the message out as forcefully as possible. It would take the frozen arrogance of a Western anthropologist to create an international scandal out of the minor fabrications.

IMPERILED AUTHORITY: WHAT IS TO BE DONE?

U.S. foreign policy is overwhelmingly a consequence of corporate policy and the economic climate for investment. When U.S. investors are "making a killing" in the marketplace, their sword arm—the military—are at the same time literally "making a killing" in the fields, in the streets, in the jungles, and in the bloodstained back alleys of foreign lands. Jennifer Harbury writes: "Whether justice is possible in Guatemala depends in part on our ability to build grassroots movements to constrain a U.S. foreign policy which is bent on terror, torture, and murder aimed at 'improving the investment climate'" (1995, p. 252).

Rigoberta most assuredly has been influenced by Marxist revolutionary philosophy, which clashes on a number of points with pan-Mayan activism (not to mention Stoll's centrist politics). Both Marxist revolutionaries and pan-Mayanists unquestionably share a selective reading of resistance, refracting their understanding of knowledge in certain political directions. Certainly, Rigoberta had an ideological agenda that attempted to create sites of solidarity and struggle with the Marxist left. The point is not to hold Rigoberta unaccountable simply because we believe that she has the "correct" political line. That would be disingenuous. While not denying either the selective tradition of Pan-Mayanism on the one hand, or the heterogeneity of the Maya *pueblo* on the other, the issue incumbent upon social justice researchers is to elaborate the context surrounding her account and to tease out its implications for the larger struggle that occupies not only Rigoberta but activist researchers in general.

Rather than consider the significance of Rigoberta's story in terms of the geopolitical light that it sheds on the history of United States imperialism, why is it that so many of us in the United States academy are more compelled to comb through the data to find minor inconsistencies and contradictions that enable the condemnation of a poor woman of color, "Rigoberta mentirosa"? A number of Latin American perspectives on the scandalous accusations by Stoll begin with a critique of the role which both the United States media and the "neutral" academy play in articulating local and international hegemonic relations of power. This critique represents an understanding of national and global politics, informed by years of U.S. propaganda and interventionism which has been consistently served by the "free" press and its journalist vigor, and even by the pristine academy in its pursuit of truth and the construction of knowledge. As Gayatri Spivak points out: "Pero mas importante aún, las intenciones del intelectual son siempre más cuestienables que las del sujeto subalterno, porque sus 'presuposiciones' . . . están condenadas a ser coherentes con el trabajo de constitución del sujeto imperialista" (Spivak, 1985, quoted in Arias, 1999, p. 3).

Lacking a high school education, Rigoberta nevertheless has been recognized throughout the world for work much more significant in the pursuit of human dignity and social justice than that carried out by most academics. The document that she, Elizabeth Burgos-Debray, and Arturo Taracena (Aceituno, 1999) collaborated to produce is a testament to the lived experience of millions of poor and marginalized people all over the world. The subsequent political conscience that Rigoberta developed and the specific choices for struggle she made may or may not reflect those made by others with similar experiences. Stoll is correct in pointing out that not all the "poor" in Guatemala or any other Latin American country actively interpret their conditions in terms set out by various incarnations of Marxist-Leninism or Maoism that have shaped armed resistance struggles against Western imperialism over the decades. Nevertheless, affirming the fact that the oppressed are capable of defining and participating in their world in a variety of ways (and we must ask ourselves; "why should this need affirmation?") runs counter to Stoll's conclusion that the poor in Latin America who have adopted a critical antiimperialist stance have been brainwashed by Communists. Hundreds of thousands of marginalized peoples living within the political boundaries of Guatemala, El Salvador, Honduras, Nicaragua, Mexico, Chile, Peru, Ecuador, Colombia, etc., have paid for imperialist and/or global neoliberal relations of power with their lives and futures. Countless others continue to take action in living and defining their own lives. It is clear that often this action manifests itself in stridently anti-Western and anti-capitalist struggles.

While this article is being written, hundreds of Mapuche people are engaged in actively reclaiming land now held by the large forestry companies. These private companies are the *dueños* of lands stolen from the Mapuche peoples. Their success and survival depend upon economic activities and are directly linked to international neoliberal relations of power through investments and sales of Chilean patrimony. The subsequent exploitation of Chilean forests, planting and harvesting eucalyptus and pine, after having decimated native trees—"la tragedia del bosque chileno"—continues to degrade the soil and exacerbate the poverty of many Mapuche communities. This is due not just to a lack of land upon which to realize their agricultural practices but also to the degraded condition of the little land still occupied by the communities—a direct result of the forestry practices of these companies. These "anti-establishment," "anti-government," "anti-development" actions—in other words, anti-neoliberal capitalist development actions—are taking place in the economic "jaguar" of South America. Chile, the "free market miracle," the shining example of the success of neoliberal economic policy, has been suffering for over a year from the worst economic depression, unemployment, and social unrest since the 1980s when the military government first imposed the economic reforms championed by the "Chicago Boys", economists who followed the neo-liberal prescriptions of Milton Friedman and Arnold Harberger. Also, during the first week of July and for the next 12 days, thousands of indigenous people occupied the capital of Ecuador; its "democracy" stands on the brink of collapse as the armed forces threaten a *coup d'état*. This in response to skyrocketing levels of unemployment and general social unrest directly linked to the government imposition of neoliberal reforms, specifically, cuts in government subsidies for fuel, and the privatization of several formally state supported services. Yet another recent example of the "poor" taking their destinies into their own hands involves the recent mobilizations of the Colombian guerrilla movements that were violently put down in a counteroffensive by the military, also in July. This counteroffensive resulted in over 200 guerrilla deaths.

In light of these recent actions taken by poor and native peoples it would seem that international norms for economic development and progress offer little in terms of bettering the conditions in which so many people must struggle to survive. Given the current historical juncture in which we have witnessed the end of the cold war and the economic decimation of socialist block countries, outdated and ridiculous arguments about a powerful "communist plot" behind every organic insurgence hold very little force. Perhaps now in this globalized and "democratic" landscape the inherent violence and oppressive practices that lubricate the international economic machine can be more easily identified as the cause of social unrest rather than foreign pawns of the "evil empire." The current unrest in Latin America, as well as many historical "facts" that one could cite representing the past 20 years of resistance and struggle by the poor and native peoples throughout the region and elsewhere, underline the importance of Rigoberta Menchú's powerful *testimonio*. According to Arturo Taracena, a Guatemalan historian who was instrumental in getting Rigoberta's text published,

> You don't see anyone else attacking autobiographies like this; there's a hidden racism. If Stoll is an anthropologist and doesn't know that Indian people speak collectively, that she expressed the voice of the collective conscience, then I don't know what he knows. If he has a point of view about Guatemala, he should write it. (cited in Canby, 1999, p. 33)

Given current global circumstances at the *fin de millénaire*, why do we focus so much attention on the least important question of all? Given the overwhelming evidence in support of the situation described in Menchú's testimony, how can we allow these "pearls" of contradiction (Liano, 1999) to negate the social and political analysis of the lived historical condition represented in her *testimonio*?

Consider some of the questions that may be raised by this analysis. One could, for instance, discuss the meaning of truth—i.e., the meaning of "truth" in autobiography versus "truth" in the "*testimonio*" genre. We could also debate the *place* of the *testimonio* and its representative voice for a certain indigenous account of historical events. We could also explore the phenomena of psychological trauma and stress on "truth." We could explore the possible influences that Rigoberta Menchú's psychological state had on the veracity of the book. These questions will be explored in several articles coming out of Latin America (Aceituno, 1999). What was the psychological condition of the young Rigoberta Menchú, having recently lost both parents, having fled her country, having to adjust to life in the hyper-urbanized megalopolis of Mexico city, and shortly thereafter her trip to Europe as the representative of the FDCR? And how did these traumas affect the now infamous *testimonio*? Perhaps the conditions of extreme stress, fear, and the knowledge that giving away certain information, specific names, places, etc. could result in the death of many of her friends, family, and co-workers played a role in certain "inconsistencies" in her account and some of the confusion that now marks this debate.

Whatever one's chosen venue of analysis, none of these debates really steps outside the academic mainstream to examine in detail what can be done about the imperialist practices of the North American academy and its trained incapacity to recognize its role in preserving the international division of labor. To do this we need to explore the significance of Rigoberta Menchú and her work both within the US academy and within the context of Latin America. In recent articles representing several points of view that have appeared in Guatemalan newspapers, the general reaction to Stoll's book ranges from anger to sarcasm to disdainful acceptance. They concentrate their critique on the "imperialist" practices in the United States, the racist, sexist, and classist relations that continue to mark everyday life within Guatemala as well as the United States. More than anything else, these critiques and reactions reflect the centuries-old struggle for autonomy and voice, and reveal a long-standing resentment; "Se ve que siempre hemos de necesitar a un antropólogo norteamericano que nos venga a explicar nuestras cosas como verdaderamente son, dado nuestro escaso intelecto y nuestra mínima capacidad analítica" (Liano, 1999).

The Latino pastiche can take many forms and represent many profound meanings. So we will stick to the blood and guts of it, literally. What do we know? What does the Guatemalan army know? What does the CIA know? What do the Guatamalan people agree upon? What does the United Nations know? The answers represent brute realities that many people have lived. Whether they choose to speak of them in the first person, or the third, thousands of people have died. Thousands of children work picking cotton and coffee, thousands of Maya and other native peoples continue to be treated as sub-humans by the racists in their own countries. This racist logic is evident too in the guilt-ridden, politically correct gringo left who thank Rigoberta for her help in titillating their voyeuristic appreciation of the suffering of others and illuminating the plight of the poor in her country. Not to mention the "puritans," like Stoll, who find fodder for their academic and publishing careers in crushing the "cult of Menchú" by locating Rigoberta's text within the prison house of instrumental rationality and a definitional and programmatic approach to the truth. In a recent Guatamalan newspaper articles (Acción Cuidadana, 1998) a writer asks, "What has Guatemala gained from this debate?" The answer is yet unclear—but according to the article there is one clear winner: Stoll. The same paper, *El Periódico*, had interviewed Stoll a couple of days earlier on December 18. In this interview, Stoll expressed the objective of his work as "desacralizar a Rigoberta Menchú, pues no es bueno que la gente considere sagrada a una figura." The author then asks: "Desacralizar a Rigoberta ante quién . . . ante los guatemaltecos, no creo." This brings up an important point: what exactly does Rigoberta represent—as a person, as an icon, as a symbol for those of us in the United States academy, for her own people, and for the larger political struggle in Latin America.

For fascists outside the academy, for whom state-supported acts of violence have always been much more immediate and less literary, David Stoll's book and its attendant critique of Rigoberta, her life, and her politics offers redemptive ground. What does Guatemala stand to gain with a now famous "apología al Ejército de Guatemala" (Liano, 1999). What does Latin America stand to gain when the acts of murderers and usurpers are justified and complex local struggles are swallowed in a racist worldview that deems "passive primitives" too powerless to construct their own history? Like the theme of the Historica Sitiada, a watercolor and installation by Guatemalan artist, Isabel Ruíz,

Guatemala participates in its won wake where the mourners themselves are missing and where the missing are not only Guatemalans but indigenous people throughout the Americas who have died over the last five centuries since the arrival of Columbus (Goldman, 1999, p. 241). The indigenous peoples are reduced to fungible components in the terrain of human capital.

Those who have mangled the bodies *y cortaron las flores* of the insurgents in constant struggle to change their historical position, those who enjoy state support as they actively pursue the elimination of the many who actively inhabit the political margins, and those who are murderers of priests and children should be afforded no concessions. This warfare continues in the form of assassinations by organized military and paramilitary forces, state-sponsored theft through systems of economic growth and development (yes, even ecotourism), and the ideological warfare waged by the academic's pen.

How can we challenge these problems? What has Rigoberta done for us? What is her legacy? How can those committed to social justice use all the master's tools to dismantle his house? The possibility that the United States academy has lost its humanity to the point that the journalistic veracity of a text is more important than the human story it accurately portrays motivates us to rally for a rethinking of our work as what Gramsci called "organic intellectuals." Is there truth without political honesty? Some of our colleagues argue for "truth", and yet claim that neutrality is possible. There seems to be a type of philosophical perversity in this stance (McLaren, 1997). Why is it so hard to accept the political nature of all the work we are engaged in? Every paper, every analysis, every department in every university is engaged in either providing ballast to the current political and economic arrangements or challenging them.

Rigoberta's "audible silence" (Sommer, 1993, p. 413) has now been amplified by Stoll, who interrogates her and attempts to humiliate her the way that the military could not. Yet Rigoberta "refuses to be redeemed from difference" (Sommer, 1993, p. 420). She stands metonymically for the oppressed, inviting the oppressed to stand with her, despite their differences. Here the reader of Rigoberta's words is interpolated "as supporter, not leader" (1993, p. 421). Rigoberta resists "the murderous Vertretung, or substitutive representation, that Gayatri Spivak protests in elite writers" (1993, p. 421). Rigoberta's words will always cut through the ontological assumptions that produce Stoll's vindictive master trope of stinging anti-alterity. The wail, the shriek of anguish, will no longer be the poor's signature at the end of history but rather a prelude to restitution. As spokesperson for both the dead and the unborn, Rigoberta's testimonio enables witnessing to occur and hauntingly demands that her voice not only be allowed to utter its cry of horror but that it not be doomed to remain alone. It claims an audience of Western sympathizers from beyond the threshold of the North-South divide, an audience who will form a choir of voices urging action and justice.

The semiotic intensity and the reality effect of Rigoberta's *testimonio* may be somewhat blunted—and the authority of her text partially undermined—by

Stoll's uncovering of the inconsistencies and fabrications of some of the evidence, but surely the real social history she is describing does not cease to exist. Do Stoll's revelations somehow neutralize—aesthetically or politically—the import of the *testimonio* for resisting state violence against indigenous populations? Does Rigoberta's *testimonio* turn suddenly and unquestionably into a simulated account? Does history suddenly stop dead in its tracks? Does the right claim victory, as they wag their kerosene tongues, shake their heads, and make infantile clucking sounds at the "tenured radicals" they despise so much? As social agents, are we obliged to return to the starting point of the debate over Guatemala's history of revolutionary struggle? Is Rigoberta's *testimonio* now compromised beyond redemption?

Stoll's academic embrace carries the imprimatur of the Western intellectual who assumes Rigoberta wants to be understood within the discourses of legal correctness and Western jurisprudence or of the "sincere" gringo with good intentions, who believes that his interest in Guatemala is too earnestly irresistible not to be responded to in kind. Rigoberta's very last words in her testimonio are: "Sigo ocultando lo que yo considero que nadie lo sabe, ni siquiera un antropologo, ni un inelectual, por mas que tenga muchos libros, no saber distinguir todos nuestros secretos" ("I continue to hide what I think no one else knows. Not even an anthropologist, nor any intellectual, no matter how many books he may have read, can know all our secrets"; cited in Sommer, 1993, p. 413).

In light of the obvious inequities and social conflicts that make up so much of the world today, we need to reconstitute our role as cultural workers who are neither comfortable in our explanations of exploitation and oppression, nor self-righteously satisfied that we are supporting the good fight without seriously stepping into the battle ourselves and being prepared to pay the consequences for our political engagement (McLaren, 1998, 1999a). As Eduardo Galeano reminds us in his recent article, "Disparen Sobre Rigoberta" (1999), "Quienes apedrean a Rigoberta, ignoran que la estan elogiando. Al fin y al cabo, como bien dice el viejo proverbio, son los arboles que dan frutos los que reciben las pedradas."

Liberation is a perpetually receding border along which engagements with otherness take place. Times change, and time runs out. For Rigoberta, time was not a winged chariot drawing near, as the metaphysical poets might conjure in a moment of romantic "carpe diem" reverie, but the sound of jackboots, the rattle of bayonets, and anonymous screams in the night. How was it possible for this Mayan voice—the voice of this K'iche Maya Woman from El Quiché—to gain legitimacy and constitute itself amidst the deafening silence of the West? If it meant embellishing some facts, then so be it. Arturo Arias (1999) writes: "Sólo los gringuitos babosos de izquierda o de derecha, puritanos todos, podrían creer de veras que todo lo que allí veían era absolutamente veraz, acostumbrados como están a que les den atole con el dedo, como si la veracidad auténtica existiera, fuera una incuestionable fórmula científica o ecuación matemática garabateada por Einstein."

Echoing this sentiment, Francisco Goldman remarks:

> Because Rigoberta Menchú's memoir was conceived as a work of propaganda and because it succeeded as one, and because so many in Guatemala have always known it was one, I've never quite understood what it is Menchú is supposed to apologize for or what the uproar is actually about. . . . What rankles is the whiff of ideological obsession and zealotry, the odor of unfairness and meanness, the making of a mountain out of a molehill. (1999, p. 67)

We need to place the contribution made by Rigoberta on a firm historical materialist basis in terms of how it provides not only a negative hermeneutics that can demystify ideology but also a positive one where the collectivity and community triumph over the alienation of labor. In this way, Rigoberta's text can continue to provide much needed openings for intervention by national-popular forces struggling for liberation. While the guerrillas have been successful in bringing about a limited form of democracy, there is still much work left to be done. The seemingly intractable forces of neoliberalism are hindering efforts to bring about a socialist victory. As Suzanne Jonas notes:

> Although successful in winning democracy, revolutionaries have generally not won the struggles for social equality. In the cases of Central America during the 1980s and 1990s, we have seen a continuation of this historical tendency. Furthermore, their ability to win social justice is even more constrained in an era dominated internationally by neoliberal policy prescriptions (privatization, dismantling of the social safety net, etc.). (1998, p. 64)

We believe that it is important to remember that Rigoberta was seized by a larger mission and was overcome and traversed by a larger truth than that which preoccupies those who would jurisprudentially condemn her as a criminal, a perjured witness to history. History will judge Rigoberta Menchú through the eyes of the Mayan toilers of the fields, of the victims of torture, of those who walk barefoot across the blood-soaked land, of those who are irrecusable witnesses to inhumanity and injustice, and not by grinning Western anthropologists bearing the gifts of their prolix cosmopolitan and ivy league insights and wielding counterrevolutionary pens.

NOTE

1. Of course there are questions raised here that the literary critics might ponder further. If Latin American discourse needs abjection to constitute itself and restitutional excess is always tropologized in the service of self-legitimization, can this self-legitimizing excess be read against the grain in the moment of testimonio? Is this moment

of resistance constitutive of an aesthetics of solidarity that gives birth, in the words of Moreiras, to a nonhegemonic postmodernity? We will leave the question open as to whether it is structurally possible for Latin American discourse to be reabsorbed into the disciplinary system of representation, to reify extraliterary experience into mere tropes for a systemic representational poetics, or whether, in the long haul, testimonio makes disciplinary necessity redundant (see Yudice, Moreiras, Sommer, Beverley). And we are not concerned here about whether we can salvage the postauratic practice of literary realism in these postliteracy times.

REFERENCES

Accion Ciudadana (1998). Rigoberta entre dos fuegos. *El Periódico*, December 21, 1998. [On Line]. (Available: http://www.quik.guate.com/acciongt/dic98.htm)

Aceituno, L. (1999). Entrevista a Arturo Taracena sobre Rogoberta Menchú: Arturo Taracena rompe el silencio. [On Line]. (Available: http://ourworld. compuserve.com/homepages/rmtpaz/Mensaja/o990110.htm.)

Arias, A. (1999). Más sobre las memorias Rigoberta Menchú. *El Periódico*, Guatemala, domingo 17 de enero de 1999. [On Line]. (Available: http://ourworld. compuserve.com/homepages/rmtpaz/Mensaja/o990117.htm)

Aznarnez, J. (1999). Los que me atacan humillan a las victimas. Entrevista, Rigoberta Menchú: Líder Indígena Guatemalteca y premio Nobel de la Paz. *El País*, domingo 24 de enero de 1999, pg. 6-7. [On Line]. (Available: http://ourworld. compuserve.com/hompages/rmtpaz/Mensaja/e990124.htm)

Beverley, J. (1996). The real thing. In G. M. Gugelberger (Ed.), *The real thing: Testimonial discourse and Latin America* (pp. 266-286). Durham: Duke University Press.

Beverley, J. (1993). *Against literature*. Minneapolis: University of Minnesota Press.

Black, G. (1997). Military rule in Guatemala. In B. Loveman & T. M. Davie, Jr. (Eds), *The politics of antipolitics: The military in Latin America* (pp. 350-363). Wilmington, DE: Scholarly Resources Inc.

Canby, P. (1999, April 8). The truth about Rigoberta Menchú. *New York Review of Books*, pp. 28-33.

Chinchilla, N. S. (1999). Of straw men and stereotypes: Why Guatemalan rocks don't talk. *Latin American Perspectives, 26*(6), pp. 29-37.

Cohen, H. (1999). The unmaking of Rigoberta Menchú. *Lingua Franca*, July-August, pp. 48-55.

Forster, C. (1999). Rigoberta Menchú unmasked? *Against the Current, xiv*(2), May-June, pp. 15-20.

Fundación Rigoberta Menchú Tum. (1999,January). Rogoberta Menchú Tum: una verdad que desafia al futuro. [On Line]. (Available: http://ourworld.compuserve. com/homepages/rmtpaz/mensajes/m990100.htm)9

Galeano, E. (1999a, January). Columna de Eduardo Galeano, Disparen sobre Rigoberta. [On Line]. (Available: http://ourworld.compuserve.com/homepages/rmtpaz Mensajes/o990100.htm)

Galeano, E. (1999b). Disparen sobre Rogoberta. *La Jornada* (Mexico City), January 16, p. 11.

Goldman, F. (1999, June 14). Reply to Stoll. *The Nation*, 268(22), p. 67.

Goldman, S. (1994). *Dimensions of the Americas: Art and social change in Latin America and the United States*. Chicago: University of Chicago Press.

Gossen, G. (1999). Rigoberta Menchú and her epic narrative. *Latin American Perpsectives, 26*(6), pp. 64-69.

Gott, R. (1999, 27 May). Sacred text. *London Review of Books*, pp. 17-19.

Grandin, G. (1999, June 14). Reply to Stoll. *The Nation*, 268(22), pp. 2, 67.

Grandin, G., & Goldman, F. (1999, February 8). Bitter fruit for Rigoberta. *The Nation, 268*(5), pp. 25-28.

Harris, R. (1995). The global context of contemporary Latin American affairs. In S. Halebsky & R. L. Harris (Eds.), *Capital, power, and inequality in Latin America* (pp. 279-304). Boulder, CO: Westview Press.

Harbury, J. (1995). *Bridge of courage: Life stories of the Guatamalan companeros and companeras*. Monroe, ME: Common Courage Press.

Horowitz, D. (1999). I, Rigoberta Menchú, liar. *Salon Magazine*. [On Line]. (Available: http://www.salonmagazine.com/col/horo/l999/01/11horo.html)

Jameson, F. (1996). On literary and cultural import-substitution in the Third World. In G. M. Gugelberger (Ed.), *The real thing: Testimonial discourse and Latin America* (pp. 172-191). Durham: Duke University Press.

Jonas, S. (1998) . Can peace bring democracy or social justice? The case of Guatemala. *Social Justice, 25*(4), pp. 40-74.

Kincheloe, J. (1991). *Teachers as researchers*. New York: Falmer Pras.

Liano, D. (1999). Artículo Dante Liano. [On Line]. (Available: http://ourworld.compuserve.com/hompages/rmtpaz/Mensajes/o990120.htm)

Marx, K., & Engels, F. (1952). *The Communist Manifesto*. Moscow: Progress Publishers.

McLaren, P. (2000). *Che Guevara, Paulo Freire, and the pedagogy of revolution*. Boulder, CO: Rowman & Littlefield.

McLaren, P. (1997). *Pedagogica critica y cultura depredadora*. Barcelona: Paidos Educador

McLaren, P. (1998). *Multiculturalismo revolutionario*. Mexico, D. F.: Siglo Veintiuno editores.

McLaren, P. (1999a). Pedagogia revolutionario en tiempos posrevolucionarios. In F. Imbernon (Ed.), *La educacion en el siglo xxi. Los Retos del futuro immediato* (pp. 101-119) . Barcelona: Biblioteco de Aula.

McLaren, P. (1999b). *Schooling as a ritual performance: Towards a political economy of educatiional symbols and gestures* (3rd ed.). Boulder, CO: Rowman & Littlefield.

Moreiras, A. (1996). The aura of testimonio. In G. M. Gugelberger (Ed.), *The real thing: Testimonial discourse and Latin America* (pp. 192-224). Durham: Duke University Press.

Rogachevsky, J. (1999). Review of *Rigoberta Menchú and the Story of All Poor Guatemalans*, 12(7/8), July-August, pp. 96-99.

Sanford,V. (1999). Between Rigoberta Menchú and la violencia. *Latin American Perspectives, 26*(6), pp. 29-37.

San Juan, E. (1999). Who speaks now? For whom? For what purpose? *Asian Reporter*, 9(18), May 4-10, p. 3.

San Juan, E. (1996). *History and form: Selected essays*. Quezon City, Manila: Philippines.

San Juan, E. (1998). *Beyond postcolonial theory*. New York: St. Martin's Press.

Smith, C. A. (1999). Why write an exposé of Rigoberta Menchú? *Latin American Perspectives*, 26(6), pp. 15-28.

Sommer, D. (1993). Resisting the heat: Menchú, Morrison, and incompetent readers. In A. Kaplan & D. E. Pease (Eds.), *Cultures of United States imperialism* (pp. 407-432). Durham: Duke University Press.

Sommer, D. (1996). No secrets. In G. M. Gugelberger (Ed.), *The real thing: Testimonial discourse and Latin America* (pp. 130-157). Durham: Duke University Press.

Stoll, D. (1999a). *Rigoberta Menchú and the story of all poor Guatamalans*. Boulder, CO: Westview Press.

Stoll, D. (1999b, June 14). "I Rigoberta . . . ". *The Nation*, 268 (22), p. 2.

Stoll, D. (1999c). Rigoberta Menchú and the last-resort paradigm. *Latin American Perspectives*, 26(6), pp. 70-80.

Warren, K. (1998). *Indigenous movements and their critics: Pan-Maya activism in Guatemala*. Princeton, NJ: Princeton University Press.

Wilson, R. (1999, January 15). A challenge to the veracity of a multicultural icon. *Chronicle of Higher Education*, pp. A14-16.

Yudice, G. (1996). Testimonio and postmodernism. In G. M. Gugelberger (Ed.), *The real thing: Testimonial discourse and Latin America* (pp. 42-57). Durham: Duke University Press.

Zimmerman, M. (1996). *Testimonio* in Guatemala. In G. M. Gugelberger (Ed.), *The real thing: Testimonial discourse and Latin America* (pp. 101-129). Durham: Duke University Press.

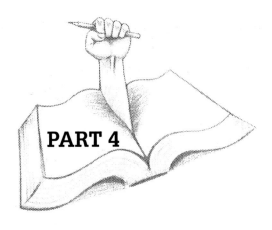

PART 4

THE POLITICS OF
POPULAR CULTURE

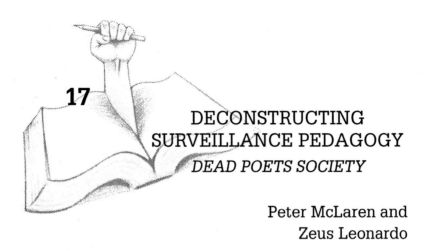

17

DECONSTRUCTING SURVEILLANCE PEDAGOGY
DEAD POETS SOCIETY

Peter McLaren and
Zeus Leonardo

In a metacommentary, we don't theorize postmodernism so much as we map the necessary conditions for the standard thought on postmodernism: why has it become so necessary to talk about a postmodern condition, what needs does that talking fulfill? The question then is not so much about the referents of postmodern discourse—what the postmodern condition is, and whether the discourse has described that condition correctly--but about what that discourse enables, and how it functions. (Stam 50)

(The human body was entering a machinery of power that explores it, breaks it down and rearranges it. A 'political anatomy', which was also a 'mechanics of power', was being born; it defined how one may have a hold over others' bodies, not only so that they may do what one wishes, but so that they may operate as one wishes, with the techniques, the speed and the efficiency that one determines. Thus discipline produces subjected and practised bodies, 'docile' bodies. (Foucault 138)

I went to the woods because I wanted to live deliberately.
I wanted to live deep and such out all the marrow of life!
To put to rest all that was not life.
And not, when I came to die, discover that I had not lived. (Thoreau)

INTRODUCTION

The current postmodern condition strongly suggests that reculturation is an important focus for educational reform. In particular, critical theories enable

This chapter originally appeared in *Studies in the Literary Imagination, XXXI*(1), Spring 1998, pp. 127-147. © Georgia State University. Reprinted with permission of the publisher.

educators to question for the "first time," the differential incorporation of high and popular culture in schools. Critical theories encourage us to identify the repressed margins of unofficial cultures, to name the struggles within the life-world of subaltern groups, and to legitimate the silenced culture of the popular in the attempt to subvert the prevailing structures of power and authority associated with high academic culture. However, if we are to observe course offerings in schools of education—especially in teacher preparation programs—not much about popular culture is taken seriously in schools. Studying it in classrooms is considered an illegitimate and ill-conceived use of pedagogical means by many educators. Popular cultural "texts" are often deemed non-academic and unworthy of scholarly pursuit, and people too closely associated with them are quickly dismissed as being undiscriminating and common. There are stratifications within popular culture as well. For example, films are usually considered inferior to books. There is a valorization of the written, as opposed to the spoken, word. As a result, when films are used in schools, they are often utilized as academic fillers, brain candy, or an electronic coping strategy when substitute teachers entertain students for a few days. Films are seen as effective pedagogical instruments to "take up time," as simple diversions, or as "special schedule" activities. Rarely do they receive extensive critique by students or are they legitimated as evidence to support historical arguments (Cohen, 1996). For these reasons and many more, popular culture, and in particular film, becomes even more important for critical educators to engage. How students live "the popular" receives such little attention in schools of education. As a result, students are denied the opportunity to learn how their identities have been constituted and shaped by quotidian forces and relations both ideological and material. Without the pedagogical space for critical dialogue about the semiotics of the everyday and what Michel Foucault refers to as the "political anatomy" of film, educators rob students of potentially transformative ways they can understand their everyday lives and work strategically toward interrogating them for hegemonic relations as well as emancipatory spaces. Through our critical analysis of the film *Dead Poets Society* we argue that understanding popular culture must become an integral part of any critical education if students are expected to understand both their location within the global economy and their situatedness within local vectors of power and privilege.

At this juncture, some definitions are warranted. For clarification, we adopt Henry Giroux and Roger Simon's (1994) statement about the status of popular culture in schools: "The dominant discourse still defines popular culture as whatever remains when high culture is subtracted from the overall totality of cultural practices. It is seen as the trivial and the insignificant of everyday life, and usually it is a form of popular taste deemed unworthy of either academic legitimation or high social affirmation" (p. 238). Because educators privilege high culture at the expense of popular culture and thus dismiss the popular in one sweeping stroke, students and educators forego the benefit of critically analyzing larger systems of social relations and entrenched interests which inform popular culture. Ironically, these are the systems of meaning many students take with them to classrooms and through which they act. Furthermore, research failing to attend to the social semiotics of the quotidian shows a bias against the "popular" and its low-brow mischief as well as a lack of engagement with "culture" in its specific articulations as opposed to Culture in its totalizing sense. We want to make clear that our interest in popular culture is not to exercise the fashionable apostasy of deconstructive analysis costumed in the academic salons of Paris but rather to analyze the ways in which education is not only embedded in its own institutional and pedagogical practices but secures its very condition of existence by requiring people to be located within the social division of labor, and now the current practices of superexploitation linked to the globalization of capital.

John Storey (1993) locates the term "popular" in those cultural practices that have a strong presence in commercial culture. Antonio Gramsci and Paulo Freire situate "culture" as a historical site of struggle over the production of meaning (San Juan Jr., 1992; McLaren, 1994). Considered together, the work of Storey, Gramsci, and Freire draws attention to an important political project: theorizing popular culture. For us, such a project must involve a search for a radical theory that neither treats the mass as Adornian dupes of popular spectacles nor celebrates the popular as "authentic" folk culture created in a revolutionary mix from below (Giroux and Simon). In addition, a critical theory of everyday life must avoid a purely rational analysis of subject positions within the circuits of semiotic economies of images, as if audience response is a purely reasoned activity involving informed consent. Moreover, following Grossberg, Giroux and Simon remind us that critical educators must work at deconstructing the ways students affectively invest in popular practices and texts. In an era characterized by the waning of affect it becomes even more imperative to construct a critical theory of popular culture that works against the totalizing and eclipsing force of reason in its monolithic sense.

For us, a specific point of theoretical importance in analyzing the popular is the way the body is portrayed in popular films. Films often oppose the ephemeral images of the carceral body with rationality's ethereal themes, favoring the latter. The body represents the site of desire, sexuality, and pleasures. In mainstream culture, somatic experimentations such as body piercing and painting become deviant symptoms of a mind gone awry. Current developments in technology, media, and marketing slogans abound on the importance of using the mind. For what exact purpose beyond exercising the mind, we are rarely told. For the capitalist class, it seems enough to announce that the mind should not be wasted. Educational propaganda about the need to use our minds is perhaps a telling sign of what Jean Baudrillard (1993) would likely suggest is an "alibi" for the general mindlessness in social life. People do not lack mindful activity, rather there is an overabundance of it to the point that it loses its specificity from that which we consider physical. To enter the debate around the mind-body split, we must first come to grips with what we mean by "mental" (Rorty,

1979). More important, intellectual labor for its own sake is never justifiable without attempting to grasp the often myriad interests that such labor serves. In our own classroom teaching we have come to understand that students benefit from discursive strategies which offer a theory of subjectivity as well as educational practices that recognize them as subjects. In short, becoming a student in the Gramscian sense of having a phronetic mind and a revolutionary disposition toward the body is a political project that can potentially transform our notions of what it means to be an active agent of history, who enunciates a pledge of emancipation in the face of current forms of capitalist superexploitation. Further, it points to the struggle for an altered historical reality where domination would cease to exist.

Appadurai (1996) notes that contemporary analyses of the body have revealed how the emotions and affect are not simply "raw, precultural materials that constitute a universal, transsocial substrate" but rather are "culturally constructed and socially situated" (p. 147). Sensory experience and bodily technique become, in this view, "parts of historically constituted regimes of knowledge and power" (p. 147). The notion of "embodied experience" or "enfleshment" has emerged as a powerful conceptual tool to understand how bodily states and experiences of the popular, and bodily techniques and affective dispositions, are inscribed upon corporeal rituals of self control and discipline that serve through everyday popular practices the material interests of the nation-state (McLaren, 1993). How are individuals motivated as body subjects through cultural and political schema that have imprinted themselves on bodily experience? How are macroconceptions of civility and dignity constructed by interests and ideologies which in turn link language and representations to the world of emotion and affect (Appadurai, 1996)?

Understanding how popular culture has structured our ideas about the body is one way to theorize our everyday practices. A critical discourse that engages the concept of corporeality affirms the micro-politics of desire as it is articulated at the level of living in the flesh. Our perspective recognizes that the body must neither be essentialized nor immaterialized. Instead, the body is an effect of ideological and discursive processes, all of which overdetermine its formation at any one time. Thus, combating a social incarceration of the body entails waging discursive battles on many fronts in order to avoid essentializing any one of its fields of articulation. This does not suggest a rejection of essentialist discourses *in toto*. Donna Haraway reminds us of the differences within essentialism (in Calhoun, 1994). In particular, she encourages radical theorists to take up the challenge of biological feminists, especially their contribution to understanding the ways in which images of women's bodies have been used in social discourse. However, it should be clear that the body is not simply an effect of discourse. Related to how the body is constructed in its specific fields are the material consequences accompanying the meanings we graft onto the body, which in turn begin physically to manifest themselves in our postures, speech, and movements: in short, our *habitus*. As opposed to a ludic interpretation of the body (i.e., viewing the body as a series of semiotic relations), we believe that material consequences follow from the regulation and appropriation of bodily techniques and dispositions which create different realities for body subjects. Critical educators are interested in the body not only to reform our ideas about the body, but to re-form the body itself as a political space of agential power.

Pedagogically speaking, teaching popular culture in the classroom is as important as theorizing about it. Teaching popular culture is simultaneously a discourse and a practice. During classroom discussions, educators must recognize the element of student voice. Problematizing student experience is a way of cultivating student voice by inviting students to problematize the routines and rituals of their daily lives and to thematize the collective and singular events that shape their self-understanding and social dispositions. In doing so, Paulo Freire (1993) suggests using problem-posing pedagogical strategies. Problem-posing education is an activity that is conducted with students, not for them. By working with students, critical educators attempt to cultivate an ethics of collectivity. Building a community of learners opposes the totalizing effect of establishing unity. Community-building is a position guided by an ethics of solidarity which recognizes differences between people. It acknowledges the pressing need to take active steps toward reconstituting the public sphere without imposing a "same page" ethos.

We recognize that popular culture consists of its own bodies of knowledge and systems of intelligibility found on street corners, playgrounds, and other embodied ways of living. In part students invest in popular practices as a result of their oppositional character to academic life and their "wastefulness" in the Baudrillardean and Bataillean sense. Educators who expect full participation from students on the basis that popular culture is about them may be thwarted by moments of resistance from the students themselves. By sanctioning popular culture as a legitimate topic of study, educators are confronting one of the important meanings that students derive from participating in traditionally non-academic practices: their opposition to schooling (McLaren, 1993). Educators risk colonizing student culture if they ignore the element of ownership. Of course essentialist ownership of popular culture must be guarded against as well. Students benefit from becoming more aware of the slippage of cultural autonomy. Popular culture is an amalgamation of hybrid practices, the original source of which escapes us.

Director Peter Weir's film, *Dead Poets Society,* is a semiotically pregnant filmic text offering a powerful examination of the ways in which the body is schooled as well as transformed. During a summer course in educational foundations at UCLA where we co-taught a class of approximately thirty-five prospective elementary and secondary school teachers, we were able to use the film for textual analysis in conjunction with theoretical pieces of writing about popular culture. Students were encouraged to assess critically the film's possibility as a critical pedagogical instrument. More important, we asked them to interrogate critically the film's assumptions about the purpose of education as well as to problematize the film's project with repect to the struggle over cultural politics. By and large, the students responded well to the film's inclusion into the course syllabus. And with the benefit of critical readings on popular culture, students gained insight on the multivalenced ways subjectivities are constituted within everyday life. Without disparaging the important role that written texts play in teaching and learning, experimenting with traditional formats by including both a film and discussing theoretical expositions of popular culture enabled the class to envision relevant and embodied pedagogies.

The process of schooling reflects Plato's concept of *idiopragein*, which is the process of harmonizing an individual's talents and interests with the needs of the social whole or larger community. Each person is given his or her place in society so that the better the fit the healthier the state. The social purpose of teaching is to bring about *idiopragein* (Blacker). In order to bring this about, Plato realized that select "guardians" would have to perpetuate the "noble lie" that some people are inherently superior to others (i.e., for Plato, this lie meant perpetuating the idea that some people are gold, silver, or bronze). We live in an era of fast, casino style, gangster capitalism in which schools are designed to give people tradable skills that are intellectual or vocational. Schools are also designed to equip people with character traits such as competitiveness and acquisitiveness (Blacker, 1996). The noble lie in this case is that only the "gold" people are destined to rise to the top of the capitalist hierarchy. The students of Welton High School—the school in the film—represent the "gold" stratum of future corporate and professional leaders. The noble lie perpetuated by their teacher, John Keating, is that the students live in a meritocratic society and that an unquestioning obedience to authority and a slavish veneration of tradition are the key to success.

Dead Poets Society makes sincere attempts to fracture the hegemonic discourse of what the school administration in the film values as a pedagogy built on the pillars of "TRADITION, HONOR, DISCIPLINE, and EXCELLENCE." Embodied in John Keating's commitment to the search for a transgressive pedagogy and the students' cry for "TRAVESTY, HORROR, DECADENCE, and EXCREMENT," the film's overt message resurrects the avatars of Romanticism by evoking the sign of *carpe diem*, or "seize the day." In doing so, Keating, played by actor Robin Williams, encourages, better yet, makes it imperative for the Welton students to pursue education to the ends of self-actualization, existential freedom, and a humanistic quest for peak experiences. For example, in one scene he spiritedly challenges the students to tear out the pages of their poetry anthology, urging them to live the verse of life rather than simply read about it, albeit from someone else's aesthetic vantage point. Keating's progressive pedagogy is an unequivocal attempt to free students from the shackles of schooling for schooling's sake in order to remind them of the richness in experience, the potential for passion, and the vitality in a life freed from a technicist mode of learning. However, critical interrogation of the film leads one to question the political project suggested by the encounter between Keating and the students. By emphasizing the cultivation of self, Keating's humanistic discourse ultimately falls short of politicizing a collective project toward cultural emancipation. Although there is much in Keating's pedagogy that is liberating, it lacks the politicized and self-reflexive discourse students need in order to combat the school's reabsorption of their fleeting transgressions. Ultimately the school serves as a flat, contiguous and homogeneous space that works to produce a compliant national citizenry. Here students are produced within modes of subjectivity most congenial to the nation-state, a lesson that is very compatible with today's uncritical patriotism. Yet while the students resist the normative charter of the school, there is little recognition in the film of the links between this charter and the manner in which schools perpetuate asymmetrical relations of power which in turn are linked to the larger social division of labor.

Keating's intervention accomplishes its initial objective of stirring up an apparently antiseptic school environment. He appropriates the discourse of *carpe diem* such that the body becomes a site of struggle. During his first day of teaching, Keating unsettles the scene by having the students follow him out into the hallway, thereby breaking the ostensible bondage between the students' bodies and their seats. Foucault (1979) reminds us of the way the body is perfected by the architecture of surveillance. Indeed, Welton students initially hesitate to leave their antiseptic, regimented, and cellularized space, perhaps out of fear of the consequences of leaving their seats. This is auto-surveillance at its most invisible. As Keating tempts the students to follow him into the hallway, they look at one another in puzzlement as if they do not own their bodies. The students seem to wait for a bell to signal their next move, as it does so many times to signal the end of a class period. Eventually, the students rise from their seats and gingerly walk behind Keating into the cold hallway.

As Foucault has shown us, the present regime of discipline regiments the body's location, temporality and behavior. In *Dead Poets Society*, Welton depotentiates the students' carnal possibilities by compartmentalizing and repeatedly sending them to their chairs, the symbolic chains of schooling. The classroom becomes a mirror of official society where resistance occurs in the cavities that separate the real from the possible. The classroom becomes the prison-house of knowledge, a site of the totalization of regulative functions, yet the site of unmarked possibility. As in the case of so many other schools, the classroom walls at Welton represent the lost horizon of possible worlds and the limit-text of freedom. Similarly, in *Discipline and Punish*, Foucault (1979) outlines the prisoners' day from their rising from sleep at six in the morning, then accounting for approximately twenty minute intervals and the activities accompanying them, until the inmates return to their cells at half past eight in the evening to return to sleep (pp. 6-7). Prison life ritualizes the inmates' bodies not only by assigning their stations at given intervals, but also by regulating a period of time for their body to be in certain locations. What results is a micro-technology of power that institutes spatio-temporal oppression.

In *Dead Poets Society* Welton ritualizes the student body by beginning the day with a lesson on poetry with the students sitting "properly" in their (apparently) assigned seats. This sets the tone for what the students can expect as normal usage of the body while learning: sitting quietly and speaking when asked to speak. Keating disrupts this arrangement by having the students follow him into the corridor, thereby transforming their potential energy into kinetic movement. Their bodies are made to relate to poetry under new circumstances by gazing at the pictures of former Welton students in the glass casing rather than being forced to engage a canonized classroom textbook. Keating's students set their poetry anthology aside and instead carry on a dialogue. Shumway (1989) explains the importance of such disciplinary controls:

> The body for Foucault is not a euphemism for the sexual, and desexualizing is only one aspect of the way the body is constructed in schooling. The body is used by Foucault to indicate the fact that disciplinary controls are not merely memorized and accepted, but actually form the body itself. One could say that they are habits in the sense that they work without the conscious choice of an individual but are ingrained in the very posture and musculature of the body. (227)

Keating unsettles the students' atomistic configuration by huddling them together in the hallway. There is tactile contact between them as their uniforms scratch against one another when they crowd around to stare at the hallway photographs. Keating encourages his students to look into past (and "dead") students' faces and identify themselves in the faces on the wall. The students stare at the Welton graduates only to find their own blank faces staring back at them in the reflections on the glass. At stake here is the moment of misrecognition, in the Lacanian sense, of locating identity in reflections other than ourselves because the students neither identify with the photographs of former students nor with their own reflections in the glass casing.

Contrast student reactivation of body zones in the hallway with their isolation from each other when sitting in their own chairs in the classroom. In the classroom, Welton student bodies are still close to the each other but maintain a critical distance that reinforces their alienation from one another. Such closeness at arm's length in the classroom is explained by John Fiske's concept of "distantiation":

> Such distance devalues socially and historically specific reading practices in favor of a transcendent appreciation or aesthetic sensibility with claims to universality . . . This distance from the historical is also a distance from the bodily sensations, for it is our bodies that finally bind us to our historical and social specificities. As the mundanities of our social conditions are set aside, or distanced, by this view of art, so, too, are the so-called sensuous, cheap, and easy pleasures of the body distanced from the more contemplative, aesthetic pleasures of the mind. (154)

Fredric Jameson explains postmodern distance this way:

> Distance in general including critical distance in particular has very precisely been abolished in the new space of postmodernism. We are submerged in its henceforth filled and suffused volumes to the point where our now postmodern bodies are bereft of spatial coordinates and practically (let alone theoretically) incapable of distanciation. (cited in Montag, 1988, p. 94)

Our bodies betray the interests of bourgeois distantiation. Whereas bourgeois distance emphasizes a certain sacred individualism that escapes the other, the body reminds us of our physical propinquity to the other. It is the point where the self is confounded by the other and (mis)recognizes itself through the other. At this juncture in *Dead Poets Society* due to the students' increased proximity to one another, statements can be felt in people's breath, heard in the slightest whisper. "Carpe diem," Keating haunts as a student feels Keating's moist breath on his neck.

But make no mistake about it. In our current viral society, distance between host, or self, and parasite, or other, is preserved only to the point that self and other fail to connect. "Touch" is approached, but never accomplished. Critical distance has been all but abolished in our tactile universe where Marshall McLuhan's dictum "the medium is the message" becomes "the massage" (Baudrillard, 1993, 123-24). Closeness is achieved only asymptotically in order to maintain the enigma of chance:

> In a sacred, ceremonial universe, things do not touch each other, and they never meet. They link up without fail, but without contact. Tact in this matter is precisely avoiding contact. Remark how ceremonial gestures, dress, and bodies roll, intertwine, brush past each other, challenge one another, but without ever touching. . . The same is true for our bodies in everyday lives. . . A very powerful force was required to break this magnetic distance where each body moves, as well as to produce this indifferent space where chance is able to put them in contact. (Baudrillard, 1983, 146)

The bodies of Welton students do not occupy any safe space on their own or a safe landscape for the functioning of the autonomous self. Critical distance does not exist at arm's length, as it were. An ecology of critical interviews between concrete voices is what remains. In this move from distantiation to implosion, the body represents what JoAnne Pagano (1995) refers to as our "radical nearness." Pagano turns the body's "attachments to the world" against the "fantasy of unfettered mind" (343). She affirms our libidinal connections which simultaneously "guarantee identity" (349) through differences between bodies. Pagano does not see the choice as merely either identity or consensus, but a critical hybrid of both difference and connection through the "specificity of the body" (352).

Keating assists in re-posturing the students' bodies in ways against which Welton's establishment has guarded. Whereas they sit robot-like with hands on their desks, with erect posture, and equidistant from one another, Keating's hallway huddles are more informal, disorganized, and flexible. Welton Academy rigidifies the body's demeanor; Keating uncoils it. Compare this with Foucault's (1979) description of embodied handwriting exercises in schools:

> A well-disciplined body forms the operationalized context of the slightest gesture. Good handwriting, for example, presupposes a gymnastics—a whole routine whose rigorous code invests the body in its entirety, from the points of the feet to the tip of the index finger. The pupils must always "hold their bodies erect, somewhat turned and free on the left side, slightly inclined, so that, with the elbow placed on the table, the chin can be rested upon the hand, unless this were to interfere with the view; the left leg must be somewhat more forward under the table than the right. A distance of two fingers must be left between the body and the table." [But there is no need to go on.] (152)

At Welton, with class seats arranged in rows that are equidistant from one another and facing the front of the room, a teacher is able more efficiently to supervise student bodies. Such a perfect arrangement of the room improves what Cohen refers to as a teacher's periscopic "super*vision*" and her technology of control.

Keating fractures Welton's surveillance pedagogy by holding class sessions in hallways, sport fields, and school quads. And when he conducts discussions in the classroom, on the importance of poetry, for example, he crouches on the ground whereas the students remain standing and looking downwards at him, thereby suggesting a disruption of their relationships vis-a-vis the body. As a result, the students are able to use the classroom as a space to experiment with what Nelson Goodman (1978) calls "ways of worldmaking." This intensifies in a scene where Keating encourages the students to stand atop the teacher's desk and take a moment to survey the room in order to see it—in a sense see the world—from a different perspective. In another outdoor scene, Keating asks the students to experiment with their style of walking in order to show "the dangers of conformity." At first the students walk like one another, almost in militia formation. Then prompted by Keating's suggestion, some students begin to strut, some waggle. Charlie sits out this exercise saying, "Exercising the right not to walk." By making the familiar strange, Keating begins the rudiments of a lesson on the unnaturalness of the classroom setting, that is, its hierarchical spatial organization and centralized arrangement.

In light of Bakhtin's (1981) insights, we can think of the body as an ideological effect of language. The body becomes a sign in discourse and communicative exchanges. In reference to Bakhtin's notion of "tact," or the codes of dialogue, Stam (1993) writes,

> In the sound film we not only hear the words with their accent and intona-
> tion, but witness the facial or corporeal expression which accompanies the
> words--the posture of arrogance or resignation, the raised eyebrow, the
> intimidating look, the ironic glance which modifies the ostensible meaning
> of an utterance. (125)

This analysis blurs the distinctions between what is cognitive and what is bodily. Eyes speak volumes. Postures communicate emotion. Speech and the body
conflate. A revolutionary discourse must not only liberate the mind, it must also
de-colonize the body. Ideologically speaking, the body houses various social
grammars and norms, not in their Durkheimian sense as accepted rules for conduct, but as discursive sites that are struggles over meaning in the Gramscian
and Freirean sense.

Keating's somatic pedagogy re-molds the students' musculatures into a formation conducive to what Bakhtin refers to as a dialogical relationship. As
such, Keating suggests that the body is social. It only gains recognition and,
more important, meaning, when juxtaposed with other bodies. Bodies, as it
were, converse on the level of signs. Similarly, Fiske (1992) observes,

> The body, its geography and history, are not empiricist facts in a Newtonian
> nature. Their natural essences are semiotically inert: they become epistemo-
> logically interesting only when they enter a social order, for only then do
> their differences become structured rather than essential; only a social order,
> therefore, can make differences signify. The concrete practices of everyday
> life are the insertion of the body into the social order, and, de Certeau would
> argue, the inscription of the social order upon that body. (163)

In *Dead Poets Society* we understand Todd Anderson's unwillingness to inject
his body into class interactions and Dead Poets events in relation to more exoti-
cized expressions of the "savage" body—e.g., Charlie Dalton's. Charlie's "yaw-
ping" behavior sets the context for Todd's reluctance to let out a "barbaric
Yawp" during Keating's class. A similar situation occurs during one of
Keating's field exercises. In an attempt to provide an embodied pedagogy of
movement, Keating takes the students out to the grass field, who then take turns
kicking a soccer ball as classical music blares in the background. One student in
particular is tentative to recite a line from a poem and weakly kicks the soccer
ball. A resounding "boo" from Keating results, strategically juxtaposed with
Charlie bellowing "To indeed be a god!" and followed by his thundering kick at
the next ball. "To indeed be a god!"—a sentiment fostered in Keating's teach-
ings—is certainly one of the repressive myths of empire and Keating leaves such
ideological impulses unchecked and free to be cathected to any movement in
search of gods to serve the empire or otherwise. Last, Knox's sexual repression
in his pursuit of the virginal Kris gains more context when we consider Charlie's
overbearing sexual and sexist comments. In one scene, Charlie unfolds a porno-

graphic centerfold; in another, he exposes a lightning bolt on his chest: according to him it is a symbol of his virility. These characters do not, as an essentialist reading might suggest, possess a transparent self independent of their social co-construction with others. The students' bodies are in constant and anticipatory dialogue with one another. Their bodies are not already formed but are always involved in a process of becoming, betwixt and between social contexts.

The issue of the body invokes the materiality of the oppression that the Welton students suffer at the hands of their teaching and administrating counterparts. We use the word "administration" to suggest a formal body of laws developed for purposes of normalization. As a backdrop, Welton's natural surroundings (e.g. the grassy fields, lakes, and wildlife) point to the unnaturalness, the ironic perversion of their schooling. When Knox rides a bike down a grassy hill, a flock of birds flood the sky to avoid getting hit. The trees, ponds, and wildlife which canopy the school grounds mask Welton's manufactured and instrumental education. This juxtaposition reminds us how instrumental reason subjugates nature for technical purposes, rather than emancipatory interests. The students' objective world sets the context for their learning. They have very little to say about the work that they do in class, on the production of knowledge that is evaluated, and on the creative directions which they would like to pursue.

Welton's official curriculum—one that the school principal, Nolan, boasts "is set, proven, and works"—follows a program of inquiry that fetishizes the production of knowledge. It concentrates more on "what works" and disregards the work which goes into knowing. On Keating's first day of class, we learn the "Prichard Scale" Welton uses to determine the "greatness" of a poem. Keating strategically sketches the Scale on the chalkboard as a two-coordinate system with the poem's "importance" on one axis and its "perfection" on another. Beauty, or what Prichard calls "artful rendition," is rendered quantifiable. We are reminded here of Immanuel Kant's (1970) compendium on beauty. Consider his words in the following passage:

> *Taste* is the faculty of judging of an object or a method of representing it by an *entirely disinterested* satisfaction or dissatisfaction. The object of such satisfaction is called *beautiful*. . . . Consequently he [*sic*] must believe that he has reason for attributing a similar satisfaction to everyone. He will therefore speak of the beautiful as if beauty were a characteristic of the object and the judgment logical. . . . Consequently the judgment of taste, accompanied with the consciousness of separation from all interest, must claim validity for every man, without this universality depending on objects. That is, there must be bound up with it a title to subjective universality. (381; emphasis in original).

For Kant, self-interest taints the ideal representation of beauty. Any purposiveness on the part of the subject renders beauty less than ideal. Any conceptualization of an object (e.g. a rose or, in our case, a poem) with relations outside of itself stains the objectification of beauty. According to Kant, such is the human capacity for reason. Kant critiques the Western obsession with ideal, sublime rationality in his attempt to synthesize the objective with the subjective, and reason with faith. The Prichard Scale reifies the neutral and ahistorical concept of beauty. It fails to note that a critic of poetry cannot divorce her values from the hermeneutics of beauty. A priori assumptions are always constitutive of our perceptions which, in turn, provide the necessary elements of our conceptual maps. This has been the staple of sociological wisdom for several generations.

In addition and in real terms, beauty is a political construct with consequences as well as liberatory possibilities. Beauty is part of a system of relations involving prior commitments to valuation of qualities between things and people, not quantifiable measures of worth. Rather than seeking consensus on the "nature" of beauty, critical educators should look for *contradictions in the aesthetic*. Keating never extends his critique of schooling to include an interrogation of Western male standards of beauty. Keating ignores the fact that different cultures have different standards of judgment. When the students ask Keating in the courtyard about the original Dead Poets, he recalls his group reading poems from Whitman, Thoreau; in sum, he says, "The biggies." Keating fails to weave his insights outside of a Western discourse on language and beauty, unabashed by the Western deletion of competing subaltern voices from the margins. Poetic verse is always imbricated with technical standards for beauty that suppress the social production of beauty in exchange for meter, rhyme, and form (e.g., Shakespearean or Italian sonnets). Keating fails to realize that the poetics of beauty never speaks for itself but is refracted by particular interests and produced by ideological imperatives that have been shaped by history.

"Seize the day," Keating advises. In effect, he is asking the students: What is it about yourselves that you no longer want to be? Keating counsels Neil Perry to practice the moral courage required to live his life in the direction he desires. Neil's longing to act in *A Midsummer Night's Dream* represents his desire to will his life in the direction he wants, to produce his life's own dramaturgy, to be autonomous as opposed to being an automaton. Keating's oppositional teaching style unsettles Welton's hegemonic relations of power, especially those that reconfirm parental authority and decision-making. Neil resists his father's impositions by circumventing and thwarting his father's control: by lying about dropping out of the play. Further, he lies to Keating about having confronted his father about his desires. Neil "seizes the day" by activating the agency he possesses in order to fulfill his destiny on stage. After his father threatens to send him to military school, Neil commits suicide. Suicide becomes his last opportunity to act, to make an existential choice that joins him with the Dead Poets of the past.

Keating's inspirational, and at times transgressive, pedagogy lacks the critical discourse necessary for liberatory practices. Resistance is primarily confined to the secrecy of the cave meetings where students privatize their dialogues. Thus, it does not threaten Welton's hegemonic hold on the student population.

The film fails to consider the fact that ideological hegemony relies upon a certain exercise of resistance. Activities such as cave meetings, tearing pages from assigned books, and reciting self-generated poetry are personalized moments of resistance that, when kept private, reconfirm hegemonic relations. Resistance is reduced to idiosyncratic acts of bourgeois transgression, performative moments of apostasy without the benefit of critical analysis.

Benedict Kerkvliet (1990) reminds us about the important differences between "everyday resistance" and "unusual resistance." Everyday resistance is usually composed of individual acts by private individuals lacking formal organization. It includes such acts as pilfering small items from a company one works for in response to low wages. Unusual resistance is characterized by a group of individuals with a chosen leadership and an agreed upon central target of opposition. Though unusual resistance benefits from the added organization, its members are also more visible to their targeted opposition and can be more vulnerable to disciplinary measures than everyday resistors. The students which comprise Dead Poets Society II celebrate resistance without the benefit of calculated actions toward a collective goal. The group also lacks what Michel de Certeau refers to as "tactics," or those acts which resemble guerrilla warfare and lack predictable sites and centers of activity (Sleeter & McLaren, 1995). Distinct from "strategies," which belong to a category of surveillance, tactics escape the gaze of official power through indeterminate strikes. Without the benefit of a discourse extending beyond a celebration of transgression and conceptions of self, students lack the political power to produce "bodies without organs" (Deleuze & Guattari, 1983). By bodies without organs, Deleuze and Guattari do not suggest bodies without hearts, lungs, and stomachs. As opposed to "full bodies," bodies free from *organ*izational territories of desire involve the discharge of institutions as excrement from humans as desiring-machines. In the film, this is semiotically accomplished when Todd vomits on the vast whiteness of snow after he learns of Neil's death. Todd's body rejects what his social conditions have made of him, a docile body. After the discharge, Todd runs wildly away, his screams reverberating against the still trees and into the white darkness of the field at dawn, as he finally lets out his barbaric "yawp."

Members of Dead Poets Society II feel they are challenging the status quo without actually transforming asymmetrical relations of power. Their actions fail to move beyond the pleasure of resistance for its own sake. Resistance at Welton takes the form of a personal revelation rather than a rebellion and actually serves to reify the alienation of the students through their absorption of the mere facticity and inevitability of defeat into their very conception of themselves. In Bakhtinian socio-linguistics, the students participate in a pseudo-carnival, a bourgeois excursion on the wild side. In Stam's (1993) words,

> Carnival in our sense is more than a party or a festival; it is the oppositional
> culture of the oppressed, the official world as seen from below; not the

mere disruption of etiquette but the symbolic, anticipatory overthrow of oppressive social structures. On the positive side, it is ecstatic collectivity, the joyful affirmation of change, a dress rehearsal for utopia. On the negative, critical side, it is a demystifying instrument for everything in the social formation that renders collectivity impossible: class hierarchy, sexual repression, patriarchy, dogmatism and paranoia. (135)

Welton students have an easy time affirming the positive side of carnival. They welcome the liberationist opportunities and controlled *jouissance* that Keating opens up for them: e.g. the tearing out of book pages, the standing atop their desks, and the cave meetings. However, they fail to self-reflect on the challenges to carnival. They fail to understand how the social logic of dominant society is actually inscribed and enfolded in the ambivalent vicissitudes of their daily life. Keating fails to enact a pedagogy that provides students with a critical vernacular which could distance them from their pleasure in participating in the act of refusing authority. Occupying a privileged linguistic capital, Charlie seduces Gloria and Tina with lines from a sonnet created, according to Keating, to "woo women." The young women's apparent amazement at Charlie's poetic sensibilities, albeit plagiarized from original authors, suggests their uneducated class background. In another scene, Charlie creates a spectacle of sexual repression when he relays a phone message from God to principal Nolan, saying "It's God. He says we should have girls at Welton." In other instances, students objectify women as sexual exploits or subject them to the male gaze, as in Knox's fixation with Kris during the pep rally. Subsequently, after having been discovered to be a Dead Poets Society II member, Cameron advises the rest of the group to cooperate with the administrators in scapegoating Keating.

Ultimately, and with Keating's assistance, the students fail to bridge Bacchic revelry with Bakhtinian transgression. They lack the ability to articulate a political project which extends beyond the celebration of self to include the transformation of their social conditions. Keating's concept of agency is ultimately naive. He seems unable to grasp the idea that real relations declare their own meanings unambiguously within the regime of the "taken-for-granted" yet are still ideological because they can only be understood within certain systems of representation. Had Keating been able to engage his students in ideology critique, he would have been able to assist them in understanding their misrecognition of themselves. Keating retains an exaggerated belief in autonomous agency and in the novelty and ludic power of personalistic transgression. In doing so, Keating simply enacts one of the most recurring *topoi* of modern education, the rejection of sameness and routine, and the celebration of the new.

Keating fails to consider how individuals are differentially enabled to act by virtue of the economic and cultural constraints they face, and by virtue of the privileging hierarchies constructed out of the discourses of race, ethnicity, class, gender, and sexual orientation. Furthermore, he fails to recognize how knowl-

edge is socially and historically constructed, and how individuals are syne-
chochically related to the wider society through asymmetrical relations of
power and privilege. Keating's position denies and obscures the politics of difference. While Keating rightly and admirably seeks to imperil the familiar, to
unsettle the certainty of Welton's sovereign regime of truth, and to render problematic the regulatory apparatuses within which proper behavior and comport-
ment and social interactions are analyzed, he is unable to analyze how student
subjectivities are rationalized and accommodated to existing regimes of truth
and social divisions of labor. Because Keating appears to adopt a quasi-
Durkheimian view according to which the social order is integrated by way of
an organic solidarity, he fails to consider sufficiently how individuals are
formed out of competing solidarities that overlap and are conflictual. Keating's
resistance is just another way of rewriting ethnocentrism as a defense of
Western civilization. He subsumes and simplifies diverse political and cultural
forms of resistance and celebrates unwittingly the ideology of individualistic
transgression which reinforces the very traditionalism and ethical quietism
which he is trying to subvert.

We are not arguing that personal responsibility should be erased by collective responsibility. Critical pedagogy requires the cultivation of a receptivity
towards a·dialogue that is rooted in everyday sensuous existence in the communal world. Such a dialogue is neither rooted in collectivism nor a Nietzschean
act of individual self-realization but rather in a community of learners which is
fundamentally dialogical. While Keating recognizes that the school requires
atomized individuals but cannot tolerate interpersonal relations based on free
association, he is unable to create a genuine community based on an openness
to the other. This is because his pedagogical dialogism is still trapped in the idea
of the self-sufficient, Cartesian cogito. He fails to notice the necessity of the
presence of the other in the self. His assertion of "seize the day" is ultimately an
arrogant conceit, a dogmatic postulate premised on the autonomous, self-centered ego. Peak experiencing by "sucking the marrow out of life" is constituted
dialogically, accompanied by the multiple consciousness of a self-other relation.
For Keating, "seize the day" becomes an enunciative act celebrating the single
consciousness and monologic desire that suppresses an understanding of the
ethical power of the self-other relation.

In fact, Keating's "essence of man" humanism ultimately betrays the boys.
His pedagogy embodies a notion of liberation which ends with the self that
merely needs to be recovered and not with the continuous transformation of
material conditions (Althusser, 1965). Humanism is limited by its reduction of
people as free and rational. It purports that through the law of reason, liberation
is realized as a fact of human nature and is an anticipated yet pre-existing
essence. Humanism, to Althusser, involves a fallacious double move characterized by an empiricist-idealist epistemology. It assumes, in one movement, that
if human essence is universal, then it necessitates a given that individuals are
concrete subjects: hence an empiricism of the subject. In another movement,

humanism locates the essence of humanity in every individual: hence an ideal-ism of the essence. Both movements affirm the individual at the cost of the col-lective. However, a negation of humanistic universals is not the same thing as a rejection of the conditions of its historical necessity as a discourse with material consequences. Humanism is a symptom of the overall social formation and its determinations. As a result of the film's classical humanism, resistances are iso-lated from one another. For instance, Charlie speaks for himself when he invites Gloria and Tina to the cave and then implicates the group during his antics in the chapel. He never fully negotiates his position with others toward a collective solidarity; resistance becomes a private decision. Consequently, it is relatively easy for administrators, teachers, and parents to "divide and conquer" the DPS II. Also, we empathize with Neil as an individual in anguish without connecting him with Charlie or the others. Neil seems to suffer alone. As a group, the stu-dents never fully shatter the micro-technological gaze that Welton's sentinels of truth and custodians of tradition use to discipline the students. This is best illus-trated when Nolan, the principal, announces that he aims to indict the culprits responsible for inserting an "unauthorized article" in the school newspaper. He warns, "Rather than spending my valuable time, ferreting out the guilty persons, [pause; tone of voice lowers] . . . and let me assure you I will find them . . . I'm asking any or all students who know about this article to make themselves known now." Isolated from one another, the subversives are cut off from each other, depotentiated as a body politic. Their resistance is regulated under the super*vision* of Nolan and company.

The film leaves unproblematized the different faces of oppression by isolat-ing one type: student oppression. The discourse on students lacking a voice in school is emphasized at the expense of gender oppression. Indeed, the film's portrayal of women during a cave meeting does not transcend their stereotypical role as sexual objects. Kris is in constant fear that her boyfriend-protector, Chet Danbury, will discover Knox's persistent effort to steal her from him. Kris is caricatured as Chet's possession. Kris is seen as morally powerless to judge Knox's actions according to her own ethical standards; she must look to Chet for accountability. Charlie contradicts his own wishes for emancipation when he attempts to seduce Gloria and Tina with the very same (Shakespearean) sonnets that the group recites during cave meetings in order to feel liberated from their teachers. This dialectic of consciousness raising points out the contradictions inherent in what we see as a discourse lacking a self-reflective apparatus.

As McLaren (1991) has said elsewhere, compared to the dictatorial approach involving rote learning and severe military-style discipline that is used by most teachers at Welton, the classroom approach used by Keating is very innovative—you could call it liberal and not be wrong—and amounts to shatter-ing mainstream conventions in the school. The students find Keating to be a charismatic leader, if not a liberating one. One of the problems that we have with this form of pedagogy is that it suggests that self-empowerment can exist without calling into question the existing capitalist social order. Issues of class, gender, and ethnic inequality are never raised. In fact, we would go so far as to claim that this form of liberal, humanist pedagogy serves to contain the political, to discursively police revolt, to equate liberation with the personal over the social, and to mask forms of domination. It is a pedagogy steeped in the romance of word at the expense of the world. This is revealed in the sexism of Keating, who claims that poetry was invented to "woo women." The students are conspicuously not invited to problematize the relationship among the authoritarianism in the school, the way power works in the larger society to silence certain groups, and its entanglements in social practices which serve the rich and the powerful.

Jim Berlin (1987) would refer to this as a form of "expressionistic rhetoric": although it includes a denunciation of economic, political and social pressures to conform—to resist the institutionally sponsored production of desire, attitude, and behavior—it is resistance in the service of the privatized ego, and the privatized male ego at that. As Berlin notes, expressionistic rhetoric reinforces the entrepreneurial virtues of individualism, private initiative, risk-taking, and subversion of authority. It is the ideology of the unique, private vision of a Donald Trump buried in the tropes of Walt Whitman, devoid of a concern with how material and social constraints prohibit other, less fortunate groups from realizing their private vision. It is as if consciousness were somehow not connected to the workings of power or as if hierarchies of power and privilege were natural hierarchies. As a teacher, Keating attempts to defamiliarize the experience which the students have of rote learning and blind obedience to adult authority and the ruling-class economies of power and privilege, and while he is intent, perhaps even insistent, on getting beyond the deformation of the individual as authorized by the discourses of tradition and the prevailing regimes of truth of the time, the result is a struggle for uniqueness—perhaps even eccentricity—of individual expression. Jim Berlin describes this kind of subversiveness as more apparent than real. It is debilitatingly divisive of political protest because it encourages individuals to achieve unique personhood in antiseptic isolation from any sense of collective struggle around the referent of difference and otherness. It is a pedagogy which operates without consideration of how power works to privilege certain groups over others on the basis of race, class, and gender, and Keating takes no pains to narrate the contingency of his own and the students' race, class, and gender privilege.

This is a soft mode of resistance easily co-opted by those forces it seeks to delegitimate; a form of resistance which actually complements the capitalist ethos of possessive individualism. In Terry Eagleton's (1990) terms, Keating's pedagogy is a form of moral technology which structures modes of desire that the society needs in order to promote capitalist social relations. It teaches what he terms a "bourgeois mode of subjectivity" precisely in the way it celebrates learning for the sake of learning, and creativity for its own sake, which is a mistaken virtue we believe, because creative learning never speaks for itself and is always inscribed by political interests and supported by relations of power.

There is a certain creativity to the Nazis' "final solution" that we dare say no teacher would ever want her students to emulate. We are not arguing that liberal humanism was responsible for the holocaust, but we are arguing that freedom and creativity should always be understood in relation to the social context in which they are engendered and put to use. Critical pedagogy poses a crucial question: Freedom and creativity for what?

Mas'ud Zavaradeh's (1994) critique of the liberal humanist classroom can be appropriately applied to the pedagogy of *Dead Poets Society*. Keating's pedagogy reveals itself as one of "fancy"—what Zavaradeh's calls a "pedagogy of pleasure." Keating's notion of liberation is personal and eminently ahistorical, and has little to do with emancipation. It is a pedagogy formally "at odds" with the "serious" workaday bourgeois world but which does not seriously question the underlying assumptions or relations of power which inform it. Questions involving power/knowledge relations are suspended, and dangerous memories of human suffering and rebellion are never raised. We leave our students with the following questions in relation to the pedagogy represented in the film: What vision of the future inheres in th pedagogy of *Dead Poets Society*? What vision of social justice? What model of the individual subject? What suppositions involving democracy? We believe that the more we attempt to clarify what we mean by "critical pedagogy," the more we will be given opportunities for discussing and elaborating the values, suppositions, and basis for practice which inform our teaching, learning, research practices, and, perhaps most important of all, the vision of the future which inheres in them.

Dead Poets Society inspires its viewers to resist oppression in schools. Through Keating, the power of a transgressive pedagogy offers alternative ways of looking at education. Keating encourages the viewer to stand within different planes of vision in order to look at the familiar from new frames of reference, or in Rorty's (1979) terms, to search for more "edifying" ways to tell stories about the world. However, the film falls short of moving beyond bourgeois forms of resistance and into a political project. The students experience moments of *jouissance*. By the end, one senses that some aspects of the school's culture have changed without transforming the culture of power. This is not an altogether hopeless state of affairs. Sporadic jolts to the system may give rise to larger political movements (Bottomore, 1993). However, without a critique of language and a language of critique, Welton students lack a powerful tool for cultural emancipation and social liberation. They are limited by the structures of signification within the discourses that they occupy.

At the film's conclusion, the viewer witnesses a triumphalistic moment as the students stand proudly atop their desks and hail their leader, Keating: "Oh captain, my captain." In solidarity, the subversives stand side-by-side. Yet if we slice through the cloud of emotions, we are left hopeful but ambivalent about their plight. A collective oppositional discourse offers hope for social justice. We can only wish that these examples of individual strands of disenchantment and resentment gradually entwine themselves into a collective struggle. Without a public, counter-hegemonic coalition, students do not muster enough power to challenge the dominant discourses of their school. What may result is their heightened marginalization.

Students who viewed *Dead Poets Society* with us were initially enthusiastic about the film. Some saw it as a definitive representation of an embodied critical pedagogy. Virtually no students were able to discern the distinction between critical pedagogy as articulated by Freire and other criticalists, and liberal bourgeois pedagogy vis-à-vis Keating. We began discussions of the film by asking students to compare their own experiences as high school students with those of the students in the film. We also asked our students to evaluate Keating's pedagogical practices in light of their pedagogical imperatives and characteristics that they would like to embody in their own teaching practices. We found that the charismatic portrayal of Keating by Robin Williams made it difficult to separate Keating's engaging personality from the pedagogical philosophy he appeared to embrace in the film. Students admired Keating's nonconformist teaching practices and described them as desirable attributes for a teacher to possess. Our attempts to contrast Keating's pedagogy with what we had been reading about critical pedagogy was described as an expression of "militant Marxism" or "dogmatic social viewpoints" by some students. Other students reacted by saying that a single teacher "can do little more than reach out to help students on an individual basis." This was followed by a reaction that stressed the vulnerability of the critical pedagogue in terms of sanctions by the administration for supporting "biased political viewpoints." In short, we found that our students reacted to our pedagogy in much the same way as Keating's students in the film did to him: they were initially hesitant, cautious, and skeptical.

After discussing with students various readings in critical pedagogy and developing with them a working vocabulary of critical terminology, students were able to point to many of the limitations in Keating's pedagogical philosophy and praxis. Critical pedagogy was identified in the final instance as the production of a pedagogical locality which can be characterized as a situated community of dialogical learners. Such a community is dedicated to generating the context for dialogical praxis whereas in mainstream pedagogies, schooling is produced or driven by the already existing context provided by the nation-state. That the students were able to make this distinction is, in our minds, one of the most essential stems in understanding both the perils and the promise of critical pedagogy.

WORKS CITED

Althusser, Louis. *For Marx.* London and New York: Verso, 1965.
Appadurai, Arjun. *Modernity at Large: Cultural Dimensions of Globalization.* Minneapolis: U of Minnesota P, 1996.

Bakhtin, Mikhail. *The Dialogic Imagination.* Ed. M. Holquist. Trans. C. Emerson and M. Holquist. Austin: U of Texas P, 1981.

Baudrillard, Jean. *Simulations.* New York: Semiotext, 1983.

___ *Fatal Strategies.* New York: Semiotext. 1990.

Berlin, James A. *Rhetoric and Reality: Writing Instruction in American Colleges, 1900-1985.* Carbondale and Edwardsville: Southern Illinois U Press.

Blacker, David. "Teaching in Troubled Times: Democratic Education and the Problem of 'Extra People'?", *The Teacher Educator* 32 (1996): 62-72.

Bottomore, Tom. (1993). *Political Sociology.* Second edition. Minneapolis: U of Minnesota P.

Calhoun, Craig. "Social Theory and the Politics of Identity." *Social Theory and the Politics of Identity.* Ed. Craig Calhoun. Cambridge, MA: Blackwell, 1994.

Cohen, Sol. "Postmodernism, the New Cultural History, Film: Resisting Images of Education, *Pedagogica Historica: International Journal of the History of Education* 32 (1996): 395-420.

Deleuze, Gilles, and Guattari, Felix. *Anti-Oedipus: Capitalism and Schizophrenia.* Minneapolis: U of Minnesota P, 1983.

Durkheim, Emile. *Moral Education.* New York and London: Free Press, 1961.

Eagleton, Terry. *The Ideology of the Aesthetic.* Cambridge: Basil Blackwell, 1990.

Fiske, John. "The Culture of Everyday Life." *Cultural Studies.* Ed. Lawrence Grossberg, Cary Nelson, & Paula Treichler. New York and London: Routledge Publishers, 1992 154-73.

Foucault, Michel. *Discipline and Punish.* New York: Vintage Books, 1979.

Freire, Paulo. *Pedagogy of the Oppressed.* New York: Continuum, 1993.

Giroux, Henry & Simon, Roger. "Popular Culture as a Pedagogy of Pleasure and Meaning." *Popular Culture: Schooling & Everyday Life.* Ed. Henry Giroux and Roger Simon. Westport, CT: Bergin & Garvey, 1989. 1-29.

___ "Popular Culture and Critical Pedagogy: Everyday Life as a Basis for Curriculum Knowledge." *Critical Pedagogy, the State, and Cultural Struggle.* Ed. Henry Giroux and Peter McLaren. New York: SUNY, 1994. 236-52.

Goodman, N. *Ways of Worldmaking.* Indianapolis: Hackett Publishing Company, 1988.

Kant, Immanuel. "Critique of Judgment: First Book 'Analytic of the Beautiful.'" *Critical Theory Since Plato.* Ed. Henry Adams. New York: Harcourt Brace Jovanovich, 1970. 379-90.

Kerkvliet, Benedict. *Everyday Politics in the Philippines.* Berkeley: U of California Press, 1990.

McLaren, Peter. (1991). "Critical Pedagogy: Constructing an Arch of Social Dreaming and a Doorway to Hope." *The Sociology of Education in Canada* 173 (1991): 137-160.

___ "Postmodernism and the Death of Politics: A Brazilian Reprieve." *Politics of Liberation.* Ed. Peter McLaren & C. Lankshear. London and New York: Routledge, 1994. 193-215.

___. *Schooling as a Ritual Performance: Towards a Political Economy of Educational Symbols and Gestures.* London and New York: Routledge, 1993.

Montag, Warren. "What is at Stake in the Debate on Postmodernism?". *Postmodernism and its Discontents.* Ed. E. Kaplan. London and New York: Verso, 1993. 88-103.

Pagano, Joanne. "Matters of the Mind." *Critical Conversations in Philosophy of Education.* Ed. Wendy Kohli. London and New York: Routledge, 1995. 340-54.

Rorty, Richard. *Philosophy and the Mirror of Nature*. Princeton, New Jersey: Princeton U Press, 1979.

San Juan, Jr., E. *Articulations of Power in Ethnic and Racial Studies in the United States*. New Jersey and London: Humanities Press, 1992.

Shumway, David. "Reading Rock 'n' Roll in the Classroom: A Critical Pedagogy." *Critical Pedagogy, the State, and Cultural Struggle*. Ed. Henry Giroux and Peter McLaren. New York: SUNY, 1994. 222-35.

Sleeter, Christine, & McLaren, Peter. (1995). "Introduction: Exploring Connections to Build a Critical Multiculturalism." *Multicultural Education, Critical Pedagogy, and the Politics of Difference*. Ed. Christine Sleeter and Peter McLaren. SUNY, 1995. 5-32.

Stam, Robert. "Mikhail Bakhtin and Left Cultural Critique." *Postmodernism and its Discontents*. Ed. E. Kaplan. London and New York: Verso, 1993. 116-45.

Storey, John. (1993). *Cultural Theory and Popular Culture*. Athens: U of Georgia Press, 1993.

Zavaradeh, Mas'ud. *Theory as Resistance: Politics and Culture After (Post)structuralism*. New York and London: Guilford Press, 1994.

18 CUBA, YANQUIZACION, AND THE CULT OF ELIAN GONZALEZ
A VIEW FROM THE "ENLIGHTENED" STATES*

Peter McLaren and
Jill Pinkney-Pastrana

Using the recent controversy surrounding Elián Gonzalez as a centerpiece, and employing a Marxian critique of United States capitalism and imperialism as a heuristic device, this essay explores the major contradictions surrounding the position taken by the Miami Mafia with respect to Elián and Cuba's communist regime. In doing so, it criticizes the US media portrayal of the saga surrounding "the miracle child." Paramount in this controversy is the campaign of misinformation directed at creating an erroneous image of life in Cuba grounded in the reactionary and virulently negative critique continually waged against Cuba's postrevolution social project. The authors explore the role played by the "Miami Mafia," the anti-Castro Cuban exile population in the United States, in conjunction with official pro-capitalist, "anticommunist" government and media apparatuses designed to create an environment of defamatory rhetoric against the nation of Cuba. In doing so, the authors bring to the surface contradictions and injustices inherent in both the rhetoric and the reality of US capitalism. In addition, this essay highlights the many achievements of the Cuban socialist project, focusing specifically on education. The authors share a concern about Cuba's recent economic experiment and put forward an argument about why market socialism should not be a viable option.

A story in nine acts

ACT ONE: THE MIRACLE CHILD

Cubans became radicalized along with their Revolution as challenges and responses, blows and counter-blows between Havana and Washington fol-

---

*This paper is dedicated to President Fidel Castro and the heroic struggle of the Cuban people.

This chapter was originally published in the *International Journal of Qualitative Studies in Education, 14*(2), pp. 201-219. © 2001 Taylor and Francis, Inc. http:/www./tandf.co.uk.

lowed one upon the other, and as the Revolution proceeded to turn its promises of social justice into solid facts . . . . The Cubans themselves have learned that revolution is no evening stroll. But after all, if the future came on a platter, it would not be of this world. . . . The revolution is forced to sleep with its eyes open, and in economic terms this costs dearly. Constantly harassed by invasion and sabotage, it does not fall because—strange dictatorship!—it is defended by a people in arms. (Galeano, 1973, p. 90)

Much has been made in the global media of Elián Gonzalez, the six-year-old Cuban boy around whom a highly publicized international custody case evolved. Elián was one of only 4 survivors among a group of 15 Cubans whose dilapidated 16-foot boat—consisting of aluminum irrigation pipes soldered together, three inner tubes from Russian truck tires that dragged along the back, and an old 50-hp outboard motor—capsized while trying to reach Miami. Elián's mother was among the victims.

Elián has been described by religious pundits, politicians, and especially his Cuban-émigre "relatives" and fellow exiles as a "miracle child" (we note sardonically that around the same time as Elián was rescued and brought to live in the United States, a boat of 400 Haitian adults and children attempting to reach the United States was forced back to Haiti). He has become a celebrated international symbol in an ideologically charged struggle over the meaning of political justice and, to a certain extent, over the meaning of "truth." This struggle has been inflected with religious and political furor that has spilled over into the realm of public debate and political accusation. It is a drama that is played out largely in the theater of Cold War rhetoric, mostly from one side of the Manichean divide separating freedom-loving citizens of the United States from those forced to endure the penal colony conditions of Cuban life and who remain in the thrall of Cuba's leader, Fidel Castro—a variant on the Cold War canard that socialism equals totalitarianism.

Conversations instigated by the Elián controversy rarely are piquantly pleasant. More often than not they evoke a toxic mixture of political invective and moral exhortation. In what follows we explore the internal fault lines of pro-capitalist discourse surrounding the Elián Gonzalez controversy by raising the following questions: What are some of the salient social and political factors that have contributed to Elián's transformation into St. Lazarus's "Mini-Me"? How can this drama be rescued from its founding binarisms (good vs. evil, freedom vs. totalitarianism), removed from the ahistorical sloganeering generated by the US corporate media, and placed into a more dialectical theater of analysis? How can the Elián controversy be undressed of right wing rhetoric and transformed into a vantage point from which social and educational conditions in Cuba—such as those to which Elián has so dramatically returned—can be critically analyzed?

As we distance this story from the acid-tongued, anticommunist invective vomited up to the nation by propagandist scoundrels within Miami's Cuban exile community—who have held a monopoly on interpreting whatever tran-spires on the "red" island (supposedly the "last Stalinist holdout") for the past 40 years, and whose fulminations against liberal politicians are well known—we discover that Cuba evidences an intriguing commentary on socialist politics and offers an example of extraordinary advances, especially in the areas of health, agriculture, and education. This paper will explore the furor over Elián and examine the allegations that his return to Cuba will inevitably result in his sacrifice to the communist "brainwashing" machine.

Try as it might, the US media could not bury the fact that the 1998 vote by the United Nations condemning the US embargo was 157 to 2, but it could cam-ouflage the Cuban government's steadfast and unwavering commitment to the education and welfare of its children. Indeed, Elián's schoolteacher and four of his classmates joined him in the United States during the last weeks of his con-finement in order to help him begin his social adjustment back into his "normal" life as well as get caught up on missed lessons. Did the Cuban government's decision to send a teacher to Elián's side while he was in custody in the United States provide unmistakable evidence of the existence of a well-oiled scheme of communist mind control that many US citizens first learned about in James Bond movies? Was this young child, arguably the most important symbol of the revolution since Ernesto Che Guevara, in danger of being reduced to zombified pulp, courtesy of the Cuban state, in a manner redolent of the characters in the film, *The Manchurian Candidate*? Or might it simply be a sign of something far more profound? Could it be that the militant and uncompromising principles of the Cuban revolution serve as a central generative mechanism animating Cuba's functional commitment to equality through education to such a degree that they transcend international crises? Could it be true that, contrary to the "experts" on Cuba trotted out before a gullible US public on Fox TV and other "impartial" US television networks, in Cuba education is fundamentally important, and teachers are highly respected members of society responsible for the nurturing and formation of academically and socially prepared citizens? Does the Elián scandal reveal the weaknesses of corporate-driven education in the United States and its depth of *coupure* with social justice? Does the outcome of the Elián scandal signal the U.S. public's anomic rupture with the right-wing asser-tions of the Miami exile community?

Unlike other "communist" countries, Cuba has adhered strongly to an alter-native vision of national development highly critical of the capitalist free-mar-ket approach which, while boasting tremendous gains for the stock market and multinational corporations, has resulted in a vast and horrific process of social deterioration throughout much of the capitalist world system. Within the capi-talist West, the potential for gathering vast quantities of accumulated capital by means of fast-track, casino-style gangster capitalism based on deregulated mar-kets and finance capital remains counterposed against a poverty of democracy and the draconian and plutocratic measures of neo-liberal development that deprives millions of people of basic needs and their right to share in the wealth of their developing nations. The priorities chosen by Cuba reflect a commitment to all of the people on the island. For educators living in advanced capitalist nations they offer a new appreciation for the Cuban project but perhaps also give us cause to question our own blighted vision of Utopia, based on a "prime time" teledemocracy peppered by doses of jacuzzi liberalism and driven by fantasies of endless market consumption in theme-park vistas that stretch as far as the eye can see.

ACT TWO: BLESS THE CHILD

The human tragedy that began in November, 1999, with the shipwreck and survival of Elián Gonzalez, ushered an unprecedented flurry of activity, adding new vigor to the fading dreams of Miami's Cuban exile community. First, news reports claimed that Elián bore few traces of injury when he was rescued and that a "normal" child surely would have died from exposure. Dalrymple and Ciancio, who had rescued Elián, claimed that they had not planned to go fishing on the day of the rescue, leaving us to wonder if some kind of divine force had beckoned them. According to some reports, dolphins, who had been protecting the miracle child from swarming sharks, had pushed Elián in the direction of his rescuers. Cuban legends contain descriptions of dolphins guided by angels, and there is the popular story of Our Lady of Charity, which portrays the Virgin Mary protecting three fishermen lost at sea (Eliott, 2000). Elián reportedly "saw" angels hovering overhead and dolphins surrounding his inner tube—stories that were gleefully circulated by Dalrymple (Eliott, 2000). Yet some reports suggest that Elián did show signs of exposure and all three survivors were treated at local hospitals for dehydration and minor cuts—and all were listed in good condition (Eliott, 2000). Family members began to circulate stories of "seeing" the image of the Virgin Mary in the mirrors of their homes (*Miami Herald*, March 26 and 28, 200). These stories could be counted on to indulge a public always ripe for the supernatural. Elián's rescue at sea eerily evokes the journey of the infant Moses recovered from the Nile in a cradle built from reeds. As bizarre and implausible as these stories seem—recounted routinely by some residents of Miami as well as politicians and religious broadcasters across the United States—they do more than hint at the notion of divine intervention.

Of the floodtide of news clips that featured Elián's Sacred Diaspora from the island of tyrants and dictators to the land of milk and honey (360 Elián stories aired on network evening news in five months [Eliott, 2000]), some showed devout Cuban Catholic women in black shawls strategically placing religious artifacts at Lazaros's home when Elián was in his custody. Local artists made paintings of Elián ascending into Heaven, reaching toward the outstretched arms of Mary, Mother of God. Frenzied bystanders tried to reach over the fence of Lazaro's yard in order to touch the miracle child in the hope that such a touch might produce some kind of a magical effect. (Today you can purchase through the Internet items that were allegedly used by Elián, such as hair combs.) If the Miami exiles could have placed a wick on the crown of Elián's head and turned him into a votive candle, they would have. In their feckless defense of American "democracy", the Miami Mafia turned the Statue of Liberty upside down, revealing its soiled undergarments, not to mention the warts and blisters upon which the weight of "*gusano* democracy" precariously rested. The drama revealed that this democracy had an odor more in common with a port-o-potty than a rosegarden.

Elián's relatives were shown as tireless defenders of freedom in their attempts to prevent him from returning to Cuba, the "land of evil," where president Fidel Castro was ideologically conjured as a monster capable of infanticide who, like the Biblical Herod, might try to "disappear" the miracle child. The US public was treated by the media to descriptions of the United States that amounted to little more than a bourgeois panegyric to a blessed and harmonious social order where "free" men and women were able to pursue and achieve their dreams—Sunday barbecue depictions of a 19th-century polis founded upon class collaborationist economic prosperity, a democratically engineered cultural unity, and personal security.

ACT THREE: PROTECT US FROM THE DEVIL AND HIS MINIONS

It would not be that far-fetched to conclude that the Cuban exile community in Miami functions collectively and cohesively as an integrated anticommunist lobby when it comes to proselytizing against Fidel Castro and the Cuban revolution (although the Elián affair admittedly took away some of its political ballast in Washington, much of the political power of Miami's Cuban Right was dramatically evidenced in the many scandals surrounding the presidential elections of 2000). Surely, few Cuban Americans, especially after their decades-long cohabitation with the petty-bourgeois thinking that has drooled out of the White House, would object to being called "anti-Castro Cubans" and would most likely embrace vigorously their role as the spearhead of open capitalist counterrevolution. Michael Moore implicates the militant, right-wing Miami exile community in a long list of politically corrupt actions (the Kennedy assassination, Watergate, Iran-Contra) and links this not only to the fact that many of them were supporters of comprador leader and ruthless dictator, General Fulgencio Batista, but also to their elitist and racist social physiognomy (Moore, 1997, pp. 177, 179, as cited in Cole, 1998, p. 148). When TNS agents in body armor grabbed Elián from the clutches of his so-called Miami "family", who were reportedly being guarded by members of the militant anti-Castro group, Alpha 66, the Miami Mafia was outraged. After all, for the past 40 years the Miami Mafia had been given the unrestrained opportunity to create in Little Havana a version of Batista's Cuba. They had been restlessly awaiting the chance to be installed again as the ruling class in Cuba after Fidel's death, when Cuba will supposedly fall to the warlords of capital. And since some of its esteemed members had served so diligently as loyal operatives for the CIA throughout Latin America, the Miami Mafia was not prepared for the US political bureaucracy to be so divided on the issue of Elián. While Senate Republican leader, Trent Lott of Mississippi, demanded a Congressional investigation, protesting that the INS raid could happen only in a place like Castro's Cuba, he was careful to make no mention of his association with the Council of Conservative Citizens, a virulent mutation of the KKK-infested White Citizens' Councils that had terrorized African Americans and activists in the South during the civil rights era. While New York City Mayor, Rudolph Giuliani, called the INS agents "stormtroopers," he failed to mention the stormtrooper squads of his own police force who killed Amadou Diallo, Malcolm Ferguson, and Patrick Dorismond, and those who continue to terrorize minority residents of the city. Indeed it is a burden to imagine that the rhetoric of democracy is often used to conceal the most heinous of crimes.

While the anti-Castro Miami Cubans undeniably function as a powerful political lobby, to what extent could the extremists among the Miami Mafia also be considered, metaphorically speaking, as members of a political cult, where ideology functions (as it so often has functioned historically) as a form of ideological imperialism linked to the imperatives of the capitalist state? Part of the answer lies both in its system of values and the know-it-all certitude of its beliefs that are constantly counterpoised to the "evil" empire of Cuba, and the matter-of-fact means by which such values are inculcated. We maintain that as the Miami Mafia continue to complain about communist brainwashing practices being employed against Elián by Cuban government operatives, including his father, they themselves are participating in the "industria del mal" (Lopez, 2000) and in ideological practices that serve to promote capitalist democracy and "furies of private interest." The ideological "forms of capture" that prevail among the Miami Mafia represent a type of fusionist triad of conservative Catholic values, pro-laissez faire capitalism, and terroristic anticommunism" (see Berlet, 1998). While it is difficult to say how much the Miami Mafia reflects the New Right's moral traditionalism, which is grounded in mainly northern European versions of traditional (Protestant) Biblical values—given that the majority of Miami Cubans are overwhelmingly devout Catholics—many of their spokespersons do mirror the "deep structure" of New Right rhetoric, articulated around the following characteristics: an apocalyptic millennialist narrative of the United States as God's chosen nation-state and defender of truth, whose efforts at world salvation are being thwarted by the Red Menace; the polarizing themes of good and evil; and forms of demonization and scapegoating that conflate church and state, especially in their traditional portrayal of communism. Post 9/11, this venomous discourse clearly defines the national rhetoric surrounding the "War on Terror." In choosing to send the miracle child back to Fidel Castro, Attorney General, Janet Reno, has abrogated the principles of US democratic justice and God's will, and has now become a torchbearer of liberal Godlessness, and a card-carrying member of Satan's Corps. The Miami Mafia has all but ostracized supporters of revolutionary Cuba, and even ghettoized those who adhere to moderate political views surrounding Cuba. Chip Berlet notes in this regard that "One of the core ideas of the fundamentalist Christian Right during this century has been that modern liberalism is a hand-maiden for collectivist, Godless communism. Many conservative Christian anti-communists believe that collectivism is Godless, while capitalism is Godly" (1998, p. 14). Many members of the Miami Mafia have personal memories of their lands being taken from them by the "barbarian guerrillas," and the historical memory of Miami's exile community is constantly being reinforced by the examples of Cubano/as fleeing the island, of people starving in the streets, and of human rights repression in Cuba today.

The cost of misinformation and the strengthening of the hegemony of right-wing discourse, exemplified by leading exponents of the Cuban exile community, has been considerable, both in the United States and in Cuba. In their excoriating message to Fidel Castro that Cuba's God-given destiny is to be rehabilitated by capital, do the Miami exiles organized around the Fundacion Nacional Cubano Americano, forget their own history? Do they forget the 1901 Platt Amendment, which gave the United States the right to restrict Cuban sovereignty in foreign affairs, the 1903 Reciprocity Treaty that tied Cuba's trade into a dependent relationship with the United States economy, and the virtual confiscation of the Cuban economy by the United States (Cole, 1998)? Cuban-Americans who may refuse to condemn Cuba and the revolution, who may wish to refunction democracy so that it serves the interests of socialism, and who may harbor alternative visions or perspectives of their homeland, are constantly harassed and relegated to the status of traitors and outcasts. Daring to break with the hardcore party line of the Miami Mafia frequently leads to violent confrontations. Many within the exile community are still furious over the loss of privileges enjoyed during the pre-revolution Batista regime. The loss of freedom of expression and freedom of information surrounding what is publicly said about the Cuban revolution and the current Cuban reality should worry United States citizens. Furthermore, it should provoke them to carefully scrutinize the paucity of information imbedded within the one-sided and ideologically-charged dogma emanating from the bars, restaurants, coffee houses, schools, and country clubs of South Florida, a Dixiecrat dogma that raspingly echoes throughout the chambers of a hypercapitalist, anticommunist, House of Representatives. Thanks to the Freedom of Information Act and the Internet, United States citizens and the rest of the world (at least those who can get access to the information) can now read the declassified CIA reports detailing economic and political atrocities waged against the national sovereignty of Cuba. Led by members of the Cuban exile community and represented by groups such as the Cuban-American Foundation, these anti-Castro attacks (both past and current) radiate the white heat of Cold War jingoism and capitalist greed.

The time-honored practice of selective dishonesty about socialist regimes that permeates the media is perfectly exemplified in the United States' relationship with Cuba. Anti-Castro public opinion surrounding the reality of life in Cuba is strategically engineered by means of a complex web of lies concocted by the Cuban American Foundation, aggravated by Cold War fears, disseminated with staggering propagandist finesse by the corporate media, promoted by relentless pro-capitalist lobbyists through out the country, and supported by petty-bourgeois government spokespersons. The Elián scandal has not only provided an opportunity to reopen the public's interest in Cuba that had lapsed in recent years, it has also opened the door to a rethinking of our disturbing, disingenuous, and reactionary foreign policy towards Cuba.

The monopoly on information concerning Cuba, which up until now has largely consisted of prime pickings from the ideological refuse heap of information conjured up by the Miami exile community and supported by the United Stated government—always eager to reinvest in the Cold War—is bent on the continual demonization of Fidel Castro and the hellification of that prickly anti-capitalist state so close to our sovereign shore. The anti-Castro cultists seek their salvation in capitalist market doctrine and their undiminished and militant faith in the frictionless character of its market laws. Such a position removes the inconvenience of having to undress such laws so as to reveal their inner workings and to evaluate the consequences of such laws in the lives of millions of poor and suffering children. It excuses them from the burden of insight into how the United States, as global imperialism's alpha male, rapaciously enforces those laws. The received doctrine of the market with its principles of classical market theory and its market value program are upheld at any price, even if it means sacrificing some people as "disposable" and, as John McMurtry notes, even if it means accepting that people will starve to death if they are not hired for profitable use in an oversupplied labor market. Here the barbarous nature of capital is vivisected and laid bare by McMurtry's Marxian analysis of its laws of motion.

Lost among the Miami Mafia is the idea that exploitation and class struggle are grounded in the objective requirements of capitalism, and in the political economy of capitalist democracy itself. Elite-based polyarchies operating as a transnationalized state work to consolidate ideological-cultural practices—and it is the combined effects of these practices that is the real wizard behind the glittering facade of OZ (see McLaren, 1999a, 1999b; McLaren & Farahmandpur, 1999a, 1999b; Robinson, 1996).

As Fidel Castro announced recently at the Group of 7 South Summit:

> Globalization has been held tight by the patterns of neoliberalism; thus, it is not development that goes global but poverty; it is not respect for the national sovereignty of our states but the violation of that respect; it is not solidarity amongst our peoples but *sauve qui peut* (every man for himself). . . . In the hands of the rich countries, world trade is already an instrument of domination, which under neoliberal globalization will become an increasingly

useful element to perpetuate and sharpen inequalities as well as a theater for strong disputes among developed countries for control over the present and future markets. . . . (2000, pp. 150, 154, 158, 159)

The Cuban leader has bravely exhorted Third World nations to liberate themselves from their financial peonage and subservience to the United States by unilaterally canceling their debts. Those nations that run the risk of being unable to qualify for short-term credit to fund imports could have their overseas accounts frozen, their assets seized, and their export markets closed (Parenti, 1995). A question rarely asked by the Miami-based adherents of this market theodicy is the price exacted in order to live in a truly "free and efficient market." In other words, what is the price that one pays for not selling one's labor to a master? Those who choose not to follow this fundamentalist market theology and its accompanying declaration of human freedom face a continual struggle for survival. In their celebration of bourgeois parvenus, and in taking up the cudgels of right-wing critique, the Miami Cultists fail to question a claim made by philosopher John McMurtry (1998), that "freedom" in capitalist democracy lies within the moral commandments of the market's rule, in particular, the command that no one is to interfere with its smooth, unfettered movement. This command takes on even more world-historical import, given the current crises of global capitalism.

ACT FOUR: SERVING THE DARK GODS OF CAPITAL: THE ARCHEOLOGY OF EVIL

McMurtry describes capitalism's value program as informed by a totalitarian master discourse in which the ultimate vehicle of value is the corporate person, and the ultimate measure of value is money profitability. In other words, what increases corporate revenues and profits, on the one hand, is perceived as good and to be approved and what decreases corporate revenues and profits is bad and to be condemned. He claims that this prescriptive duality of Good and Bad is no less absolute and binding than religious commandments. Our argument is that the "free market" decrees absolute commandments of nonintervention. The "invisible hand," that lies at the center of market command and to which all must submit, is, in reality, the blocfortunes of several hundred billionaires who own as much wealth as almost half the globe's population put together, the interlocking directorates of multinational corporations, and global intrafirm trading empires that dominate the market's base of supply and demand. These ruling positions of the global market hierarchy participate in a regulating paradigm of mind and reality in which the ultimate value system supporting democracy comprises the laws of capital accumulation, which seemingly exist prior to and independent of society. In other words, they ARE the laws of nature and of God (McMurtry, 1998).

While Margaret Thatcher's TINA acronym (There is No Alternative) seemingly has captured the attitude of most government pundits in the industrialized West towards free trade, free enterprise, and market-based economies, neoliberalism does not yet constitute an inevitable future for the planet (Azad, 2000). The challenge that progressive citizens face is truly a daunting one. What is most frightening about these "new times" is that most governments the world over are allowing—even encouraging—the market to make major social and political decisions. Correlatively, trade unions are under attack and citizens increasingly are told that their own social protection is a liability created by the myopia of Keynesian economics and bad for the health of the global economy—hence, the world-at-large—and that economic salvation can occur only when elites and corporations allow everything public to be privatized. We are told that democracy will flourish only when the market mechanism is firmly embedded in the structural unconscious of advanced capitalist countries and when the corporate priesthood is allowed to reap profits at historically unprecedented levels while the numbers of the poor in all countries increase in proportion to the internationalization of competition, the remuneration of capital to the detriment of labor, the downsizing of the public sector—where union support is strongest—and the privatization of "natural monopolies" such as public services. Neoliberalism relies on a social Darwinist philosophy that blames the poor for their poverty. Neoliberalism justifies eliminating nonunionized jobs by arguing that unions are ultimately self-serving and harm the economy. It supports overall job reduction because the few workers you have, the less they will impinge on shareholder value (George, 2000, p. 5). During the 1980s the top 10% of U.S. families increased their average family income by 16%, the top 5% of families increased their income by 23%, and the top 1% celebrated a 50% increase. The bottom 80% all lost something; the bottom 10% of U.S. citizens lost 15% of their incomes (George, 2000).

Today, in the United States, nearly US$200 billion is spent each year on advertising. Globally, advertising spending exceeds the growth of the world economy by one-third (Morgan, 2000). In fact, people live on behalf of—or die as a result of—their allegiance to the signs and symbols of corporate life. For instance, the Nike "swoosh" has more power than the flags of numerous nations, as decisions made in the boardrooms of some of the world's leading transnational corporations affect the fate of a growing number of governments. Of the 100 largest economies in the world, 51 are now global corporations, while 49 are national states (Morgan, 2000).

The value system of the market doctrine before which Miami's anti-Castro cultists kneel in reverence supports the efforts of free marketeers and global carpetbaggers to harass, to torture, and to murder union and community organizers who fight for legislative protection of citizen rights. Do these Cultists for Capital know that they are supporting a value system that is purposively eroding job security and protection from hazardous working conditions? The Miami cultists have attempted to inject their anti-Castro invective into a pro-American discourse, without revealing that the source of their hatred towards the Cuban government is the fact that their class privileges, their property ownership and their accompanying ability to exploit the poverty-stricken who labored under the murderous iron fist of Batista, were unceremoniously taken away by the revolution. Fidel Castro will never be forgiven for closing down the casinos and brothels and nationalizing all business, depriving the US Mafia and US-based multinationals of a profitable cash cow. He will never be forgiven for surviving the many assassination attempts (that some claim number in the hundreds) carried out by the CIA. In their paeans directed at Elián, the miracle child, the anti-Castro cultists deflect attention from the 40-year economic war waged against the people of Cuba. The blockade imposed by the United States denies food, medicine, and other supplies whose lack the cultists rejoice in pointing out in endless tirades condemning conditions of poverty in Cuba.

Capital breathes most freely the more ruthlessly its overseers succeed in mystifying the population. Criticisms of capitalism and capital are so far removed from the hegemonic centers of knowledge production that they seem uncomfortably out of place in a bourgeois democracy such as ours. Especially in the United States, capital has entrenched itself into the very subjectivities of its servant population, perhaps due to the fact that commodity exchange has been more valorized and spectacularized there than in any other country. What the process of commodity exchange eclipses from view is the value-form of labor. The value-form becomes "objectified' in a product, "condensed" into an object of exchange. The process of exchange is what, as quotidian observers, captures our view, and we are engineered to misrecognize social relations between people as a purely commercial exchange of things. It is not the machinations of the market (fluctuations in price) that is the important instrument of exploitation here, but the social relations of production that result from the materialization of human labor—from the productive relations. Concealed in the product of human labor is the value-relation made manifest through the process of exchange. But we need to undress the process of exchange and peer beneath its shimmering surface. To do so is to rupture the regulative dialectics of the bourgeois public sphere and capital's quest for self-certainty, peace of mind, and a safe public terrain from which to negotiate the working-class peace accord. The answer is not to transform exchange relations but to dismantle existing social relations of production—the very act of laboring itself. This acknowledges that the problem is within capital itself. The architects of the Cuban Revolution understood this. Present day revolutionaries in the field of critical pedagogy understand this too, as they fight for the collective ownership of the means of production by the associated producers by creating a federation of popular bodies organized worldwide.

ACT FIVE: SALVATION FROM THE FALLEN ANGEL OF CAPITAL

Cuba has developed a booming tourist industry, but it has refused to succumb to client state servitude. While it is true, notes Parenti, that tourists are given accommodations that few Cubans can afford, in pre-Revolutionary Cuba the profits from tourism were devoured by big corporations, generals, gamblers, and mobsters, while today the profits are divided between the foreign investors who build the hotels and the Cuban government so that the government can pay for health clinics, education, machinery, powdered milk, the importation of fuel, etc. (1995, p. 85). The people also benefit from the export earnings of Cuban coffee, sugar, tobacco, rum, seafood, honey and marble (Parenti, 1995).

Some critics on the left argue that it is possible to ameliorate the debilitating impact of globalization by forcing capital to become democratically accountable. They have suggested that while Cuba will likely not move towards a competitive market option, it may one day embrace a form of market socialism. We reject this option because the purpose of capital is to reproduce itself, and any effort to control capital without fundamentally transforming its basis of value production will only serve to strengthen capital and its power to exploit (Cole, Hill, McLaren, & Rikowski, 2000). Until value and surplus value are both targeted for elimination by social reformers and revolutionaries, capital will continue relentlessly to self-expand. Socialism's stringent rejection of class hierarchy is allied with its demand that all persons be provided with the conditions of creative and collective self- and social empowerment as they are transformed into subjects of history. While many socialists have tried over the years to control capital by ameliorating its more destructive capacities through the establishment of state planning or market socialism, these efforts have been limited because, even though the working class is granted an ontological primacy of place, value production is allowed to persist. Cuba is currently experimenting with changes in its economic structure. It is unclear to what extent this experiment could lead to the restoration of capitalism in Cuba (Alfonso, 2000). We agree with Dilla Alfonso that "Cuba has another opportunity to become an integral part of the shaping of an anti-capitalist project. This project, although having various national outlooks, can be viable only on an international scale" (2000, p. 40). Alfonso calls for a redesign of Cuba's political system that meets three requirements: "guaranteeing the unity of the Nation against imperialist interference, strengthening the popular subject and its organizations in the light of their increasing complexity, and taking social diversity into account on the basis of popular hegemony and the negotiated subordination of the emergent sectors not included under this rubric" (2000, p. 42).

Ken Cole provides a cogent explanation as to why market socialism is untenable as an option for Cuba, given Cuba's unwavering commitment to the principles of the revolution. Market socialism will not work because the social basis of exchange value is flawed; in fact, it is a fundamental contradiction in terms. Value cannot be evaluated in quantitative terms only. This is because value is a social relation—it is both qualitative and quantitative. What is valued is not just labor time but labor power (the abstract value of the concrete labor time that is worked). This, of course, will vary according to the social demand and social supply of the commodity that is produced as well as the laborer's control of the means of production. With a model of development founded upon commodity exchange, there will be qualitative changes in the value of the quantitative measure of labor time worked by wage labor, a value that varies with the process and practice of exploitation.

Cole argues that the terms of reference of the debate should be how the market and the state are integrated: the dialectic of the abstract labor theory of value. In doing so, Cole makes some important points. The well-known turning points in the evolution of the Cuban Revolution—the commitment to the Sistema de Dirección y Planificación de la Economía in 1970; the beginning of Poder Popular in 1974; the Rectification Campaign of 1986—have now given way to the challenge of socialist development in the face of the globalization of capitalism, structural adjustment policies of the WTO and IMF, the economic blockade and the collapse of Consejo de Ayuda Mutua Económica and the Eastern bloc states. Cole notes that socialist development in Cuba must include a skilled and empowered labor force that actively participates in the organization and purpose of production. This cannot happen, Cole notes, if Cuba allows itself to be a source of cheap labor to be exploited by foreign investment (i.e., the strategy of comparative advantage where national development strategy becomes a by-product of the fluctuation of international prices) or, in the longer run, if it becomes a reflex of the technocratic management of the economy through market socialization which simply adheres to the logic of commodity exchange through a "mixed economy" that works to ensure "the profitability of private enterprise and the income of a functionless class of rentiers" (Cole, 1998, p. 142). As Ellen Meiksins Woods argues:

> Once the market is established as an economic "discipline" or "regulator," once economic actors become market-dependent for the conditions of their own reproduction, even workers who own the means of production, individually or collectively, will be obliged to respond to the market's imperatives—to compete and accumulate, to let "uncompetitive" enterprises and their workers go to the wall, and to exploit themselves. . . . [W]herever market imperatives regulate the economy and govern social reproduction, there will be no escape from exploitation. There can, in other words, be no such thing as a truly "social" or democratic market, let alone a "market socialism." (1999, p. 119)

A socialist development strategy should be founded on participation through the institutions of the Poder Popular, moving beyond "The Special Period in Time of Peace," marked by shared shortages and austerity and economic decisions based on available resources. With the Rectification Campaign come new possibilities for asserting the political over the economic and extending the process of socialist development. For instance, Cole notes that horizontal links need to be made between enterprises as an antidote to vertical relations of planning and commercial decision making that is independent of social priorities. The defense of the class interest of the proletariat, which is increasingly threatened by exploitation through globalized commodity exchange, must be sufficiently flexible to adapt to the evolving needs and potentials of the Cuban people.

Cole emphasizes that the objective of a large-scale investment program must be premised on a strategy independent of imperialism, a strategy, in other words, of sustainable development and "widely distributed benefits for the people as a whole" (1998, p. 149). This implies decentralization and community participation as well as creative, sustainable technologies, respect for a diversity of ecosystems and societies, and an emphasis on social justice. What is clear is that Cuba must not adopt a comparative advantage investment strategy that would turn it into a low-wage, low-productivity economy and society where the imperatives of commodity exchange swallow the rational, participative imperatives of socialist development. As Cole warns, when commodity exchange underwrites the economy, power becomes concentrated in international agencies such as the World Bank and International Monetary Fund that worship at the altar of accumulation where the blood of the lamb protects only the rich. Here, consumer choice and the universal rule of property replaces the imperative of citizen's power and social justice. Again, market socialism is not an option, especially, as Cole notes, when nation-states are competing more ferociously than ever to attract foreign capital and when the powers of the state to manage the economy are being renegotiated, as the internationalization of capital grows stronger. The Cuban strategy must de-fund and decommission capital, putting the enterprises of the global robber barons into receivership with the larger purpose of decommodifying and destratifying everyday life. Unlike the former communist nations of Eastern Europe that no longer utilize the public sector to redistribute a (major) portion of the surplus value to the common people, who allow the productive surplus wealth to be pocketed by a few rich private owners, and who are returning the factories and lands to a rich capitalist class, Cuba continues to resist client-state servitude (Parenti, 1995).

ACT SIX: THE CORPORATE MEDIA MACHINE: SATAN'S INSTRUMENT OF PUSILLANIMOUS PROPAGANDA

The media constitute the greatest pedagogical device known to humankind. Their power lies in the fact that they play to the basic instincts of viewers and their visual catechism works best when its emotion is unvarnished and wiped clean of causal reasoning. The media were quick to report assertions that Elián's father was abusive (there was never a shred of evidence produced) but rarely mentioned the incident that took place outside the home of Elián Gonzalez's Miami relatives, when radio talk show host Scott Piasant of Portland, Oregon, display a T-shirt reading "Send the boy home" and "A father's rights," then was physically assaulted by a nearby exile crowd before police came to the rescue. The media also failed to report that two cousins who had spent time with Elián at the house of great-uncle Lazaro had been previously arrested on felony charges, including burglary, grand theft, robbery, petty larceny, and felony firearms and prowling charges. The public was also left in the dark as to the man responsible for directing much of the on-camera media coverage of Elián's Miami relatives, someone who is known in Miami for running dirty political campaigns (Macpherson, 2000).

Of course, in covering the Elián story, news commentators and reporters could have talked about what "freedom" means in the United States. For instance, they could have reported on how much more free pupils are in the United States to murder their classmates and, in the case of Florida and California, to be arrested and tried in the judicial system as adults. They could have talked about how less burdensome it is in the U.S. to establish a judicial system underwritten by racist and class-driven protectionism. They could have talked about how much easier it is for the US Government to plunder the world's resources in a demented effort to accumulate capital. They could have talked about how much easier it is in the United States for agents of the ruling class and its junior partners in imperialism to terrorize and punish working-class movements world-wide. They could have talked about how less difficult it is for African-Americans and Latino/as than for Euro-Americans to enter the penal system. Reporters seem to suffer memory loss when it comes to mentioning the numerous clandestine attempts by the US government to destabilize freely elected socialist regimes throughout Latin America and the Caribbean. They quickly forget the war crimes of Richard Nixon and Henry Kissinger and countless acts of imperialist aggression on the part of the US military and its NATO allies (Such as the recent destruction of Yugoslavia). There is also a motivated amnesia or structured silence surrounding the plight of Haitian refugees. As Michael Parenti reveals, Cuban refugees have been granted entry in the United States— enjoying special treatment through the extraordinarily lopsided "wet-foot," "dry-foot" policy, so named for the immigration law that allows Cubans immediate residency once their feet actually make contact with US soil, while Haitian refugees are routinely turned away. According to Parenti, "of the 30,000 Haitians who applied for political asylum in 1993 only 783 were accepted. Since many Cubans are white and almost all Haitians are black, some people have concluded that the differences in treatment can only be ascribed to racism" (1993, p. 85).

Providing context is not a big part of the media's function, which is to generate ballast for the existing status quo. All of these televised "memory lapses" can be best attributed to the value system that inscribes our everyday social life, values linked to the laws of the market. Viewed from the vantage point of the Miami exile community, the United States must surely betray a greater fidelity to God's will than any other country on the planet, considering its claim that its standard of living is the highest in the world. What would Gloria Estefan, or Andy García say to the charge that, given the disparity of wealth between the rich and the poor, the United States is the most unequal country in the world? We think we know the answer. What is perfectly clear is that the Miami exile community does not want a normalization of relations between the US and the Cuban government since the future of Cuba, must, in their view, be linked to their right-wing organizations in Miami. Regrettably, the media largely abandoned the Elián saga to the Manichean struggle between those who argue for family values (e.g., return Elián to his father) versus those who vehemently oppose communism (Elián must remain in the US because in Cuba's supposedly totalitarian regime he will lose his autonomy and become a member of the group mind).

Not surprisingly, the capitalist media mindset have systematically failed to acknowledge the many conditions that exist within this small island which challenge the model of capitalist development, from both a practical and a moral standpoint. While the US media have occupied themselves with a one-sided, decades-long attack on the mini "evil empire" and the "dictator" who eats children and practices black magic, other countries in the world—relatively free of the ideologically oppressive and violent force of the exile community—have enjoyed a more balanced consideration of the Cuban reality. Indeed, virtually all the countries in the world have engaged in trade and sociopolitical conversations with Cuba. Even within the United States there have always been various groups who, defamiliarized with their own anti-communist, pro-capitalist colonization, have fought the imperialist practices of US foreign policy and have attempted to cut the Gordian Knot that has tried to keep Cuba in a brutal reservation-style system, condemned to isolation, and stalked by poverty.

ACT SEVEN: HONK IF YOU SUPPORT CAPITALIST INVESTMENT AND SUPER-EXPLOITATION IN YOUR NATIVE COUNTRY, AND REPEAT AFTER ME: "GOD BLESS AMERICA"

While Washington has supported some of the world's most brutal right-wing counterrevolutionary groups, such as Savimbi's UNITA in Angola, RENAMO in Mozambique, the mujahideen in Afghanistan and Pinochet in Chile, it hypocritically and chauvinistically justifies its "embargo,"[1] sabotage, and other hostilities against Cuba as a reaction to the autocracy of the Cuban government and its human rights record. The real reason for US ire is that Fidel abolished private corporate control of the economy, nationalized US holdings, and made impressive gains in abolishing the clan structure through an emphasis on collectivization (Parenti, 1995). What other reason could account for the fact that the

U.S. would give most favored nation status to China, while at the same time condemning its human rights violations? Even though China is routinely condemned, it has been rewarded because it has "opened itself to private capital and free market 'reforms,' including enterprise zones wherein corporate investors can super-exploit the country's enormous and cheap labor supply with no worry about restrictive regulations" (Parenti, 1995, p. 84). In the final instance, it does not matter if a nation plays by the rules of democracy. If it is hostile to capitalism and refuses to open up its borders to foreign investors, it will be treated as a hostile nation by the United States. This is a constitutive feature of life in the world's mentor democracy.

ACT EIGHT: PEOPLE KEEPING THE FAITH IN THE PEOPLE

Cuba has developed many remarkable social advances despite the economic hardship that the island faces. The areas of education, health, and agriculture stand out as examples of Cuba's success in creating superior systems without the material wealth that defines the United States. Agricultural practices have been developed that utilize biologically friendly methods, free from the massive overuse of chemicals that has spurred on the "Green Revolution" (Shiva, 1991). Cuban agriculture is recognized by many as far superior, less expensive, and more "earth friendly" than the corporate agricultural model that is dependent on expensive pesticides, fertilizers, and biogenetically engineered seeds that have been developed by multinational US firms, such as Monsanto and Cargil. It is partly because of these agricultural practices, and partly because no US firms have ventured onto the island to exploit Cuba's natural wealth and biodiversity over the past 40 years, that Cuba remains an ecological paradise unequaled by any other Caribbean nation. One can only imagine the devastating consequences that an export-oriented capitalist development model, such as that championed by free market policy makers and followed by the rest of Latin America, would have had (and could have) on this fragile island ecosystem.

Not surprisingly, the Cuban exile Mafioso fail to mention that the health system in Cuba supports a population with free national medical coverage available to all of its citizens. This remains the case despite the severe limitations imposed by the longstanding blockade and the more recent Helms-Burton Act. Cuba is lacking many of the technological advances that define the North American and Western European healthcare systems, and does not have access to many of the designer medicines that have been developed by US pharmaceutical companies. Yet it boasts infant mortality rates lower than many sectors of the United States and a more equitable distribution system. In fact, Cuba is renowned for is own independently developed pharmaceuticals and medical treatments, so much so that travel for medical treatment to Cuba is a well-known source of income for the country. The recent case of Argentine soccer superstar, Diego Maradona (who proudly wears a tattoo of Che on his arm), underlines the international fame of Cuban medicine. Maradona, in urgent need of treatment for a series of medical problems, most stemming from his addiction to cocaine, chose treatment in Cuba over the United States. Another recent example is the case of a well-known Chilean politician, Andres Allamand, who served as the General Secretary of the ultra-right Renovación Nacional party during the early 1990s. Allamand sent his son to Cuba for medical treatment rather than to the more "developed" West. The case of Allamand seems hypo-critical when you consider that it has been the Chilean right that has enthusiasti-cally cut public expenditures in healthcare and embraced free-market reforms and the creation of the system of ISAPRES—the elitist healthcare/medical insurance system that defines access and coverage in the supposedly "advanced" Chilean medical system.

Perhaps the most impressive development of all in Cuba is the educational system. While many countries are succumbing to the pressure (as outlined by international development organizations, such as the World Bank and IMF) to follow a specific model of education reform, Cuba has stood alone in its contin-uing commitment to education as a fundamental human right enjoyed by all its citizens, a right that is guaranteed by a national educational system unsurpassed by any other Latin American country. This stands in stark contrast to the global trend in education reform of applying the logic of the free market to educational systems, thereby turning schooling into another means of production in an effort to improve capitalist development (Puiggrós, 1996). In the United States and elsewhere, we see this trend in the form of voucher proposals, the de-skilling of teachers, the move towards choice and charter schools, the continual push for national standards and testing, and teacher accountability measures, such as merit pay. All these policy reform trends reflect the free-market myth that gov-ernment bureaucracies can never function as efficiently as private enterprise. These criticisms of public schools and their accompanying formulae to fix the system through measures that encourage business-like competition among schools, reflect a weakening commitment to public schools and represents noth-ing less than a thinly veiled attack on public education itself.

In November of 1998, UNESCO released the initial results of a major com-parative study "Primer Estudio Internacional Comparative sobre Lenguaje, Matemáticas y Factores Asociados en Tercero y Cuarto Grado." A second report was released on July 18, 2000. According to the research discussed in these reports, the state of education throughout most of Latin America is at a dismal level. The 13 countries that participated in the study showed remarkably low lev-els of achievement in both math and language arts. According to the report:

The students exhibited a fragmentary comprehension of the reading process, they recognize the specific information within a text but they are not able to determine how the text says what it does or why. This indicates that in the region, children are learning to read but not to understand the significance of a text, neither to interpret what they are reading. They learn to read but not to learn reading. . . . The results of Math . . . are generally even lower and more unequal. The students have not assimilated the understandings nor have they developed mathematical competencies. They recognize signs and structures but with a poor capacity to solve simple mathematical problems of everyday life. (UNESCO, Segundo reportaje, July 2000, p. 11)

The results of this study report only one exception to these findings—education in Cuba.

In marked contrast to every other country in the region, Cuba showed remarkable levels of performance in both Math and Language Arts. The levels were so high as to have effected the median scores measured by the study. In a region where class inequities have contributed to degenerated public schools and an elite system of private educational institutions favored by Latin America's capitalist class, the Cuban educational system includes no private schools. Cuba has not experimented with excellence through competition, pitting schools with fewer resources against those in wealthier neighborhoods, and furthering the degeneration of schools in marginal sectors within urban and rural areas. Rather, in Cuba all schools are held to the same high standard.

Doubtless there are differences between individual schools throughout Cuba, but the ethically deplorable, and violently inequitable situation found throughout Latin America and within the United States, does not exist. The effectiveness of Cuba's educational system is so far superior to the performance of other educational systems throughout Latin America that even the supposedly excellent, elite private schools of the region do not come close to the achievement measured within the lowest level scoring schools in Cuba's economically challenged public school system. When this report was first announced in 1998, many Latin American countries found themselves in the midst of extensive educational reforms. While increasing the economic commitment to public schools in recent years, they have refused to reconsider the free-market infrastructure underlying their educational system that reinforces competition through national testing, voucher systems, and merit pay for teachers. Elite private schools continue their pull as desired commodities within a population eager for capitalist, consumer-driven advancement. Yet this atmosphere does not nurture children and families or create the conditions for educational advancement. This is a hardscrabble truth that US citizens are reluctant to face. A lack of addressing the structural contradictions within capitalist education remains a perdurable reality that delimits the possible avenues that educational reform can take.

ACT NINE: LA LUCHA CONTINUA

"Our agent advised against flying to Miami. Much too dangerous, she said.
Why didn't we consider flying to Havana for our holiday? Much safer
there."
   comments by a Canadian tourist (Nordheimer, 1994).

Despite severe economic hardships, despite a lack of high-tech resources, and
despite the anticommunist rhetoric that spews from the bowels of neoliberal
regimes throughout Latin America (not to mention punitive economic sanctions
instigated by the United States), Cuban advances in education cannot be disputed, though they are systematically silenced. Not surprisingly, the UNESCO
study and its revolutionary findings were rarely reported in the US. Admitting
that a Cuban model for education may be far superior, more equitable, and more
effective than the neoliberal model aimed at improving national economic
capacity within a global marketplace would amount to political suicide in any of
the Latin American countries dependent on their patriarchal neighbor to the
north for increased trade and other assistance, such as military support in the
"war on drugs."

   As conservatives and entrepreneurs act to influence public opinion on what
makes effective and efficient schools—namely competition, improved standardized test scores, and economic efficiency—Cuba remains implacable in its model
of education and commitment to educating all of its citizens. The results of this
commitment cannot be disputed and should be made public and central to discussions concerning public schooling, such as the contradictions of capitalist ideology to models of equitable education and the exploration of alternative visions of
education—namely authentic projects of national, equitable education.

   Elián has been released from captivity in South Florida and can again enjoy
the benefits of growing up in a country committed to its children. Meanwhile,
President George W. Bush continues to promulgate his feckless plan for educational vouchers and the corporatization of public education through school and
business partnerships and the disastrous No Child Left Behind Act. Though the
UNESCO report was obligated to publish the (possibly unexpected) results of
its study, which in essence condemns capitalist models of education, it in no
way engages these results. Instead, the report concentrates on the generally poor
performance of Latin American schools and laments the long-range negative
consequences the region is sure to face in terms of economic development, with
its population unprepared to "compete" in the global marketplace. We ask if the
funders and other supporting agencies of the UNESCO study, namely the Banco
Interamericano de Desarrollo, the Ford Foundation, and Secretaría del Convenio
Andrés Vello, OCDE, IEA, Educational Testing Service, and the World Bank,
found the results unworthy of detailed analysis. Cuba was continually mentioned as the extraordinary outlier in the data, but little attention was paid to

why this could possibly be the case, especially considering that many of the other countries actually spend more per capita on education than Cuba.

Cuba has not strayed from its political vision that continues to emphasize the values of its socialist revolution. In terms of education this means, first and foremost, "sensitivity to social problems, love of learning, modesty, unpretentiousness, solidarity . . . and intransigence against injustice and formalism" (Turner Martí, 1999, p. 3). Within the capitalist context, these ideals may appear romantic and even foolish. However, considering Cuba's adherence to these ideals within its educational system and the concrete results that have followed, perhaps our moralistic and shallow calls for "family values" and "accountability" embedded within late capitalism need to be critically examined. We would do well to cast aside the information blockade against Cuban social policy and reconsider the advances of socialist models of education, health, and development.

As we penned the final words to this essay, one of us (McLaren), born and raised in Canada, and now a US citizen, recalled the 1976 visit to Cuba of Canada's then Prime Minister, Pierre Elliott Trudeau. While very critical of Trudeau's politics, McLaren none the less appreciated how he challenged the US government, the Miami Mafia, and NATO, by shouting in the streets of Havana: "Viva Cuba y el pueblo cubano!" "Viva el Primer Ministro Commandante Fidel Castro!" The surge of pride that Trudeau's remarks created among the Canadian left was immeasurable. Both Trudeau and Fidel were educated at elite Jesuit schools in the 1940s. Moulded by similar curricula, and profoundly influenced by the same teacher, Father Jean Chadwick [Trudeau was taught at St. Jean de Brebeuf in Montreal, and Fidel at Colegio Belen [Bethlehem College, re-named The Lenin School] in suburban Havana), Trudeau and Fidel became fast friends. The friendship was strengthened when Trudeau maintained that US multinationals operating in Canada could do business with Cuba because they were Canadian-registered companies and thus not subject to the (now 40-year-old) US embargo (Harbron, 2000). It appears fitting that, only months after Elián was returned from captivity in Miami to the loving embrace of his fellow countrymen, Commandante Fidel Castro made his first official visit to Canada where he served (along with ex-President Jimmy Carter and singer/songwriter Leonard Cohen) as an honorary pallbearer at Trudeau's funeral, a momentous event in Canada that attracted world media coverage but that received only scant attention (if at all) in the US media.

The Elián Gonzalez controversy cannot be potted neatly into ideal typical narratives of accusation and guilt. The elder statesman of hyperreality, Jean Baudrillard, might say that the Elián saga never happened at all, since it consisted of the fabricated products of corporate media in response to the directives of multinationalists whose capitalist-class Weltanschauung they support. Elián became a powerful signifier caught in the net of capital and turned into a powerful commodity selling Yanqui ideology by way of the transnational media circuits. Yet as a politically embattled signifer, his meaning-making potential was mainly—but not always secured and anchored to the dominant message of the

Miami Mafia. However, in the hands of some progressive US journalists the tragic saga of Elián became momentarily entangled from the hitching-post of anticommunist invective and resignified in opposition to the Miami Mafia's position, partly as a result of the end of the Cold War and partly because the Miami Mafia's attempt to keep Elián from his father collided with the cult of family values so dear to mainstream US identity.

Perhaps this was a postmodern spectacle of sorts. But—at least in Cuba—it was not so much fuelled by irony or pastiche, or the proliferation of hybrid identities as classified and vomited up by cosmopolitan, bourgeoisified anthropologists. Rather, in Cuba the struggle over Elián became an endogenous cultural defense against yanquización and against the empires of capital that have come knocking on Cuba's door, feigning the white-shirted innocence of Mormon evangelists but unable to conceal their bad breath or hide their forked tongues behind their glistening fangs.

NOTES

1. We reject the term "embargo" used exclusively in the United States to define several policy mandates—the terms by which trade, travel, and other business and humanitarian relations between the United States (this includes attempts to regulate relationships other nations also forge with Cuba in the case of the Helms Burton Act) and Cuba are mandated. The embargo is in reality an inhumane and unethical *blockade* against the economic and political sovereignty of the Cuban nation.

REFERENCES

Azad, B. (2000). *Heroic struggle: Bitter defeat.* New York: International Publishers.

Alfonso, H. D. (2000). The Cuban experiment: Economic reform, social restructuring, and politics. *Latin American Perspectives, 27*(1).

Bardach, A. L. (2000). The untold story. *George Magazine*, May.

Berlet, C. (1998). Dances with devils: How apocalyptic and millenialist themes influence right-wing scapegoating and conspiracism. *The Public Eye, xii*(2/3), 1-22.

Calzadilla, I. (July, 7, 2000). El mayor acierto de la Revolucion rue confiar plenamente en Juan Miguel. *Granma* [Havana, Cuba].

Castro, F. (2000). Address to the South Summit. *Monthly Review, 52*(3), 149-160.

Cole, K. (1998). *Cuba: From revolution to development.* London and Washington: Pinter.

Cole, M., Hill, D., McLaren, P., & Rikowski, G. (2000). *Red chalk.* London: Tufnell Press.

CNN (March 28, 2000). Image of Virgin Mary said to Appear in Elián's Miami Home. Available online: http ://www.cnn.com/2000/US/03/28/virgin.mary/o

Davies, C. (2000). Surviving (on) the soup of signs: Postmodernism, politics, and culture in Cuba. *Latin American Perspectives, 27,* 103-121.

Eliott, J. (2000). Debunking Elián. Monitor. http://www.monitor.net/ monitor/ 004a/Elián.html

Galeano, E. (1973). *Open veins of Latin America: Five centuries of thc pillage of a continent.* New York: Monthly Review Press.

George, S. (2000). *History of neo-liberalism: Twenty years of elite economics and emerging opportunities for structural change.* ZNET. http://www.milleniumround.org/

Granma (May 8, 2000). Manifiéstanse miles de personas en Miami en apoyo al retorno de Elián a su padre. *Granma* [Havana].

Harbron, J. (2000). The Cuban connection. *Thc Globe and Mail,* October, 4, A21.

Hudis, P. (1997). Conceptualizing an emancipatory alternative: Istvan Mészaros's *Beyond Capital. Socialism and Democracy, 11,* 37-54.

Hudis, P. (2000a). Can capitalism be controlled? *News & Letters,* www.newsandletters.org

Hudis, P. (2000b). The dialectical structure of Marx's concept of 'revolution in permanence'. *Capital & Class,* No. 70, 127-142.

López, F. (June 6, 2000). Triunfó la verdad sobre la industria del mal. *Granma* [Havana, Cuba].

Macpherson, M. (2000). All in Elián's family. *Salon Magazine* [online]: http://www.salon.com/news/features/2000/04/08/family/print html [2000, May 1]

Marquez Garcia, S. (March 26, 2000). Mary appears near Elián. *Miami Herald.* Available online: http::://www.herald.com/content/sun/docs/025573.htm

McDonald, J.A. (2000). Forty years after the revolution: A look at education reform in Cuba. *International Journal of Education Reform, 9*(1).

McMurtry, J. 91998). *Unequal freedoms: The global market as an ethical system.* West Hartford, CT: Kumarian Press.

McLaren, P. (1999a). Contesting capital: Critical pedagogy and globalism: A response to Mike Apple. *Current Issues in Comparative Education, 1*(2), April 30: www.tc.columbia.edu/cice.

McLaren, P. (1999b). Che Guevara, globalization and leadership. *International Journal of Leadership in Education, 2,* 269-292.

McLaren, P., & Farahmandpur, R. (1999a). Critical multiculturalism and the globalization of capital: Some implications for a politics of resistance. *Journal of Curriculum Theorizing, 15*(4), 27-46.

McLaren, P., & Farahmandpur, R. (1999b). Globalization and contraband pedagogy. *Theoria,* No. 93, 83-115.

McLaren, P., & Farahmandpur, R. (2000). Reconsidering Marx in post-Marxist Times: A requiem for postmodernism? *Educational Researcher, 29*(3), 25-33.

Marx, K. (1973). *Grundrisse.* Harmondsworth, UK: Penguin Books.

Mora, P. (July 2, 2000). El caso de Elián aumentó la conciencia del pueblo de Estados Unidos acerca de las relaciones entre ambos paises. *Granma* [Havana, Cuba].

Morgan, P. (2000). *Socialist Review,* Issue 243 (July/August). Available online: http :// www.callnetuk.com/home/socrevitext/pubs/sr243/morgan.htm

Moore, M. (1997). *Downsize this!* London: Booktree.

Nordheimer, J. (1994, 2 September). The Gold Coast fights for its image. *New York Times,* p. A-16.

Parenti, M. (1995). *Against empire*. San Francisco: City Lights Books.

Parenti, M. (197). *Blackshirts and reds*. San Francisco: City Lights Books.

Puiggrós, A. (1996). World Bank Education Policy. *NACLA Report on the Americas*, XXIX, (6, May/June).

Robinson, W. (1996). Globalization: Nine Theses on our Epoch. *Race & Class, 38*(2), 13-29.

Shiva, V. (1991). *The violence of the green revolution*. London: Zed Book Network.

Turner Martí, L. (1999). *Del pensamiento pedagógico de Ernesto Che guevara*. Habana, Cuba: Editorial San Luis.

UNESCO (1998). *Primer estudio internacional comparative sobre lenguaje, matemática y factores asociadoes, para alumnos del tercer y cuarto grado*. Santiago, Chile: UNESCO, Laboratorio Latinoamericano de Evaluación de la Calidad de la Educación.

UNESCO (July, 2000). *Primer estudio internacional comparative sobre lenguaje, matemática y factores asociadoes, para alumnos del tercer y cuarto grado de la educación básica. Segundo Informe*. Santiago, Chile: UNESCO, Laboratorio Latinoamericano de Evaluación de la Calidad de la Educación.

Van Natta, D. (April 24, 2000). The Elián Gonzalez case: The tactics; debate over a decision to seize the boy by force. *New York Times*.

Wilkinson, S. (1999). *David and Goliath*. London: Cuba Solidarity Campaign.

Wood, E.M. (1999). *The origin of capitalism*. New York: Monthly Review Press.

Woods, E.M. (2000). Kosovo and the new imperialism. In Tariq Ali (Ed.), *Masters of the universe? NATO's Balkan crusade* (pp. 190-200). London and New York: Verso Books.

19 RATED "CV" FOR COOL VIOLENCE

Peter McLaren, Zeus Leonardo
and
Ricky Lee Allen

Hay que hacer la opresión real todavía más opesiva añadiendo a aquella la conciencia de la opresión haciendo la infamia todavía, mas infamente, al pregonarla. [Real oppression is made still more oppressive by adding to it the consciousness of that oppression, making infamy even more infamous while proclaiming it.]
—Marx and Engels[1]

This is how one pictures the angel of history. His face is turned toward the past. Where we perceive a chain of events, he sees one single catastrophe which keeps on piling wreckage upon wreckage and hurls it in front of his feet.

The angel would like to stay, awake and dead, and make whole what has been smashed. but a storm is blowing from Paradise, it has got caught in his wings with such violence that the angel can no longer close them. This storm irresistibly propels him into the future to which his back is turned, while the pile of debris before him grows skyward.

The storm is what we call progress.
—Walter Benjamin[2]

In recent years, violence in U.S. schools has taken on increasing importance as parents, educators, and students experience unparalleled structures, if not the physical threat, of daily assaults. Gun control in schools has inspired a bunker mentality as urban campuses throughout the country institute weapon checkpoints when students enter the site of learning. Real, physical violence has become a possibility in the daily lives of many students, especially those whose schools represent a symptom of structural inequalities at the local level.

This chapter originally in Stephanie U. Spina (Ed.), *Smoke and Mirrors: The Hidden Context of Violence in Schools and Society*, pp. 67-92. © 2000 Rowman & Littlefield Publishers, Inc. Reprinted with permission of the publisher.

However, and without downplaying the painful reality of physical violence, we want to focus on the individous and infectious consequences of discursive violence, to construct a language of critique that unseams the representation of violence and the violence of representation. That is, we want to explore the ways in which schools propagate violence at the level of the sign and at spaces of struggle over meaning.

VIOLENCE AS A "GIFT"

Discursive violations often escape critical scrutiny due to their often less-than-immediate effects and the ways they symbolically inscribe student subjectivities. We are arguing that because of its commonsense association with communication, discourse becomes normalized as a natural exchange. Yet, according to Foucault, this represents the power of discourse.[3] Discourses normalize the codes of knowing and render them legitimate as part of an overall rationalization process. What Foucault's resistance postmodernism lacks in terms of a strategy to subvert the power of violence (since power begets power) can perhaps be found in Jean Baudrillard's theory of the gift.[4] Originally the gift was an anthropological import developed by Marcel Mauss to explain aspects of Melanesian and Polynesian symbolic cultures. He explains their rituals this way:

> Many ideas and principles are to noted in systems of this type. the most important of these spiritual mechanisms is clearly the one which obliges us to make a return gift for a "gift received." Refusing to give is like a "declaration of war." . . . No one was free to refuse a present offered to him. Each man and woman tried to outdo the others in generosity. There was a sort of amiable rivalry as to who could give away the greatest number of most valuable presents. . . . The objects are never completely separated from the men who exchange them. . . . Failure to give or receive, like failure to make return gifts, means a loss of dignity.[5]

Mauss's observations of gift rituals inspired Baudrillard's theory of the gift as a "symbolic exchange." Baudrillard prefers the indeterminacy or ambiguity of symbolic exchange to the economic determinism of political economy. On some level, material violence has become an alibi for our general lack of attentiveness to discursive violence. Baudrillard's rearticulation of the gift should not be taken as a literal offering. It represents a fundamental *challenge*. As Pierre Bourdieu puts it: "If it is not to constitute an insult, the counter-gift must be *deferred* and *different*, because the immediate return of an exactly identical object clearly amounts to a refusal (i.e., the return of the same object)" (italics in original).[6] Failing to appropriately receive or return a "gift" institutes power in favor of the giver. For as Bourdieu reminds us, giving is a form of possessing.[7] The intent behind the gift is very important; the gift is meant to honor those with noble motivations and to relegate others to an ignominious status. In order to preserve equilibrium in symbolic exchange, one must reciprocate a gift with a counter-gift.

By using Baudrillard's theory of symbolic exchange (and to a lesser extent Bourdieu's), we understanding discursive violence to be a form of "gift." In schools, subaltern discourses and their carriers are given the "gift" of silence. This is manifest in various ways. For example, in order to become full participants in classroom discourse, students of color must forfeit their cultural capital in exchange for a white, patriarchal, and heterosexual perspective. This produces an identity crisis in students who find themselves having to choose between academic "success" and cultural integrity.[8] This gift of silence is sometimes returned by marginalized students in the form of nonparticipation. That is, silence begets silence as these objectified subjects relatively penetrate the ideology behind success and disqualify themselves.[9] In fact, this form of censored voice leads to other forms of violence because it denies subjects their right to name the world.[10]

In his study of the "mass," Baudrillard salvages silence as a strategy which engenders violence in its own right. He theorizes the silence of the mass as such:

> [T]heir strength is actual, in the present, and sufficient unto itself. It consists in their silence, in their capacity to absorb and neutralise, already superior to any power acting upon them. . . . The mass absorbs all the social energy, but no longer reflects them. For every question put to it, it sends back a tautological and circular response. It never participates.) (Italics in original.)[11]

In addition to the more conventional interpretation of silence as a sign of alienation from the total process of labor or due political process, we must consider seriously Baudrillard's suggestion that transgression is to be found in silence. One only has to recall the aggressiveness engendered by a person who refuses to participate in an argument by enacting the "silent treatment." The non-verbal, yet semiotically aggressive, message from such a response is unequivocal in its attempt to subvert the power of speech. The overbearingness of argumentative perspectives is canceled out and thrown back to itself with the apathy of the object(ified). Thus, the violence instituted by a curriculum that dismisses the Other's perspective is compromised (at times canceled) by the power of those who do not wish to participate in its language games. The challenge for transformative educators is to redirect this return gift of silence toward the desire for collective transgression, an organic hush over the administrative gaze.

Discursive violence is often the subtle maintenance of more overt forms of violence. Theorizing the mechanics of covert violence, Bourdieu has activated a concept of "symbolic violence."[12] According to Bourdieu, symbolic violence is veiled in rituals and symbolic interactions. He writes:

> [W]hen domination can only be exercised in its *elementary form*, i.e.,
> directly, between one person and another, it cannot take place overtly and
> must be disguised under the veil of enchanted relationships, the official
> model of which is presented by relations between kinsmen; in order to be
> socially recognized it must get itself misrecognized.[13] [Italics in original.]

We arrive at the "legitimate" use of authority at the level of the symbolic and
soft violence. In other words, symbolic violence is the *cool* and "euphemized"
version of material, economic violence. In contrast to the hot violence of material exploitation, cool violence functions under the pretenses of guiles and ruses,
of which the gift (e.g., obligations) is only one of many. The object of violence
falls victim to its machinations, not so much through coercion, but through *complicity* and by embodying the objective structures of violence vis-à-vis the *habitus* (Italics in original).[14] The power behind sanctioned violence is administered
more efficiently when it can cloak itself as other than itself; that is, as an objective structure. Symbolic violence works best in the absence of outright oppressive consequences, but through disciplinary mechanisms that make it the precondition for participating in symbolic interactions. According to Bourdieu,
power, like symbolic violence, is often misrecognized for what it is. Of power,
Foucault writes,

> Power is tolerable only on condition that it mask a substantial part of itself.
> Its success is proportional to its ability to hide its own mechanisms. . . .
> New methods of power whose operation is not ensured by right but by tech-
> nique, not by law but by normalization, not by punishment but by control,
> methods that are employed on all levels and in forms that go beyond the
> state and its apparatus.[15]

Symbolic violence and symbolic power work side by side. They inscribe our
actions without at the same time producing them. The legitimation of power is
generated as a symbolic surplus value which is secured by reifying differences
into distinctions through equally reified rituals and customs.[16]

Thus, we arrive at the relative importance of discourse in liberating students from violent regimes of signification supporting and supported by material social relations of capitalist exploitation. Critical educators must recognize
the important role that discourse plays in inscribing the subjective choices of
students. Discursive violence occurs when the historical *work of meaning* is
obscured and meaning is fetishized as natural and not recognized as being produced in historical struggle. Or as John Thompson suggests, discursive violence
is the power to make certain meanings or significations *stick*.[17] Violence here is
a product of the struggle over the signified. Although we are arguing for the relative importance of ideas at the level of discourse, we are not suggesting that
ideas themselves are real, but that they produce real consequences.

Discourses in themselves do not produce material realities, as if utterance by itself gives rise to the existence of its contents. However, this does not negate the historical effects of reification whereby narratives told over and over again (and supported by institutional structures) become reified material realities, as in the case of educational tracking. Oakes has found that despite negligible *academic* differences at a young age between children from different races, narratives regarding who is intelligent, for example, and who is not (and supported by tracking practices) produce real, material consequences such that children from different races exhibit disparities in test scores as they advance in age.[18] In turn, this form of narrative violence manifests itself in social and economic outcomes, limiting the life chances of many students of color. However, we have seen the pitfalls of the position that there is "no outside" to discourse, as if "monsters are as real as material things."[19]

Certain discursive repertoires are a direct result of material forces and realities. We tell narratives because we have experienced something and desire to communicate its meaning. In this manner, discourse is based on a slice of material reality. Students create discourses about school life and the myriad interests which inscribe them as they make sense of experience through language. We want to make it clear that experiences never speak for themselves, as if language captures their essential, transcendental meaning. Meanings are concomitant with the limited constellation of discourses to which subjects have access (e.g., their concepts, epistemic rules, and ideological interests). Educators can provide students with the gift of critical discourse, a condition where meanings are neither arrived at through semiotic closure in order to leave signifieds in historical abeyance nor are they indeterminate to the point where students fail to find the agency to act. Hence, though language alone cannot negate violence, a change in discursive structures produces change *effects* that become available for counter-hegemonic purposes. We hope to make this line of reasoning clearer as we proceed.

At the very least, radical discourses allow students to "see" social life in more critical ways so that they can ask questions which may, in turn, lead to an increased desire for social justice. The violence of dominant discourses buries underneath their interests a mound of meanings associated with marginalized voices. Yet, these subaltern voices subvert hegemony when recovered for revolutionary purposes. Students need to interrogate critically those memories, voices, and perspectives in history that the current episteme has repressed in order to recognize that the history of U.S. education has been built upon the backs of the oppressed.

If the act of seeing is a de facto act of violence because there is much that is veiled from our view, then critical educators must forge a new discourse around what it means to "see" the world. Upon our *perception* of them, ideas are said to be registered by the body. That is, they are grasped by the experiential senses as these are inscribed by discourse. At their *inception*, ideas are signified through language; they are given shape through linguistic imprints and terms. This is the moment when an idea becomes a linguistic sign. At their conception, ideas become part of mental schema in the Kantian sense of fitting them into *a priori* categories. Through deception, ideas produce forms of false consciousness which, according to Marx, obscure the objective basis of social life in commodity production, that social existence produces human consciousness, not vice versa.[20] Inception, perception, conception, and deception are all ways of (mis)viewing an idea. Moreover, they are all part and parcel to the process of hegemony at the level of the sign.

If the act of seeing is, on some level, a recapitulation of hegemony—and therefore, a form of violence—then a transformation of our construction of worldviews is necessary. Critical educators must forge a new discourse around *contra-ception*, or those sensibilities and strategies which are counter-hegemonic, in order to assist students in a radical critique of the ways they currently "see" the social order. Contra-ception enables us to understand, as structured social beings, that subjects *do not only read signs but that signs also read them.* Through contra-ception, progressive teachers can proceed to deconstruct the "political economy of the sign," or how commodities are produced as sign and the sign as commodity.[21]

Contra-ception builds a language of critique around the ways violence is perpetrated on the Other and simultaneously commodified for profit. Take the event of Mike Tyson's biting Evander Holyfield's ear. There was much discussion in the media around the violence manifested in this single act at the expense of critical reflection over the *general* violence in the sport itself. In Baudrillardean terms, the ear biting becomes an *alibi* for boxing's violent political economy. At the infamous fight, a spectator picked up a piece of cartilage which had fallen onto the mat from Holyfield's ear. It is estimated that the piece of flesh has a market value of $30,000. Mainstream discussions of the event have failed to critique the commodification of the spectacular image found in men of color pummeling each other, almost to the point of physical discordance, for a living. Contra-ception would work toward a critical re-view of these and other violent relations.

However, contra-ception also guards against essentialist readings of social life. Any reading is at best partial. Social life is not an unmediated relation, or a simple correspondence between the real and the experience. Rather, subjects live daily life as an imagined relation to the real relations of production.[22] That is, worldview (or Althusserian ideology) comes to subjects in the form of representations of the real. Contra-ception partakes of a discursive function that disaggregates and disarms violent representations from potentially transformative ones. It constitutes a way of seeing the social that provides students with the basis for a critical pedagogy of everyday life—a life never fully present to itself, but one that is represented through particular interests and specific ends.

THE SOCIO-SPATIAL CONSTRUCTION OF
COOL VIOLENCE REGIMES

Within what Foucault calls modernistic *govern/mentalities*, an institutionalized scenario privileges a view where violence is quantified and historicized, individuals and their communities are vilified, places (such as inner-city schools) are demonized, bureaucratic plans are rationalized and legalized, and seemingly violent "Others" are marginalized. From this perspective, violent "Others" become objects of panoptic space where the disciplinary gaze of govern/mentalities cellularizes their bodies into "private" places: e.g., prison cells and detention rooms in schools. For instance, consider the new program of territorial surveillance instituted by the Los Angeles Police Department (LAPD). In a low-income Latino section of Los Angeles' San Fernando Valley, bright red banners on the light poles of Parthenia Street signal to passing motorists that they are entering an "LAPD Video Zone, Buy Drugs, Go To Jail." There are two images at the bottom of the LAPD Video Zone banners. One is the outline of a camcorder and the other is a person behind prison bars. Commenting critically on the way LAPD police officers manipulate the spatial significance of sending people to prison, Steve Herbert states:

> Jailing is the most satisfying way in which the police can cleanse a dirty area; it is a surgical dislodging of the cancerous agents that pollute the lives of the good people. It is in this sense, a satisfying moral act, a clear victory of good over evil, an active removal of the problem and a restoration of peace and tranquillity. . . . Space is thereby purified of its moral pollution.[23]

Meanwhile, across the street from the Latino community is the upscale commercial center of the city of Northridge with its signs of invitation that welcome wealthy and desiring consumers. There are.no state-produced signs warning of the oppressive dangers of capitalism and whiteness, at least not "obvious" ones.

Curiously, violence is a signifier conflated in an identification and location that is too settled. Typically, the subjectivity of violence is narrowly defined around psychosocial consequences of violence, rather than an engagement of differing understandings of violence. In the mid 1990s, there was a national debate over a television ratings system that resulted in TV programs being labeled with a "V" for "violent content." The arguments in the mainstream media focused exclusively on the rationalized psychological effects that these supposedly violent images have on children rather than on what constitutes violence in the dialogue and electronic images of TV programming. The symbolic violence in the *criteria* used to justify the ratings themselves are hidden from view. A contra-ceptive discourse moves the recognition of violence from the occasional act of physical harm or property damage towards a critical awareness of the pervasive and "violent" conditions of oppression operating at the level of everyday life. Moreover, an examination of subjectivity might shed conceptual light on the fixed and natural state of objective violence in public discourses.

The exploration of subjectivity has been dominated by questions of meaning such as "What is violence?" This type of reflection is often imbued with the political belief that governmental action can only succeed if the nature of a problem is definitively understood. However, this line of inquiry is problematic if the vision guiding the search seeks a singular subjectivity that has analytically concocted a transcendental truth as to the ultimate presence and meaning of violence. Postmodern, poststructural, postcolonial, and feminist theorists have struggled to deconstruct universal knowledge claims for their mythical and monolithic tendencies. These contestations have also problematized relationships between knowledge and identity such that assumptions of essentialized subjects are giving way to notions of decentered subjectivities that represent partial knowledges within situated totalities.[24] Since knowledges of violence have been constructed in this same modernistic milieu of definitive meanings, essentialized subjects, and techno-rational bureaucratic responses, this milieu must be deconstructed as well for its relationship to hegemonic constructions of both subjectivity and objectivity. Or as Althusser puts it, it is not people's thoughts that are necessarily alienated, but the social formation itself that produces an alienated subject.[25] Alienation is the violent separation of objective reality from subjective experience which results from the contradictions between labor and capital. Although material violence is certainly important, the objective realities of violence are related to differentially positioned conceptualizations, or "imaginaries," that are socially represented in discourses which allow people within particular communities to discuss violence. In other words, there are communities whose occupants share a sense of a common reality relative to their experiences with violence which they signify to each other. However, powerful communities are able to institutionalize their discursive renditions of violence, thus dominating marginalized people at multiple geopolitical levels, such as in the establishment of the LAPD Video Zone.

Moreover, these power differentials in the discourses of violence are not simply naturally occurring events. Relationships of domination are social constructions with histories and geographies that are often reified (which maintains the same power relationships between communities over time and space even as meanings and language may change or "slip") in part by the ideological processes found within discourses. As Derrida and Saussure have argued, language is governed by rules that are not so much about "positively" defining what something is as they are about "negatively" defining what something is not.[26] Saussure recognizes that identity is never merely an issue of positive presence but one of relation with the other terms in its environment.[27] To Derrida, identities are negatively defined by their Other which completes their supplementarity.[28] This undeniable absence which supplements the metaphysics of presence both gives form to identity while subverting its certainty. For example, one cannot make sense of the center without its margins, white without black, or master without slave. Although the first terms in the binary are privileged signifiers or are parasitic on the second terms, they are internally divided identities and achieve their register interdependent with their repressed Other. Human thought and experiences are so complex and varied that every attempt to "understand" the world through language necessarily and simultaneously involves "misunderstanding" the "worlds" of others.[29] Since all that is human cannot be synthesized into linguistic representations, language is a social process that is product and producer of both presences, which are spatial and temporal realities, and absences, which are spatial and temporal occlusions. Violent absences must be contra-ceptively recovered as they are continually produced and reproduced by hegemonic discourses. A contra-ceptive discourse recognizes the "not yet discoursable" and works to excavate these "private" perspectives into public spheres of political discourse; all the while trying to avoid what Ryan calls "semiotic positivism," or the over-reliance on signs.[30]

A contra-ceptive discourse recognizes that the public spheres of political discourse are surveilled and bordered by logocentrisms and structurations that inscribe and delimit subjectivity and legitimate particular expressions of reason. The logocentrism of violence communicated through hegemonic discourses hide or mask representations of violence that exist outside of conceptual and perceptual borders, yet are given presence by those same borders. As a transgression of representational borders, resistance to discursive violence occurs when the object of violence begins to *own* the violence produced by the process through which she has been signified and engages in an act of *resignification.* Judith Butler describes this form of resistance as a "mobilization against subjection."[31] She writes, following Foucault, that signs can be used for purposes counter to those for which it was designed:

> Even the most noxious terms could be owned, that the most injurious interpellations could also be the site of radical reoccupation and resignification. But what lets us occupy the discursive site of injury? How are we animated and mobilized by that discursive site and its injury, such that our very attachment to it becomes the condition for our resignification of it? Called by an injurious name, I come into social being, and because I have an inevitable attachment to my existence, because a narcissism takes hold of any term that confers existence, I am led to embrace the terms that injure me because they constitute me socially. The self-colonizing trajectory of certain forms of identity politics are symptomatic of this paradoxical embrace of the injurious term. As a further paradox, then only by occupying—being occupied by—that injurious term can I resist and oppose it, recasting the power that constitutes me as the power I oppose . . . any mobilization against subjection will take subjection as its resource, and that attachment to an injurious interpellation will, by way of a necessarily alienated narcissism, become the condition under which resignifying that interpellation becomes possible. This will not be an unconscious outside of power, but rather something like the unconscious of power itself, in its traumatic and productive iterability.[32]

Subject formation involves reworking injury and subjection through resignification, which can challenge the subject's attachment to subjection in order to reform subjectivity.

What our poststructural critique of violence and language suggests is that the question of "What is violence?" is itself hiding the more spatially overt question of "Where is violence?"[33] Regimes of power are also constitutive of and constituted by space. Subjects come to occupy places and spaces by the workings of power and discourse. Space, in other words, scripts subjectivity. As Sibley explains:

> The processes of social segregation observable in the modern city, for example, are mirrored in the segregation of knowledge producers. The defense of social space has its counterpart in the defense of regions of knowledge. This means that what constitutes knowledge, that is, those ideas which gain currency through books and periodicals, is conditioned by power relations which determine the boundaries of "knowledge" and exclude dangerous or threatening ideas and authors.[34]

Through a spatially conscious contra-ceptive discourse; a critical spatial theory of violence seeks to bring into view representations from the margins that question and transform the cool, distanced, and dominant centers of violent spatial logics. We argue that violence should be examined spatially because it is typically sensed as an act that not only needs a space in which to occur but also is a disruption, or "violation," of the rules and order of that space. Sibley contends that the rules which order space follow a hegemonic desire for "purity" and "defilement" in the social construction of self and community, leading to the exclusion of deviant others. Speaking on the relationship between alienation and physical space, he states that:

> thus, the built environment assumes symbolic importance, reinforcing a desire for order and conformity if the environment itself is ordered and purified; in this way, space is implicated in the construction of deviancy. Pure spaces expose difference and facilitate the policing of boundaries. The problem is not solely one of control from above whereby agents of an oppressive state set up socio-spatial control systems in order to remove those perceived to be deviant and to induce conformity. . . . [E]xclusionary tendencies develop in the individual and . . . exclusionary practices of the institutions of the capitalist state are supported by individual preferences for purity and order. . . . A rejection of difference is embedded in the social system.[35]

The consequences of violating pure and ordered spaces of a particular spatial territory, whether it be a school district, city, or nation-state, usually result in being socially "assigned" to repressive or oppressive "residual" spaces such as prisons, housing projects, or "low-track" educational programs.

Furthermore, the power to control the purification and ordering of spatial territories is related to notions of "community" that both exclude and occlude. This is especially salient and problematic when powerful communities experience a "moral panic" caused by a perceived disjuncture of and threat to their pure and ordered spaces. Such moral panics are expressed spatially by casting out offending "Others" from valued territory or by reappropriating violent "residual" spaces of the Others in order to reform it.[36] For example, the San Francisco Unified School District has implemented a program of "reconstitution" whereby schools scoring low on district evaluations have had most of their faculties and administrations transferred to other school sites in an effort to spatially "cleanse" school cultures. Of course, the reconstituted schools are typically located in neighborhoods where poor students of color reside. When exclusionary and occluding communities achieve state, media, and institutional power, the consequences of their representations of Others can be devastating.

A critical spatial language opens possibilities for contra-ceptively transgressing the borderations imposed by privileged communities that exclude and occlude. For example, the spatial term "region," as opposed to local, nation, or global, is a flexible way of contextualizing examinations of sociospatial relations that wish to consider the productive relationships between community, territory, and power. Region and regionalization are especially important concepts for a critical understanding of the spatialness of violence. A region is not simply a natural topographical area associated with a river valley, desert, or mountain range. Derived from the Latin root *regis*, which means "of the king," a region is a space, such as land, body, or mind, that is territorialized through the rationalization and enforcement of regulations. Regionalization is maintained through the regimentation of a state of governance and logocentrism known as a regime which produces subjectivities that make the spaces of everyday life appear to be regular. In modernistic regimes of liberalism, for example, regions and their regulations have been structured into, among other things, laws that are normative and normalizing forces in the maintenance of govern/mental territories such as nations and cities.[37] The existence of "criminality" demonstrates that constructions of spatial violence have been institutionalized as part of legal systems and territorial rule. For instance, in 1993 conservatives in the British government proposed a bill which sought to restrict the presence of Gypsies in the English countryside because they are seen as "nomadic spatial deviants" and "filthy." Invoking nostalgic images of a bucolic English utopia with redcoated huntsmen and quaint cottages that is now being violated by the presence of Gypsies, Sir Cranley Onslow, a supporter of the measure, decried that:

> [This section of the bill strengthens] the position of those people who want law and order to prevail in the countryside. The creation of a new offense of aggravated trespass is a significant step forward that will be widely welcomed in all parts of the country *where people have become all too used to disorder, intimidation and violence prevailing and interrupting the lawful*

*pursuits of those who live in the country, value it and want to continue with
their countryside sports.* (Italics in original)[38]

As this quote illustrates, the primary problem of the normalization and naturalization of regional rules is that they structure an impression that there are
both times and places that are free or detached from violence, that is, that exhibit the banality of "everyday life," whereas violence occurs only in traumatic,
extraordinary instances. Moreover, in the world of Onslow's English countryside, Gypsies are the ones who endure conditions of violence simply by being
present in a region where they are not welcome. Yet Onslow has the audacity to
claim that it is the Gypsies who violate his space by supposedly disrupting his
fox hunts. Unfortunately, Onslow is in a position of power to promote a law to
regulate his violent spatial imaginary by criminalizing Gypsies.

Through its partnership with the production of blinding regionalizations,
violence is rarely perceived as an ongoing presence or condition perpetuated by
acts of representational injury. A violent condition is only acknowledged when it
is imagined as a natural association with isolated, irregular, and demonized subregional space, such as a "barrio" or "inner city school." Children who grow up
in these denigrated subregional spaces are said to be "living in violence" whereas
other spaces, such as white suburbs, are read as being nonviolent and "safe."
This Manichean dichotomy of good versus bad spaces is itself symptomatic of a
society that is violent at its roots. A contra-ceptive discourse on the spaces of
violence must interrogate dominant conceptualizations of space itself, particularly those that disconnect different spaces and spatialities from their interrelated,
interreactive, and interdependent social constructions. Conceptualizations of
space, or conceived space, dictate perceptions of spatial reality and sociospatial
relations such as govern/mental policies on violence through the legitimation and
institutionalization of appropriate spatial knowledge. Conceived space has the
potential to be both product and producer of spatial violence. It can also be a colonizer of subjectivity as it is inscribed and implemented in spaces such as the
explicit and hidden curriculum of schools. The interplay between
knowledge/space/power at microgeopolitical levels, such as the classroom,
serves to reify blinding regionalizations and territories of surveillance.

Like violent discourses, space and spatial knowledge should be scrutinized
for their modernist tendencies to produce and occlude violence. A contra-ceptive discourse on violence must correspondingly name and deconstruct the dominant ways in which spatial knowledge is conceived and practiced. Western
(educational) institutions are closely associated with views of space that are
trapped in binary opposition between objective and subjective space. Objective
space, or the spaces of everyday life that are often identified as "reality," have
been overemphasized, especially by those who are almost exclusively structural
and scientific, such that the names and meanings of objective spaces are
assumed to be naturally occurring and obviously understood. This rigid view of
space is affiliated with a scientific, modernist project of quantifying or describ-

ing objective space so that "evidence" can be gathered to create a convincing argument in the public spheres. This desire for evidence collecting constructs epistemologies which seek information that will influence an audience of the powerful, that is policy makers and bureaucrats. For example, racial and ethnic identities of body spaces are frozen into categories on census forms in an effort to produce disciplined "demographics" while many completing these forms must struggle to decide which box to check for their own identity. Special education and bilingual education students must be officially categorized and identified by state agendas in order to receive funds for their programs. These same categories also act to normalize the mainstream curriculum and perpetuate their own existence in what are often marginalized programs. In modernist forms of objective space, violence is also quantified as crime statistics, reinforcing the notion that violence is limited to "known" typologies such as murder rates or percentages of students in gangs, thereby masking a critical consideration of the oppressive conditions and acts of representational violence targeted at exploited people. The fixed views of objective space can be particularly violent because they are discursively enacted by those with institutional power in ways that deny and structure the alternative realities of marginalized people.

On the other side of the modernist epistemological binary, the discourse of subjective space is often used to counter rigid views of objective space by offering different meanings and interpretations. Soja describes subjective space, or, as he calls it, "imagined space," as the site of the mental contemplation of space, or the conceptual and subjective spatial plans of the mind.[39] For instance, before the LAPD implemented its Video Zone program, first it had to perceive a problem in particular spaces and then it had to devise a plan to "solve" the problem. This process was mediated through the imaginings of space held by those in the LAPD. Jill Leovy of *The Los Angeles Times* describes how the spatial imaginations of the police have even been accommodated in plans to develop disciplined spaces in "unruly" neighborhoods:

> Burbank police were losing the turf war with gang members over West Elmwood Avenue. So the city rolled out a weapon against which gangs couldn't compete: Money. Lots of it. . . . Using the millions of dollars at its disposal, the city staged a wholesale takeover of one of its worst areas, the notorious 100 block of Elmwood, buying 11 buildings and performing drastic surgery on a cul-de-sac that was once a magnet for trouble. . . . "We took away their homeland," one police officer said. . . . The new street design has a distinctive law enforcement stamp. Officers reviewed blueprints at every step. Police recommended a 14-foot-high wrought-iron fence be erected just behind the buildings, blocking the normal escape routes used by gang members when police cruised down the block. The city built curbs too high to drive over, but not so high they become inviting places to sit. The new decorative plants are covered with spines and thorns to discourage the hiding of guns or contraband.[40]

Educators and educational planners also use manipulations of space to discipline "unruly" students and students from "unruly" places, whether through a "basic skills" curriculum, seating arrangements, expulsions and transfers, or busing programs. In fact, many public schools in Los Angeles have prison-like fences such as those recommended by the Burbank Police for Elmwood.

Discursively structured systems of spatial metaphors that stand in place of the real are closely tied to abstract representations of space or "imagined space."[41] For example, "school" is a spatial metaphor in the way it represents a place where formalized acts of education take place. However, the meaning and purpose of places called "school" is far from settled because schools are implicated in sociospatial struggles over knowledge and power. When Paul Willis describes how the curriculum of a school reproduces class stratification[42] he is conveying a very different political image and understanding of what a school is than someone who imagines the school to be an appropriate "sorter" of capital into their rightful social locations. Imagined space is representationally violent when it is idealized as a utopian space of agency, such as when education is discussed as a space that opens the benefits of society to everyone. There is a tendency in modernist subjective space to solidify or fix spatial metaphors such as "school," "nation," and "inner cities," and to veil their sociospatial production from our view. After all, nations, schools, and inner cities have not always existed, particularly as they are in their current forms.[43]

The irony of the spatialities of modernist epistemologies is that an emphasis on objective space cannot be elaborated without invoking a subjective spatiality, and an emphasis on subjective space cannot be realized without experiencing objective spaces. As Soja argues, spatial thinking is not a question of being *either* real *or* imagined because it is always *both* real and imagined.[44] In other words, the perceptual is always interreactive and interdependent with the conceptual. The focus of critical spatial analysis should then be more concerned with *social space*, which is the realm where the differential and ideological production of real-and-imagined spatialities are socially constructed such that some spatialities are legitimated and regionalized in ways that both produce and mask subaltern spatialities.[45] Critical spatial analysis seeks the representational violences in social space that are hidden in the hot margins of the cool, abstract, and idealized modernist spaces of violence. Social space is where we should question the constructed spatial regimes that both allow and limit our perception of violence. Since social space is structured primarily through language, a critical semiotics of violence needs to articulate a theory of semiotics that embraces critical spatial theory.

Working towards a description of a critical semiotics of violence, we begin with a brief description of "semiotics." Saussure's theory of signs (or semiotics) held that language could be broken down into two fundamental elements, the signifier and signified; the first a linguistic form (e.g., a written or spoken word—*parole*), the second its intended meaning.[46] Together, the signifier and signified create the sign. Signifiers are not necessarily articulated forms, but invocations of "the psychological imprint of the sound," as in a sound-image or thought. Signifieds are "mental representations of the meaning" attached to signifiers.[47] As such, Saussurian linguistics opposes the naturalists' claim that there exists an essential relation between things and words.

A critical semiotics of violence releases the sign "violence" from its symbolic functioning and disrupts its unitary meaning. It reveals the textuality of violence and the unnamed logocentric practices that are its conditions of possibility. It displaces the sanctioned and often sanctimonious ways in which violence as a realm of meaning delimits itself. It problematizes the status of violence as self-evident and natural. A critical semiotics of violence problematizes various sites of violence as marked by space/power/knowledge production systems. It recognizes that the symbolic structuring of dominant spatialities of violence necessarily produces counterspatialities of violence that should be represented, although they will never be fully present for discussion. Conversely, violence should not be isolated solely to a critique of discourse on the topic of violence because the discursive act and condition of masking subaltern representations is violent regardless of the topic in question. The logic that produces subaltern spaces is related to their denigrated state of "readiness" or "preconditioning" for capitalistic exploitation.

So, *cool violence*, in contradistinction to the detached and detaching views of space as seen from within modernist epistemologies of violence, is an ever-present condition of representational acts and disjunctured spaces that are significant in that they relate to material consequences of oppression. Cool violence is an institutionalized regime in that it ideologically regulates blinding regionalizations of violence associated with modernist, capitalist, masculine, and white supremacist ways of seeing space. In cool violence regimes, violence is itself a spatial metaphor that signifies harm perpetrated on a given space by the violation of the commonsense rules of that space. Acts of violence are located in spaces that have been socially constructed as mostly existing in a state of nonviolence.

For instance, residential suburbs are rarely considered violent as opposed to the often demonized "barrio." Spatial nonviolence is partially perpetuated by "violent memories" of past places that are dictated by a nostalgia which obliterates any sense of the production of difference through cool violence. By omitting past relationships in the racialization, genderization, and capitalization of spaces, violent memories act normatively to delegitimate knowledges that emphasize the interconnectedness of spatial differentiation and power, thereby reifying the conditions of cool violence. In the discourse of cool violence, normative conditions of nonviolence in a protected space may be referred to and maintained by allegedly "neutral" evaluative signifiers such as "safe," "healthy," "sound," "clean," or "well managed." Cool violence also masks constructed notions of "privacy" or spatial "ownership."

Through the construction of privacy, the act of violence is not just to the space but also to the owner(s) "in charge" of that space. In the capitalist regime of cool violence, groups or individuals are allowed to maintain private spaces as long as they remain within the "commonsense rules of ownership." Violence is then said to occur when nature or other people commit an act (not a produced condition) that breaks the socially constructed rules of safety and privacy for that space. Conditions of violence are identified when certain places become symbolically attached to "Others" who are seen as breaking the rules of ownership. LAPD Video Zones, school reconstitution reforms, and urban renewal projects are just a few examples of the spatial logic and practice of cool violence. Through the detached and detaching spatialities of modernistic epistemologies, these situations of supposedly "improper" or "dirty" ownership are blamed on those who inhabit "violent places."

Embodied space is one of the specific sites located in cool violence regimes. The body is a contested site of the blinding regionalizations of cool violence and modernist spatial epistemologies that must be contraceptively recovered through a space-conscious critical semiotics. Constructed in relation to the metaphors of industrial and techno-capitalism, the body is a machine for the production of value, thus making it the atomistic unit of social agency in a field of free market competition. The capitalist body as value-production machine has been simultaneously regionalized by medical and biological discourses that regulate the normalized, "systems" view of the body. These discursively structured, scientific logics of normalized bodily "functions," "safety," and "health" cloak the capitalist body in an illusion of mechanistic form and purpose that validates the belief in and the desire for an optimum state of nonviolent body conditions. Additionally, a common sense of self-ownership regulates a region of seemingly natural bodily privacy. However, the mere fact that society does not allow you to do what you want with your own body should suggest that this privatization of the body is socially constructed (e.g., prostitution, suicide, abortion, and sodomy are often subject to legislation). From this perspective, bodily violence is the result of an act that disrupts the regulated functions, safety, and health of the body in a way that threatens the value of the body. Through cool violence, the body is regimented such that it reflects the current regime of capitalism; the form of the body closely follows the function of capitalism.

This capitalist and modernist construction of the body disguises the general condition of cool violence. The body as commodity is constantly being produced and consumed through capitalist regionalizations of differential value. Systems of capitalist enfleshment commodify bodies through multiple social constructions such as race, class, gender, sexuality, and citizenship. The body is real in that it inhabits material space, but it is also imagined as a sign constructed in disjunctured ways that are interrelated to sociospatial struggles over power and reason. The body serves as an image machine of sorts that is continually read, consumed, and reproduced through the regional discourses inscribed by regulatory logocentrisms. For example, modernist governmentalities that produce a "nation" also enflesh all human bodies as either "citizen" or "alien" such that aliens within the traditional national boundaries are more likely to be marginalized, especially in core capitalist nations like the United States. Enfleshment is an ongoing state of cool violence in modernism because problematic logocentrisms precondition and essentialize social gazes that correspond to the reification of marginalization for denigrated "Other" bodies, thereby reproducing them as regions of capitalist exploitation that are implicit in nation-state formations. This symbolic and material cool violence also has representational significance in that the lived spatialities of marginalized bodies are made to appear irrational and non-sensical to the oppressors, thus violating the real-and-imagined spatial knowledges of the disenfranchised.

Another region of cool violence is property. Within capitalist regimes of exploitation, property consists of a regionalization of the ownership of objects, which in various times and places has included human beings, land, ideas, buildings, consumer goods, and signs. Sensibilities of privacy have been constructed around commonsense rules on the procurement of property and its sound, safe, and organized maintenance and management. The metanarrative of property ownership in capitalism suggests that property is obtained through a meritocratic system of individual ability and perseverance in a free-market economy. When property continues to be read as functioning within the logic of capitalism, a state of cool violence goes unrecognized. In other words, property becomes a condition of nonviolence. However, when the property regulations of capitalism are violated to the extent that property has been significantly devalued, the term "violence" is often used to describe this occurrence.

For example, news media often follow perceived "outbreaks of violence," such as that associated with storms or rioting, with estimates of property "loss" or "damage" quantified through the capitalist objectification and regionalization of space. In the United States, Hurricane Andrew, which passed over Miami in 1992, is described as the "most costly disaster" in U.S. history. Certainly the enslavement of blacks and the genocide of native peoples are "greater" U.S. disasters. Even so-called public spaces are still considered as property in that they are owned by the same state that regulates and is regulated by modernist notions of privacy and cool violence. The quick and blatant sacrifice of Koreatown by the police during the 1992 Los Angeles uprisings shows the selective engagement of capitalist state protection with public spaces.[48] Considered unprofitable by the local state apparatuses, the police left Koreatown to burn and Korean merchants were forced to protect themselves.

Of course, what the regime of cool violence masks is the ever-present condition of violence associated with the differential production of "property" in both its real and imagined connotations. Capitalism relies on the possibility of locating and owning spaces of exploitation that provide surplus value. However, spaces for production do not exist naturally and are socially constructed.[49] "Ownership" of production spaces is subject to sociospatial power differences in the struggle to define and regulate property "rights." This struggle cannot be separated from previous historical and geographical conditions and regulations. In the case of property, violence exists in the logocentrism of ownership and the reproduction of differential abilities to own in a regime of a reified meritocracy. Since capitalism is also related to the logics of whiteness and masculinity, spaces also become differentially commodified and valued as they simultaneously become associated with particular racialized and gendered bodies.[50] When these differences become hegemonically rationalized as separate and natural, conditions of violence persist. The marginalization of certain people's lived spatialities in this system of property demonstrates cool violence because their representations of property are absent from the discourses of social institutions.

Consider the discursive violence involved in media treatment of gang violence. Wayne Mellinger has analyzed the manner in which the *Los Angeles Times* covered street-gang murders between 1994 and 1995.[51] We wish to extend some of Mellinger's insights into our own analysis of a recent four-part series the *Times* ran from Sunday, May 25, 1997, to Wednesday, May 28, 1997. Working his way through a montage of journalist reporting on gangs, Mellinger argues that we read these stories as postmodern "channel surfer," as "decentered and distracted" spectators, as "textual flaneurs whose eyes stroll through this spectacular pagescape rapidly scanning for juicy stories, shocking images, and useful information."[52]

He further argues that these stories comprise little more than "emotion rousing stories," and "public spectacles of private troubles,"[53] and that few of these murders are reported in any sociological detail in the *Times*. They are mostly "brief, detail-depleted one paragraph stories banished to the second page of the Metro section."[54] The saturated "moral panics" that are *not* suppressed in the *Times* include stories on "welfare queens," serial murderers, and acts of terrorism. Mellinger speculates that whereas sensational gang stories were once needed in order to "whip up fear and build consensus concerning the need for police intervention," the police and the media no longer consider gang murders to be as newsworthy as in earlier years, perhaps out of fear that crime will be amplified or the image of the city worsened. In an era of "post-Fordism in which the boundaries between reality and simulation are blurred,"[55] what we see more and more in the *Times* is the implosion of information into entertainment. The *Times* risks substantially hurting tourism if too many gang homicide stories are run. Furthermore, the necrophiliac logic which teaches that death can come from anywhere, anytime, ruptures the postmodern sensibilities of Angelino valley dwellers who prefer Los Angeles to be associated with majestic palm trees, placid swimming pools, and endless shopping spaces. When stories of gang members can be found sandwiched between advertisements for the Broadway, Robinson's, Von's, and Ralph's, few of them deal with the structured and sociogeographical aspects of gang violence. Mellinger writes:

> In demonizing gang members, media representations fail to understand the real problem and its political economic origins. To understand this epidemic of youth violence we must acknowledge and condemn the political economy and lived reality of poor youth in the inner city. The cause of much juvenile crime can be found in me rampant youth poverty that exists in many parts of Los Angeles.[60]

The *Times* series on gang life focused on life at a thirty-six-unit building at 8960 Orion Avenue, one block east of the San Diego Freeway in North Hills, at the center of the San Fernando Valley. Once a working-class community that housed California State University Northridge students, the area surrounding the Orion Avenue complex was now home to the Langdon and Columbus street gangs. The housing complex has become both a refuge and a prison to immigrants from Mexico, Guatemala, El Salvador, and Puerto Rico. In order to cover the stories, two of the three *Los Angeles Times* journalists lived in an apartment at the complex that, we are told, was enclosed by iron gates and barbed wire. During their three month investigation, they managed to meet the building's many residents including gang members, factory workers, welfare recipients, "scavengers who collected cans and bottles," and even one "bounty hunter" who worked for a medical clinic and got eight dollars for each customer she delivered. But the most detailed descriptions were of gang members. We learn for instance:

> There was Woody, stabbed by a drunk. Crazy killed himself, as he predicted, playing Russian roulette. Blanca was shot in the mouth by a San Fernando gang. Chatto was gunned down on his way to church. There were Leon, Gordo, Downer, Joker and finally, Pee Nut, a mischievous artist who climbed onto the roof of Langdon Ave Elementary School one Yule season and wrote, "Have a Pee Nutty Christmas."[57]

On August 7, 1997, Matea Gold reported in the *Times* that "classroom drop-and-cover routines" which were used during the cold war in preparation for a nuclear attack were now being used in area schools to "teach children to sprawl flat at the sound of shots." They are called "drop drills," "crisis drills," or "bullet drills." Usually, school lockdowns are initiated during the drills as well. One nearby school in Lennox has monthly "drop exercises" and an "annual outdoor sniper drill." Principal Anna McLinn of Marvin Avenue Elementary School is quoted as saying:

> If students heard a loud noise, they were trained to drop to the ground and crawl as if they were in the service, keeping their bodies flat. . . . If you stand up, the bullet could hit you. . . . This was an area where Uzis would go off next door. . . . It's nothing for my youngsters to see a shooting a couple of blocks from school. When you're looking at a community where this is almost normal, you have to be prepared.[58]

"Drop drills" are credited with saving the life of students at Figueroa Street Elementary School in February 1996 when Alfredo Perez was seriously injured by a stray bullet. Of course, "drop drills" are approaches that react to the symptoms of a violent society and do little to make the streets a safer place. When capitalist social relations accord certain people the status of deviants, it is not surprising that little is done to provide the necessary social and economic conditions for young people to acquire dignity and hope in their lives.

Although many residents were described as hard-working but down on their luck, the journalists noted that, in general, "we found people . . . living lives of paralyzing deprivation."[59] While the journalists described efforts by local residents to build a sense of community, attempts by police to fight drug-dealing, and actions by the local church to provide spiritual and social services, they conceded that little could be done outside of small incremental successes. Not one of the four parts in this series seriously linked life on Orion Avenue to larger economic relations in the wider society or attempted to situate crime in the context of the way in which Los Angeles has been ravaged by capitalism. Wayne Mellinger offers the following statistics:

> 16 percent of the city's 3.6 million people live below the poverty level, 333,000 are officially unemployed. . . . Massive reductions in social services in the city have left parts of the city with shattered school systems with dropout rates over 50 percent, the poor with virtually no emergency care, the streets packed with thousands of homeless, and infant mortality rates approaching third world levels.[60]

While the series often offered sensitive and heartfelt accounts of family life at the apartment complex on Orion Avenue and chronicled both the despair and the hope for a better future of many of the people who live there, it failed to connect the lives of individuals to worldwide economic conditions and the internationalized profit-making conditions under global capitalism. For the journalists, personal attributes determine whether or not a gang member escapes Orion Avenue and is able to rebuild his or her life outside of the neighborhood. Failure to do so is also individualized or psychologized, as it is connected to pathological family life, lack of work skills, or the habitual lure of gang solidarity and quick profits. The lives of inner-city poor are seemingly unconnected to the fact that half a million employees have been laid off each year for the last six years, while on a worldwide scale direct investment (mostly by United States) in creating foreign plants and operations has soared to $325 billion. The distribution of incomes between capital and labor is unsettling, especially in the United States. While workers' wages in terms of real hourly wages and family incomes have taken a downward turn between 1983 and 1992, the net worth of the top 1 percent of the nation has increased by 28 percent. Such greed, avarice, and indifference to human misery has created a "Judas economy" of betrayal and destruction.[61]

Discursive violence is about the density of discourses and multiple economic interests they serve, and the emancipatory knowledges that are displaced or submerged. Here the *Los Angeles Times* partakes of cool, discursive violence in its attempt to portray the reality of gang violence. Here the neighborhood is primarily seen visually as a space of decay. The journalists write from a position of logocentric occularcentrism in which the mark of the social disappears under a claim of access to the unmediated presence of the neighborhood. There is a latent system of signification at work here that stresses only that which can be seen. They remain blind to the social codes that legitimate their particular acts of seeing and nonseeing. Exploitation is more than an epistemological phenomenon; it is an economic, social, and cultural set of relationships. The systems of intelligibility that inform the analysis of the Orion Avenue neighborhood remain insensitive to their own historical conditions of production. The inhabitants of Orion Avenue are assumed to be responsible for their own condition. They live in crowded facilities behind a barbed wire fence. Outside the fence is the "street," a space of drug corruption, violence, and death. It is a tangible space that is out of control, even with regular police monitoring, surveillance, and periodic arrests. The description of this "material space" is really a negative image of the garrison of the colonial mind that sees itself in the middle of conquered territory that it has to suppress forcefully in order to defend civilization. The fact that the journalists remark that Beverly Hills residents would never tolerate the time it takes for police to respond to complaints on Orion Avenue locates the residents on Orion Avenue as lacking the necessary symbolic capital as well as property value to warrant the same kind of protection under the law as residents who occupy spaces of ruling-class interests. This double standard with respect to law enforcement illustrates the alarming disjuncture between neighborhoods produced within an episteme of community that is regulated by binary oppositions such as innocent/criminal, sane/pathological, worthy/unworthy. These opposed, yet interdependent pairings become: the dichotomous codifications of difference or grid upon which oppression and domination are coordinated in a regime of truth.

There is a false assumption at work which suggests that empirical data in the form of selected interviews combined with a physical description of people and surroundings is sufficient to explain the psychodrama of their lives, why these people are poor, and why they seemingly will remain so. Such forms of cool violence journalism, while making well-intentioned efforts at "thick description" are unable to locate urban dwellers within the social totality and ensemble of social structures in which they are produced, and within the abstract space (local, regional, and national) in which their subjectivities are formed. A critical semiotics of space, we are arguing, will be able to foreground the imperial imaginary in which space is produced and enable new "mappings" of urban space that will intervene in the subject formation of individuals such that they will be able to reconquer the "spaces" of their lives through the development of a new spatial imagination, a new cartography of subjectivity. In this sense, spatial practice becomes a form of political intervention,[62] an instance of counter-hegemonic praxis.

So, where is violence? It exists not just in the regular forms of the occasional act or isolated condition, but in the cool violence perpetrated by the conceptual space of modernist epistemologies and their associated logics of whiteness, masculinity, and capitalism. Cool violence is slippery and cannot be easily regulated by bureaucratic solutions without committing more violence. In terms of schooling, educators, educational researchers, and educational technocrats must conceptualize and counter the cool violence that differentiates educational spaces into systems of power. Imagine that a so-called model school in Beverly Hills, California—one of the most affluent municipalities in the world—is perceived as violent because it serves to rationalize a view that sees it as an "exemplary, ordered educational condition." Do you imagine this school as racialized? The "model-ness" of this school would most likely be studied through modernist spatial epistemologies and fashioned into "visions" for "educational reform" through the fixed, naturalized, and essentialized spatial metaphors associated with cool violence.

Meanwhile, cool violence is reinforced as a demonized school somewhere in Los Angeles is given "*the* model" to follow, hoping this will curb the violence in a "barrio" or "inner-city" school. Powered by the force of spatial legitimation, the model bulldozes over local spatialities. Unfortunately, local spatialities of the disenfranchised are often themselves caught in colonized conceptions of violence that lead to hopelessness and self-hate. Although our bodies and possessions are marked with it, cool violence remains out of sight, and out of mind. Cool violence is a form of discursive domination, one which diffuses itself at the level of the political economy of signs. It is a gift which can only be canceled through a critique of the work of educational texts. As the oxygen of state repression, cool violence is invisible yet life-sustaining in a social order dependent upon capitalist exploitation.

NOTES

This chapter was previously published in *Discourse* (Spring 1999). It is reprinted here with permission.

1. Karl Marx and Fredrich Engels, *The Sacred Family and Other Texts* (Mexico: Editorial Grijalbo, 1962), 6.

2. Walter Benjamin "Theses on the Philosophy of History" in *Illuminations* (New York, Schocken Books, 1979).

3. Michel Foucault, *Discipline and Punish: The Birth of the Prison* (New York: Vintage Books, 1979).

4. Jean Baudrillard, *The Mirror of Production* (St. Louis: Telos Press, 1975); *Seduction* (New York: St. Martin's Press, 1979); *Symbolic Exchange and Death* (Thousand Oaks, Calif.: Sage Publications, 1993).

5. Marcel Mauss, *The Gift* (New York: Norton, 1967), 5-40; See also P. McLaren and Z. Leonardo, "Jean Baudrillard's Chamber of Horrors: From Marxism to Terrorist Pedagogy," in *Revolutionary Multiculturalism: Pedagogies of Dissent for a New Millennium*, ed. P. McLaren (Boulder, Colo.: Westview Press, 1997), 114-149.

6. Pierre Bourdieu, *Outline of a Theory of Practice* (Cambridge: Cambridge University Press, 1977), 5.

7. Bourdieu, *Outline*, 195.

8. Signithia Fordham, "Racelessness as a Factor in Black Students' School Success: Pragmatic Strategy or Pyrrhic Victory?" *Harvard Educational Review* 58, no. 1 (1988): 54-84.

9. Peter McLaren, *Schooling as a Ritual Performance: Towards a Political Economy of Educational Symbols and Gestures* (New York: Routledge, 1993); P. Willis, *Learning to Labor* (New York: Columbia University Press, 1977); J. MacLeod, *Ain't No Makin' It* (Boulder, Colo.: Westview Press, 1987).

10. Paulo Freire, *Pedagogy of the Oppressed* (New York: Continuum, 1993).

11. Jean Baudrillard, *In the Shadow of the Silent Majorities* (New York: Semiotext, 1983), 3, 28.

12. P. Bourdieu, *Outline*; P. Bourdieu, and L. Wacquant, *An Invitation to Reflexive Sociology* (Chicago: The University of Chicago Press, 1992).

13. Bourdieu, *Outline*, 191.

14. Bourdieu and Wacquant, *An Invitation*, 167.

15. M. Foucault, *The History of Sexuality*, Vol. 1 (New York: Vintage Books, 1978), 86, 89.

16. Bourdieu, *Outline*, 195.

17. Cited in T. Eagleton, *Ideology* (London: Routledge, 1991), 195.

18. Jeannie Oakes, *Keeping Track* (New Haven: Yale University Press, 1985).

19. D. Macdonell, *Theories of Discourse* (Oxford: Basil Blackwell, 1986), 73.

20. K. Marx, "Selected Texts," in *Ideology*, ed. T. Eagleton (London and New York: Longman, 1994), 23-30.

21. J. Baudrillard, *For a Critique of the Political Economy of the Sign* (St. Louis: Telos Press, 1981).

22. L. Althusser, *Lenin and Philosophy* (New York: Monthly Review Press, 1971).

23. S. Herbert, *Policing Space: Territoriality and the Los Angeles Police Department* (Minneapolis and London: University of Minnesota Press, 1997), 155.

24. Donna Haraway, *Simians, Cyborgs and Women* (London: Routledge, 1991).

25. Althusser, *Lenin and Philosophy*.

26. G. Biesta, "Deconstruction, Justice and the Question of Education." *Zeitschrift fuer Erziehungswissenschaft* 1, no. 3 (1989): 395-411.

27. Jacques Derrida, *Of Grammatology*, trans. G. Spivak (Baltimore: Johns Hopkins University Press, 1976).

28. Ferdinand de Saussure, *Course in General Linguistics* (Chicago: Open Court Classics, 1983).

29. Biesta, *Deconstruction*.

30. M. Ryan, "Foucault's Fallacy," *Strategies: A Journal of Theory, Culture and Politics* 7 (1993): 132-154.

31. Judith Butler, *The Psychic Life of Power: Theories in Subjection* (Stanford: Stanford University Press, 1997).

32. Butler, *The Psychic Life of Power*, 104.

33. See also G. Biesta, *Where Are You? Where am I? Identity, Intersubjectivity, and the Question of Location*. Paper presented at the University of California, Irvine, 1997.

34. D. Sibley, *Geographies of Exclusion* (London and New York: Routledge, 1995), xvi.

35. Sibley, *Geographies*, 86-87.

36. Sibley, *Geographies*.

37. N. Blomley, *Law, Space and the Geographies of Power* (New York: Guilford Press, 1994).

38. Cited by Sibley in *Geographies*, 107.

39. E. Soja, *Thirdspace* (Cambridge, Mass.: Blackwell Publishers, 1996).

40. J. Leovy, "Burbank Buys Turf to Clean Out Gang," *Los Angeles Times*, 31 August 1997, A1, A30.

41. Soja, *Thirdspace*.

42. Willis, *Learning to Labor*.

43. S. N. Haymes, *Race, Culture, and the City: A Pedagogy for Black Urban Struggles* (Albany: SUNY Press, 1995).

44. Soja, *Thirdspace*.

45. E. Soja and B. Hooper, "The Spaces that Difference Makes: Some Notes on the Geographical Margins of the New Cultural Politics." in *Place and the Politics of Identity*, eds. M. Keith and S. Pile (London: Routledge, 1993): 183-205.

46. Saussure, *Course in General Linguistics*.

47. F. Gadet, *Saussure and Contemporary Culture* (Great Britain: Hutchinson Radius, 1986), 32.

48. P. Ong, K. Park, and Y. Tong, "The Korean-Black Conflict and the State." In *New Asian Immigration in Los Angeles and Global Restructuring*, eds. P. Ong, E. Bonacich, and L. Cheng (Philadelphia: Temple University Press, 1994), 264-292; S. Cho, "Korean Americans vs. African Americans: Conflict and Construction." In *Reading Rodney King: Reading Urban Uprising*, ed. R. Gooding-Williams (New York: Routledge, 1991), 196-211; E. Kim, "Home Is Where the Han Is: A Korean-American Perspective on the Los Angeles Upheavals." In *Reading Rodney King*, 215-235.

49. J. Urry, *Consuming Places* (London: Routledge, 1995).

50. Haymes, *Race, Culture, and the City*; D. Massey, *Spatial Divisions of Labor*, 2nd ed. (New York: Routledge, 1995).

51. W. Mellinger, "Reading the News in the Age of Postmodern Mass Media: Gang Murders in the *Los Angeles Times*," *Cultural Studies* 2 (1997): 217-236.

52. Mellinger, "Reading the News," 222.

53. Mellinger, "Reading the News," 222.

54. Mellinger, "Reading the News," 223.

55. Mellinger, "Reading the News," 225.

56. Mellinger, "Reading the News," 233.

57. J. Johnson and C. Cole, "Gang Life's Grip Proves Hard to Escape," *Los Angeles Times*, 27 May 1997, A22.

58. M. Gold, "Urban School Drill: Duck and Cover for Gunfire," *Los Angeles Times*, 2 Aug. 1997, A20.

59. J. Johnson, "Surviving on a Block Ruled by a Gang," *Los Angeles Times*, 25 May 1997, A30.

60. Mellinger, "Reading the News," 233.

61. W. Wolman and A. Colamosca, *The Judas Economy: The Triumph of Capital and Betrayal of Work* (New York: Addison-Wesley, 1997).

62. S. Pile, *The Body and the City: Psychoanalysis, Space and Subjectivity* (London and New York: Routledge, 1996).

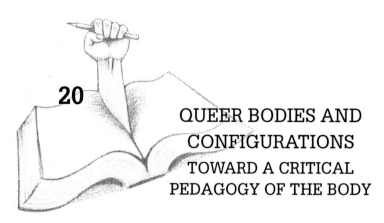

20

QUEER BODIES AND CONFIGURATIONS
TOWARD A CRITICAL PEDAGOGY OF THE BODY

Cindy Cruz and Peter McLaren

BODIES AND PEDAGOGY

In his affirmation of and admiration for the body, anthropologist Marcel Mauss (1934, p. 456) observes the pedagogy of swimming:

> Previously, we were taught to dive after having learned to swim. And when we were learning to dive, we were taught to close our eyes and then to open them underwater. Today the technique is the other way around. . . . Thus, even before they can swim, particular care is taken to get the children to control their dangerous but instinctive ocular reflexes: before all else they are familiarized with the water, their fears are suppressed, a certain confidence is created, suspensions and movements are selected.

Mauss studiously noted that the body trains for an efficiency of movement, a creation of an action that succeeds in its efforts to control involuntary reflexes. "One of the reasons why these series may more easily be assembled where the individual is concerned," Mauss noted, "is precisely because they are assembled by and for social authority" (p. 473). Famously concluding that bodies are nothing less than instruments used in an process of acculturation, Mauss asserted that not only is there an educational dimension to the process of adapting the body to its use (as worker, as student, as member of a civil society), but there also exists a pedagogy of normalization, a "mechanism inhibiting disorderly movements" (p. 474). But what do we make of the body that refuses to acculturate? Is a queer body one that, according to the dominant discourses of queer the-

This chapter originally appeared in Sherry and Svi Shapiro (Eds.), *Body Movements: Pedagogy, Politics and Social Change*, pp. 187-207. © 2002 Hampton Press Inc. Reprinted with permission of the publisher.

ory that take post-structuralist critiques of humanism as their point of departure—adheres to "disorderly conduct"—a conduct that resists the social mores
of its respective communities? Or is it more?

The observations of Mauss sheds some important light on the constitutive
elements of a pedagogy of the body in this era of the crisis of late capitalism.
The body techniques we inhabit—such as walking, sitting, or gesturing—are
comparable to but not synonymous with other corporeal or somatic forms of
mediation such as writing or speaking. They serve as both sign and agency. In
this sense, it is imperative that we view the physical body as a site of meaning-
making; and that we read the body's contradictory and often agonistic discourses as a social relation linked to the forces of revolution, rather than as a signifying apparatus of some "free range" transcendent and self-birthing Self that can
only function in tandem with its repressed other—the dark, the crippled, mis-
shapen, and context-dependent Queer Subject.

It is the queer body—the body that not only refuses and rejects the inscriptions of dominant discourses of gender and sexuality, but also the sovereign citations of race and class—where the implications of Mauss' observations of a body
pedagogy is most compelling. For our purposes, it speaks to the possibility of constructing a provisional anatomy of queer configurations that can bridge the dis-
tances between disciplinary interests and community alliances. Our work on this
project is a collaborative one, an affiliation that crosscuts contradictory positions
on—and sometimes radical departures from—normalized racial and gendered
positions. Our focus is to critically interrogate the narratives of the "effeminate
boy" and the "masculine girl" in an attempt to undress conceptually the existing
conditions that produce such narratives—the developing corporeal significations
of young queer bodies and their intersection with social relations of production.

THE QUEERED BODY

In Simon Leung's 1995 essay, "Squatting through Violence," the author narrates
a conversation he had with his younger brother, who comments on the squatting
bodies of Vietnamese immigrants at a San Jose, California, bus stop. It was not
only the incongruity of the scene of squatting bodies that Leung related, but also
of bus stop seats that were left empty. Leung states: "Squatting, as a form of
inscription, cannot in and of itself figure the abjection of its occupants. Yet, when
it functions as a signifier which inversely reflects one's own servitude to (a sitter's or a citizen's) identity, such signification secures the citation of sovereignty
in the sitter while exiling the squatters from the realm of identity" (p. 96). The
gesture of squatting signals a resistance to the process of cultural assimilation in
the broader U.S. context, which according to Leung, is nothing less than a "continual grasping of fragmented information, displacing old habits—an ecology of
the Self in which differences are enacted against the terms of the self" (p. 94).

Like the gesture of squatting, a queer gesture can also function as signifier of a body that may or may not reflect complicity with a gendered or sexualized order. Judith Butler argues that the body constitutes a ludic arena of linguistic performance, a public proscenium of "play" where the categories of male and female act out dramas of misrecognition. Punch and Judy have taken to cross-dressing and have taken over our structural consciousness. "As a corporeal field of cultural play," Butler argues, "gender is basically an innovative affair, although it is quite clear that there are strict punishments for contesting the script by performing out of turn or through unwarranted improvisations" (1993, p. 415). Strict punishments, like the labeling of an act as "disorderly conduct," reflect the undialectical dualisms of self/other and male/female. The official designation of "unwarranted improvisations" not only illuminate the mechanisms that delineate and order gender/sexual difference, but give visibility to the disproportionately harsher punishments meted out to African Americans, indigenous peoples, and members of working-class communities. For example, Proposition 21, the "Gang Violence and Juvenile Crime Prevention Act" initiative on California's March 2000 ballot sponsored by former Governor Pete Wilson, strips youth of protections—such as extending the "three strikes law"—currently granted to them by law. With recent media attention on young offenders engineering the manifest illusion of the adolescent "superpredator"—urban troglodytes with shaved heads, neck tattoos, and baggy pants intent on violence and mayhem—it is little wonder that laws redefining "gang member" specifically target youth of color, granting police the right to assume that any suspicious-looking group of three or more young bodies is "gang affiliated." In this instance, the "improvisations" of race and class can be severely restricted by law, further illuminating the repressive apparatuses of capital that help to produce the widening gap between rich and poor (and those who benefit from this) in the state of California.

The notion of "improvisations" creates categorizes of gender and sexuality as "corporeal style, an act, as it were, that is both intentional and performative" (Butler, 1993, p. 415), not only challenging the constructions of gender but also the primacy of heterosexist assumptions. But a body is not so easily manipulated. Performativity, as Butler argues in her landmark 1993 essay, "Critically Queer," becomes the "compulsory repetition of prior and subjectivating norms, ones which cannot be thrown off at will, but which work, animate, and constrain the gendered subject, and which are also the resources from which resistance, subversion, displacement are to be forged" (p. 22). It is within this space of possibility that a body's resistance to regimes of stability and power emerges. The techniques of the body, as Mauss so eloquently and presciently defines them, are assembled by and for "social authority." Here a space is provided for the restraint of "disorderly movements," gestures that, as Jean-Claude Schmitt (1989) suggests, refuse to "avoid excess" (p. 130). Excessive gesture reflects a less ordered state of mind, a degeneracy and effeminacy that becomes "too much" for the custodians of normality. In this way we can begin to see how, in

Foucault's terms, power manufactures the lineaments and discursive ligaments of the docile body.

> The judges of normality are everywhere. We are in the society of the teacher-judge, the doctor-judge, the educator-judge, the social worker-judge; it is on them that the universal reign of the normative is based; and each individual, wherever he may find himself, subjects to it with his body, his gestures, his behavior, his aptitudes, his achievements. (Michel Foucault, 1994, p. 181)

Power, for Foucault, is never contraceptively seamless, "but always spawning new forms of culture and subjectivity, new openings for political resistance to emerge" (Bordo, 1993, p. 254). While recognizing the limitations of Foucault's theory of power (in particular, his studied inattention to capitalist social relations of production and his dispersal of power into a multicausal stream of discursive effects), we appreciate a founding gesture of his politics, which directs attention to the role of critical social agents in the creation of new forms of associative capacities and formations. As Kenn Gardner Honeychurch (1996, p. 350) suggests, "Forced to ponder our bodies by a culture startled by gender non-conformity and sexual diversity, social researchers who claim a queered position may best be suited to interrogating the sexual in social inquiry." Recognizing that the queer gesture—the excessiveness of the arms and hands, the broken wrist, exaggeration of a walk (for a male) and the defensive posturing of arms crossed at the chest, the heavy tread of walking heel-to-toe, and the unabashed gaze that refuses to turn away (for a female)—is, as David Gere (1997, p. 73) perceptively argues, the "bold strategy to resist arbitrary societal restrictions." The cultural practice of the queer gesture offers the possibility—but not the assurance or insurance—of a radical representational practice, a practice that not only is about developing a critical politics of corporeal significance, but also is about creating a dialectical understanding that is not only performative, but pedagogical.

CORPOREALITIES

It is here that we need to brush queer theory up against the conceptual limits of performativity. In so doing, we must engage the body, not as a site of immanent desire, but as a site for the enfleshment of capitalist social relations—as social relations of production metaphorized in the flesh, and as nondiscursive "products" through which ideological relations and concrete social practices are lived. Here we draw attention to the materialism of the body, its irreducibility of labor, and its constitutive implication in practical-material activity. Capitalist social relations punish bodies, forcing them into brute conditions of abstraction and conditions of alienation linked to their reduction to relations of exchange. What must be acknowledged is "not so much the desiring body and how it is cusped by the couplet of identity/difference, but rather how to emancipate the body that is crushed under the weight of capitalist extraction and produced within the iron jaws of profit" (McLaren 1997, pp. lv-lvi). In this sense, we contend that the queer body must be re-positioned for consideration within the political economy of the sign in so far as the sign can be located within its historical production in the arena of class struggle.

Radhika Mohanram asserts that "bodies become visible or invisible only through the vectors of power and economies and the meaning systems imparted to these within cultural knowledge systems" (1999, p. 387). Consequently, an understanding of our bodies and the bodies of others cannot be isolated from the concrete materiality of social relations within late capitalism. As Mohanram remarks about the victims of capital, "Poverty drains one of identity, as identity in its purest form is seeped in consciousness, which brings about detachment and objectivism. Poverty reverts us to being the visible body and as being subject to the body, and as object, without padding, protection or consciousness" (1999, p. 37). It is in this context that Mohanram asserts that the "racialized body" and the "poor body" can be used relatively interchangeably because neither "has an idealized, invisible body, nor do they have a proper identity. The proper ideal subject is one with property but no body" (1999, p. 38). There is no subject position for the gay man or lesbian from which to speak loudly and indignantly, except through the ventriloquism of heteronormative discourse; there is no "unmarked" positionality from which the queer body (or any body) can enunciate itself. Homophobic heterosexuals attempt to fashion their identities in a pure consciousness of being through the making of the gay, lesbian, or transgendered body—the latter of which, like murdered transgender youth, Brandon Teena, are rendered both brute and mute. The violence of such marking leaves the heterosexual body more invisible and, paradoxically, its heterosexist identity more secured.

Queer bodies bespeak markings of a subterranean alterity. The markings of the queer bodies are read or "world-ed" as "deviant" not only because they are read by heterosexual eyes, but also because the mechanisms of capitalist society underwrite a "self/other" dichotomy, whose intractable gridlock we know as queer/straight. Only the heterosexual "self" has property. The homosexual "other" is property-less. The queer subject names her marked body only to find that she recuperates the general economy of otherness produced by technical demands of established systems of intelligibility and the tropology of the subject inscribed within the logic of capital. Similarly, in her attempt to "unmark" her body, clamorously disavowing the interpretation given to it, she is able to affirm only those subject positions or acts of naming or unnaming bestowed upon her (or withheld from her) by the "straight" patriarchal capitalist society. In other words, even the act of resisting heteronormative discourse affirms the already available systems of intelligibility through which we are able to locate "self" and "other."

Cruz: My queer body is unable to strip off its defensive postures. I pose
         my arms across my chest to disguise myself. I bind my breasts. I
         crop my hair short to the scalp and in these ways, I shape my body to
         defend itself against the ravages of excessive heterosexuality.

McLaren: My straight body is irrefragably crooked. It arches towards other-
         ness but is bent from both gravity and regret. It glistens pink and is
         invisible. The opposite of a vampire, it can be seen only in the mirror.

Cruz: I look for others like me, acknowledge our occupation of public
         space. My queer body is masculine, a body shaped by a history of
         colonization and resistance. Looking into the mirror I see my face—
         my wide mouth, bronze skin, and almond-shaped eyes—my indige-
         nous ancestry, my mestiza features. Histories of conquests lie just
         underneath skin. Strip this first layer and I reach another narrative of
         insurgency, only this discourse is inscripted on my body, written in
         blood. I learn to embody resistance. I survive.

McLaren: My flesh is scarred by history. It slips furtively in the form of a
         white body from occupied spaces to unoccupied places. Like one of
         Dickens' ghosts, it drags a long, always lengthening chain of mistakes
         and transgressions. It is a time machine that takes me back through my
         genetic code to life in the swamp. Very much like contemporary Los
         Angeles. Swamp Thing enjoying a caramel latté at the Coffee Bean on
         Sunset Boulevard. I am a licensed opium-eater in a den of heterosexu-
         als, a subterranean voluptuary with a bodily affliction. Ingesting the
         ololiuqui plant transforms my body into a jaguar.

Cruz: My queer body is marked to display to other queers my own plea-
         sures and desires. It is a butch language that I embody where others
         who have similar cultural experiences can read in the stride in my
         walk, the swing of my arms, the rigidity of my shoulders. I am the
         pollutant of my race—the hybrid of perversity and my rebellion
         against rampant nationalism. But I have yet to refuse this peripheral
         state of existence outside the heterosexual norm. In fact, I revel in it.
         Perhaps this is what makes it queer.

McLaren: Pursued by no one except lawyers, I am constantly on the run.
         With an awkward grace, I skin my dead, white self with a whimsy
         and a glee that would make Hannibal Lecter envious, adding on
         layer upon layer of talismanic inscriptions. Like a drunken bricklay-
         er with a trowel heaped with significations from the Museum of the
         Revolution, I seal a wounded soul behind a wall of regrets. I regular-
         ly have tea with Norman Bates. Zapata and Che stand guard from the
         portals of my shoulders. They are my guardian santos. I hide from
         the sunlight and my cultural mistakes. I was conceived on Cobra
         Island, by a demon and a robber baron. I bear the stigmata. I am hid-
         ing from priests.

Cruz: My body is space where discourses wage battles over a territory of
           flesh and blood. "Your body couldn't be the land," says poet Cherrie
           Moraga (1993, p. 13), even as our attachment to Aztlan is used against
           us, colonized along with and through our desires. Race intersects with
           gender intersecting with the history of steel plant closures and seventh
           generation Mexicano families on one body to create this post-human
           fusion called queer. Volatile and transgressive, not only do I perform
           gender, I perform race and history. My body remembers.

McLaren: I owe my body to the farmlands of Cornwall, Canada. They nour-
           ished four generations of McLarens, many of whom are buried in a
           family cemetery in Apple Hill. My Scottish, Irish, and English ances-
           tors—going farther back than those who made their way down the St.
           Lawrence River—were drunken brawlers in the pubs of Glasgow,
           Liverpool, and Dublin. Many of them were ne're-do-wells. I owe my
           thick skull—perfect for head butts—to these wonderful louts. Masters
           of the black-thorns and shilaleaghs, which they used to wield at
           Donnybrook Fair in Dublin, they would have cursed the cheekbones I
           inherited from Fourier, my broad forehead from Proudhon, my jaw-
           bone from Trotsky—even the carbunkles I inherited from Marx. And
           while I'm trying to re-make my body here in Hollywood, it seems a
           lost cause. Hollywood might seem "liberal" to those who believe the
           press. But California witnessed the unravelling of the left in the 1950s,
           as the ruling class sought to consolidate its political power from the
           coffee klatches in suburban Orange County, through the church base-
           ments across the Sunbelt and the bridge clubs of the Midwest to the
           Klan rallies of the Old Confederacy of Mississippi and Alabama. While
           Fred Schwarz was preaching to 7,000 impressionable young men in his
           School of Anti-Communism in Anaheim's La Palma Stadium, while
           Aimee Semple McPherson was staging elaborate spectacles of reli-
           gious worship at her Foursquare Church in Echo Park, while the public
           was morbidly transfixed by the stabbing by Lana Turner's fourteen-
           year-old daughter of her mother's suitor, Johnny Stompanato, a cohort
           of Mickey Cohen, the police were raiding African-American and
           Latino clubs in a drive to "purify Los Angeles." They were raiding the
           "drag balls" and busting the young men at Dreamland, the
           Hummingbird Black and Tan Cafe, the Morocco, the Saw Dust Trail,
           Jimmy's Backyard on Ivar, and The Barn on Cahuenga Avenue. The
           (mainly) white ruling class has been engaging in a war against commu-
           nists, African-Americans, Latinos, Asians, and gays and lesbians that
           continues to this day. Despite the mask that history has given me and
           the ocean of blood it has placed at my feet, I will do whatever it takes
           to smash the objective conditions and class locations and relations that
           made me.

QUEER CONFIGURATIONS

There is nothing new about Kroker and Kroker's (1987) insistence that the body is the new zone of surveillance. Feminists have charted this line of inquiry into body politics since the second wave of feminism in the early 1960s (Bordo, 1999, p. 247). Judicial apparatuses, such as the 1986 upholding of the Georgia sodomy law in Bowers v. Hardwick and routine locker/body searches and drug tests in schools and in the work place, represent contemporary strategies of capture that have directly affected lesbian and gay bodies.

School is a particularly difficult terrain to be negotiated for lesbian and gay youth—sexuality is not easily discussed without parental consent and rampant homophobia is usually left unchecked by administrators. Lesbian and gay youth are routinely institutionalized as mentally ill or forced out of homes that will not tolerate "deviance" in their own children. In "How To Bring Your Kids Up Gay," Eve Kosofsky Sedgwick (1993) argues that although homosexuality as a pathology has been removed from the American Psychiatric Association's *Diagnostic and Statistical Manual* in 1973, a new diagnosis, "Gender Identity Disorder of Children," another pathologizing diagnosis attacking the effeminate boy and (less frequently) the masculine girl, has surfaced. It comes as no surprise that lesbian and gay youth account for a gross disproportion of attempted and successful suicides in the United States.

Overtly effeminate boys and masculine girls have always existed in our hyper-heterosexual households, yet our categories of cultural experience have neglected to look at strategies employed by youth to develop their bodily significations. As Eve Kosofsky Sedgwick suggests, "the eclipse of the effeminate boy from adult gay discourse would represent more than a damaging theoretical gap; it would represent a mode of annihilating homophobic, gynephobic, and pedophobic hatred internalized and made central to gay-affirmative analysis" (1993, p. 72). In an era where lesbian and gay political movements work hard to become part of the mainstream—as parents, as nonpromiscuous partners, and as good capitalists—the effeminate boy and (perhaps to a lesser extent) the masculine girl have little to offer when their "deviancy" is assured to impede lesbian and gay assimilation.

Understanding how "tomboy" and "sissy" identities are "performed" within cultural experiences of gay or lesbian identities may be helpful to researchers attempting to document queer resistance. In our own research into the transgressive potential of queer bodies, we have discovered (and helped to create) the pedagogical power of video narratives. Video work, as a means of choreographing a narrative, allows young people to explore complex strategies and tactics of performance for developing transgressive corporeal meanings. According to Susan Leigh Foster, "bodies do not only pass meaning along, or pass it along their uniquely responsive way; they develop choreographies of signs through which they discourse. . . . They narrate their own fate" (1996, p. xi).

STORYING THE FLESH

The interrogation of corporeal narratives of queer youth is more than an exploration of the self or a deconstruction of the legacies that inform the construction of our bodies. Ivor F. Goodson argues that "storying the self" can be a means of making sense of new conditions of working and being. The self becomes a "reflexive project, an ongoing narrative project" (1998, p. 16). In this context, storying the body becomes an examination of the role of corporeality in the production of a queer narrative, in the articulation of a queer gesture, and the enactment of queer configurations. In short, it becomes the movement towards a queer identity. The movement toward a queer pedagogy is, as Debra Britzman suggests, "a reading of the world [that] is always about risking the self, and about the attempt to exceed the injuries of discourse so that all bodies matter" (1998, p. 187), where young people not only can begin the construction of a critical queered consciousness but also push beyond individual self and body towards collective radical social transformations and queer liberatory practices. The latter move, we argue, is more than an attempt to *épater la bourgeoisie* in terms of its elevation of hysterical heteronormativity to a sacerdotal status; rather it stipulates an understanding of how the ideological manufacture of queer identities is intimately related to the historical struggle between the bourgeoisie and the working-class.

THE ERASURE OF THE TOILING BODY

Using the body as the centerpiece of analysis, David McNally has recently published a powerful critique of Saussure, Derrida, and the post-structuralists. His basic argument is that certain problematic economic concepts figure centrally in their approaches to linguistic science. He illustrates how postmodern theorists model language on their specific understanding of the capitalist marketplace. McNally makes a strong case that, in the process of such modeling, formal linguistics turns language into the dead labor of fetishistic commodities. It does this by decapitating signifiers and their meaning-making process from their fundamental connection to living labor, in other words, from their connection to the toiling body, the body that labors under capitalism. For example, Saussure and Derrida equate the general phenomenon of linguistic value with the role of "money" as a general equivalent of exchange. Derrida, it turns out, had criticized Saussure for positing an invariant or transcendental signified, or what McNally calls a "gold standard" against which signs can be measured or interpreted. Derrida, as readers familiar with his writings will recall, argues that there is only *differance*, that unknowable form prior to language, that condition of undecidability and the very condition of possibility of that undecidability that permits the endless play of reference that Derrida famously discusses in his large corpus of work (Derrida seems enraptured by difference and enraged by sameness, norms, standards). When Derrida makes the claim that *differance* is the most general structure of the economy he denies the praxis and labor that ground economic relations. That is because, according to Derrida, money lacks a referent. It has no material foundation; money circulates without any referents. You can, for instance, have bad checks, a fraudulent credit card—and these function as money. Credit and speculation become a form of "fictitious" capital. For this reason, McNally describes Derrida as the philosopher of fictitious capital.

McNally goes on to discuss Baudrillard and how, in his system, sign values are independent of external referents; they refer, in other words, only to *themselves*. Baudrillard's is an economy of internal relations, following its own code. Baudrillard lives in a techno-crazed universe of techno-mediatic power where labor is always already dead, where political economy is dead, where everything is virtual, the economy is virtual, and where use values have disappeared. Use values do not transcend the codes that encapsulate them and give them live.

There is something compelling about Baudrillard's argument as long as you realize it is science fiction. Baudrillard maintains that we consume fictitious identities by purchasing the sign value of, say, an Armani suit, or a pair of Guess jeans. We dress ourselves up in abstractions—literally. Contrast this with what Marx had to say, that in capitalist societies, concrete labor is reduced to a quantum of total social labor, as something translated into socially necessary labor-time—a process that is part of the circuit of production and exchange. The key point here, according to McNally, is that, for Marx, abstract labor is not a mental abstraction but the *real social form of labor* in capitalist society. This is an absolutely crucial point. When labor-power itself becomes a commodity (a special kind of commodity) in the very act of laboring itself, then this abstracting process becomes generalized. McNally recognizes that what we are talking about here is surely more than a linguistic phenomenon. Consequently, McNally is very critical of Derrida's linguistification of life. If everyday life were just a linguistic phenomenon then we would have to go along with Wittgenstein and perhaps in the process have to concede that Marxist theory was the result of a linguistic error! Contra Baudrillard and Derrida, signifiers do not replace use value in a virtual economy of signs. True, capitalism entails an abstracting process, but it is one in which concrete labor is translated into abstract labor—into a labor that resembles interchangeable bits. But this is not just a concept, or a signifier—it is a real social form within the process of production; it is, as McNally notes, a systematic process of abstraction wherein capital compels the translation of concrete labor into abstract labor. Labor-power becomes value only when it assumes a value-relation, an objective life as a commodity, an abstraction from the body-work of the laborer, and hence from the use-values produced by the efforts of laboring subjects. This is alienated labor, the subsumption of concrete labor by abstract labor. McNally writes that no matter how abstracted things become, the exchange between money and a commodity always entails exchanges of labor. Capital is not self-birthing; it is never an independent source of value. For instance, interest-bearing capital does not except a connection with human labor but is merely the purest fetish of them all. In their rage against Marx's obsession with decidability, poststructuralists deny the origin of value in labor, in the life-giving, toiling, body in labor.

McNally describes historical materialist critique as a politics that reclaims the origins of the body in labor in its struggle against idealism, against the subordination of the world of bodies, nature, objects, and labor to subjectivity, and in its struggle against objects being subsumed by concepts. It is a direct challenge to the autonomy of thought, that is, to objective, concrete, sensuous life being subsumed by the self-movement of thought.

While McNally praises Bakhtin, or Volosinov, as seeing class struggle embodied in the struggle over the meaning of signs, it is to the polymath Walter Benjamin that his praise is most clearly and enthusiastically directed. Benjamin's understanding of the redemptive possibilities within the de-mythified and barren landscape of capitalism is what makes his work especially valuable in the struggle against capitalist social relations. In his work on the *flaneur*, for instance, Benjamin conveyed that everyone in capitalist society is a prostitute who sells his or her talents and body parts. We live in the charred world of capital, a dead zone inhabited by smoldering corpses and decaying commodities. Such a critical understanding can help break through the naturalization of history and the domestication of our individual agency and enter the terrain of historical action. In this way we become agents of history, and not pawns in the hands of a historical destiny written by the powers that be. At the same time, Benjamin ruptures the myth of the self-made individual. We are all dead objects awaiting the meanings we have yet to write, as McNally puts it. McNally sees Benjamin as establishing a political project in which the oppressed class must reclaim the libidinal energies it has cathected onto commodities and rechannel them into a revolutionary praxis, a praxis of historical struggle towards emancipation, towards liberation. It was Benjamin, after all, who said that "*money stands ruinously at the center of every vital interest.*" Revolutionary action involves the dialectics of remembering and forgetting, of challenging the repressed bourgeois desires linked to the rise of capitalism and embodied in the collective dreams of a pathological culture, a society gone mad. Benjamin, asserts McNally, considers the body to be the primary site for a transformative type of knowing, one that arises through physical action, through a type of praxis not unlike that discussed by the great Brazilian revolutionary, Paulo Freire. Revolutionary practice, for Benjamin, means cultivating a "bodily presence of mind." It is this to this type of revolutionary praxis that our work on the body is directed.

THE PRODUCTION OF A QUEER SELF

In video artist Andrew Becerra's narrative, *Alone Once Again* (1996, VHS 2 min.), the last camera shot reveals an androgynous looking youth, gender undetermined, with plucked eyebrows and close-cropped hair, staring wistfully into the camera for just an instant. Yet, this moment expands into a look of regret, then confusion, and finally, resignation. But it is in this instant that the youth's slow and measured turning away from the camera confronts the viewer with a performed instanciation of a gay or lesbian corporeal experience. This short video "poem" may be said to mark the beginning of the narration of its own fate.

Artist Rhiannon Pollock's (1995, VHS, 3 minutes) *Gabbing with God* offers an insight into a corporeal schema that resists and refuses a patriarchal discourse. Pollock's work starts with the camera settling into an image of a Bible, a novena candle, and a Catholic rosary. A young woman's voice spins the tale of her encounter with God:

> I faxed a letter to God and surprisingly,
> He answered me.
> So we set up a time to meet and discuss how I felt about life. I got
> To the cafe on time, four p.m.

In this next shot, God is no more than a talking head, the screen filled with the creased, pock-marked and stained flesh of an older white male mouth and nose, with just the suggestion of eyes above pale, pulpy cheeks. Pollock has created her God in the image of the wizened white patriarch, a specific species of masculinity, the weather-beaten and rust splotched face of an aging Marlboro Man (who, incidentally, the actor portrayed at one time). Juxtaposed with the image of God's mouth is a side shot of the mouth of the narrator, our first image of her. Her lips are slightly opened, almost trusting, a duet of teeth and tongue. This image is youthful, with fair skin and rosy cheeks dotted with a faint trace of acne, underscoring the adolescent impishness of the narrator.

The most arresting image of the narrator's face is an isolated shot of her pierced lower lip. A silver hoop pushes deliciously through pursed red lips with a double women's symbol suspended outside of the hoop. The next image of the narrator shows her standing directly in front of the camera. Our eyes are drawn to her close-cropped hair, nose, mouth, and muscular neck anchored by a black tee-shirt freighted with necklaces of silk and silver chain. The image of the lesbian mouth takes up most of the frame. Unafraid and looking straight into the camera, the narrator's face questions the ultimate authority:

> I understand we have to learn our lessons but
> why do you torture us?
> I'm sick of seeing people die, I'm sick of the racism, sexism, and homophobia.

Pollock's emphasis on testimonial imparts a special emphasis to the images of mouths, lips, tongues, and throats. The mouth plays a critical role in Pollock's project, suturing together those gestures that are considered prohibited to women—females speaking out and lesbian sexuality. The second close-up of God's face is much closer to the camera than the previous shot, showing more enlarged pores, more dry creases along the jawline and mouth. God's lips are cracked and weathered, chapped from too much exposure to the elements of His universe. God replies to the narrator's questions, but the close-up creates a face that is monstrous.

> Well, Rhiannon, you should know that white people will always be superior. Men are more important and more knowledgeable than any woman can ever be. . . . Intimacy is meant for procreation, not pleasure.

For Pollock, organized Christian religion becomes an oppressive instrument of the ruling class in its attempt to purge bodies that fail to exhibit the inscriptions of the dominant white supremacist, heteronormative and patriarchal culture. This challenge to God constitutes the narrator's structured refusal to allow God's values to infect her body and to trouble her identity. The next image is of the young narrator, with Pollock angling her shot up and into the narrator's face, suggesting that she is taller than God. For the first time we see the narrator's entire face—dark hair and dark eyes on a slightly rounded jawline. Her cropped and colored hair, the suggestive stance of her body, the imperious camera angle, and the tone and inflection of the narrative voice become "too much" for God. The excessiveness of voice and alignment of the body is a direct, and literal in-your-face confrontation with God. In an arcane gesture to Wiccan spirituality, the narrator's hand pulls out a small charm in the shape of a winged woman. The hand caresses the fairy, fingers moving lovingly over the glistening metal charm. This affiliation with the symbols of Wiccan religion reasserts the narrator's women-centered lesbian spirituality, neutralizing the spiritual despotism of a patriarchal Christianity. The video effectively becomes a challenge to Christian ideology, confronting a system of beliefs and values that render women invisible, deviant, and silent. In opposition to the Christian symbols in the opening images, fairies become nothing less than a connection to a queer cultural past where Pollock can begin the construction of her own lesbian histories.

In another personal narrative project, artist Andrew Becerra documents the isolated reality of a young Latino youth in his experimental video poem, *Alone Once Again*. Beginning with a montage of images of industrial Los Angeles, Becerra begins his *testimonio* as a young gay Latino living his life recklessly through a culture of clubs, drugs, and unsafe sex. The first image in the video is of a young person scurrying up a flight of stairs. Wearing jackboots, knee socks, and revealing waif-like legs, the gender of this figure remains, temporarily, very ambiguous.

I was only 16, going on 17
All I wanted to do was have some fun.
Looking for fun in all the sleaziest places.
Dark alleys, dark clubs, dark stairways,
Strange strangers and strange places.

Becerra leads the audience through a world of anonymous sex, "dark alleys/dark clubs/dark stairwells" that reflect a desire for intimacy so strong that the protagonist, like many young gay men, risks all for those fleeting moments of sex.

Home at sunrise
Staggering up to my room
Staring at the wall
Feeling so careless.

With HIV infection rampant among young Latinos and young gay men of any ethnic group, Becerra's narrative is meant to disturb viewers who might believe that there exists in advanced western metropolitan societies sufficient information about AIDS and safer sex behaviors. Far from an individual story of loneliness, Becerra's narrative elicits the voices of other young gay men who, exhibiting similar behaviors, and using crystal meth and other drugs popular with young club communities, combine these with unsafe sex—with deadly results. Sporting a flouncing walk, with swinging arms emphasizing his/her gender ambiguity, the narrator takes careful and deliberate steps in his/her movement down a hallway. A brief moment of unsteadiness suggests perhaps a delicate inebriation.

The camera follows the narrator into a room and finally we are able to see the face, make-up trowelled onto eyelids and fierce plucked brows; his (and we now establish that he is a young man) movements suggest exhaustion and a drama of regret. This is not a posture of traditional masculinity. The boyish striped shirt and long shorts and knee socks contribute to our reading of this narrator as a young effeminate man. It is a contradiction that allows us to forget that he is living a life that is much too adult.

Both Pollock and Becerra establish a connection by means of contradiction between the audience and their young queer protagonists who are casualties of late capitalism, who inhabit canceral space where neo-liberal freemarketeers, captains of industry, and Washington cartels of global carpetbaggers enact trans-border mergers and mega-deals that produce both gay and straight victims of carrion capitalism. The straight members of the audience, in this sense, are forced to confront a reality that is very distant and unfamiliar in the context of their own immediate experiences. For Pollock and Becerra, this type of testimonial narrative proves to be one of the few genres readily available to young lesbians and gay men for the articulation of experiences that may engage an audience at the level of a possible political and cultural solidarity.

A QUEER CONCLUSION

Locating the queer body within a framework of radical agency is a difficult task. The ethnography of gesture is a study of the body's choreography against a stage of capitalist production—transforming the horizon of normalcy into a pirouette of difference—that betrays the "excessiveness" of a mouth that defies its inscription of silence, the exaggeration of the eyes that reorient our view of the body in space, the mannered fluidity and lyricism of a gesture that transcends new geographies of meaning both on and beneath the surface of the flesh and that reveals the image of desire as well the pain of memory. The video narratives are examples of bodies that adhere to a "disorderly conduct." Not only do these queer configurations resist the normalizing judgements discussed in Foucault's conception of power, but they begin the groundwork for a radical project of queer agency and emancipation. But how can we extend this groundwork? This excess, we argue, is an abrogation of the labor-power needs of capital, a flouting of those attributes of capital demanded by patriarchal capitalism, such as work-conducive habits linked to productive labor. Excess in this sense signals a rupture in the valorization of the statist project of labor-power enhancement. This excess marks the ferocious biting of the hands of God that deliver queer youth into the jaws of capital.

The irrecusable truth of capital is that it is relentless in its pursuit of profit and its commodification of all pleasure zones that constitute subjectivity, including those zones that are created in the very act of contesting capital and its control over the direction of our desiring. Capitalism, to put it bluntly, colonizes our desire in a macabre dance of unrelenting immiseration. Desire, in this case, cannot be reduced to the object of desire; neither can it be limited to the desiring subject. Rather, desire can be located in the social relations that are constitutive of and that constitute the need and dependency produced by the productive consumption of labor-power and the global political economy of accumulation. The narratives of these queer youth in many ways can be seen as efforts to negate the exchange values that define them as "commodities," that confine them within the larger economy of differences, and that mark them as deviant, unproductive, and criminal. A queer pedagogy that dematerializes the social, that disenables investigation into dependent hierarchies of power and privilege linked to private property and capitalist relations of exploitation, and that, in the process, dehistoricizes desire, is a pedagogy that enshrines the reigning value system of white supremacist capitalist patriarchy. Too often a queer pedagogy of embodiment recuperates the worst aspects of postmodern theory, creating the evacuated space of the simulacrum, a fissure in the void, a structured absence, a mimesis that has lost its pants. A queer pedagogy of embodiment must insist on a universal moral minimum linked to what Marx referred to as the evolution of human capacities and powers and the actualization of human potentialities. In doing so, it must be remembered that human capacities are always in a process of social and historical development. They are never "performed" in a social vacuum. Nor can they been understood in terms of the logic of citationality or performativity alone. Rather, they need to be understood in terms of the development of the social forms that give rise to them. In this way our invocation of the "esemplastic" imagination will generate an anticipatory, utopian thrust based on collective praxis, rather than a reactionary drive based on bourgeois illusions of ego-centered liberty. A queer pedagogy of the body is one that rematerializes the social such that the queer subject comprehends the social dialectically, as a knowable totality where the rich become rich at the expense of the ever-expanding ranks of the poor, whom capital is structured to destroy.

Constructing a story about lesbian, gay, bisexual, and transgender youth in the mean streets of Los Angeles is part of constructing a memory for many of us who have come out as teenagers and older (sometimes a painful coming out) and for others, a celebratory remembering of difference. The critique of a political economy of gesture is a mode of understanding queer experience that forces both participants and researchers to rethink corporeality, including their own constructions of their bodies. For Pollock and Becerra, queer bodies become the battleground where discourses struggle for dominance in a highly contested, demarcated territoriality. Artist Rhiannon Pollock, in her study of the lesbian mouth, forces the viewer into multiple considerations of the functions of lips, tongue, and throat in her choreographed depictions of desire and transgression. Andrew Becerra documents a choreography of risky behavior. The narrator in the Becerra piece projects the discourses of AIDS and self-abuse on the body, realizing that he is left with no ground from which to mount a project of resistance except through a resignification of the dominant tropes and conceits of hetero-normativity.

TOWARDS A MARXIST QUEER THEORY

The answer to the challenges of Pollock and Becerra is not to deregulate desire, even though this may lead to the development of a "queer desire." What we need to understand is that desire does not emerge from some opaque, transcendental territory of pure intensity that has no referent points, and thus all reference points are given equal weight as terminals of signification that "fire up" desire. Desire is socially and historically produced within specific social relations of production under capitalism and serves both to occlude and displace "needs." The emancipation of the queer body is not linked to revalencing "disorderly conduct," to give the "unwarranted" gesture official legitimacy, to bringing unconventional behavior into the center of heteronormativity, to unleashing unmediated desire; rather, it is to understand the production of power relations within the totality of capitalist social relations and economic conditions (Morton, 1996, p. 19). It also means moving beyond analysis to a politics and pedagogy of praxis where the unmet needs of queer youth can become part of the constituent ground of revolutionary struggle. What is the link between liberation as a queer identity, and a politics of social justice? Donald Morton (1992) puts the issues this way:

> If—in inter subjective terms—the space of the queer is the space of the "quirky outcasts" who "fight among themselves with a degree of affection," this is because it is a libidinal space for exchanges of self-evident utterances needing no conceptual argument or explanation. It is therefore what was described previously as a dialogical, rather than dialectical, space. In other words, it is the space where subjects can only engage in what is now known as (post)modern performance, which stands in contrast to the historical materialist understanding of practice. (p. 13)

We are arguing for a reinsertion of the political into the pedagogy of queer theory. We are arguing for reconnecting the queering of the body to a larger politics of liberation that does not simply critique heteronormativity from inside the text of the queer body. The queer body cannot be understood solely within the terms it generates because the language it uses to speak (or perform) its transgression (whether discursive or nondiscursive) is unable to achieve transparency. What is necessary is a conceptual understanding of how the oppression of the queer body is located within the larger exploitation of bodies under capitalism, a process of exploitation that reduces bodies to commodities given worth by their ability to extract surplus value, by their ability to become servants of exchange value and owners of property. In so far as the substance of the social universe of capital is value (Rikowski, 1999), and the form that labor-power assumes within this social universe is that of human capital, we need to locate queer youth within state-sponsored forms of capital development required for the reproduction of capitalist social relations. As Morton argues:

> Rather than working indefatigably—as ludic (post)modernism and its bourgeois proponents do—to mystify the very category of the "other" (as an interminable and basically unknowable—and unexplainable, but only describable—series of emerging difference), a materialist queer theory will account—within a rigorous (but not eternally fixed) conceptual frame of understanding—for existing, historically produced "othernesses" of all kinds. (1992, p. 30)

We have found it necessary to situate queer bodies within a conceptual vocabulary that not only embraces some of the important insights from theories of indeterminacy, performativity, and citationality (i.e., Butler) but that, most importantly, also attempts to locate queer identity within forms of resistance to the determinate social relations of the larger white supremacist, racist, heteronormative, capitalist society. Queer identity (as in the case of al identity formations) must be situated within a concept of the social totality that is capable of explaining the specificity of its historical production, that is, in relation to the determinations that produce queer identity. In this way we can assign queer identity an authority beyond its renunciation. Ultimately, what is needed is an historical materialist approach to queer practice that links such practice to its historical formation within the unmet needs of capitalist social relations of production.

We want to conclude by sounding a caution that gestural or corporal "excess" is not inherently transgressive. Similarly, queer "excess" is not, *in itself*, contestatory. It becomes politically transgressive to the extent that queer gesture is self-reflexively connected to the laboring body as a necessary value form that binds our social universe through the blood, sweat, and tears of the working-class. The production of the body as a commodity known as labor-power is historically specific. Under capitalism labor-power becomes the supreme commodity. It's concrete particularity is subsumed by its existence as value-in-motion or what we call capital (Rikowski, 2001). In so far as the queer body attempts to unchain itself, to break out of its constitution of value within existing relations of production, it can break the hold that capital has upon it. By choosing not to labor, under the imperatives that capital has laid down for it, it can slice open the veins of capital and search for freedom within objective conditions capable of producing it. This stipulates developing new forms of human sociability and a new sociocultural order outside of the social universe of capital and its attendant value formations. Once the queer subject is able to lay bare the contradictions that is inherent in the labor-capital relation, it is possible to reclaim the libidinal energies it has cathected onto fetishized commodities and the dead gods of divinity—including its own body-as-supreme-commodity—and rechannel them into a revolutionary praxis. These are not free-floating or spontaneous energies but educated energies. They constitute the social formation of affect put into the service of critique. They are not de-fanged feelings linked uncritically to experiences, but critical agency educated by an historical materialist understanding of how investment in revolutionary struggle at the level of one's unmet needs can be linked to larger projects of anti-capitalist struggle that are international in scope. This is more than a counter-hegemonic project that simulates the emancipatory impulses of the working-class but leaves them to function merely as substitutions for the dismantling of capitalist social relations. Counter-hegemony is the offspring of impotent mutineering among the bourgeois postmodernists and locates its transgressive practices in the unsettling of bourgeois norms, as if undressing the contradictions of commodity forms can (unjoint) the body of capitalism. In contrast, the queer revolutionary praxis to which we ascribe constitutes a "dialectics of awakening" that steers itself towards the construction of a proletarian hegemony that will bring about the abolition of capital, the esablishment of a freely associated labor, and the enrichment of human capacities. Queer workers of the world have nothing to lose but their chains. They have a world to win.

Queer workers of all countries, unite!

REFERENCES

Bordo, Susan (1993). "Feminism, Foucault, and the politics of the body." In Caroline Ramazanoglu (Ed.), *Up against Foucault: Explorations of some tensions between Foucault and feminism* (pp. 179-202). New York: Routledge.

Bordo, Susan (1999). "The body and the reproduction of femininity." In Katie Conboy, Nadia Medina and Sarah Stanbury (Eds.), *Writing on the body: Female embodiment and feminist theory* (pp. 90-111). New York: Columbia University Press.

Butler, Judith (1993). "Critically queer." *GLQ*, 1, 17-32.

Foster, Susan Leigh (Ed.). (1996). "Preface." *Corporealities*. London: Routledge.

Foucault, Michel (1994). *Maturity and modernity* (Trans. David Owen). London: Routledge.

Gere, David, (1997). "Effeminate gestures: Choreographer Joe Goode and the heroism of effeminacy." In Jane Desmond (Ed.), *Queer theory and the dancing body*. Middletown, CT: Wesleyan University Press.

Goodson, Ivor F. (1998). "Storying the self: Life politics and the study of the teacher's life and work." In William Pinar (Ed.), *Curriculum: Toward new identities*. New York: Garland.

Honeychurch, Ken Gardner (1996). "Researching dissident subjectivities: Queering the grounds of theory and practice." *Harvard Education Review, 66*(2), 339-354.

Kroker, Arthur and Kroker, Marilouise (Eds.). (1987). *Body invaders: Panic sex in America*. New York: St. Martins Press.

Leung, Simon (1995, Spring/Summer). "Squatting through violence." *Documents, 3*(6), 92-101.

Mauss, Marcel (1992). "Techniques of the body" [1934]. In Jonathan Crary and Sanford Kwinter (Eds.), *Incorporations. The Zone, 6* (pp. 455-477).

McLaren, Peter (1997). *Revolutionary multiculturalism: Pedagogies of dissent for the new millenium*. Boulder, CO: Westview Press.

McNally, D. (2001). *Bodies of meaning: Studies on language, labor, and liberation*. Albany: SUNY Press.

Mohanram, Radhika (1999). *Black body: Women, colonialism, and space*. Minneapolis: University of Minnesota Press.

Moraga, Cherrie (1993). *The last generation*. Boston: South End Press.

Morton, Donald (1992). "Changing the terms: (Virtual) desire and (actual) reality." In Donald Morton (Ed.), *The Material queer: A LesBiGay cultural studies reader* (pp. 1-35). Boulder, CO: Westview Press.

Rikowski, Glenn (2001). *The battle in Seattle: Its significance for education*. London: Tutnell Press.

Sedgwick, Eve Kosofsky (1993). "How to bring your kids up gay." In Michael Warner (Ed.), *Fear of a queer planet: Queer politics and social theory* (pp. 69-81). Minneapolis: University of Minnesota.

Schmitt, Jean-Claude (1989). "The ethics of gesture." In Michael Fether (Ed.), *Fragments for a history of the human body* (Part Two, pp. 128-147). New York: The Zone.

PART 5

**INTERVIEWS WITH
PETER McLAREN**

21 CAPITALISM, CRITICAL PEDAGOGY, AND URBAN SCIENCE EDUCATION
AN INTERVIEW WITH PETER MCLAREN

Angela Calabrese Barton

INTRODUCTION: THE QUESTIONS THAT FRAME URBAN SCIENCE EDUCATION

We have prepared this discussion of capitalism, critical pedagogy, and urban science education in conversation format in order to keep problematic the contextual realities of privilege, power, and knowledge in urban settings. The conversation begins with a discussion of key issues in education in general and then leads into a critique of the relationships among capitalism, science, and education. This more general beginning is important because it enables the argument that we are not looking in the right places in science to bring about meaningful reform based on social justice. Only when we see the problems in science education as problems at a societal level, which always mediates the other problems, can we aspire to any hope. Indeed, McLaren makes three key claims here: (a) that the relationship between capitalism and urban education has led to schooling practices that favor economic control by elite classes; (b) that the relationship between capitalism and science has led to a science whose purposes and goals are about profitability rather than the betterment of the global condition; and (c) that the marriages between capitalism and education and capitalism and science have created a foundation for science education that emphasizes corporate values at the expense of social justice and human dignity. We conclude this conversation by describing the implications that critical pedagogy might have for productively confronting these three main issues in urban settings.

This chapter originally appeared in *Journal of Research in Science Teaching, 38*(8), pp. 847-859. © 2001 National Association for Research in Science Teaching. Reprinted with the permission of Wiley-Liss, Inc., a subsidiary of John Wiley & Sons, Inc.

Calabrese Barton: Urban science education raises several challenges for science educators because of the vast inequalities in terms of resources, social privileges, and capital control which play out in inner-city settings, in general, and inner-city schools, in particular. You have been writing about education and inequality for over 20 years. In particular, a major theme of your work over the past two decades (in particular in your book *Life in Schools*) has been to understand teaching in cultural, political, and ethical terms with the goal of building strong links between the classroom and our efforts to build a more just world through critical pedagogical practices and analyses. From your critical theory perspective, what would you say are the key issues with which the science education community must come to terms in urban settings?

McLaren: For me, the key questions about urban science education raised by a critical approach include: How is the social practice of science organized? Or of education organized? How are social classes constituted through these practices? How are social practices constituted prior to these practices, since capital works to limit and control intellectual and scientific activity? What kind of scientific knowledge or school-based knowledge has the greatest exchange value in society? How is labor-power—the selling of one's ability to work—implicated in the reproduction of scientific knowledge? What type of science has ownership of the most prestigious research capital? What happens to scientists or the science teachers who have become alienated by the corporate community?[1] Since the discourse of science relies on the world outside of science, it needs to be analyzed critically from the social, cultural, and historical determinations that influence it.

THE RELATIONSHIP BETWEEN CAPITALISM AND EDUCATION

Calabrese Barton: The problems of science education are just a small subsection of the problems endemic to education and capitalism. It seems to me, then, underlying your key issues, or rather your key questions, is the claim that school science reform has aligned itself to the imperatives of the capitalist marketplace rather than the goals of a democratic socialist struggle. In other words, science education has become more about presenting students the science they need to fit into society rather than about educating students about how they might produce, use, and critique science to work with and transform society. Going to school does not enhance one's chances of success because even if everybody was learning something, schooling is still about stratifying students.

McLaren: Yes. Perhaps the best way for me to expand upon these points you raise is to share with you and your readers some serious concerns I have that shape my present perspective on education in general, science in general, and then urban science education in particular. The first point that I want to make is about the relationship between education (generally) and capitalism. Our society's unfettered capitalism has become a dangerous prejudice in the U.S. and worldwide and has impacted our social, political, scientific, and education structures. Everywhere you look today, learning is being marginalized by its stress on capitalist accumulation. Scientific research, education, and capitalism serve each other so intimately that it is hard to think of one without the other. Nowhere is this more dangerous than in economically and politically oppressed communities. While capitalism, having emerged victorious from the shadow of Marx's incubus with the fall of the former Soviet Union, continues to make good on its promises of providing considerable consumer advantages available to large numbers of people in advanced industrial nations, it also functions systematically as a form of global pillage. The neoliberal economic politics of the developed capitalist states (marked by the elimination of the public sector, the imposition of open-door free trade policies, and a draconian curtailing of state subsidies, compensations, and social protections) have created staggering disparities in wealth among populations in advanced democracies. They have also intensified and expedited the flow of surplus values from poor countries into the U.S., leaving unprecedented levels of poverty, starvation, disease, and homelessness in those very countries that the U.S. ostensibly attempts to assist (McLaren & Farahmandpur, in press; McLaren, forthcoming).

Calabrese Barton: Yet some argue that education will become more efficient and productive in a fiercely competitive marketplace and that this is just what urban school systems need. Indeed, this relationship between capitalism and education seems to be the central thesis in the Bush administration's recent approach to school reform.

McLaren: And this link is reinforced by profitability coinciding with the educational system, transforming it into a billion-dollar marketplace ripe for corporate investment and profit. An education which is subordinate to transnational capital can only be detrimental to any attempts to bring about social justice through education (McMurtry, 1998). I want to be clear here, Angie, that as a Marxist I am not advocating social justice in the sense of equalizing resources under capitalism. I am not trying to make capitalism more "compassionate"— although that would certainly be a step in the right direction. I am for the abolition of capitalism both in its private property form and its state property form. In other words, I support the transformation towards a socialist alternative. A democratic socialist alternative, I might add, and what Marx referred to as the new humanism. I have labeled my position, revolutionary materialist pedagogy, multiculturalism, etc. Let us step back for a moment to sketch out how this relationship between education and capitalism has developed because how this relationship developed (and continues to develop) is just as important as its outcomes.

In many respects the deregulation of markets and the marriage between knowledge production and profit making has taken on the form of a transcultural prejudice, underwritten by capitalism's law of value, and what appears to be the unstoppable march of capital accumulation. Never in the history of human wealth-creation have fortunes been amassed so quickly by so many. The U.S. now has 300 billionaires and approximately 5 million millionaires. Silicon Valley alone adds about 64 new millionaires every day, according to recent reports. Nine million Americans have household incomes above $100,000 a year, up from just 2 million in 1982, with many of the new millionaires profiting from the science/technology industries (i.e., Bill Gates or Hendrik Verfaille [CEO of Monsanto]). It has been said that if Great Britain was the first country to produce a mass middle class, the U.S. is the first country to produce a massively large ruling class.[2] But let's not forget that the majority in the U.S. are not rich or middle class—but are working class. The working class, in the broadest sense, are those who have to sell their labor powers to survive, those people who can't just live on assets. In a more pointed sense, the working class is comprised of those workers that produce surplus value for capital. There are three issues important to how our society makes a distinction between the working and professional classes besides the kind of labor which occupies people. First, there is the issue of control over work (its content, pace, conditions, and so on)—the working class is lacking in this area of social life. Second, there are the cultural aspects of class: dress codes, speech, mannerisms, and so on—more significant in countries like England perhaps than here in the U.S. but relevant nonetheless. Political power, of course, is the third issue and is particularly significant when analyzing the ruling class, as C. Wright Mills pointed out many years ago. As Michael Zweig (2000) and other commentators have noted, the political power of the economic elite is at least as great as it was in the 1920s, perhaps even more so, since today there are fewer challenges from other class interests. Contrary to the popular claims of the postmodernists, class struggle has not disappeared; it is simply being reconstituted. In fact, while class struggle from below may have temporarily disappeared from the discourses of many scholars, class struggle has strengthened from above. Since the early 1980s, under the leadership of Reaganomics and Thatcherism, the ruling classes have waged an all-out class warfare from above against the working class. These continued struggles around class must remain central analytic themes in our work in urban centers.

Calabrese Barton: Democracy and capitalism in many ways seem opposed. and yet in the popular imagination they appear indissolubly linked.

McLaren: To argue that capitalism is fundamentally democratic is like saying Harry Potter is a Trotskyite or Leninist on the basis of his wearing round-rimmed glasses.

Calabrese Barton: Or a Lennonist!

McLaren: Right. Lenin—the Russian, not the Beatle—was correct when he wrote that bourgeois democracy, which was invaluable for educating the proletariat, was also narrow, hypocritical, spurious, and false and always remained a democracy of the rich and a swindle of the poor (Lenin, 1943). The structural inability of capital to provide for the majority of the world's population and its creation of historically structured systems of inequalities between men and women, social classes, and developed and undeveloped countries mark the imperialist character of its current efforts to dominate the globe. What you are seeing today is the result of economic policies that date back nearly a decade. Capitalism's revanchist ascension to public education in recent years, under the guise of a neoliberal restructuring of the educational system through education-business partnerships, privatization, school choice, accountability schemes, and standardized tests, and the like, can be traced back to the early 1990s.

Calabrese Barton: At least to 1994.

McLaren: Exactly. My central claim is that you can't divorce educational policy from the transmogrification of the world economy because the global financial system is overrun by speculators and modern-day robber barons who are concerned with profit at any cost rather than social justice. Take the World Trade Organization [WTO], for example. In 1994, the World Trade Organization replaced the General Agreement of Tariffs and Trade [GATT]. This program established the framework and political architecture necessary for the U.S. to acquire free access to the global market. Consequently, the WTO, the World Bank, and the International Monetary Fund created a barrier between the poorest and must vulnerable of the world's population and big Western capital, mostly U.S. capital. Those in power in the U.S. hold onto the best jobs and export the most menial, low-wage, polluting industries.

In such a climate of outlaw capitalism and corporate orthodoxy, is it any wonder that education has been reduced to a subsector of the economy—a zone of free capital investment? Indeed, the corporate agenda for public and higher education fundamentally contradicts education in principle. Any value system that maximizes the private monetary interests of major stockholders without opposition or resistance is both anti-educational and complicit with superclass interests. One of the urgent projects of critical pedagogy is to urge educators to keep the veneration of capital and the sacerdotal status of corporate rule out of the classroom. We must provide students with opportunities to develop "robust reflexivity" (Harding, 1998). We must also exercise a in critical agency that moves beyond competitively selling knowledge as priced commodities for profit and private returns. Take, for example, the more than 1,000 corporate scientists in Monsanto headquarters building genetically engineered food systems—this is more about turning a profit than about real food safety. I am not suggesting that genetically altered food is unsafe—indeed, I do not think we actually know the long-term impacts of adding new genes and proteins to plants, to our bodies, or to the larger global ecosystem. What I am suggesting is that we find ways to critically examine the relationship between corporate power and the knowledge we label for our students as "objective" and "true."

The rude contradiction in all of this is that where for-profit enterprises have been introduced in education, there is little evidence that students actually perform better or that high school graduates are getting better jobs (Zweig, 2000).

What do you think of the fact that the leading private education company, Edison Schools, Inc., is consistently losing money? When private firms successfully compete with the government, it is usually because they take only the most potentially profitable segments of the market. In addition, private schools often screen out students who often need more attention (i.e., cost more money). In the final analysis private schools are a "niche item" that allows some students to do better (Zweig, 2000). Thus, once we realize that capitalism's link to democracy is really a chimera, we can begin to examine how urban science educational policy and practice is largely controlled by superclass political dominance (Perrucci & Wysong, 1999).

THE RELATIONSHIP BETWEEN CAPITALISM AND SCIENCE

Calabrese Barton: Are you saying that science and education serve primarily the superclass? In other words, the oppressors, to use Paulo Freire's term?

McLaren: Yes, and your question brings me to my second major point: the relationship between capitalism and science has led to "corporate science." More and more these days capitalism and science are moving into a shared orbit, as the earlier Monsanto example shows. If we conceptually undress the role science plays in the larger society, we can see how it stabilizes dominant social relations. If we make problematic the commonplace notion that science equals progress, we can begin to develop a different view of how science works. When I talk about science serving the interests of the dominant class, I am not only talking about paradigmatic historical exemplifications of scientists participating with, say, fanatical regimes of power, such as the Nazi scientists who helped to advance the "final solution" or members of the medical profession who have proved indispensable to military juntas for their work in perfecting "interrogation techniques" to be used during "information-gathering sessions" with dissidents and political prisoners. I am also talking about the ways in which corporate life and profitability shape and influence the directions and products of science.

Calabrese Barton: This all sounds very abstract.

McLaren: But the consequences are decidedly not. As underscored by Canadian philosopher John McMurtry (1998), the fact that corporate-directed science and medicine devotes little or no research funds to resurgent malaria, dengue fever, or river blindness (whose many millions of victims lack market demand to pay for cures), while it invests billions of dollars into researching and marketing dubious and often lethal drugs to treat nondiseases of consumers in rich markets, reveals a principle of selection of problems that is highly suspect. How else do you make sense of the millions dying in Africa from treatable diseases, such as tuberculosis, malaria, and sleeping sickness or the fact that the country that spends the most on AIDS research—the U.S.—is ignoring the plight of Africans who account for 70% of new AIDS cases worldwide. The reason that U.S. scientists are searching for a vaccine for a subtype of AIDS present in the northern hemisphere is that drug companies don't find it profitable to sell drugs to dirt-poor Africa.

As David Trend (2001) has recently noted, university research has been transformed into a privately sponsored affair driven mainly by industries in bioscience and information technology. Projects that can produce new drugs, genetically engineered cotton, and faster microprocessing chips are reaping huge profits. In the pharmaceutical industry large research projects are no longer dedicated to saving lives of millions of people in the developing world but to creating lifestyle drugs for impotence, obesity, baldness, and wrinkles. Trend mentions that new resistant strains of malaria, tuberculosis, and respiratory infections killed 6.1 million people last year. Yet of the 1,223 new medications introduced last year, only 1% was developed for those specific illnesses. Viagra sales totaled more than $1 billion its first year alone. But total global expenditures for malaria treatment stand at $84 million.

Calabrese Barton: And you could also have mentioned the biotech revolution—such as the recent case in South Africa where the drug companies backed down on suing the country for attempting to import cheap drugs to deal with their AIDS epidemic.

McLaren: Absolutely. Approximately 38 million people are currently infected with HIV, 25 million of them live in sub-Saharan Africa and 7.2 million in Asia. Since the International AIDS Conference was held in Barcelona in 2002, 6 million people have died of AIDS and 10 million people have become newly infected, even though antiretroviral drugs have become available to more and more people infected with HIV. Most of these drugs are made by European and U.S. pharmaceutical corporations, costing as much as $5,000 per person per year, whereas generic copies of these drugs can cost as little as $150 per person per year.

While Thailand, India, and Brazil are making cheap generic drugs, not enough of the drugs are being produced to make a huge impact on effectively combating AIDS worldwide. In addition, the $15 billion over fives years for AIDS treatment programs which George W. Bush has pledged to be made available through a series of bilateral agreements—known as the President's Emergency Plan for AIDS Relief—has come under fierce criticism as the United States is accused of blackmailing poor countries by asking them to relinquish rights to make the generic drugs in return for free-trade agreements (an accusation they deny). While the World Trade Organization gives developing countries the flexibility to ignore foreign patents and produce their own generic brands in times of health crises, nothing prevents a country such as the United States from imposing patent restrictions when negotiating a bilateral trade agreement. Clearly, such bilateral agreements need to be scrutinized carefully by the world community.

Currently, the money that the United States gives to AIDS research, treatment, and prevention goes to countries that support its abstinence-first policy; presently, the money can only be used to purchase brand-name drugs, because Washington has insisted that only drugs approved by the U.S. Food and Drug Administration can be endorsed. This is what we are up against.

Think about the vast amounts of capital poured into genetic engineering research, the genetic manipulation of corn and soybeans, not to mention the "modification" of animal reproduction or the human genome project. The point I am trying to make is that advances in science and technology are firmly lashed to the mast of capital's value form. Indeed, scientific value has been engineered, not for the improvement of the quality of life for all but for profit. Can you imagine sometime in the near future, the CEO of a biogenetic corporation calling his or her corporate quislings into the office and announcing: "We need to recall several life-forms that may be flawed." This scenario is unlikely, especially when products are so intimately connected to the next quarter earnings. Perhaps I appear squalidly pessimistic here, but the stakes are too high. Let me be clear, Angie. I don't want to collapse innovations in technology into social and political institutions. As Callinicos (1999) points out, technology can be improved without changing its nature, but the same cannot be said about capitalism. To improve capitalism would require a fundamental change of its nature since it has as a constituent feature an inherent tendency towards crises. The major problem today is the widely held belief that there is no alternative to capitalism.

CORPORATE URBAN SCIENCE EDUCATION

Calabrese Barton: So, it seems then that the corporate approach to urban science education might not be so different from the corporate approach to science. Let me be more specific. The challenges in urban science education are layered, and these layers are deeply connected to each other and to issues of power and control. I am concerned that science education has not incorporated the needs or concerns of children in poverty and children from ethnic, racial, and linguistic minority backgrounds. These "gaps" can be seen in high-stakes tests, mandated curricula, and daily school practices. I am also concerned that science—as a culture and practice—has developed along elitist lines resulting in a knowledge base and a cultural practice reflective of those already in power and uses the unobtainable ideals of truth and objectivity to hide its singular focus. Finally, I am concerned that schooling itself and the workaday practices of low-level worksheets, discipline through humiliation, and teacher-student bargaining (to name only a few) in urban centers strips children of their cultural identities, their right to learn, and their dignity as human beings. In short, I see schooling practices and the practice and content of science as potentially oppressive and schools and science as contributors to the colonization of people's minds (whether that be students, teachers, or anyone else). Are you arguing that the neoconservative agenda of implementing standards, assessing students' technical knowledge and understandings, and engaging in cross-national comparisons of student achievement ignores the ways in which the practice of schooling and the organization and intent of school science are structured to support capitalist goals? Isn't this what the "weeder" introductory college science courses are supposed to accomplish anyway?

McLaren: Yes, and this brings me to my third major point: that the marriages between capitalism and education and capitalism and science have created a foundation for science education that emphasizes profitability and control at the expense of social justice and human dignity. As long as society uncritically accepts the relationship between capitalism, science, and education, then science educators will continue to be bound to discourses and social practices responsible for needless human suffering. Instead, science education needs to be directed to assisting an educated population with managing a large-scale investment program for a sustainable future for humanity. The wealth of our nation should be measured by the elimination of class exploitation, racism, sexism, homophobia, and other forms of oppression; by the health of a people, their creative capacities, their social relations, their forms of labor, their standard of living, and their well-being. I feel strongly that a corporate approach to science in our classrooms has failed to raise questions dealing with what knowledge counts most, for whom, and for what purposes. I also feel that it has distanced science from confronting the objectifying and mediating functions of capitalist production and exchange relations, deflected attention away from how the advanced imperialist order of contemporary capitalism actually works in the production of knowledge, swept away contradictory class interests, and cultivated an engineered misunderstanding of how the geography of capital accumulation helps perpetuate bourgeois power and suppress workers' rights and aspirations.

Calabrese Barton: I can link your point about distancing science from class interests to, on the one hand, how we "teach" about developing countries in science class. The rare moments when developing countries are described in typical science textbooks tend to be in relation to disease and pollution (i.e., the typical biology textbook picture of the poor African woman with a goiter). The sad parallel is that, on the other hand, I can link this very example to how little mention (or no mention) is given in these same texts to how these poorer countries often serve as the first clinical test beds for new drugs. Let us not forget what is also happening in our poor centers in the U.S.—Hispanic and African American children were immunized with the EZ measles vaccine in Los Angeles, and their parents were not informed that the vaccine was not licensed in the United States (Trafford, 1996). How would you say these ideas translate pedagogically?

McLaren: The issue for me is to create pedagogical sites where educators and students collectively can "speak truth to power." One of my goals is to develop learning contexts—both in schools and in community settings—where the local habitation of such a struggle for socialism can take root. For me, the educational system is an important possibility in this regard. It is here that critical pedagogy can be employed in the teaching of science. At present there is a haunting absence of critical approaches to the teaching of urban science, an enigmatic silence with respect to attempts at conscripting teaching science into the service of social justice. Here, Angie, I need to emphasize what I mean by social justice. I mean, who would ever admit that they are against social justice? I am not referring here to a liberal bourgeois notion of social justice, of dividing up the spoils of surplus value more equitably. Because this agenda is still premised on the logic, the practice, and the rule of capital. The very creation of surplus-value turns human beings into human capital—in short, it "capitalizes" them, as my friend Glenn Rikowski would say. I am against capital's law of value altogether. Social justice for me can only be achieved through the abolition of capitalism, and through the forging of new human relations through a socialist alternative by means of a Marxist-Humanism.

Calabrese Barton: Can you expand a bit on what you mean by critical pedagogy and why this approach may help to foster social justice and "science for all" in urban settings?

McLaren: I believe that a critical pedagogy of urban science approached from a Marxist perspective[3] evaluates educational policy and practice using the following criteria as a yardstick: Does it mobilize the working class to engage in activities that address those contemporary dynamics of advanced capitalism that place education in a subordinated partnership with imperialist capital? Does it promote unity of political purpose within a diversity of experiences (race, gender, class, and sexuality)? Does it promote gender equality and the destabilization of patriarchal structures of oppression? Does it promote racial/ethnic equality and dismantle the hegemony of White privilege? Does it improve the overall lives of the working class? Does it provide leadership in challenging the injustices that are constitutive of capitalist accumulation? Does it provide opportunities for an analysis of the contradictions between the forces and the relations of production?

Calabrese Barton: So how do you see critical or, rather, revolutionary pedagogy intersecting with the production of scientific knowledge in classrooms? And, how might we think about this intersection in our work with urban youth? In other words, you have outlined a stance towards science and a stance towards education, both of which emerge from a critique of the democracy-capitalism couplet. My concern now is: so what does it mean to bring these ideas together in our efforts to build a more socially just science education in urban settings, especially in the daily practice of classroom life?

McLaren: Although it is hard to speak about the practicalities of classroom life because students and teachers are situated differently from day to day and from place to place, I will share some general thoughts on the kinds of classroom practices in urban settings that may underpin these more abstract ideas. It seems important that the practice of teaching has to be constructed differently.

Urban teachers are confronted, on the one hand, with "being accountable" to district and state standards, with the expectation that they are there merely to transmit the epistemologies and cultural practices foundational to these standards. On the other hand, urban teachers interact daily with diverse groups of students who may, as cultural groups, be semiotically and physically excluded from the very assumptions which drive those standards at the same time that they are confronted with limited resources, time, or decision-making authority to do anything serious or systematic about what or whom they need to be accountable to or serve. To think about teaching differently means that we must think about what it might look like in classrooms to reject this structured and regimented practice and begin to question what or how it is that teachers are supposed to teach. We must also begin to question how the very structure of schooling also works to silence any kind of critical conversation about what or how teachers are supposed to teach. In other words, teaching becomes about not only critically assessing the science and how it may intersect with the lives of students who are most often on the fringes of science but also critically assessing why it is that conversations about power and authority—at both local and global levels—are generally not allowed in science class.

Take, for example, the case of Beta, a Grade 8 teacher in a major urban center. As part of a unit intended to teach her students about temperature gradients and the function of insulators, she had her students design the "ideal cooler," big enough to fit a six-pack of soda. She had prepared a set of experiments to test out different materials for their ability to insulate. She also prepared different activities to help the students think about size, scale, measurement, and design. Although her students would have to work in groups because she did not have access to a wide swath of resources, she believed that this experience might at least get them thinking about science outside the text. Her implementation of the unit was not as she anticipated. Her students verbally and physically indicated their disinterest in the project. Yet Beta took their resistance and turned it into a class-long discussion about "what the class should do with the topic of insulators," given that she was bound by certain district learning standards and limited resources. She learned that her students preferred to design insulated lunch bags that held their lunches rather than a six-pack cooler, and they preferred to make individual bags because they wanted to keep them and use them. She also learned that the aesthetic quality of the materials was also important as the students intended to actually use these bags for their lunches. Through the story of one student's experiences with their family's icebox in the Dominican Republic, she also learned that they had ideas, more complicated real-world simulated experiments to test out the viability of the lunch-bag design. Students' concerns about inequalities, both local and global, also emerged: differences in the availability of insulating and cooling devises in different places, such as refrigeration in the U.S. versus the poorer communities of the Dominican Republic, or the differences in air-conditioning systems between the affluent and poor school districts in the city entered the conversation.

Finally, the students voiced their belief it was more important for the school to spend money on better and more materials than the kinds of things the school typically purchased (paper for too many worksheets, overhead projectors, and metal detectors).

This seems like a simple story, but indeed it raises questions about what it means to think about teaching and science differently. By allowing her students to see "inside" the expectations that schools place on teachers—by turning the classroom talk about why build lunch bags over coolers into talk about the science standards for the quarter—Beta's students turned science class into a political space, where the learning of science was coupled with learning about (and critiquing) the schooling process and the purposes and goals of doing science and its connections to social control, economic trade-offs, and human welfare. Beta and her students not only created new spaces to design and build lunch bags—something that was important to them in their day-to-day lives but also critiqued the purposes behind why making lunch bags was a necessary and important project for them to engage in as students. It made public the profound differences between learning a regulated list of science standards for the purposes of fitting into a particular mold of scientific literacy and engaging in a practice of science for the purposes of youth development.

This story also helps us to begin to reflect upon what it means to interrogate how science education is framed through profitability and control at the expense of social justice and human dignity. The youth recentered the goals of science class as about agency and learning to use and produce science in situationally meaningful ways rather than as about good studenting and capitulating to the contemporary dynamics of advanced capitalism that place education in a subordinated partnership with imperialist capital (i.e., where learning to be an obedient student is more important than learning to be critical of how power, knowledge, and culture interact to facilitate particular definitions of science and schooling). Here the difference is more powerful yet more subtle: The youth enacted a critique of "do we do science in ways and times set out by others in order to keep systems moving smoothly or do we do science in ways that turns those systems on their heads—in ways that uncover just how much the process of learning science is embedded with issues of hegemonic control, as can be the very construction of science itself." Yet even more could have happened and may still happen in Beta's class—the youth could see their actions as students building lunch bags and as students critiquing their school and science as part of a larger global effort to better understand how structures like school and science help to perpetuate global inequalities and social injustices.

This example also shows the ways in which transforming what it means to teach positions students and science with and among each other differently. It makes asking questions about why some ideas are taught at the expense of others or how it is that some scientific practices elevate certain cultural beliefs and practices over others a part of the discursive practices of the science classroom. Indeed, it creates the kinds of spaces that allow students and teachers to inter-

rupt the practice of learning and doing science in order to uncover the unacknowledged aspects of culture that historically underwrite and shape the social
practices out of which science education is produced through experiences like
end-of-year exams, textbooks, or state and local curriculum objectives. Think
about it. This story could have turned out many ways. Beta could have made her
students make the coolers. She could have listened to her students and allowed
them to make the lunch bags without exploring the deeper intentions in such a
decision. Rather, she chose to politicize the students' choices as a vehicle for
helping her students (and herself) to uncover the assumptions that guide the
practice of schooling in urban centers.

Calabrese Barton: Your point that position matters in the science we teach,
and how we choose to teach it centralizes both the importance of how we think
about the purposes and goals of science education as well as the roles that students and teachers play in that process.

McLaren: Yes, and indeed, one of the keys for me is vantage point
(Althusser, 1975) and how this ideal in light of revolutionary pedagogy shapes
classroom practices. For Foucault (1972, 1973), local knowledges must be reac-
tivated against the scientific hierarchy of knowledges. Harding (1991, 1998) has
made some important advances in this regard in her development and refine-
ment of "standpoint epistemologies." For Harding standpoint epistemology sets
the relationship between knowledge and politics at the center of its account. It
explains the effects that different kinds of political arrangements have on the
production of knowledge and knowledge systems. Empiricism tries to "purify"
science. Yet Harding has shown that these empirical methods never reach
greater objectivity, for they exclude thought from the lives of the marginalized.
For Harding—who draws upon postcolonial, feminist, and post-Kuhnian social
studies of science and technology as well as Latour's notion of technoscience,
with its tension between local and global science practices—all attempts to produce knowledge of any kind are socially situated, and some of these objective
social locations are better than others as starting points of research. Harding
points out that, for instance, when physics is permitted to set the standards for
what counts as nature and what counts as science, knowledge becomes truncated and is often misapplied, limiting our ability to produce knowledge in ways
that can assist aggrieved populations.

So the question arises: What are the knowledge opportunities for the marginalized and disenfranchised, especially for those youth who live and go to
school in poor urban settings? To use Harding's terminology, these groups
occupy the "borderlands" as "outsiders within." The dominant conceptual
frameworks, criteriologies, systems of intelligibility and classification don't
reflect their input or their interests. When decisions are made as to what kind of
scientific studies should be undertaken, these groups rarely have a voice.
Similarly, when decisions are made as to what kinds of science should be taught
in school, these groups again rarely have a voice. Indeed, the example of Beta

involving her students in her decision-making process was not the norm, and if Beta continued this practice throughout the school year, she may even have found herself in trouble with her administration. The dominant epistemologies and truth claims exercised by the bourgeois science establishment dehistoricize knowledge conflicts within science and fetishize them as permanent and unavoidable features of the scientific enterprise instead of seeing them as conflicts produced by class struggle, by patriarchal oppression, by heteronormative and homophobic perspectives. But doing science, both in the scientific workplace and at schools, from the perspective of the oppressed—whose lives bear a disproportionate share of the costs of these activities—can bring a wealth of important knowledge to the table. In Beta's case it wasn't that making the lunch bags that was so important—rather it was that the youth questioned the process of how decisions to make a cooler or a lunch bag get made, why they get made, and the implications this has for what students learn and do in school. This questioning pulled into the public discourse their lives, the intentions of the school system (i.e., the standards), the issues faced by urban schools (the lack of resources, the distance between the prescribed curriculum and the students' lives, and the overwhelming focus, at least in her district, on passing the test), and the larger connections between science, schooling and the perpetuation of inequalities—why the difference between availability of cooling and insulation systems in affluent versus poor communities?

In urban science education circles—both in schools and in universities—we must begin to ask hard questions about what and how we teach and research: How is science integrated with and across diverse communities such that scientific advantage accrues to some but not to others? How do we interrupt this process? What are the unacknowledged aspects of culture that historically underwrite and shape the social practices out of which science is produced or about which science education is produced through experiences like end-of-year exams, textbooks, or state and local curriculum objectives? How are women, racial/ethnic minorities, and the working class functionally excluded from the dominant practices of doing science? Of course, for me the struggle is not only about a more just and equitable distribution of resources but transforming existing contradictory capital-labor relations in such a way that the system itself does not generate such contradictions.

Calabrese Barton: Yet some have described standpoint epistemology as relativist, and, indeed, some have argued that this only further oppresses youth in marginalized settings because it denies them opportunities to "learn the canon" or to "have access to the culture of power." After all, with the push towards greater accountability, how much will it matter to students if they learn to see the intersections between science and culture yet fail to learn the Western canon of science?

McLaren: "Learning the canon" and learning/critiquing/revisioning how culture and science intersect are not mutually exclusive. Indeed, finding ways to access the canon is a central part of critique and revision. It is that the focus is different. Harding points out that this kind of diametric thinking confounds power with cultural differences. Differences are historical and material. They also stem from a confusion that empiricism is politics-free, that the canon is apolitical, ahistorical, and acultural. Standpoint epistemology is more sophisticated than this in that it constitutes a powerful sociohistorical analysis of how dominant discourses of science work to serve the interests of the powerful by masking their claims in a neutral view-from-nowhere position. What I like about the way Harding uses standpoint epistemology is that she doesn't assume that because a standpoint is articulated from the position of the oppressed that it is necessarily the best position. Freire (1978) used the term *basism* to describe this. In other words, consciousness is not determined by social location but it is greatly influenced by it. Just because somebody is oppressed does not mean their statements or opinions are exempt from critical scrutiny. But the political underplot of Freire's work (1978, 1993) opens up the process of becoming literate to the idea that the oppressed are in a unique position to reclaim authority for their experiences in the struggle to end exploitation on the basis of race, class, and gender. My position is not to reduce science education solely to politics. Rather, I want to assert that position does matter, both in terms of the science we teach and in the ways we choose to engage students in a critical understanding of that science. Adam Katz (2000) articulates the relationship between science and politics that I am trying to underscore here:

> If the service science provides to politics is in explaining its conditions of possibility, eliminating as many false paths as possible, and demystifying obscurantist ideological generalities, this is, first of all, in the interest of a science that itself depends upon a politics that defends its conditions of possibility by opening spaces previously closed to scrutiny; furthermore, this displays before science the limits and terms of its own tasks, and it sets science in motion by opening itself for critique. Politics, likewise, is interested in a science that protects the foundational political categories upon which politics and science both depend—categories, in the case of Marxism in particular, whose demystification stands at the origins of the science itself and whose various appearances, semblances, and mystifications set the terms for science or revolutionary theory. (2000, pp. 24-35)

My struggle to promote socially just education, especially for children and youth in poor urban settings, stems from a critical analysis of my own experiences as an elementary school teacher and from the discourses that legitimate *and* interrogate such experiences. Indeed, I know the very ideas I present here are difficult to live in the big machine of schooling. Yet if we do not try, we will have given over ourselves as educators to a future filled with inequality, oppression, and unlived lives. I believe deeply that we must commit in urban science education circles to work with and for youth to make the science they learn and they science they do a part of the practice of working towards social justice in our urban centers here in the U.S. and especially in developing countries. No other goal will bring us closer to science for all.

NOTES

1. I need to add this qualification: I don't agree with some of the Frankfurt School theorists who reduce the physical sciences to instrumental rationality. In other words, I don't believe that the sciences are only forms of domination, bourgeois impulses seeking to master the laws of nature and the physical environment. The epistemological critics of science—Lakatos, Bachelard, Popper, Canguilhem—postulate a relative autonomy of theoretical science through the idea that sciences serve as a type of heuristic (Callinicos, 1999). What interests me is how scientific knowledge is integrated into private corporate power.

2. These figures are the May 20, 2000, article "The Country-Club Vote" in *The Economist*, page 42.

3. In looking at critical pedagogy, it is important to demarcate its staging ground and political trajectory (McLaren & Baltodano, 2000). It is primarily a dialectical approach to understanding the contradictions within social life grounded in a commitment for encouraging each group—defined in racial, ethnic, gender, or other ways—to claim a notion of the good. My particular approach to critical pedagogy is Marxist, and I have often chosen to refer to it as "revolutionary" pedagogy. The critical pedagogy that I am seeking bears a kinship to the Marxist humanism developed by Raya Dunayevskaya and, more recently, by Peter Hudis (see Dunayevskaya, in press). It emphasizes the way in which Marx's work was deeply immersed in the dialectics of the revolution. It is grounded in Marx's notion that capital is a form of congealed abstract labor and that the transcendence of alienation proceeds through a "second negativity" (Hudis, 1997; Marx, 1975). The first negation would be the negation of private property—that is, to get rid not only of the capitalists but capital itself. The negation of the negation—that is, the negation of the negation of private property and the political overthrow of the bourgeoisie—must occur if capital is truly to be abolished (Dunayevskaya, 1989). This notion of self-movement through absolute negativity is what Marx meant as the basis of permanent revolution (Hudis, 1997).

REFERENCES

Althusser, A. (1975). *Lenin and philosophy and other essays.* New York: Monthly Review Press.

Callinicos, A. (1999). *Social theory: A historical introduction.* New York: New York University Press.

Dunayevskaya, R. (1989). *Philosophy and revolution, from Hegel to Marx to Mao.* New York: Columbia University Press.

Dunayevskaya R. (in press). *The power of negativity: Selected writings on the dialectic in Hegel and Marx* (Kevin Anderson & Peter Hudis, Eds.). Lanham, Boulder, New York, and Oxford: Lexington Books.

Foucault, M. (1972). *The archaeology of knowledge and the discourse on language* (Sheridan Smith, Trans.). New York: Pantheon Books.

Foucault, M. (1973). *The order of things: An archaeology of the human sciences.* New York: Vintage.

Freire, P. (1978). *Pedagogy in process: The letters to Guinea-Bissau.* New York: Seabury.

Freire, P. (1993). *Pedagogy of the oppressed.* New York: Continuum.

Harding, S. (1991). *Whose science? Whose knowledge?* Ithaca, NY: Cornell University Press.

Harding, S. (1998). *Is science multicultural? Postcolonialisms, feminisms, and epistemologies.* Bloomington: Indiana University Press.

Hudis, P. (1997). Conceptualizing an emancipatory alternative: Istvan Meszaros's beyond capital. *Socialism and Democracy, 11*(1), 37-54.

Hudis, P. (2000a). The dialectical structure of Marx's concept of "revolution in permanence." *Capital & Class, 70,* 127- 142.

[1]Hudis, P. (2000b). Can capital be controlled? *The Hobgoblin, 2,* 7-9.

Katz, A. (2000). *Postmodernism and the politics of culture.* Boulder, CO: Westview Press.

Lenin, V.I. (1943). *What is to be done?* New York: International Publishers.

Marx, K. (1975). *Early writings.* Harmondsworth, UK: Penguin.

McLaren, P. (in press). *Capitalists and conquerers.* Landham, MD: Rowman and Littlefield Publishers.

McLaren, P., & Farahmandpur, R. (in press). Teaching against globalization and the new imperialism: Towards a revolutionary pedagogy. *Journal of Teacher Education.*

McLaren, P., & Farahmandpur, R. (forthcoming). Class, cultism, and multiculturalism: A notebook on forging a revolutionary politics. *Multicultural Education.*

McLaren, P. & Baltodano, M. (2000). The future of teacher education and the politics of resistance. *Teaching Education, 11*(1), 31-44.

McMurtry, J. (1998). *Unequal freedoms: The global market as an ethical system.* West Hartford, CT: Kumarian Press.

Perrucci, R., & Wysong, E. (1999). *The new class society.* Boulder, CO: Rowman and Littlefield.

Trafford, A. (1996, July 2). Bitter medicine. *Washington Post,* p. Z-6.

Trend, D. (in press). *Welcome to cyberschool.* Boulder, CO: Rowman and Littlefield.

Zavarzadeh, M., & Morton, D. (1994). *Theory as resistance: Politics and culture after (post)structuralism.* New York: The Guilford Press.

Zweig, M. (2000). *The working-class majority: America's best-kept secret.* Ithaca, NY: Cornell University Press.

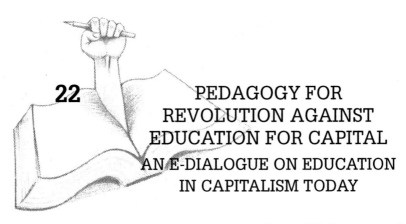

22 PEDAGOGY FOR
REVOLUTION AGAINST
EDUCATION FOR CAPITAL
AN E-DIALOGUE ON EDUCATION
IN CAPITALISM TODAY

Peter McLaren and
Glenn Rikowski

This dialogue between Peter McLaren (UCLA) and Glenn Rikowski (University of Central England, Birmingham) was conducted by e-mail during January-February 2001. References added.

INTRODUCTION

Peter: Well, Glenn, it's great to have the opportunity for this e-dialogue with you. We've corresponded by e-mail now for nearly four years and this situation is set up well for me to bring together a number of points I would like to ask you about your work and politics, your 'project' maybe—if you're not offended by the Blairite connotation!

Glenn: It's wonderful to share this platform with you, Peter, and we both owe it to *Cultural Logic* for giving us this slot. I have read your work closely over the last few years, and I have used it to try to radicalize further my outlook on education and its place in social transformation. And most certainly this is a magical opportunity to pose some questions to you with these ends in view. For me, this kind of thing is really about pushing our own views further and in new directions, to go beyond where we have gone in our published work, and also seeking to move the other person on that basis too. It's also about giving explanations and accounts of aspects of our own work, to show why we are doing what we are doing and in the style that we are doing it. On all these fronts it's about taking risks for an open future.

Peter: Yes, Glenn, I'm with you on your account on what we are doing here. Certainly, one thing we have both done in various ways is to have taken risks, risks that some have criticized us for—and we'll get on to those later. Also, Glenn, despite the range of topics you address in your work, the various empirical studies you have done, there are some strange silences too. I hope to kind of 'flush you out' on some of those gaps. I'm intrigued as to why you don't write about certain issues. I first became aware of your work through that monster article you did for *British Journal of Sociology of Education*, the *Left Alone* (Rikowski, 1996) article. Your honesty in that article was exemplary. You seemed to be facing the crisis within Marxist educational theory head-on, trying to grasp the depth of the crisis resulting from the deficiencies of what you called the 'old' Marxist educational theory that was based on Sam Bowles and Herb Gintis's *Schooling in Capitalist America* (1976) and Paul Willis's (1977) *Learning to Labor*. You also launched an attack on me in that article, on the more 'postmodern' moments within my work!

POSTMODERNISM

Glenn: Indeed I did, Peter, as you've reminded me from time to time! Perhaps it would be useful if you could take me through where you stand now on postmodernism. I mean, without rehearing your objections to postmodernism, which would take several articles to do the job, can you give me some of your recent thinking on the subject—something, say, that you have not yet written about?

Peter: Let me begin to answer this by trying to give you a sense of where I situate my own analysis, first.

Glenn: Fine. It's a good way in.

Peter: I pretty much follow some of your ideas on where to begin my critique. I take the position that capital grounds all social mediation as a form of value, and that the substance of labor itself must be interrogated because doing so brings us closer to understanding the nature of capital's social universe out of which our subjectivities are created. Because the logic of capitalist work has invaded all forms of human sociability, society can be considered to be a totality of different types of labor. What is important here is to examine the particular forms that labor takes within capitalism. In other words, we need to examine value as a social relation, not as some kind of accounting device to measure rates of exploitation or domination. Consequently, labor should not be taken simply as a 'given' category, but interrogated as an *object of critique*, and examined as an abstract social structure. Marx's value theory of labor does not attempt to reduce labor to an economic category alone but is illustrative of how labor as value form constitutes our very social universe, one that has been underwritten by the logic of capital. As you have underscored in your own work, Glenn, value is not some hollow formality, neutral precinct, or barren hinterland emptied of power and politics but the *'very matter and anti-matter of Marx's social universe'*, as Mike Neary and yourself have indicated (in Neary and Rikowski, 2000). The production of value is not the same as the production of wealth. The production of value is historically specific and emerges whenever labor assumes its dual character. This is most clearly explicated in Marx's discussion of the contradictory nature of the commodity form and the expansive capacity of the commodity known as labor-power. In this sense, labor power becomes the supreme commodity, the source of all value. For Marx, the commodity is highly unstable, and non-identical. Its concrete particularity (use value) is subsumed by its existence as value-in-motion or by what we have come to know as 'capital' (value is always in motion because of the increase in capital's productivity that is required to maintain expansion). Raya Dunayevskaya (1978) notes that *'the commodity in embryo contains all the contradictions of capitalism precisely because of the contradictory nature of labor'*. What kind of labor creates value? Abstract universal labor linked to a certain organization of society, under capitalism. The dual aspect of labor within the commodity (use value and exchange value) enables one single commodity—money—to act as the value measure of the commodity. Money becomes, as Dunayevskaya notes, the representative of labor in its abstract form. Thus, the commodity must not be considered a thing, but a social relationship. Dunayevskaya identified the 'soul' of capitalist production as the extraction from living labor of all the unpaid hours of labor that amounts to surplus value or profit. I think that too much stress is being placed on the market and not enough on the process of production itself. There needs to be more analysis of the fetishism of the commodity form.

Glenn: I agree. You see this in 'Left' educational theorizing especially. A garage full of emphasis on education markets and quasi-markets, but not much recognition of education as production or the products of education.

Peter: Yes, Glenn, the issue here is not simply that workers are exploited for their surplus value but that all forms of human sociability are constituted by the logic of capitalist work. Labor, therefore, cannot be seen as the negation of capital or the antithesis of capital but capital's human face. Capitalist relations of production become hegemonic precisely when the process of the production of abstraction conquers the concrete processes of production, resulting in the expansion of the logic of capitalist work. We need to move beyond the fetishized form of labor (as organizational forms of labor such as labor movements or new forms of work organization) and concentrate instead upon new forms of human sociability. The key question that drives much of my work can be captured in the following question: How is labor constituted as a social relation within capitalism?

Glenn: So the key here is that teachers need a better grasp of the inner dynamics of capitalism? Is that it, Peter?

Peter: Yes, that's it precisely, Glenn. Living labor creates the value form of wealth that is historically specific to capitalism. What drives the capitalist machine, in other words, is the drive to augment value. We need to explore the inner dynamics of capitalism, how it raises social productivity to a level of mind-numbing enormity yet that does nothing to limit scarcity. Paula Allman talks about how capitalism's relations of distribution are simply the results of the relations of production, placing a limit on consumption by limiting the 'effective' demand of the vast majority of the world's population. She reveals, in turn, how material use values are only available in the commodity form, and how use-value is internally related and thus inseparable from the exchange-value of the commodity, which is determined by labor-time. She writes that the wealth that is constituted by capitalist societies is not just a vast array of use values (it appears as this), but value itself. Wealth in capitalist society takes a perverted form. I agree with her that capitalism is perhaps best understood as a *global quest to produce value*. We need to focus our attention on capitalism's totalizing and universalizing tendencies. Its forms of global social domination are, of course, historically specific. Allman uses some of the insights of Moishe Postone (1996) to argue some very important points. One is that while capitalist exploitation through the production of value is abstract, it is also quasi-objective and concrete. Allman notes, correctly in my view, that people experience abstract labor in concrete or objective formations that are constituted subjectively in human actions and in human feelings, compulsions and emotions. Value produced by abstract labor can be considered objective *and* personal. How else can you account for the 'hold' that abstract labor has on each and every one of us?

Glenn: I concur on that point. A lot hangs on it; the capitalization of humanity flows from that point.

Peter: Furthermore, Allman reveals how the value form '*moves between and binds all the social relations and habituated practices of capitalism into an interlocking network that constitutes what is often referred to as the social structure of capitalist society*'. All critical education endeavors need to address the antagonistic terrain of capital that is inherent in the labor-capital relation itself, and to lay bare the contradictions that lay at the heart of the social relations of production. The value form of labor which gives shape to these internal relations or contradictions not only affects the objective conditions within which people labor, but also the domain of subjectivity or human agency itself. This mediative role is far from innocent.

Glenn: This is the deep horror of capitalist reality. The difficult thing is to acknowledge that horror in a process of overcoming it—collectively, and on a world scale.

Peter: Yes, at the level of individual psychology the fact that our personalities are penetrated by capital is not that appealing! Of course, many Marxist educators advocate a fairer distribution of wealth, arguing that the current inequitable distribution that characterizes contemporary capitalist societies results from property relations, in particular, the private ownership of the means of production. For Paula Allman, and others, including yourself, Glenn, this doesn't go nearly far enough. The real culprit (as both you and Paula Allman have maintained) is the internal or dialectical relation that exists between capital and labor within the capitalist production process itself—a social relation in which capitalism is intransigently rooted. This social relation—essential or fundamental to the production of abstract labor—deals with how already existing value is preserved and new value (surplus value) is created. It is this internal dialectical relationship that is mainly responsible for the inequitable and unjust distribution of use-values, and the accumulation of capital that ensures that the rich get richer and the poor get poorer. It is this relation between capital and labor that sets in perilous motion the conditions that make possible the rule of capital by designating production for the market, fostering market relations and competitiveness, and producing the historically specific laws and tendencies of capital.

Glenn: But what about private property? 'Traditional' Marxists make a big deal of that, Peter.

Peter: True, private property is a concern, I don't want to downplay this. But private property, commodities, and markets all pre-date the specific labor-capital relations of production and serve as pre-conditions for it. And once capital develops they are transformed into the results of that relation. This is why you, Paula Allman, Mike Neary and others emphasize as fundamental the abolition of the labor-capital relationship as the means for laying the groundwork for liberation from scarcity.

Glenn: The abolition of capital, as a social relation and social force, is crucial, as you say, Peter. To get rid of private property and the capitalist without abolition of capitalist social relations clearly leaves a vacuum into which the state can enter, making for a pernicious *state* capitalism. Okay, Peter, now that you have situated your own work firmly within the Marxist tradition, how does your position enable you to criticize postmodernism? We still haven't got to my original question on where you stand on postmodernism today!

Peter: For me it is important to be able to help students understand various postmodern theories as contributing to a re-functioning of capital. Rather than rehearse—even briefly—my critique of postmodernism, I'll start somewhere specific.

Glenn: You are never brief, Peter!

Peter: Okay, right. Okay, instead of itemizing my general criticisms of postmodern theory, it might be more productive to share my recent reading of the work of David McNally, because I think he has done a tremendous job of deepening the critique of postmodern theory from a Marxist perspective.

Glenn: Shoot!

Peter: McNally has recently published a wonderful critique of Saussure, Derrida, and the post-structuralists—as well as a celebration of Volisinov/Bahktin, and especially Benjamin—in a book called *Bodies of Meaning* (McNalley, 2001). His basic argument, since I can't recall all the details without reference to my notes, is that economic concepts figure centrally in their approaches to linguistic science. I recall that he argued the following points. Postmodern theorists model language on their specific understanding of the capitalist marketplace. McNally makes a good case that, in the process of such modeling, formal linguistics turns language into the dead labor of fetishistic commodities. It does this by decapitating signifiers and their meaning-making process from their fundamental connection to living labor. For example, Saussure and Derrida equate the general phenomenon of linguistic value with the role of 'money' as a general equivalent of exchange. McNally calls Derrida the philosopher of fictitious capital. Derrida criticizes Saussure for positing an invariant or transcendental signified, or what McNally calls a 'gold standard' against which signs can be measured or interpreted. Derrida, as you will recall, argues that there is only *'differance'*, that unknowable form prior to language, that condition of undecidability and the very condition of possibility of that undecidability that permits the endless play of reference that Derrida famously discusses in his large corpus of work (Derrida seems enraptured by difference and enraged by sameness, norms, standards). When Derrida makes the claim that *'differance'* is the most general structure of the economy he denies the praxis and labor that ground economic relations. That's because money lacks a referent, according to Derrida. It has no material foundation; money circulates without any referents. You can, for instance, have bad cheques, fraudulent credit cards—and these function as money. Credit and speculation become a form of 'fictitious' capital.

Glenn: Sounds a lot like Baudrillard. Smells like postmodern virtual spirit.

Peter: Exactly. Actually, McNally goes on to discuss Baudrillard, and how in his system sign values are independent of external referents; they refer, in other words, only to *themselves*. Baudrillard's is an economy of internal relations, following its own code. Baudrillard lives in a techno-crazed universe of techno-mediatic power where labor is always already dead, where political economy is dead, where everything is virtual, the economy is virtual, and where use values have disappeared. Use values do not transcend the codes that encapsulate them and give them life.

Glenn: Right, the sign economy. We don't have exchange value or use value in the Marxist sense anymore, we have an information economy that trades in images, and status, and all of that. It's a good story if you can get people to believe it. A lot of Internet magazines seem convinced: *Fast Company*, *Business 2.0* and the like.

Peter: There is something compelling about it, I admit, as long as we realize it's science fiction. Scientologists beware! You have competition for Battlefield Earth! Baudrillard maintains that we consume fictitious identities by purchasing the sign value of, say, an Armani suit, or a pair of Guess jeans. We dress ourselves up in abstractions—literally. Contrast this with what Marx had to say, that in capitalist societies, concrete labor is reduced to a quantum of total social labor, as something translated into the socially necessary labor-time—a process that is part of the circuit of production and exchange. The key point here, according to McNally, is that, for Marx, abstract labor is not a mental abstraction but the *real social form of labor* in capitalist society. This is an important point. It's an absolutely crucial point. When labor-power itself becomes a commodity (a special kind of commodity) in the very act of laboring itself, then this abstracting process becomes generalized. But what we are talking about here is surely more than a linguistic phenomenon and McNally is very critical of Derrida's linguistification of life. If this were just a linguistic phenomenon then we would have to go along with Wittgenstein, and maybe in the process have to concede that Marxist theory was the result of a linguistic error! *Contra* Baudrillard and Derrida, signifiers do not replace use value in a virtual economy of signs. True, capitalism entails an abstracting process, but it is one in which concrete labor is translated into abstract labor—into a labor that resembles interchangeable bits. But this is not just a concept, or a signifier, it is a real social form within the process of production; it is, as McNally notes, a systematic process of abstraction wherein capital compels the translation of concrete labor into abstract labor. Labor-power becomes value only when it assumes a value-relation, an objective life as a commodity, an abstraction from the body-work of the laborer, and hence from the use-values produced by the efforts of laboring subjects. This is alienated labor, the subsumption of concrete labor by abstract labor. McNally writes that no matter how abstracted things become, the exchange between money and a commodity always entails exchanges of labor. Capital is not self-birthing; it is never an independent source of value. For instance, interest-bearing capital does not escape a connection with human labor but is merely the purest fetish of them all. In their rage against Marx's obsession with decidability, post-structuralists deny the origin of value in labor, in the life-giving, toiling, body in labor.

Glenn: Which is why we need materialist critique.

Peter: Precisely. McNally describes historical materialist critique as a struggle against idealism, against the subordination of the world of bodies, nature, objects, and labor to subjectivity, and a struggle against objects being subsumed by concepts. It is a direct challenge against the autonomy of thought, that is, against objective, concrete, sensuous life being subsumed by the self-movement of thought.

Glenn: So, then fetishes are not a figment of the imagination?

Peter: No, they are tangibly real. Marx believes that they are necessary forms of appearance of alienated life. McNally brilliantly notes that in Derrida's economy of fictitious capital, our birth into language is—how did he say it?— right, our birth into language is detached from our origin in the bodies of others. This is very important for us to grasp. He likens Derrida's approach to language to the way that money-capital is treated as self-generating, without an origin in labor.

Glenn: And how do we abolish these fetishes?

Peter: By undressing them, and undoing them, and through revolutionary praxis, abolishing capitalist social relations.

Glenn: But developing revolutionary praxis surely means uncovering redemptive possibilities within the commodity form, too? I mean, you can't escape the commodity form entirely, you can't work fully outside the seductive thrall of capital, altogether?

Peter: That's an excellent point, Glenn. Let's follow some of McNally's observations further. He notes that Walter Benjamin realized the redemptive possibilities within the de-mythified and barren landscape of capitalism. In his work on the *flaneur*, for instance, Benjamin conveyed that everyone in capitalist society is a prostitute who sells his or her talents and body parts. We live in the charred world of capital, a dead zone inhabited by corpses and decaying commodities. Such a realization can help break through the naturalization of history and enter the terrain of historical action. According to McNally, Benjamin ruptures the myth of the self-made man. We are all dead objects awaiting the meanings we have yet to write, as McNally puts it. McNally sees Benjamin as establishing a political project in which the oppressed class must reclaim the libidinal energies it has cathected onto commodities and re-channel them into a revolutionary praxis, a praxis of historical struggle towards emancipation, towards liberation. It was Benjamin, after all, who said, '*money stands ruinously at the center of every vital interest*'. Revolutionary action involves the dialectics of remembering and forgetting, of challenging the repressed bourgeois desires linked to the rise of capitalism, and embodied in the collective dreams of a pathological culture, a society gone mad—something we don't have time to explore here. But it is something I have touched upon in my earlier work, especially in my *Critical Pedagogy and Predatory Culture* (1995). In other words, we need to have a theory that helps us to resist the social practices of exploitation linked to the social relations of production, but, dialectically, our resisting also helps us to have theory. In fact, this resisting is in many ways the basis of our theory.

Glenn: What about modes of resistance that you and I are more familiar with in our everyday praxis: the strike, protest rallies, and the like.

Peter: Yeah, Benjamin writes very little about these. But in his *One-Way Street*, Benjamin does stress the centrality of physical action. According to

McNally, Benjamin views the body as the site of a transformative type of knowing, one that arises through physical action. Revolutionary practice, for Benjamin, means cultivating a 'bodily presence of mind'. We need to locate new energies—in hip-hop, in art, in protest demonstrations (like the Zapatistas)—without being re-initiated into the giddy whirl of bourgeois subjectivity, its jaccuzzi reformism, and its lap-dog liberalism. That can only happen when you have a collective political project to give direction and coherence to your struggle. For me, that direction comes from a commitment to defeat the capitalists, but also capital. Admittedly, we are consigned by history to live in the disjunction between the defeat of capital and the recognition that such a defeat is not likely to happen soon. Glenn, you have quizzed me about how I now see postmodernism, but I am puzzled by your *own* attitude towards it. I know you have critiqued postmodern theory with Mike Cole and Dave Hill in your 1997 article (Cole, Hill and Rikowski, 1997), but what exactly is your own position on it?

Glenn: Well, you're correct that I haven't written as much on the critique of postmodernism as yourself, or as much as Dave Hill and Mike Cole. This does need some explaining, perhaps. It's not just a case of slothfulness! In the late 1980s and early 1990s I read a shed full of material in education journals written from various postmodernist and poststructuralist perspectives. At the time I thought I could see where it was all leading: to various doors labeled 'Nihilism', 'Relativism' or 'Solipsism'. With hindsight, I think that gut judgement was validated by what actually occurred. Also it seemed that educational postmodernism was on the road to totally eclipsing Marxist educational theory by absorbing any form of potential radicalism and spitting it out as a fashion statement. But I formulated a particular reaction—a strategy if you like—to the situation. I decided I would stop reading all the secondary, derivative stuff and go straight to the heart of the postmodernist beast by reading the postmodern Godfathers: Foucault, Deleuze, Baudrillard, Lyotard, Derrida and the rest. That was a very short phase, for I realized that Nietzsche had heavily influenced all these theorists. Thus: I needed to dive deeper to get to the real roots of postmodernism. So from 1992 to around 1996 I read most of the works of Nietzsche. Some I read twice. I pretty much continued to ignore the postmodernist stuff written after 1992—though for the Cole, Hill and Rikowski article (1997) I had to backtrack and read a bit in order to make my contribution to that article useful. Then in 1996 Geoff Waite published his monumental and masterly critical study of Nietzsche (Waite, 1996). Waite got right to the core of Nietzsche's *intentions*, what the philosopher with a hammer was really up to. According to Waite, Nietzsche's Project was to attempt to bring about an eternal rift within humanity between an elite (that would venerate Nietzsche as one of its own) and the mass. The mass would have the role of sustaining the elite in conditions where their creativity could remain vital and flourish—which was why Nietzsche was obsessed with the state of culture and society in his own day. For

Waite then, the Eternal Return of the Same is the Eternal Return of the elite/mass duality. The doctrine is an attempt to engineer a future where the corpse of Nietzsche would be continually rejuvenated as the elite lived an idealized Nietzschean existence and his corpus (the body of his work) venerated in the process.

That's not all. Waite explains that Nietzsche obviously needed the help of intellectuals, politicians, media people and educators to bring this about. He had to *seduce* us. Nietzsche had to write in an esoteric way that recruited us to the project of realizing his abominable Eternity. Furthermore, Waite indicates the forms and processes of Nietzschean textual, conceptual and discursive seduction; the many tactics he used, and the fishhooks and tests he put in our way. On this account, Nietzsche's corps has two main officer blocs overlaying a postmodernist infantry. First, there is what Waite calls the Nietzsche Industry—those apologists and so-called 'interpreters' of Nietzsche who avoid or sanitize Nietzsche's real game. Second, there are the postmodern Godfathers—Derrida, Lyotard and the rest. These are the upper tiers of Nietzsche's corps. The interpreters of postmodernism are the footsoldiers, the infantry, of Nietzsche's corps. They are legion, and they cast a huge cloak of obfuscation, denial, mind-fucking mediocrity and inverted pomposity on the question of the implication of themselves within the realization of Nietzsche's Project of Eternal Return. For me, postmodernism does not just collude with Nietzsche's project for humanity and his resurrection through his followers; it is a vital force within that project. So, through the work of Geoff Waite, I wish to simultaneously uncover the roots of postmodernism and Nietzsche's dangerous project for humanity's future. I'm more interested in exposing this—because I think it's more important—than just criticizing postmodernism *per se*.

Peter: You said there were two aspects to your outlook on postmodernism: what's the other one, Glenn?

Glenn: Yes, there is a second aspect of my take on postmodernism. I do believe postmodern thinking has inadvertently hit on something with its foregrounding of a de-centered, fragmented and multi-faceted 'self'. Basically, the postmodernists and poststructuralists are interesting on this. But the key task is the *explanation* of this fragmentation. Now, for me, the role theorists of the 1960s and early 1970s and the work of Erving Goffman and R.D. Laing had explanations of the 'divided self' that surpass any stuff on 'discourse' produced by most postmodernists and poststructuralists. This work is largely forgotten nowadays. For me though, the task is to explore the 'divided self' through Marxism as an exercise in developing Marxist science. Thus, the analysis of 'the human' as a contradictory phenomenon, where these contradictions are generated by value relations as they flow through labor power, is the starting point. Labor power is inseparable from personhood, though labor recruiters and personnel managers necessarily reify it as a collection of attributes in the recruitment process. This impossibility of separation is a problem for capital, as the single commodity that can generate more value than that constituted at the moments of its own social production—labor power—is an aspect of the person of the laborer that is controlled by a potentially hostile will. Holding 'that the will has no existence' sidesteps the issue, as acts of willing (whether there is a 'will' or not) have the same effect. The 'will' itself, moreover, can also be explored as a set of contradictory forces. Of course, I can see the inevitable objection; that whilst I have criticized forms of Marxist educational theory that embrace determinism, I have opened the door to a reconfigured determinist embrace. But I hold I've done the opposite; the clash of contradictory drives or forces within the 'human' engenders *indeterminacy*, openness. One could, of course, introduce a new determinism on the basis of some presupposition regarding the relative *strength* of particular social drives and forces as they come into contradiction within the 'human'. Not only would this be undesirable, but also for Marxist science it would avoid the problem of explaining changes in the power and strength of these contradictory drives and forces. Furthermore, the core dynamic antagonism is denied on such determinism: the contradiction between our 'selves' as labor and ourselves as *capital*, human-capital. I am capital. We are human-capital, the human-as-capital, but this is constituted by and through ourselves as labor; we haunt ourselves in a creative loop within the constitution of our personhoods. We are inherently contradictory life forms, but these very contradictions drive us on to try to solve them within our everyday lives (including within 'ourselves'). On an individual basis this is impossible. Marxist psychotherapy is pointless. We require a *politics of human resistance*. This is a politics aimed at resisting the reduction of our personhoods to labor power (human-capital), thus resisting the capitalization of humanity. This politics also has a truly negative side: the slaying of the contradictions that screw-up, bamboozle and depress us. However, only collectively can these contradictions constituting personhood (and society: there is no individual/society duality) be abolished. Their termination rests on the annihilation of the social relations that generate them (capitalist social relations), the social force that conditions their development within social phenomena, including the 'human' (capital) and the dissolution of the substance of capital's social universe (value). A collective, political project of human resistance is necessary, and this goes hand-in-hand with *communist politics*, a positive politics of social and human re-constitution. This is the collective process of re-designing society, revolutionary socialist transformation as Paula Allman (1999) has it. We need to simultaneously engage in this as we struggle for abolition of the social domination of capital. As I see it, Marxist science and politics and a politics of human resistance to capital are forms and aspects of each other. Communist society already exists on this view; it is a suppressed and repressed form of life within capitalism.

Peter: And where does this leave postmodernism, Glenn?

Glenn: Well, Peter, postmodern thinking just becomes a liability, a block, on even raising these sorts of issues and questions, let alone getting any kinds of answers. Postmodernists don't like answers, it seems to me; as you said earlier they celebrate 'undecidability', and hence they fight shy of explanation. But this disarms us. These are big hang-ups that we can't afford. We need to move on. The development of Marxist science (a negative critique of capitalist society) and a politics of human resistance are just more important, and also more interesting, than criticism of postmodernism. Though, on the basis of forestalling a Nietzschean future, we have to expose postmodernism as the blight on humanity that it is, whilst also using it if we actually do find something worthwhile residing within it.

Peter: Well, your answer raises a lot of issues, questions and problems, Glenn, and I want to take some of these up later. You packed a lot of punches into a few rounds there! But where do you stand on those who have tried to leave postmodernism through Nietzsche? I have people like Nigel Blake and his colleagues in view here (Blake et al., 2000). You sent me an unpublished paper of yours, *Nothing Becomes Them: Education and the Nihilist Embrace* (2001a) where you lavish fulsome praise on Nigel Blake and his pals for moving from postmodernism to nihilism through Nietzsche. This seems weird when Mike Cole, Dave Hill and yourself castigated Nigel Blake in an earlier article (Cole, Hill and Rikowski, 1997) for supporting postmodernism that, on the analysis there, was on track to run into nihilism which the three of you thought was the last stop before hell! Secondly, on what you said previously, moving from postmodernism to Nietzschean nihilism looks to have thrown Blake and company smack into the arms of something far worse than postmodernism: Nietzsche's Project of Eternal Return! Where's the redeeming features of the track taken by Blake and friends? I must admit, I can't readily see them!

NIHILISM AND NIETZSCHE

Glenn: Straight for the weakest link, Peter, nice one! I know what I've said seems strange, but I'll try an explanation. When I moved back from reading derivative postmodern writings to reading the postmodern Godfathers and then to reading Nietzsche, this was, in my view, a kind of progression. Nigel Blake, Paul Smeyers, Richard Smith and Paul Standish have made a similar movement in their book *Education in an Age of Nihilism* (2000), though I get the impression that they didn't actually engage with the first base (the derivative stuff) as much as I did. So, by the same token, they have moved in a productive direction. It should be noted, however, that they have not moved wholly away from the postmodern Godfathers, so their *Nihilism* book is transitional. Secondly, through the concept of nihilism, they have forged a deep and wide-ranging critique of many aspects of contemporary education and training in England. They indicate how the abyss of nothingness (the de-valued values) at the core of education policy, where discussion about the purposes and goals of education is substituted by instrumentalism and managerialism, is the centrifugal (but negative) force conditioning developments in contemporary education and training. The 'crisis of value' in education is a precondition for the generation of such phenomena as the school effectiveness/improvement movements, targets, funding systems umbilically tied to outputs, the drive to produce human capital and much else in this gloomy educational landscape. Thirdly, they contrast this state of affairs with Nietzsche's affirmative attitude towards life. The quest to overcome nihilism in education parallels Nietzsche's attempt to transcend nihilism through a process of self-overcoming. Blake and colleagues seek to show how education can be made more vital, intense, interesting and worthwhile when the overcoming of nihilism radicalizes educational processes, forms and content. They aim to bring moral *commitment* back to the educational enterprise. Thus, for Blake and co-writers, education after Nietzsche is implicated in the quest to overcome nihilism by creating the conditions where new values can emerge, values that do not de-value themselves as we attempt to realize them (as did the old, tired values underpinning modernism). Fourthly, Blake and company note that they wish to *use* Nietzsche, not just interpret him, not just be part of the Nietzsche Industry. I too argue that Nietzsche needs to be used, used to subvert his own goals! I now don't go along with Geoff Waite (1996) that we should just not mess with Nietzsche at all; that gives Nietzsche too much respect. Waite seems almost paranoid, or at least fearful, about what Nietzsche's texts can do to us. After I read his book I could understand why he held this. But on reflection I think I was wrong, and that Blake and colleagues' attitude towards Nietzsche is healthier.

Peter: Explain why and how this is so, Glenn.

Glenn: Well, now, for me, it seems that Blake and associates have produced a serious and important critique of certain trends and developments within contemporary education and training that Marxist and socialist educational analysts have also highlighted. Indeed, their critique is deeper and more interesting than in some Marxist and socialist accounts. They attack the very *roots* of education policy and change—not just the effects of these. Unlike a standard postmodern 'deconstruction' of education policies, Blake and his collaborators have a dreadful, but strangely productive, vantage point—nihilism— from which to illustrate the dread at the heart of contemporary education. In doing this, they make critique of today's education significant and interesting whilst offering an apparent way forward through Nietzsche. For me, this is preferable to infinite deconstruction and 'questioning of concepts' from no position whatsoever (as positions are denied). Blake and colleagues face up to the fact that postmodernism entails nihilism; they are honest. Once they face this they creatively turn this insight into conceptual dynamite for the critique of education and society.

Peter: I see, but there's a downside? I mean, I've seen some of your unpublished stuff on Nietzsche.

Glenn: Yes, there is. Their avoidance of Nietzsche interpretation also insulates them from the growing anti-Nietzsche. Most of all, they seem oblivious to Geoff Waite's critical analysis. The implications of their analysis is that 'the strong should be protected from the weak' in education and society as a whole. The weak masses are sacrificed to the potential for creativity and innovation of the strong, the elite whose heroic members are capable of forging new values. This becomes the ultimate new value of the education system. They say: '*The strong—those who can affirm life—need to be protected from the life-sapping nihilism of the weak, and this is not to be realized through the nostalgic restating of values, through the monitoring and rubber-stamping of standards, for these are only guises of the Last Man. It must reach its completion by passing through the Last Man, but going beyond him to the one who wants to perish, to have done with that negativity within himself: relentless destruction of the reactive forces, of the degenerating and parasitic, passing into the service of a superfluity of life*' (Blake et al., 2000, p. 63) For Marxist science and Marxist educational theory, the hope is precisely in those 'reactive forces' incorporated within the masses collectively expressing themselves as concrete forms of definite danger to the social domination of capital. In running counter to this possibility, Blake and his collaborators open themselves up to the full force of Geoff Waite's critique. Furthermore, their analysis of nihilism does not go deep enough; they fail to raise the question of the *form* that nihilism takes in contemporary capitalist society, to explore the relation between *value*, values, nothingness and meaninglessness (they tend to see nihilism in terms of meaninglessness). This work has yet to be undertaken. Thus, I am suggesting that their critique can be radicalized further through engagement with Marx, and that taking this route can neutralize Nietzsche's program for humanity as we come to grasp that there is no 'self-overcoming' without dissolution of the capitalist universe. Self-overcoming is synonymous with overcoming capital, as the 'self' is a form of capital, human-capital.

Peter: This last point of yours, Glenn, fits in with something that you have raised in your work, and which you hint at in this e-dialogue previously: the relation between labor power and human capital. What is that relation? Also, you have stated on a number of occasions, that education policy in England rests on human capital development. Perhaps you could illustrate how these pieces fit together.

HUMAN CAPITAL AND LABOR POWER

Glenn: Well, I'll try. The first bit's controversial. First, although I am interested in Marx's method of working and in his method of presentation, I am not one of those who believe that there is a 'Marxist method' that can simply be 'applied'. I'm certainly not one of those who believe in some 'dialectical' Marxist method (deriving from a Hegelian reading of Marx) that we can take ready-made off-the-peg either. Certainly, I learnt a tremendous amount from reading the works of Derek Sayer (1979, 1987), but I tend to start from asking a simple question: what is the *form* that this social phenomenon assumes within the social universe of capital? Now, labor power is in the first instance a transhistorical concept. There must be labor power of some sort or another; a capacity to labor that is transformed into actual labor within a process of laboring—the labor process—for any human society to exist. However, labor power takes on different forms as between social formations. Marx talks about labor power in ancient societies based on slave labor, and the feudal form of labor power. Marx was most interested in the *historical social form* that labor power assumed in capitalist society. In capitalism, I have argued, following Marx, labor power is a commodity. Furthermore, it takes the form of *human capital*. Human capital production and enhancement is at the heart of New Labor's education policy (Rikowski, 2001c).

But it is not strictly accurate to say that human capital and labor power are *identical*, though as convenient shorthand they can be viewed as such. The form of labor power varies between social formations, whereas human capital is a phenomenon tied to capitalist society, but when we refer to 'labor power within capitalist society' then *de facto* this fixes the form of labor power as human capital. In my *Education, Capital and the Transhuman* article I demonstrate their virtual identity in capitalism in detail, with reference to Marx's work (Rikowski, 1999).

Secondly, labor power also has the potential to be expressed in non-capitalist, anti-capitalist modes, and in the transition from capitalism to socialism it will be. This point indicates the fact that labor power can exceed its contemporary social existence as human capital. Finally, the possibility for internal struggle, within the person of the laborer, *against* the capitalization (i.e. the subsumption) of her/his personal powers and capacities under the domination of capital for value-creation, is a potential barrier to the capitalization of labor powers. For me, *this is the class struggle within the 'human' itself; a struggle over the constitution of the 'ourselves' as capital through the practical definition of labor power.* Today the class struggle is everywhere, as capital is everywhere. Human capital is labor power expressed as capitalist social form. As labor power is intimately linked to personhood then 'we are capital' to the extent of its incorporation within our personhoods and its expression in our lives. Thus, a really useful *psychology of capital* would be an account of our 'selves' as capital. This would be a parasitic psychology, for capital is a blind social force (created by us) that has no ego of its own (as noted by Moishe Postone, 1996), but is given life through us, as we become (are taken over, transformed into) it.

What I call 'liberal Left' critics object to this account on two main fronts. First, they argue that labor power is not a commodity as people 'are not sold on the market or produced for sale on the market', and if they were that would be a society based on slave labor, and not essentially capitalist society based on formally 'free' labor. Humans, therefore, cannot be 'capital'. Secondly, some have put it to me, in private conversations that I am quite perverse in taking the concept of 'human capital' seriously at all. After all, they would say, is this not just a hopeless bourgeois concept? Does it not just reduce education to the production of skills and competencies? And is this not what we are *against*?

Peter: So what are your replies to these critics, Glenn?

Glenn: Let's explore the first point: labor power is not a commodity. Well, labor power is in the first instance, within the labor market, the capacity to labor, not labor itself. It is this capacity that the laborer sells to representatives of capital as a commodity, *not her or his total personhood*, nor 'labor' as such. We have many skills, abilities and knowledges, but from the standpoint of the capitalist labor process, only those that are significant for value-creating labor have direct social worth, validity or relevance. Representatives of capital buy labor power, but not the whole person. However, it is most unfortunate for capital's managers that this unique value-creating power is incorporated within a potentially volatile and living body—the laborer. There is no getting round this. The task of getting the laborer to yield up her or his special power, labor power, for value-creation, to channel the laborer's talents and capabilities into the process of generating value, is the material foundation of business studies, human resource management and other branches of management studies. Furthermore, the sale is made only for a specific duration and the laborer can take her/himself off to another employer, subject to contractual procedures. In all of this, the fact that labor power is incorporated within the personhood of the laborer is a source of much vexation and frustration for representatives of capital. On the other hand, the flexibility that this implies, where the constitution of labor power changes with demands made upon the laborer within the capitalist labor process, is an aspect of labor power that capitalists appreciate. Management 'science' is littered with eulogies to flexibility and adaptability. Indeed, a study I made of the UK Institute of Personnel Management's and also the Industrial Society's journal going back to the First World War showed that flexibility and adaptability in school-leavers were attributes that employers were looking for in youth recruits right back to that time. They also expected schools and colleges to play their part in producing such forms of youth labor. Thus they were looking for labor power, or human capital, of a certain kind.

Peter: And the second point, Glenn, what's your reply there?

Glenn: Yes, on the second point: this is that 'human capital' is a bourgeois concept therefore we should have nothing to do with it. For me, this constitutes an abandonment of serious critical analysis of society. Marx remember, in his *Capital*, was not giving a better 'socialist' form of political economy, but a *critique* of political economy. Marx held that political economy was the most highly developed and condensed form of the expression of the social relations of society within bourgeois thought. It was society viewed from the 'standpoint of capital', as capital. The critique of political economy was simultaneously a critique of the social relations, and especially the form of *labor* (the value-form), within that society. I maintain that the concept of 'human capital' expresses something quite horrific; the *human as capital*! The critique of this concept is, therefore, of the utmost urgency. It is precisely because 'human capital' is a bourgeois concept, and one that expresses such deep horror, that critical analysts of capitalist society should place it center stage. Running away from it, like superficial liberal Left critics, gives capital and its human representatives an easier time and avoids the potential explosiveness that its critique can generate for unsettling capitalist thought and social relations. We should take the concept very seriously indeed. In fact, I would argue that human capital theorists do not take their own master concept seriously. This is because they cannot, for to do so would explode the full horror of the phenomenon the concept expresses. There is real horror lurking within this concept of human capital; Marxists have a special duty to expose it, as no other critical analysts of society seem to have the stomach for it. The politics of human resistance is simultaneously a *politics of horror*, as it includes fighting against the horrific forms of life that we are becoming. For although 'we are capital' the process is historical; it develops in intensity over time. Fortunately, the more it occurs the greater its obviousness, and the more paranoid supporters of the system (those who gain millions, billions, of dollars on the foundation of suppressing this insight) will become.

Peter: The thing with reading this stuff, Glenn, is that I find myself seeing your explanations of my questions and then I also find that there are further ideas that you use to give the explanations that are also interesting, and that I would like to follow up! It would be great to read more about what you say on capital as a 'social force', what your views are on the nature of the 'human' in capitalist society and what you have to say on the 'social universe of capital'. But for now, could you expand on what elsewhere you have called the 'social production of labor power' in capitalist society—in your conference paper for the British Educational Research Association, *That Other Great Class of Commodities* paper (Rikowski, 2000a). Because this seems to me to be the point where your Marxism connects directly with education, and in quite specific ways, Glenn.

THE SOCIAL PRODUCTION OF LABOR POWER IN CAPITALISM

Glenn: Yes, Peter, what I have called the social production of labor power in capitalism is crucial for the existence and maintenance of capitalist society today, and education and training have important roles to play in these processes of social production. For Marx, labor power is defined as the aggregate of those mental and physical capabilities within a human being which they exercise when they produce a use-value of any kind (Marx, 1867). Now, the significant issue, for me, is what is included in 'mental capabilities'. The standard response is to view these as skills, competencies or the ability to draw upon different knowledges in labor power performance. But I argue (in Rikowski, 2001b, for example) that 'attitudes', personal values and outlooks and personality traits are also included within 'labor power'. I argue this on a number of counts. First, empirically, recruiters of labor search for work attitudes and personality traits above all other categories of recruitment criteria (and many recruitment studies show this). Second, the first point indicates a key feature of labor power. This is that a laborer can have three PhDs, a bunch of IT qualifications and a Nobel Prize in physics, but from the perspective of capital the key questions is whether s/he is motivated and committed to expending all these wonderful capacities and capabilities within the labor process. For representatives of capital this is the essential point—and why I include attitudes to work and work-related personality traits within the orbit of labor power. Third, at the global level, it is essential that labor power is expended sufficiently to create surplus-value; thus not only must the 'wills' of individual workers be subsumed under their own labor power in the service of capital (value-production), but the working class *in toto* must be. It is therefore an aspect of social domination, and that indicates reconfiguration of the collective social life of the laborers on the foundation of capital. Fourth, and most important, including attitudes, values and personality traits within labor power both *radicalizes* Marx and *radicalizes* the concept of labor power.

Peter: But again, it could be argued that you have produced another form of determinism—with no escape. Aspects of our very personalities 'become capital' as they are incorporated within labor power. So, what happens to agency? Where is the space for self-activity? And where does education come into this? You still have to explain that.

THE PROBLEM OF AGENCY

Glenn: The incorporation of aspects of 'personality' (attitudes, values and personality traits) changes nothing. Remember earlier that I said it is clashes of contradictory forces and drives within the 'human' that make determinism impossible. These oppositional forces within personhood ensure *openness* within the social universe of capital; a universe that moves and expands on the foundation of the clashing of drives and forces within its totality. This openness does not exist within postmodernist *aporias*, or in some social spaces 'in the margins', or in the borders of this social universe. There are no such social spaces, in my view. There is nowhere to hide. The social universe of capital *is all that* there is. Rather, the openness results from the clash of social forces and drives. This partly contradicts what I said earlier, for although none of these forces and drives are inherently stronger or superior there is one that has the capacity to destroy the whole basis of the social universe of capital. This is the collective social force of the working class acting on a global scale to destroy capitalist social relations, to annihilate *capital* itself, and this is the *communist impulse* at its most vital, when there is a massive movement of social force and energy. The capitalist social universe, whose substance is value, *implodes* when this social force to move human history on from pre-history generates sufficient pressure. In the routine running and expansion of the social universe of capital, this force is *suppressed*—it only has virtual existence. But it is our hope for the future.

Peter: Yeah, but, pressing you still: what is agency in the social universe of capital?

Glenn: Well, first I'll get the mess out of the way. The conventional agency/structure problem, so-called, is insoluble. Basically, it's a recasting of the freedom/determinism problem within social life, capitalist social life in fact. Thinking 'agency' has the effect of dissolving 'structure' and vice versa. An experiment: just try to think both at the same time! Purported solutions such as Anthony Giddens's 'structuration theory' evade the impossibility of simultaneous existence of agency and structure. I explain all this in more detail in my 'Which Blair' Project article (Rikowski, 2000b), so I won't enter into it here. Agency, for me, can be understood like any other social (and it is social, not an individual) phenomenon within the social universe of capital: by inquiring into its social *form*. I haven't followed this through in detail, so I'm literally 'thinking on the keyboard' here, but I would probably argue that agency in capitalist society exists to the extent that individuals partake in a social project of human emancipation through imploding the social universe of capital. This implosion *opens up* human futures to possibilities where agency can have real (not just virtual, or repressed, or suppressed) social existence. This applies to many other 'moral' or 'social value' phenomena too, such as social justice. In the struggle against capitalist social existence, the abstract and virtual begins to take on real social form, but its substantive reality is repressed and suppressed. Thus, 'agency' and 'social justice', for example, in capitalist society, are only ever virtual. In this sense, agency in capitalism can only be the *struggle* for agency, the struggle to make it substantively *real*—as opposed to the abstract reality (as real abstraction) it attains in capitalist society. The same for social justice: in capitalist society, social justice is the *struggle for social justice* (as I explain this in greater depth in an experimental paper I wrote a year ago: Rikowski, 2000c). Capital, as Moishe Postone tells us (Postone, 1996), is 'without ego'. There is therefore, not just an absence of any standpoint on which to base *values*, but no *substance* that can make values possible. The postmodernists and nihilists are expressing something at this point. In capital's social universe, 'values' have no substance, but value *is* the substance. Morality, is the *struggle* for morality, the struggle to make it real, and this can only be a possibility (still only a possibility) in the movements of society post-capitalism. Moral critiques of capitalism are in themselves insufficient, as Marx held (though they are understandable, and may energize people and make them angry against the system, and this anger may lead to significant forms of collective struggle). However, the *struggle to attain morality*, the struggle to make values possible, continually crashes against the fabric of society. It is this that makes struggles for gender equality, 'race' equality and so on so explosive. In capitalist society, these forms of equality (like all other forms of equality) are impossible. But the struggle for their attainment exposes their possibility, a possibility that arises only within a post-capitalist scenario.

On this analysis, collective quests for gender and 'race' equality are a threat to the constitution of capitalist society; they call forth forms of equality that can have no social validity, no existence, within the universe of capital—as *all forms of equality are denied except for one*. This is equality on the basis of *exchange value*. On the basis of exchange-value we are all equal. There are a number of aspects to this. First, our *labors* may be equal in terms of the value they create. However, as our labor powers have different values, then 10 weeks of my labor may be equal to a single day of the labor of some highly paid soccer player. Equality here, then, operates on the basis of massive substantive *inequality*. Secondly, the value of our labor powers may be equal; so one hour's labor of two people with equal labor powers (in terms of labor power quality) creates the same value. In a paper of last year, I go on to show that although these are the only forms of equality socially validated within the social universe of capital, practically they are unattainable as other social drives break these forms of equalization (Rikowski, 2000c). For example, the drive to enhance labor power quality as between different capitals, national capitals and between individuals pursuing relative 'self-investment' in their own labor powers would constantly *disrupt* any systematic attempt to create equality of labor powers through education and training. Although forms of equality on the basis of exchange-value are *theoretically* possible, the first (equality of labor) is abominable as it is compatible with massive inequalities of income and wealth, whilst the second (equality of labor powers) is practically hopeless. The outcome of all this is that struggles against inequalities in capitalist society are struggles for forms of equality that cannot exist within capitalism. Yet they nevertheless constitute struggles against the constitution of capitalist society, and also *for* equality than *can* attain social existence on the basis of the dissolution of the social universe of capital.

Peter: So now we get round to the 'social production of labor power' in capitalism? We seem to keep churning out new issues. In your published work, as far as I can see, you have not really expanded tremendously on this, though you have hinted that it is at the foundation of what you want to say about education and training in capitalist society, Glenn. How would you sum up what you call the 'social production of labor power,' Glenn? What are the main characteristics and features?

RETURN TO THE SOCIAL PRODUCTION OF LABOR POWER

Glenn: Sure! This is a big topic. First I want to summarize why labor power, and then education and training, are so crucial in capitalist society. Labor power is transformed into labor in the labor process, and in this movement value, and then at a certain point surplus value, is generated. There are two aspects to labor: it is a process of producing use-values and also value (a valorization process). There are not two separate processes going on here; they are both expressions of the one and same set of acts within the labor process. If the product is useless then value is not realized at the point of sale. Labor power consists of those attributes of the person that are used in creating a use-value (the use-value aspect of labor power), but labor power also has a quantitative, *value*-aspect too. Through the activity of the worker (labor) in the labor process, some of our personal powers (labor power) also become expressed as value-generation. Thus: labor power is the unique, living commodity that is the foundation of value, the substance of the social universe of capital. We create the social universe of capital.

Now, I have argued (e.g. Rikowski, 2000a) that education and training play a key role in the *social production* of labor power. Definite productive forms of this can be located empirically. Empirical studies I have undertaken, on apprentice recruitment for example, illustrate this. However, processes of labor power production are extremely fragmented on an institutional and organizational basis (between forms of education and training, work-based learning). Thus, we see relatively 'weak' forms of *labor power production.* But this misses the key historical point, which is that over the last fifty years processes of the social production of labor power have become socially defined and delineated more clearly and definitely. This is because the social drive to reduce all education and training to labor power production has gained ground historically. This reflects the deepening capitalization of the whole of social life. Thus, education and training increasingly operate as systems and processes of labor power production, and it is labor power that generates value. Value is the substance of the social universe of capital. In this chain of transformation and production we can see that education and training, therefore, have a key role to play in the *maintenance and expansion of the social universe of capital.* The social power of teachers, trainers and all those involved in socially producing labor power rests on this fact.

Representatives of capital in business, state bureaucracies and government are fundamentally aware of the significance of education and training in terms of labor power production, though they call it 'human capital', but we know what that means! Indeed, read any UK Department of Education and Employment report of the last twenty or more years and they illustrate the intense concern regarding the quality of UK labor power. It is, of course, all wrapped up in such euphemisms or proxy concepts as 'employability', 'human capital', 'work-ready graduates', school kids who are able to 'meet industry's needs' and the like. Teachers and trainers have huge strategic importance in capitalist society: they are like 'angels of the fuel dump', or 'guardians of the flame', in that they have intimate day-to-day responsibility for generating the fuel (labor power) that generates what Marx called the 'living fire' (labor) (Marx, 1858, p. 361). Their roles start to explain the intense efforts of representatives of capital in state bureaucracies, government, business and the media in attempting to control the labor of teachers and trainers. Teachers' and trainers' labor is channeled into labor power production, and increased pressures arising from competition to enhance the quality of labor power within nation states (as one response to globalization), spurs on efforts to do this. The implications are massive: control of curricula, of teacher training, of education unions, training organizations and much more. There are many means of such control, and empirical and historical investigations are important here. Letting the law of money loose (though education markets) is just one strategy. Attempts to control the processes involved is another, but increasingly both are used in tandem (though these strategies can come into conflict).

So, there are strong forces at work to ensure that teachers' and trainers' labor is reconfigured on the basis of labor power production. But also, teachers and trainers are in a structural position to *subvert* and *unsettle* processes of labor power production within their orbits. Even more, they can work to enshrine *alternative* educational principles and practices that bring into question the constitution of society and hint at ways in which expenditure of labor power does not take a value form. This is a nightmare for representatives of capital. It is an additional factor making for the control of teachers' and trainers' labor. And this highlights, for me, the central importance of radical or critical pedagogy today, and why your work, Peter, has such momentous implications and consequences for the anti-capitalist struggles ahead.

Peter: And for me, it highlights the significance of education for today's anti-capitalist movement. As you have put it, radical pedagogy and the anti-capitalist struggle are intimately related: that was also one of the messages I aimed to establish in my Che/Freire book (McLaren, 2000).

Glenn: Your Che/Freire book really consolidated the relation between anti-capitalism and radical pedagogy for me. You see, Peter, when I was younger, I used to think that it would be better being in some industrial situation where the 'real action' was going on, rather than in education. However, labor power is capital's weakest link, as it is incorporated within personhood. Labor power is the commodity that generates value. And education and training are processes of labor power production. Give all this, then to be in education today is to be right at the center of the action! There is no better place to be. From other things I have said, it follows that education and training, insofar as they are involved in the production of labor power, that, in capitalism, takes the form of human capital, then they are also involved in the capitalization of humanity. Thus: a politics of human resistance is necessary *first of all* within education and training. These are the places that it goes on in the most forced, systematic and overt way. Radical pedagogy, therefore, is an aspect of this politics, an aspect of *resisting processes within education and training that are constituted as processes of reducing humans to labor power (human capital)*. On this account, radical pedagogy is the hot seat in anti-capitalist struggles. The question of pedagogy is critical today, and this is where our work productively collides.

You have written extensively on Pedagogy for Revolution (though also increasingly, and more directly on the critique of capitalist schooling in recent years). I have concentrated more on the negative analysis of Education for Capital, and said little about pedagogy, though I now realize its absolute importance more clearly after reading your wonderful *Che Guevara, Paulo Friere, and the Pedagogy of Revolution* (McLaren, 2000). Both are necessary moments within an exploration of what Paula Allman (1999) has called socially transformative praxis. My negative critique of Education for Capital exposes the centrality of the question of pedagogy, I believe. From the other direction, your work on the centrality of pedagogy for the anti-capitalist struggles calls for an exploration of the constitution of society and a negative critique of education as labor power production. This also provides an argument about the necessity of radical, transformative pedagogy as a key strategy for use in terminating the capitalization of humanity and envisioning an open future. It grounds the project of radical pedagogy; shows its necessity in capitalism today. We can contrast Education for Capital (as an aspect of the capitalization of humanity) with Pedagogy for Revolution (that transforms social relations and individuals, and seeks to curtail the horror of capital within the 'human'). I was wondering if that was how you saw it, Peter. Although we have come at things from different angles, we have arrived at the same spot. Capital is like a labyrinth.

Peter: That's a good way of putting it. I think you have spelled out the connections between our work from the development within your own ideas and experience. I might see it slightly differently in some respects. I think I have a stronger notion of Marxism as a *philosophy of praxis* than you have in your own work, is that fair and accurate?

Glenn: I think it is in the sense that is I would not place so much store by the notion of philosophy, though *praxis* is hugely significant for me. You may say the two go together. My Marxism was learnt largely through debates within the Conference of Socialist Economists, their journal *Capital & Class*, participating in the (now defunct) Revolutionary Communist Party and going to Socialist Workers Party meetings in the mid-to-late 1990s, but most of all through reading Marx. Theorists such as Derek Sayer, John Holloway, Simon Clarke and Kevin Harris were very important for me, and more recently Moishe Postone and the works of Michael Neary (Neary, 1997; Neary and Taylor, 1998). But what do you think, Peter? How do you see Marxism as, for lack of a better word, a philosophy? And how does it link up with your work on pedagogy for revolution?

MARX, MARXISM AND METHOD

Peter: Yes, Glenn, as I see it Marxism is a philosophy of praxis. This is so in the sense that it is able to bring knowledge face-to-face with the conditions of possibility for its own embodiment in history, into contact with its own laboring bodies, into contact with its forgotten life-activity, its own chronotype or space-time co-ordinates (i.e., its constitutive outside). Knowledge, even critical knowledge, doesn't reproduce itself, for to assert this much is to deny its inherence in history, its insinuation in the social universe of production and labor. But I guess that's okay with some post-structuralists who tend to reduce history to a text anyway, as if it miraculously writes itself. Postmodern theory is built upon the idea of self-creation or the fashioning of the self. Self-creation assumes people have authorized the imperatives of their own existence, the conditions in which they form or create themselves. But Marxism teaches us that people make history within, against, and through systems of mediation already saturated by a nexus of social relations, by a force-field of conflicting values and accents, by prior conventions and practical activities that constrain the possible, that set limits to the possible. Raya Dunayevskaya (1978) describes Marxism, as I recall, as a 'theoretical expression of the instinctive strivings of the proletariat for liberation'. That pretty much captures the essence for me. Paula Allman (1999) notes that Marx's efforts were directed at exposing 'the inherent and fundamental contradictions of capitalism'. I agree with her that these contradictions are as real today as they were in Marx's time. She enjoins readers to dismiss the criticisms of Marxism as essentialist and teleological and to rely not on the perspectives of Marxists but on the writings of Marx himself. After all, Marx's works constitute a critique of relations historically specific to capitalism. We need to try to understand not only the theoretical concepts that Marx offers us, but also the manner in which Marx thinks.

Glenn: It sounds as if there is a role for philosophers in the revolution then.

Peter: I think the concrete, objective crisis that we live in today makes philosophy a matter of extreme urgency for all revolutionaries, as Dunayevskaya puts it. You may not be interested in philosophy, but I am sure philosophy is interested in you. Well, the specific ideologies of capitalism that frame and legitimize certain philosophical approaches and affirm some over others are interested in your compliance, perhaps that is a better way to put it. My own interest here is in developing a philosophy of praxis for educators. The key point for me is when Marx broke from the concept of theory when he wrote about the 'working day' in *Capital*. Here we see Marx moving from the history of theory to the history of the class struggle. The workers' struggles at the time shifted the emphasis of Marx's work. Dunayevskaya (1978) notes that '*From start to finish, Marx is concerned with the revolutionary actions of the proletariat. The concept of theory now is something unified with action. The ideal and the material became unified in his work as never before and this is cap-*

tured in his struggle for a new social order in which "the free development of each is the condition for the free development of all."'

Glenn: Certainly, the role that something called 'philosophy' plays in my own work has not been clarified—which is ironic really, as philosophy was my major subject for my first degree and I taught philosophy in the early 1990s. On Dunayevskaya, I am a Marxist-Humanist of sorts; the problem I have with it is the notion of the 'human' and humanism, but I won't go into that here. Just to say that Marxist-Humanism is the struggle to attain an open future for humanity: that's how I see it.

Peter: You see, Glenn, I think that this is one of the silences in your work — the role of philosophy. Let's recast the issue, so we come at it at an angle that more clearly does crash into your work. You have given me an idea of some of the general forces flowing through what you call the 'social universe of capital', and I can see your points about how our work meets up, and so on. What puzzles me though is how you see all this meeting up with what some might call the 'level of appearances', or 'everyday life'. I mean, you make your living as an education researcher (though you research training processes too, if we want to make that distinction). But what are the connections between your work as an education researcher and your Marxist educational theory, or your 'labor power theory', as you might prefer to call it? Can connections be made? What is the role of 'education research' in relation to what you have said so far in this dialogue?

Glenn: From my perspective, those questions have colossal significance today, Peter! The connection between the phenomena structuring life within capital's social universe and 'everyday life' in capitalism has been a key issue in Marxist theory since Marx's death. The usual starting place is to make the distinction between essence and appearance, and then try to show that what we observe empirically, on the surface of society, can be explained with reference to the deeper phenomena (value, abstract labor and so on). For me, this suggests that, ontologically, there are two realms of existence: the real and the abstract, or essence and appearance. This allows some to argue that we can understand things like competition, price and money without recourse to any 'deeper reality' (value, abstract labor, surplus value, and so on). It is a short step from there to exploring 'everyday life' in terms of markets, price and competition without recourse to value, abstract labor and others ideas central to Marx's analysis of capitalism.

A concrete example of this is the work on education markets and the marketization of education. In the UK there is a massive literature on education markets, quasi-markets and related empirical studies of the marketization of schools and colleges. These studies, however, are extremely superficial in that they incorporate no sustained analysis of what the 'products' of education are. Thus, we have 'education markets and missing products', as I explained in a paper to the Conference of Socialist Economists in 1995 (Rikowski, 1995). However, I would not wish to say that production, value and labor power and so on constitute some kind of 'deeper *reality*'. I read Marx as saying that the phenomena pinpointed as key by the educational marketization writers are *phenomenal forms* of essential relations. There is no 'analytic dualism' involved here, or a Critical Realism that is founded on such a dualism, as in the writings of Robert Willmott in England (e.g. Willmott, 1999). The phenomenal forms are an *expression* of value, not some radically different ontological 'level' or order. I would want to argue that this is so even for the phenomena of 'everyday life' too. So when I say 'I am money', or "I am capital", or 'I am value' I am heralding the ways in which money, capital and value literally are 'me' and flow through my life as aspects of observable things that I do and say. But the former (capital, value, and money) does not constitute some analytically distinct level apart from 'everyday life'. 'Real life' is abstract. Although we can use the power of abstraction to abstract *from* reality, to indicate generalities, a really radical approach to abstraction demonstrates and indicates how concrete, 'real life' is also abstract. We are indeed 'ruled by abstractions', but these abstractions are not separate from lived experience; we live the abstractions through the concrete (and *vice versa*). It's as with labor. The same labor has two *aspects*: first, the concrete, qualitative, use-value aspect; and secondly the quantitative, abstract value-aspect. There are not two different acts of labor going on. Now, I want to argue that the whole of social, 'everyday life' is like that. There are concrete and abstract aspects to social phenomena in capitalist society. One of the tasks of Marxist science is to explore these aspects as 'living contradictions'. Of course, getting funding for this type of 'Marxist research' will not be easy. Furthermore, if it is to have any real value then the lessons learnt from this research must be fed into the wider anti-capitalist movement, and ways for disseminating it have to be addressed.

Peter: But have you done this, Glenn? I mean have you actually examined particular social phenomena in capitalism in this way? And if you have, how have you done this?

ASPECTS OF LABOR POWER

Glenn: Yes: labor power. I have attempted to uncover various aspects of labor power: the use-value, exchange-value, value aspects in particular, but also the collective and subjective aspects (Rikowski, 2000a). And this work shows that it is not a case of 'applying' concepts to reality; aspects of capitalist social life are expressed in such a way that these ideas are produced in thought at the moment of grasping the aspects and essential relations. In capitalism, social reality writes itself through us, as *ourselves*, as we live its forms and aspects. There is no determinism involved here; as there is no duality. The phenomena are not separate in capital's social universe (its totality) in the way that determinism in the classical sense presupposes. Causality also has no purchase either on this outlook; the phenomena are aspects and forms of each other within the totality. There is no separation of phenomena as in bourgeois social science. What is required is a communist scientific language adequate to the expression of movements, transformations and metamorphoses of phenomena within a social universe whose substance is value. Thus, we talk of totality, social universe, infinity, relativity, process, transformation, movement, metamorphosis, morphing, aspect, contradiction, generation, form, intensity, density, force, implosion, explosion, dissolution and other concepts, that explain social transformations and relations. The processes of labor power formation or surplus-value generation, when examined through these ideas, rather than notions of cause/effect, determination, base/superstructure and the ideas of what Moishe Postone (1996) called 'traditional Marxism', are *radicalized*. Unlike 'postmodern thinking', this process truly unsettles through exposing the bareness of capitalist social relations as we live them. The gap between lives lived and lives theorized about closes.

Peter: A couple of points. First, this must make the social production of labor power a tricky process! If labor power incorporates various 'aspects', as you call them, presumably these are in contradiction. Secondly, what's the role of empirical research? Do Marxists do that? Is there any point to it? After all, will not analysis of our own lives be sufficient? Why research anyone else when we can research ourselves with the same degree of validity?

Glenn: Yes, the social production of labor power is made difficult by the fact that labor power incorporates aspects: use-value, exchange-value, value, collective and subjective aspects—that do express a whole bunch of contradictions. Schools are in the business of producing a living commodity that incorporates contradictions! You can see the enormity of what they are up against! This conditions contradictions in education policy; state functionaries have to try to make sense of the absurd. Result: education policies that reflect the contradictions, or skip around from one prong of the fork to the other. Of course, sometimes they are suppressed too. This is fascinating stuff, as you can see these contradictions playing themselves out within people's lives, within government policies and thinking—everywhere! Empirical studies can give these insights power and relevance. Secondly, the social production of labor power, *as a process*, crashes against social *re*-production and maintenance of laborers and their families through the wage form. I show this contradiction in relation to the phenomenon of the student-worker, nominally full-time students who work to survive (Rikowski, 2000d). Education policies are riddled with contradictions flowing from these considerations also. Mainstream academics attempt to make sense of, to rationalize these concepts, these processes, at war! Empirical and historical studies are crucial for uncovering the forces that we are up against.

And this gets on to your second point, Peter, the point of doing empirical research. First, it's true that 'researching ourselves' can get us a lot further than previously envisaged. Autobiography attains importance; we can locate the contradictions within our own personhoods as they are transformed and flow throughout our own lives. However, the *intensity* of some of the contradictions within personhood as capital and between persons and groups varies. Sometimes these living contradictions can be illustrated and demonstrated more easily by exploring the lives of others, rather than merely examining your own 'self' as contradictory social entity. But most importantly, from what I have said previously, the concrete is also the abstract, so an empirical exploration of some aspect of education is never just empirical and concrete. There is a place, therefore, for Marxist research in education and in other areas of social life. The obvious problem is getting resources and time to do this work. In the UK, the school and college effectiveness and improvement are being driven increasingly strongly from the centre through the Department for Education & Employment (DfEE). The Economic and Social Research Council (ESRC), the premier funding body for serious social science research, is under increasing pressure to narrow the limits for 'acceptable' education research. A National Educational Research Forum is being established which is dominated by the school/college effectiveness/improvement industry. Of course, you can try to get something through this system—but it's getting extremely difficult. There are some big programmes (such as the Teaching and Learning Research Programme) and the megabucks research centers through the DfEE that make any critical research program difficult to get off the ground in any substantial manner. There are ways round this; hidden agendas and so on, but it's tough. I'm reading Russell Jacoby's book, *The Last Intellectuals* (Jacoby, 2000)—the new edition—and he's great at showing the processes through which even mildly critical research, let alone any Marxist research, gets squeezed out, and how Left academics get marginalized, victimized and worse.

Peter: You said that empirical studies can give us insight and also relevance into the ways that contradictions within personhood and within processes of the social production of labor power itself—within which education and training are implicated heavily—through empirical studies. On the 'relevance' aspect, what did you have in mind exactly?

Glenn: *Political* relevance, principally. In my pamphlet, *The Battle in Seattle: Its Significance for Education* (Rikowski, 2001c), I show how the WTO agenda for education is related to New Labor's education policy. However, for me, the really important part is the second half of the book where I explore the significance of education for anti-capitalism post-Seattle. At that point, the links between labor power, radical pedagogy and the need for organisations that can seriously take on the kind of politics of human resistance to processes of our capitalization—in particular, the key role that education plays in these processes, these links can all be made. They can be made for political strategy. That is the full force of the 'relevance' I am thinking of. In England, sadly, I have received criticism from some who hold that we should not mix up writing about

Marx with writing about something like the WTO's education agenda and New Labor education policy—and these criticisms from the Left too! These criticisms come from elements within what I call the liberal Left, and they induce us to separate theory from empirical study, radical pedagogic practice and education politics (and politics in general). I have been called a 'radical poser' (and worse) on the basis that I dare bring Marx up front into education analysis and politics. It will 'put people off', I am told, and I 'will make a fool of myself'! Obviously I care about 'putting people off'. My answer is that in education theory, analysis and politics we really ought to be trying to *radicalize* Marx, to make him more relevant and *exciting*. That is a project for writing, analysis, critique and practical politics to demonstrate. As to 'making a fool of myself', let history decide! Marx didn't seem to worry about that very much; he took tremendous risks with his own personae and public image—on the basis that he believed that it would be for the good of the movement. Surely, the goal is to bring Marxist analysis, theory and politics together within the sphere of education together—I argued this years ago (Rikowski, 1996). Marx is neither an embarrassment nor an idol. He is there to be used, as still the greatest critic of capitalist society today. Anyway, I tried to bring this all together in *The Battle in Seattle* booklet; to give a materialist analysis of today's new anti-capitalist movement that would indicate how social movements are engaged in *one fight, one struggle*—for only on this basis can they win out.

Peter: Establishing the unity of diverse struggles is important, surely. Seattle brought that to the fore with tremendous practical force. The key point is that we collectively crash through the walls of capitalist society.

Glenn: Yes, Peter, but in what direction is it possible to move in order to transcend the entrapment of capital? In other words, in what direction should we labor?

Peter: There are specific modes of production, some of which are historically bound up with capitalism. Not all modes of production are capitalist. A core feature of the capitalist mode of production is that the labor that is operative within it contains a duality, as use value and exchange value. Living labor therefore incorporates concrete and abstract labor. Abstract labor, for capital, is the foundation of value. Bruno Gulli (1999) mentions the fact that labor is an ontological power, a creative power, which is why capital wants (must have) it for its social existence! Living labor is turned into productive labor because of its special relationship with objectified labor. Peter Hudis (2000a-b) poses the crucial question: What kind of labor should a human being do? It seems to me that strategizing against capital means working with those in the technologically underdeveloped world, and part of the challenge stipulates that we go beyond empirical treatments of categories developed by Marx and engaging them dialectically. Capital, as Marx has pointed out, is a social relation of labor; it constitutes objectified, abstract, undifferentiated—and hence alienated—labor. Capital cannot be controlled or abolished through external means without dispensing with value production and creating new forms of non-alienated labor. Creating these new forms of non-alienated labor is the hope and promise of the future. This is something that you have talked about in your own work, Glenn.

Let's consider for a moment the harsh reality of permanent mass unemployment, contingent workforces, and the long history of strikes and revolts of the unemployed. It is relatively clear from examining this history that the trajectory of capitalism in no way subsumes class struggle or the subjectivity of the workers. We can relate this to the work of Raya Dunayevskaya and Peter Hudis and bring Hegel into the conversation here. What for Hegel is Absolute knowledge (the realm of realized transcendence), Marx referred to as the new society. While Hegel's self referential, all-embracing, totalizing Absolute is greatly admired by Marx, it is, never the less, greatly modified by him. For Marx, Absolute knowledge (or the self-movement of pure thought) did not absorb objective reality or objects of thought but provided a ground from which alienation could be transcended. By reinserting the human subject into the dialectic, and by defining the subject as corporal being (rather than pure thought or abstract self-consciousness), Marx appropriates Hegel's self-movement of subjectivity as an act of transcendence and transforms it into a critical humanism. The value form of labor (abstract labor) that has been transmogrified into the autonomous moment of dead labor, eating up everything that it is not, can be challenged by freely associated labor and concrete, human sensuousness. The answer is in envisioning a non-capitalist future that can be achieved, as Hudis notes, after Dunayevskaya, by means of subjective self- movement through absolute negativity so that a new relation between theory and practice can connect us to the idea of freedom. Hudis (2000b) argues that the abolition of private property does not necessarily lead to the abolition of capital. We need, therefore, to examine the direct relation between the worker and production. Here, our sole emphasis should not be on the abolition of private property, which is the product of alienated labor; it must be on the abolition of alienated labor itself. Marx gave us some clues as to how to transcend alienation, ideas that he developed from Hegel's concept of second or absolute negativity, or 'the negation of the negation'. Marx engaged in a materialist re-reading of Hegel. In his work, the abolition of private property constitutes the first negation. The second is the negation of the negation of private property. This refers to a self-reflected negativity, and what Hudis refers to as the basis for a positive humanism.

Bruno Gulli makes a similar point when he notes that the 'both/and' bourgeois logic used to resolve contradictions is not an alternative to capital. The possibility of change does not reside in a 'both/and' logic but rather can be located in a 'neither/ nor' logic. He writes that

> In reality, the *both/and* modality enjoyed by the few is the condition for the *neither/nor* modality of a growing majority. *Chiapas* is an example of this. The possibility of a change does not reside in the acceptance of the

both/and mentality but in the creation, out of a double negation, of a new radicality, one in which the having become of becoming is resurrected again to return to the immediacy of its subject . . . The logic which breaks that of capital is a logic of *neither/nor*, a logic of double negation, or, again, a logic of double resistance and absolute affirmation. Through this logic, labor returns to itself, not posited by capital as valorizing labor, but posited by itself as *neither productive nor unproductive* labor: as living labor or form-giving fire (Gulli, 1999, note 28; paragraph 35).

Glenn: Absolute negativity in this sense is a creative force.

Peter: Yes. Of course, Marx rejects Hegel's idealization and dehumanization of self-movement through double negation because this leaves untouched alienation in the world of labor-capital relations. Marx sees this absolute negativity as objective movement and the creative force of history. Absolute negativity in this instance becomes a constitutive feature of a self-critical social revolution that, in turn, forms the basis of permanent revolution. Hudis raises a number of difficult questions with respect to developing a project that goes beyond controlling the labor process. It is a project that is directed at abolishing capital itself through the creation of freely associated labor: The creation of a social universe not parallel to the social universe of capital (whose substance is value) is the challenge here. The form that this society will take is that which has been suppressed within the social universe of capital: socialism, a society based not on value but on the fulfillment of human need.

Glenn: This brings us together, facing a common enemy in order to struggle for the realization of those human needs. At this point, the question of social movements asserts itself: different struggles it appears, but do they form just *one* struggle from the perspective of anti-capitalism? For me, the social movements have a common enemy: capital—and the ideologies (especially neo-liberalism) that sustain it. But what is your perspective on social movements, Peter? You indicated by e-mail some while back that you where rethinking the significance of social movements. What are the problems with social movements?

SOCIAL MOVEMENTS AND CRITICAL PEDAGOGY

Peter: I find the creation of multi-class formations exceedingly problematic for a number of reasons, several of which I would like to mention, without excessive adumbration. Others have gone into this in capillary detail but for the purposes of this discussion I want simply to mention that, for the most part, such movements serve mainly the petit-bourgeoisie and their interests. Secondly, these groups rarely contest the rule of capital. The laws of motion of capital and social relations of production do some seem the central objects of their attack, and, frankly, too often they are not even regarded as the central issues around which their struggle coalesces. Their efforts are too often reform-based, calling for access to capitalist forms of democracy, for redistribution of resources. Thirdly, in their attempt to stitch together a broad coalition of groups, they often seem rudderless. Should we be for 'social justice' that works simply to re-institute capitalist social relations of production? Of course, these are issues that we need to debate in schools of education. The whole issue of rights-based justice is predicated on capitalist right to property. Can we shift the focus to the abolition of private property? I don't see these discussions occurring with any consistency within the tradition of critical pedagogy in the United States.

Glenn: How so?

Peter: What seemingly gives them ballast—emotional, conceptual, political—is their all-encompassing rallying cry for 'counter-hegemonic struggle at all costs' without, as it were, ever specifying what they mean. There is a lack of contextual specificity in tying their interests together. In other words, is all counter-hegemonic struggle a good thing? It reminds me of the clarion call of the multiculturalists for diversity, for social justice. Is the struggle for diversity always transparent, always self-evident? I think not. Today the great benefac-tors of diversity are the multinational corporations. Especially when you consid-er that we have arrived at a point in our history where democracy and social inequality proceed apace, in tandem. In today's global plantation, diversity—ethnic, gender, sexual—functions in the interests of capital accumulation. The questions we need to raise are: Diversity for what purpose? In whose interests? By what means? Who benefits? Just look at the Republican Party and the calls for diversity during its national convention. Diversity for 'compassionate' con-servatism? Diversity for boosting big business? For taking money from the poor and putting it in the pockets of the rich? Is this what we mean by 'diversity'? Is this what we mean by counter-hegemony? What are we countering, precisely?

I should think that the strategic centrality of counter-hegemony very much depends on what you are attempting to counter. I would much prefer to see the various new social movements linked by a singular commitment towards a pro-tracted, all-embracing assault on capital, not just capitalism. Wouldn't it be more productive for the center of gravity in such a project to be the struggle for mass, collective, working-class struggle, for proletarian hegemony? So that we can create conditions that captures Marx's concept of 'from each according to their ability, to each according to their need.' As Marx and Engels noted, our concern cannot merely be the modification of private property, but its abolition, not the amelioration of class antagonisms, but the abolition of classes, not the improvement of society but the establishment of a new one. This is no easy task but it requires working-class internationalism at a time of a powerful diversity within the international division of labor.

Glenn: I would see things slightly differently. Whilst I agree with you that the struggle against capital is *the* struggle, the critical engagement, I don't think this is a majority position within the post- Seattle anti-globalization movement.

However, I do think its appeal is growing within that movement, as the various fragments come to realize the impossibility of findings real solutions within the framework of capitalist society. For me, the issue is to bring the anti-globalization movement towards its constitution as an anti-*capitalist* movement. The arguments for that transition have to be continually made. But Peter, backtracking a tad, you said that critical pedagogy has the potential to become a challenge to private property rights, and a challenge to the domination of capital itself. It can also articulate social injustices as they relate to education and the wider society. Yet, for you, it is clear that the so-called Critical Pedagogy School has to date signally failed in realizing its potential. The issue of critical pedagogy is where our contributions meet up—as I indicated earlier. My work on labor power shows that critical or radical pedagogies have the potential to disrupt the smooth flow of the social production of labor power by raising issues of social justice and inequalities in capitalist society. Further, radical pedagogy is an essential moment within revolutionary social transformation; it is at the heart of truly revolutionary transformative praxis, as Paula Allman (1999) convincingly argues. So what, Peter, in your view, has gone so wrong with the Critical Pedagogy School? I am afraid if we don't center our question on pedagogy now then we might not have time enough to do it justice. Specifically, where is the problem with critical pedagogy in the United States?

Peter: I like to say there exist critical pedagogies, in the plural, because the few of us who write about it, and practice it, have definite ideas about what makes a pedagogy critical, or vulgar and domesticating, or reproductive, or what I have been calling of late, revolutionary. I won't give a nuanced rendition of these debates, but offer you my simple but straightforward impression of what's wrong.

Glenn: Okay, just the outline of the tragedy then.

Peter: Critical pedagogy has, in the main, been defrauded of its legitimacy, defunded of its revolutionary potential, at least the critical pedagogy that I am thinking about. In my discussions last year with my dear comrades in Finland, Israel, Brazil, Mexico, Australia, and Taiwan, I noticed that there was a great enthusiasm surrounding the possibilities of critical pedagogy, and a misperception that it was finding its way into the classrooms of the United States. In the United States, it is has been sadly vulgarized and emasculated to what I call 'the democracy of empty forms'—seating arrangements in circles and semi-circles, teachers serving as 'facilitators' and promoting informal discussions of students' experiences, and the like. On the one hand, when critical pedagogy is taught in university settings it is dismissed as being elitist. There are constant attacks on the language of critical pedagogy as it is used in the academy, for instance. On the other side of the debate is populist elitism. This is a heavily-charged feeling among some activists that the closer in proximity that you are to the oppressed (that is, if you are a teacher in South Central or Watts or East Los Angeles) then the closer you are to the 'truth' of the teaching enterprise. It also puts you nearer to interpreting the experience of students. Hence, professors who teach critical pedagogy are accused of being ivory tower intellectuals who offer theoretical approaches that make little sense in actual classroom situations.

Glenn: The 'ivory tower' no longer exists, if it ever did. Studies of higher education show that it too is increasingly under the truncheon of capitalist social relations. I have David Harvie's excellent article in *Capital & Class* in mind here (Harvie, 2000), but also I also have in view important work in this journal by Teresa Ebert, Deb Kelsh and others.

Peter: Absolutely, Glenn, but on the specific issue of classroom teachers, I do believe that this proximity gives the teacher a unique vantage point for interpreting their experiences, but I don't think it guarantees the truth of their own experience or that of their students. There are a lot of teachers and students who work in the barrio who don't betray—or strive for—what might be called 'critical consciousness'. We can apply the same criticism to professors of education, of course. But I do think that the teachers and students from aggrieved communities have the potential to build a powerful revolutionary movement. The pressing question for me—whether we work in inner-city areas in classrooms or whether we work in the precincts of the academy—is whether or not our approach to making sense of experience is a dialectical one. That is, that it locates students, schools, curricula, policies and pedagogical and social practices within the larger social totality or social universe of capitalist social relations. My focus here is not on analyzing schooling from the perspective of social relations of exchange or consumption as much as it is analyzing the schooling process and the formation of students within it from the perspective of the social relations of production. Behind the exchange of things—knowledge, information, and commodities—there is always a relationship to production. Students are not only consumers, they are also casualties of a perverse production process. They therefore become casualties of history. When I talk about interrogating our experiences as learner-practitioners or teacher-learners, I am trying to find ways of forging a collective revolutionary praxis and creating contexts where students can shape history through their own actions in, through and against the world. Language and experience are not pristine, unmediated, fully transparent, or sealed off from society but rather are refracted by dominant values as well as stabilizing and conventional discourses. Experiences need to be both affirmed and critically interrogated, but the point behind our affirmation of and challenge to the 'common sense' character of our experiences is the commitment to transform our experiences. We need to make a connection between our collective revolutionary aspirations and personal experiences of oppression. But our attempts at the transformation of social relations of exploitation must pay attention to the appropriate forms that our cultural action should take as a mode of revolutionary praxis. Paulo Freire underscored the notion that cultural action in order to be transformative must also be a preparation for cultural revolution. And such a revolution is most fully developed when we are engaged in the struggle to bring about the dictatorship of the proletariat. The point I want to make here is that we can't be passively bound by our experiences—even populist ones (perhaps especially populist ones when you consider the fact that it is a form of populism that is currently informing the politics of George W. Bush). This is because critical knowledge means an encounter with dialectical analysis in order to smash the oppressor within. Paula Allman reads Freire brilliantly—and 'bodily'—when she notes that *'dialogue enables us to experience the alternative or certain aspects of it for a period of time and in a specific context'*. The structure of society resides in the structure of experience. We carry this in our musculature, in our gestures, our emotions, in our dreams and desires. Our subjectivities are commodified (a process that Lukacs described as 'reification').

Glenn: This was a central theme of your *Schooling as a Ritual Performance* (McLaren, 1999), was it not?

Peter: Yes, I was trying to find a way of exploring the link between labor and the language of symbolic gesture, between knowledge and the commodification of desire. Unfortunately I was not schooled in the work of Marx as much as I should have been when I wrote that book. But let's get back to the idea of commodification. The whole process of commodification should be more central in discussions and practices of pedagogy. These commodities, these reifications are not illusions but objective social processes. Commodification regulates our social lives. We can't just 'think' away the commodification of our subjectivities, our 'structures of feeling' as Raymond Williams put it. We need to find our freedom in our actions, in new sets of actions that explode the prison-house forged out of the grammar of capitalism. Our truth will be found in our actions, in our praxis. Marx wrote, *'man must prove the truth, i.e., the reality and power, the this-worldliness of his thinking in practice'*. That is, the truth of our ideas exists only in practice. Lukacs quotes Lenin thus: *'the concrete analysis of the concrete situation is not an opposite of "pure" theory, but—on the contrary—it is the culmination of genuine theory, its consummation—the point where it breaks into practice'*. Lukacs follows this with the remark: *'Without any exaggeration it may be said that Marx's final, definitive thesis on Feuerbach — "The philosophers have only interpreted the world in different ways; the point, however, is to change it"—found its most perfect embodiment in Lenin and his work'*. In other words, Lenin's revolutionary struggle is illustrative of what is meant by a philosophy of praxis. All critical educators need to become philosophers of praxis. So that to summarize and give you the gist of my argument, and I fear that I have been meandering terribly, here, Glenn—I believe that critical pedagogy needs to focus on interrogating and transforming the constituent results of the complex and concrete social totality. We need to explore the 'fertile dungheap' of capitalism's contradictions, through which all of us live and labor. We need to get back to this messy work of historical materialist critique in order to build momentum in our revolutionary praxis. This is so especially given the often grave misperceptions about Paulo Freire's pedagogy that have proliferated over the last several decades, following in the wake of what has been a steady domestication and embourgeoisment of his work.

Glenn: This is a key element in your Che/Freire book, Peter (McLaren, 2000). You exhibit the tragedy beautifully but with an obvious sadness of heart.

Peter: Yes, Glenn, what I aimed to show in that book was why a dialectical critique of capitalism needs to underlay the development of critical consciousness. This point is essential, and, in part, it can be achieved through the act of decoding everyday life, and, in the process, liberate students to deal critically with their own reality in order to transform it. Students need to understand that they do not freely choose their lives, that their identities, their dreams, their actions in and on the world, as well as their objects of consumption are adaptive responses to the way that the capitalist system manipulates the realm of necessity. Commodification regulates social lives. Something Paula Allman points out is exceedingly important: that Freirean educators are unwaveringly directive. Paulo confirmed this in numerous discussions with me. Teachers have something to say, something to offer in creating the context for students to name their world, and through dialogue come to creatively reshape their historical reality. Freire did not approve of attempts to turn teachers into passive facilitators. To ask students to 'read the world' critically in order to transform it in a way that will foster humanization is, after all, prescriptive. To demand that the world needs transforming and that education should play a critical role in this effort is, again, prescriptive. Educators should use their authority that comes from their own critical reading of the world as well as their understanding of Freire's philosophy of education in their work with students. As Paula Allman asks: Isn't the most facilitative, non-prescriptive and non-directive form of progressive teaching doubly prescriptive in the sense that it is a prescription for non-prescription as well as for political domestication and adapting successfully to the social universe of capital and the law of value? Freirean educators direct and prescribe, but do so in a spirit of co-operation and mutuality, with an eye to collective action and with a Marxist grasp of the fact that the truth of thinking exists only in practice.

Glenn: I detect a deep disappointment in what you say, Peter, and this flows from your account of really existing critical pedagogy as, more or less, a renunciation of its *criticality* so that it has become more of a liberal pedagogy. That is, it is severed from the social drive of the working class to transform society. Is that correct?

Peter: Critical pedagogy must be tied irrevocably and implacably to our faith in the ability of the working class to shape society in the interest of freedom and justice. How do we enjoin our students to create conditions for escaping from the capitalist compression that necessarily splits value-preserving labor (that reproduces use value) from value-creating labor (exchange-value that gives shape to capital)? It seems to me that we need to focus with students on how they can become active social agents in shaping the sphere of revolutionary political praxis. How can we get them interested in anti-capitalist political praxis: including mass strikes, establishing workers' councils, overthrowing the state, and establishing a revolutionary party? These are questions that are currently challenging my thinking and my praxis. How can we make the anti-capitalist project (the struggle for working-class hegemony) a salient, coherent, and viable project, one with a force that will make history explode? How can we generate new horizons of experience, language, and struggle? These are issues that brush against the grain of most efforts at establishing critical pedagogy projects in classrooms.

Glenn: Although you emphasize the collective moment here, Peter, yet, at the same time, I get the impression that, for you, truly radical pedagogy is also a very *personal* thing. I have in mind your work on Che Guevara's pedagogy in your *Che Guevara, Paulo Freire and the Pedagogy of Revolution* (McLaren, 2000)—and also the stuff on Freire too. The co-operative moment, the mutuality that you speak of is manifested through the lives of individuals. So, although Che did not write huge tomes on pedagogy, his life was lived as pedagogic form for others. We just have to know how to 'read' it, and that is where radical educators come in. Is that how you see it, Peter? Of course, at that point, personal histories, biographies become the 'texts' of the collective learning that aims to transform social existence. How does the personal life link in with life as critical educator? Perhaps you could say a bit on this in relation to your own trajectory.

PERSONAL HISTORY, INTELLECTUAL LIFE, AND EDUCATION

Peter: My intellectual life had lowly origins; my body kept getting in my way of my mind. No, I'm not talking about a preoccupation with sex, but with the 'event', with the fusion of idea and action, argument and activity. Pivotal ideas meant that you crouched on them and used them as a springboard for action. Sometimes they were too slippery or two narrow to get a good footing. But reading Malcolm X, and Frantz Fanon lit a fire under me and I leap-frogged into the streets. Those two figures built a launching pad for urban action that was as large as an aircraft carrier. And Che Guevara, well, his was a platform the size of a continent. At the end of the 60s, my activities became more bookish, starting with attempts to engage the existentialism of Sartre, really. Merleau-Ponty was a strong influence for years, as was Pierre Teilhard de Chardin, especially in my early engagement with Catholicism and Catholic mysticism, and, for a brief period, the theosophical tradition.

Glenn: Are you serious?

Peter: Yes, all that bourgeois muck, as they say. And I felt no sense of shame in luxuriating in the metaphysics of Krishnamurti and indulging in the self-scrutiny of Thomas Merton with an unappeasable frenzy, but in the case of

Merton, I was starting to sniff a little Catholic triumphalism in the air and so I backed off.

Glenn: We were all young once, I suppose.

Peter: Don't tell me, Glenn, that you have never thumbed through a deck of Tarot cards! Or I suppose you used them as bookmarks in your readings of *Capital*!

Glenn: Well, there was the ouija board thing, and that put me off the Tarot. Okay, what was next?

Peter: Then the pastoral tradition of liberation theology swept through my life like a Kansas tornado. That is what spirited me away in the 1960s and 70s. Then I was introduced to Althusser and Balibar. There was not much of a link for me at that time with the tradition of Hegelian Marxism, although I was alerted to Lenin's shift to a Marxian dialectics, and encouraged by friends to indulge his ideas with some serious reading. From Althusser it was a brief engagement with Lacan, at first through the influence of Anthony Wilden's work. I worked my way back to the dialectic through the Budapest school, Lukacs, Heller, and, of course, Korsch. There was little discipline attached to my reading here, but I recall a rather dutiful engagement with the Frankfurt School, Fromm and Marcuse mostly, and only later Adorno, Horkheimer and Benjamin. Of course, Gadamer, Habermas, Ricoeur, they all made an impact. By that time I was working in education and had to engage Dewey, which was quite a worthwhile endeavor. But not as worthwhile as discovering Freire. Of course, Foucault came next, followed by Eco; next up, the post-structuralists and the intellectual high fashion at the time—what a competitive enterprise it was!—and still is— and then, well, I've pretty much rehearsed that part of my intellectual history elsewhere. I think most people will find this boring, so let me conclude by saying that my journey back to Marx, and hence my journey forward politically, carefully sidestepped rational-choice theory and analytical Marxism—to which I was temperamentally averse but begrudgingly respectful—as I made an effort to re-engage the Hegelian Marxist tradition. I read Karil Kosik, and Lenin, and Luxemburg, and, of course, the great Marxist-humanist, Raya Dunayevskaya. Of course, I am leaving out the Birmingham School here, and my subsequent engagement with the cultural turn brought about by a specific reading of Gramsci; a turn which I now find highly problematic, and believe it to be a significant vulgarization of Gramsci's radical politics. Suffice it to say that I am still very much a student of Marx and the Marxian tradition. Just when you think the old bearded devil is down for the count, he rises up stronger than ever. Marx was uncannily prophetic—and eerily prescient—about the internationalization of capital. But there is more to Marx than his ability to anticipate crisis. I am currently very much impressed with the work of Terri Ebert, E. San Juan, James Petras, Mas'ud Zavarzadeh, Ellen Meiksins Wood, Terri Eagleton, Alex Callinicos, well, I will stop there because if I try to list everyone, I'll inevitably leave some important names out.

Glenn: Yes, Peter, but how much of what you have read has informed, or continues to inform, your activism?

Peter: Glenn, the issue isn't what you've read. I've often been asked what influences have been vital to my intellectual formation, as if they all appear in the pages of a book. It really is a question of *what you actually do with the knowledge that you have*: what concrete events you helped shape, but also what concrete events helped to shape the contours of your subjectivity, of your action both in and on the world, within the social order and against it. I remember in the 1960s when I was arrested for the first time. After being thrown against a black-and-white, I was taken to the police station, and into a cell, alone, and beaten with a flashlight by a sadistic cop. It was that sense of feeling the arm of the state (literally and concretely) on my skull that helped to shape the direction of my life. And wearing the scars of the encounter months later was a reminder, as was—and is—the memory, still. I had similar experiences in school—the strap, of course, on the palm of my hand—but my most powerful memory of corporal punishment is the slashing ruler brought down in hacking motions on the top of my hand, below my knuckles, by a sadistic industrial arts teacher.

Glenn: Given the current context of global capitalism, how would you describe your current contribution to educational debates and struggles in the US? I'm thinking of a quotation from your *Preface* to Paula Allman's new book:

> *The vagaries and vicissitudes of capitalist domination and the conceptual apparatuses that yield our means of rationalized it are unceremoniously exposed. It is revealed as a world-system, an abundant and all-permeating social universe that, in its endless and frenetic drive to expand, co-operates in implacable and irreparable denials of social justice and shameless practices of exploitation. Such is the pervasive reach of capital that no aspects of the human condition are left untouched. Indeed, our very subjectivities are stuck in the 'muck' of capital. And the momentum capitalism has achieved makes it unlikely that it can be derailed without tremendous effort and sacrifice. It constitutes a resplendent hemorrhaging of the labor-capital relation, where commodities vomited up from the vortex of accumulation are hungrily consumed by tormented creatures, creatures who are deliriously addicted not only to new commercial acquisitions, but to the adrenaline rush of accumulation itself. Here the individual 'essence', in Gramsci's sense, is equivalent to the totality of social relations within global capitalist society. (McLaren, in Allman, 2001)*

Peter: If you'll permit me to express myself—with decidedly less dramatic flair—let me share the fact that, unlike many postmodernists, I don't believe that humanity has entered a qualitatively new epoch. I don't subscribe to the picture that we are breaking away from the (Fordist/industrial) era of modernization and entering the new world of globalization where the economy is operating at a transnational level and where the nation state is no longer the political formation

seeking to regulate the economy. I don't maintain—as do many left-liberal educationalists—that the major actors can be found in the realm of civil society in
the form of new social movements and NGOs who work to expand, extend,
defend, and strengthen civil society, as well as to render it more inclusive. In
other words, I don't assume that civil society is relatively autonomous from the
state, capital and the market, even when you consider the ongoing informal and
non-formal efforts of the new social movements and their accompanying NGOs,
to advance the cause and the practice of citizenship. It is misguided to view the
arena of civil society as a space where public policies of social justice can be
pursued in a spirit of co-operation and civic participation, and where a critical
education approach can be enacted within a reform-oriented politics of inclusion, influence, and democratic accountability. Those of us who have attempted
an activist politics in the domain of civil society know it isn't inherently benign.
It's not a warm or co-operative space of dialogue and identity-formation. John
Holst correctly notes that civil society is not antiseptically removed from the
social relations of production. In fact, it is perfectly compatible with the emphasis that the free marketeers place on self-sufficiency, enterprise zones, 'capacity
building' and grassroots empowerment initiatives. But what is worse is that it
simply transfers the costs of structural reform onto civil society. Radical pluralists, for instance, in arguing for personal and community responsibility, in
schemes like the self-management of public housing and public schools and the
privatization of welfare, derail the guaranteeing of basic social services by the
state. My recent work has been an attempt to challenge the reformists from a
classical Marxist position. Thus, I have of late being trying to re-ignite politically and conceptually some old debates that need to be exorcised from the musty
North American vaults of the educational imagination. I suppose that if I am
making any kind of contribution to the field, and I dare say it is a modest contribution at that, then it's in the area of challenging this radical pluralist/radical
democracy school (you can also read this as the postmodernist school of educational criticism) in terms of its considerable and ongoing impact on critical theory and critical pedagogy. I would like to re-route educational theory away from
its secure precincts in civil society and back to Marx. Well, actually, it really
hasn't made much of an engagement with Marx to begin with. There are scat-
tered about the field some good Marxist educators, but for the most part the field
is pretty much empty of Marx. But I would say that my work—especially recent
work with Ramin Farahmandpur—is attempting to spark an interest among educators in Marx and the Marxist tradition. There are others, like Richard Brosio,
and Holst, and a handful of others in the United States, who are writing against
the liberal grain. I suppose, then, what I am attempting to do is to renovate educational theory in terms of Marx's value theory of labor and to make some
Hegelian Marxist incursions into the educational literature.

   Glenn: Your Che/Freire book has made a significant impact, Peter. I know
that it has been reaching young readers in their early twenties and readers in

their teens. They are relating to your work, I think, on a number of levels, and are initially drawn to your work by the way you present yourself. You mentioned to me recently that you read a book review that attacks you personally for the Che tattoo you display in the author's photo but also for the prefaces to the book written by distinguished scholars.

Peter: That's right. In failing to deal substantively with the ideas, concepts, and arguments in the book, Ken Zeichner, a teacher educator, focussed instead on my physical appearance, as well as on the series editor's preface and a preface by an internationally respected Latin American scholar—two prefaces that, I might add, were published word-for-word, and title-for-title, exactly as they were sent to the publisher (mercifully, he omitted any commentary about the *Foreword* written by Nita Freire, Paulo Freire's widow). Prefaces of introductions by a series editor are standard fare in academic publishing and in this case the editor, Joe Kincheloe, complimented my writing style. My unorthodox style has received quite a bit of critical commentary over the years because it is considered by some educators to be overly literary and too esoteric to be of much practical use for teachers or pre-service students seeking to improve the educational system. I guess Zeichner feels that I should have asked the publishers to halt the presses so that Joe could have time to write a less-flattering preface, maybe asking readers to put the book down and read something by somebody who professes to have more humility, somebody perhaps like Zeichner. Zeichner also found it self-indulgent of me to be in a book graced by a second preface, written in the form of a poem by Chilean Marxist, Luis Vitale. Vitale entitled his poem 'a salute to Peter McLaren' (a poem, by the way that mentions me only once). Webster's Unabridged New Universal Dictionary defines 'salute' as 'to greet or welcome in a friendly manner.' So, in Zeichner's mind, to be 'greeted' by a respected Latin American Marxist in a poem that mentions the author only once, and to be complimented on one's writing by the series editor somehow illustrates a character flaw in the author. Zeichner finds the ultimate index of my lack of humility in the fact that a tattoo of Che Guevara is visible on my arm in the author's photo.

Glenn: So what should you have been wearing in your author's photo?

Peter: Whatever Zeichner wears, I guess. Maybe a tweed or corduroy sports jacket and a turtleneck? A patch pocket blue blazer with an embroidered gold wire crest from a private university? Coffee-stained Dockers and button-down cotton Levis shirts? A shark skin suit? I have never seen him so I have no idea what he wears and, frankly, don't care, but I'd put money on the fact that he doesn't wear leather pants or sport a tongue stud. You can tell he doesn't live in Hollywood. Here I pretty much blend into the crowd. The point is that if you take Zeicher's logic about glowing prefaces a bit further then even blurbs about one's book should equally earn censure for self-indulgence. That would apply to every author whose book is festooned with the usual endorsements.

Glenn: Or a tattoo.

Peter: My advice to authors: cover those arms and keep the blurbs tame.

Glenn: In addition to commenting on your appearance, Zeichner infers that you rarely leave your university campus in Westwood so you couldn't know the real world of teachers and teaching.

Peter: I am not impressed by Zeichner's knowledge of Los Angeles. It might be interesting to put him in my shoes for a week, and see how he holds up. Then again, maybe that isn't such a good idea, he might not feel comfortable wearing Doc Martens.

Glenn: The point of the Che/Freire book then?

Peter: The point of the Che/Freire book was to launch an all-out critique of capitalism from an historical materialist perspective and to encourage educators to consider socialist alternatives. The global restructuring and retrenchment of capitalism should be the starting point for any serious analysis of and engagement with teacher education. My work since the Che/Freire book has gone even further in postulating what this might mean in terms of revolutionary class struggle.

Glenn: For some, this might sound a bit 'fundamentalist'. I mean, I have heard it said by some educators in the United States, that in your work, in particular, critical pedagogy at its best is too preoccupied with issues of social class. Your Marxism in your current work swamps concerns with 'race', gender—with the social movements in general. Is there any truth to this?

TOO MUCH CLASS?

Peter: I am glad you raised this question, Glenn. What do we mean by social class? That's part of the issue. You, Dave Hill, and Mike Cole all have objected strenuously—and courageously—to the way that the official classification of social class in Britain is based upon status and associated consumption patterns and lifestyles. If you say somebody is upper class and then designate somebody else as lower class, the assumption is that there is a middle-class and the upshot of this classification system is the naturalization of the notion of progress within capitalism. All you do is too lend credence to the myth that it is possible for everyone to move up the ranks on the basis of hard work, fortitude, and perseverance. This justifies the social division of labor and class differentiation and mystifies the agonistic relation among the classes. When we talk about 'white collar' and 'blue collar' workers, we hide the existence of the working class and the fact that this class has common class interests. We hinder the development of a common class-consciousness among fractions within the working class. I prefer the term 'ruling class' or 'capitalist class' on the one hand, and 'working-class' on the other.

Glenn: Okay—so not much room for the predominant neo-Weberian view of class there. I'm totally with you on this. Last summer I went to a conference at Kings College London on education and social class and all the presentations presupposed a neo-Weberian stance that reduces 'class' to status, income and consumption groups (with the usual cultural overlay — which is important in England). Anything approaching a Marxist class analysis of education was lacking, sadly. I think there are serious problems in Marxist class analysis. Marx never left us a developed class theory. *Capital* volume three ends with, well, basically a neo-Weberian 'box people' approach that today's sociologists of education feel very at home with. But Peter, I do feel you have sidestepped the issue of an apparent prioritization of social class in your work—above gender, 'race' and so on. I'll press you on this one!

Peter: Well, it is important that we continue this discussion. But let me shift here to your comment about privileging class oppression over other forms of oppression. I hold that in general class struggle modifies the particularities of other struggles, that there is a strategic centrality to class struggle in that capitalism is the most powerful and far-reaching process of commodification imaginable. I hold, too, that the working class does pose a credible threat to the viability of the capitalist system. The charge that I privilege class exploitation over other forms of oppression is usually leveled at me by bourgeois left-liberals (some with pretensions to neo-Marxism). These people claim that advocating for anti-capitalist struggle is mere rhetoric. They also maintain that a stress on class detracts from anti-racist efforts in education, or efforts to de-claw patriarchy. This is an insult to feminists and to activists of color who have historically played an important role in the struggle against capitalist exploitation. I see an indissoluble link among 'race', class, and gender forms of oppression.

Glenn: I totally agree on this, Peter. I indicated earlier in our dialogue that it is difficult to make the links, but we shouldn't duck the responsibility for making them.

Peter: Yes, Glenn. My point is that capitalism will find ways to survive the challenge of multiculturalism and feminism by co-opting these struggles. Many of the new social movements are seeking resource re-distribution, not the overthrow of capitalist social relations. That's my point, plain and simple. I support projects that undress the conspiracy between capitalism and racism, and capitalism and sexism, and capitalism and heteronormativity. But there is a strategic centrality to my work that I won't deny, or apologize for, that seeks to unite new social movements with the old social movements, so that anti-capitalist struggle becomes a unifying priority.

Glenn: This is interesting, on how the social movements relate to the anti-capitalist struggles of the future. It touches on the old, but still significant debate about reform *versus* revolution and the 'problem of centrism'. This debate is playing itself out in the emerging anti-capitalist/globalization movement post-Seattle. Furthermore, there are problems of leadership and strategy, and these problems are being discussed within the anti-capitalist/globalization movement throughout the world. How do you see things, Peter? Can social movements congeal into a force for anti-capitalism?

Peter: I find the creation of multi-class formations exceedingly problematic for a number of reasons, several of which I would like to mention, without excessive adumbration. Others have gone into this in capillary detail but for the purposes of this discussion I want simply to mention that, for the most part, such movements serve mainly the petit-bourgeoisie and their interests; secondly, these groups rarely contest the rule of capital. The laws of motion of capital and social relations of production do not seem the central objects of their attack, and, frankly, too often they are not even regarded as the central issues around which their struggle coalesces. Their efforts are too frequently reform-based, calling for access to capitalist forms of democracy, for a redistribution of resources. Thirdly, in their attempt to stitch together a broad coalition of groups, they often seem rudderless. Should we be for a form of 'social justice' that works simply to re-institute capitalist social relations of production? Of course, these are issues that we need to debate in schools of education and elsewhere. The whole issue of rights-based justice is predicated upon capitalist rights to property and entitlement to the extraction of surplus value in measures unimaginable. Can we shift the focus of such a struggle to the abolition of private property and the abolition of the private ownership of the means of production? To new social relations, political cultures, and forms of free, creative, and collective association not trapped within the social universe of capital? I don't see these discussions occurring with any consistency within the tradition of critical pedagogy in the United States.

Glenn: But this, for me, is not just an issue for the United States. In your own work, Peter, you have continually stressed the international dimension when thinking through how critical pedagogy, social movements and anti-capitalist struggles relate.

Peter: Yes, this is important, absolutely essential. What you see, for instance, in Eastern Europe and the Soviet Union is not a disappearance of the hidebound and monolithic structures of power, or the disappearance of the previous socio-economic orders—i.e., centrally planned socialism—of the old regime, so much as its transmogrification: the capitalist consolidation of power over markets and property — i.e., via spontaneous privatizations or voucher privatizations, and the like; power over the means of the extraction of surplus value; the power to merge civil society more fully into capital; the power to increase dependence on Western economic systems; the power to legitimize what amounts to a swapping of elites in the name of democracy. A capitalist revolution without capitalists, a bourgeois revolution without the bourgeoisie, as some commentators note. Attempts at integration into the capitalist world economy have increased misery and poverty—through a vertical international division of labor—on a world-historical scale, and this also relates to Latin

American economies in general. In fact, in light of the restoration of the comprador elites, many of the present-day Eastern European countries, by means of their prolonged austerity and increasing unemployment, the exacerbation of the rifts between the ruling class and labor, and the deepening of class divides, are beginning to resemble the peripheral capitalist countries of Latin America. Here the dreams fuelled by the consumer promise of a better life in capitalism fall and shatter on the pavement of hard truths: that the so-called 'transition to democracy' will see the authoritarian regimes of Eastern Europe come in through the back door. A class system riven with such disparities — even when overhauled by neo-liberalism—cannot afford a real participatory form of political representation, but must rely more and more upon brute state repression or authoritarian populism. Witness also recent events in Spain with respect to government policies on immigrants.

Glenn: These facts point to some of the tasks ahead for the anti-capitalist movement. People like to point to Seattle, Washington, Prague, Nice and so on —but in some countries the anti-capitalist movement and working-class action are at lower levels. Basically, though, are you optimistic about the future?

THE FUTURE

Peter: Occupying the horizon of the future—the immediate future, at least —is the continuation of life as warfare, of war against the poor, against women, against people of color, against gays and lesbians and transgendered peoples. I lament the continuing contempt that the ruling class betrays towards those who do not mirror its values. I mourn daily for the revolution that has not yet come to pass. How can one not recoil from the refuse of history that litters the charred path to emancipation, to freedom? So much agony, so much bloodshed and misery. I may not be able to summon optimism, but I still hold on to hope, as fragile as my grasp might be. I am careful to reject a facile optimism, so prevalent in the current craze of bourgeois self-fashioning, yet I refuse to be burdened by a politics of despair. Nor do I seek to aestheticize despair and turn it into a coffee klatch therapy session for academics, or to make it an art-form—or forum to succor more bourgeois self-indulgence for the metropolitan art scene crowd. Now is the time to become intoxicated with the struggle for freedom, to get drunk on the possibility that comes from the horizon of the concrete. Look at the general strikes that have occurred in countries all over the world. Look at Seattle, Washington, and beyond. Look at the revolutionary movements that continue to forge a new politics of the possible. But before we in the North become drunk by such anticipation we need to become awakened to the tasks ahead. The tasks that Freire, Gramsci, Lenin, and Luxemburg have put before us. If we accept the terms of capital, then one has already conceded defeat at its hands. That's where critical education comes in and that is where I believe I have been granted a special gift. The gift of being able to work with teachers and students from all walks of life, and being given the privilege to fight along side of them for working-class power.

Glenn: What about the struggle, the pragmatics of it. Take the Zapatistas. You have written about their struggle and admire it. But does it go far enough?

Peter: You mean, are the 'cuernos de chivo' just postmodern props today? No, the ammunition is ready to be chambered, if necessary. The question is this: Is it the correct time? That depends, of course, upon where you happen to be standing when you are asking that question. Take the recent split between the Revolutionary Party of the Insurgent People (ERIP) and the Popular Revolutionary Army (EPR) in Oaxaca and Guerrero.

Glenn: You have written about them in a recent book, correct?

Peter: Yes. I am also encouraged in hearing about the Armed Ecologist Group who are defending communal forests from timber exploitation, and the National Indigenous Guerrilla Triple Alliance (TAGIN), a joint command of three armed groups in the Sierra del Sur, Morelos, and Mexico state: the Indigenous Campesino Revolutionary Party (ERIC), the Nationalist Army of Insurgent Indigenous Mexico (ENMII) and Armed Capesino Command of Indigenous Liberation (COACUAUHTLI). There is an interesting and informative article on all of these groups by Bill Weinberg in a recent issue of *Native Americas*. A major concern Weinberg identifies is the whole issue of the drug war as counterinsurgency. Here the Pentagon has played a role in advancing what it has called 'Guerra de Baja Intensidad' or low-intensity warfare that consists of limited and protracted politico-military struggle designed to put economic, psychological and diplomatic pressure on insurgent groups. The Pentagon has imparted this doctrine to the Mexican National Army. Weinberg notes, for instance, that 1,500 Mexican military officers received training from 1996 to 1997. The training is supposedly for counter-drug interdiction operations, but it is obvious that it is for counterinsurgency against the guerrillas. There are clear signs of tension between and within some guerrilla factions. For instance, the ERPI basically split from the ERP on the grounds that the ERP was becoming too militantly orthodox, too messianic. The EPR and Comandante Jose Arturo refuses to dialogue with the Mexican government and criticizes the Zapatistas 'armed reformism'. The ERPI wants to operate in a bottom-up fashion, with the direction coming directly from the people. They want to be the Army of the People, not the Army of the Party. The guerrilla command should obey the will of the people, and not the other way around. The question of organization is crucial, and always will be. Weinberg cites an exchange by Arturo and Subcomandante Marcos. Arturo criticized Marcos by arguing that 'poetry cannot be the continuation of politics by other means' followed by Marcos's reply: '*You fight to take power. We fight for democracy, freedom and justice. It's not the same thing. Even if you are successful and win power, we will go on fighting for* *democracy, freedom and justice'.* This really reflects a lot of the debates around issues of organization, of how revolutionary movements can become authoritarian and despotic once they take power. On the other side of the issue is the difficult task of achieving real, structural change by operating in the civil sphere. This brings us to the debates around the relationship of civil society to the state.

Glenn: Where do you stand on this issue, Peter?

Peter: It has a lot to do with the issue of how hegemony is forged. Radical pluralists, neo-Marxists and post-Marxists rely a great deal on the democratizing potential of civil society. They wish to portray civil society as largely free from the tentacles of the state. Like Marx, I view civil society as an arm of the state. Hegemony is forged there, too, as well as at the site of production. Individuals consent to the dominant ideology because of the position the dominant group in the world of production attains. The class that constitutes the ruling material force in society forges the dominant ideology. Gramsci, as far as I know, didn't use the concept of counter-hegemony because it speaks overwhelmingly to a reformist politics. I think that operating in the civil sphere alone is problematic. I believe that as a result of each and every solution that is put forward by liberal democratic pluralists, or NGOs, or liberal or left-liberal multiculturalists, to the suffering of labor, labor will continue to suffer, precisely because these solutions don't directly challenge the rule of capital.

Glenn: You can, of course, trace this back to Hegel.

Peter: Yes, for Hegel the state becomes the site where alienation experienced in civil society is overcome. But Marx criticized Hegel's notion of civil society and the state as an imaginary idealist relation. For Marx, the state was another form of alienation, a central site of ruling class oppression. The state becomes a means for civil society to create the natural cosmopolitan citizen. John Holst has some provocative things to say about this. According to Holst, rejecting as outmoded and romantic Lenin's dream of taking over the state, and skipping around Marx's project of overthrowing capital, radical pluralists merely champion the cause of the new progressive social movements and organizations dealing with feminism, anti-racism, sexuality, and environmental issues whilst leaving capitalism intact. Nevertheless, they view this as a necessary defense of the lifeworld and a courageous deepening of democracy through their engagements with civil society. On the other hand, notes Holst, revolutionary socialists seek alliances between the old (community-labor organizations/trade unions) and new social movements. They reject, for the most part, the new social movements as the center of progressive change on the basis that they cleave away from the basic tenets of classical Marxism, especially when read directly against the work of Marx and Gramsci.

Glenn: And what's your view on it, Peter?

Peter: I believe that forging a counter-hegemonic bloc with new social movements could be problematic, and should be encouraged only when the primacy of working-class struggle against capital remains the overwhelming objective. Of course, let me say without further qualification that I believe today's dialectics of liberation, of self and social transformation, must include all forces of revolution: proletarian, women, gays and lesbians, people of color. Of course, Marx famously put it that 'labor in the white skin cannot be free so long as labor in the black skin is branded'. But I believe fervently that such forces should always be united against capital. I think it is possible to address the heterogeneities and differences in society based on, for example, race, gender, age, ability, locality, religion, culture, and the like, and still concentrate on class struggle. This brings us—does it not—to the inevitable discussion of Antonio Gramsci, and don't all educational roads always seem to lead to Gramsci?

Glenn: Well, for me they never did! Gramsci has played virtually no part in my intellectual development. Peter, we come from very different intellectual traditions, and that has to be acknowledged. I think that gives our conversations a certain edge. In the States, it seems that critical/radical pedagogy came principally through Gramsci and Freire, with Dewey sometimes in attendance. In Britain, the critical/radical pedagogy phenomenon has always been very much weaker as compared with the United States. Direct reading of Marx, labor process theory, Marxist critiques of education policy and Marxist historical writings on education (I have the work of the legendary Brian Simon in mind here) have been the main referents.

Furthermore, I don't really go along with the notion that we have to work only with the 'maximum program' (abolition of capitalism). I've seen too much of what happens with that in England. The key issue is how you build for anti-capitalism, and I'm not convinced that 'taking the message neat' necessarily works best. I witnessed the early history of the Revolutionary Communist Party (as the Revolutionary Communist Tendency in its early years) as indicating the weakness of the 'all or nothing' approach. Maybe I'm being unfair. But please go on, Peter, on Gramsci.

Peter: We shall take those points down-line, Glenn, for sure!

Glenn: Okay!

Peter: We, all those involved in anti-capitalist practice, need to discuss these vital issues. But yes, back to Gramsci, and I believe this is something we both agree on. It is important to expose those left liberals and radical reformists who have emasculated and vulgarized the political center of gravity that informs Gramsci's revolutionary theories, thereby distorting his legacy as a committed communist.

Glenn: Yes, absolutely with your there, Peter. In both our countries the liberal left approach to critique of education policy is dominant.

Peter: Right, Glenn. The crucial point is this: John Holst's reading of Gramsci is similar to the position held by British scholars such as Paula Allman and John Wallis (1995). Allman and Wallis contend that Gramsci did not have in mind loose coalitions of social movements when he spoke of creating an historical bloc in civil society. The war of position and the creation of proletarian hegemony means that the majority of the working-class population needs to be mobilized by class alliances. And this mobilization is directly undertaken to challenge the state. It is crucial to locate Gramsci within the historical context of his attempt to forge proletarian hegemony. He was interested in bringing forth a revolutionary class. We need only examine his emphasis on the pedagogical dimensions of the revolutionary party. Holst re-situates Gramsci— including his ideas of the state, the political party, organic intellectuals, spontaneity, hegemony, and alliances—within Marx's problematic. Gramsci saw civil society as a fundamental aspect of the state. I realize there are major debates on this issue but even if we should concede that Gramsci saw private, civil society as distinct from the state, or political society, we have to agree that he saw both as the domain of ruling class economic power and political interest. The ruling class exerts its authority over the social order in the arena of civil society. So while I agree that you can't foist socialism on workers, I have not abandoned the notion of the vanguard. The issue for me is what such a vanguard should be like. Ideally, the entire people should comprise the vanguard.

Glenn: Right, I think we are nearer on the account you are giving now, Peter.

Peter: For me, Glenn, the key issue is the central role that can be played by education. Socialism must first be 'embodied' or 'enfleshed' by workers in a type of struggle-in-motion, a collective internal dialogue, one directed towards emancipation from capital. After all, as Gramsci notes, historical acts can only be performed collectively. And this is to occur through the creation of a cultural-social unity in which toilers who reflect '*a multiplicity of dispersed wills*' are welded together on the basis of a heterogeneous, single aim: that of '*an equal and common conception of the world, both general and particular*'. This is the future that inspires and powers my work and life.

Glenn: Well, from Europe, the notion of vanguard party building has perhaps a different resonance. In Britain, we have witnessed the fortunes of many far left groups that have in one way or another subscribed to the notion of a 'vanguard party' deriving from Leninist principles of organization. Examples are the Workers Revolutionary Party, the Revolutionary Communist Group, the Revolutionary Communist Party, Workers Power, and the Socialist Workers Party—and many smaller groups. On the whole, the results have not been impressive. We have seen examples of brilliant critique and analysis (the early writings of the Revolutionary Communist Tendency—their *Revolutionary Communist Papers*, for example, stuff by the Revolutionary Marxist Tendency, which I still use now). There have been some fantastic campaigns and solidarity building (around many strikes), and so on. But no real big anti-capitalist party or group has emerged that has posed a really substantial threat to the British state and capital. The Leninist model has not been that successful in enabling these parties and groups to hold on to members either. The Socialist Workers Party has clearly been most successful, and I have great respect for them. When Ruth Rikowski and Howard Bloch were victimized by the managers of Newham Library Service in the mid-1990s (both were librarians at the time), the SWP's campaigning was impressive. At the college I worked at up to 1994 (Epping Forest College), it was the SWP members who were really great at organizing the fightback against management—over new contracts, staff appraisal and other issues. Maybe, Peter, I have not made the distinction you might wish to make between a vanguard *party* and vanguard anti-capitalists, where the latter are not necessarily members of a particular party.

A concrete example may help develop this last point. Last weekend (4th February) Ruth Rikowski and I attended the 'Globalize Resistance' Conference in London. What impressed us was the way that the SWP were becoming a part of the anti-capitalist movement, rather than trying to dominate or get it 'oriented' in classical Leninist mode. In terms of the future, that Conference demonstrated that there is indeed 'something in the air': it brought the Greens, the SWP, Workers Power, the Revolutionary Communist Group, the environmental movement, Jubilee 2000, Drop the Debt and other organizations together to work for what Kevin Danaher calls the 'People's Globalization'. There was a wonderful finale with a speech by a striking London Underground worker being cheered to the rafters! I admit that there are problems and debates around the organization of the movement against capitalist globalization. Ruth Rikowski summarizes the event in *Link-up* (Rikowski, R. 2001—a journal for Third World information workers) and argues that the movement has come a long way in a short time. But obviously, it needs to attend further to organizational and democratic forms, and left political parties are in a process of discovering their role *vis-à-vis* this rapidly developing movement. The SWP in particular are really trying hard to do this. People talked about a 'new politics' in relation to postmodernism, and in relation to Blair's New Labor. The former was a kind of anti-politics, the latter a continuation of Thatcherite neo-liberalism with a home-spun gloss. But the rising anti-capitalist movement is a genuinely new politics; it places the future of capitalism itself on the chopping block of history. The anti-capitalist movement that has developed throughout many countries in the last five years also—given a massive boost post-Seattle—points towards an open future. This is a future no longer dominated by capital. It is a future worth fighting for. More than that: we are *driven* to fight for this future by capitalist development itself. We must not fail; the survival of our planet depends on the success of the anti-capitalist movement and the abolition of capital.

Peter: There are clearly issues requiring further discussion, Glenn, especially in relation to the notion of vanguardism. I've enjoyed this e-dialogue and look forward to further discussions with you.

Glenn: It's been great, and I feel that I've clarified and deepened some of my own ideas. I have also deepened my understanding and appreciation of your work, Peter. In addition, I've also got a clearer grasp of where our work interlocks most strongly for the project of human liberation. I look forward to developing our dialogue some more in other contexts with this project in view.

REFERENCES

Allman, P. (1999) *Revolutionary Social Transformation: Democratic Hopes, Radical Possibilities and Critical Education* (Westport, Connecticut: Bergin & Garvey).

Allman, P. (2001, in press) *Critical Education Against Global Capital: Karl Marx and Revolutionary Critical Education* (Westport, Connecticut: Bergin & Garvey).

Allman, P. & Wallace, J. (1995) Gramsci's Challenge to the Politics of the Left in 'Our Times', *International Journal of Lifelong Education*, 14(2), pp. 120-143.

Blake, N., Smeyers, P., Smith, R. & Standish, P (2000) *Education in an Age of Nihilism* (London: Routledge/Falmer).

Bowles, S. & Gintis, H. (1976) *Schooling in Capitalist America: Educational Reform and the Contradictions of Economic Life* (London: Routledge & Kegan Paul).

Cole, M., Hill, D. & Rikowski, G. (1997) Between Postmodernism and Nowhere: The Predicament of the Postmodernist, *British Journal of Educational Studies*, 45(2), pp. 187-200.

Dunayevskaya, R. (1978) *Marx's 'Capital' and Today's Global Crisis* (Detroit, Michigan: News & Letters).

Gulli, B. (1999) The Labor of Fire: On Time and Labor in the *Grundrisse*, in *Cultural Logic: An electronic journal of marxist theory & practice*, Spring, 2(2), at: <http://eserver.org/clogic/2-2/gulli.htm>.

Harvie, D. (2000) Alienation, Class and Enclosure in UK Universities, *Capital & Class*, summer, no.71, pp. 103-132.

Holst, J. (2001, in press) *Social Movements, Civil Society, and Radical Adult Education* (Westport, Connecticut: Bergin & Garvey).

Hudis, P. (2000a) The Dialectical Structure of Marx's Concept of 'Revolution in Permanence', *Capital & Class*, Spring, No. 70, pp. 127-142.

Hudis, P. (200b) Can capital be controlled? *News & Letters Online*, at: <http://www.newsandletters.org/4.00_essay.htm>.

Jacoby, R. (2000) *The Last Intellectuals: American Culture in the Age of Academe*, 2nd Edition (New York: Basic Books).

Marx, K. (1858) [1973] *Grundrisse: Foundations of the Critique of Political Economy* (Rough Draft), Trans. M. Nicolaus (Harmondsworth: Penguin).

Marx, K. (1867) [1977] *Capital: A Critique of Political Economy-Volume 1* (London: Lawrence & Wishart).

McLaren, P. (1995) *Critical Pedagogy and Predatory Culture: Oppositional Politics in a Postmodern Era* (New York & London: Routledge).

McLaren, P. (1997) *Revolutionary Multiculturalism: Pedagogies of Dissent for the New Millennium* (Boulder, Colorado: Westview Press).

McLaren, P. (1999) *Schooling as a Ritual Performance: Towards a Political Economy of Educational Symbols and Gestures*, 3rd Edition (Lanham, Maryland: Rowman & Littlefield).

McLaren, P. (2000) *Che Guevara, Paulo Freire, and the Pedagogy of Revolution* (Lanham, Maryland: Rowman & Littlefield).

McNally, D. (2001) *Bodies of Meaning: Studies on Language, Labor, and Liberation* (Albany, New York: State University of New York Press).

Neary, M. (1997) *Youth, Training and the Training State: The Real History of Youth Training in the Twentieth Century* (Basingstoke: Macmillan).

Neary, M. & Rikowski, G. (2000) *The Speed of Life: The Significance of Karl Marx's Concept of Socially Necessary Labour-time*. A paper presented at the British Sociological Association Conference 2000, 'Making Time-Marking Time', University of York, April.

Neary, M. & Taylor, G. (1998) *Money and the Human Condition* (London: Macmillan).

Postone, M. (1996) *Time, Labor and Social Domination: A Reinterpretation of Marx's Critical Theory* (Cambridge: Cambridge University Press).

Rikowski, G. (1995) *Education Markets and Missing Products*, a paper presented at the Annual Conference of Socialist Economists, University of Northumbria, Newcastle, 7-9th July.

Rikowski, G. (1996) Left Alone: End time for Marxist educational theory? *British Journal of Sociology of Education*, 17(4), pp. 415-451.

Rikowski, G. (1999) Education, Capital and the Transhuman, in: D. Hill, P. McLaren, M. Cole & G. Rikowski (Eds) *Postmodernism in Educational Theory: Education and the Politics of Human Resistance* (London: Tufnell Press).

Rikowski, G. (2000a) *That Other Great Class of Commodities: Repositioning Marxist Educational Theory*, a paper presented at the British Educational Research Association Conference 2000, University of Cardiff, Wales, 9th September.

Rikowski, G. (2000b) The 'Which Blair' Project: Giddens, the Third Way and Education, *Forum for Promoting Comprehensive Education*, 42(1), pp. 4-7.

Rikowski, G. (2000c) *Education and Social Justice within the Social Universe of Capital*, a paper presented at the British Educational Research Association Day Conference on 'Approaching Social Justice in Education: Theoretical Frameworks for Practical Purposes', Faculty of Education, Nottingham Trent University, Clifton Hall, 10th April.

Rikowski, G. (2000d) The Rise of the Student-Worker, in: M. Gokulsing and C. DaCosta (Eds) *A Compact for Higher Education* (Aldershot: Ashgate).

Rikowski, G. (2001a) *Nothing Becomes Them: Education and the Nihilist Embrace.* Unpublished paper, Faculty of Education, University of Central England, Birmingham, 14th January.

Rikowski, G. (2001b) Education for Industry: A Complex Technicism, *Journal of Education and Work*, 13(1), pp. 27-47.

Rikowski, G. (2001c) *The Battle in Seattle: Its Significance for Education* (London: Tufnell Press).

Rikowski, R. (2001) Globalise Resistance Conference, forthcoming in *Link-up: the newsletter of LINK—a network for North-South library development*.

Sayer, D. (1979) *Marx's Method: Ideology, Science and Critique in 'Capital'* (Hassocks: The Harvester Press).

Sayer, D. (1987) *The Violence of Abstraction: The Analytical Foundations of Historical Materialism* (Oxford: Basil Blackwell Ltd.).

Waite, G. (1996) *Nietzsche's Corps/e: Aesthetics, Politics, Prophecy, or, the Spectacular Technoculture of Everyday Life* (Durham & London: Duke University Press).

Willis, P. (1977) *Learning to Labor: How Working Class Kids Get Working Class Jobs* (Farnborough: Saxon House).

Willmott, R. (1999) Structure, Agency and the Sociology of Education: Rescuing analytical dualism, *British Journal of Sociology of Education*, 20(1), pp. 5-21.

23

THE PATH OF DISSENT
AN INTERVIEW WITH
PETER MCLAREN

Marcia Moraes

The work of U.S.-Canadian Peter McLaren has assumed a central place in the debates over the role of critical pedagogy in North America; less known among North American educators is that his work has sparked considerable interest in South America for more than a decade and has received special attention in Brazil, the birthplace of Paulo Freire. McLaren is one of North America's most significant ambassadors of Freire's work; in recent years, he has also moved into a pedagogical terrain uninhabited by the majority of North American educators—that of Marxist theory and analysis. Of course, this may account for the increased interest in his work throughout many Latin American countries (as evidenced by the creation of La Fundacion McLaren de Pedagogia Critica by a group of Mexican researchers and activists), but it is sure to alienate McLaren from many of his long-standing supporters in the United States. It is clear that McLaren is dedicated to developing schools into sites where students can begin to imagine socialist alternatives to capitalism. Although the vast majority of educators in the United States are calling for a redistribution of economic resources within a more "compassionate" capitalism, McLaren is convinced that only within a socialist society can democracy be achieved.

This interview began with McLaren over the Internet and continued in person during a recent trip McLaren made to Rio de Janeiro to speak to teachers and professors. It has taken on the form of a guided essay.

Marcia: In Brazil, despite the brilliant contributions of Paulo Freire, it is quite difficult to say that teacher education programs are totally related to the philosophy of critical pedagogy. On the other hand, teacher education programs in the United States have been dealing with critical pedagogy for several decades now. What progress has been made on the critical pedagogy front?

This article originally appeared n *Journal of Transformative Education, 1*(2), pp. 117-134. © 2003 Sage Publications, Inc. Reprinted with the permission of the publisher.

Peter: This is an excellent question to begin our conversation. Let me begin by challenging the term "critical pedagogy." I much prefer the term that British educator Paula Allman has christened "revolutionary critical pedagogy." It raises important issues that more domesticated currents of critical pedagogy do not. For example, it draws attention to the key concepts of imperialism (both economic and military) and the value form that labor assumes within capitalist society. It also posits history as the mediator of value production within capitalist society. In political partnership with educationalists such as Allman, Glenn Rikowski, Dave Hill, Ramin Farahmandpur, and Mike Cole, and in comradely conversations with Peter Mayo, Rich Gibson, Richard Brosio, John Marciano, Wayne Ross, and others, I have made some modest efforts to revive the fecundity of Marxist critique in the field of education, since I believe Marxist theory, in all of its heteronomous manifestations and theoretical gestation for well over a century, performs an irreplaceable analytical and political function of positing history as the mediator of human value production. By pivoting around the work of Karl Marx, Paulo Freire, and Antonio Gramsci, and by maneuvering and tacking around the work of contemporary continental philosophers and critical theorists, critical revolutionary pedagogy brings some desperately needed theoretical ballast to the teetering critical educational tradition. Such theoretical infrastructure is absolutely necessary if we are to create concrete pedagogical spaces in schools and in other sites where people struggle for educational change and transformation.

The critical revolutionary pedagogy I am envisioning here operates from the premise that capital in its current organizational structure provides the context for working-class struggle. My approach to understanding the relationship between capitalism and schooling and the struggle for socialism is premised upon Marx's value theory of labor as developed by British Marxist educationalist Glenn Rikowski and others, including scholars such as Enrique Dussel (especially his commentary on Marx's manuscripts of 1861-1863). In developing further the concept of revolutionary critical pedagogy and its specific relationship to class struggle, it is necessary, I believe, to focus on labor's value form. This focus will unlock a path towards a Marxist-humanist approach to educational struggle. There are many approaches to Marxist humanism, and here I look to the writings of Raya Dunayevskaya, the works of Erich Fromm, C.L.R. James, and various and varied works within the Marxist-Hegelian tradition. As I have argued in my conversations with Glenn Rikowski, critical revolutionary educators follow the premise that value is the substance of capital. Value, it should be understood, is not a thing. It is the dominant form that capitalism as a determinate social relation takes. Within the expansive scope of revolutionary critical pedagogy, the concept of labor is fundamental for theorizing the school/society relationship and thus for developing radical pedagogical imperatives, strategies, and practices for overcoming the constitutive contradictions that such a coupling generates. The larger goal that revolutionary critical pedagogy stipulates for radical educationalists involves direct participation with the masses in the discovery and charting of a socialist reconstruction and alternative to capitalism. However, without a critical lexicon and interpretative framework that can unpack the labor/capital relationship in all of its capillary detail, critical pedagogy is doomed to remain trapped in domesticated currents and vulgarized formations. That's precisely why it is important to bring the various languages of Marxist analysis into schools of education. Why? Because the process whereby labor-power is transformed into human capital and concrete living labor is subsumed by abstract labor is one that eludes the interpretative capacity of rational communicative action and requires a dialectical understanding that only historical materialist critique can best provide. Historical materialism provides critical pedagogy with a theory of the material basis of social life rooted in historical social relations and assumes paramount importance in uncovering the structure of class conflict as well as unraveling the effects produced by the social division of labor. Today, labor power is capitalized and commodified, and education plays a tragic role in these processes. According to Rikowski, schools therefore act as vital supports for, and developers of, the class relation, at the core of capitalist society and development.

Here is a crucial point. Insofar as schooling is premised upon generating the living commodity of labor-power, upon which the entire social universe of capital depends, it can become a foundation for human resistance. This is a main point stressed by Rikowski. In other words, labor-power can be incorporated by the forces of capital only so far. Workers, as the sources of labor-power, can engage in acts of refusing alienating work and delinking labor from capital's value form. As a relation of general commodification predicated on the wage relation, capital needs labor. But I emphasize that labor does not need capital. Labor can dispense with the wage and with capitalism and find different and more autonomous ways to organize its productive relations. I am thinking of social forms and human relations that draw from, but are not limited to, the rich tradition of socialism.

Inasmuch as education and training socially produce labor-power, this process can be resisted. This is because labor power is never completely controllable. Glenn Rikowski has made the important point that people can learn something other than that which capital intends them to learn. Critical educators push this "something other" to the extreme in their pedagogical praxis centered around a social justice, anticapitalist, antiracist, and anti-imperialist agenda. One key—and I am not suggesting it is in any way sufficient—is to develop a critical pedagogy that will enable the working class to discover how the use-value of their labor-power is being exploited by capital but also how working-class initiative and power can destroy this type of determination and force a recomposition of class relations by directly confronting capital in all of its hydra-headed dimensions. Here I am talking of an anti-imperialist, internationalist, gender-balanced, and multiracial social movement that addresses issues related to education, but not limited to education. Efforts can be made to break down capital's control of the creation of new labor-power and to resist the endless subordination of life to work in the social factory of everyday life. Students and education workers can ask themselves, What is the maximum damage they can do to the rule of capital, to the dominance of capital's value form? I have raised this question in much of my writing: Do we, as radical educators, help capital find its way out of crisis, or do we help students and educational workers find their way out of capital? And as I have phrased this in a number of my recent writings, the success of the former challenge will only buy further time for the capitalists to adapt both its victims and its critics; the success of the latter will determine the future of civilization, of whether or not we will have one.

Possibility often hides its liberating force within contradictions. The struggle related to what Marx called our "vital powers," our dispositions, our inner selves and our objective outside, our human capacities and competencies and the social formations within which they are produced, ensures the production of a form of human agency that reflects the contradictions within capitalist social life. Yet these contradictions also provide openness regarding social being. They point towards the possibility of collectively resolving contradictions of "everyday life" through what Allman has called revolutionary/transformative praxis or, if we prefer, "critical subjectivity." Critical subjectivity operates out of practical, sensuous engagement within social formations that enable rather than constrain human capacities. Here, critical revolutionary pedagogy reflects the multiplicity and creativity of human engagement itself: the identification of shared experiences and common interests; the unraveling of the threads that connect social process to individual experience; the rendering as transparent the concealed obviousness of daily life; the recognition of ourselves as both free and conditioned; an understanding of the future as both open and necessary; the recognition of a shared social positionality; the unhinging of the door that separates practical engagement from theoretical reflection; the changing of the world by changing one's social nature, one's social subjectivity. It achieves this through an understanding of Marx's dialectical approach. While I don't have space to go into these, I would like to point to Bertell Ollman's analysis of Marx's dialectical approach and repeat Ollman's warning here that the laws of dialectics do not in themselves explain, prove, or predict anything in themselves or cause anything to happen. What they do is organize the most common forms of change and interaction that exist on any level of generality so that we might be able to study and intervene into the world of which they are a part.

The work of Bertell Ollman has proved valuable in explaining how Marx's dialectical analysis can bring out the differences between two or more aspects of an interactive system in order to highlight the asymmetry in their reciprocal effect. For instance, take Marx's example of abstracting social reality into objective and subjective conditions. By abstracting a vantage point first in objective conditions, and then in subjective conditions, Marx can see these conditions as two distinct forms of the same essential conditions, and thus he can uncover the objective aspects of what is generally assumed to be subjective and vice versa.

Critical revolutionary educators seek to realize in their classrooms democratic social values and to believe in their possibilities—consequently, we argue that they need to go outside of the protected precincts of their classrooms and analyze and explore the workings of capital there as well, to workplaces, to neighborhoods, to urban zones, to rural communities, and so forth. Critical revolutionary pedagogy thus sets as its goal the reclamation of public life—what has been called by Canadian philosopher John McMurtry the "civil commons." It seeks to make the division of labor coincident with the free vocation of each individual and the association of free producers. At first blush, this may seem a paradisiac or radically utopian notion in that it posits a radically eschatological and incomparably "other" endpoint for society as we know it. Yet this is not a blueprint but a contingent utopian vision that offers direction not only in unpicking the apparatus of bourgeois illusion but also in diversifying the theoretical itinerary of the critical educator so that new questions can be generated along with new perspectives in which to raise them (I emphasize this point because it is precisely here that the postmodern pundits argue that, as a Marxist, I must be trying to impose some kind of totalitarian vision on unsuspecting educators). Here, the emphasis is not only on denouncing the manifest injustices of neoliberal capitalism and serving as a counterforce to neoliberal ideological hegemony but also on establishing the conditions for new social arrangements that transcend the false opposition between the market and the state.

In contrast to a number of incarnations of postmodern education, critical revolutionary pedagogy emphasizes the material dimensions of its own constitutive possibility and recognizes knowledge as implicated within the social relations of production (i.e., the relations between labor and capital). I use the term materialism here not in its postmodernist sense as what Teresa Ebert would refer to as a resistance to conceptuality, a refusal of the closure of meaning, or whatever "excess" cannot be subsumed within the symbol or cannot be absorbed by tropes; rather, materialism is being used, after Teresa Ebert, in the context of material social relations, a structure of class conflict, and an effort of the social division of labor. Historical changes in the forces of production have reached the point where the fundamental needs of people can be met—but the existing social relations of production prevent this because the logic of access to "need" is "profit" based on the value of people's labor for capital. This is a position stressed in Ebert's important work. Consequently, critical revolutionary pedagogy argues that without a class analysis, critical pedagogy is impeded from effecting praxiological changes (changes in social relations).

As I often discuss the term, critical revolutionary pedagogy includes what might be perceived as a three-pronged approach: I have called the first moment a pedagogy of demystification centering around a semiotics of re-cognition, where dominant sign systems, tropes, conceits, discourses, and representations are recognized and denaturalized, where commonsense understandings of social and institutionalized spheres of everyday life are historicized, and where signification is understood as a political practice that refracts rather than reflects reality, where cultural formations are understood and analyzed in relation to the larger social factory of the school and the global universe of capital. The second moment could be called a pedagogy of opposition, where students engage in analyzing various political systems, ideologies, and histories, but with the emphasis on students developing their own political positions that, in time, they are able to both extend, deepen, and refine. They are also able to defend their political positions, perspectives, and philosophies within, alongside, and in opposition to other positions. Inspired by a sense of ever-imminent hope, students move to a third moment, which includes developing a philosophy of praxis, where deliberative practices for transforming the social universe of capital into noncapitalist alternatives are developed and tested, where theories are mobilized to make sense of and to deepen these practices, and simultaneously where everyday practices help to challenge, deepen, and transform critical theories. How this occurs within the classroom will vary from individual to individual, from group to group, depending upon the sociopolitical context and the historical and the geopolitical spaces in which such pedagogies are played out. Revolutionary critical pedagogy supports a totalizing reflection upon the historical-practical constitution of the world, our ideological formation within it, and the reproduction of everyday life practices. It is a pedagogy with an emancipatory intent. It looks towards the horizon of the future from the vantage point of the present while simultaneously analyzing the past, refusing all the while to form a specific blueprint for change. Practicing revolutionary critical pedagogy is not the same as preaching it.

Revolutionary critical pedagogy is not born in the crucible of the imagination as much as it is given birth in its own practice. That is, revolutionary critical education is decidedly more praxiological than prescored. The path is made by walking, as it were. Revolutionary educators need to challenge the notion implicit in mainstream education that ideas related to citizenship have to travel through predestined contours of the mind, falling into step with the cadences of common sense. There is nothing common about common sense. Educational educators need to be more than the voice of autobiography; they need to create the context for dialogue with the other so that the other may assume the right to be heard. But critical pedagogy is also about making links with real, concrete human subjects struggling within and against capital and against the structures of oppression that are intimately linked to capital: racism, sexism, patriarchy, and imperialism.

The principles that help to shape and guide the development of our "vital powers" in the struggle for social justice via critical/revolutionary praxis discussed at length by Allman include principles of mutual respect, humility, openness, trust, and cooperation; a commitment to learn to "read the world" critically and expending the effort necessary to bring about social transformation; vigilance with regard to one's own process of self-transformation and adherence to the principles and aims of the group; adopting an "ethics of authenticity" as a guiding principle; internalizing social justice as passion; acquiring critical, creative, and hopeful thinking; transforming the self through transforming the social relations of learning and teaching; establishing democracy as a fundamental way of life; developing a critical curiosity; and deepening one's solidarity and commitment to self and social transformation and the project of humanization. These principles are not enough by themselves. They must be accompanied by dialectical investigations of the social relations of production in which all of us toil.

Marcia: Your own work has helped to define the tradition of critical pedagogy not only in North America but in South America as well.

Peter: The tradition of critical pedagogy in North America is not an easy history to trace. But yes, it most certainly grew out of Freire's path-breaking work in the early 1980s and its adaptation to North American contexts by Henry Giroux, Donaldo Macedo, and Ira Shor (and later by others such as Antonia Darder and Pepi Leistyna), and we can see in its varied inflections the birthmark of John Dewey and the social reconstructionist movement in the United States that developed after the Great Depression in the 1930s; I think it is fair to say that major exponents of critical pedagogy in North America were influenced by the sociology of knowledge that was emerging from England in the early 1980s as well as the pioneering work that was produced by Raymond Williams and the cultural studies that was being undertaken at England's Birmingham School of Contemporary Cultural Studies. We would have to include the work of U.S. economists Sam Bowles and Herb Gintis, especially their book, *Schooling in Capitalist America*, but admittedly there was never much of a Marxist tradition in North American instantiations of critical pedagogy. Certainly, there were neo-Marxist interpretations and, of course, an interest in Western neo-Marxism, particularly the Frankfurt School. As in the early days of critical pedagogy, we don't in today's incarnations of critical pedagogy see much influence from Soviet Marxism and very little reference to Lenin or Trotsky. But we do see a strong Gramscian—albeit watered down—presence. Today, we see on North American shores the influence of recent and very sophisticated and important international work on critical pedagogy, and I am thinking of the work of Peter Mayo and Carmel Borg in Malta as one important instance and the work of Colin Lankshear and Mike Peters from New Zealand. I have already mentioned the work of Rikowski, Cole, and Hill, as well as Allman, and for me these are the most urgent voices because of their grounding in the Marxist tradition. If we examine critical pedagogy within the graduate schools of the United States, for in stance, we notice that it is highly transdisciplinary, and there are few theoretical perspectives that you can't find these days among its many exponents. Today, critical pedagogy has been cross-fertilized with just about every transdisciplinary tradition imaginable, including theoretical forays into the work of Richard Rorty, Nietzsche, Jacques Lacan, and Jacques Derrida. I have been highly critical of much of the postmodernized versions of critical pedagogy, as I am sure you have gathered from much of my recent work.

Marcia: Brazilian educational legislation, for instance, points to the relevance of critical pedagogy but never in a political sense of the term; never as a way to better understand the complexity of our social (dis)organization. Unfortunately, *critical* means celebrating diversity and being prepared for the work market. After all, each educational law addresses critical pedagogy within a very narrow view.

Peter: While I have been very critical of much that has been going on in the academy in the name of critical pedagogy, I do not see myself as a self-appointed guardian of the term. To echo something I wrote several years ago, and to borrow from some of my articles to help be more precise, critical pedagogy was once considered by the guard dogs of the American dream as a term of opprobrium, but now its relationship to broader liberation struggles seems quite threadbare if not fatally terminated. While its urgency was difficult to ignore, and its hard-bitten message had the pressure of absolute fiat behind it, critical pedagogy seemingly has collapsed into limitations placed on it by its own constitutive limitations. Force-fed by a complacent relativism, it has all but displaced the struggle against capitalist exploitation with its emphasis on a multiplicity of interpersonal forms of oppression within an overall concern with identity politics. It fights capitalism's second-hand smoke without putting out the cigar. I am scarcely the first to observe that critical pedagogy has been badly undercut by practitioners who would mischaracterize or misrepresent its fundamental project. In fact, if "critical pedagogy" is examined in the context of current educational debates and reform efforts, we see the very manifestation of its forms of domestication to which Paulo Freire drew attention. I think it is not useful to try to trace this history in order to try to find the "cause" of how this pedagogy has become decanted of its revolutionary potential; it is more important, at least in this present historical conjuncture, to develop a comprehensive approach to pedagogy that can touch on the central issues around which teachers and students are currently struggling. Critical pedagogy is very much a living tradition, one that needs to be reanimated with each successive generation, who face new and historically specific challenges.

Marcia: How do you conceptualize your work in critical pedagogy?

Peter: For me, that is, in my own work, I employ a concept of critical pedagogy that has Hegelian-Marxist origins to it—critical pedagogy in this regard is essentially a philosophy of praxis, one that acquires its emphasis within the contextual specificity of particular class struggles. Unlike many North American critical educators who are mainly concerned with subjective or discursive manifestations of oppression (which, in themselves, surely are not unimportant), I am more concerned with the structural and relational or conjunctural foundations or conditions upon which various antagonisms take root (racism, sexism, etc.): the exploitation of human labor within capitalism. Whereas between 1985 and 1994 I was primarily concerned with cultural production, since that time I have been concerned with the conditions under which humans materially reproduce themselves, including their cultural formations.

Marcia: Can you expand on this?

Peter: To make this idea clearer, it is necessary to place the question of praxis within the larger question of consciousness in general and the development of class consciousness in particular. I have recently had the opportunity to read some interesting work on the biological roots of consciousness by Maturana and Varela, work that is making quite an impact among friends and colleagues of mine in Latin America. There is certainly something useful in their approach to human biology as grounded in autopoietic systems. According to Maturana and Varela, we enter into language through our linguistic coupling with others; we know, for instance, those linguistic interactions play a role in the recurrent coordination of social actions. Language arose through the process of socialization, particularly cooperation, as humans continued to increase their capacity to make distinctions and engage in linguistic reflection, and the appearance of the self is essentially a distinction in a linguistic domain. Surely, it is in language that the "I" or the "self" arises as a social singularity defined by the operational interaction in the human body of the recursive linguistic conditions in which this singularity is distinguished—as Maturana and Varela so presciently note—since this accounts for the way that we are able to maintain linguistic operational coherence by means of a descriptive recursive identity as the "I." We need to admit, too, that our "languaging" is a social phenomenon; it is performed as a social coupling within the historical context of human interaction. There is no pre-given consciousness, in other words.

This is very compatible, I believe, with the way I approach the concept of human consciousness/praxis within my practice of critical pedagogy. Language, in this sense, does not reflect knowledge as much as it refracts it. That is, in Maturana and Varela's terms, language is not a tool to reveal the objectivity of an outside world as much as it is a form of behavioral coordination—a social-structural coupling—that brings forth the world as an act of knowing. Here, it is co-ontogenetic coupling that produces our identities as essentially a "continuous becoming" through a permanent linguistic trophallaxis. In this case, it becomes necessary not to presuppose an objective world with a fixed point of reference in order to adjudicate the descriptions of the world that we continually bring forth in our coexistence with others. I would amend this perspective somewhat. In doing so, I would turn to historical materialist analysis and Marx's notion of consciousness. Maturana and Varela's perspective is essentially that "knowing is doing" and that to presume a fixed objective point of view by which to judge our actions is essentially untenable since it is tantamount to assuming a view from nowhere. Here, we see an emphasis on knowing as experience, where experience is in the same sense both a poesis and praxis. Norman Fairclough makes the point that language figures in material social process as an element of these processes dialectically related to other elements; in other words, it figures in the reflexive construction of these processes, which social actors produce as an inherent part of these processes. Discourse analysis can help us to understand, for instance, how language functions in hegemonic struggles over neoliberalism and how struggles against neoliberalism can be partly pursued in language.

Surely there is some truth to this, but the problem is that many postmodernist educationalists stop here and thus remain mired in the trap of an ethical relativism out of which they find it hard to escape. Too often, they study the representations of the world as if they were the things that they represent. It is not the signs that produce capitalist culture; clearly signifiers are as much the products of capitalist society as they are representations that help shape it. Surely, the whole process of consumption is not the prime mover of capitalism but a result of the forces and relations of production. The fact that all theories of the world are partial and provisional—to cite a mantra of many postmodernists—does not make the world unknowable. Surely, there are approximations of the truth that are invaluable in knowing the world. In my view, critical pedagogy becomes a means not only of acknowledging language as a complex system of mediation through which we glean approximations of the world but also of developing a historical understanding of how social structures work as mechanisms of such mediation.

I agree that social structure mediates—in a multifaceted and multilayered sense—language and consciousness and that modes of production of material life condition the language we use to make sense of our everyday social life. Modes and relations of production condition all of our social, cultural, and intellectual life, which is not the same thing as arguing that all of social existence can be reduced to them. In this way, I believe we should work towards developing a general theory of social reality by analyzing the process of historical development. It is interesting to note some parallels that Maturana and Varela have with Marx, and also Freire, who believed that knowing was a form of doing, knowing that comes from concrete activity of being in the world.

Marcia: Your early work was already related to Marxism, but now it seems much more connected to it. Some of your works locate the weaknesses of postmodernism and replace them with Marxist perspectives. How would you explain your shift from postmodernism back to Marxism? What were the issues that, let me say, had pushed you back to Marxism?

Peter: In answering this question, let me say that I don't want to reject—in the main, at least—my former work, which was informed by a critical postmodernist perspective. While this work had its limitations, I always attempted to address the importance of struggling against capitalist exploitation, racism, sexism, and homophobia, as well as other issues; neither do I want to denigrate the work of other postmodernists unfairly. I have a new book that I edited with Mike Cole and Glenn Rikowski and Dave Hill that delves into most of the central limitations of postmodernist perspectives. To be fair, postmodern theory enabled me to think through the many and variegated issues of identity construction within the context of contemporary U.S. culture and lifestyle issues. But over the year, I became increasingly concerned that if we are simply little more than an "other" to somebody else's "other," staring at each "other" in an endless hall of mirrors, as a surfeit of differences produced in the "tain" of these mirrors as some unending signifying chain that descends from the sky like Jacob's Ladder in the middle of nowhere, we need to do more than affirm our right to difference as a call for dignity and respect.

I began to critique postmodern rebellion as a rebellion without a rationality, without an argument, where signs are set in motion in order to shape consciousness at some "raw" (as opposed to "cooked") incarnation of unreason, where significations hustle the signifiers for the cheapest (i.e., most simple) meaning, and where social life is reduced to barroom conversations among political drunkards trapped in a sinkhole of slumbering inertia and collapsing heresies. That is not to say that I don't believe there is a place for an aesthetics of rebellion or that we cannot venture into the nonrational (or even the irrational) in order to challenge the system. But we need an overall philosophy of praxis to give our rebellion some conceptual and political ballast. We need to engage in something more fundamental, which I take to be class struggle, to create the conditions in which dignity emerges from the material conditions of having enough to eat, a place to sleep, and the possibility of becoming critically literate about the world in which we inhabit, a world where resources such as oil are determining the future of global relations between nations and affecting the lives of millions of innocent people killed in imperialist wars and who are forced to migrate to other countries or who are forced to suffer because of embargoes and other forms of economic terrorism—a place where cowboy capitalism enflames an unprincipled frenzy of economic deregulatian causing financial impoverishment and insecurity for the vast majority of the world's poor. In this way I am opposed to the imperialism of George Bush, and, of course, imperialism in any and all of its current incarnations of destruction and death.

In postmodernism's rejection of grand historical narratives, of central struggles that ideologically define history, of the pure historical subject, and in its argument that knowledge is constituted in diffuse power relations—that is, in discourse (which is for postmodernists the sole constitutive element in social relations)—has helped to pave the way for important discussions of the role of language in the ordering and regulation and reproduction of power. But the work of postmodernism and its perfumed vocabulary of "difference" has been in the main insufficient in helping me to understand in a more nuanced way the historical shifts within the globalization of capitalism—and I am talking here about transnational finance capitalist enterprises, those ungovernable and anarchistic capitalist movements, and the permanent structural unemployment—conditions that are cruelly manifesting themselves everywhere today and which are devastating the entire globe. There are some postmodernists who have written with great sensitivity and erudition about issues of globalization but many others who have betrayed an understanding of contemporary capitalism that is, I believe, woefully rife with misconceptions and fundamental errors. Most of them are unable or unwilling to make the connection between globalization and imperialism, which I think is a crucial flaw. For me, it is important to operate from a critique of political economy within an international framework of opposition to U.S. imperialism, an imperialism that is grounded in super-exploitation (especially of colonial and female labor) through economic, military, and political aggression in defense of the interests of the United States "Homeland" (a very Teutonic-sounding word).

For me, the postmodernists all too willingly, but by no means in all cases, detach cultural production from its basis in economic and political processes; that is, culture as a signifying system is all but sundered from its constitutive embeddedness in the materiality of social life. To put it yet another way, the relationship between cultural artifacts or commodities and their material basis is viewed by many postmodernists as little more than epiphenomenal, or only tenuously connected to the production of value. Difference is rendered opaque in that it is often unhinged from its historical embeddedness in colonial/imperialist relations. Signification doesn't take place is some structural vacuum, frozen in some textual netherworld, defanged of capitalist alienation. It is a process that occurs in historical contexts, through modes of production and circulation tied to specific social relations that produce and reproduce value formations. Anyway, I found that the work by many postmodernists devalued or downgraded and in some instances scuppered altogether the material basis of cultural production.

Of course, Marcia, I agree that culture cannot and should not be reduced to its material base, but neither can it be dis-embedded from it. That is the crucial issue. With this in mind, Marxism is indispensable in challenging the ideology of capitalism—i.e., the imperial hegemonic bloc of the transnational capitalist class—through both counterhegemonic struggle and the struggle for proletarian hegemony, through attempts at creating a united front against imperialist capitalism and the internationalization of slave labor—a united front that has as its goal the redistribution of power and resources to the oppressed. The key here is to understand that capitalism is no longer self-reinforcing; it needs to expand its markets constantly, invading each nook and cranny of the globe through colonization, war, competition, and military aggression. Imperialism is the carotid artery that enables capital to flow to the farthest reaches of profit maximization.

I don't want to knock everything about postmodern theory since clearly there have been important insights in this work. My overall perspective is that postmodernism often reduces class struggle to a Nietzschean "will to power" which expunges the whole notion of necessity out of history, out of temporal progression. Many postmodernists in the United States are engaged in "identity politics" where they center their struggle around their racial, gender, or sexual identities. While these struggles can be very important, many of the new social movements based on race and gender identities sever issues of race and gender from class struggle. I find that this conveniently draws attention away from the crucially important ways in which women and people of color provide capitalism with its super-exploited labor pools—a phenomenon that is on the upswing all over the world. Postmodernist educators tend to ignore that capitalism is, according to Eileen Wood, a ruthless "totalizing process" which shapes every aspect of our lives and subjects all social life to the abstract requirements of the market through the commodification and fetishization of life in all of its myriad dimensions. This makes a "mockery" out of all aspirations to autonomy, freedom of choice, and democratic self-government.

Marcia: How does your version of critical pedagogy situate Marxism?

Peter: As Valerie Scatamburlo-D'Annibale and Greg Martin and I have argued, for well over two decades we have witnessed the jubilant liberal and conservative pronouncements of the demise of communism. History's presumed failure to debar existing capitalist relations has been read by many self-identified "radicals" as an advertisement for capitalism's inevitability. As a result, the chorus refrain "There Is No Alternative to Capitalism" chimed by liberals and conservatives has been buttressed by the symphony of post-Marxist voices recommending that we give socialism a decent burial and move on. Within this context, to speak of the promise of Marx and socialism may appear anachronistic, even naive, especially since the postmodern intellectual vanguardist antivanguard has presumably demonstrated the folly of doing so. Yet we stubbornly believe that the chants of "there is no alternative" must be challenged for they offer as a *fait d'accompli* something about which progressive leftists should remain defiant—namely, the triumph of capitalism and its political bedfellow, neoliberalism, which have worked together to naturalize suffering, undermine collective struggle, and obliterate hope.

I make the point here that Marxism is not built upon an edifice of all-knowing totality. It does not offer a blueprint for an alternative to capitalism. It is a form of revolutionary praxis insofar as it explores the contradictions within capitalist social relations, knowing full well that the abolition of class society is not a certainty, it is only one possible outcome of many. Critical revolutionary pedagogy, for me, adopts a perspective that knowledge is praxis; it is transforming action. In this sense, objective truth becomes a practical question. What concerns me more is the value form in which our labor is exercised. How do we produce value? Surely, it is the value form of our labor that produces capitalist ideology—in that the value form of our labor within capitalist social relations is what conditions human thought at its roots. This ideology is fostered by the imperial-sponsored circulation of market ideologies through right-wing think tanks and NGOs (nongovernment organizations). Thinking and consciousness arises from our interactions with the material world, the world in which we labor. Our social existence—embedded as it is in the material world—is what produces our consciousness. This is a fundamental insight of Marx. Critical agency becomes, then, from this perspective, a form of revolutionary praxis, knowing the world by bringing it forth and bringing it forth by interacting with it, by changing it.

The question is: In what direction should we move? And that question constitutes the present debate. Well, it isn't much of a debate in the U.S. since questions about socialism and alternatives to capitalism are the kinds of questions that are raised by those who are now called "enemies of civilization."

Marcia: How does all of this factor into your rethinking of critical pedagogy?

Peter: The larger goal that revolutionary critical pedagogy stipulates for radical educationalists involves direct participation with the oppressed in the discovery and charting of a socialist reconstruction and alternative to capitalism. However, without a critical lexicon and interpretative framework to unpack the labor/capital relationship in all of its capillary detail, critical pedagogy is doomed to remain trapped in domesticated currents and vulgarized formations. The process whereby labor-power is transformed into human capital and concrete living labor is subsumed by abstract labor is one that eludes the interpretative capacity of rational communicative action and requires a dialectical understanding that only historical materialist critique can best provide. Historical materialism provides critical pedagogy with a theory of the material basis of social life rooted in historical social relations and assumes paramount importance in uncovering the structure of class conflict as well as unraveling the effects produced by the social division of labor. Today, labor-power is capitalized and commodified, and education plays a tragic role in these processes. According to Rikowski, education represents what he refers to as the links in the chains that bind our souls to capital. That's a powerful way to put it. It constitutes the arena of combat between labor and capital—a clash between titans that powers contemporary history we know as the class struggle. Schools therefore act as vital supports for, and developers of, the class relation, the violent capital-labor relation that resides at the very heart of capitalist society and development.

Marcia: Can you share your thoughts on your idea of teachers as transformatory intellectuals? What is needed to be done in this regard, and how are we to do it?

Peter: Well, there is a problem with how educators have domesticated the work of Gramsci on the topic of organic intellectuals. Postmodernists overestimate the "partially autonomous" space created by civil society, and while their intentions are often laudable, they have no program for socialist struggle; in fact, many of them abhor the very idea of socialism. They have effectively remade Gramsci in terms more acceptable to the bourgeoisie. It becomes very important in this regard to examine Gramsci's use of the term "civil society" within his overall analysis of the state. According to educators such as John Holst, Gramsci viewed civil society as part of the "hegemonic" aspect of the state that essentially worked to balance the coercive aspect of the state. Civil society, while clearly a contested terrain, is a site where the ruling class exerts its hegemony over the social totality.

It is not a form of complete control. From this perspective, the most radical elements of civil society must work to build working-class solidarity in a postrevolutionary society. For Gramsci, working-class organic intellectuals are challenged to bring socialist consciousness to the working class, that is, to give the proletariat a consciousness of its historic mission. If there were spontaneous rebellion, then according to Gramsci, this should be an educated spontaneity. As Holst points out, Gramsci's conception of the long struggle for proletarian power is one that mandates an organically devised ideological and political education and preparation, including the creation of a system of class alliances for the ultimate establishment of proletarian hegemony as well as the development of workers councils. Holst does an excellent job of summarizing Gramsci here. These developments are part and parcel of what Gramsci called the historical bloc, consisting of organizations and alliances as well as a permanent organization of specialists (organic intellectuals) coordinated by the party who are able to assist the working-class move from a class in itself (the objective class created by relations of production) to a class for itself (a subjective understanding of its position in production and its political mission). So, essentially, revolutionary pedagogy is committed to revolutionary praxis against the power of the state.

Now, I am not saying that the struggle to build organic intellectuals today is identical to the struggle that Gramsci articulated in his day. We inhabit quite different historical and sociopolitical contexts. I see the challenge of transformative (organic) intellectuals today as developing strategic international alliances with anticapitalist and working-class movements worldwide, as well as with national liberation struggles against imperialism (and I don't mean here homogeneous nationalisms but rather those that uphold the principles of what Aijaz Ahmad calls multilingual, multidenominational, multiracial political solidarities). Transformative intellectuals should be opposed to policies imposed by the International Monetary Fund and the World Bank on "undeveloped" countries because such measures are the actual cause of economic underdevelopment. Transformative intellectuals should set themselves against that which the Community/Labor Strategy Center here in Los Angeles links to the systematic cultivation of racist ideology, reactionary nationalism, xenophobia, male supremacy, and misogyny. Of course, racism and sexism spreads independently of the material basis for imperialism.

I elaborate further on your question, Marcia. In discussing responses to the imperial barbarism and corruption brought about by capitalist globalization, James Petras makes some very useful distinctions. For instance, he distinguishes stoics, cynics, pessimists, and critical intellectuals (categories that encompass those who serve the hegemony of empire, from the prostrated academics who bend their knees in the face of capitalism while at the same time denouncing its excesses to the coffee-sipping intellectuals of Soho) from what he refers to as irreverent intellectuals (who serve the cause of developing revolutionary socialist consciousness and a new internationalism). The stoics are repulsed by the "predatory pillage of the empire" but, because they are paralyzed by feelings of political impotence, choose to form small cadres of academics in order to debate theory in as much isolation as possible from both the imperial powers and the oppressed and degraded masses. The cynics condemn both the victims of predatory capitalism and their victimizers as equally afflicted with consumerism; they believe that the oppressed masses seek advantage only to reverse the roles of oppressor and oppressed. The cynics are obsessed with the history of failed revolutions where the exploited eventually become the exploiters. They usually work in universities and specialize in providing testimonials to the perversions of liberation movements. The pessimists are usually leftists or ex-leftists who are also obsessed with the historical defeats of revolutionary social movements, which they have come to see as inevitable and irreversible, but who use these defeats as a pretext for adopting a pragmatic accommodation with the status quo. They have a motivated amnesia about new revolutionary movements now struggling to oppose the empire (i.e., movements by militant farmers and transport workers) and use their pessimism as an alibi for inaction and disengagement. The pessimists are reduced to a liberal politics that can often be co-opted by the ideologists of empire. Critical intellectuals frequently gain notoriety among the educated classes. Protesting indignation at the ravages of empire and neoliberalism and attempting to expose their lies, critical intellectuals appeal to the elite to reform the power structures so that the poor will no longer suffer. This collaborationist approach of critical intellectuals creates a type of indignation that appeals very much to the educated classes without asking them to sacrifice very much.

In contrast to all of the above categories, the irreverent intellectual, Petras argues, respects the militants on the front lines of the anticapitalist and anti-imperialist struggles. Petras describes them as "self-ironic anti-heroes" whose work is respected by activists working for a basic transformation of the social order. He notes that irreverent intellectuals are "objectively partisan and partisanly objective" and work together with intellectuals and activists involved in popular struggles. The irreverent intellectuals admire people such as Jean-Paul Sartre, who rejected a Nobel Prize in the midst of the Vietnam War. Irreverent intellectuals are careful to integrate their writing and teaching with practice, and in this way they are able to avoid divided loyalties. I think these descriptions by Petras hold a lot of merit and are pretty much accurate.

Marcia: Can the existing schooling system, which prepares selfish capitalist pseudo-humanitarian professionals, lead us to a struggle for social justice?

Peter: For those of us fashioning a distinctive socialist philosophy of praxis within North American context, it is clear that a transition to socialism will not be an easy struggle, given the global entrenchment of these aforementioned challenges. Joel Kovel argues that the transition to socialism will require the creation of a "usufructuary of the earth." Essentially, this means restoring ecosystemic integrity across all of human participation—the family, the community, the nation, the international community. Kovel argues that use value must no longer be subordinated to exchange value, but both must be harmonized with "intrinsic value." The means of production (and it must be an eco-centric mode of production) must be made accessible to all as assets are transferred to the direct producers (i.e., worker ownership and control). Clearly, eliminating the accumulation of surplus value as the motor of "civilization" and challenging the rule of capital by directing money towards the free enhancement of use values goes against the grain of the existing capitalist society.

Marcia: Now, I ask you, is class struggle relevant today?

Peter: That depends on what you mean by class struggle. Critical revolutionary educators believe that the best way to transcend the brutal and barbaric limits to human liberation set by capital is through practical grassroots movements centered around class struggle. But today, the clarion cry of class struggle is spurned by the bourgeois left as politically fanciful and reads to many as an advertisement for a Hollywood movie. The liberal left is less interested in class struggle than in making capitalism more "compassionate" to the needs of the poor. What this approach obfuscates is the way in which new capitalist efforts to divide and conquer the working class and to recompose class relations have employed xenophobic nationalism, racism, sexism, ableism, and homophobia. The key here is not for critical pedagogues to privilege class oppression over other forms of oppression but how capitalist relations of exploitation provide the backdrop or foundation from which other forms of oppression are produced and how postmodern educational theory often serves as a means of distracting attention from capital's global project of accumulation. I am arguing that capitalism is not inevitable and that the struggle for socialism is not finished—it has barely begun.

Marcia: What are some of your concluding thoughts?

Peter: I would like to comment briefly again on the role of teachers and how it needs to change in a world rife with war and terror brought about by a number of forces that include but are no means limited to religious fanaticism, globalized capitalism, overproduction, neoliberalism, and the resource wars engaged in by the leading imperialist powers, with the United States serving as the most carnivorous Alpha Male of all these "civilized hyenas" (Lenin's term). Because there appears to be no outer perimeter to capital's destructive overreach, I see the role of teachers as that of transforming the world, not just describing or interpreting the world. It is constantly reshaping it self to meet the challenges of harmonizing relations among human beings with each other and with nature in a world convulsing in chaos. How much more chaotic can it be with George Bush and his militant evangelicism, his claim to be a vehicle for God's will, his fascist ideology, his imperialist machinations? Critical educators must increasingly confront at both regional and global levels the crisis of overproduction, the continuing use of surplus value as the key to historical acceleration and social progress, ecocidal development policies and practices, and economic, cultural, and military imperialism that holds much of humanity in the combustible thrall of violence and terror. The role of the critical educator follows Marx's clarion call to transform the world and not be content with describing or interpreting the world from some frozen hinterland of presumed objectivity; Marx's call requires a complex understanding of the ideological dimensions of teacher work and the class-based, racialized, and gendered characteristics of exploitation within the capitalist economy and its educational, administrative, and legal apparatuses. And it demands from us a living philosophy of praxis. What is the use of critical revolutionary pedagogy if it can not help us to discover ways of feeding the hungry, providing shelter for the homeless, bringing literacy to those who can't read or write, struggling against the criminal justice system to stop it from its war on Blacks and Latinos who are imprisoned in this country in numbers that are staggering when their percentage of the overall population is taken into account—in fact, the prison population of the U.S. is the largest in the world. We need to create spaces and sites for the development of critical consciousness and grassroots social activism both within the schools and outside of them and in both urban and rural spaces where people are suffering and struggling to survive on a daily basis. And we need to discover ways of creating—and maintaining—a sustainable environment.

I have described critical pedagogy as the performative register for class struggle. It is praxiological and is occupied with real bodies, toiling bodies, sensuous bodies, bodies bearing the weight of generations of suffering under capital and as a result of imperialist wars and racism, sexism, and homophobia. Consequently, revolutionary critical pedagogy sets as its goal the decolonization of subjectivity as well as its material basis in capitalist social relations. It seeks to reclaim public life that is currently under the relentless assault of the corporatization, privatization, and businessification of the lifeworld (which includes the corporate academic-complex) and to fight for new definitions of what public life should mean and new formations that it can take. We need to realize that civic public life (as distinct from the state) itself is in a crisis situation with all kinds of conflicts between workers and their bosses. We can't just exhume some notion of public from the past and apply it to the present. We need to struggle for qualitatively new and different forms of public life, while we gain some sense of direction from past struggles and accomplishments. As we lurch along the battered road towards socialist renewal, we edge closer to the social universe of which Marx so famously spoke. Our optimism may be sapped by literally centuries of defeats, yet we need to keep our spirits alive and our vision of what must be done clear-headed and measured. Of course, my success in this struggle has been modest. I am attempting to refine a philosophy of praxis on groundwork already set by people such as Paulo Freire and Raya Dunaveyskaya. I am only trying to walk modestly behind their far-reaching reflections.

I advocate one more point in closing—it is this: As we begin the task of removing Marx from the museum of history, we need to affirm the central role that class struggle plays in the determination of history. We also need to remember that there are no guarantees that socialism will win the day. That will depend upon us.

REFERENCES

Allman, P. (1999). *Revolutionary social transformation: Democratic hopes, political possibilities and critical education*. Westport, CT: Bergin & Garvey.

Allman, P. (2001a). *Critical education against global capitalism: Karl Marx and revolutionary critical education*. Westport, CT: Bergin & Garvey.

Allman, P. (2001b). Education on fire! In M. Cole, D. Hill, P. McLaren, & G. Rikowski (Eds.), *Red chalk: On schooling, capitalism and politics*. Brighton, UK: Institute for Education Policy Studies.

Bensaid, D. (2002). *Marx for our times: Adventures and misadventures of a critique* (G. Elliott, Trans.). London: Verso.

Bowles, S., & Herbert Gintis. (1976). *Schooling in capitalist America*. New York: Basic Books.

Cole, M., & Hill, D. (1999) *Promoting equality in secondary school*. London: Cassell.

Cole, M., Hill, D., McLaren, P., & Rikowski, G. (2001) *Red chalk: On schooling, capitalism and politics*. Brighton, UK: Institute for Education Policy Studies.

Cole, M., Hill, D., McLaren, P., & Rikowski, G. (2001). *Red chalk: On schooling, capitalism & politics*. London: Tufnell.

Davies, S., & Guppy, N. (1997). Globalization and educational reforms in Anglo-American democracies. *Comparative Education Review, 41*(4), 435-459.

De Lissovoy, N., & McLaren, P. (in press). *Towards a contemporary philosophy of praxis: Radical relevance* (L. Gray-Rosendale, Ed.). Albany: State University of New York Press.

Dunayevskaya, R. (in press). *The power of negativity*. Boulder, CO: Lexington.

Ebert, T. (2002). *University, class, and citizenship*. Unpublished manuscript.

Freire, P. (1998). *Pedagogy of the heart*. New York: Continuum.

Gramsci, A. (1971). *Selections from the prison notebooks*. London: International Publishers.

Hill, D. (2001). State theory and the neo-liberal reconstruction of schooling and teacher education: A structuralist neo-Marxist critique of postmodernist, quasi-postmodernist, and culturalist neo-Marxist theory. *British Journal of Sociology of Education, 22*(1), 135-155.

Hill, D., & Cole, M. (2001). Social class. In D. Hill & M. Cole (Eds.), *Schooling and equality: Fact, concept and policy*. London: Kogan Page.

Hill, D., Sanders, M., & Hankin, T. (2003). Marxism, social class and postmodernism. In D. Hill, P. McLaren, M. Cole, & G. Rikowski (Eds.), *Marxism against postmodernism in educational theory*. Lanham, MD: Lexington Books.

Lenin, V. (1951). *Imperialism: The highest stage of capitalism*. Moscow: Foreign Language Publishing House.

Luxemburg, R. (1919). *The crisis in German social democracy: The Junius pamphlet.* New York: The Socialist Publication Society.

Marx, K. (1972). *Theories of surplus value—Part three.* London: Lawrence & Wishart. (Original work published 1863)

Marx, K. (1973). *Critique of the Gotha program.* New York International Publishers.

Marx, K. (1976). *Results of the immediate process of production* (Addendum to Capital, Vol. l). Harmondsworth, UK: Penguin. (Original work published 1866)

Marx, K. (1977). *Capital: A critique of political economy* (Vol. 3). London: Lawrence & Wishart. (Original work published 1865)

Marx, K. (1977). *Economic and philosophical manuscripts of 1844.* Moscow: Progress Publishers. (Original work published 1844)

Marx, K. (1993). *Grundrise* (M. Nicolaus, Trans.). New York: Penguin. (Original work published 1857-1858)

Marx, K., & Engels, F. (1850, March). Address of the Central Committee to the Communist League, London.

Maturana, H. R., & Francisco Varela. (1987). *The tree of knowledge: The biological roots of human understanding.* Boston: New Science Library.

McLaren, P. (1995). *Critical pedagogy and predatory culture: Oppositional politics in a postmodern era.* London: Routledge.

McLaren, P. (1997). *Revolutionary multiculturalism: Pedagogies of dissent for the new millennium.* Boulder, CO: Westview.

McLaren, P. (1998a). *Life in schools: An introduction to critical pedagogy in the foundations of education* (3rd ed.). New York: Longman.

McLaren, P. (1998b). Revolutionary pedagogy in post-revolutionary times: Rethinking the political economy of critical education. *Educational Theory, 48*(4), 431-462.

McLaren, P. (2000). *Che Guevara, Paulo Freire, and the pedagogy of revolution.* Lanham, MD: Rowman & Littlefield.

McLaren, P., & De Lissovoy, N. (2002). Paulo Freire. In J. W. Guthrie (Ed.), *Encyclopedia of education* (2nd ed.). New York: Macmillan.

McLaren, P., & Farahmandpur, R. (1999a). Critical pedagogy, postmodernism, and the retreat from class: Towards a contraband pedagogy. *Theoria, 93,* 83-115.

McLaren, P., & Farahmandpur, R. (1999b). Critical multiculturalism and globalization: Some implications for a politics of resistance. *Journal of Curriculum Theorizing, 15*(3), 27-46.

McLaren, P., & Farahmandpur, R. (2000). Reconsidering Marx in post-Marxist times: A requiem for postmodernism? *Educational Researcher, 29*(3), 25-33.

McLaren, P., & Farahmandpur, R. (2001a). Educational policy and the socialist imagination: Revolutionary citizenship as a pedagogy of resistance. *Educational Policy, 13*(3), 343-378.

McLaren, P., & Farahmandpur, R. (2001b). Teaching against globalization and the new imperialism: Toward a revolutionary pedagogy. *Journal of Teacher Education, 52*(2), 136-150.

McMurtry, J. (2002). *Value wars: The global market versus the life economy.* London: Pluto.

Mészáros, I. (1995). *Beyond capital.* New York: Monthly Review Press.

Mészáros, I. (1999). Marxism, the capital system, and social revolution: An interview with Istvan Mészáros. *Science & Society, 63*(3), 338-361.

Mészáros, I. (2001). *Socialism or barbarism: From the "American century" to the crossroads*. New York Monthly Review Press.

Neary, M. (2001). *Travels in Moishe Postone's social universe: A contribution to a critique of political cosmology*. Unpublished paper, forthcoming in Historical Materialism: Research in Critical Marxist theory.

Neary, M., & Rikowski, G. (2000, April 17-20) T*he speed of life: The significance of Karl Marx's concept of socially necessary labour-time*. Paper presented at the British Sociological Association annual conference, University of York.

Ollman, B. (1976). *Alienation: Marx's conception of man in capitalist society* (2nd ed.). Cambridge, UK: Cambridge University Press.

Ollman, B. (1993). *Dialectical investigations*. New York: Routledge.

Ollman, B. (2001). *How to take an exam and remake the world*. Montreal, Canada: Black Rose.

24

RAGE AND HOPE
THE REVOLUTIONARY PEDAGOGY OF PETER MCLAREN:
AN INTERVIEW WITH
PETER McLAREN
Mitja Sardoc

Peter McLaren is an internationally acclaimed educator and critical social theo-rist and one of North America's pioneers of critical pedagogy—an approach to teaching and learning that invites students to become politically active and socially conscious agents of history. Influenced by the work of the famous Brazilian educator Paulo Freire, who was imprisoned and exiled for his contro-versial approach to teaching peasants to resist their ruling class oppressors, criti-cal pedagogy encourages students to become educated not simply to adjust to the norms of society but to actively re-shape society in the interests of social justice for all. Professor McLaren began his teaching career in his hometown of Toronto, Canada, teaching in an inner-city school in one of the most highly pop-ulated housing projects in the country. His elementary school diary, *Cries from the Corridor*, held the number seven position on bestseller lists in Canada in 1980. McLaren completed his PhD at The Ontario Institute for Studies in Education, University of Toronto, in 1983. In 1984 he held the position of Special Lecturer in Education at Brock University's College of Education where he taught in the undergraduate and graduate programs. In 1985 McLaren worked with Henry Giroux to create the Centre for Education and Cultural Studies, at Miami University of Ohio, where he served as both Associate Director and Director. While at Miami he became the youngest professor ever to be awarded the title of Renowned Scholar in Residence, School of Education and Allied Professions. A Fellow of the Royal Society of Arts and Commerce, and Associate of Massey College, Professor McLaren is the author and editor of over 40 books. He began teaching st the University of California in 1993, where he serves as Professor, Division of Urban Schooling, Graduate School of

This chapter originally appeared in *Educational Philosopy and Theory, 33*(304), pp. 411-439. © 2001 Philosophy of Education Society of Australasia. Reprinted with the permis-sion of the publisher.

Education and Information Studies. Professor McLaren lectures worldwide and his work has been translated into 17 languages. His most recent books include *Schooling as a Ritual Performance* (3rd edn, Rowman & Littlefield, 2003), *Critical Pedagogy and Predatory Culture* (Routledge, 1995), *Revolutionary Multiculturalism* (Westview, 1997), *Che Guevara, Paulo Freire, and the Pedagogy of Revolution* (Rowman & Littlefield, 2000), *Teaching Against Globalization and the New Imperialism* (with Ramin Farahmandpur), and *Capialists and Conquerors.*

Mitja: I first became aware of your work through *Schooling as a Ritual Performance*, which combined a structuralist, post-structuralist and Marxist analysis of Catholic schooling. Since that time your work (I am thinking of the third edition of *Life in Schools, Critical Pedagogy and Predatory Culture, Revolutionary Multiculturalism, Che Guevara, Paulo Freire, and the Pedagogy of Revolution*) has become much more informed by postmodern theory but also has been moving—quite noticeably in your last book, *Che Guevara, Paulo Freire, and the Pedagogy of Revolution*—towards a re-engagement with histori-cal materialist analysis, a critique of the globalization of capitalism, and a pre-occupation with class struggle. Class struggle and other Marxist ideas seem to be outdated with the fall of the Berlin Wall and what Francis Fukuyama called the 'end of history' or the 'end of ideology'. But if we read, for example, *The Communist Manifesto*, we find some parts of it even more relevant today than when it was originally published in 1848. Why are Marxist ideas still haunting mainstream western educational discourse despite the apparent closure of the Marxist legacy in history's cabinet of lost revolutionary dreams?

Peter: I agree with you, Mitja, that Marx's ideas are still haunting Western educational discourses, but I don't agree that educationalists in North America have been affected by these ideas to any substantive degree. Postmodern theory seems to be holding sway—at least it has become the most fashionable form of educational criticism. While many of my erstwhile Marxist colleagues are embracing postmodern theory and its post-Marxist variants, and the work of Foucault, Lyotard, Virilio, Baudrillard, Kristeva, Butler, Derrida, Deleuze, Guattari, and the like, my work is becoming more centred in Marxist critique. A number of my colleagues have said to me: 'Why, when postmodern theory is at the cutting edge of critical social theory, would you want to re-join the dinosaurs of historical materialism? My answer is that one does not have to be a postmodernist to work on the cutting edge of social theory. Perry Anderson, Ellen Meiksins Woods, James Petras, John Bellamy Foster, Raymond Williams, Eric Hobsbawm, Robert Brenner and Alex Callinicos—who work in a Marxist tradition—are hardly theoretical slackers. If one follows the trajectory of my work over the last several decades one will quickly discover a constant motion. Sometimes it is a steady march, perhaps even militant; sometimes a swaying motion from idea to idea, as in my former dalliance with left postmodern theo-ry; more often than not lumbering gestures towards a definitive line of reasoning; and on too many occasions recently I find myself staggering across the intellectual firmament like a drunken sailor after a night out on the town. I become, in other words, intoxicated by the possibilities of linking revolutionary theory to political praxis. The motion, however direct, purposeful or erratic, is always towards Marx and the Marxist tradition. The work of Marx is continually being revisited in my work. For instance, in the new edition of *Schooling as a Ritual Performance*, I updated my work on the ethnography of symbols, with a short discussion of Marx. Basically I argued that class exploitation within capitalist societies occupies a strategic centrality in organizing those very activities that make us human, including our sign and symbol systems. Volosinov and others have maintained—rightly in my view—that speech genres themselves are determined by production relations and the machinations of the sociopolitical order. This is an important assertion especially in view of the fact that, as John McMurtry notes, the market system is being applied to democracy itself: where democracy is seen as occurring at the sites that market intervention occurs the least; where abstract law overrides concrete determinations and abstracts real existence into nothingness; where distributive principles overrule concrete struggles for new freedoms; where a successful democracy is defined in terms of its ability to become self-legitimating and self-justificatory; and, where the market is permitted to remain impersonal and omnipresent and is encouraged and facilitated in its efforts to totalize and fetishize the field of social relations in which it has become a central force. Surplus extraction occurs through processes that are dialogical and simultaneously economic, political and ideological. These are not ontologically privileged processes but rather become central in the way that they organize the constitutive processes of everyday life. In other words, the class struggle is also a language game. And one that in some fundamental way co-ordinates all the other language games. All language games and symbol systems are accented by class power. If this is the case, then living in a capitalist social order demands the continual affirmation of a working-class struggle not only against capitalism, but against capital itself. Marx, after all, held that capital was a social relation: the abolition of capital, then, requires us to abolish a particular form of social relation. Volosinov goes so far as to argue that the sign becomes the very arena of class struggle because the continual accumulation of capital can only continue through an unequal exchange between social agents—an exchange that favours one social agent while the other is reduced to scrounging out of mere necessity. So I have tried to amend some of my earlier insights in *Schooling as a Ritual Performance*, with an engagement, however brief, with Marx.

Mitja Some scholars and researchers have remarked that Marx is returning with a vengeance to the social sciences? Why, in your opinion, isn't this the case, as you claim, among educationalists in the United States?

Peter You could say that Marx is returning with a vengeance, yes, Mitja, I would agree. To a certain extent you are correct. While anti-capitalist struggle and Marxist analysis has an indistinct and relatively undigested place in the field of educational theory, there is some movement towards Marx in the social sciences here in North America. With one glaring exception being the educational left in the United States, I would say that Marx is being revisited by social scientists of all disciplinary shapes and sizes even, and perhaps most especially and urgently today, when capitalism is in a state of severe organic crisis. While hardly on their way to becoming entrenched and pervasive, Marx's ideas are taking their significance most strikingly from the particular and varied contexts in which his ideas are being engaged. In the face of the cultivated arrogance and pitylessness of the post-Marxists, the unabashed triumphalism of the apostles of neo-liberalism, and the tight-lipped solemnizers of bourgeois democracy as they choose to ignore the precariousness of the current triumph of capitalism over communism—not to mention the unprecedented gravity of the crisis of neo-liberalism's death-squad capitalism—it is not easy to recover the soiled mantle of Marx from the gravesite where it had been derisively and capriciously flung in those ecstatic moments of bourgeois revelry and spiteful, tongue-wagging glee, when the ruling classes watched from their princely Western heights the 'popular democracies' of Eastern Europe trembling alongside the wobbling pillars of communism that were collapsing across that crimson space of historical memory we know as the Soviet Union. There have been times when I have coquetted with postmodern theory, with the voguish apostasy of post-structuralist brigandry, or deconstructionist outlawry—even to the point where I have been identified as the first to introduce the term 'postmodernism' into the lexicon of education criticism (a dubious claim, but one made of my work none the less)—but I have found there to be insuperable limitations to postmodern theory, not to mention a growing confederacy of academic sycophants who these days appear to overpopulate North American and European critical studies. As Callinicos has noted, much of what we find in French post-structuralism in many ways is a continuation of the thought of Nietzsche, reformulating it by way of Saussure's theory of language and Heidegger's philosophy of Being. And he also notes that much of the critique of the Enlightenment undertaken by Foucault and other postmodern theorists had already been anticipated by the Frankfurt School theorists—Adorno, Horkheimer, Benjamin, and others. This is not to disparage their work—I think that it is immensely important—although I also think that, for the most part, postmodern theorists and critical theorists (in the tradition of the Frankfurt School) are too pessimistic about the possibilities of social revolution. I have found that there exists a strategic centrality in Marx's work—the work that, as Callinicos puts it, 'survived the debacle of Stalinism'.

Mitja: Strategic centrality?

Peter: Yes, in terms of linking educational theory to a political project that can address the onslaught of globalization, in particular the globalization of capital. However 'disorganized' capitalism has become, I don't believe that we live in an era of capitalism without classes.

Mitja: There is some irony, living in the United States—in Hollywood no less!—and working as a Marxist?

Peter: Yes, many people outside the United States find it a bit—how should I put it?—strange. But it might surprise you how many Marxists I've met in Hollywood. More than you might think. But we are certainly outnumbered by the postmodernists! Though many criticalists in education are reluctant to descend from the topgallant of postmodern theory into the heated 'red' engine room of social analysis, I find that practicing sociology below-the-water line, in the 'hatch', so-to-speak, has its distinct advantages. Marx's work enables me to explore with fewer theoretical constraints, in more capillary detail, and with more socio-analytical ballast, the dynamic complexity of the social totality. Marxism provides me with the conceptual tools necessary to navigate between the Scylla of positivism and the Charbydis of relativism. It also provides an approach to praxis that, in these world historical times of the epochal dominance of capital and the reworking of forms of global capitalist imperialism, is fundamentally necessary.

Mitja: What theorists have influenced your recent turn towards historical materialism?

Peter: Well, I could extend the list I gave earlier to include Marx, Gramsci, Lukacs, Althusser, Trotsky, Malcolm X, Istvan Mezsaros, Raymond Williams, Walter Benjamin and the Frankfurt School, Terry Eagleton, Aijaz Ahmad, James Petras, Frantz Fanon, Albert Memmi, Paulo Freire, Stuart Hall, Rosa Luxemburg, Epifinio San Juan, Slavoj Zizek, and a host of others too numerous to mention. Of course, I have learned much from Foucault, whose lectures I was able to attend (in Canada) a few years before he died. And Lyotard, certainly, and Baudrillard. I can't deny that there was a time when the postmodern thinkers played a central role in my work. Not to mention the important work of Mauss, Victor Turner and Pierre Bourdieu (I still follow Bourdieu's work), to cite but three examples from the anthropological literature. Through my current re-engagement with Marx, and the tradition of historical materalism, I have enjoyed the company of British colleagues—Glenn Rikowski, Mike Cole and Dave Hill—whose work is paving the way for new generations of educationalists to encounter Marx. I have also been influenced by the Marxist Humanism of Peter Hudis and Raya Dunayevskaya, the 'red feminism' of Teresa Ebert, and Rosemary Hennessey, the Marxist-Leninism of Mas'ud Zavarzadeh, and Donald Morton, and the work of Canadian philosopher, John McMurtry, and others. Ramin Farahmandpur and I have been working together on a number of projects related to rethinking Marxist educational praxis.

To repeat my previous comment, Marx is being re-evaluated on numerous fronts today: sociology, political science, philosophy, economics, ethics, history, and the like. It is perhaps more difficult for such a re-evaluation to take place in education here in North America, mainly because his work was never very important in the education debates here to begin with.

Mitja What about the early 1980s? Wasn't there interest in Marxist analysis among critical educators in the United States during that time?

Peter Yes, that's true, there was a handful of educationalists who incorporated some Marxist insights into their work—I am thinking of the important contributions of Henry Giroux, Mike Apple, Phil Wexler and Jean Anyon (who are still turning out splendid work)—but the influence of Marxist and quasi-Marxist analysis (mostly influenced by British educationalists) lasted about five years. Then postmodern theory started to be taken up. And . . .

Mitja: And?

Peter: And . . . well . . . for the most part this has led to a stress on identity politics—a proliferation of issues dealing with race, ethnic and sexual identities and waning and supersession of discussion around social class. The interest in identity politics is understandable enough, especially given the burgeoning migration of immigrants to the United States over the last several decades.

Mitja: So I take it that you are a dyed-in-the-wool Marxist?

Peter: Let me make this qualification before I continue. I am not one of those die-hard leftists who regard Marxism as a religion that explains everything that needs to be known about humanity. Marxism is not a faith; it is not a sibylline discourse. I have no truck with solifidianism—Marxist or ecclesiastic. In fact, Marxism puts its stock in good works rather than in faith. It puts an emphasis on denouncing and transforming the world, not wrapping doctrinal tentacles around its major texts, or clinging steadfastly to historical materialism as if it admitted a pristine purity or sacerdotal truth. There is a denunciatory aspect to Marxism that is crucial here. If the language of analysis that informs your work does not enable you and encourage you to denounce the world, then you would be wise to reconsider the language that you are using. Even Pope John Paul II, in his encyclical, *Centesimus Annus*, admits to at least some 'seeds of truth' in Marxism.

Mitja [laughing] Please, Peter, you're not saying the Pope is a Marxist, are you?

Peter: I believe in the power of salvation, but this, I fear, is asking too much of God, and of Marx, I am afraid!

Mitja; What about the post-Marxist movement? You mentioned identity politics—isn't that part of it?

Peter: As I said previously, I find the efflorescence of identity politics problematic but it is nevertheless understandable. The problem is that identities are often framed within a discourse of militant particularism, and there are ways that a stress on identity politics can sabotage class struggle, especially when it is uncoupled from the larger social totality of advanced capitalism. In a class I taught this summer, the students didn't want to discuss the exploitation of the working class. They thought that issues of race and gender were more important. And while all identities are racialized, sexualized and gendered, and located in class relations—in a non-synchronous way, as Cameron McCarthy has pointed out—I think that we have forgotten how social class works in our everyday lives. I think that recovering class struggle is essential in creating wider political solidarities necessary in the current movement against global capitalism. Class exploitation is not to be 'privileged' over racism or sexism or homophobia—please let me underscore that point again—but I feel that capitalist social formations often co-ordinate and organize and reify these other, equally important, forms of oppression. It's a more central and wholly social form of oppression, but that doesn't mean it is more important. I hope that I am making myself clear.

Mitja It's clear to me.

Peter: Let's move away from identity politics specifically for a moment and return to your question about post-Marxism. I find much about post-Marxist theory—and postmodern theory—to be functionally advantageous to the status quo. In fact, I find a thunderous resonance in the work of the postmodernists with that of the New Right. The work of Laclau and Mouffe is a case in point. I have great respect for their scholarship, but they tend to look at social contradictions as semantic problems whereas I see social contradictions as anchored in the objective nature of things; they are part of the structural determinations of the social. For the most part Laclau and Mouffe reject dialectical thought, and have abandoned the notion that capitalist exploitation is linked to the law of value and the extraction of surplus value. Exploitation is not a linguistic process only—it takes place objectively, in the bowels of everyday contradictions which expel relations of equality and I do not believe that resistance has to be conscious on the part of workers in order for exploitation to take place. As the Argentine scholar, Atilio Boron, provocatively notes, relations of subordination are antagonistic in relation to an ideology [a logic of capital] that rationalizes this relationship. Boron has revealed how the work of Laclau and Mouffe, far from constituting a supercession of Marxism, is, in effect, reproductive of some of the fundamental expressions of United States sociology of the 1950s, as found in the work of Talcott Parsons, for instance. Unlike Laclau and Mouffe, I do not believe hegemony is purely an articulatory device, but a politico-ideological process that is grounded in class relations.

Mitja: But how feasible is class struggle today?

Peter: That is a point of real contestation among social theorists and political activists. On the one hand I agree, Mitja, that there is no guarantee that a class *in itself* will be transformed into a class *for itself*; there is no metaphysical guarantee hovering over the outcome of class struggle. There is no secret structure of predestination, no teleological certainty On the other hand, Mitja, I agree that there is today the necessity of class struggle. It is a concrete necessity. Look at what happened in Seattle. Forty thousand young people protesting the World Bank and the global economic interests of the ruling class! I think that a new generation of young people is waking up to the injuries of globalized capitalist relations. Making politics practical is what is driving my work these days. I am not so much interested (as are many postmodern educators) in decentring capitalist social relations, relations of exchange, or consumer culture, although I do think it is important to analyze the objective determinations that have given rise to the complex ensemble of dislocated and dispersed identities that we find in contemporary postmodern necropolises—hybridized and creolized identities that have resulted from the unequal and combined character of capitalist development. I am more interested at this point in time in how education can play a fundamental role in developing new forms of non-alienated labor through the dismantling of capitalist social relations and capital itself. I am trying to develop ways of encouraging students to think of such a possibility through the creation of what I have called, after Paula Allman, a 'revolutionary critical pedagogy'. By extension, I am interested in the role that education can play in the wider society by dismantling capital's law of value as a central form of mediation between human beings

Mitja: While you have made it clear in recent work that you are not a postmodernist theorist, or a postmodern Marxist . . .

Peter: How about a classical Marxist?

Mitja; Ok. A classical Marxist. You have, nevertheless, mentioned that postmodernism has helped deepen our understanding of the way that ethnic and racial identities have been constructed. Traditionally excluded 'social groups' as blacks, women and other minority social groups, generally defined as 'others' in opposition to the mainstream discourse, were traditionally excluded from the curriculum. How productive do you find their inclusion in the curriculum, thus making it multicultural? Following that, do you think that multiculturalism's replacing of universalism with the call for diversity and tolerance has contested the the conservative agenda that disempowered and depoliticized the powerless and the marginalized? And one final question related to this issue: What do you think is the difference between 'inclusion'—the integration of previously marginalized groups into the mainstream culture on terms that secure their freedom and equality—and 'assimilation' which can be associated as its negation? How do those two practices differ in educational policy?

Peter: These are important questions, Mitja, that have to do with what has been called 'the politics of difference'. I have tried to address such politics in a number of books that I have co-edited with Christine Sleeter, Carlos Ovando and Henry Giroux. You are correct when you note that postmodern theory has helped educators to understand how identity formations are constructed within various social and institutional formations within capitalist consumer society. Yet much of this work locates power in discourse and 'representations' rather than social relations. The issue of mediation has been replaced by representation. Contradictions between labour and capital are replaced by issues of conflicting epistemologies. The problem with understanding discourses as epistemologies of oppression is that too often they are stripped of their historical specificity by bourgeois/postmodern theorists—what is of singular importance to the critical educator is not their formal link to Eurocentrism, but the way that they have been used by capitalists to exploit the objective world (as opposed to the lexical universe) of the working-classes. The fascism of the Third Reich has been defeated, and the communism of the Soviet Union has been brought to its knees, it seems, mainly so that transnational identities can be constructed by developed nations with the promise of a thousand years of uninterrupted shopping and watching re-run episodes of Baywatch. Our subjectivities are being created out of the detritus of productive forces, the expelled vomit of overaccumulation, and the bloated promise of globalized capitalist relations. The economies of desire linked to capitalist social relations are myriad, and complex, and it would take too much time to explore them here. Suffice it to say that identity construction is a process that cannot be ignored by those of us in education. In fact, it is a key challenge. But the challenge has to be greater than surfing for identities within hybridity, and among spaces opened up by the furious clashes in the Fight Clubs of culture. For me, such identity construction must take into account the relationship between subjective formation and the larger totality of globalized capitalist social relations. Capitalism here must not be perceived as anodyne, but rather as a brakeless train that is smashing all that is in its path, continuing to savage the possibility of constructing free associative forms of labour and the flourishing of human capacities. Look at the marriage of the neoliberal globalization of capital and the military industrial complex that took place in the imperialist and criminal invasion of Iraq by the United States.

Let me address your comment on universalism. Yes, the general critique of the post-colonial theorists is that asserting universal claims is tantamount to exercising disciplinary power in putting forward a hidden particularism. There is much to be said for this criticism. But Callinicos argues, and I agree with him, that abjuring appeals to universal principles on the basis of a particular standpoint, of, say, the community, ignores the asymmetrical relations of power and privilege in local situations and in the end truncates the form of social criticism you are able to muster. Rather than dismissing universalisms; as masked particularisms (which leaves you the choice of ranking your particularisms on some scale of preference), I would side with Callinicos, Eagleton, and others, in arguing that what is needed is a genuine universality in which everyone is included and there are no 'Others'. In this way, the Enlightenment project is called upon to live up to its name. This is ultimately what I believe the project of Habermas is all about. My position is that if we are to deepen the project of the Enlightenment rather than jettison it, we need to decide if capitalism has a place—central or peripheral. In my opinion, it doesn't have a place. I do not believe it is justifiable on ethical grounds or political grounds. Here we need to replace analyses by neoclassical economists with that of Marx. And we need to develop a coherent political and pedagogy theory that takes this factor into account. But I could go on . . .

Mitja Let me ask you how what you have been saying fits with your ideas on multiculturalism?

Peter: Let me try. Calls for diversity by politicians and educators and social reformers have brought historically marginalized groups—Latino/as, African-Americans, Asians, indigenous populations—to the centre of society in terms, at least, of addressing the importance of addressing their needs, rather than *actually* addressing their needs, or addressing their *actual* needs. In other words, this call for diversity has been little more than Enlightenment rhetoric certainly not practice. However, motivated by a lack of opposition to capitalist exploitation that has been fostered by neo-liberal policies worldwide, multicultural education continues to defang its most emancipatory possibilities by initiating what I believe are, for the most part, politically 'empty' calls for diversity—calls for diversity carried out in antiseptic isolation from an interrogation of capitalism's centre. This centre is what gives ballast to the production of sameness that I call the *eternal recurrence of whiteness*. This sameness constitutes the distillate of colonialism, imperialism and the ether of white lies that spikes the very air we breathe. It means that pluralism is secretly aligned with assimilation. To be brought 'into the centre' without being permitted to critique that centre is tantamount to internalizing the codes of whiteness—without being granted the benefits of actually assuming the 'social position' of whiteness. There is a parallel here with some of the debates on social exclusion in the European Union. Eurocapitalist states advance a rhetoric of social inclusion—of the unemployed, of adults who can't read, of the disabled and other groups— that simultaneously stigmatizes the 'excluded' as either victims or lacking in certain skills or attitudes, whilst claiming to want to include them as *equals* (with the whole question of equality left up in the air). But this is cruel fantasy. In a sense, there are no 'socially excluded': everyone is included into capital's social universe—but on differentially, obscenely unequal grounds. Possession of capital in its money form excludes people—to vastly differing degrees— from buying all manner of goods, real human need going by the board. On the other hand, capital includes us all, only to generate incredible differences between us on the basis of money. Gender, 'race' and other social and cultural differences are grounds within bourgeois metaphysics and 'ethics' for differentiating and fragmenting us on the basis of money. Capital drives us, therefore, against ourselves.

Going back to postmodernism, postmodernists given over to identity politics frequently overlook the centrality of social class as an over-arching identity that inscribes individuals and groups within social relations of exploitation. What identity politics and pluralism fail to address is the fact that diversity and difference are allowed to proliferate and flourish, provided that they remain within the prevailing forms of capitalist social arrangements, including hierarchical property arrangements. Of course, I agree that class relations are most certainly racialized and gendered. I do not want to subordinate race, gender, or sexuality to that of social class; rather I want to emphasize that without overcoming capitalism, anti-racist, anti-sexist and anti-homophobic struggles will have little chance at succeeding. Slavoj Zizek has said that in the Left's call for new multiple political subjectivities (e.g., race, class, feminist, religious), the Left in actuality asserts a type of all-pervasive sameness—a non-antagonistic society in which there is room made for all manner of cultural communities, lifestyles, religions and sexual orientations. Zizek reveals that this Sameness relies on an antagonistic split. As far as this split goes, I believe that it results, at least to a large degree, from the labour-capital relation sustained and promoted by white supremacist capitalist patriarchy. In other words, I do not see the central tension as one between the autochthonous and the foreign but between labor and capital. As you might be aware, am very sympathetic to the movement here in the United States known as the 'new abolitionists'

Mitja: Tell me about this movement—it relates to the politics of whiteness, correct?

Peter: Correct. Scholar-activists such as Noel Ignatiev, David Roediger, and others are calling for the abolition of whiteness, or the abolition of the white race. What they mean by this is that at there is no positive value that can be given to the social position known as whiteness. The term cannot be recovered or given a positive spin. White people need to disidentify entirely with the white race since it is constitutively premised on the demonization of all that is not-white. To seek any kind of positive identity with a white race—or political detente—is ill-conceived at best. This is because the white race was an historical invention born in the ovens of racial superiority and European caste. We have to un-invent the white race, and not re-invent it!

Theodore Allen and other scholars have noted, and rightly so, that the social function of whiteness is social control, a practice which has colonial origins that can be traced back to the assault upon tribal affinities, customs, laws and institutions of Africans, native Americans and Irish by English/British and Anglo-American colonialism. Such insidious practices of social control reduce all members of oppressed groups to one undifferentiated social status beneath that of any member of the colonizing population. With the rise of the abolitionist movement, racial typologies, classification systems and criteriologies favouring whiteness and demonizing blackness as the lowest status within humanity's 'great chain of being' spread throughout the United States. These typologies or myths (in Barthes' sense) were used to justify and legitimize the slavery of Africans and ensure the continuation of lifetime chattel bond-servitude. Today 'whiteness' has become naturalized as part of our 'commonsense' reality. Ignatiev has noted that whiteness is not a culture. There is Irish culture and Italian culture and American culture; there is youth culture and drug culture but, he asserts, there is no such thing as white culture. He points out that Shakespeare was not white; he was English. Mozart was not white; he was Austrian. According to the new abolitionists, whiteness has nothing to do with culture and everything to do with social position. Ignatiev notes that without the privileges attached to it, there would be no white race, and fair skin would have the same significance as big feet.

Ignatiev further notes that identification with white privilege reconnects whites to relations of exploitation. The answer to this plight, is, of course, for whites to cease to exist as whites. He claims that the most challenging task is to make it impossible for anyone to be white. This entails breaking the laws of whiteness so flagrantly as to destroy the myth of white unanimity.

What is also needed—and here the work of Marx becomes crucial—is an acute recognition of how the ideology of whiteness contributes to the reproduction of class divisions—particularly divisions between working-class Anglo-Americans and ethnic minorities—in order to reinforce existing property relations and reproduce the law of value as a mediatory device *par excellence* in reifying and fetishizing social relations in general.

Along with efforts to abolish the white race (not white people, there is, of course, a distinct difference) we must mobilize efforts to abolish capital. Capital is a social relation, as I noted earlier, not a 'thing'. It is a relation between all of us and value, which is the substance of capital, its lifeblood. The very existence of the capitalist class rests upon surplus value; unrequited labour-time, our sweat, our mental processes and our domestic labour (to bring up and maintain the next batch of labourers), our education (as generator of the attributes of labour-power: capacity to labour) and every other sphere of social life. Capital is a global virus that finds its way (mediated by our labour—that is the tragedy) into all areas of contemporary human life. It is nurtured by the New Right and all those who stand to gain millions, billions of dollars from the expansion of this demon seed. We need to reclaim human life from capital.

Mitja: What about the politics of globalization? How does that feature in your work?

Peter: The richest tenth of households in the United States own 83 per cent of the country's financial assets, while the bottom four-fifths own about 8 per cent. As Cuban Foreign Minister Felipe Roque exclaimed recently: Are the 4.5 billion human beings from underdeveloped countries who consume only 14 per cent of the world's total production really as free and equal as the 1.5 million living in the developed world that consume the other 86 per cent? What are we to think of the globalization of capitalism when the combined assets of the three richest people in the world exceeds the combined GDP of the 48 poorest nations; and when the combined assets of the 225 richest people is roughly equal to the annual incomes of the poorest 47 per cent of the world's population? What indeed! I link globalization—or what has been described as 'capitalism with the gloves off'—to its governmental bed-fellow, neo-liberalism. We have seen neo-liberalism at work in the oppression by the State of non-market forces, in the dismantling of social programs, in the enthronement of a neo-mercantilist public policy agenda, in the encouragement of social life—almost every inch of it!—to be controlled by private interests, in the scrapping of environmental regulation and in its interminable concessions to transnational corporations. While globalization has been used to describe social, political and economic shifts in late capitalism, such as the deregulation of the labour market and the globalization of liquid capital, I prefer a more close-to-the-bone definition that links it to a form of imperialism. This might seem a rebarbative exaggeration, but I see it as a recomposition of the labour and capital relationship that subordinates social reproduction to the reproduction of capital.

Mitja: How would you assess the politics of resistance in opposition to the conservative obviousness of predatory culture?

Peter: Mitja, I like the way that you framed that question. The obviousness of conservative culture is precisely why it is so hidden from view. Much like those who controlled the *paradis articificels* of everyday life in the film, *The Truman Show*, I am struck each day by the manner in which predatory capitalism anticipates forgetfulness, nourishes social amnesia, smoothes the pillows of finality and paves the world with a sense of inevitability and sameness. I am depressingly impressed by what a formidable opponent it has proven to be, how it fatally denies the full development of our human capacities, and inures us to the immutabilily of social life. In other words, it naturalizes us to the idea that capital is the best of all possible worlds, that it may not be perfect, but it certainly is preferable to socialism and communism. Many leftists have unwittingly become apologists for capitalist relations of domination because they are overburdened by the seeming inability of North Americans to imagine a world in which capital did not reign supreme. To address this situation, I have turned to critical pedagogy.

Mitja: You are very much identified with the field of critical pedagogy. How would you define critical pedagogy? What is your position within this field today?

Peter: As you know, Mitja, critical pedagogy has been a central liberatory current in education of the last two decades. Critical pedagogy has served as a form of struggle within and against the social norms and forces that structure the schooling process. Most approaches to critical pedagogy are limited to disturbing the foundations upon which bourgeois knowledge is built, placing the term 'schooling' itself under scrutiny. Questions that arise in critical pedagogy often have to do with the relationship among schooling and the broader array of publics constructed by the marketplace and brought about by the secularization and the internationalization of the politics of consumption. In other words, critical pedagogy most often deals with cultural manifestations of capital, and the norms and formations that are engendered by means of relations of exchange. This is a good strategy as far as it goes. However, the revolutionary pedagogy that I advocate, that I have built from the roots of Freire's and Marx's work and the work of many others, such as the great revolutionary Che Guevara, involves the uprooting of these seeds of naturalization—planted through the reification of social relations and the subsumption of difference to identity by means. of the law of value—and this means undressing the exploitative, sexist, racist and homophobic dimensions of contemporary capitalist society. But it also means more than simply 'uncovering' these relations, or laying them bare in all of their ideological nakedness. It stipulates—and here it is important not to mince words—the total uprooting of class society in all of its disabling manifestations. Revolutionary pedagogy refers to taking an active part in a total social revolution, one in which acting and knowing are indelibly fused such that the object of knowledge is irrevocably shaped by the very act of its being contemplated. That is, the very act of contemplation (I need to emphasize that this act of contemplation is collective and dialogical) shapes—and it shaped by—the object under investigation. The knowers are shaped, through dialogue, by the known. Revolutionary pedagogy attempts to produce an excess of consciousness over and above our conditional or naturalized consciousness, to create, as it were, an overflow or supplement that outruns the historical conditions that enframe it and that seek to anchor it, so that we might free our thought and, by extension, our everyday social practices from its rootedness in the very material conditions that enable thinking and social activity to occur in the first place. In other words, revolutionary pedagogy teaches us that we need not accommodate ourselves to the permanence of the capitalist law of value. In fact, it reveals to us how we can begin to think of continuing Marx's struggle for a revolution in permanence. A number of thinkers have helped to unchain the revolutionary implications of Freire's thought in this regard—Donaldo Macedo, Henry Giroux, Antonia Darder, Ira Shor, Peter Mayo, among others. I have attempted to do this by iterating the protean potential of his work for social revolution and not just the democratizing of capitalist social relations. So much contemporary work on Freire has inflated its coinage for transforming classroom practices but devalued its potential for revolutionary social change outside of the classroom in the wider society. Revolutionary pedagogy requires a dialectical understanding of global capitalist exploitation. Freire is often brought in to illuminate debates over school reform that are generally structured around the conceit of a dialogue over equality of opportunity which rarely go beyond momentous renunciations of corporatism or teeth-rattling denunciations of privatization. But such debates studiously ignore the key contradictions to which history has given rise—those between labour and capital. Such debates are engineered in the United States to avoid addressing these contradictions.

Mitja; What do you see as the most important challenge in the future for educational researchers?

Peter: The key to see beyond the choir of invisibilities that envelope us, and to identify how current calls for establishing democracy are little more than half-way house policies, a smokescreen for neo-liberalism and for making capitalism governable and regulated—a 'stakeholder' capitalism if you will. I do not believe such a capitalism will work, nor am I in favour of market socialism. We need to chart out a type of positive humanism that can ground a genuine social-ist democracy without market relations, a Marxist humanism that can lead to a transcendence of alienated labour. Following Marx, Eagleton claims that we are free when, like artists, we produce without the goad of physical necessity; and it is this nature which for Marx is the essence of all individuals. Transforming the rituals of schooling can only go so far since these rituals are embedded in capi-talist social relations and the law of value. There are signs that research in the social sciences might be going through a sea-shift of transformation. I think we need to take the focus away from how individual identities are commodified in postmodern consumer spaces, and put more emphasis on creating possibilities for a radical reconstitution of society. I like the public role that Pierre Bourdieu advocated before his untimely death—a role that sees the social agent taking his politics into the streets and factories, fighting the structural injustices and eco-nomic instabilities brought about by capitalism and neo-liberalism—fighting what, in effect, are nothing short of totalitarian practices that are facilitating the exploitation of the world's workers. Bourdieu realizes that we haven't exhaust-ed all the alternatives to capitalism. If that is the case, we need, as researchers, to bring our work to bear on the seeking out of new social relations around which everyday life can be productively and creatively organized. In my view, this is social science—and politics—the way it should be practiced. Hence, I will continue to struggle for a socialist society.

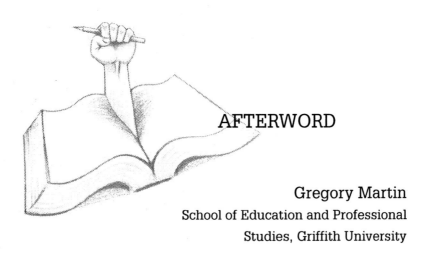

AFTERWORD

Gregory Martin

School of Education and Professional
Studies, Griffith University

As an unapologetic Marxist, the best thing I can say about *Red Seminars* is that it represents a trenchant intervention in the production of knowledge in the bourgeois academy. Appalled that public schools and universities are being transformed into self-interested zones of free enterprise, the scholars in this book theorize knowledge, its organization and its effects not just in terms of "content" but also as a social process of production, reproduction, distribution and consumption that perpetuates capitalist relations of exploitation. This point deserves attention. Contrary to popular opinion, schools are part of class society and the history of what and how ideas are taught is part of the struggle between classes. One of Marx's greatest contributions is that he showed how the production process (the economic structure) is at the heart of this struggle, which is why he dedicated his life to inquiring into its conditions. Keep in mind that every act of production is dependent on human labor and the development of knowledge, which spawns creativity and technology.

On this note, if there is one thing that the analysis and political exposures in *Red Seminars* make abundantly clear, capitalism is dependent on the economic role of education and particularly its value-added product, which is knowledge. Faced with a crisis of stagnation and decay, the ruling class has privileged knowledge production not just for developing fixed capital (e.g., machinery systems) but also for producing the appropriate ideologies and socialized subjectivities required to secure competitive advantage in a globally competitive market. Today, the management mantra is all about the "knowledge" people carry in their heads and how to get employees not only to work more effectively but also how to extract that knowledge to improve productivity and profit. What matters here is that the economic role of educators is to shoulder responsibility for teaching the skills and attitudes that ultimately ensure the quality of labor power for all the differing national capitals (Martin, 2002; Rikowski, 2001).

As Peter has explained to his students, this brings us to a problem that all pedagogues dedicated to revolutionary educational praxis must eventually confront, especially as the politics of our beleaguered public schools, colleges and universities become deformed by the patronage of multinational corporations or any other entity that has funds. Clearly, the servility associated with this entrepreneurial activity is bound to get worse, with large numbers of public intellectuals already transformed into their opposite: self-serving administrative clerks of the ruling class. Witness the rush of careerist academics to "update" their course offerings and research with a pro-business agenda in order to facilitate the flow of surplus value and profit into their pockets (often as a side benefit), whether by way of tenure, a good review, or external sources of funding. At the other end of the spectrum, the radical pedagogue is confronted with the challenge and contradiction of being an alienated and marginalized laborer, albeit one in the final analysis, with the authority to dispense work-related "competency" and "knowledge."

Of course, to dare speak out and combat these tendencies is to risk outright hostility not only from the right but also the liberal left, which falling toward illusions of reformism is blithely content with helping the system correct itself and now likewise sharing in the spoils. A good illustration of what can happen to intellectual renegades is Peter's estrangement from the academic establishment that has been the result of his headlong dive into a forbidden critique of the relationship between schooling and its capitalist agents, whose dirty secret is that it feels good to be on the side of money and prestige. Expanding on Marx, he argues that this pathology has contributed to the evolution of the neoliberal model of education, which is immune to the plight of millions of the world's poorest people. With this stage-managed shift, the power structure of the academe resembles a shop-floor production line, especially with its emphasis on efficiency (cut backs on "inefficient" programs), commodification (prepackaged, online courses, videos and CDs), and performance (standardized testing) (Tabb, 2001).

For students and new faculty such as myself, who are engaging this re-enchanted field of Marxist educational inquiry, the glaring class character of such one-sided pedagogical techniques defines our tasks and perspectives—whether teaching, publishing, or doing research. In my case, this is not purely a theoretical matter but directly linked to developing my own pedagogical praxis. Over the past year, I have been working "hands-on" with a local grassroots political organization, which has organic roots based in multiracial, multilingual working-class communities throughout Los Angeles, a city that exhibits all the contradictions of modern capitalism. With the support of Peter, my learning objective has been to better understand how educators, broadly defined, can intervene in the production of labor power to build a new range of literacies, knowledges, social competencies and cooperations that are capable of challenging the highly organized corporate practices of Big Business, while building support for a potentially broader revolutionary movement that addresses the pressing realities of race, class and gender formation within the circuits of global capital.

Thus, like other forms of social investigation, education has the latent but explosive potential to change the world for the purposes of attaining human freedom. Yet, the business-like pragmatism that pervades the academe has transformed it into a vulgar form of human resource management. This functionalist and technocratic approach has made it appear to students and new faculty alike that it is no longer realistic or even desirable to engage in critique of these practices, which acts in turn to preserve the structural subordination of labor to capital. Critique, according to Marx's theory of praxis, is the marking of this social contradiction (i.e., relating the situation of the exploited with the exploiting) for the purpose of changing it (Katz, 1991). But such critique is antithetical to the corporate ethos of the university and the aspirations of many graduate students toward professionalism and the academe's hidden architecture of power.

What matters here is that if education is to become a stronger intellectual framework for people struggling for liberation, then students will need to decide on the type of education they will practice and whose interests they will serve. This is a daunting choice for anyone about to enter the academe, especially given the pressure placed on graduate students and new faculty during this phase of purgatory to do conventional teaching and research. Yet, the examples of work in this book should dispel the pervasive myth that "there is no alternative" to this present crisis in education that has only served to fuel blind pessimism and despair.

One of the most refreshing things about Peter's radical aesthetic and blatantly political work is that it displaces the received notion that there is no room left for intellectual independence and radicalism in the academy. On the one hand, Peter *is* relatively isolated at UCLA. On the other, the ever-present invitations to speak abroad, and the expanding translations of his articles and books, indicate that his work attracts a loyal audience, even if it does infuriate his colleagues on the right as well as those lulled to sleep by the apparatus on the left. Inspired by the ideas of Freire, who introduced a whole generation of pedagogues to revolutionary Marxist concepts of radical citizenship such as "ideology," "class consciousness," and "revolution," Peter has chosen to dedicate his life to re-activating a pedagogy on the side of the oppressed. The result is a legacy of work, which is impressive in its scope and impossible to spur, even if he did experiment along the way with postmodern-left epistemologies before reaching his final Marxist position.

With a keen eye to the parlous state of critical pedagogy, Peter's recent work has sought to advance an explicitly Marxist conception of *revolutionary critical pedagogy*, a term coined by Paula Allman (1999, 2001). Despite the ideological counterclaims of his leftist critics who have discarded Freire like a burnt match, such pedagogy does not stem from utopian optimism but rather from radically democratic praxis. Here, concepts such as "co-operation," "dialogue," and "problem solving" are not objectified and capitalized activities but rather forms of revolutionary praxis harnessed to promote democratic social action. In fact, as a product of Peter's ongoing struggle to overcome what Freire called the teacher/student contradiction, *Red Seminars* contains within it at least one concrete expression of such social praxis. Viewed in isolation, each co-authored article tells a different story but all are also essential points of a fuller radical and activist tradition, which hails students and Marxist educators as interventionists in the production of knowledge.

Still, the decision to devote one's energy to such a politically supercharged pedagogy does not occur in a social vacuum. Students and new faculty such as myself who want a life in higher education must consider the need to earn tenure to ensure the means of subsistence for themselves, and, in many cases, their families. In this regard, what is particularly alarming, and this is generally conceded, is the anti-intellectual thuggery that runs rampant in teacher training programs. This tyranny is often an effect of pedagogical strategies that discomfort students who occupy positions of privilege in the classroom (e.g., white, straight males) but is also reinforced by senior faculty, who vested in the system, have the best paying and stable jobs (i.e., tenure) (Martin, 2002). The political consequences of calling into question and reckoning with, either directly or indirectly, these captains of pedagogy can be dire. On a more optimistic note, it is perhaps a testimony to Peter's tutelage, if not the informal "underground railway," that every one of his Leftist students is now working in university positions. It may already be apparent to the reader that we face enormous challenges, but opportunities *are* emerging and what I want to say is that the academe is as good a space as any to deepen the struggle.

REFERENCES

Allman, P. (1999). *Revolutionary social transformation: Democratic hopes, political possibilities and critical education.* Westport, CT: Bergin & Garvey.

Allman, P. (2001). *Critical education against global capitalism: Karl Marx and revolutionary critical education.* Westport, CT: Bergin & Garvey.

Katz, A. (1991). The university and revolutionary practice: A letter toward a Leninist pedagogy. In D. Morton & M. Zavazadeh (Eds.), *Theory/pedagogy/politics: Texts for change* (pp. 222-239). Chicago: University of Illinois Press.

Martin, G. (2002). What is to be done? Toward a revolutionary praxis. *Journal of Critical Inquiry into Curriculum and Instruction, 3*(3), 42-45.

Rikowski, G. (2001). *The battle for Seattle: Its significance for education.* London: Tuffnell Press.

Tabb, W. (2001). Globalization and education as a commodity. Retrieved May 1, 2003, from http://www.psc-cuny.org/jcglobalization.htm

CONTRIBUTORS

Estanislao Antelo earned his PhD at the Universidad Nacional de Rosario). He is professor of pedagogy at the School of Humanities and Letters, Universidad Nacional de Rosario and at the PhD Program of FLACSO. He has published several articles and three books: Instrucciones para ser Profesor. Pedagogía para aspirantes. (Editorial Santillana. Colección dirigida por Graciela Frigerio. Bs. As, 1999), *El Renegar de la Escuela* (Con Ana L. Abramowski. Editorial Homo Sapiens. Rosario, 2000), *La Escuela Más alla del bien y el mal* (Ensayos sobre la transformación de los valores educativos [Comp.] Editorial A.M.S.A.F.E., 2001).

Ricky Lee Allen is an assistant professor of educational thought and sociocultural studies at the University of New Mexico. His scholarship focuses on the sociology of education, critical studies of whiteness, critical race theory, and critical pedagogy. His major scholarly focus is on the white racial identity politics of critical theories.

Marta P. Baltodano is an assistant professor at the School of Education of Loyola Marymount University in Los Angeles. Her current work focuses on teachers' beliefs about social justice and the impact of the anti-bilingual legislation (Prop. 227) in the process of identity formation of second language learners in California. She is the current chair of the Committee on "Anthropological Studies of Schools and Culture" of the American Anthropological Association, and one of the founding members of the California Consortium for Critical Educators (CCCE). She recently co-edited the book *The Critical Pedagogy Reader* (Darder, Baltodano, & Torres, 2003).

Angela Calabrese Barton, received her PhD in Curriculum, Teaching and Educational Policy from Michigan State University in 1995. Drawing from critical and feminist perspectives, her research focuses on the means by which and the reasons for which high poverty urban youth construct science practices outside of school and how they apply those practices toward promoting social justice and community empowerment. Her work also focuses on the role that community-based and case-based learning experiences can play in the development of science teachers' understandings of urban youth and their own science teaching practices. She has extensive experience conducting research with students, parents, and teachers in high poverty urban communities. She also has extensive experience teaching in after-school programs in high-poverty urban centers and working with teachers in their studies to become science teachers. Her research has been funded by the National Science Foundation, the National Institutes of Health, and the Spencer Foundation. Her work has been published in *Educational Researcher, Educational Policy and Practice, the Journal of Research in Science Teaching, Science Education*, and *Curriculum Inquiry*, among others. Her most recent book, *Teaching Science for Social Justice* (Teachers College Press), won the 2003 AESA Critics Choice Award.

Rebecca Clark currently lives in Seattle, WA, and has been doing participant-observation research on global technology development and the international IT worker at Microsoft for the past 5 years. Her recent work and interests focus on South Asian women, critical autobiography, and how to theorize and organize around the possibilities for love and spirituality in the pursuit of radical democracy and justice. Her work has also been published in the journal *Race Traitor*. A graduate of the University of California, Davis and the University of Washington, she intends to pursue a PhD in women's studies or a related field in the near future.

Philip Craft is a communications strategist in New York City working for the reform of federal law and policy. He has been involved in campaigns to distribute disaster recovery aid to low-income communities more fairly, to use DNA evidence in the prosecution of sexual assault cases more effectively, and to prevent the erosion of affordable housing in the city. A graduate of Emerson College and the University of Washington, Philip also teaches at the Baruch College Graduate School of Public Affairs (CUNY).

Cindy Cruz describes herself as an "old school butch dyke". She is a doctoral candidate in education at UCLA, where her interdisciplinary work focuses on the queer body, memory, and epistemology. She is currently an HIV street outreach worker for homeless youth and teaches revolution as Core Faculty at Pacific Oaks College. In her own words: "Eclectic, transdisciplinary, and an Aquarius, I try my best to honor the histories of my family who have been in the San Gabriel Valley since we walked across the Bering Straits."

Zeus Leonardo earned his both his BA in English and PhD in Education from UCLA. He has published articles and book chapters on critical education and social theory with special attention to issues of race, class, and gender. He is the author of I*deology, Discourse, and School Reform* (Praeger) and co-editor (with Tejeda and Martinez) of *Charting New Terrains in Chicana(o)/Latina(o) Education* (2000, Hampton). His recent work can best be described as the political integration of ideology critique and discourse analysis. Formerly an assistant professor of education at the University of St. Thomas in St. Paul, MN, he is currently an assistant professor in the College of Education at California State University, Long Beach.

Noah De Lissovoy is a doctoral candidate at the UCLA Graduate School of Education and Information Studies. His research interests include the investigation of processes of oppression and resistance in public schooling and society, as well as the development of theories of anti-imperialist pedagogy. His articles have appeared in several journals and edited collections. He is co-editor of *InterActions: UCLA Journal of Education and Information Studies.*

Manuel Espinoza is a fifth-year doctoral student in the UCLA Graduate School of Education. He has spent the last decade working as an educator. Manuel is currently a member of the UC Links After-School Computer Club research program and the Statewide Migrant Leadership Institute at UCLA.

Ramin Farahmandpur is an assistant professor in the Department of Educational Policy, Foundations and Administrative Studies at Portland State University. His research in education encompasses globalization, imperialism, neoliberalism, Marxism, and critical pedagogy

Gustavo Fischman earned his PhD at UCLA. He is an assistant professor in the division of Curriculum and Instruction at Arizona State University. His areas of specialization are comparative and international education, gender and education, and the development of participatory and action-oriented research programs with educators and communities. He is the author of *Imagining Teachers: Rethinking Teacher Education and Gender* (Rowman and Littlefield, 2000), and has co-authored with Isabel Hernández (1991) *La Ley y La Tierra: Historia De Un Despojo En La Tribu Mapuche De Los Toldos* (Centro Editor para América Latina/Centro de Estudios Avanzados-UBA, Buenos Aires, Argentina). He has also co-edited two books and written several refereed articles and invited chapters in books on politics of education, teacher education, and gender issues in education. In addition to serving on several editorial boards, he is the associate editor for Spanish and Portuguese of *Education Review* and *Educational Policy Analysis Archives.*

Nathalia Jaramillo is a doctoral student in the UCLA Graduate School of Education and Information Studies. Her research interests include feminist theory, education policy, and globalization studies.

Gregory Martin is lecturer in education and student diversity at the School of Education and Professional Studies at Griffith University, Gold Coast Campus, Australia. His research interests include Marxist educational theory, socially critical action research, and revolutionary multiculturalism.

Peter McLaren is professor at The Graduate School of Education and Information Studies, University of California, Los Angeles. He is the author and editor of over 40 books. His works have been translated into 15 languages. He lectures worldwide on the politics and pedagogy of liberation. Recently, La Fundacion McLaren de Pedagogia Critica was set up by a group of Mexican educators to advance critical pedagogy throughout Latin America. His most recent works include (with Ramin Farahmandpur) *Teaching Against Globalization and the New Imperialism* (Rowman and Littlefield), and *Capitalists and Conquerors: Critical Pedagogy Against Empire* (Rowman and Littlefield).

Marcia Moraes is professor at Universidade do Estado do Rio de Janeiro (UERJ-Brazil). During her first years in the field of education, she was an elementary, secondary, and high school teacher. She is also a former associate professor at the University of St. Thomas-Minnesota. Her publications include diverse articles in education and the books *Bilingual Education: A Dialogue with the Bakhtin Circle* (SUNY) and *Ser Humana: Quando a mulher está em discussão* (Brazil: DP&A).

Juan Sanchez Munoz is an associate professor at Texas Tech and assistant editor of the *Journal of Latinos in Education*. His work has examined the educational opportunities extended to urban students in general, and, in particular, students placed at-risk as a result of their race, class, and culture. Currently, he is working on a manuscript investigating the climate of alternative education for at-risk students in urban public school districts.

Jill Pinkney Pastrana is currently an associate professor in Social and Multicultural Foundations of Education, California State University, Long Beach. She has spent extensive time researching education reform in Chile, and served as an invited guest Lecturer in La Programa de Innovación en la Formación Inicial de Profesores, Universidad de la Frontera, Temuco. She continues to collaborate with a number of colleagues in Chile in the area of emancipatory pedagogy and democratic participation in traditionally marginalized populations, exploring linkages between such populations in solidarity across community and national boundaries. Her research focuses on the contradictions between purportedly democratic principals of schooling and neoliberal education reform framed within the context of globalization.

Carlos Tejeda is associate director of the UCLA Migrant Student Leadership Institute and associate professor at the California State University, Los Angeles, where he teaches courses in the social foundations of education, the history of education, the sociology of education, and human development. He is also a researcher at UCLA's Center for the Study of Urban Literacies, where he is currently working on an emerging line of theorization, research, and practice defined as decolonizing pedagogy. He is a coeditor of the text *Charting new terrains of Chicana(o)/Latina(o) Education.*

Glenn Rikowski is a senior lecturer in education studies in the School of Education at University College Northampton, England. Previous to that, he was a supply teacher in schools in London (2001-2002), a Senior Research Fellow in Lifelong Learning at the University of Central England (1999-2001), and a Research Fellow in Post-compulsory Education & Training at the School of Education, University of Birmingham (1994-1999). From 1985-1994, Rikowski taught in schools and vocational colleges in London and Essex. His latest books are, *The Battle in Seattle: Its Significance for Education* (2001, Tufnell Press), *Red Chalk: On Schooling, Capitalism & Politics* (with Dave Hill, Mike Cole and Peter McLaren, 2001, Institute for Education Policy Studies), and an edited collection (with Dave Hill, Mike Cole and Peter McLaren) *Marxism Against Postmodernism in Educational Theory* (2002, Lexington Books). With Tony Green, Rikowski runs the bi-annual (May and October) Marxism and Education: Renewing Dialogues seminars at the University of London, Institute of Education.

Aimee Carrillo Rowe is an assistant professor of rhetoric at the University of Iowa. Her research and teaching focus on third world feminisms, whiteness and antiracism studies, critical pedagogy, and the politics of spirituality and justice. Her recent writing appears *Feminist Media Studies* and *Radical History Review.*

Mitja Sardoc works at the Educational Research Institute in Ljubljana, Slovenia, where he is currently engaged in research projects on citizenship education, human rights, school autonomy, and inclusion. He earned his MSc in Anthropology from the Ljubljana Graduate School of the Humanities. His research focuses on political theory and philosophy of education, specifically addressing questions of citizenship education, equality, inclusion, and diversity in public education. Over the last five years he has edited and co-edited a number of journal special issues on citizenship education, social justice, human rights, and inclusion and has interviewed some of the most renowned contemporary political philosophers on the topic of education and political theory (e.g., Michael Walzer, Iris Marion Young, Stephen Macedo, Martha C. Nussbaum,

Harry Brighouse, Peter McLaren) and citizenship education (e.g. Robert K. Fullinwider, Eamonn Callan, Kenneth A. Strike, Bernard Crick, Richard Dagger). He is executive editor of *Theory and Research in Education*, a quarterly journal published by Sage, a correspondent for the *Politeia Newsletter* and member of the editorial board of the *Journal for Critical Education Policy Studies*. He is doing his MPhil/PhD study on citizenship education in contemporary liberal political philosophy at the Institute of Education, University of London.

María Silvia Serra, Magíster in Social Sciences, is pursuing a PhD in education at FLACSO (Argentina). She is a faculty member and research director of the College of Education at the Universidad Nacional de Rosario. She has published several articles on critical pedagogy and is also a founding member of the Centro de Estudios en Pedagogía Crítica de Rosario (Center for Critical Pedagogy of Rosario) and co-editor of the journal *Cuadernos de Pedagogía* (Pedagogy Notebooks).

Juha Suoranta is a professor of adult education at the University of Joensuu, Finland. In 2003, he worked as a senior researcher in the Academy of Finland and as a visiting professor at the University of California at Los Angeles. His research interests include research methodology, critical (media) education, and revolutionary life-long learning. He has some 200 scientific publications in his record.

AUTHOR INDEX

SUBJECT INDEX